Adaptive Hardware Infrastructures for SAP®

SAP PRESS

SAP PRESS is issued
by Bernhard Hochlehnert, SAP AG

SAP PRESS is a joint initiative of SAP and Galileo Press. The know-how offered by SAP specialists combined with the expertise of the publishing house Galileo Press offers the reader expert books in the field. SAP PRESS features first-hand information and expert advice, and provides useful skills for decision-making.

SAP PRESS offers a variety of books on technical and business related topics for the SAP user. For further information, please also visit our Web site: *www.sap-press.com*.

Mißbach, Gibbels, Karnstädt, Stelzel, Wagenblast

Adaptive Hardware Infrastructures for SAP®

SAP PRESS

German Edition first published 2005 by
Galileo Press.

Translation Lemoine International, Inc.,
Salt Lake City, UT
Copy Editor Nancy Etscovitz and John Parker,
UCG, Inc., Boston, MA
Cover Design Silke Braun
Printed in Germany

ISBN 1-59229-035-3

Contents

Foreword

In safeguarding their competitiveness, many companies today face the challenge of having to constantly adapt their business processes to the ever-changing requirements of the market. The main issues that companies must address are the increasing internationalization of markets and production locations, the creation of new partner networks (due to decreasing vertical integration within companies, for example), and the timely introduction of new products and services.

With the continuing development of its software solutions—from R/2 and R/3 to the multi-tier, Internet-enabled architecture of the mySAP Business Suite—SAP makes a significant contribution to helping companies meet this challenge. In particular, SAP's latest measure, in which it brought together its existing solutions in a Web-based services architecture, was intended to address the aforementioned needs for adaptation. This new architecture enabled the combining of individual function modules (for example, a module for creating a customer order) in order to create new solution modules and therefore support changing business processes quickly and cost-effectively while maintaining high quality.

Today, IT managers in most companies are faced daily with the question of how to reconcile the need for cost-cutting in the implementation and operation of SAP solutions with the demand to make these solutions more flexible. The most frequently asked questions are:

- What significance do the changing SAP solution architectures have for underlying IT infrastructures?
- What does an SAP IT infrastructure have to do in order to be able to adapt quickly to changing requirements?
- How do we ensure that issues such as high availability, performance, and scalability are not neglected?
- What can we expect from operating these 'adaptive SAP solutions' in terms of their running costs?

This book provides real-world answers to these questions. The team of authors, under the leadership of Dr. Michael Mißbach, Senior Consultant at Hewlett-Packard (HP), has several years' combined experience dealing on a daily basis with international clients and various SAP development and consulting departments in solving similar questions. His wealth of experience is reflected in this book, which focuses on current developments in platform and network technologies, and on technologies and concepts for operations optimization such as virtualization, IT Service Management (ITSM), and Total Cost of Ownership (TCO).

Moreover, this book highlights the close cooperation that has existed between SAP and HP for 15 years now, both in various technological developments and the daily joint support of thousands of clients worldwide.

Dr. Wolfgang Oskierski
SAP Business Manager EMEA

Foreword

The argument for using IT to support enterprise processes is stronger than ever today.

While managers in enterprises usually have little or no understanding of the concepts and specifics of information technology, they will still articulate what they expect from IT: to provide a measurable business value. However, they do so in their own specific "business-language" vernacular. The ability to translate these expectations expressed in business-speak into IT requirements is an art in itself; however, it is one that we must master if we want to position technology in its rightful place in our enterprises.

A situation where employees have to spend an indefinite amount of time in front of a static input screen to search for the information they require (and possibly never find it) is not the way to demonstrate the efficiency that is always demanded of IT in day-to-day business operations. A far better way to show the usefulness and value of IT is to have the interface open up a communications portal that can adapt itself to very specific individual requirements. SAP refers to it as a "role-based user interface" and it is considered to be a result of an Enterprise Services Architecture (ESA). This kind of architecture clearly demonstrates the value proposition of IT, because it enables users to access the information they require quickly and directly.

That's the theory.

For this kind of application layer to be feasible in the real world, a stable and solid basis is a must. SAP has its own name for this too—SAP NetWeaver—which is the foundation of the ESA structure. SAP NetWeaver forms a basis that consolidates and provides information about the people, information, and processes in an enterprise. Only if the basis is strong enough does the added value of the overlying application and communication landscape become apparent. An added difficulty is that besides being solid, the basis must be also highly flexible—two factors that may initially appear to be mutually exclusive.

In business-speak, this means that in the coming years we'll see an increased demand for solutions that promise quick interchangeability and ease of integration into existing landscapes. Shorter roll-out times and lower process costs will be expected as well, and the demand for contributions from IT solutions to value creation and the fulfillment of enterprise strategies will be, in a word, uncompromising.

This book is intended to help you lay the foundation for successful process design and visible added value in your enterprise. It will assist you in mapping out your own strategic path, along which enterprise visions can become a reality. Economizing in the wrong places in this context simply provides fertile ground for risks and errors rather than value creation, and this book thus makes a significant contribution to the success of ESA strategies.

May you have many hours of enjoyment reading this book and may you have success in creating solid solutions that bridge the gap between IT and business.

Andreas Kerbusk

Chairman of the German SAP User Group (DSAG e.V.)

Introduction

Adaptive IT infrastructures for agile enterprises

While most IT projects in recent years have been dominated by the need to cut costs, today enterprises are enhancing their competitiveness by using IT to adapt their business processes to markets that are changing evermore rapidly.

This is because thinking purely in terms of costs makes sense only up to a point. Without any doubt the cheapest IT system is the one which is completely written of and is running without any change, however continually changing market conditions mean that enterprises are forced to modify their processes, including their IT, on an ongoing basis. Therefore, enterprises have a clear competitive advantage if their IT is flexible enough to be able to implement new processes quickly.

However, it is not just the markets that are changing. Company mergers and acquisitions indicate that enterprises themselves are becoming increasingly agile. For example, steel companies can turn into mobile telephone operators or tourism enterprises, and it is not always the big fish that swallow the small fish. In these cases, too, it is the speed at which the IT infrastructure can be adapted to the new circumstances that determines the success or failure of an enterprise.

SAP NetWeaver and ESA

With SAP NetWeaver, and especially the Enterprise Services Architecture, SAP has developed products and concepts that will have a dramatic effect on how IT is used to benefit enterprises. These concepts form the basis for quickly introducing and adapting business processes. However, for this to be possible, enterprises need an infrastructure that is as adaptive as the software, while still providing a stable technology basis.

Technologies for adaptive infrastructures are not a completely new concept. For some time, many hardware manufacturers have been working on consolidation concepts that include the "virtualization" of server and storage resources.

SAP Adaptive Computing Controller

One new concept, however, is the idea of incorporating the application, which creates an holistic, all-around solution. With the introduction of SAP Adaptive Computing, this kind of solution is beginning to make its mark. For the first time, the SAP Adaptive Computing Controller provides an interface between the infrastructure and the application, and therefore implements the preliminary steps toward integrating two previously separate worlds.

Availability The increasing predominance of SAP solutions in enterprise processes proves that enterprises are becoming increasingly more dependent on these systems. High availability is therefore gaining more importance than ever before. Because business processes in SAP NetWeaver environments are distributed across several SAP systems, the processes can work only if every system is functioning perfectly. Similarly, Enterprise Services Architectures (ESA), which can integrate functionalities from different systems in an overlying business process in a very short space of time, can work only if all the connected systems are equally available.

However, high availability does not depend on technology alone. Besides unified management and monitoring tools, running adaptive infrastructures also requires the consistent and carefully planned use of IT Service Management (ITSM) methods.

Adaptivity After many discussions with customers, the authors have learned that there is a demand for a guide to adaptive infrastructures. However, everyone has his or her own idea about the meaning of "adaptive"—from simple load distribution mechanisms to the virtualization of whole data centers or automatic recognition and monitoring of resources. Intrinsic to all definitions is the goal of enabling infrastructures to adapt flexibly to business requirements. This book provides an outline of all the aforementioned topics.

The great demand for our two existing books, which deal with the infrastructure and the operation of SAP systems, encouraged the authors to produce this third book, which deals with the latest developments and challenges and their corresponding solutions. We also outline trends for the future, where appropriate. Therefore, this book is an addition to the books we previously authored, and not simply an update.

To ensure that readers who do not regard themselves as "gurus" in each area can still derive benefit from reading this book, the most important technologies are explained in detail. Practice-oriented guidelines are provided throughout the book in order to make the reader aware of essential but often less obvious facts. The book concentrates exclusively on the technical aspects of IT infrastructure; the details of how to install and adapt SAP software to business processes are beyond the scope of this book.

The solutions presented here refer to the latest releases at the time of printing. However, although the laboratories are constantly producing new hardware and software, the underlying technologies and architectures change much more slowly, and so the concepts presented here can be used on a long-term basis. Also, many of the technical solutions presented here are also suitable for other enterprise-critical software systems.

The book has intentionally taken a neutral stance in terms of manufacturers. Nonetheless, the authors are employees of the SAP HP International Competence Center and their expertise is largely based on the numerous solutions that have been developed there since 1989. For this reason, SAP and HP products, and solutions from partner companies, of which the authors have positive experiences, are used as examples for a class of solutions. However, references to any product do not represent an evaluation of that product.

Structure of the Book

Each chapter of this book contains a short introduction that outlines the goals of that particular chapter. Wherever possible, the detailed descriptions of the solutions are addressed in terms of performance, availability, and flexibility, and are illustrated by real-world examples. The closing section of each chapter consists of a short summary of the main recommendations.

The first two chapters provide a brief description of the functionalities of the SAP software components and of the underlying technical components involved in each case from an IT point of view to establish the foundation for the subsequent chapters. **Chapter 1** gives an overview of the functionality and use of the SAP NetWeaver components. It also describes the software lifecycle of the SAP solution and user management solutions.

Chapter 2 presents the solutions of the mySAP Business Suite and places them in the context of the Enterprise Services Architecture.

Chapter 3 introduces the architecture of the SAP Web Application Server, which is a platform for the process execution of almost all SAP solutions. In doing so, it deals with the ABAP and the Java stack and considers the various aspects of Unicode implementation. Lastly, it looks at aspects of grid computing.

Chapter 4 deals with dimensioning computer systems. The focus here is on explaining the most important parameters used for designing a hardware landscape. This chapter ends with an examination of the level of exactness that can be achieved with a standard approach to sizing.

Chapter 5 presents computer systems for SAP applications. It describes the available technologies with particular emphasis on the design of the processor and main memory, and describes the advantages and disadvantages of blade concepts. It also presents the various operating systems, with a special focus on Linux.

Chapter 6 deals with the disk storage sub-systems of the SAP database server. It describes the various files in an SAP system and explains how to dimension and structure storage sub-systems. It also deals with how Network Attached Storage (NAS) can be used with SAP.

Chapter 7 tackles the subjects of availability and downtime in integrated systems of mission critical systems. All aspects of high availability are presented here, from protecting a computer center from disasters, to cluster technologies and shadow databases, to system operation.

Chapter 8 describes the various user interfaces of the SAP solutions, as well as print and output management solutions. It also presents the new Interactive Forms and SAP Web Dynpro.

Chapters 9 to 12 deal with network infrastructures for SAP system landscapes. The specific requirements that an SAP system has in terms of network bandwidth and latency, as well as the specific aspects of local-area and wide-area networks are each dealt with in their own separate chapters. Another chapter deals with protecting enterprise data and systems from unauthorized access via the Internet.

Chapter 13 shows how the virtualization technologies presented in the previous chapters can be used to build flexible SAP infrastructures. It also describes the SAP Adaptive Computing Controller and 10 different application scenarios for adaptive infrastructures.

Chapter 14 addresses the management of Enterprise Services Architectures. It also presents the IT Service Management (ITSM) reference model and the various management system concepts for monitoring, analyzing, and optimizing the infrastructure. An example of a vendor-managed inventory scenario illustrates the various points.

Chapter 15 explores the cost aspects of operating an SAP system. It briefly describes the most common scientific models and a model for structuring the overall operating costs. Lastly, using two practical examples, it discusses the costs and benefits of a system integration scenario, and compares the operating costs of a scale-up concept with those of a scale-out concept.

Acknowledgements

This book is the product of voluntary work done in our free time during many nights and weekends. We therefore dedicate it to our wives and children, who have had to spend a lot of time without our undivided attention.

We would also like to thank all the customers and colleagues who selflessly provided much help in the form of tips, contributions, and constructive criticism. Without their support, we would not have been able to write this book. In particular, we would like to mention Helmut Fieres, Sebastian Buhlinger, Marina Marscheider, Roland Wartenberg, and Markus Meisl at SAP; Monika Reitmeier and Michael Weber at Munich Re-Insurance; Friedel Manus at Capgemini, Paul Hammersley at EPI-USE Limited and Rob de Maat and Peter van Eijk at Deloitte Consulting; Uwe Hoffmann at Microsoft; Gerd Kammerath at Citrix; Nils Bauer from Network Appliance, Lothar Zocher and Andreas Epple at EMC; Dan Ellenbogen at Spaceline; Christian Schult at Norasia; and Andreas Schweizer, Jens-Uwe Walther, and Horst Jacobi at Carl Zeiss Jena (now HP Managed Services) and Andreas Kerbusk at STEAG.

Thanks are also due to those colleagues who patiently answered so many of our questions: Eric Martorell, Gene A. Burke, Laurie Ford, Chuck Desostoa, Fanny Osorio, Filip Van Grembergen, Michael Wiseberg at HP USA and Canada, Nigel Edwards at HP Labs Bristol, Heiderose Doms, Bernd Klopsch, Carsten Helmers, Jörg Schade, Mike Wenner, Peter Weiler, and Friedrich Kilian at the SAP HP Competence Center, Werner-Wolfgang Gaertner, Georg Storz, and Rudi Grom at the HP SAP Center of Excellence, David Adelmann, Arne Hartmann, and Holger Zecha at HP Managed Services, Peter Holzmann at HP Service, Michael Igel at LinuxLab, our Microsoft experts Horst Kanert and Erik Rieger, Dr. Christoph Balbach at HP Storage, Thilo Domsdorf, Engelbert Epple, Andreas Koch, Volker Empl, Bernhard Zimmermann, Markus Berg, and Dirk Schneider at HP Consulting & Integration, Matthias Precht, Dirk Benecke, and Peter Schenk at HP OpenView, and the countless others who contributed to this book with commitment and dedication.

We would also like to thank in particular Mr. Robert Riemann at Porsche, whose detailed comments made a major contribution to the content of many chapters, and Ms. Susanne Jansen at SAP, who provided much valuable information. The practical experience of all our advisors greatly added to the value of this book, and their support was a great source of encouragement.

Lastly, our thanks go to Florian Zimniak, Nancy Etscovitz, John Parker and the rest of the staff at Galileo Press and Wellesley Information Services, who made it possible for us to bring this book to life.

1 SAP NetWeaver

"It is not the strongest of the species that survive, nor the most intelligent, but the one most responsive to change."
Charles Darwin, The Origin of Species

Never touch a running system?

IT departments always strive to keep the systems they operate as stable as possible, and with good reason. In the past, it was common for IT departments to acquire hardware and software for a particular project, to run this hardware and software for several years without making any significant changes to the application, and to completely replace it on the occasion of a new project. That way, the stability of the systems was ensured, and the norm of using the hardware until it is completely depreciated to help to keep costs under control was observed. Investment cycles were mainly determined by innovations both in hardware and software that enabled new improved business processes not possible before without these innovations in many cases.

The survival of the most adaptable in the context of enterprises

The global competitive environment forces today's enterprises to quickly adapt their business processes to the constantly changing market conditions. In addition, the life span of Enterprise structures and cultures is becoming progressively shorter all the time due to company mergers, acquisitions and spin-offs. As a consequence of these two trends, the requirements of IT have also undergone a dramatic change.

The change in the requirements of IT infrastructures is illustrated by examining what has to be adapted when any of the following happens:

- A new product is about to be introduced
- A new sales channel is established
- A new partnership is established
- A new location is set up
- Another company is acquired, merged, or spun off

Usually, the IT systems that support the associated processes have to be adapted first, creating a clear need for more flexible IT systems, processes, and infrastructures.

1.1 The SAP Product Portfolio

From R/2 to R/3 SAP has also risen to the challenges outlined above. In response to the strategic initiatives and customer requirements, the range of SAP enterprise products has expanded and changed over the years. R/2 was intended to automate the core business processes of large enterprises. R/3, which was originally conceived for small and midsize businesses, extended this functionality to include processes to support sales, distribution, materials management, and production planning.

New dimensions The demand for increasingly complex analytical solutions was the motivation in the "New Dimension" initiative for introducing special technologies such as InfoCubes and memory-resident databases. This led to the creation of self-contained products such as SAP Business Information Warehouse (SAP BW) and SAP Advanced Planner and Optimizer (SAP APO). The Internet Transaction Server (ITS) also came into existence, providing the first gateway to the Internet.

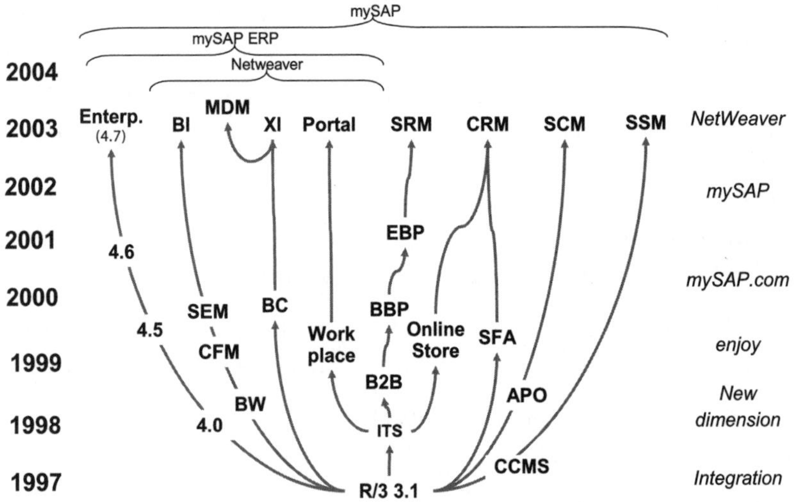

Figure 1.1 The mySAP "Family Tree" (Unofficial and Incomplete)

EnjoySAP The EnjoySAP initiative heralded not only a new, user-friendly user interface, but also applications for sales support, an online store, a solution for electronic trade between enterprises, and more. Figure 1.1 shows the "roots" of some SAP products and their development.

mySAP.com With mySAP.com, every department manager in a typical enterprise now effectively had his or her own specific enterprise application: The R/3 Enterprise Resource Planning System was for the CEO and the CFO, the HR manager had mySAP Human Resources (mySAP HR), the Sales manager had mySAP Customer Relationship Management (mySAP CRM), the head of production had mySAP Supply Chain Management (mySAP SCM) system, and the head of development had mySAP Product Lifecycle Management (mySAP PLM).

This organic development brings some advantages to the customer as his investment in training remains protected, and so is the wealth of experience from his employees, their know-how of configuring, optimizing, and operating R/3 which could also be applied to other mySAP solutions. Another benefit is the usability of the IT service management processes originally set up for R/3.

However, even for an expert, it is not always easy to keep current with this ever-changing plethora of components, solutions, and functions, especially since some of the terms used to describe them tend to have a very short lifecycle. Also, the data integration that had been achieved in R/3, through the usage of a single database, was now lost in these new developments, as each of the new applications needs its own database.

Operating system for enterprises

In a sense, we can think of SAP products as an "operating system for enterprises." Parallels can be drawn here with Microsoft's development of an operating system for Intel computers. In the beginning, there was DOS, which primary function was to start programs. It had very basic functions and the user controlled it by entering cryptic abbreviations in the command line. Windows, on the other hand, provided the user not only with an easy-to-use interface, but also with an increasingly extensive portfolio of productivity-enhancing functions.

With R/2, SAP provided the most important business processes right from the start, but similarly, only with a very basic user interface (the 3270 screens of the "Mainframosaurus" era). R/3 ushered in a user-friendly interface that was continually improved as part of the Enjoy initiative and in step with new Internet technologies. The functionality, too, was enhanced with every new release and product, and with SAP NetWeaver, it became a complete operating system for enterprises.

SAP's current range of software solutions can be divided as follows:

- The mySAP Business Suite, which supports cross-industry core business processes
- The industry solutions, which provide typical processes specific to each industry

- SAP NetWeaver, which provides a common technology basis and integrates employees, information, and processes across all applications
- SAP xApps, which are cross-component applications (Composite Applications)
- Solutions for small and midsize enterprises (SMB)

1.2 The Components of SAP NetWeaver

Figure 1.2 shows a logical view of the components of SAP NetWeaver.

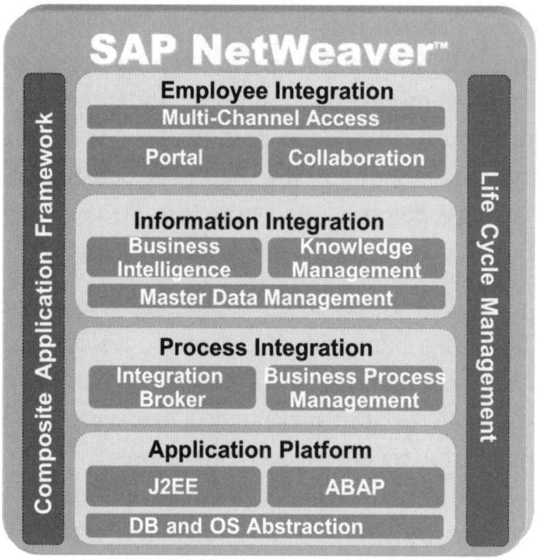

Figure 1.2 The Components of SAP NetWeaver (Logical View)

Employee integration The term employee integration refers to technologies that bring together all the relevant functions and information for each employee in an interface that can be configured on an individual basis. This technology is implemented using the following NetWeaver components: SAP Enterprise Portal (EP), the Portal Collaboration Package for team collaboration, and the SAP Mobile Engine (ME). The TREX search engine is the technology that allows employees to search for information.

Information integration Information integration refers to the analysis of structured data (Business Intelligence) by the SAP NetWeaver component SAP Business Intelligence (SAP BI), and the administration of unstructured information, such as text files, audio files, and presentation by the SAP Knowledge Management (SAP KM). Another part of the responsibility of information management is the problem of managing master data in a consistent way across system boundaries. The NetWeaver component SAP Master Data Management (SAP MDM) handles this area.

Process integration

Process integration is defined as enabling business processes to be executed across a number of different systems and is supported by the NetWeaver component SAP Exchange Infrastructure (SAP XI).

Figure 1.3 shows the technical components of SAP NetWeaver.

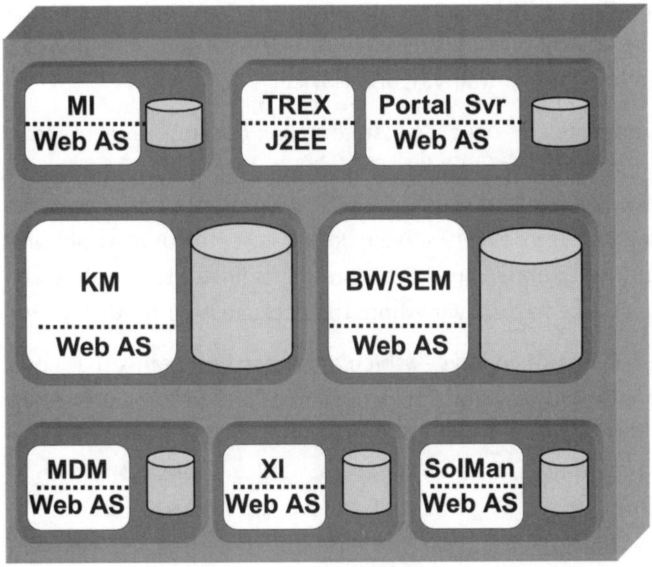

Figure 1.3 The Components of SAP NetWeaver (Technical View)

The basis of all these components is the SAP Web Application Server (Web AS), the common application platform for J2EE (Java 2 Enterprise Edition) and ABAP[1] programs. The Lifecycle Management Suite also provides tools for software design, development, implementation, and change management, and the Composite Application Framework (CAF) enables developers to create Composite Applications, a new class of applications for cross-function business processes.

1.3 SAP Enterprise Portal

Because users today access content in several IT systems, rather than just triggering transactions in a single system, portals are becoming increasingly important as universal information sources. Like the display screens

1 Advanced Business Application Programming, SAP's proprietary programming language for business applications.

in an airport, portals are the first thing that users look for in order to orientate themselves.

With the SAP Enterprise Portal (SAP EP), SAP provides personalized access to a wide range of back-end systems (SAP solutions as well as solutions from other manufacturers and based on other technologies), file storage systems (such as the Windows file system), and Internet information sources (such as Yahoo). Access can be achieved from any terminal with a browser. Besides the classic desktop and laptop computer, terminals can include any mobile device such as a PDA (Personal Digital Assistant), a mobile telephone, or any hybrid device.

Drag&Relate

Features like Drag&Relate make it possible to link business objects across different systems and even across different enterprises. A frequently quoted example is linking an order in SAP R/3 Enterprise with the delivery number in a package delivery service. In this case, the user would simply 'drop' the order number onto the icon that is linked to the Web site of the package service to discover where the package is currently located.

iView technology

A portal page consists of "iViews," which are special programs that communicate with other applications or data sources and present the results to the user in his specific context on the portal (other portal manufacturers call these programs "portlets"). Even MS Office applications such as Excel are among the applications that can be used interactively in the browser in this way.

A portal page can also contain other portal pages, since technically these pages are really other iViews. iViews can also communicate with and even modify each other.

The arrangement of iViews on the page and their content are defined for a specific layout in the SAP Page Builder and are stored to the database via the Portal Content Directory (PCD).

With the Enterprise Portal Business Content, SAP provides several thousand ready-made iViews.[2] Customers can use the Portal Development Kit (PDK) to create their own iViews in several programming languages (such as JSP, Java, XML, Microsoft.NET, SAP Business Server Pages (BSP), and SAP Web Dynpro) with minimal effort.

iFrames

The portal can also display iFrames, which are typical URLs that don't allow the layout to be changed or the data to be selected or changed.

2 You can also download them at *www.iViewStudio.com*.

iFrames enable you to include the user interface of an application, such as HP OpenView, in the SAP Enterprise Portal in Figure 1.4.

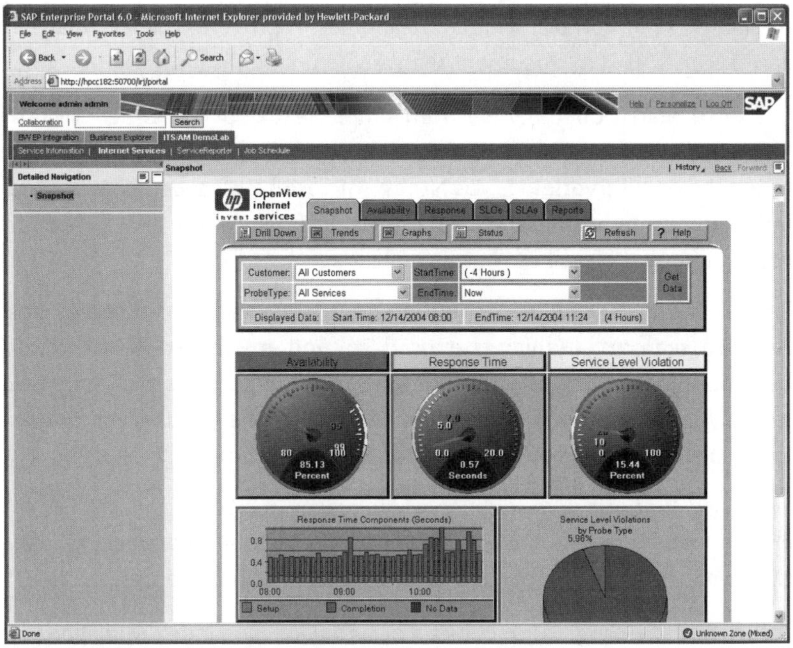

Figure 1.4 Example of an iFrame in the SAP Enterprise Portal

The optional Unification Server enables Drag&Relate between back-end systems from different manufacturers. A connector is required for every non-SAP system that cannot be accessed via a URL, such as Microsoft's Sharepoint and Lotus Notes. Connectors are Java applets that usually run in the portal and are based on the J2EE Connector Architecture (JCA) standard. Partners like iWay provide connectors for Siebel, Oracle, and PeopleSoft (separate licenses are required).

Knowledge Management

With the continual growth in the volume of data in enterprises, finding the information we need is becoming increasingly time-consuming. According to studies conducted by the market research service iwd, employees spend an average of 2.5 hours a week searching for documents. To combat this, in addition to the portal platform itself, the SAP Enterprise Portal features the optional Knowledge Management (KM) platform, which consists of the Text Retrieval and Information Extraction (TREX) search engine and Content Management functionality.

A sniffer dog called TREX

SAP provides the TREX server for quickly finding relevant documents (text mining). Although TREX was originally designed for indexing mass data, it is currently also used for searching mySAP CRM Internet Sales catalogs, the Expert Finder in SAP Human Resources, High Performance Analytics and the mySAP PLM document management system.

TREX can search documents—from simple text documents to HTML to Microsoft Word or PowerPoint—and index files that are stored on file servers or Web servers, in Lotus Notes, Microsoft Exchange, a EMC^2 Documentum[3] system, or in the Content Management of the SAP Enterprise Portal, among others.

Error-tolerant search

Besides the usual search engine functions, such as "error-tolerant" and "similar" searching, which are used to find misspelled terms (fuzzy search), and the inclusion of different grammatical forms (linguistic search), TREX also provides functions for automatically classifying documents into taxonomies (i.e. hierarchically-structured categories).

Multilingual search

TREX also supports a wide range of languages, including Danish, Dutch, English, Finnish, French, German, Italian, Portuguese, Norwegian, Spanish, Swedish, Korean, Japanese, and Chinese (traditional and simplified).

Technically speaking, TREX consists of two parts: the Index Management Server (IMS) and the TREX search engine (or another index server software that fulfils the specifications of the SAP search server API). The IMS saves its indices in the file system as simple files. If several parallel Index Management Servers are used, operating-system tools have to be employed to synchronize the indices.

TREX is one of the few exceptions to the rule that all SAP NetWeaver components use the SAP Web AS as the standard runtime platform. This is because it comes with its own Java engine and therefore, it only requires a Java environment.

The TREX Web server accepts requests via HTTP. A TREX queue server manages the queue, and the TREX processor provides the linguistic functionality and converts the documents to a unified format (mime type filtering) before the indexing occurs. The TREX index server saves the search and classification indices, and processes the actual index, search and classification requests. All these components can be installed either together or separately. In case of a distributed installation, the TREX name server forwards requests to the correct computer.

3 *www.documentum.com.*

TREX is purely a service provider for other applications, and therefore does not have its own user interface (except for the TREX administrator). Clients for Java, ABAP, Python, and C++ are available so that it can also be called by other applications.

Other optional KM components are the Content Management component, which supports the creation (authoring, workflow, storage) and display of content, and its distribution (subscription, publishing) across different repositories; and the Repository Manager, which enables access to the various file storage locations (and on which the TREX Java client runs). Although this multitude of options may sound somewhat complex, a single shared set-up routine means that installing the whole system is actually quite simple.

Business packages

The Collaboration Business Package supports collaboration in geographically dispersed teams via discussion forums (collaboration rooms) and mechanisms for feedback, reviewing, real-time collaboration (application sharing, chat, instant messaging, and so forth), and synchronous collaboration (task-lists, group calendar, etc.). An application sharing server is used for this very purpose.

Other Business Packages consist of collections of roles, relationships, and iViews, relevant to the specific business scenarios at hand. The large-scale modifications and in-house development inherent in other portal products are simply rendered unnecessary with the introduction of these business packages. Included with these packages is the PDK, which supports the development of Java and .NET applications.

Portal infrastructure

Both the Enterprise Portal Server and the components for Content Management and collaboration are fully implemented in Java and therefore run on the J2EE Engine of the Web AS (see Figure 1.5).

SAP Enterprise Portal data (pages, iViews, personalization and access authorization data of the user) is stored in a database. The Portal Content Directory provides the necessary storage environment. The Portal Content Studio and tools such as iView Wizard, iView Catcher, Unifier Wizard, and the other parts of the PDK allow developers to create portal content without writing a single line of code.

SAP Enterprise Portal is Unicode-enabled and supports Web services. This allows connectors and portal services—such as user management—to be called as Web services, for example. Conversely, iViews can use Web services.

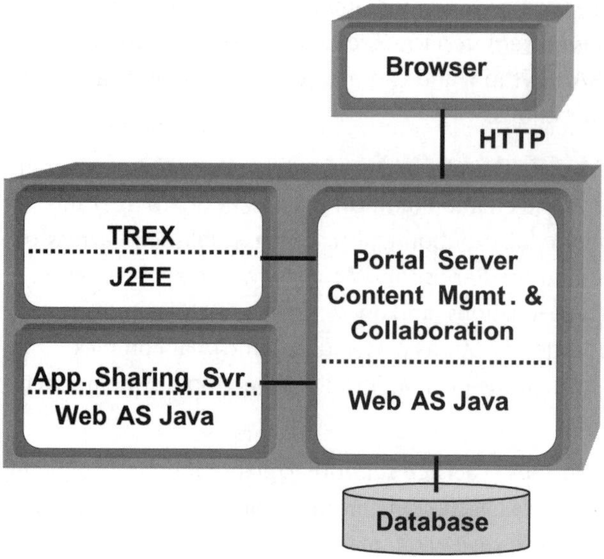

Figure 1.5 Components of the Enterprise Portal

Because the SAP Enterprise Portal is one of the central components in a mySAP system landscape, the infrastructure design of its components should include some redundancy. In live systems, the Application Sharing Server, as well as the TREX, should be installed on a separate Java instance for performance reasons.

1.4 SAP Mobile Infrastructure

The SAP Mobile Infrastructure (MI) uses replication mechanisms to enable mobile access to NetWeaver components and the mySAP Business Suite, even without an online connection.

Mobile applications

SAP provides a range of mobile applications as part of mySAP Mobile Business:

- Mobile Sales for Handhelds is a CRM solution for salespersons. Mobile Sales for Handhelds is also available as an independent ERP solution.
- Mobile Services for Handhelds is the Customer Relationship Management (CRM) solution for service and sales staff.
- Mobile Time and Travel is an Employee Self Service (ESS) for time management and travel costs management.
- Mobile Procurement controls the procurement process.

- Mobile Asset Management (MAM) supports service technicians in managing and updating maintenance data. There are two forms of MAM: one for Customer Service (CS), and the other for Plant Maintenance.
- Mobile Supply Chain Management (SCM) is intended for mobile integration into the logistics chain.

In addition, enterprises can also use the SAP NetWeaver Developer Studio (NWDS) to develop their own mobile applications. As a client programming model, SAP Mobile Infrastructure (SAP MI) supports Java Server Pages (JSP) and the Abstract Window Toolkit (AWT, part of the Java Foundation Classes, JFC). It also supports the microITS model from SAP ME 1.0. This provides a range of Java APIs, such as APIs that enable connections to peripheral devices, and APIs that enable tracing and XML parsing.

SAP MI is made up of MI clients, the MI server, and a database (see Figure 1.6).

The SAP MI client runs on the local mobile terminal and has a Web server, a database, and its own process logic. **SAP MI client**

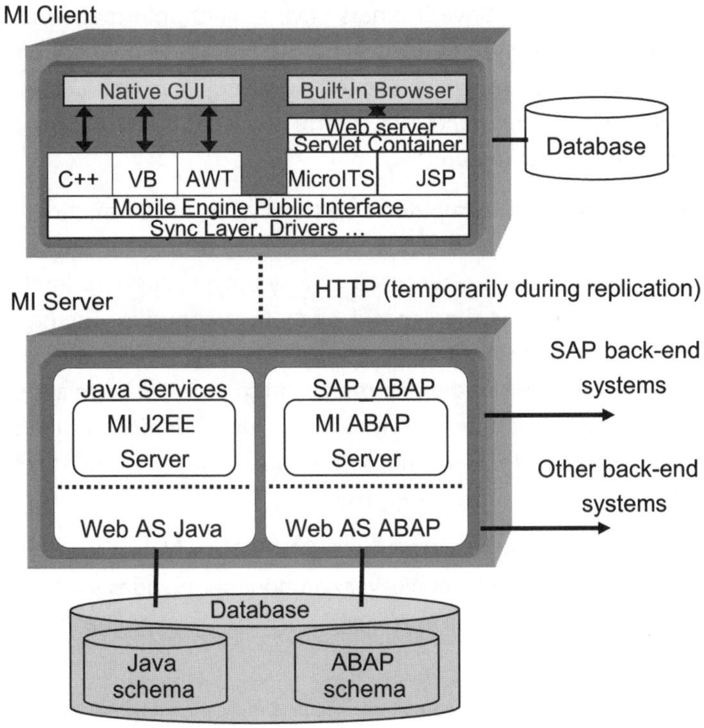

Figure 1.6 Components of the Mobile Infrastructure

SAP MI server The SAP MI server is based on the SAP Web AS and has both a Java and an ABAP component.

The SAP MI Java server is responsible for automatically installing the SAP MI client when the user logs on the first time. When doing so, it determines which components and drivers are needed by each device. It also gives the system administrator the option of centrally managing the mobile devices.

The SAP MI ABAP server is responsible for synchronizing the applications and for replicating the data between the mobile device and the back-end systems. In this process, an individual data package is compiled for each device ("data allocation"), the system determines which data has to be replicated and when this should occur (delta comparison), and any conflicts that may be detected are resolved (conflict management). The data is transferred in compressed form and is encoded using 128-bit RDS encryption[4].

1.5 SAP Business Intelligence

In today's intensely competitive business environment, information is a central factor in the success of enterprises. The fund of know-how and information in an enterprise, which has to be properly managed and utilized, is called *Business Intelligence* (BI), a term coined at the beginning of the 1990s by the Gartner Group.

Business Intelligence It refers to the process of computer aided analyzing of information in order to support business decisions within the enterprise. Management Information System (MIS) is often used as a synonym. Business Intelligence is implemented using the concept of data warehousing. The basic principle of data warehousing is quite simple: collecting data from all the various transaction systems in the enterprise, putting this data into a separate database, and formatting it so that it provides a unified, seamless and consistent view of the customers, business processes, and other aspects of the daily work of the enterprise.

A warehouse for information The SAP Business Information Warehouse (SAP BW), which is the most proven and most widely used NetWeaver component, provides the technical foundation of SAP Business Intelligence. SAP BW is an online analyt-

4 Remote Data Services (RDS) is a completely secured replication and synchronization solution for authenticated and encrypted data transfer. RDS' security mechanisms allow using the Internet without the concerns of data loss, pilferage or malicious impersonation.

ical processing (OLAP) system. It enables multidimensional analysis of large volumes of current and historical data from various business perspectives.

OLAP systems that are used for the differentiated analysis of data sets, the size of which can often be measured in terabytes, are very demanding on the infrastructure, especially on the database server and the storage subsystems. Therefore, an intelligent database design and the selective creation of indices and pre-aggregated data have a considerable effect on performance. The loading processes are another area with great optimization potential.

The extracting, transforming, and loading (ETL) is an important part of SAP BW functionality. SAP BW is not restricted to SAP systems for its sources; it can also use many other enterprise applications, such as Oracle and NCR Teradata[5] databases. Relying on its pre-defined data structures and analyses (Business Content), the extensive modifications and in-house development that are necessary with other data mart products are largely superfluous in SAP BW.

The comprehensive SAP BW Business Content contains preconfigured, role-based, and task-based information models. These models contain roles, workbooks, queries, InfoSources, InfoCubes, ODS objects, key figures, characteristics, update rules, and extractors for mySAP solutions and other selected applications.

This way SAP BW Business Content makes rolling out the solution quicker and more cost-effective, and it also comes with a model that can be used as a guide in the rollout process, giving the customer the advantage of benefiting from past rollout experiences.

What are InfoCubes?

Unlike an OLTP system, where all data sets are stored in standardized form for the sake of consistency, BW, being an OLAP system, is based on entities known as InfoCubes, which are special data structures that provide a multidimensional view of data.

Technically, an InfoCube consists of fact tables and dimension tables, which are stored in a relational database. The fact tables contain numerical data (such as quantity, price, and discount) and keys that reference an associated combination of characteristics. The dimension tables contain all existing combinations of characteristics, with one entry for every combination. Characteristics can be articles, customers, or buyers, for exam-

5 *http://www.teradata.com.*

ple. The dimension tables are sorted according to related characteristics, to ensure that the tables do not become overly large. One dimension table could contain, for example, customer, region, and industry, while another could contain article number, color, and size.

For example, if a query is started for all articles sold in a particular region and in a particular color, all matching entries are first selected in the dimension tables. Then, the system returns all the matching keys in the fact tables, which can then be rapidly searched for suitable entries. This pre-filtered data model allows reports to be executed in BW much faster than in an OLTP system. This data model is also referred to as a star schema, because of the star-shaped arrangement of dimension tables around a fact table.

A store of key figures

Unlike the historical original data, which is loaded directly from the source systems, BW calculates and stores key figures derived from the underlying data. These figures are known as aggregates. Thus, for example, costs and turnover can be calculated from sales data. One could say that an aggregate is the same as a classic report, because it answers the question: Who sold what, when, and where?

Aggregates do not have to be newly calculated ad-hoc for every query. Instead, they are calculated directly after the data is loaded and are available immediately after a query is made. Another advantage of key figures is that all the original data sets do not have to be accessed when analyses or reports are run where only individual totals are required.

The conception and implementation of multidimensional InfoCubes is very time-consuming. Therefore, SAP provides industry-specific, predefined InfoCubes as Business Content with SAP BW. These InfoCubes cover the typical issues specific to each industry, such as the automobile industry.

Neither live R/3 systems nor SAP BW InfoCubes can store all original documents indefinitely, as this would place an enormous burden on the storage systems and computing infrastructures. Therefore, data is compressed when it is loaded into the InfoCubes, and the source data is deleted from the system after a specified storage period (for example, after a fiscal year).

Operational Data Store

In certain cases, a detailed analysis of up-to-the-minute data is required with such a high level of detail (in other words, a high level of granularity) that the capacities of InfoCubes are exceeded. For example, a retail firm may want to analyze its sales figures for the previous day. To do this, it would use the Operational Data Store (ODS) provided by SAP BW. Unlike InfoCubes, ODS objects consist of normal (that is, flat) tables.

Therefore, InfoCubes are optimal for analyzing large historical datasets in order to use the results in making strategic decisions, while ODS objects are optimal for analyzing smaller current datasets "fresh from the catch" in order to use the results in making day-to-day operational decisions.

Relieving the load on live systems

In live R/3 systems, the database server and its I/O systems can become severely overloaded when analyses of large data sets are carried out. SAP BW relieves the load on such systems. For example, if monthly financial reports are created in the R/3 system, every table has to be accessed that contains cost accounting data. These tables contain millions of data records, each of which has to be read in its entirety, because this data has a flat structure. This process can take several hours in a large system.

For typical mass data, such as cash register data for retail systems, outsourcing the process to BW is a significant step that helps keep the R/3 system database at a manageable size.

Compressing data

The granularity of the data is a central factor in allocating the required disk space in SAP BW. When data is extracted from live R/3 or third-party systems, the data records should be compressed (aggregated) if possible. If the data is not compressed, the SAP BW database would exceed the source system, because it contains derived and redundant data as well. For example, cash till figures for the sales of certain articles can be compressed into a daily sum. Should the original data records still be required for individual analyses, they can be accessed in the source system using a drill-down function.

Strategic Enterprise Management

Enterprises can use BW as a planning tool as well as for reporting purposes. SAP Strategic Enterprise Management (SEM) is a function that is integrated into SAP BW as an add-on. It provides a Management Cockpit with Balanced Scorecards (BSC) and Key Performance Indicators (KPIs). SEM also provides planning and simulation tools, a Shareholder Information Management system, and the functionality to consolidate financial information, according to legal requirements of GAAP, IAS, HGB etc.

Precalculation Service

The optional SAP BW Precalculation Service accelerates the creation of reports as the necessary calculations are not ad-hoc, but are carried out in advance. It is used only with the Business Explorer Analyzer (BEx Analyzer) and BI Information Broadcasting.

Information Broadcasting SAP BI Information Broadcasting is not the electronic form of the "company grapevine" for spreading rumors! It consists of Web services for automatically distributing individual reports via email or portal. It provides functions such as subscriptions, feedback, discussions, evaluations, and TREX-supported searching.

BW frontend The Business Explorer (BEx) is the SAP BW user interface for reporting and analysis. It consist of the SAP GUI for Windows and a BW extension, and allows you to create and save analyses and their results as Excel workbooks.

Also, the SAP BW Web Application Designer can be used to create reports that can be displayed as Web applications in the browser, or as iViews in the SAP Enterprise Portal. Here, too, the increasing interweaving of SAP NetWeaver components is evident in the many predefined iViews for reporting within the scope of BI Business Content.

BW infrastructure In terms of infrastructure, BW consists of the SAP Web AS and a database instance.

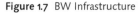

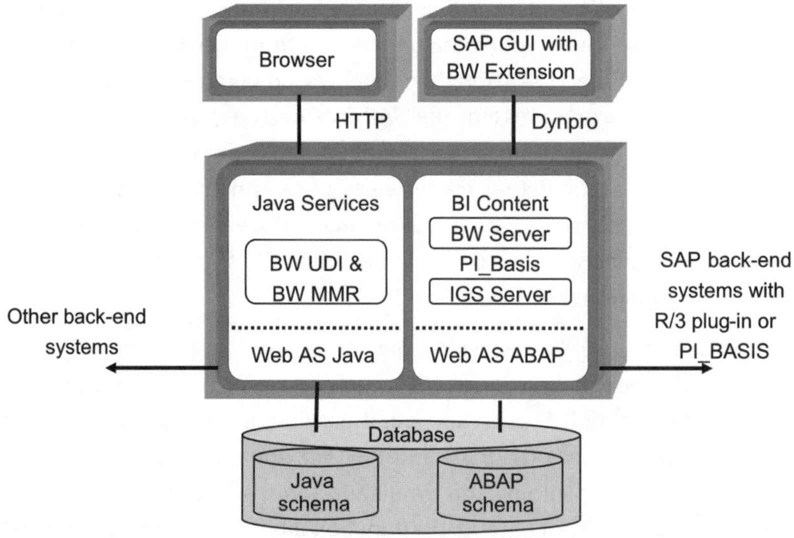

Figure 1.7 BW Infrastructure

ABAP components SAP BW, as one of the first "spin-offs" of R/3, is fully programmed in ABAP. Therefore, if only SAP systems are to be used as data sources, the ABAP part of the SAP Web AS is sufficient as a platform for the BW server. You also have the option of installing BW Business Content (see the right-hand side of Figure 1.7). The R/3 plug-in or PI_BASIS has to be installed on the SAP R/3 systems used as data sources.

In order for BW to connect to non-SAP data sources, the Java part of the SAP Web AS (see the left-hand side of Figure 1.7), and the BW components SAP BI Universal Data Integration (BI UDI) and SAP BI Meta Model Repository (BI MMR) are required. UDI provides connectors for XMLA, JDBC[6] drivers, and a BI Java Development Kit.

Java components

The Business Content provided with BW comprises plug-ins and extractors as well as preconfigured InfoCubes and reports. The costs of connecting source systems, which usually constitute two-thirds of the budget in conventional data warehouse projects, are therefore significantly reduced.

High Performance Analytics for SAP NetWeaver

To provide the ability to query greater amounts of data with an easy to use interface and to further enhance the deployment of business analytics; SAP introduced High Performance Analytics (HPA) for SAP NetWeaver. The solution based on SAP Netweaver04s release and the TREX 7.0 engine, extracts information from BW InfoCubes and "massages" the data into rows and indexes for analysis which is stored in Linux file systems. During the "data massage" process the data is reduced to about 1/3 of it's original data size. The data is then sliced and loaded into the memory of multiple small computer nodes (for example blades). Note that data change in the BI 7.0 InfoCubes then incremental changes can be sent to TREX and the incremental changes are uploaded into memory.

BW 7.0 automatically determines which queries can be performed on the HPA engine, and which ones have to go to the normal BW OLAP engine. HPA queries are then sent to TREX which executes the query across all the nodes available to provide for outstanding performance. Results from the query are then sent back to BW and displayed on the GUI tool in use (e.g. SAP GUI or Portal iView, all supported BW GUI tools can be used).

If an existing BW cannot be upgraded to version 7.0, it is possible to install a BW 7.0 with HPA as a "black box" besides the existing BW. Data that should use the HPA mechanisms will then be extracted from the existing BW to BW 7.0.

The ability to load this data into memory across the nodes is made possible by the extended memory capability of the Intel XEON technology

6 Java standard API for databases. *www.java.sun.com* contains over 200 JDBC drivers for ADABAS, Clipper, DB2, dBase, Excel, FoxPro, Informix, Ingres, InterBase, LDAP, MS SQL Server, MS Access, Oracle, Paradox, Redbrick, SAS, Sybase, Teradata, Text (CSV, tab-separated etc.), TinySQL, VSAM, XML, and others.

coupled with software from Intel that allows for sharing of query load across multiple blades. A key feature is that to expand or provide more processing power you just plug in more blades which when configured to work with the solution then expand the processing capability of the TREX solution. Initial tests have shown a near linear scalability for the TREX servers.

This allows for very large tables with billions of rows to be analyzed extremely fast. The TREX index is stored in a file system. Using this process once the index is created, there is no access to any database. The OLAP processor will get all required data from the index file.

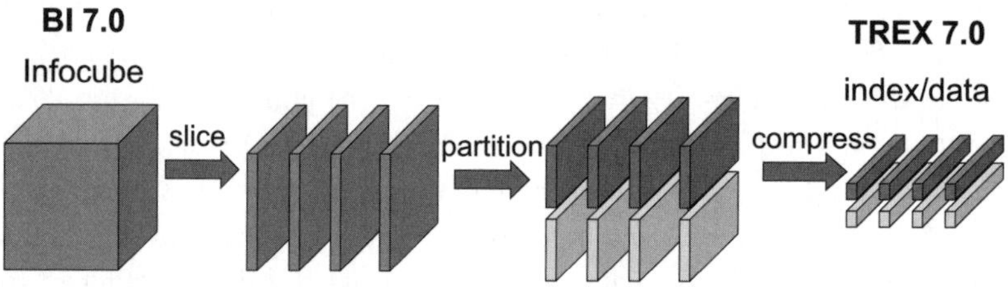

Figure 1.8 High Performance Analytics Concept

HPA for NetWeaver is not a replacement of BW, it is an appliance which provides the capability to do ad hoc reporting of selected data from BW Infocubes. The BW environment will continue to be required to support a majority of analysis and data aggregation. Also the normal data extraction and transformation process that collects data from the source systems and transforms them into info cubes does not change.

However the reporting in HPA is indeed high performance and provides users with an ability to look at data in ways that wouldn't have been feasible before. For example the ability to analyze an Infocube[7] with 1 Billion rows, select 1 Million, and aggregate data into 60 or so rows in less than 1 second as demonstrated at Sapphire Boston 2005.

1.6 SAP Knowledge Warehouse

SAP Knowledge Warehouse (KW) is another of the Knowledge Management components of the SAP Enterprise Portal (TREX, Content Management, and so forth). It is used to create, manage, and distribute documentation, training materials, and manuals, especially in the areas of quality management, training, and online help.

7 Real live data provided by HP for the development partnership with SAP for HPA.

A warehouse for knowledge

Many companies use KW to hold SAP training courses, since SAP provides the materials for its training courses, including Instructor Guides, as a (fee-based) extra with KW. This means that original SAP training materials can be used for both in-house and company-specific training courses. On a specific day once every quarter, SAP KW customers receive, free of charge, new and updated documentation for all solutions in the mySAP Business Suite or SAP training materials (which requires a separate license).

By integrating the Microsoft Office applications Word, PowerPoint, and Visio, all content stored in SAP KW can be created and adapted quickly and easily. SAP KW also features functions that provide translators with version management functions and access to the SAP terminology database.

You can also use KW to create a quality manual in accordance with EN ISO 9000 and 14000, for example, for which SAP provides suitable templates.

KW infrastructure

KW infrastructure consists of the SAP Web AS, a database instance for the content structures, and the associated user permissions, and the Knowledge Provider (KPro). If the KW is relatively small and is mainly used to store information such as training courses, the data itself can be stored directly in the KW database.

SAP Content Server

For large Knowledge Warehouse installations, a separate maxDB Instance (formerly SAP DB) is used to store the information (such as large documents, CAD files, and so on). The SAP DB in this case is managed by the Content Server. Alternatively, a normal file system can also be used as a file storage system for the SAP Content Server.

With distributed systems, the information can also be distributed on local cache servers. If a requested document is not available on the cache server, it is then requested from the Content Server. This process increases the speed for accessing large files and reduces the network load on remote connections (see Figure 1.8).

Performance Assessment Workbench

The Performance Assessment Workbench (PAW) is a tool for evaluating the success of training courses. It records the performance of course participants in the form of tests or assessments, and also provides for instructor feedback from participants via a form.

SAP Internet Knowledge Servlet

The SAP Internet Knowledge Servlet (IKS) controls how content is displayed, and the communication between the SAP Web AS and the SAP Content Server.

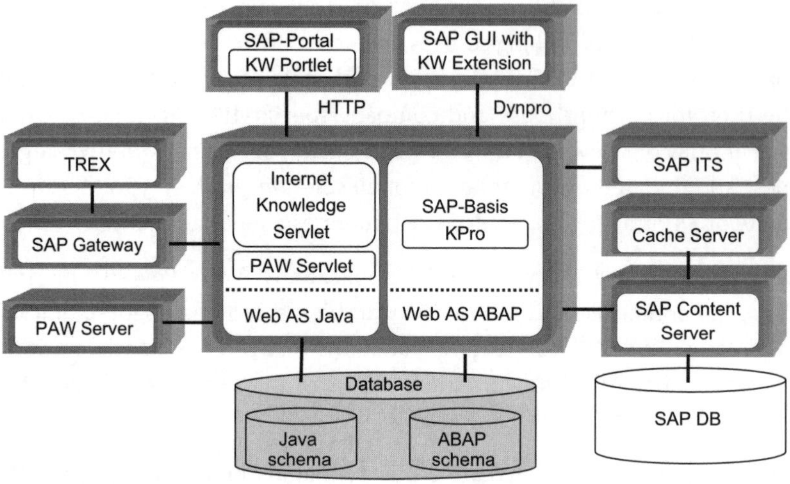

Figure 1.9 Knowledge Warehouse Infrastructure

The SAP Gateway is required only for the connection to the TREX search engine unless the SAP Content Server is installed on its own computer.

1.7 SAP Master Data Management

Maintenance of Master Data

Master data is data that is not connected to any specific transaction, such as customer addresses and product descriptions. Enterprises usually have several different IT systems and thus several different master data management systems, which often leads to a situation where the master data in the various systems is redundant and in incompatible formats.

The process of comparing master data from the different systems in order to ensure consistency involves complex distributed processes. Typically, no comparisons are carried out; the data is simply entered multiple times. This process results not only in unnecessary duplicate work, but also, almost invariably, in inconsistent master data with different spellings; for example, of customer addresses or names of parts.

For example, if every subsidiary of a company has its own purchasing system, there is the risk that subsidiaries may purchase the same part from the same supplier at a different price in each case. The company cannot bargain in an optimized way, as the part may have a different name or number in each system, with the result that company-wide reports show several individual totals rather than the total sum for the part.

SAP Master Data Management (MDM) is designed to tackle this problem. MDM allows companies to consolidate, harmonize and centralize their entire stock of master data. Its main benefit is the reduction of costs for master data maintenance and repair. It also ensures the consistency of enterprise data and thus enhances the quality of the information in an enterprise.

Master Data Consolidation

Master data consolidation (Content Consolidation, CC) involves identifying duplicate master records in the various systems in an IT landscape and eliminating the duplicates where necessary. The master data records have to be extracted from the source systems (Master Data Clients, MDC) and loaded to the Master Data Server (MDS). The Periodic Inbound Collector (PIC) is used for regular load processes.

One possible use of MDM Content Consolidation would be to compare lists of suppliers with the goal of identifying identical or duplicate master data. The data that is used for the comparison could be the name and address, the VAT ID number (in Europe), or the Dun & Bradstreet number. These "dependencies" (supplier X in system A equals supplier Y in system B) can be transferred to the SAP Business Information Warehouse (SAP BW) in the form of ID mapping data and used there for a Global Spend Analysis, for example (to answer the question: "How much are we spending in total on products from this supplier?").

Master Data Harmonization

Master Data Harmonization (MDH) is used to ensure that master data is universally consistent in all systems of an enterprise. To do this, the master data that was consolidated in the previous scenario is replicated back to the source systems.

In this process, master data attributes that are relevant only to a specific system or systems can be maintained in those systems. For example, the name and address of a customer could be made consistent across the whole enterprise, while individual price conditions could be entered in the CRM system only.

Central Master Data Maintenance

Central Master Data Management (CMDM) is suitable for enterprises whose organizational structures do not permit master data objects to be created or modified locally.

For example, if an employee needs to create a new customer in CRM or a new material in R/3, he uses the SAP Enterprise Portal to send a request that the master data in question be created. MDM automatically checks the request and stores it in the workflow inbox of the responsible person, who fills in any missing data. The system then checks that no identical object already exists, and if everything is in order, creates the complete data record. A confirmation message is then sent to the person who created the request.

MDM infrastructure

The master data server is the central component of the MDM. It centrally controls the master data of the whole enterprise and is based on an SAP Web AS with Unicode.

The Content Integrator interconnects master data objects in different systems via object characteristics, and ensures that identical master data objects can be identified and duplicate records eliminated.

MDM adaptors are used to connect different systems.

MDM requires the SAP Exchange Infrastructure (SAP XI) and the SAP Enterprise Portal. While MDM configures and controls the publish-and-subscribe mechanism for the data comparison, SAP XI converts the data and ensures that it is distributed in a consistent manner. The portal is the user interface; the Enterprise Portal plug-in provides special MDM iViews for this purpose. The Integrated Product and Process Engineering (IPPE) function is also required.

SAP recommends the use of an SAP Internet Transaction Server (ITS) to support the Customizing of the ID mapping. The ITS is an integrated component of the Web AS from Release 6.40.

MDM has its own database. An SAP BW is also required for MDM Content Consolidation, but is optional for the other scenarios. Portal Content Management (CM) and the Text Retrieval and Classification (TREX) search engine are required for MDH and CMDM.

We also recommend that you install the MDM master data server and the Content Integrator on one server (add-in installation) to minimize the number of Remote Function Calls (RFCs).

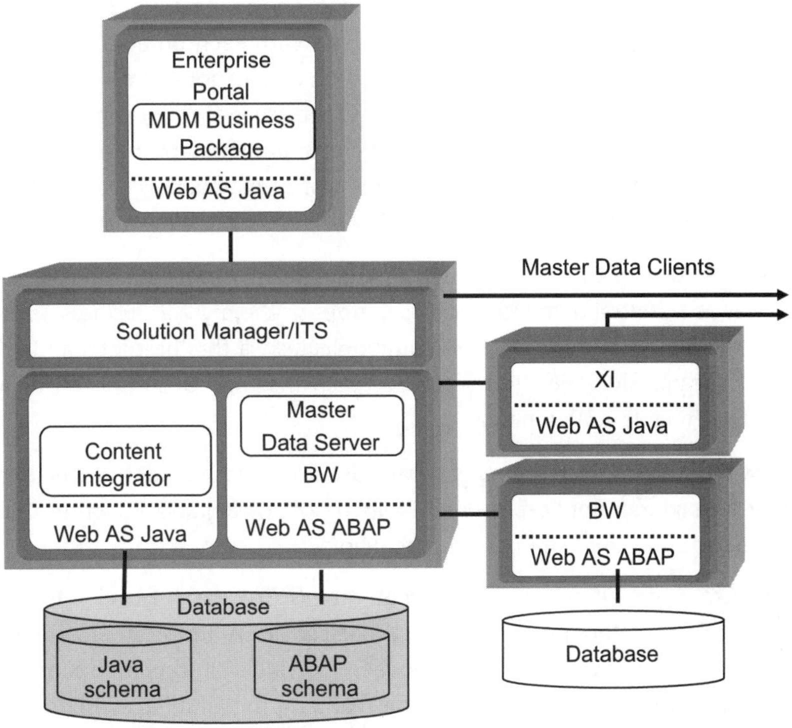

Figure 1.10 Master Data Management (Technical View)

1.8 SAP Exchange Infrastructure

The problem of communication between the different applications in an enterprise (known as Enterprise Application Integration, EAI) is not a new one. It has existed as long as companies have used computers for anything more than accounting. R/2 and R/3 tackled the problem by providing all the business functions of an enterprise in one monolithic application.

However, for both organizational and technical reasons, more than one SAP system is often necessary. Also, the high level of company mergers and acquisitions in recent times has meant that many IT departments wanted to ensure that ERP systems from different manufacturers could communicate with each other. With the advent of department-specific applications such as CRM and SCM, the increase in the number of enterprise applications that need to be integrated has multiplied.

Costly point-to-point connections

In most cases, a dedicated point-to-point connection has to be set up for every communication relationship, and an application-specific interface has to be programmed for each end of every connection. Even if the number of applications that exchange data with each other is relatively small, this still creates a large number of connections and interfaces. Despite standards such as Electronic Data Interchange (EDI) and RosettaNet,[8] the time and money required to create and operate these connections is considerable. Estimates put the cost of maintaining just a single point-to-point connection up to $120,000 per year.

SAP's answer to this problem is the SAP Exchange Infrastructure (XI). It serves as a central data hub for all solutions in the mySAP Business Suite and third-party systems. SAP XI communicates via the Internet standard HTTP. Application-specific content of each message is transferred as a freely-definable XML schema.

New SAP developments now generally use SAP XI instead of the previous SAP procedures Application Link Enabling (ALE), Remote Function Call (RFC), and Intermediate Documents (IDoc).

Data pipelines and information silos

The Exchange Infrastructure concept moves SAP far beyond the EAI approaches of other manufacturers. While classic EAI tools can be used to create communication channels between individual "information silos" in an enterprise (although much of the manual programming work is still required for the "pipework" within the silos), SAP provides a platform for integrating business processes across enterprise boundaries. This enables the internal connections between SAP systems to be provided as standard via Business Content.[9]

Enterprise Process Integration

This approach allows a significant reduction of implementation costs and, in particular, the time and effort required to modify business processes in EAI scenarios. SAP XI is therefore the basis of Enterprise Process Integration (EPI).

The SAP XI Integration Builder is a development environment that enables developers to design business scenarios that are made up of various integration processes. The technical parameters of a business scenario, such as the rules for routing and for transforming message content (mappings), can be described independently of a specific system landscape. In the case of routing, SAP XI checks which system sent a particular message and to which system the message is to be forwarded. The map-

8 An initiative of the high-tech industry set up in 1998, named after the Rosetta Stone, which enabled the decoding of Egyptian hieroglyphics.

9 The authors of the book *SAP NetWeaver for Dummies* have aptly described this as "pre-packaged integration".

ping function ensures that the data is translated into a format that the recipient system can understand. This "integration know-how" about the processes ("shared collaboration knowledge") is stored in the central integration builder (Integration Repository and Integration Directory).

Connections made easy

There are various methods for connecting SAP solutions to XI. For older SAP systems, the Integration Engine relies on adapters to communicate with these systems. Adapters convert IDocs and RFCs to the XI-specific XML/SOAP[10] protocol and vice versa.

Proxy programs

Since Release 6.20 of Web AS, SAP systems can communicate with other application via proxies, which are programs that receive messages as a 'substitute for the application, like a gateway. The concept of proxy generation enables developers to build new interfaces simply and easily. For this purpose, a platform-independent description of the interface is created in Web Services Description Language (WSDL) format in the Integration Repository. From this description, a source code prototype is generated in either ABAP, or Java. The proxies created in this way are then installed on the source and target systems. From then on, these proxies handle the communication with XI.

Proxy framework

The proxy framework can also be used without XI for simple integration scenarios. If both business partners have an XI system, they can communicate directly with each other via the XI Message Protocol.

Adapters for every occasion

With XI, SAP provides a wide range of adapters for specific applications:

- The RFC adapter is used to connect systems that have an RFC interface.
- The Plain HTTP Adapter is used for systems that can exchange XML messages via HTTP.
- The file adapter connects systems that can communicate only by exchanging flat files. This adapter converts the files to XML messages.
- When the JDBC adapter is used to connect a system or a database, it also converts the data to an XML message.
- The Java Message Service (JMS) adapter connects systems via a JMS provider such as MQSeries or SonicMQ.
- The SOAP adapter is used to connect Web service providers or clients.

10 SOAP stands for Simple Object Access Protocol. It is based on XML and is used to call services remotely. To do this, parameters are converted to an XML text format (marshalling) and vice versa.

- The marketplace adapter connects electronic marketplaces.
- The SAP Partner Connectivity Kit (SAP PCK) is intended for smaller business partners.

SAP partners such as Seeburger (industry-specific EDI adapters), Webmethods (Oracle, Siebel, PeopleSoft, Baan, and so on), and iWay (UCCnet) provide adapters for connecting third-party systems or individual applications. SAP provides adapters for RosettaNet and CIDX.

XI infrastructure SAP XI is based on the Web AS, and requires both Java and the ABAP Engine. Because the Internet protocols used in XI (HTTP, XML, SOAP, and so on) are based on Unicode, as is the Internet itself, a Unicode Web AS is a prerequisite for installing and operating XI. Since Release 3.0 of SAP XI, a System Landscape Directory (SLD) is also required.

As purely an infrastructure component, XI has no users (except for the applications to which it is connected). Therefore, a SAP GUI is required for administration purposes only.

XI components SAP XI comprises the following components: Integration Builder (Integration Repository and Integration Directory), Integration Server (Integration Engine, Adapter Engine and Business Process Engine), Runtime Workbench and System Landscape Directory. The Integration Engine identifies recipients (routing) and converts the message content that is transferred between sender and recipient (mapping).

Adapter engines The IDoc adapter and the Plain HTTP Adapter are installed as standard in a Web AS installation. Adapter engines provide other adapters, such as the following:

- The Plain J2SE Adapter Engine supports file adapters, and JMS, JDBC, and SOAP adapters.
- The adapter engine also supports marketplace, RFC and RNIF adapters (for RossettaNet and CIDX), and Java proxy servers and Java proxy runtime.

Both engines have various advantages and disadvantages, depending on the scenario. While the adapter engine must always be installed on the J2EE Engine of the Web AS, any standard Java runtime is sufficient for the Plain J2SE Adapter Engine. Therefore, the adapter engine is better integrated into NetWeaver and can be centrally configured and monitored.

Both adapter engines can be installed centrally on the XI server or on their own Web AS instances (see Figure 1.10).

An XI server installation (which is the default) has the advantage that no further installation work is required, and it is very suitable for development and test systems.

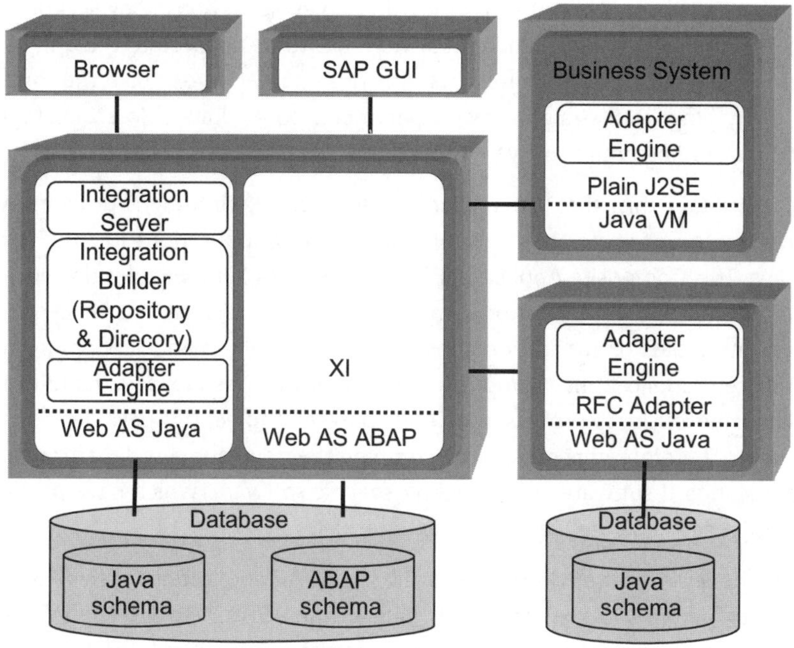

Figure 1.11 Exchange Infrastructure (Technical View)

Installing the adapter engines on their own machine can improve performance, although a complete Web AS J2EE Engine must also be installed in this case.

If the J2SE Adapter Engine is installed on the target system, only an HTTP connection between the adapter and the Integration Server is required. This is a good idea in heterogeneous system landscapes with different operating systems and authorization concepts, or for connections on WAN networks with firewalls.

Partner Connectivity Kit

Another option is the SAP Partner Connectivity Kit (PCK), which can be used to connect systems of partner enterprises that do not have their own XI installation. The PCK consists of a Web AS Java platform and the XI Adapter Engine, and provides a file adapter, a JMS adapter, and a JDBC adapter. The system must be installed in the partner enterprise's system and is licensed separately by SAP.

1.9 SAP NetWeaver Development Environment

One of the main reasons for using standard software solutions is to avoid as much as possible the time and costs involved in in-house development. However, it is not usually possible to avoid in-house development altogether, since even standard software has to be adapted to the unique environment of each business system. This adaptation can take the form of anything from straightforward parameter configuration (customizing) to developing entire software modules.

Composite Application Framework

To facilitate this, the NetWeaver development environment provides a complete system for the development of Web applications in ABAP or Java. This Composite Application Framework (CAF) also enables developers to develop combined or composite applications such as SAP xApps. This new class of application consists of functionalities and services from different applications. Composite applications can be flexibly adapted to changing business processes without the need for costly new development. Therefore, it is possible to combine the development departments for standard software and company-specific software, which have previously been separate areas in many enterprises.

Developing ABAP applications

The development environment for classic ABAP applications is the ABAP Development Workbench, which runs on the ABAP Web AS. The Workbench is a robust, integrated development environment for business applications in SAP. In order to use it, the developer only needs access to a SAP GUI.

Developing Java applications

Java is based on open standards, and, thanks to its platform-independence, it is very widely used. However, when used to develop mission-critical applications for enterprises, J2EE shows its limitations quickly. Developers who write Java applications also have to be aware of details on the system level, and these are a distraction from the actual task at hand. Most importantly, however, development and quality assurance are different for enterprise-critical applications than they are for small applets for the PC.

It is for this reason that SAP provides the NetWeaver Developer Studio (NWDS), a professional development environment for Java applications. The Developer Studio is based on the open-source software Eclipse[11] and on tools that have been developed in collaboration with SAP partners. It

---

11 *http://www.eclipse.org/*.

also features all the proven, tried-and-tested concepts of the ABAP Workbench, replicating them for developing enterprise-critical applications in Java form.

Building blocks of software development

SAP provides software development kits (SDKs) for the various technical components of NetWeaver. One example is the Portal Development Kit (PDK), which is a plug-in for the NetWeaver Developer Studio. The Mobile Development Kit (MDK) provides a Java Server Pages library for developing mobile applications, and the BI Java SDK Java provides class libraries and APIs for SAP BW.

The SAP NWDS enables you to create proxy classes for calling ABAP functionalities or BAPIs by simply selecting the relevant ABAP module or BAPI in the target system. The SAP Java Connector (JCo) is a middleware component that facilitates communication between Java and ABAP programs. It supports ABAP program calls by Java (inbound calls) as well as calls in the opposite direction (outbound calls).

Developing Web services

Developers can also use the SAP NWDS to provide the functions of applications that run on the Web AS (publishing, discovering, and accessing) as Web services. For example, a Web service interface could be created for Enterprise Java Beans (EJB). This kind of Web service can be executed directly on the J2EE Engine of the Web AS. Because standards such as XML, SOAP, WSDL, and UDDI (Universal Description Discovery and Integration) are supported, these programs can then access Web services.

Using the WSDL file as input, the Web service proxy generator generates a platform-specific client proxy. The proxy concept enables the developer to concentrate on the functionality, while technical aspects such as the creation of a SOAP message are handled automatically in the proxy implementation.

Software quality assurance

For the purposes of quality assurance, SAP recommends the use of a multi-level quality assurance concept. This is usually based on three separate SAP system installations.

Customizing, parameterization, and all development are carried out in the development system (DEV). To ensure that the development code does not adversely affect the stability of the production system, we strongly recommend that you first conduct a test using a copy of the live data in a preparatory production system. This kind of system is usually referred to as a quality assurance system (QA) or a test system. It is in this system that the release tests for transport requests are carried out before they are transferred into the production system. The QA system is used to perform stability tests on upgrades, and patches to operating systems, databases, SAP releases, and new system drivers.

The actual production system (PRD) contains only released developments for all applications. To ensure that you do not jeopardize the functionality and data consistency of the production system, no development or testing work should be carried out in this system.

Separation ensures stable production systems

This approach of separating systems according to their purpose makes it possible to develop applications and ensure their quality without compromising the integrity and stability of the production system. The separation concept for development, test, and production environments allows each system to evolve in an orderly fashion, but only if the concept is strictly adhered to. Even in very small SAP installations, a system landscape that comprises a development system and a productive system is an absolute minimum requirement. Even if this system landscape causes costs to increase initially, comparisons with the stability of software products that do not have this kind of "built-in" quality assurance show that the costs are worth it.

Non-production systems are free of charge

While license keys are required for non-production systems, the licenses for these systems are free of charge. Such systems also include training systems and so-called evaluation or sandbox systems.

The Transport Management System (TMS) is the link between the various parts of an SAP system landscape and is used to transfer released development work to the next level of the SAP system landscape; for example, from the development system to the test system, and after a successful test to the production system (be aware that no code will be transported from test to production). The TMS also features a sophisticated authorization and tracking system that records information about who makes what changes, and when. This ensures that only checked and released code enters the production SAP systems. Also, the extended Transport Management System (eTMS) allows developers to create a workflow of authorization steps for transports.

Technical infrastructure

In principle, the SAP NetWeaver Developer Studio can be installed on a simple PC, provided that the PC has the required resources. For a complete development system, however, a Java Web AS is required to test the development work.

There are several options here, which depend on the size of a particular development project and the number of developers involved.

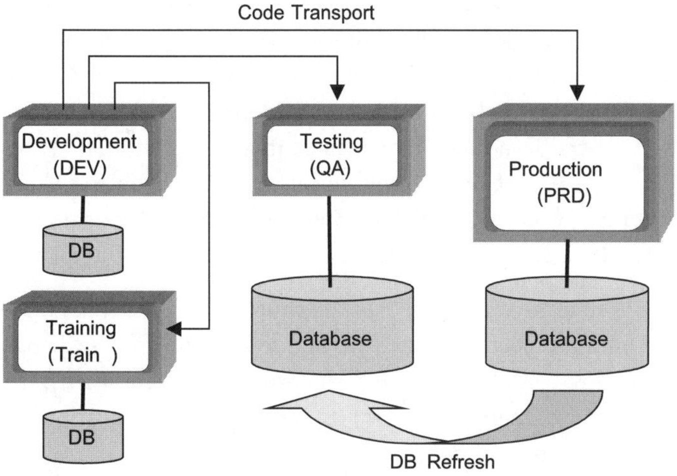

Figure 1.12 Complete System Landscape with Systems for Development, Quality Assurance, and Production, and an Optional Training System

An installation of the Developer Studio with a Java Web AS on a developer's PC provides the developer with a self-contained development and test environment. However, this option can cause problems that impact both the coordination and integration of individual projects.

An installation of the Developer Studio on the developer's PC—with a central Java Web AS that functions as a shared test environment—ensures the interoperability of the various developments (sees Figure 1.12). Another option is to combine the Developer Studio and a Java Web AS on every developer PC with a central Java Web AS as a shared test system.

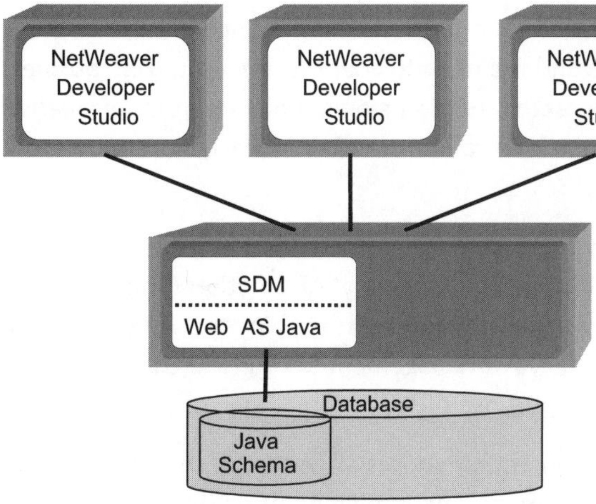

Figure 1.13 Distributed NetWeaver Development Landscape with Shared Java Web AS

Team-oriented development

With this concept, local installations of the SAP NetWeaver Developer Studio use a central Design Time Repository (DTR) for storing the source code. The DTR has a source versioning function and a conflict detection and resolution function; the latter can be used when assigning file names, for example. A central Java dictionary ensures that tables and data types are defined in a consistent way. Communication is based on the Web-Based Distributed Authoring and Versioning (WebDAV) standard, an extension of HTTP.

The Component Build Service (CBS) uses the sources in the DTR to create the required runtime objects (Java archive and so on), which the Change Management Service (CMS) installs on the central J2EE server. Lastly, the Software Deployment Manager (SDM) is responsible for distributing components in the system landscape.

Component-oriented development

The team-oriented concept can be extended to become a model for developing re-usable components. What is most important here is that you clearly define the dependencies between components.

As before, every developer has his or her own development environment with a SAP NetWeaver Developer Studio and a Java SAP Web AS. The Developer Studio is configured for the component model, and the DTR is used as a version control system. A name reservation service helps to avoid name conflicts. This service is provided by the SAP System Landscape Directory (SLD), which is described in the next section.

1.10 SAP Solution Manager

Solution Lifecycle Management

Although a software component is not subject to the same wear and tear that erodes a mechanical part, nonetheless, it does "age" due to ongoing technical developments and the need to adapt to ever-changing business requirements. Therefore, software has its own lifecycle, from its creation to implementation and repair to its eventual replacement by a new, improved version.

The Lifecycle Management function in NetWeaver is implemented in the SAP Solution Manager (SSM). Unlike the mySAP solution Product Lifecycle Management (PLM), which is described in the next chapter, NetWeaver's Solution Lifecycle Management pertains to the lifecycle of software solutions for the purpose of supporting business processes.

Solution Lifecycle Management comprises all phases of the software lifecycle, from design, development, and implementation, to versioning and testing, to daily operations, including administration and change management.

The SAP Solution Manager was developed on the basis of the Computer Center Management System (CCMS), which has existed since R/3 4.0. It's implemented based on a stripped down SAP CRM core. In Chapter 14 we will explain how to integrate SAP Solution Manager into an Enterprise Management environment.

However, while CCMS was a system for monitoring individual SAP systems, the SAP Solution Manager monitors the entire system landscape and the business processes that run on it.

System implementation

The SAP Solution Manager for implementation is an extension of the Accelerated SAP (ASAP) concept and provides configuration guides, documentation, best practices, and scenarios for application configuration. The Test Workbench is used to create and implement test scenarios.

In addition to process-oriented documentation, the Solution Manager also provides mechanisms for project management and distributed customizing across system boundaries. It is also possible to "bend" the use of distributed Customizing in order to adapt authorization roles across the entire system.

System operation

After the implementation phase, SAP Solution Manager supports functions such as system operation handling. Here, the Solution Manager uses the CCMS of the individual SAP systems to implement centralized monitoring of the entire, enterprise-wide SAP system landscape, including all sub-systems, components, databases, proxy servers, and Web servers. The Adaptive Computing Controller (ACC), which is described in detail in Chapter 13, can be used to actively control the process of distributing SAP applications and their components in the system landscape.

Landscape descriptions

The SAP System Landscape Directory (SLD) serves as a central repository for all technical parameters in the system landscape. An important factor here is the description of the possible combinations and interdependencies of the systems and applications.

In accordance with the Common Information Model (CIM) of the Distributed Management Task Force,[12] SLD provides a description of the system landscape (Landscape Description; corresponds to the Core and Systems

12 *http://www.dmtf.org/home*; industry organization for developing and distributing standards for managing desktops, servers, and networks.

Model in CIM) and a description of the installed and installable software (Component Information, corresponds to the Application Model in CIM).

The content of the Landscape Description is created during implementation and is then automatically updated on the individual systems on an ongoing basis; for ABAP components, this is done by CCMS agents with an SLD plug-in, and for Java, via the Data Supplier. The content of the component information, on the other hand, is provided by SAP and is regularly updated via the SAP Master Component Repository via downloads from the SAP Service Marketplace (see Figure 1.13).

Help desk The SAP Support Desk is the third functionality in the Solution Manager, and enables workflow-based handling of error messages within the framework of Problem Management. Information about the relevant system files in the affected systems is automatically included in trouble tickets, so that the support staff member who is dealing with the problem does not waste any time searching for this information. Also, a database containing solutions to known problems is another aid to problem-solving. The SAP Note Assistant supports the implementation of SAP Notes.

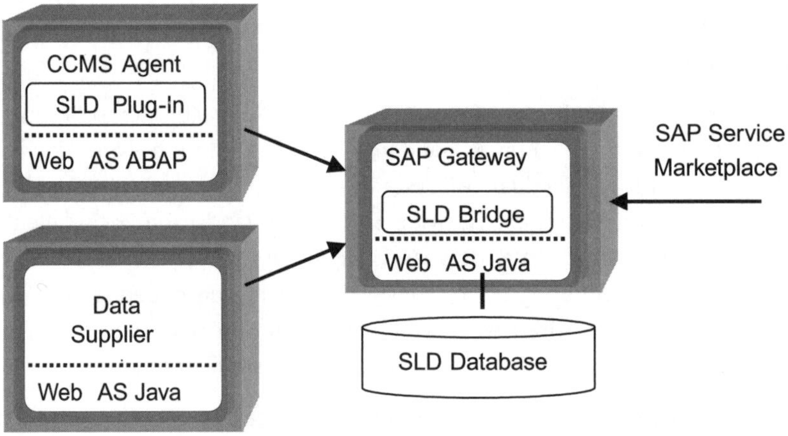

Figure 1.14 Updating the System Landscape Directory

Technical infrastructure The Solution Manager and the SLD are central components that control geographically and logically distributed system landscapes, even if the landscapes are separated by different sub-networks. The benefits for the whole system landscape of a shared Solution Manager and SLD server are simpler administration and consistent data. In principle, however, multiple servers can also be installed in a system landscape.

While the Solution Manager is based on ABAP, the SAP SLD is implemented solely in Java and runs on the Web AS as a J2EE component. It is delivered as standard with the Web AS from Release 6.40.

1.11 User and Authorization Management

As we have seen, NetWeaver systems comprise a range of individual systems and components. Whether each system and component is installed on its own computer, or whether the system is a consolidated one is of little significance. In every case, the user and authorization management is a real technical and organizational challenge on its own.

In the mySAP concept, every user fulfils a specific role that defines which systems, functions, and services he or she needs to access in order to perform his or her tasks within the enterprise. Single Sign-On (SSO) allows users to use various mySAP components without having to log on separately to every system.

The Java and the ABAP personalities of SAP NetWeaver each have their own system for managing the roles and authorizations of the various user groups.

Java—User Management Engine

The SAP User Management Engine (UME) is based on the J2EE Engine of the Web AS and is administrated using the Java tools of the Web AS. The SAP UME provides a centralized user management system for all Java applications, and can be configured for use with data from existing sources, such as the ABAP-based Central User Administration (CUA) or an LDAP directory.

In cases where only Java programs without a connection to ABAP or non-SAP systems are executed on the SAP Web AS, it is worthwhile configuring the UME for use with a database as the data source, for example, Java development systems.

ABAP—Central User Administration

The Central User Administration (CUA) function is based on the ABAP engine of the SAP Web AS and enables developers to replicate user authorizations to other ABAP-based components. For the purposes of integrating Java-based components, such as the Enterprise Portal, the Java User Management Engine (UME) of the Java SAP Web AS is configured in such a way that it can use the CUA system as a data source (see Figure 1.14).

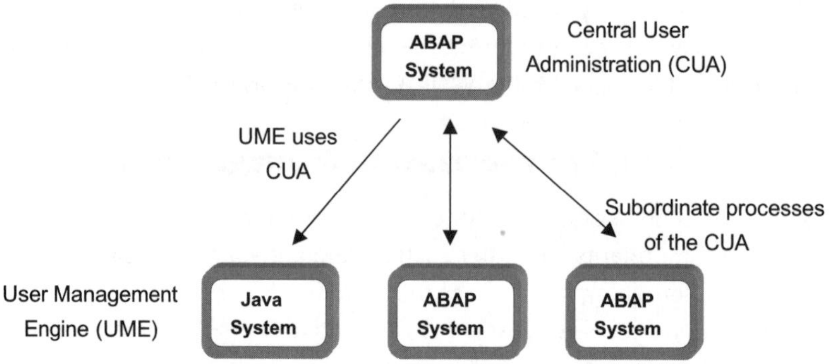

Figure 1.15 Integrating the Central User Administration System

ABAP and Java components can either run on a shared Web AS instance or be installed on separate instances. An example would be an Employee Self-Service (ESS) system (as a Java-based Web dynpro) that is installed on the same computer as an (ABAP-based) HR system.

In the SAP Enterprise Portal, roles and authorization assignments can be managed in the portal and then distributed to the ABAP systems.

If a Java application on a SAP Web AS uses the service of only a single ABAP component, it makes sense to configure the UME in such a way that the user authorizations of the ABAP system are used.

However, if no ABAP services are used in addition to the Java application, installing the ABAP personality of the Web AS—for the sake of user administration only—is of absolutely no benefit. Instead, the Java UME should be configured to use a database.

LDAP

For their cross-application user and authorization administration purposes, many enterprises use products that are based on the Lightweight Directory Access Protocol (LDAP), such as Novell eDirectory, iPlanet from Sun, or Microsoft Active Directory (AD).

The UMEs of various Java components can directly use this kind of corporate LDAP directory as a data source. From SAP Web AS Release 6.10, ABAP CUA data can be exported to an LDAP directory and synchronized on a regular basis, which means that authorizations can then be distributed on other ABAP components (see Figure 1.15). However, passwords cannot be synchronized between CUA and LDAP directories. To avoid a situation where passwords are entered non-centrally in the CUA and the UME, we recommend that you use centralized password entry on the LDAP server and logon tickets on all connected systems.

Using an LDAP directory makes particular sense in system landscapes that include non-SAP systems. LDAP is highly recommended in systems with more than 5,000 users, because integrating ABAP roles as groups in UME has a negative effect on system performance.

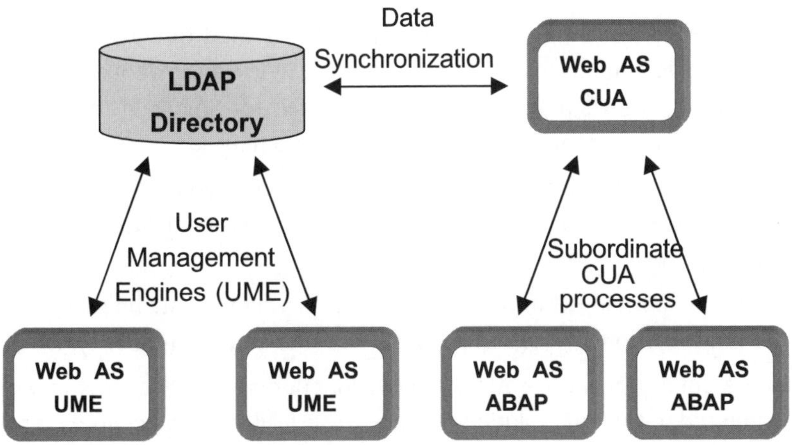

Figure 1.16 Integrating User Administration with LDAP

1.12 Summary

In previous decades, enterprises concentrated mainly on gaining control of their internal business processes. However, in the current economic climate of intense competition, the real challenges today are integrating all the different business applications in an enterprise, and using these applications in a flexible manner. It was in response to this challenge that SAP revamped its range of solutions, turning the monolithic, all-purpose SAP application into a portfolio of modular software components. SAP NetWeaver is the shared technology basis for this suite of software, and it provides components for integrating employees, information, and processes:

- The SAP Enterprise Portal (EP) will remain the standard user interface for all SAP solutions in the mid-term. Particular features include Drag&Relate and iView technology. Other options are TREX, a multilingual search mechanism for unstructured information, and Collaboration, a solution for facilitating team-based work.
- The SAP Mobile Infrastructure (MI) is responsible for mobile use. A replication mechanism is also available so that MI can be used offline. SAP MI is made up of MI clients, which are installed on the mobile device, and the MI server, which runs on the Web AS.

- The SAP Business Information Warehouse (SAP BW) is a system for the multi-dimensional analysis of large volumes of historic and current data. SAP Strategic Enterprise Management (SAP SEM) is an add-on for financial information. It also provides the optional Precalculation Service and Information Broadcasting.
- The SAP Knowledge Warehouse (SAP KW) is used to create and distribute documents and manuals, especially in the areas of quality management and training. The training materials for SAP training courses are available for the purposes of in-house training.
- SAP Master Data Management (MDM) enables you to consolidate, harmonize, and centrally oversee the entire master data stock of an enterprise.
- The SAP Exchange Infrastructure (SAP XI) is a central data hub between all the solutions in the mySAP Business Suite and third-party systems.
- The Solution Lifecycle Management function in NetWeaver is implemented in the SAP Solution Manager. This facilitates the central monitoring and control of entire SAP system landscapes.
- The SAP NetWeaver Development Environment with the NetWeaver Developer Studio (NWDS) is the basis of the Composite Application Framework (CAF). The CAF makes a whole new class of composite applications possible that can be flexibly adapted to changing business processes.

2 mySAP Business Applications

Flexible assembly lines for business processes

Integrated business processes are the indispensable basis for business success in a networked world. However, integration alone does not fulfill orders, produce goods, or pay invoices. While the SAP NetWeaver components described in Chapter 1 are used, as we have seen, for integrating employees, information, and processes, the actual business processes are carried out by the solutions in the mySAP Business Suite. These solutions are high-performance, scalable assembly lines that are sufficiently flexible to facilitate almost any process that may occur in day-to-day business operations. Their scope of functions is so extensive that it will take years to describe each individual functionality as a Web service in the Simple Object Access Protocol (SOAP). The underlying technology of these solutions is described in the next chapter, where we discuss the SAP Web Application Server (SAP Web AS), which is the standardized "power unit" for the mySAP Business Suite and the SAP NetWeaver components.

This chapter presents the overlying business functions of the software solutions in the mySAP range. A brief overview of the purpose, the underlying technology, and the requirements for the IT infrastructure are given for each function. However, a detailed description of the business functions of each SAP application is outside the scope of this book.

Universal versus special applications

The classic R/3 solution was conceived as an online transaction processing system (OLTP), however, it also evolved as an application for functions for which the architecture of an OLTP system was not ideally suited, such as reporting, and extended material requirements and distribution planning.

Then, with its New Dimensions initiative, SAP departed from the concept of monolithic all-purpose applications in favor of modular solutions whose architectures were optimized in accordance with the requirements of the line-of-business departments in which they were used. However, due to the ever-changing nature of the requirements of the individual departments and industries, the mySAP solutions became like "Swiss army knives" for their users. As we saw in Figure 1.1, the mySAP solutions and the industry solutions arose out of the standard R/3 system, and consist of one or more SAP instances for the application logic and a relational database instance for data storage. Some mySAP solutions also use special components, such as the liveCache and Optimizers in SAP APO.

Enterprises are under no obligation to roll out all the mySAP solutions immediately. Usually, the components that are first implemented are those that are required to support the fundamental business processes of the enterprise; then, the other solutions are introduced gradually.

mySAP versus best-of-breed

The cross-component integration of the mySAP solutions with SAP NetWeaver provides significant benefits compared to the so-called best-of-breed concept, which involves considerable costs for connecting interfaces in order to exchange information between the different software packages.

With the best-of-breed concept, the customer is responsible for carrying out the integration work. Various studies show that the conception and implementation of interfaces with a best-of-breed solution require up to 50 % of the project budget. Also, some parts of the system architectures of the various providers are so different that a separate team of administrators, each with its own know-how, is required to operate and optimize each specific application.

2.1 mySAP ERP

The most important solution in the mySAP Business Suite is and has always been mySAP Enterprise Resource Planning (mySAP ERP). This is because this solution deals with the most fundamental business processes in every enterprise: accounting, production, and human resources. In other words, mySAP ERP ensures that orders are accepted, fulfilled, and, of course, paid for.

Once almost promoted to death during the era of "e-hype," today ERP systems are more vital than ever and are the backbones of enterprises that rely on integrated, streamlined, and transparent business processes.

Components

mySAP ERP consists of the Enterprise Core Component (ECC), the SAP NetWeaver components that we have already discussed, and additional functions for Collaborative Business (see Figure 2.1). In SAP NetWeaver '04, the long-established functions of SAP R/3 were integrated into the ECC. ECC is a new ERP engine that has the functions of R/3 Enterprise, but that is better modularized and comes with Web interfaces. For example, SAP's FI application component is modularized into Asset Accounting, General Ledger, and Dispute Management. The latter can also be used as a self-contained component in other CRM functions.

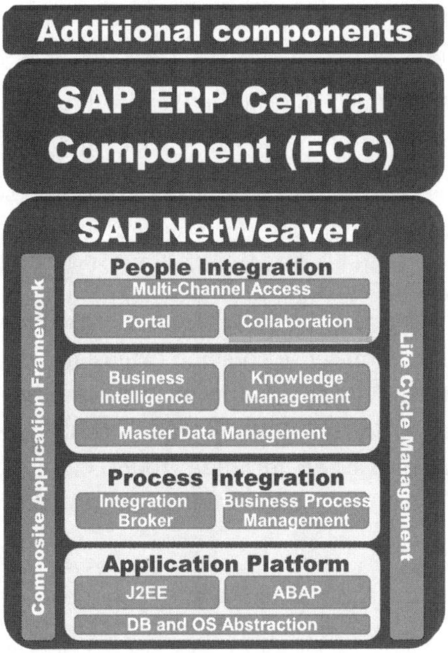

Figure 2.1 mySAP ERP (Logical View)

The SAP Enterprise Portal provides all employees with the business functions of the core system via a browser. This is even possible for employees who are traveling, thanks to the mobile infrastructure. (The traditional, locally installed SAP GUI is still supported, but not for new components.) SAP Business Information Warehouse (SAP BW) provides reporting and complex analyses, SAP Master Data Management (SAP MDM) provides consistent, enterprise-wide master data management, and SAP Exchange Infrastructure (SAP XI) allows the individual technical components to communicate with each other and with third-party systems. The SAP Web Application Server (SAP Web AS) serves as a shared, unified process platform.

Collaborative Business

The following additional functions are available for Collaborative Business (in some cases, a usage-related or volume-related surcharge may apply to the license):

- SAP Strategic Enterprise Management (SEM)
- SAP Financial Supply Chain Management (FSCM)
- SAP Employee Self-Service (ESS) and SAP Manager Self-Service (MSS)
- SAP E-Recruitment
- SAP Learning Solution

- Collaborative Projects (cProjects)
- SAP Internet Sales (R/3 Edition)
- SAP Supplier Relationship Management (SRM) (Self-Service Procurement only)

The combination of SAP NetWeaver and SAP Enterprise Core Component in mySAP ERP therefore makes up an enterprise with a complete business solution.

Unlike in earlier R/3 releases, the actual business process logic programmed in ABAP is split up into an enterprise core and extension sets. Also, SAP ECC is divided into function groups rather than the module concept in R/3. This function groups described below are self-contained (sub-)solutions by there own and are available for these groups.

2.1.1 mySAP Financials

The mySAP Financials solution contains the fundamental components of accounting, including the following areas:

- Financial Accounting for transaction processing, accounting, and reporting
- Financial Supply Chain Management (FSCM) for outgoing and incoming payment processes in accounting and liquidity planning
- Management Accounting
- Corporate Governance

mySAP Financials allows enterprises to access the whole range of accounting functions, including extensive reporting. The current balance sheet is always available in real time. This solution takes into account the requirements of globalization by making available different currencies, units, and languages, and national taxation and legal regulations (such as the IAS, the US GAAP, and many other national accounting standards like the German HGB). Thus, the solution facilitates the consolidation of subsidiaries in countries with different legal systems.

With ECC a new general ledger with a standardized data structure was introduced. The option to extend the general ledger in any way has made it no longer necessary to keep separate ledgers and make manual postings to them. So, for example, ledgers for GAAP and HGB reporting can be kept at the same time as an IAS ledger (as a "leading ledger" in which all postings are made). And since financial and management accounting are now integrated, you no longer have to keep a special reconciliation ledger. Also, the solution supports online splits in accounting. All these functions are intended to support fast month-end and year-end closes (Fast Close).

The Sarbanes-Oxley act

In the area of corporate governance, SAP Management of Internal Controls (MIC) supports US stock exchange-listed enterprises in fulfilling the requirements of the Sarbanes-Oxley Act[1] and similar regulations in other countries (such as the KonTraG[2] in Germany). It also supports enterprises in complying with Basel II, the guideline on shareholders' equity for banks, which establishes criteria for lending. Besides having financial consequences, Basel II can also affect the requirements of an enterprise's IT. SAP Management of Internal Controls (MIC) also supports the control efficiency assessments recommended in the COSO's Internal Control Framework[3]. Similarly, it supports—in a workflow-driven way—the whole process of documenting companies' internal control mechanisms and the relevant assessments, right up to the point when the CEO signs off the quarterly and annual reports.

Using SAP BW for reporting is optional. Users access the system via the portal, using a browser-based interface. The system can be run either on a separate Web AS instance or jointly with another SAP component: SAP BW and MIC can be combined on one server, for example. However, for auditing reasons, we recommend that you activate table logging; therefore, a separate client will be required for MIC.

2.1.2 mySAP Operations

mySAP Operations consists of projects, logistics, and production functionalities, including plant maintenance and quality assurance. It is therefore one of the most extensive areas of mySAP ERP with one of the largest numbers of components.

Simultaneous order costing

Sales & Distribution (SD) covers the whole sales cycle—from quote to order to delivery and transport to invoicing. Other useful features include immediate product availability and delivery schedule information by inte-

1 U.S. law dealing with balance sheet fraud, which is named after two senators. This law tightens controls on corporate procedures and requires that corporate decisions be well-documented and clearly traceable.

2 Law governing monitoring and transparency in the corporate world.

3 Committee of Sponsoring Organizations of the Treadway Commission, a voluntary private sector organization dedicated to improving the quality of financial reporting through business ethics, effective internal controls, and corporate governance, go to *http://www.sox-online.com/coso_cobit_coso.html*.

gration with MM and PP. Due to seamless integration with FI and CO (and connections with bank accounts), receivables and revenues are immediately updated. A simultaneous order costing process supports the user at all stages—from the initial inquiry to making a quote to taking a customer order. A comprehensive foreign trade processing function handles the export processes.

Production planning

Operational Production Planning (PP) runs on the basis of sales planning. PP provides a whole palette of production methods ranging from make-to-order production to repetitive manufacturing/mass production for discrete, batch oriented and continuous production. Operational Production Planning provides all necessary functionality for classical Material Requirements Planning (MRP) or Distribution Requirements Planning (DRP) along with material requirements marking in daily operations. Bottleneck and simulation planning functions cover any special cases.

Internal and external Kanban processes ensure that materials are always replenished. The results of the capacity requirements planning (CRP) are fed into the procurement process. Simultaneous costing for production orders, a cost collector for a run schedule header, and the complete integration of quality assurance (Quality Management, or QM) into individual operations are all equally possible. For the latter, an inspection lot is automatically created in the background. The results of the inspection lot analysis—from the defects recording process and the appraisal costs determination data—flow directly into the activity allocation process.

Warehouse functionality

Along with Logistics Execution System (LES), and the Transport Management System[4], the full functionality of the Warehouse Management (WM) system covers all warehouse requirements. With Inventory Management, warehouse stock can be organized based on quantities or values. Warehouse Management is integrated with financial accounting and is responsible for mapping goods receipts and goods receipt confirmations in the system. Inventory Management also enables users to manage multiple warehouse categories (such as "freely available" and "reorder point") and special warehouse types (such as "vendor consignment stores"). It supports the various inventory variants and assists the user in controlling specific warehouse stock. The logistics modules are used to manage all processes belonging to internal logistics chains, from raw material procurement to delivery to the customer. Its seamless integra-

4 Don't confuse this with the SAP transport management system TMS which takes care of software change management.

tion with mySAP Financials allows receivables and receipts to be updated immediately.

Procurement

The production requirements trigger the purchasing processes, while quality assurance is linked to goods receipt. The system also handles the process of posting to the stocks in question and the required inspections. The next stages are invoice verification and release, and any bonus rebate settlements.

Project planning

The integrated project management system (PS) allows the project structure plan and the network plan to be included in the sales order. The associated network plans, including materials and resources, the required documents, and project texts can also be integrated. In addition, SAP Plant Maintenance (SAP PM) supports time scheduling, project costs planning and project revenue, and project finance planning, including unit costing and base object costing, if necessary.

Preventive maintenance

The plant-maintenance functions that are integrated into mySAP Operations (Plant Maintenance, PM) go far beyond the simple task of keeping the machines running. PM's integrated approach to maintenance increases the availability of machines and plant via preventive repairs and maintenance, with the added benefit of transparent costs.

2.1.3 mySAP Human Capital Management

In this age of information, non-material values such as corporate culture and the skills of employees are decisive factors in the success of enterprises. Effective human resource management therefore involves more than just managing employees; it is also about getting them to fulfill their potential, that is, their skills, relationships, talents, and goals. As one of the main components in mySAP ERP, Human Capital Management (HCM) links operational components for developing employee potential with collaborative components that enable employees to do their jobs better.

Functions

HCM in mySAP ERP supports all processes in human resources management, from recruiting to hiring to qualification and loyalty-building. The following functions help develop employee potential:

- Performance Management (management by objectives, appraisals, remuneration)
- Talent Management (internal and external recruiting, following up applications and supporting applicants, career and succession planning, profiling)

- Skills Management (e-learning, management training, and employee qualification)

The integrated functionality for payroll, organization management, time management, bonuses, reporting, and cost planning makes it possible to keep down the transaction costs associated with human resource management.

HCM is globally-oriented; for example, it reflects different local legal systems. The corresponding information is contained in a central database. Enterprises can therefore manage their global employees more efficiently and reduce the costs of maintaining employee data. Users can access all HCM processes via the SAP Enterprise Portal, in accordance with their role (such as employee, manager, and manager with personnel responsibilities).

2.1.4 mySAP Analytics

mySAP Analytics is divided into the following tactical components:

- Financial Analytics with sales and profitability management and activity-based costing/management (ABC/M), for identifying the costs of individual processes and activities
- Workforce Analytics with personnel cost planning and fluctuation analysis
- Operations Analytics with campaign planning, supply chain performance analysis, and concurrent costing
- Strategic Enterprise Management/Business Analytics (SAP SEM/BA)

Enterprise management

SAP SEM/BA (Business Analytics) is SAP's solution for enterprise management within mySAP Analytics. SAP SEM is the solution that supports strategic planning and investor relations, while Business Analytics involves the operational management loop and has the following components:

- Strategy Management with balanced scorecard and risk management
- Performance Measurement with management cockpit and value driver tree
- Business Planning with financial planning applications
- Business Consolidation with statutory and management consolidation
- Stakeholder Relationship Management with investor relations applications

Typical usage scenarios of SAP SEM/BA include balance sheet planning and operational planning, especially planning for cost of sales, resulting costs planning, and overhead costs planning, and consolidation and financial reports (primarily statutory consolidation, then management consolidation). Strategy Management and Performance Measurement (management cockpit and balanced scorecard), and customer-based profitability analyses are also common uses.

From a software standpoint, the separation of transactional processing and analytical processing has become standard. For this reason, the analytical functions of mySAP ERP are provided by the NetWeaver component SAP BW with the SEM add-on, which is optimized for this purpose (although ECC 5.0 also makes available a BW that is technically integrated into the core system). Because analyses consolidate and aggregate large data volumes, they usually place a heavy load on system resources. Therefore, unless the system has some method of distributing existing resources across separate instances, the performance of transaction processing in operational business processes may suffer.

2.1.5 mySAP Corporate Services

Corporate Services supports the management of central matters such as travel costs, real estate, treasury, and bonuses and commissions. These processes are necessary, but are not usually part of core business. Corporate Services enables enterprises to reduce their costs in these areas by simplifying processes and providing Self Services. A good example of this is travel expenses management.

Processing business trips

Due to the increasing globalization of economies, business trips are becoming increasingly more numerous. Not only does a business trip cost time and money, but the administrative work that goes along with it is also significant. First, the employee in question has to apply for the business trip, and his or her boss has to approve it. Then, the necessary reservations have to be made. Once the employee has returned from the trip, the costs must be calculated and refunded.

SAP Travel Management is an integrated component of mySAP ERP and links human resources, accounting, and controlling. All the business processes involved in business trips can therefore be processed efficiently. The electronic travel application makes paper forms obsolete, and the direct connection to Amadeus and Sabre, the two leading global reservation systems, reduces planning costs substantially. The travel expenses component provides a simple means of calculating these expenses and accelerates the process of refunding expenses to the employee. It also comprises a wide range of country-specific versions, and the mySAP ERP implementation guide contains the legal requirements associated with business trips, as well as regulations on average costs and allowed maximum costs.

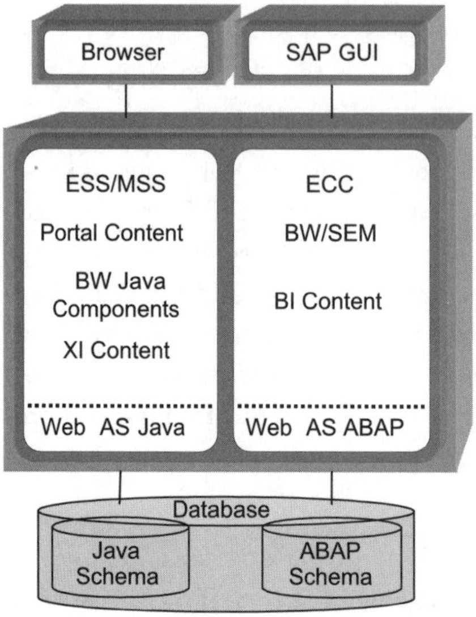

Figure 2.2 mySAP ERP Infrastructure (Without Options)

2.1.6 Additional mySAP ERP Components

In addition to the functionalities in SAP ECC and SAP NetWeaver, mySAP ERP also comprises a range of other components, as we saw in Figure 2.1.

Employee Self-Service

SAP Employee Self-Service (ESS) enables employees to maintain and manage their own master data via the Internet without the need for the involvement of the Human Resources (HR) department. This master data includes name, address, telephone number, and other similar data. In addition to HR functions, SAP ESS also provides every employee in the enterprise with some logistical, financial, and office functions via the Enterprise Portal. SAP NetWeaver '04 provides additional time recording functions.

Manager Self-Service

SAP Manager Self-Service (MSS) supports management staff with approval processes, Equipment Lifecycle Management, hiring (this function is integrated with SAP E-Recruiting), and cost-center monitoring, among other things.

Audit trail

The audit trail tool is a cross-application component whose function is to document changes made to business objects in a format that can be audited. Internal or external auditors can therefore reconstruct changes in the business processes supported by SAP, as required by regulations such as General Rules for Accounting, the Sarbanes-Oxley Act, GDPdU, IRS, JFMIP, the Code of Federal Regulations, the PIC/S Guidance, the Japanese MHLW, the EU General Food Law, as well as various other EU directives. The audit trail is particularly important in the pharmaceutical industry, because it helps enterprises in this industry to fulfill the requirements of 21 CFR Part 11[5] of the Food and Drug Administration (FDA).

2.2 Industry Solutions

SAP offers a wide range of industry-specific solutions (Industry Solutions, IS) for several industries, each of which provides functionalities specific to that industry. These industry solutions comprise modified and extended R/3 standard components, and the technical architecture of the IS solutions is the same as that of R/3 standard systems.

A good example of the industry solutions is mySAP Retail. The business process mapped in this solution covers the daily transfer of sales data, which is collected at the cash register at the point of sale (POS) at the various branches, to the SAP system at the company's headquarters. This function is called POS Upload. Next, the system calculates the volume of products required to replenish the stores in each branch. The results of an optimization run are used to create picking orders. These orders are sent, and the delivery notes for the trucks are generated in accordance with the route plan, and printed. POS Upload and the replenishment runs are extremely resource-intensive processes, and must be carefully considered when the hardware for the SAP system is being set up.

Every industry solution is developed by specially established expert teams. In the past, this created a situation whereby each solution had its own release cycles, and in many cases, modifications made to individual solutions led to the incompatibility of solutions, both with each other and with the R/3 standard system. Also, Support Packages (for standard program maintenance) could be integrated into an IS system only once there was a Conflict Resolution Transport (CRT) for the Support Package level in question. CRTs resolve incompatibilities with industry-specific modifica-

5 21st volume of the Code of Federal Regulations, Chapter 11, which deals with electronic records and electronic signatures.

tions. Therefore, a dedicated system had to be installed for many industry solutions. The idea behind SAP NetWeaver is to have unified release cycles and full compatibility.

For example, SAP for Discrete Industries and Mill Products (DIMP) combines the following industry solutions:

- SAP for Aerospace & Defense (including Maintenance and Service Planning, MSP)
- SAP for Automotive (including integrated product and process engineering (iPPE), Kanban control circles, Just in Time (JIT) or Just-In-Sequence processing, Vehicle Management System, and so on)
- SAP for High Tech (including Distributor Reseller Management, DRM)
- SAP for Engineering, Construction & Operations (including equipment, and tools management (ETM), bill of services, homebuilding, and so on)
- SAP for Industrial Machinery & Components
- SAP for Mill Products (including multiple output planning)

2.3 mySAP Customer Relationship Management

"king customer"

Despite the differences between enterprises and industries, they all have one goal in common: to sell their products and services to "his majesty—the customer". In order for enterprises to achieve this goal, they have to build up and maintain thriving relationships with their customers. This is because experience has shown that every satisfied customer generates three new customers by word-of-mouth, while a dissatisfied customer, on the other hand, can lose a company nine customers by the same method.

Customer Relationship Management (CRM) is an area that comprises the planning, creation, and maintenance of customer relationships. CRM processes support all phases of the "customer interaction cycle," from the initial contact to closing the contract to order fulfillment and after-sale services.

Many enterprises have also recognized that customer data is not just something that contributes to more administrative work; it can also be leveraged to actively build customer relationships and therefore, create more revenue. SAP CRM systems are thus also used as information and management instruments by managers in enterprises.

Therefore, mySAP Customer Relationship Management (CRM) comprises several scenarios that are tailored to each type of interaction with the customer. The central component is the operational part, which provides processes for marketing, sales, service, support, and enterprise management from the CRM point of view (operational CRM). It also includes functionalities for cooperation with partners and customers (collaborative CRM) via the Internet and for analyzing customer-related data (analytical CRM). Technically speaking, mySAP CRM is based on the SAP CRM server (which is run on the SAP Web AS), a relational database, and various additional components from SAP and its partners.

Sales

Personal contact with the customer is, and always has been, the cornerstone of customer relationship management. Unfortunately, it is also the most expensive form of selling. So there is nothing more frustrating for a salesperson than being prevented from closing due to a simple lack of information. This information could be: What has this customer bought before? Can we supply the quantity he requires? With the discount this customer wants, will this order (or customer relationship) even generate a profit for us?

mySAP CRM helps sales staff manage their business partners by providing them with information about interested parties, customers, partners, and suppliers. The various activities involved in selling—from arranging appointments for customer visits to managing everything involved with closing—are managed in the activity management function. The opportunity management function distributes information about known sales opportunities to the sales staff, who can then use the order management function to create an order, including the price and a digital signature, on the spot.

Similarly, mySAP CRM supports customer service staff with managing appointments to do with the various activities in the task management function. Service staff can use a mobile device on the customer's premises to call up problem messages and information about the order and the installed equipment, to enter information about the services performed and the materials used, and possibly also to create new service orders.

Mobile solutions

SAP CRM Field Sales and Field Service supports sales staff and service technicians in the field. A replication mechanism ensures that the product catalogs or repair instructions, for example, that are stored on the employees' laptops or other mobile devices are always kept current. At the same time, orders that were created offline or time statements for repairs, for example, can be forwarded to the relevant modules in mySAP ERP.

In the mid-term, this functionality will be covered by the SAP Mobile Infrastructure (MI) in SAP NetWeaver.

2.3.1 mySAP CRM Interaction Center

Call centers Call centers are a tried-and-tested method of cost reduction. However, long wait times and incompetent (or contradictory information) from call center staff can drive customers away. The mySAP CRM Interaction Center (IC) supports call center and sales support staff by providing them with the information they need in order to function competently and reliably, thereby increasing customer satisfaction.

Interaction Call Centers provide call center agents with access to service orders and contracts, and a solution database. Functionalities such as interactive conversation threads, order management, and product proposals help staff to manage the telesales process. Furthermore, outbound call functions, interactive scripting, and call lists support marketing campaigns and telemarketing. In addition to the telephone, other communication media such as email, fax, Chat, Voice-over-Internet Protocol (VoIP), and callback functions can also be used to enhance communication with the customer (multichannel support). Call center agents can also search for solutions to known problems in the solution database.

The IC supports the various scenarios such as the following:

- Inbound telesales (order acceptance)
- Outbound telesales (sales campaigns)
- Information helpdesk (processing customer queries and requests)
- Service (processing repair requests)
- Complaint handling

The IC is based on the SAP CRM server, which runs on the SAP Web AS and has its own database. The user interface is implemented on the basis of Web Dynpro technology.

SAPphone Together with a private branch exchange (PBX), SAPphone can be used for functions such as taking and forwarding calls, and predictive dialing[6]. A telephony gateway, a telephony server, and an interface to the tele-

6 System is dialing down a list automatically.

phone system are required for advanced voice functions (Computer Telephony Integration, CTI). A Broadcast Messaging Server allows messages and announcements to be distributed to individual call center agents.

SAPconnect provides an interface to mail servers[7] that allows it to integrate email functions. With the SAP Email Response Management System (ERMS), incoming email is automatically fed into the call center workflow for processing, its progress is tracked, and personalized responses are sent. Information is filtered out of the messages and used in the automatic response. **SAPconnect**

The IC also provides interfaces to call center solutions from other providers. This allows other functions such as session management, automatic call distribution, and other intelligent optional functions to be added to existing Call Centers.

2.3.2 SAP Internet Sales

The e-selling scenario is the most technically demanding business scenario in CRM. SAP provides two different e-selling scenarios:

- The SAP Internet Sales R/3 Edition deploys the functionality available on an R/3 system to sell over the internet .
- The SAP Internet Sales uses the mySAP CRM system to process almost all e-selling processes

Besides mySAP CRM and the J2EE Engine of the Web AS, the mySAP CRM Internet Sales infrastructure also consists of a number of extra products that can also be used with SAP Internet Sales R/3 Edition.

Online customization

The SAP Internet Pricing & Configurator (IPC) enables customers to create configurable products online, from a PC to a car. The IPC checks the interdependencies between components (for example, whether the desired configuration is technically feasible) and calculates the prices online. In this process, the IPC accesses the prices that are stored in the CRM database.

The IPC is a self-contained Java application and consists of a dispatcher and one or more server instances. The IPC is based on a multi-threaded Java architecture that can be implemented on the J2EE Engine of the Web AS, but is also suitable for grid computing. To ensure appropriate load distribution and to guarantee availability, at least two IPC's should

7 As well as fax and X400 products.

always be installed, which are then accessed in a round-robin process. The SAP Java Connector (JCo) is required to connect to the mySAP CRM system.

SAP Internet Sales R/3 Edition uses its own self-contained SAP IPC. For this reason, the SAP IPC has its own database and extracts the required data from the R/3 system at regular intervals.

Online billing

Another solution in the area of customer relationship management is SAP Biller Direct (SAP BD), part of SAP FSCM in mySAP ERP. This solution allows customers to process billing, billing inquiries, and complaints online in the portal. SAP Biller Direct formats accounting data so that it can be displayed in the browser, and transfers data input by the customer via the Java Connector (JCo) to the mySAP ERP system. SAP BD is a Java-based Web application that runs on the J2EE Engine of the SAP Web AS.

Online catalogs

Web shops are usually based on one or more catalogs. Graphics, images, and video sequences can be automatically stored in the SAP Knowledge Provider (KPro) and published on the Web server. If the volume of documents in the product catalog is very large, the SAP Content Server can be used.

Searching and browsing

To support catalog browsing, accelerate search processes in a Web catalog, and reduce the load on the CRM system, product catalog data can be replicated via the Index Management Service (IMS).

IMS saves its indexes in the file system; however, for the actual indexing process, IMS requires the TREX of the Enterprise Portal or another type of index server software. Only one IMS can be configured in the mySAP CRM system. In situations where multiple parallel Index Management Services are used, the indexes must be synchronized via operating system tools.

Permanent shopping basket

Another option is a permanent shopping basket. This function is based on a local database, to which the basket can be saved and from which it can be called. Also, via the BackWeb server and push technology, additional information such as marketing material can be transferred to a suitable BackWeb client laptop.

Interactive product advice

Third-party products can also be incorporated, such as the Intelligent Product Advisor (IPA) from UBIS,[8] which enables interactive product advice, and TeaLeaf,[9] which filters customer interactions in the Web shop

8 Go to *http://www.ubis-ag.com/125_content.htm*.

9 Go to *http://www.TeaLeaf.com*.

out of the HTTP data flow and sends it in the form of collected data to SAP BW.

Internet shops make high demands on the adaptability of an infrastructure, because their performance must be acceptable 24 hours a day, with an unpredictable number of users. Internet shops must also ensure a high level of security in order to protect business data and customers' personal data, while making their services available to the entire Internet community.

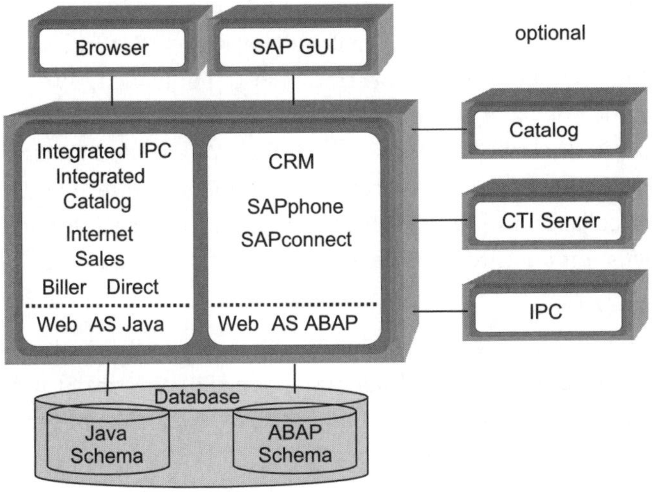

Figure 2.3 mySAP CRM Infrastructure

The "minimum" scenario—all in one

In principle, all components can be installed on a single computer. However, in this scenario, all users have direct access to the host, on which the application logic and the database are stored. Therefore, we definitely do not recommend that you link this kind of system with the Internet, even if it is protected by a firewall. An all-in-one system is therefore not suitable for an operational Internet shop. The smallest operational system consists of at least two computers, one of which hosts the Web server, and the other, the Web middleware and the back-end systems. Both hosts are separated by a firewall.

For an Internet shop, the user names and passwords have to be stored on the middleware server, which has access to the mySAP CRM or mySAP ERP system, so that you can use the shop anonymously. For this reason, the middleware host should be located in the internal network rather than in the demilitarized zone (DMZ).[10] Also, the user should have only very restricted access to the back-end system.

For extra security, a firewall can be placed between the middleware host and the internal back-end systems such as SAP CRM, SAP ECC, SAP APO, and SAP BW.

mySAP and SAP NetWeaver integration

Besides the basic CRM components, functionalities from other mySAP components can also be used to enhance Internet sales scenarios. For example, the availability of products or an expected delivery date for a customer-specific configuration (Available to Promise—ATP) can be determined by SAP APO. Similarly, materials-related and accounting functions for Internet sales can be processed in ECC. For its part, BW is a data source on the one hand, while on the other, it consolidates and analyzes CRM data (analytical CRM). SAP EP and SAP MI are used for user integration, and SAP XI is used for process integration. Therefore, a portal is available for collaborative CRM that allows partners to be informed about campaigns, products to be ordered, and the status of an order to be tracked.

Industry-specific CRM

CRM processes are usually very different in different industries. Therefore, as with mySAP ERP, there are also industry-specific versions of CRM. The following list gives a brief explanation, based on keywords, of some of the over 280 industry-specific functionalities:

- mySAP CRM for the automotive industry provides data about customers and vehicles, including fittings, for the lifecycle of the vehicle, for the dealer, the customer, and vehicle management (Vehicle Management System, VMS).
- mySAP CRM for discrete manufacturing provides a dealer portal, among other things, and an Installed Base Management function supports the handling of warranty claims.
- mySAP CRM for the consumer goods industry supports trade promotion management and consumer service, in order to strengthen brand loyalty.
- mySAP CRM for process industries supports batch tracing, from production to delivery, compliance with statutory requirements in template assignment, and analysis of indirect sales (such as IMS data).

10 In networks, the area between the access router to the Internet and the firewall to the intranet.

- mySAP CRM for financial services providers support functions for processing claims (Case Management), among other things.
- mySAP CRM for services companies provides functions for resource planning on the basis of freely-definable requirements profiles, and functions for complaints processing.
- mySAP CRM for media companies supports the management of rights, licenses and royalties for authors and other artists.
- my SAP CRM for the utilities industry provides information about the usage patterns of important customers, and therefore makes it possible to provide individual, tailored supports for commercial customers and other special customers. This functionality is completely integrated into SAP for Utilities and thus allows prices to be correctly determined and seamlessly transferred to the billing department.

2.4 mySAP Supply Chain Management

The supply chain is one of the key factors in today's competitive environment, both in retail and production companies. The goal of any supply chain is to keep lead times and warehouse stock to a minimum while maintaining maximum availability, even with fluctuating levels of demand. Therefore, supply chain management has to encompass the whole logistics chain, from raw material and parts suppliers, subcontractors and carriers, to the end-customer. The widely-distributed and complex supply chains and networks that are the norm today require automated methods for planning, optimization, monitoring, and management. Therefore, the network has to be able to react quickly and allow the parties involved to collaborate in real time. The mySAP Business Suite for Supply Chain Management (SCM) covers all these requirements.

SCM Components

The SCM application area comprises business and logistics functions whose purpose is to optimize the flow of goods and finance in the value chain, inside and outside enterprise boundaries. The components in question are the core component, SAP Advanced Planner and Optimizer (APO), as well as SAP Event Manager and SAP Inventory Collaboration Hub (ICH); the latter is the solution for supplier and vendor-managed inventories.

Because different industries have different requirements of their logistics chains (for example, companies could use make-to-order, batch, or repetitive manufacturing), SAP provides industry-specific SCM solutions for the automotive industry, plant engineering and construction, mechanical engineering, process industry, retail, consumer goods industry, logistics services provider, and the public sector.

2.4.1 SAP Advanced Planner and Optimizer (APO)

The SAP Advanced Planner and Optimizer (SAP APO) provides a complete portfolio of planning instruments and optimization algorithms for real-time planning and decision support. It combines sophisticated planning algorithms, object-oriented data structures, and a main memory-resident database, in order to solve complex logistical optimization problems in the various sub-areas of supply chain management shown in Figure 2.4.

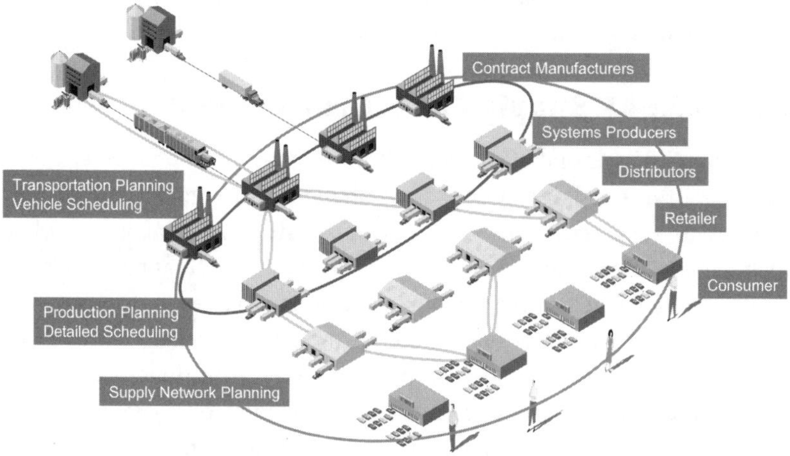

Figure 2.4 The Various Areas of Supply Chain Management

APO modules SAP APO supports all areas of strategic, tactical, and operational planning. The Demand Planning (DP) module forecasts future requirements on the basis of historical data, while Supply Network Planning (SNP) optimizes the distribution of orders, in view of the available cross-plant transport and production capacities.

While the production planning (MRP) in mySAP ERP is necessarily restricted to the data available in individual R/3 systems, SAP APO Production Planning—Detailed Scheduling (PP-DS) is used to optimally distribute production orders across the available machines in an individual plant. The detailed planning function optimizes the order of processing. The production timeframe determines the point at which supply network planning stops and production planning and detailed planning or recipe transfer in processing industries begins.

The Transportation Planning—Vehicle Scheduling (TP-VS) function factors in warehouse and transport restrictions, combines optimal truck loads, and manages in-house and third-party stock (Vendor Managed Inventory, VMI).

Global ATP check

While the availability check in mySAP ERP is necessarily restricted to the individual R/3 systems, the global Available-to-Promise (ATP) function in SAP APO provides a multilevel availability check that can verify material stock, production capacity, warehouse capacity, and transport capacity, and cross-plant and cross-company costs. The Supply Chain Cockpit has a configurable GUI for maintaining the advanced logistics chain model (plants, distribution centers, etc), factory plans (machines, storage locations, and so on), deadlines, exceptions rules, and so on.

None of this affects the operational handling of the processes (order entry, delivery, billing documents, production order processing, goods receipt, and goods issue) in mySAP ERP in any way. The master data and transaction data are exchanged between systems, depending on the process.

Technical infrastructure

The technical infrastructure of APO is based on the standard SAP Basis components (the ABAP engine of the Web AS and a database), plus the APO specific components SAP liveCache (APO LC) and the Optimizer. The SAP liveCache is a database that is optimized for APO and that is completely contained in main memory. It is based on MaxDB (previously SAP DB). This is necessary so that complex optimization runs can be processed efficiently in real time, including those with many characteristics combinations. For this to be possible, very fast data access, as well as an object-oriented data model, is required, something that is not guaranteed with disk-stored data.

With the liveCache, almost no transaction processing data is copied between the hard disk and the main memory during the planning runs. Also, the MaxDB has been extended for liveCache, with the result that, for example, a bill of materials (BOM) is no longer displayed simply as a join (a set-theoretic operation); rather, the BOM items (as we know from procedural programming languages) are represented as a tree structure via pointers. Thus, along with LCApps (previously COM routines—C++ programs that are executed in the memory at runtime), the processing rate for BOMs, orders, and so on is now 50 times greater than before. However, once the BOM items and orders (which have to be stored in the memory) reach a certain volume, the maximum addressable main memory for 32-bit systems is reached very quickly. Therefore, we recommend that you use 64-bit platforms with APO in live systems.[11]

APO Optimizers are special optimization algorithms from the company ILOG[12], each of which is executed on its own (small) server. They range from linear algorithms (such as simplex procedures), to dynamic and stochastic search procedures, to heuristic procedures. If these algorithms are not sufficient, you can also implement your own procedures using the ABAP Workbench.

APO uses a plug-in to extract the required data from SAP BW (or another Data Warehouse solution), which gets the data from a mySAP ERP system (or another ERP system). For this purpose, the APO system has its own data mart made up of InfoCubes in which the data and planning results are stored. If there is a dedicated BW system, this can be used as the data mart for demand planning.

SCOR model

SAP BW is also used for Supply Chain Performance Management, on the basis of performance indicators. For this reason, BW information models such as workbooks, queries, and key figures are delivered with mySAP SCM Business Content in the form of preconfigured objects. Many of the over 300 preconfigured key figures are based on the Supply Chain Operations Reference (SCOR) model of the Supply Chain Council[13].

2.4.2 SAP Event Management

Exception-based management

It is an unfortunate fact that the reality often does not correspond to the plan. Delays, interruptions, breakdowns, and accidents can never be completely ruled out, which is why supply chains must always be in a position to recognize and counteract deviations from the plan as quickly as possible. Supply Chain Event Management (SCEM) tools check the network of logistical processes on the basis of predefined events on a continuous basis. An "event" in this context is the occurrence of a fact or situation in the supply chain at a predefined point in time. If a specific event occurs too late, whether or not this is unexpected, the Event Manager reports this deviation from the plan. The enterprise can then react immediately, before the event triggers an avalanche of subsequent events.

11 See SAP Note 622709.
12 Go to *http://www.ilog.com*.
13 Go to *http://www.supply-chain.org/index.ww*.

In mySAP SCM, SAP Event Management (SAP EM) provides a deviation management function with threshold values between execution and planning. It is used to recognize interruptions to the logistics chain in real time, thus enabling the enterprise to react without delay to these interruptions.

To do this, SAP EM monitors activities such as the start of production, the departure of a truck, or the arrival of a container ship, all in real time. When an event report arrives in SAP EM, the system first checks it for plausibility and issues warning messages if there are any delays, if the order of steps is not adhered to, or if an event is missing altogether. Thus, critical situations are recognized and responded to as close to the event as possible, before costs are incurred due to delays or interruptions to production. In certain cases, the system can even automatically trigger standard procedures in response to defined events.

SAP EM is based on the ABAP engine of the Web AS and on SAP XI. The SAP Enterprise Portal is used to issue warning messages to the intended users, based on their roles, and SAP BW generates performance key figures.

RFID

The traditional article management function draws a static picture of the articles in the warehouse or shop. Radio Frequency Identification (RFID) assists in this process by identifying and booking in the article when it is still on the loading ramp. RFID technology is one step ahead of its siblings, barcodes, and magnetic strips, in that it can identify an object without seeing the object. While a barcode scanner can recognize the pattern of lines in a barcode only if the item in question is held right against its lens, RFID tags can be detected even if they are deep inside a box. Thus, RFID scanners are the ideal external "feelers" for SAP EM, and render obsolete one of the classic gaps in the goods receipt process.

Also, RFID can store more data than a barcode, so that even individual batches can be tracked back to the production stage. There are even RDIC chips that can store specific environmental data, such as fluctuations in temperature during a transport.

SAP Auto-ID

The SAP RFID Solution Package consists of the SAP Auto-ID Infrastructure (AII) on the basis of the Web AS, and special AII content for SAP XI, SAP BW (optional), and SAP EM (optional). SAP XI is required to connect AII and ERP systems in order to route the data from the RFID scanners to the various components and to convert the data to the required formats. Depending on which SAP ERP version is used (R/3 4.6C, R/3 Enterprise Extension Set 2.0, or ECC), there are different additional AII add-ons and plug-ins that have to be installed.

2.4.3 SAP Inventory Collaboration Hub

Supplier-Managed Inventory

Increasingly more enterprises are transferring responsibility for warehouse stocks to their suppliers, along with the capital tie-up for the stocks. This kind of scenario requires transparency on both sides—for the customer, in the quantity of articles that are available at any time, and for the supplier, in the forecast requirement for an agreed replenishment control run. Thus, the supplier can contribute to the goal of cost reduction by optimizing stocks in accordance with demand, by having the logistics chain ready so that it can be included in the planning process, and by being able to guarantee the supply.

SAP Inventory Collaboration Hub (ICH) is the SAP solution that allows suppliers to manage stocks (Supplier-Managed Inventory, SMI). With SAP ICH, all the suppliers involved in a delivery network can view warehouse stocks in real time and across company boundaries. Like Vendor-Managed Inventory (VMI), SMI supports a process for replenishing warehouse stock that is based on minimum and maximum limit values.

The "release processing" scenario supports buyer-driven replenishment planning via delivery schedules that are usually triggered by the Material Requirements Planning (MRP) runs in the customer systems.

SAP ICH is based on SAP NetWeaver and the SAP Exchange Infrastructure (SAP XI). Thus, SAP ICH can be integrated into the various transaction and planning systems of the suppliers and manufacturers. A plug-in takes care of the integration of APO, ICH, and EM with mySAP ERP. Since mySAP SCM 4.0, the respective APO, EM, and ICH components can be run together on one instance of the SAP Web AS, with one database instance.

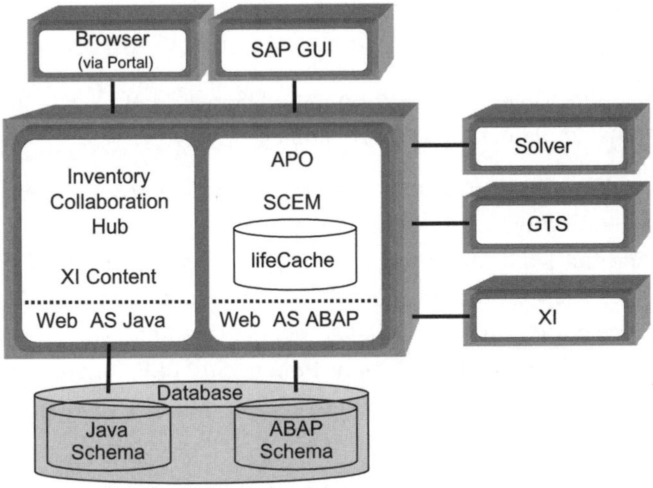

Figure 2.5 mySAP SCM Infrastructure

2.5 mySAP Supplier Relationship Management

Today, online communication with suppliers is taken for granted as much as online communication with consumers and customers.

Supplier Relationship Management (SRM) is the mySAP component for purchasing and procurement. The concept of mySAP SRM goes far beyond the scope of traditional desktop purchasing systems (DPS), since it involves suppliers in the procurement process in real time. With SRM, end users can process the entire procurement process in a Web browser—from placing the order to paying the invoice. Flexible approval procedures and tracking functions ensure that spending levels are monitored and controlled. Therefore, staff in the purchasing department no longer have to perform operational purchasing tasks, and consequently can focus their attention and time on strategic acquisitions and contractual negotiations. Along with interfaces to other online catalog systems and external content aggregators such as Aspect, Harbinger, and Commerce One, the SAP catalog is integrated into SRM.

From a technical point of view, SRM is based on SAP Web AS plus an additional catalog server. From a logical point of view, mySAP Supplier Relationship Management comprises the following components (in addition to the SAP NetWeaver components SAP EP, SAP BW, and SAP XI):

- SAP Enterprise Buyer Professional (EBP)
- SAP Content Integrator

- SAP Bidding Engine for online auctions
- SAP Supplier Self-Services (SUS)
- SAP Live Auction Cockpit Web Presentation Server (LAC WPS) for online auctions (implemented as a Java applet)

Similar to the catalog tools eMerge and BugsEye from Requisite[14], with mySAP SRM 4.0, SAP provides its own catalog solution with an authoring environment and the TREX search engine. The process of loading catalog content in formats such as BMECat and XML can be automated using SAP XI. For acceptance of delivered goods, inventory management, and financial accounting, mySAP SRM uses functions from mySAP ERP; for production planning, functions from APO are used; and for reporting, functions from BW are used.

In terms of its development history, mySAP SRM harks back to SAP Business-to-Business Procurement (B2B, later BBP). While the goal of SAP BBP was to procure materials such as auxiliary materials and factory supply materials, and services, in a cost-effective way, SAP Enterprise Buyer Professional (EBP) as the core component of mySAP SRM supports all procurement processes for all materials, right up to electronic negotiations, auctions management, and contract management.

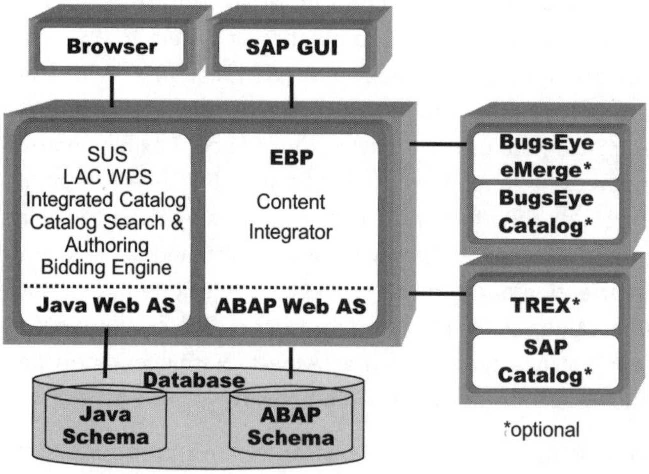

Figure 2.6 mySAP SRM Infrastructure

14 Go to *http://www.Requisite.com/*.

2.6 mySAP Product Lifecycle Management

Today, it is not enough to simply develop innovative products of outstanding quality. Enterprises also have to bring these products to market as quickly as possible, and provide a reliable maintenance service and customer service to go with them, all from the moment that the product idea is conceived, right up to the point at which it is taken from the market. mySAP Product Lifecycle Management (PLM) is the mySAP component for inter-enterprise product development, plant maintenance, quality assurance, hazardous substance management, industrial hygiene and safety, and environmental protection.

While mySAP PLM is a self-contained solution, it is not a component in and of itself; rather, it makes combined use of functions from ECC, CRM, SCM, BW, SCM, CO/PS, EP, and others. Therefore, PLM does not require its own infrastructure, and is usually installed simply as an add-on to SAP Enterprise Core Component (ECC). The Knowledge Warehouse infrastructure can be used for storing and distributing "disk space-intensive" files (scanned files, CAD drawings, video files, and so on). Files can also be stored in the ECC database, however, this does increase the size of that database.

2.6.1 Product Development and Product Launch

Program and project management

The program and project management function enables users to plan, manage, and control the development of new products and their launch on the market (New Product Development and Introduction, NPDI). Project managers can therefore monitor project structures, deadline planning, costs, and resources.

Development teams can use the digital mock-up functions (DMU) in mySAP PLM to simulate and analyze the product design before the prototype is built. The integrated viewer in mySAP PLM enables users to create 2D drawings and 3D models, even without the use of CAD systems. WebFlow, SAP's Internet-based workflow system, and redlining functions accelerate the product development process.

Inter-enterprise collaboration

Lifecycle Collaboration supports cross-enterprise product development with cProjects, a Web-supported tool for managing collaboration projects. cProjects uses the integrated cFolders function for communicating with external project partners.

mySAP PLM cFolders enables data to be exchanged with business partners, without having to give those partners access to the back-end system. Objects such as materials, bills of material, CAD drawings, PowerPoint presentations, table calculation files, and Word documents that are stored in mySAP PLM can be published in cFolders. Data that has been added or modified by external partners can again be seamlessly transferred from cFolders to the back-end system.

Separate suppliers' work areas can be set up with individual authorization settings on the cFolders object level. If an enterprise's security policy does not permit partners to access the intranet, a reverse proxy can be used in the demilitarized zone (DMZ).

External users with low-bandwidth Internet access can upload and download larger files using FTP on the cFolders server. The cFolders function is a component of the mySAP PLM cProjects function portfolio and runs on the SAP Web AS.

Portal integration

The cFolders project structure is displayed as an iView in the SAP Enterprise Portal. Team members can use WebEx[15] to invite themselves to virtual meetings. These invitations contain a hyperlink that the meeting participants can click on to view project information relevant to the meeting.

Product data management

The product data and document management solution, SAP Lifecycle Data Management, provides integrated functions for managing specifications, bills of material, task lists, resource data, CAD models, and technical documentation (like MS Office files). In this solution, a document master record contains metadata for the document (number, description, status, version, and so on). The link to the material masters and bills of material allows the constructor to access business data as early as the development stage. Also, the integrated change service (Change and Release Management) ensures that all changes are thoroughly documented over the whole lifecycle, from construction to maintenance.

Documentation by Drag&Drop

With SAP Easy Document Management, the whole mySAP PLM document management system is displayed in the user's Windows Explorer as a separate hard disk. The users check documents into the PLM document management system by simply dragging and dropping them from an Office application directly onto the mySAP PLM screen. Additional metadata can then be assigned to each document. Users can create private and public folders in order to control how their documents are accessed. SAP Easy Document Management can be used either as a self-contained application or with the whole mySAP PLM system.

---

15 Go to *www.WebEx.com*.

SAP Recipe Management is a sophisticated recipe management system developed to meet the requirements of process industries. It is used to document multilevel recipes and the changes that these recipes undergo in accordance with specific countries and production lines. SAP Recipe Management can be used either as a stand alone, or as part of mySAP PLM.

Recipe management

2.6.2 Asset and Buildings Management

The PLM asset and buildings management solution, SAP Asset Lifecycle Management (ALM) is used to schedule inspections, maintenance and repairs to technical assets and buildings, and to calculate the cost of the work involved. ALM manages maintenance lists and task lists for plant maintenance (PM task lists), which consist of a series of individual plant maintenance activities. Confirmation messages regarding the time and materials used in plant maintenance automatically change the status of the order. If a task is externally assigned, service orders can be created with or without service specifications as early as the plant maintenance planning stage.

Breakdown management

If worse comes to worst, SAP ALM provides a comprehensive messaging and request system for quickly fixing any breakdowns. Catalogs are used to define the extent, cause, and location of the damage. At the same time, the system checks the resources, such as the availability of materials and personnel, from a scheduling viewpoint.

Mobile plant maintenance

With SAP Mobile Asset Management (MAM), building services engineers can call up and enter the data they need—such as information about technical objects or the tasks they have to complete—on-site using a mobile device. MAM uses the SAP Mobile Engine to synchronize and replicate the data between the PLM system and the mobile device.

Real estate management

Integration with the commercial real estate management solution (mySAP Financials Real Estate) creates the ideal environment for planning and handling plant maintenance and modernization activities for real estate and any associated technical assets.

2.6.3 Quality Management

Unlike conventional, isolated computer-aided quality (CAQ) systems and laboratory information and management systems, mySAP PLM supports continuous quality improvement by integrating information from the whole lifecycle of a product. It is for this reason that mySAP PLM facilitates seamless integration with production, data control, and data acquisition systems (Supervisioning, Control and Data Acquisition, SCADA), allowing for statistical process control, and integration with other mySAP components. Quality certificates can be automatically generated and made available to the customers on the Internet under the relevant order.

The audit management function helps enterprises with planning, executing, and evaluating benchmarks according to ISO 9000:2000, QS 9000, GMP, ISO 14011, ISO 19011, and so on.

2.6.4 Hazardous Substance Management, Industrial Hygiene and Safety, Environmental Protection

The SAP Environment, Health and Safety (EH&S) component also belongs to the mySAP PLM area. The core of EH&S is a materials and specifications database, in which objects such as materials (substances, preparations, and so on), agents (noise, climate, hazardous substances, and so on), packaging, dangerous goods classifications, and waste codes are described in a flexible manner.

Material safety data sheets

On this basis, all the documents required for industrial hygiene and safety, and environmental protection—such as material safety data sheets, standard operating procedures, labels and waste manifests—can be dynamically created in any language. The rule engines EH&S Expert and EH&S Easy Expert can be used to derive further data from these documents, or to automatically modify existing data, if this is necessary due to statutory changes.

Dangerous goods transports

Similarly, various papers are required for the transport of dangerous goods. The Dangerous Goods Management component of EH&S automatically adds data regarding the dangerous goods to delivery notes and packing notes in other solutions in the mySAP Business Suite. In doing so, when the system is creating an order or a delivery, it checks whether it is permitted that a certain dangerous good can be transported using the planned means of transport (truck, rail, ship, airplane), taking into account any mixed loadings prohibitions.

Waste management

Many processes do not just create products; they also create varying amounts of dangerous waste. The waste management functions of mySAP PLM EH&S help enterprises to comply with all regulations and laws regarding waste disposal, such as Volume 40 of the Code of Federal Regulations (CFR) in the US, the Waste Avoidance, Recovery and Disposal Act (KrW-/AbfG) in Germany, and EU regulation 259/93. The documents required for transporting waste, such as hazardous waste manifests, can be created via a few simple mouse-clicks.

Safety at work

EH&S makes work easier not only for people who work with hazardous substances, dangerous goods, and waste, but also for industrial hygiene and safety experts, and occupational physicians. Accidents are recorded in the electronic injury and illness log and archived, and health surveillance protocols are automatically proposed, taking into account the level of exposure in the workplace, and the activity and age of the employee in question. Accident statistics and analyses help employers to identify focal points of accidents.

2.7 An Example of SAP xApps: SAP Global Trade Services

The process of exchanging goods and services must often overcome national borders, especially in the global economy. At these borders, a range of customs regulations has to be complied with, in addition to various sanctions and embargos. By means of its SAP Customs Management and SAP Compliance Management components, the SAP Global Trade Services (SAP GTS) SAP xApps supports enterprises with handling customs formalities and ensuring compliance with embargo regulations.

Anything to declare?

SAP Customs Management supports the regulatory classification of products for which duty is then calculated. Trade Document Services ensures that the required import and export documents are created. The Customs Communication Service enables you to connect to the IT systems of national customs offices, such as the Automated Export System (AES) in the US and the New Computerized Transit System (NCTS) in the EU.

Sanctions and embargos

SAP Compliance Management helps enterprises to comply with embargos and sanctions. For example, for every order that is entered into a mySAP ERP system, the system can trigger a process in which the ordering party's address is compared against a "sanctioned party list" (SPL) in the SAP GTS system (SPL Check).

The GTS system can use the Import/Export Control and Embargo Checking function to automatically verify whether a delivery is permitted, and, if necessary, create the license number. The transaction is automatically blocked if the combination of the export list number and the destination country are not permitted.

SAP GTS is based on the J2EE Engine of the Web AS and interfaces to mySAP ERP or another ERP system. The sanctions lists can be loaded into the GTS system in XML format.

2.8 Solutions for Small and Midsize Enterprises

All-in-One With mySAP All-in-One, SAP and various partners with industry know-how have provided approximately 80 preconfigured, industry-specific solutions. Besides classic ERP functionality, mySAP All-in-One also provides additional CRM and SCM functions. All its components use the same database, which reduces rollout and operating costs. However, these solutions have been pared down to the core processes of each industry. Because mySAP All-in-One is based on SAP NetWeaver technology, it can be converted to a complete mySAP solution, if required.

Business One SAP Business One is a business management software solution that is tailored to sales-oriented retail and small to midsize enterprises (SMEs). Because it is not based on SAP NetWeaver, we do not deal with it in this book.

2.9 Summary

The mySAP Business Suite comprises specialized components that provide business functionality for the various areas of an enterprise. Together with the SAP NetWeaver components, which provide the functionality for integrating employees, information, and processes, the mySAP Business Suite components form the basis of a service-oriented architecture and the technical foundation for developing and operating Composite Applications. It is thus an integrated software ecosystem that meets almost all the business requirements of an enterprise in an era characterized by globalization and the Internet. Figure 2.7 shows the logical arrangement of a complete SAP system landscape (without Industry Solutions and PLM).

Even though the individual components of the mySAP suite are self-contained software systems, they should not be regarded as isolated systems in the context of corporate IT landscapes. These systems are technically interconnected due to their close links with each other and the high volume of data exchange between them. Problems in one component can affect business processes running on another system. Therefore, a mySAP system landscape requires a stable foundation, which is manifest in the form of an IT infrastructure that combines high performance and availability with the need for the lowest possible total cost of ownership (TCO).

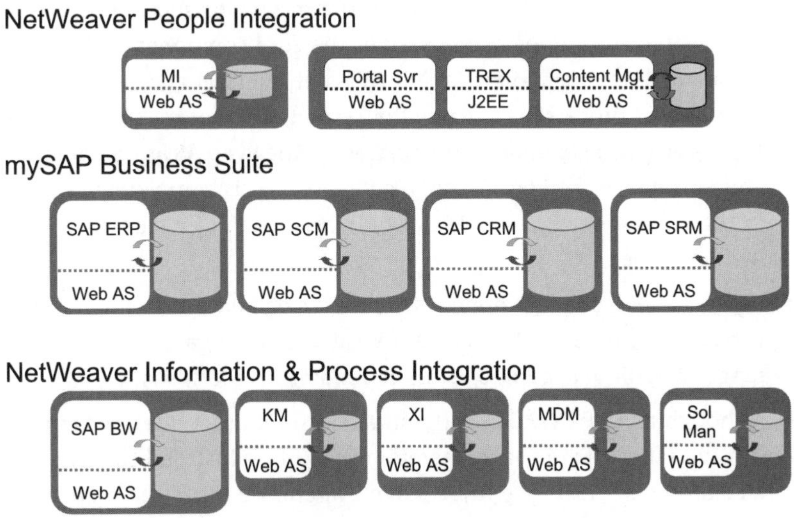

Figure 2.7 Complete mySAP System Landscape (Logical View)

The most important points in this chapter are as follows:

- mySAP ERP remains the most important solution in the mySAP Business Suite. It is here that the most fundamental business processes in every enterprise are run. It also forms the basis for a whole range of industry solutions.
- mySAP ERP consists of the long established SAP R/3, the NetWeaver components described in the previous chapter, and additional functions for Collaborative Business. In mySAP ERP '04, the core R/3 functions are absorbed into the ERP Central Component (ECC). This is a new modularized ERP engine with Web interfaces.
- The analytical functions of mySAP ERP and the reporting function are provided by SAP BW with the SEM add-on (although ECC 5.0 also provides a BW that is technically integrated into the core system).
- mySAP CRM contains applications for marketing, sales, service, and support, as well as functionalities for cooperating with partners and customers via email, a call center, or directly via the SAP Enterprise Portal. mySAP CRM is based on the SAP Web AS and a relational database. Depending on the scenario, the IPC components, catalog systems, the mobile infrastructure, and a range of other additional components can also be included. SAP BW is used to analyze customer-related data.

- mySAP SCM comprises functions for optimizing logistical processes in cross-enterprise value chains. Besides the core component, SAP APO, these functions include the SAP SCM Event Manager and the SAP ICH. Operational processing remains the responsibility of mySAP ERP. The technical infrastructure of APO is based on the Web AS and a database, and also on the SAP liveCache, a database that is completely resident in the main memory, and APO Optimizers, each of which runs in its own instance.
- mySAP SRM is the component for purchasing and procurement. SRM is based on the SAP Web AS and a catalog server, a database, and a range of additional components, depending on the scenario.
- Although mySAP PLM is a self-contained solution, it does not require its own infrastructure, and therefore, it is often installed simply as an add-on to SAP R/3. The Knowledge Warehouse infrastructure can be used for storing CAD drawings, video files, and so on. mySAP PLM cFolders enables enterprises to exchange data with business partners without granting those partners access to back-end systems. The cFolders project structure is displayed as an iView in the SAP Enterprise Portal.
- All components of the mySAP Business Suite can run together on one computer, provided that this computer is adequately dimensioned.

3 SAP Web Application Server

A unified technology base for SAP NetWeaver, the mySAP Business Suite, and in-house development

Before development work began on SAP R/3, there was no suitable programming language and no adequate processing environment for real-time business applications. Thus, SAP had to create them, and ABAP and the SAP Basis (also often referred to as the kernel) were born. Functionalities that are programmed in ABAP are completely independent of the hardware on which they run or the database program in which the information is stored. It is the job of the SAP Basis to ensure that ABAP commands can be executed by the operating system in question and that the database system can process data queries and data storage. The SAP Basis also provides an overlying transaction monitor, a mechanism for load distribution within the network of computers, and many more functions. It thus functions as a hardware abstraction layer, as a data flow platform, and, to a certain extent, as middleware. Therefore, even in those early days, the runtime environment of an ABAP engine was a virtual machine, long before the term came to be associated with Java.

An application server before the term existed

Early on, individual customers began to exploit the benefits of this system by using the SAP Basis not only for SAP applications, but also for complete in-house developments.[1] SAP had therefore created an application server long before the term was appointed for products that, in many cases, often had less extensive functionality. Then, once support for Java and open Internet standards was implemented as part of NetWeaver, it made sense to rename this new, extended SAP Basis as the SAP Web Application Server, or Web AS for short.

The Web AS forms the technology base for nearly all NetWeaver and mySAP solutions and is therefore a component of every NetWeaver and mySAP installation. Besides the processing environment for ABAP and J2EE processes, it also provides a development environment, user management functions, an authorization concept, system monitoring functions, and communication protocols.

1 One example is the Swiss company Interhome/Hotelplan, which used the R/3 Basis to develop a complete travel agency system.

3.1 The Classic SAP Architecture

Technically, the classic R/3 system is designed as a three-tier client/server architecture, with a specific function assigned to each tier (also known as layers). The *presentation layer* provides the user interface, the *application layer* processes the business logic, and the *persistence layer* stores the business data. This architecture provides a high level of scalability and flexibility, and supports heterogeneous environments.

Presentation layer

The presentation layer, which is usually installed on the local workstation, provides the SAP Graphical User Interface (SAP GUI). Because the visual elements of the user interface are provided by the local computer, only the actual reference data has to be transferred via the network, for which a compressed format is used. The concept of this design indicates that, from the beginning, SAP R/3 had the lowest bandwidth requirement of all ERP offerings.

Application layer

The application layer executes the business logic, processes transactions, generates output requests, creates reports, coordinates database access, and establishes connections to other applications. This layer is the heart of the SAP system. The programs in the application logic can run in parallel, and therefore, if the resource requirements ever exceed the capacity of an individual computer, the load can be distributed over multiple servers.

Persistence layer

The persistence layer stores the business data of the application and the code for the SAP application programs. The individual software modules are loaded from the database to the SAP application server only if necessary.

All the business data that belongs to an individual SAP solution is stored in a single database. This has the advantages that data consistency is automatically guaranteed, and the users do not require operating system authorization.

On the other hand, the database server is also the component that sets the maximum performance capacity of an SAP system.

SAP supports several common database platforms[2], so customers can select their own database manufacturer. The database license is usually part of the SAP license agreement, and the database software is delivered with the SAP installation package.

2 Oracle, Microsoft SQL Server, DB2, Informix and maxDB (the former SAPDB).

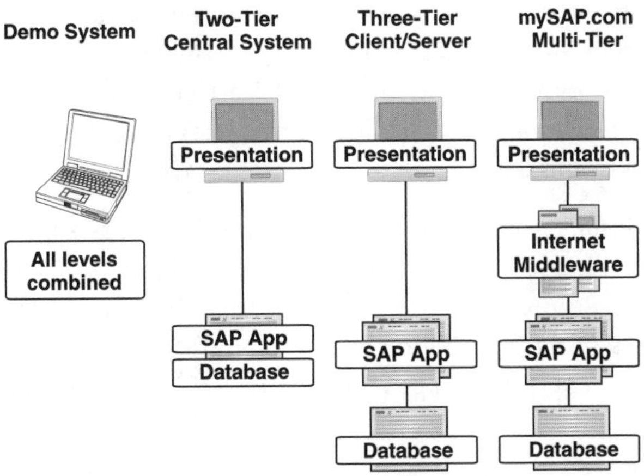

Figure 3.1 The Multilayered Architecture of the SAP System

While the presentation layer is usually installed on the user's workstation (or on a terminal server), the application and persistence layers are installed either on a single computer (central or two-tier system), or on a single database computer and on multiple application servers, depending on the required performance. Understandably, for economic reasons, one should always try to make do with as few servers as possible (server consolidation). In demonstration and development systems, all software layers can be easily installed and run on a single computer.

An interim solution for the Internet

The first solution for accessing SAP systems via Internet protocols was an extra middleware layer known as the SAP Internet Transaction Server (ITS). For every SAP transaction, the ITS dynamically generates an HTML page that can be displayed by any of the common browsers.

Despite its name, the ITS does not usually process any transactions; all incoming data originates from the application servers of the SAP solutions and all outgoing data is sent to these computers. SAP ITS was previously installed on dedicated servers, however, since NetWeaver '04 (Web AS 6.40), it is part of the Web AS.

3.2 The Anatomy of the Web AS

Processes, instances, and clients

The SAP Web AS consists of various programs that provide services for handling business logic. These programs are executed in a range of software processes. All processes on the SAP Web AS and the shared memory that they use are collectively called an SAP instance (similarly, there are also database instances).

All the components of an instance are parameterized via a shared instance profile, and are started and stopped together. Multiple instances can be used in an SAP system. There must be at least one instance per computer, but a single computer with sufficient resources can easily handle several instances at the same time.

While process and instance are IT terms, the term client also has a business meaning. A client is a self-contained commercial, organizational, and IT entity within an SAP system. Due to the special data structure of the SAP system, business settings can be made in customizing that apply to only specific clients. There is also a repository for cross-client settings and objects.

3.2.1 ABAP Engine

The classic ABAP engine of the SAP Web AS consists of several work processes, each of which has its own specific tasks, and a dispatcher process, which distributes the tasks among the work processes.

- Dialog work processes execute the user's transactions in real time. A dialog work process can handle requests from multiple users.
- Batch work processes execute tasks in the background that do not require any online action.
- Update work processes (known as update tasks) update the database asynchronously with the dialog and batch processes so that system performance is not affected by a synchronous process of writing data to the database.
- Spool work processes are responsible for printing and other forms of output.
- Gateway work processes regulate communication between the applications inside the system, and communication with external systems.

In principle, these processes can be executed any number of times on any number of application computers. All the Web AS installations that belong to an SAP system also have one each of two other processes:

- The enqueue process manages an overlying enqueue table in order to ensure the consistency of data on the business level, even across different database transactions.
- The message process controls communication between the various Web Applications Servers and distributes the load across computers.

The instance that runs the enqueue and message processes is called the central instance (CI) (strictly only the message process). All other work processes can run on the CI (see Figure 3.2).

Central instance

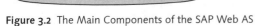

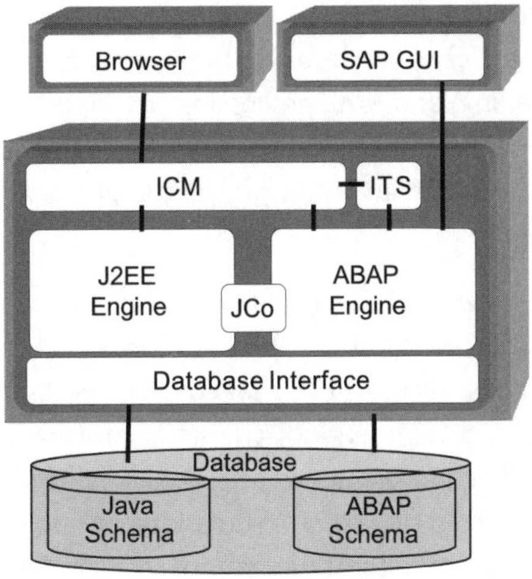

Figure 3.2 The Main Components of the SAP Web AS

If more than one SAP instance is running on an application server, there is one dispatcher per instance. However, if these SAP instances all belong to one SAP system, only one message and enqueue server runs on the central instance. If SAP instances from several SAP systems are running on the server, there is a dispatcher for every SAP instance, and a message and an enqueue server for every SAP central instance.

3.2.2 J2EE Engine

Java applets and servlets

Java is a programming language developed by Sun Microsystems, whose syntax and semantics, like ABAP, are based on C and C++. The story goes that the name came from the large amounts of Java coffee that the developers liked to drink. Thanks to the Java Virtual Machine (JVM) concept, Java programs are independent of the hardware and operating system on which they run. Of all the various Java editions, only the Java 2 Enterprise Edition (J2EE) is relevant to business applications.

Enterprise coffee beans

J2EE can handle different types of application components: application clients, Applets, Servlets, Java Server Pages (JSP), and Enterprise Java Beans (EJB). Java applets are downloaded directly to and run on the user's PC. To run them, you need a client runtime and a GUI (usually a Web browser). Java servlets, on the other hand, run on a server that has a J2EE runtime environment. EJBs are modules that are used to create the business process logic of an application.

Java is considered to be the method of creating a service-oriented architecture. The Java platform provides a wide range of standardized services for database access, connections to legacy systems, security, transaction management, mail delivery, messaging, and XML processing. The application logic is embedded in standardized, modular components. The J2EE variant of Java is intended to provide the availability, security, and scalability that business applications require.

As we already mentioned, the Web AS is a further development of the tried-and-tested SAP Basis, with the addition of Java components. The Java Engine of the SAP Web AS goes back to SAP's takeover of ProSyst and its In-Q-My technology, which SAP extended, adapted, and made J2EE-compliant. Elements of the SAP Basis that were retained were its reliability and scalability, which had been developed over a long period of time, and its independence of operating systems and databases. The SAP Web AS also provides functions that are not comprehensively covered by either the Java standard or by most providers of J2EE application servers.

One core—two personalities

Because of the additional Java components, Web AS has two personalities: the ABAP personality and the Java personality. However, unlike Dr. Jekyll and Mr. Hyde, the classic example of a split personality, the Web AS can use both these personalities concurrently. Therefore, it can not only run as a pure Java or a pure ABAP system, but as a dual ABAP-Java system.

Two heads are better than one

The benefit of this combination of J2EE and ABAP is that, for example, the presentation logic can be used for a Web application with Web Dynpro technology on the basis of JSP, while the existing ERP system runs in the ABAP environment, using SAP Java Connector (JCo) for straightforward access to the relevant Business Application Programming Interfaces (BAPIs). Both the ABAP and the Java personalities communicate within the Web AS using fast Remote Function Call (RFC) connections. The Internet Communication Manager (ICM) handles Internet requests and distributes them across the components.

The middleware component JCo enables communication, that is, method calls, between Java and ABAP applications and vice versa.

The shared transport and correction system, which is part of Software Lifecycle Management, and a shared translation process ensure consistency between J2EE and ABAP.

.NET

Unlike J2EE, with .NET, Microsoft provides a Windows-specific architecture made up of manufacturer-specific components such as *.NET Framework Classes* (a collection of functions for application development), *ADO.NET Data Sets* (Active X data objects, in which database content, for example, is stored) and *.NET Remoting Protocol* (a mechanism for client access to distributed servers). The Windows server and the development environment Visual Studio.NET are the technology base for .NET.

The SAP .NET connector, which connects the .NET world to SAP NetWeaver, basically consists of a wrapper around the standard Win32-RFC librfc32.dll library and some additional services for communication via Simple Object Access Protocol (SOAP) or RFC. The older DCOM connector is still supported, but is no longer being developed.

With Java now part of the long established SAP kernel, enterprises can use their in-house SAP knowledge to operate Java-based applications. The potential synergies of this SAP-Java relationship are fully realized if all J2EE applications are implemented on a Web AS as part of a platform consolidation drive. From the viewpoint of IT managers, this type of strategy helps to cut costs and promotes improvements in the quality of system support.

We should emphasize that business processes can be implemented in a SAP system with Java as well as with ABAP. Depending on the requirements, either programming language can be used in any situation. This opens up new possibilities for the development of Web applications, without the need for enterprises to invest in additional software systems.

However, experience shows that ABAP-based development is still considerably easier on resources than Java applications.

A platform for In-house Development

The SAP Web AS can also be used to develop in-house Java applications using existing SAP knowledge. Unlike conventional Java development environments, the SAP Web AS provides all the benefits of the SAP system, such as transaction security, user management, multiuser capability, version control, a transport mechanism, and interfaces to the SAP system. These benefits, plus the short training period for business process developers, underline the suitability of the SAP Web AS as an in-house development platform. Many enterprises now use the Web AS in this way; one example is an online recruiting system of a large retailer, which is implemented on a Linux server. The development and implementation times for this website were significantly lower than what would have been the case with other Web development environments such as WebSphere and Intershop.

Dispatchers and server processes

Similar to the ABAP engine, the Java part of the SAP Web AS, known as the J2EE Engine, is made up of a dispatcher and several J2EE server processes:

- The Java dispatcher accepts queries from the user and distributes them to the Java server processes.
- The Java Server Processes are responsible for executing the required functionality.
- The Java Enqueue Service is the overlying transaction monitor and is responsible for ensuring consistency.
- The Java Message Service handles internal communication.

The Java part of the SAP Web AS also has a central service instance as does the ABAP part. Here, too, the Java dispatcher and server can be distributed across multiple servers.

Load distribution with the SAP Web dispatcher

SAP provides a Web dispatcher for distributing the load of HTTP requests between multiple Web Application Servers. With the help of a session cookie, the SAP Web dispatcher can always forward all the requests of a particular user to the same application instance, as is necessary in stateful applications. The Web dispatcher also correctly assigns Java and ABAP requests.

While the user's requests are always directed to the Web dispatcher as the single point of contact, and the dispatcher then forwards them to the ICM of the application instances, the work processes' responses always go directly to the user.

The technical structure of the Web dispatcher is largely identical to that of the ICM, and so it can easily be installed on the central instance. Moreover, if the central instance is running in a cluster, the availability of the Web dispatcher is guaranteed.

To increase security, the Web dispatcher can also be installed on a computer in the demilitarized zone (DMZ). In this case, however, it should be designed to be redundant, so that it is not a single point of failure (SPoF). For more information on this topic, see Chapters 7 and 10.

In theory, HTTP load balancers from other providers could also be used, but there are a number of disadvantages to this (bookmarks cannot be used, and re-authentication is carried out if another application server is assigned, among others).

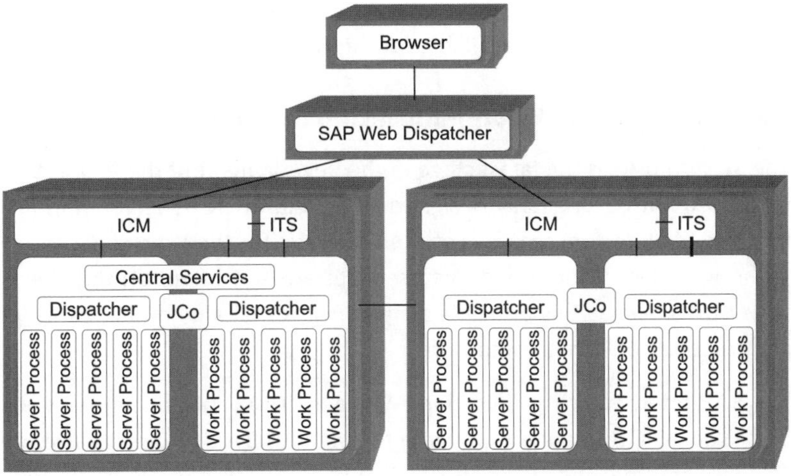

Figure 3.3 Processes of the Central Instance (Left) and of an Application Instance with Load Distribution by the Web Dispatcher

3.2.3 Buffer

Every instance has a memory buffer area for various objects; for example, program code, dictionary objects, screen structures, and table content. This buffer is created at runtime and is optimized on an ongoing basis. Various algorithms ensure that the most frequently required data is stored in the buffer. Every time a Web AS is stopped and re-started, the buffers have to reestablish their optimal state.

3.2.4 Database Layer

Open SQL interface

Applications that are programmed in ABAP access the database system via the Open SQL interface, which converts ABAP statements to the corresponding database commands. This method ensures that the business process logic is completely independent of the database and the operating system. When interpreting statements, the interface carries out a syntax check and ensures that the load is optimally distributed across the buffers for SQL statements and SQL data.

These functionalities have been carried over from ABAP to an Open SQL for Java. Database-independence is ensured by the use of standards such as Java Database Connectivity (JDBC).

The Java part of the SAP Web AS requires a separate database schema. Therefore, to install a pure Java Web AS instance, a database instance has to be installed as well. To install a Web AS with a Java and an ABAP part, a shared database instance for the Java and the ABAP schema is sufficient. (Note: no Java schema is available for Informix.)

3.2.5 SAP Internet Communication Manager

An evolutionary development

The SAP Web AS is the latest stage in the development of the long established SAP Basis. Originally designed in the era of client-server computing, it is the latest incarnation of the SAP Basis for the Web services age (although experts know that Web services are also based on the client-server principle, as this principle simply means that a computer can trigger processes on other computers).

The SAP Internet Communication Manager (ICM), introduced with the SAP Web AS 6.20, made it possible for the SAP Basis to directly use the standard Internet protocols HTTP, HTTPS, SOAP, and SMTP. It supports Internet document standards such as HTML, XML, and XLST, and server-side scripting with ABAP and JavaScript.

The ICM can function either as a server or as a client for external communication partners. It functions as a server when an application or a client, such as a Web browser, initiates communication by establishing a connection to the ICM, and it functions as a client if the Web application server initiates communication. Note at this point that although the term "client-server technology" is now regarded as old-fashioned by the marketing people, the Internet and all its services nonetheless still function according to this paradigm.

Thanks to its integration with the Web AS, the ICM is very fast (~ 35,000 hits/minute on a four-way Linux system). The parallel multithread architecture[3] supports simultaneous read and write access. The use of caching means that the quantity of server resources required to build the required

3 Threads are series of commands. They are the smallest subset of a process and can run simultaneously on different CPUs of a system.

pages is significantly reduced, and frequently requested sites do not have to be called anew from the server every time.

3.2.6 Internet Graphics Service

The SAP Internet Graphics Service (IGS) enables you to display data from an SAP system or another source as graphics in a Web browser. The IGS is a component of the Web AS, but can also be installed on a separate computer. This can prove to be paradoxical in terms of the network load, because there is no direct communication between the IGS and the browser. For example, if an application server sends data to the IGS, the IGS creates a graphic that is then sent back to the application server, which then forwards it to the user's browser.

3.2.7 The Achilles' Heel of an SAP System

Single points of failure

Almost all technical systems have an Achilles' Heel, also known as a single point of failure (SPoF). These are components that are not designed to be redundant (and cannot be redundant) and when they fail, so does the whole system.

A classic ABAP system has two SPoFs: the Message Service and the Enqueue Service. Admittedly, the message service is not as big a problem, because if its central instance fails, it can be restarted within a few milliseconds on another computer. The Enqueue Service, however, is more complicated.

Systemwide Lock Management

All databases that are certified for use with SAP have a lock mechanism. This mechanism ensures that transactions are executed either completely or not at all. Thus, the database is always in a consistent state, even if the database computer breaks down.

However, the database cannot ensure the consistency of overlying business transactions, that is, the task of transaction monitors such as SAP's Enqueue Service. While multiple enqueue server processes can occur in a system, there can be only one enqueue table for systemwide lock management.

Therefore, the system has to be restarted if the enqueue table is not available. All transactions that were not fully completed must be returned to their initial state and then restarted.

Because the J2EE Engine is structured similarly to ABAP processes, it experiences the same SPoFs. Until Web AS 6.30, there were four SPoFs: two message servers and two enqueue servers. The distribution of the J2EE Engine in cluster mode, as it is known, does not help in this case, since it is only intended for scaling. Then, with Web AS 6.40, the central instance was replaced by the SAP System Central Services (SCS), which unites the message server and the enqueue server for the ABAP kernel and the J2EE Engine.

Replicated enqueue

The introduction of the SAP Enqueue Replication Service also solves the problem of the enqueue table as an SPoF, because this table is now replicated to a second computer. Therefore, along with a cluster solution, a new enqueue service can be activated fast enough so that transactions do not break down under normal circumstances. The Enqueue Replication Service does not make the system unsinkable, however, when combined with a cluster solution, it does provide very effective protection against the consequences of a system breakdown.

3.3 Internationalization

The fast pace of the convergence of international markets is a necessary by-product of globalization. Nonetheless, the global business world is still made up of different countries, each with its own rules, laws, and languages. Despite the fact that multinational enterprises assume that all their employees can communicate in English, customers still expect quotes and invoices to be in their own language, or at least that their name and address be spelled correctly. Phonetic transliterations (such as "Missbach" instead of the correct German "Mißbach") are not a satisfactory solution. Right from the start, SAP has taken these country-specific aspects of business into account; its support for multiple currencies in the Accounting solution is just one such example.

Legal aspects

Country-specific versions address the various legal aspects that apply in each country. SAP provides an extensive library and templates that make it easier for customers to implement typical business processes tailored to their own country. Special date display options, country-specific calendars of public holidays and factory calendars, and country-specific format settings such as settings for value-added tax (VAT) numbers all help customers to fulfill the requirements of their respective country.

Multilingual capability

All parts of an SAP application can be displayed in a country-specific version. For example, names of input fields can be automatically displayed in the required language, on the basis of the translated texts contained in the data type repository. If necessary, an application can also have country-specific views in order to display a different text orientation (such as right-to-left like in Hebrew), for example.

SAP provides the translations of user interface texts (dynpros, menus, messages, online Help, and so on) with the installation pack. It is of course the customer's responsibility to organize the translation of master data, texts associated with in-house development, print-outs, and so on.

Code pages

If an SAP system is to contain multiple languages, a number of requirements have to be considered. Every language requires a specific character set, and character sets are displayed via code pages. As long as the required languages can all be displayed by the same code page, there is no problem. Figure 3.4 shows the languages that are covered by the standard ISO code pages. All the languages contained in a single ellipse can be combined in an SAP system.

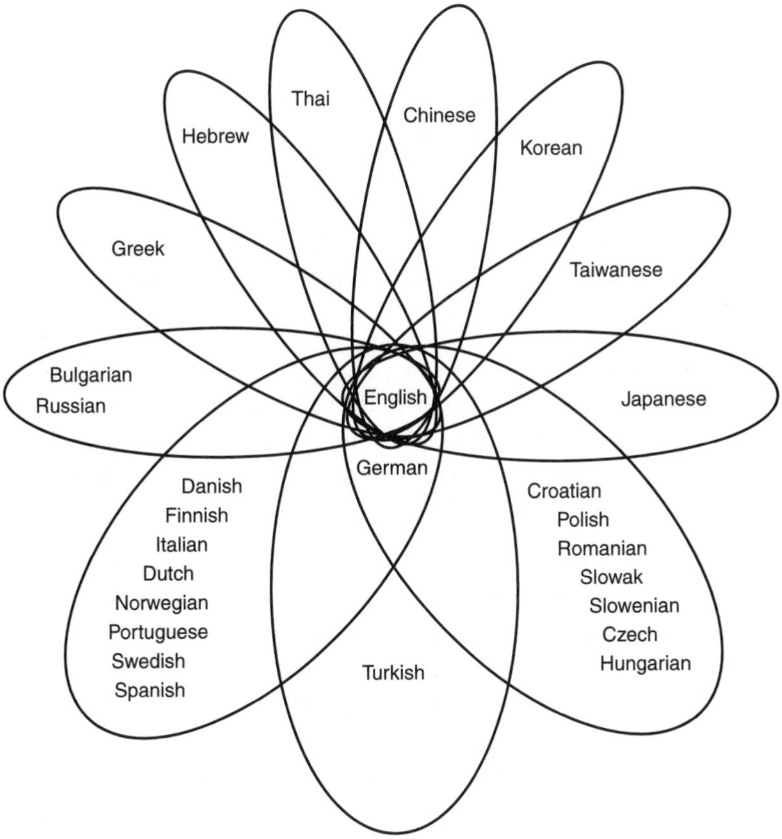

Figure 3.4 Language Combinations with Standard Code Pages

However, not every required language combination is supported by an ISO code page. For this reason, SAP developed its own SAP code pages for frequently required language combinations. It also created the option of combining multiple code pages in an SAP system for situations where the SAP code pages were not sufficient.

3.3.1 Unicode

Why Unicode?

Computers work only with numbers. Letters and other characters are assigned to numbers in a coding system so that computers can process and store them. In the days of punch cards, memory space was limited, and so people tried to restrict themselves to as few bits as possible. For example, in the widely used ASCII code, only seven bits are required for character display. The downside of this is that only 128 characters (2^7) can be uniquely encoded. This is more than enough for English, which requires only 60 characters (uppercase and lowercase letters, figures, punctuation marks, and special characters).

However, all the languages of the EU member states, not to mention the Asian languages, require more than the 256 characters that can be displayed with the usual 8-bit (that is, one byte) code pages (hence the different ellipses for Western and Eastern Europe in Figure 3.4). Korean, for example, has approximately 12,000 syllables, and Chinese has approximately 50,000 characters. The so-called CJK languages (Chinese, Japanese, Korean) have therefore always required 16-bit (double-byte) code pages.

Unlike the many different ISO and SAP code pages, Unicode defines a unified character set that covers almost all the world's languages. Unicode has been in existence since 1988 and is managed and developed by the Unicode Consortium.[4] Unicode Version 3.0 is largely identical to ISO/IEC 10646 and various national standards.

All the languages of the world

Thanks to its universal nature, Unicode was destined to be used on the Internet. Internet standards such as HTML, XML, and LDAP were based on Unicode from the start. Programming languages such as Java, JavaScript, C#, Perl, and Python are also based on Unicode. Both Linux and Microsoft operating systems and applications have been Unicode-enabled for a while, which is evident by the fact that Google sometimes returns Asian pages in its hit lists. Although not all users may have the lan-

4 *http://www.unicode.org*.

guage skills to understand them, the Internet can transport them and display them in the browser.

Unicode Scripts

A Unicode script combines multiple languages that share a common character set. The Latin script, for example, contains English and German, and also Vietnamese, among others; the Arabic script contains Arabic, Farsi, and Urdu. Some languages, such as Korean, require their own script (Hangul), and Japanese requires a number of scripts (Han (Kanji), Hiragana and Katakana).

Unicode supports the following scripts: Latin, Greek, Cyrillic, Armenian, Hebrew, Arabic, Syriac, Thaana, Devanagari, Bengali, Gurmukhi, Oriya, Tamil, Telegu, Canadian Aboriginal Syllabics, Malayalam, Sinhala, Thai, Lao, Tibetan, Myanmar, Georgian, Hangul, Ethiopic, Cherokee, Ogham, Runic, Khmer, Mongolian, Han (Japanese, Chinese, Korean), Hiragana, Katakana, Bopomofo, and Yi. It also supports mathematical symbols, musical notation (modern and Byzantine), technical symbols, and Braille.

So far, of the 4,294,967,296 characters available in Unicode, a little over 90,000 are currently assigned.

3.3.2 SAP and Unicode

In principle, the process logic of SAP applications was always Unicode-enabled. Java is Unicode-enabled since its inception. The ABAP engine, however, is based on C/C++ and therefore must be adjusted before it can work with Unicode. For this purpose, SAP developed new data types for C/C++ and incorporated them into the ISO standard.

Unicode is an installation option from SAP R/3 Enterprise on, and Unicode will gradually be made available in all solutions in the mySAP Business Suite. In particular, Unicode capability is required for SAP XI by default, due to the reliance of XI on Internet standards such as XML and SOAP.

Double-byte—double the storage capacity?

Since the characters have doubled to two bytes with Unicode, do the hardware requirements double as well? Not necessarily. For one thing, not all Unicode characters require two bytes, and not all information that is processed in an SAP system and stored in the database is in the form of texts. Also, in the Asian languages, for example, a word may be expressed by a single two-byte character, while other languages may require several single-byte characters for a word. For example, the English word locomotive requires 10 bytes, while the equivalent Chinese word requires only four bytes.

Unicode encoding schema

Not all characters require 32 bits (four bytes); in many cases, eight bits or one byte are sufficient, while some require 16 bits or two bytes, and even some Asian languages only require three bytes. Therefore, the Unicode standard defines various coding schemas and algorithms for converting characters from one schema to another.

The UTF[5]-8 schema, for example, uses a variable number of bytes; it stores ASCII characters as single bytes, Latin letters including European accent characters as double bytes, and many Asian characters as triple bytes. Therefore, there are no additional memory requirements for converting US ASCII code, only a small percentage for ISO-8859–1, 50 % more for Chinese, Japanese, and Korean, and 100 % more for Greek and Cyrillic characters. Thus, while UTF-8 is very efficient at data storage and transfer, the variable coding means that more computing resources are required for the decoding process. UTF-8 is used by UNIX systems, HTML, and most Web browsers.

With 32-bit coding (UTF-32 and UCS[6]), all characters have a fixed length. This makes them easier to process, but is very demanding on memory space: 100 % more is required for Chinese, Japanese, and Korean, and 300 % more is required for US-ASCII, ISO-8859–1, Greek, and Cyrillic.

Sixteen-bit coding (UTF-16 and UCS-2) represents a compromise, since it does not require as much memory space as UTF-32, but still uses a fixed character length. In this case, Chinese, Japanese, and Korean do not require any extra memory space, but US-ASCII, ISO-8859–1, Greek and Cyrillic require 100 % more. Both Java and Microsoft from Win95/NT 4.0 use UTF-16.

Because of the balance between CPU and memory requirements, and its compatibility with Java and Microsoft systems, SAP has also selected UTF-16 as a platform for the Web AS.

An increase in CPU resource requirements of between 30 % and 35 % can be expected when a single-byte code page system is upgraded to Unicode. Modern CPUs can easily handle this increase.

5 Unicode Transformation Format.

6 Universal Character Set.

The main memory requirement, however, usually increases by around 50 %[7] and can therefore exceed the limits of a 32-bit operating system, even in medium-sized systems. Therefore, it is probably not a coincidence that SAP only introduced Unicode once 64-bit systems for Linux and Windows—such as Itanium and, later, Opteron CPUs—became available.

The amount of extra disk space required depends on the Unicode Encoding Schema of the database system. Databases that use UTF-8 or CESU-8, such as Oracle, MaxDB (from Version 8.0) and DB/2 for AIX, require 33 %; and UTF-16 databases such as Microsoft SQL Server, DB/2 for AS400, and MaxDB (up to Version 7.0) require between 60 % and 70 %.

The network load increases by approximately 7 % for Latin-1, approximately 15 % for Japanese, and 25 % for other Asian languages.

Changing over to Unicode

Most existing ABAP programs should have no problems running with Unicode. When a mySAP solution is updated to a Unicode-enabled version, all customer extensions are automatically subject to a Unicode compatibility check and are also checked for compliance with the stricter syntax and semantics. This also applies if a solution is upgraded to a non-Unicode version. Thus, the same source code can be used for Unicode and non-Unicode, and new developments can be easily swapped between the two systems. A special version of R3Trans enables transports between the systems.

Automatic code page conversion has been added to the interfaces (such as RFC), and systems can thus communicate with other Unicode-based and non-Unicode-based systems.

Because the Web AS always uses UTF-16, data can be easily transferred between databases with different coding systems; for example, between an R/3 system with a UTF-16 database and a SAP BW with a UTF-8 database. However, you cannot save Unicode data in a non-Unicode system. Therefore, Java data cannot be stored in a non-Unicode system without first being converted to the relevant code page(s).

3.4 SAP System Landscapes

In the business world, nothing is certain except change. Therefore, the configuration settings of the enterprise software systems that support business processes have to be adapted to change on a continuous basis.

7 Except for Asian-language systems, which were always double-byte in any case.

However, these adaptations should not be made directly in live systems, for obvious reasons.

Usually, enterprises run the main production systems, plus separate development systems (DEV) for new and continuing development work. However, it would be careless to simply copy any changes made in the development systems to the business-critical production system without checking them first. Reason dictates that all necessary changes and new development must first be transferred to a special upstream system with a copy of the real data, for the purposes of quality assurance and testing (test system or quality assurance system, QA), before they are used in the real system. Once the tests have run successfully, the changes can then be released for transfer from the development to the production system.

Customizing

Customizing is used to adapt the predefined business settings in the system to the requirements of the real-world business processes of the individual enterprise. These settings have to be made during the implemantation process of the SAP system, and are then adapted to changes in the enterprise's requirements during productive operations. Examples of Customizing settings are company codes, plants, warehouses, and so on, and also factory calendars. Customizing changes are also usually necessary if any changes are made to the relevant statutory framework conditions.

The Quality Assurance (QA) system is also often referred to as the consolidation system and is also used to conduct stability tests on patches to the operating system, the database, and the SAP system, and so on, before these patches are copied to the production system.

There can also be training, evaluation, and *sandbox systems*, which are used for user training, to collect feedback on people's experiences with mySAP, and for feasibility studies for customer-specific requirements. If there is a large project in which multiple development teams are working in separate development systems, a separate integration system is used to ensure that the development work of each team is compatible with the work of the other teams.

While these systems and the development systems are usually very small, the QA system should be large enough so that the results it produces can be reliably tested to accurately reflect the performance of the production system. Duplicates of the data in the production system are used for this purpose, so that the test results are based on realistically large datasets.

Test Automation

The Test Workbench has been delivered by SAP with the Web AS for some time now. This tool is used to automate functionality and scaling tests. It comprises the Test Organizer, which manages test case catalogs and test projects, and the Extended Computer Aided Test Tool (eCATT), an automation tool. Consequently, if modifications need to be made to business transactions due to updates or new support packages, the necessary regression tests can be automated in complex system landscapes. In this process, the user input of transactions to be tested are recorded right up to the printing stage, and can be *replayed at any time on a test system*. In addition to its other benefits, the main advantage of eCATT is that the time spent on testing by key users in the individual technical departments is kept to a minimum.

The minimum recommended configuration for a landscape consists of a DEV, QA, and PRD system for every SAP NetWeaver and mySAP solution in the enterprise. However, not all these systems have to be always active. It is sufficient to keep installations of the non-production systems in reserve, using the methods described in Chapter 13, and then to deploy them onto a computer when and if necessary. No license fees apply to non-production systems.

Software logistics

Any changes and new development work completed by the customer have to be transported to all these systems. These transports are also subject to the rules of quality assurance for software systems, as defined in the quasi-standard Information Technology Infrastructure Library (ITIL) and the IT Service Management Reference Model (ITSM) an adoption of ITIL for client/server systems.

The Web AS provides change management functions and transport services for this purpose. The configuration system contains all changes, and transports them to the quality system, where they are then tested.

IT Service Management Reference Model

In principle, operating an SAP system landscape is no different from operating any other multiuser application. However, the availability of SAP systems and the consistency of the data they contain is usually of fundamental importance in enterprises. Therefore, the same principles apply to SAP systems as those that generally apply to enterprise-critical applications in the Information Technology Infrastructure Library (ITIL). ITIL was originally developed by the Central Computer and Telecommunications Agency (CCTA) for mainframe environments, and is now further developed by HP for distributed computer environments in accordance with the IT Service Management Reference Model (ITSM). Today, ITSM is regarded as the industry standard for the professional operation of distributed computer environments.

Change Management

A professional Change Management is one of the cornerstones in ITIL as well as in ITSM. The SAP Change and Transport System (CTS) is part of SAP's software logistics system and is used to manage quality assurance procedures. All the data and structural information contained in the changes is stored in a central transport directory on the operating system level. All systems in the system landscape have access to this directory. The Transport Management System (TMS), which manages all import queues, is used for importing data in to the target system. A transport consists of the phased export from the source system to the central transport directory, and the import to the relevant target system.

With the SAP Web AS, the functionalities of the CTS are now also available for Java developments. This greatly improves the quality of the daily operation of a Java application, and allows the costs and development times of Java projects to be significantly reduced.

Transport requests and routes

Changes to the repository or the Customizing are recorded in transport requests. Transport requests are distributed via transport layers, which combine all the development projects that are to be transported to the same target systems. There are two types of transport routes, which have to be created in the transport route editor of the TMS before the development project starts:

- The consolidation route is used to transport changes from the development system to the quality assurance system. There can be only one consolidation route per SAP system and transport layer. Changes to objects for which a consolidation route has not been created cannot be transported to other SAP systems. These changes are recorded in local change requests.

- The delivery route is used to transport changes from the development system to the production system, after the tests have been successfully completed. Changes can also be transported to multiple SAP systems. This may be necessary if, for example, a system is set up so that multiple production systems at various locations get changes from one central development system. Training systems are another example. Depending on the structure of the SAP system landscape, multiple delivery routes can be set up with the same source system and different target systems (parallel delivery), or multiple delivery routes can be concatenated (multilevel delivery).

The Transport Organizer supports the development team with creation and documentation functions, functions for releasing change requests, and functions for reorganizing the development landscape up to the point of releasing a change request. The TMS also supports the subsequent processes of transport execution, monitoring, and logging.

3.5 Grid Computing

Scientific grids

Grid computing is the distribution of an application across multiple computers, which are themselves distributed in a network (or grid). The grid concept has its origins in the world of academia, in which there are some tasks that require computing power that exceeds the capacity of even supercomputers. Because these kinds of tasks can (relatively) easily be performed in parallel with each other, they can be distributed across individual computers. Provided that a relatively small amount of information is exchanged in the calculations, and the latency time does not have any particularly negative effects, in theory, these computers can be located anywhere. For example, the workstations of an enterprise's employees could be used for intranet applications (or even, in theory, those of all the Internet users who make their computers freely available, as is the case with SETI, a project whose purpose is to look for extraterrestrial life).

Industrial grids

Grids are also used in industry for computing-intensive tasks that lend themselves to parallel processing, such as analyzing seismic data for oil prospecting, crash simulations in automobile development, and, in particular, molecular modeling in bioinformatics.

The specifications and standards for an open grid services architecture (OGSA) are formulated by the Grid Forum, while the Globus tool group provides freely available grid middleware software in its Globus Toolkit.

The Grid services concept

Grid services are applications that run on a computer in the grid platform. This computer, in turn, is equipped with special management software. Grid services must have very specific interfaces (APIs) and be able to use such interfaces as well. These include interfaces for finding and loading, and for the whole Lifetime Management process. They also have to provide events for the overall management of the services and interoperate compatibly in this process. Because there are no regulations governing the implementation of the services—for example, the language used for the implementation—the interfaces are provided in the form of client-specific proxies.

Web services and grid services

To be able to use a grid and its computing power, the architecture of an application has to be suitable for distribution, and the calculation task at hand must lend itself to segmentation. Grid computing is thus similar to remote batch processing, while Web services are used more for distributed processing with asynchronous communication.

Contrary to Web services, in a grid system, you cannot process business processes in the classic sense, because the grid architecture cannot ensure transactional integrity. For example, message receipts that get lost in the network cannot be recovered.

Currently, standards for Web services and grid service interfaces are converging in the Web Service Remote Framework (WSRF) from OASIS. In this framework, Web services are responsible for the state management and lifecycle management of the Open Grid Service Interface specification (OGSI 1.0). Both standards use the extended version of Web Service Definition Language (WSDL) for grid services as a shared interface definition language.

SAP and grids

SAP has already developed some grid services on the basis of Web service technology. However, due to technical restrictions, these services are limited to applications that exchange a relatively small amount of data, such as the SAP Internet Pricing and Configurator (IPC), the mySAP CRM Workforce Management (WFM) Optimizer, the SAP APO Optimizer and SAP High Performance Analytics (HPA).

For example, the grid-enabled IPC can be used to dynamically adjust the number of IPC servers to meet current requirements. The application is automatically installed, configured, and activated on computers that conform to the OGSI specifications. Once it is started, the service is monitored by the IPC Manager Service. If the load falls below a predefined threshold value, an IPC server is removed from the grid.

The limits of the grid

With grid computing for technical and academic purposes, the goal is to bundle computing resources to enable large-scale, parallel calculations. However, these calculations must lend themselves to parallel processing.

For business solutions, on the other hand, the focus is on I/O-intensive database operations. Usually, you cannot relocate large data sets to a remote computer before processing; therefore, fast networks have to be used to make large data sets accessible at a location close to the processors.

Because of the high I/O rates and the influence of signal latency on performance, the use of grid computing in classic business scenarios is largely restricted to hosting centers. If the database and the application software were adapted accordingly, as is currently in progress, then these enterprise grids could fulfill their enormous potential for increasing flexibility, provided that the complexity of the application is kept under firm control.

3.6 Summary

With the Web AS, SAP provides an integrated data flow and development platform that addresses almost all enterprise requirements in the Internet age. The most important points in this chapter are as follows:

- A SAP system comprises a database and at least one SAP instance. Because the programs in the application logic run in parallel, the process can be distributed over SAP instances on different application servers. However, there can be only one database per mySAP component.
- Provided that the computing resources and main memory are sufficient, the database and application levels can be combined on one central system, or alternatively, multiple central systems can be consolidated on one computer.
- A typical mySAP system landscape consists of at least one development system, a test system, and a production system for every mySAP component.

4 System Dimensioning and Service Level Agreements

The art of prediction and budgeting

Performance versus total cost of ownership

Although investment in server infrastructure is not usually the largest part of the total cost of ownership (TCO) of an SAP system, dimensioning and architecting the IT systems so that they provide optimum performance is still central to every SAP project. This is because the response times of a system that is dimensioned to be too small are, at best, unsatisfactory, causing the users to be less productive. At worst, there can be a total system breakdown, usually at the most inconvenient time (such as when the year-end accounts are being drawn up, or, worse, just before Christmas).

The process of dimensioning a system is referred to as *sizing*, and involves estimating the maximum expected system load, and deciding on the minimum hardware configuration requirements that can handle this load. Sizing is not an exact science, however. There are many reasons why, but the main one is that at the time when the sizing process is most needed (for budgeting and bid invitations), the data required to determine the system load is not yet precise enough to make the necessary calculations. In this case, as in many others, the adage "garbage in—garbage out" applies (in other words, if you input nonsense, you get nonsense back).

However, you can still make a sound estimate of the required system performance, using the experience of other real-life customer situations and sizing-oriented performance measurements, which are known as *scalability measurements*. Besides in-depth knowledge of sizing methods and the tools to go with it, practical experience is one of the most important prerequisites for a sizing process that most accurately reflects the customer's requirements.

Sizing tools

Generally, hardware providers offer a free sizing service as part of their presales process. While an experienced consultant can certainly do a sizing estimate with pen and paper, hardware providers and SAP have created a range of tools for system sizing. Tools from hardware providers can create a realistic system configuration with computers from the manufacturer's portfolio; however, these tools are usually only available to the manufacturer's sizing experts and those of their partners.

SAP Quick Sizer

The SAP Quick Sizer is available via the Internet[1] to every SAP customer. The output of the SAP Quick Sizer are calculated values for CPU capacity, memory requirement, and disk requirement, which hardware providers can then convert into actual hardware systems. Because all SAP partners have access to the Quick Sizer, you only have to specify the customer number and the project name in a bid invitation. Therefore, the manufacturer can create a proposal simply by using the relevant information in the Quick Sizer; however, in doing so, the customer assumes responsibility for the correctness of the data that he or she enters. It is therefore advisable that customers learn the definitions of the individual input fields in the Help function very carefully.

The SAP Quick Sizer is constantly extended and optimized on the basis of practical feedback from customers' experiences. Consequently, if the same values are entered at different points in time, the output may differ on each occasion. To ensure that old versions are not unintentionally used, the Quick Sizer does not have an offline version. If you're designing a system on the basis of Quick Sizer results, you should always note the date on which the analysis was carried out.

This chapter is not intended as a detailed guide to the sizing of SAP systems. Rather, it is meant as a way to foster an understanding of the processes involved in dimensioning, and their limitations, in order to make it easier for you to collaborate with the sizing experts at SAP and their partners. The first section provides an overview of the various methods of determining system load, and explains how to draw conclusions from this data regarding the CPU, memory, and disk space requirements. The second section shows how these requirements can be reconciled with the existing hardware configurations.

4.1 The Meaning of Service Level Agreements

IT is service

As we know, computer systems and applications in an enterprise are not operated for their own sake; their purpose is to support business processes. Making information available is thus a service that is the response to a demand from the line of business departments and management of the enterprise. Therefore, in principle, there is no particular difference

1 Go to *http://service.sap.com/quicksizing*.

between this service and the services provided by an outsourcer or an application service provider.

Internal customer-vendor relationship

As in every customer-vendor relationship, it is advisable to define the type and quality of the service to be provided, using measurable criteria. This is the task of Service Level Management. The resulting Service Level Agreements (SLAs) form the planning basis for how the system landscape is designed in terms of capacity and availability.

It is obvious, that a system landscape that is required to ensure very short response times, even under extreme loads, and to tolerate breakdowns of individual components, has to be designed differently from a training system. The task of Service Level Management is to ensure that the gap between the user's expectations and what the system landscape is capable of doing under the given conditions and restrictions don't open too wide.

SLAs for business applications make sense only if they are jointly drawn up by the various business areas along with the application development team and the IT department. The goal is to create an unambiguous and mutually acceptable definition of the services to be provided, and to define parameters for the quality of those services, such as the following:

- Transaction load
- Response time behaviour
- Retention period (period of time in which the data has to be directly accessible)
- Required availability of the service, and the maximum tolerable number and duration of planned and unplanned downtimes (Maintenance windows and unplanned downtime)
- Reaction times for incidents, and target recovery times

Response time influences productivity

The productivity of a user of a real-time business system, such as SAP NetWeaver and the solutions in the mySAP Business Suite, is largely determined by the response time of the system in question. Therefore, the goal of every SAP infrastructure is to make the system's response times as short as possible. However, high performance in the form of low response times comes at a price, namely that the infrastructure must be sufficiently dimensioned to ensure that the system can process the business processes in question in an acceptable time frame.

System metrics

It's clear that if the system metrics are changed, the system design must be adapted accordingly, and the required budget must also be made available accordingly. For this reason, the system metrics, which are the basis of the sizing process, have to be part of the SLA. This ensures that the IT department is not held accountable for any deterioration in the response times of the SAP system due to an increase in the number of users or additional modules.

Besides the required response times, the necessary system resources are mainly determined by the type and scope of the business processes that the SAP system is expected to handle. In order for the dimensioning experts to determine the optimal configuration, the specific performance requirements of the business processes have to be known with as much detail as possible. However, this is made very difficult by the enormous range of functionalities in R/3 and the other mySAP components, along with the almost limitless customizing options. Any extensions to the system that the customers themselves may make add to the complexity of sizing.

Customer-specific load tests

Therefore, an exact calculation of the performance requirements for the specific business processes of the different business departments is possible only via a customer-specific load test. The customizing and all extensions must already be in place. These kinds of tests are very resource-intensive. If you're not prepared to invest in such tests, you will have to accept that the result of the sizing process will only be an estimate, based on general values, and that real-world values may differ significantly from these in individual cases.

The price of openness and flexibility

To ensure maximum flexibility when the customer's business processes have to be adapted, plus the greatest possible level of standardization of the system core, only the SAP Web Application Server (Web AS) is compiled in a platform-specific manner, with a small number of exceptions. Conversely, most of the application logic programmed in ABAP or Java is interpreted. Also, in order to remain independent of any one manufacturer, SAP does not use any proprietary functionalities of the hardware or database systems. This approach requires much higher processor performance than an approach where the software is compiled for one single application and one platform.

4.2 User-Based Sizing

At the very least, the number of users for which the system is intended should be known from the beginning. Assuming that the number of business processes that a user can process within one working day will not exceed a certain amount, the expected transaction load can be calculated on this basis. However, remember that not all users will be active at the same time and to the same degree.

What is a user?

In the SAP context, the term *user* can be defined as follows:

- A *named user* is a user with a user account in the system. In most cases, the number of named users is the same as the number of SAP licenses. Because it is highly unlikely that all named users will be active in the system at the same time, this definition of a user does not yield any useful information for the purposes of sizing. The same basic principle applies to installed SAP Front-Ends.
- Every *logged-on user* occupies a certain amount of main memory. Therefore, even though not all logged-on users are active at the same time, the estimated number of users who are logged on at the same time is information that can be used to size main memory.
- The number of *concurrent users* in a system is the most important information for dimensioning, since these users execute business processes that require CPU power and generate data that has to be stored to the disks. The maximum number of concurrent users is therefore very important for sizing processor requirements.

Load factors for business processes

When executed, the business processes supported by the various solutions result in very different CPU and memory loads. These differences are caused by the different levels of complexity, integration with other modules, and the number of database tables that have to be accessed. These different resource requirements are standardized using a unified basis for every solution via load factors. Therefore, the users must be assigned to the solution that they use most frequently for the sizing process.

Degree of activity of the user

If possible, the number of active users in the different modules should be further differentiated, because experience shows that not all users are active in the system to the same degree. The degree of activity, also known as the transaction profile, provides important information about how frequently a user working with the different components sends a request (user interaction step) to the system per hour.

The user needs a certain amount of time between inputs in order to think about what he or she will enter next, and so the transaction profile can be defined using this "think time" of the user. In other words, by using the think time, you can roughly classify the concurrent users into three categories:

- The *user with a low degree of activity* executes at least one interaction step every five to six minutes. This could be a manager or a user whose main activity is to call up information.
- The *user with a medium degree of activity* executes a interaction step every 30 seconds. This is the most common active user profile in the SAP Enterprise Core Component (ECC) system and is the default profile; that is, this profile is used if no specific details on a user's degree of activity are available.
- The *user with a high degree of activity* executes a user interaction step every 10 seconds. Such a high degree of activity reaches the limit of human capability, and occurs only for users who are entering mass data.

Thus, we see that "low users" generate 10 user interactions steps per hour, while "medium users" generate 120 steps per hour, and "high users" generate 360 steps per hour. Using this data, small to medium-sized standard SAP ERP systems can be dimensioned with a degree of precision that is adequate for budgeting purposes.

4.3 Transaction-Based Sizing

A user based sizing produces valid numbers only for standard SAP processes. For installations whose processes are very different from the standard, especially for industry solutions, the dimensioning process must use as its basis the number of transactions in the various components that are processed in the SAP system.

Transactions

A transaction is defined as an event in which a document (or object) is displayed, created, or updated.

This quantitative approach takes into account the number and size of the objects of the business processes in the individual components. Thus, the load from transactions that are generated by connections to other systems can be included in the sizing calculations. In addition, the different "weights" of the different solutions are considered via load factors. However, to determine the size of main memory, the number of concurrent users is also needed.

In order for transaction-based sizing to be able to provide realistic estimates, much more information is required than with user-based sizing. Even if it isn't possible to obtain data for every individual transaction, the relevant technical department has to provide estimates of the quantity and scope of the main transaction data and master data for every component.

In the Financial Accounting area, for example, this data would consist of invoices, payments, general ledger journals, asset postings, internal cost allocations, and so on. In the Logistics area, typical objects would be sales orders and sales inquiries, orders and goods movements, production orders, and MRP runs, among many others. In Human Resources, time recording and travel expenses, which come under the payroll area, are the main activities in which documents are displayed, created, or updated. A difference also has to be drawn between the two types of time recording: positive and negative time recording.

Virtual users

Because SAP systems exchange data with other systems frequently and on an ongoing basis, appropriate resources are required for processing the transactions generated in the data exchange process. These required resources must be taken into account either as virtual users or directly via transaction-based sizing in the hardware-sizing process.

Online and offline batches

Besides user-initiated online transactions, the sizing process also has to consider batch jobs. The general assumption is that batch jobs are usually run offline, at night, and that they therefore require fewer system resources than online transactions. However, these assumptions may not apply in all cases. Moreover, in systems that are distributed over several different time zones, there is no day and night in the traditional sense.

In certain industries, the nightly batch load can actually be much greater than the maximum load caused by online users. A typical example is the retail industry, in which it is imperative that the nightly replenishment planning run finishes in time so that the trucks can be loaded and depart early in the morning. In this case, the transaction load of the night-time batch jobs is several times greater than that of the online users. Therefore, the transaction load of the batch job runs, and the time window available for these runs must be defined in the SLAs, so that the system can be designed accordingly.

Activity patterns

When considering how to manage the performance and capacity of a system, the system designers have to consider the uneven distribution over time of the system load. After all, real users complete transactions in a much more sporadic fashion than machines. A realistic activity pattern contains typical daily and yearly maximums.

Load peaks at the end of the month

In almost all business applications, the system load peaks at the end of each month. This is usually because large data sets have to be consolidated via batch jobs at the end of the month, quarter, or year.

This is certainly the situation that exists in Human Resources departments. During the month, the system load is relatively low, as the system is used only by a comparatively small number of HR staff, and possibly by employees spending short periods of time using Employee Self-Services (ESS). In contrast, at the end of the month, resource requirements soar due to the sudden surge of activity by the payroll department, and also by time administrators making time corrections and so on.

Seasonal peak loads

Regardless of the industry in question, the system must be able to handle seasonal peak loads. Examples are ice cream manufacturers, whose peak season is summer, and gift item manufacturers, whose busiest time of the year is at Christmas. For the purposes of CPU sizing, information regarding the maximum number of orders that the system must be able to handle, and in what time frame, is much more important in such cases than information about the number of orders input over a year. A system sized according to the average load, while less expensive, will fail to fulfill the business demands of the enterprise.

Industry solutions

In the case of the SAP industry solutions (IS), the special business processes of each industry have to be considered. Therefore IS-specific sizing questionnaires for SAP Retail, SAP Utilities, and so on have been developed. The transaction load is calculated based on measurements of the key processes and specific benchmark tests. As the study quoted below shows, the resource requirements of the industry solutions can be very different from the standard requirements, depending on the specific business processes used in each case. It is advisable to seek the advice of a consultant with proven experience of the processes specific to the industry in question when carrying out a sizing assessment for a large IS implementation.

Sizing questionnaire

The competence centers of the hardware manufacturers provide extensive questionnaires for compiling all the data relevant to the sizing process. Although it takes time to answer all the questions, you should still do so as fully and with as much detail as possible. Note that it is more important to define potential loads than to specify individual figures in exact detail. If later on, it turns out that the system has been underdimensioned, the manufacturer will point to the information specified in the questionnaire.

4.4 The Limits of the Sizing Process

In-house development

Despite the greater precision of transaction-based sizing, this method of sizing has its limits.

Although the range of functions in the SAP solutions is wide and varied, special requirements can still arise that are not (yet) covered by the SAP standard. In such cases, the customer in question can extend the standard solution by adding his or her own in-house development work. As is the case with all program development, in-depth knowledge and experience are prerequisites for writing high-quality ABAP and Java code.

Because "homemade" code is not subject to SAP's quality assurance process, in-house programs can often cause serious performance problems in SAP systems. The cause is not usually insufficient system resources; rather, factors such as queries that return entire tables, for example, are more often at the root of these kinds of problems. If the code of an ABAP or Java program is of very low quality, it can exhaust the performance of even the most powerful computer landscape.

In many cases, performance problems can be solved by reformulating a single SQL statement. The book *SAP Performance Optimization Guide*[2] by Thomas Schneider is a valuable aid on this subject. However, the most important thing is to correct the code in question, whatever correction method you choose, before the problem causes performance bottlenecks and "red alert" signals, not to mention unhappy users, in a production system. SAP also provides a performance optimization service.[3] Some system manufacturers offer holistic services of this kind, covering every-

2 Thomas Schneider: *SAP Performance Optimization Guide*. SAP PRESS, 3rd edition 2003.

3 Gerhard Oswald: *SAP Service and Support*. SAP PRESS, 2nd edition 2003.

thing from the application to the database and the operating system to hardware and storage.

If in-house development cannot be avoided, tests have to be carried out on a copy of the production database in order to establish whether the existing system resources are adequate. For this reason, a quality assurance system is part of the SAP standard system landscape. The database server of this system should be dimensioned to be as large as that of the production system.

However, at the beginning of the project, the complete system landscape does not even exist yet. Therefore, the major hardware manufacturers provide test centers for stress tests and feasibility studies. For more information on performance tests, see the SAP White Paper *Conducting Customer Performance Tests*.

Load-based sizing

If an existing system landscape has to be extended due to new users or an upgrade, you can base the sizing figures on the current system load, rather than relying on an estimate. This kind of load-based sizing requires reliable measurements of the peak system load during critical periods. A typical period would be the end of the month, when the load is high.

In most cases, data about the current IT landscape (number and type of processors, and so on), the number of active users, and peak load figures for the processor and main memory, is enough to allow a good customer-specific user profile to be created. This individual profile automatically factors all the specific requirements of the customer's business processes, including hot spots and in-house developments.

Load-based sizing can therefore be used for adding new users to a system, and for consolidation projects and platform migrations.

The method that you select to measure the current load depends primarily on how the application reacts to peak loads. If the main goal is simply to achieve a specific throughput per hour or day, the figures documented in SAP EarlyWatch reports are sufficient. If, on the other hand, there are predefined response times that have to be adhered to, even during short peak load times (possibly even only for a few minutes), a detailed measurement at the operating-system level is necessary. With these kinds of measurements, the shorter the measurement interval, the more precise the information about peak loads.

4.5 Response Time

The central performance criterion for the user of an SAP system is the response time. An average response time of one second is generally perceived as good, while anything longer than two seconds is generally regarded as disruptive. However, it always depends on the current business process; for example, in a call center that is based on the mySAP Customer Relationship Management (mySAP CRM) Interaction Center (CIC) solution, the response times should be significantly less than one second. On the other hand, with online analytical processing (OLAP) solutions such as SAP Business Information Warehouse (SAP BW) and SAP Advanced Planner and Optimizer (SAP APO), there is no point in defining average response times.

Response time from the system's viewpoint

From the viewpoint of the system, response time is defined as the average length of time required to process a transaction. In other words, what is measured is the time that elapses between the arrival of the processing request in the application server, and the moment when the application server sends the system response to the network. Note that, in an SAP system, the response time is always defined as the average response time over an hour. This definition is also the basis for proposed configurations and bids from the hardware manufacturers.

Response time from the user's viewpoint

From the point of view of the user, response time is the period of time that occurs when the user presses ENTER and the requested information appears on the screen. The network infrastructure therefore has a considerable effect on the response time as perceived by the user. This subject is discussed in more detail in Chapter 9. Where a SAP GUI is in use, the response time is also affected by the computing power of the PC.

Response time depends on CPU load

Every transaction has a minimum response time (depending on the system configuration) that must be maintained. This ideal value can be achieved only within a certain amount of time after the system starts up, however, when all the buffers are full (when the system has 'warmed up') and not many users are active in the system yet. As the number of users increases, so does the probability that multiple user processes will access the same CPU simultaneously. When this happens, wait periods are incurred that prolong response times. Therefore, the CPU load, or more precisely the CPU wait time, has a direct effect on the response time.

As Figure 4.1 shows, even with a moderate CPU load of only 50 %, the random distribution of user activity over time causes a recurring short-duration CPU load of 100 %, which causes wait periods for the user—although, these periods are usually so short that they go unnoticed by the user.

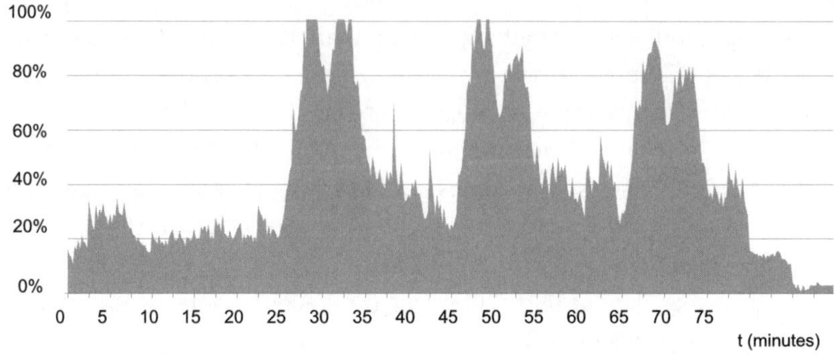

Figure 4.1 Example of the Temporal Distribution of the CPU Load with an Average Hourly Value of approximately 50 %

Figure 4.2 shows the situation that occurs with an average CPU load of approximately 70 %. Here, the 100 % peaks are actually minor plateaus, resulting consequently in a little longer system response time for the user.

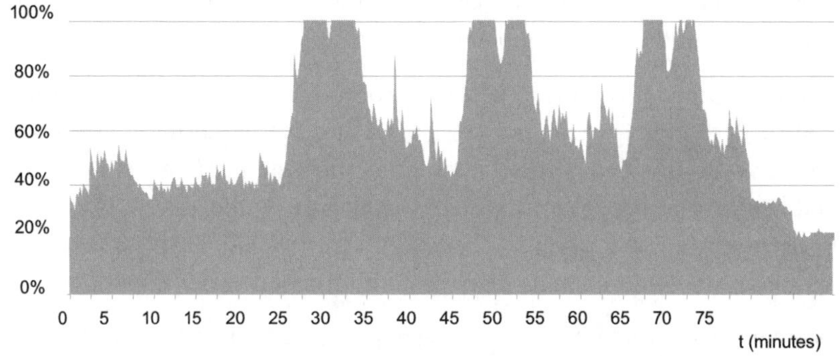

Figure 4.2 CPU load with an average value of approximately 70 %

In Figure 4.3, the 100 % plateaus are so widespread that, despite an average CPU load of ca. 80 %, long periods of unsatisfactory response times and, hence, dissatisfied users, can hardly be avoided.

Note

With an average CPU load of almost 100 %, maximum use is made of the hardware, but the response times will be absolutely unacceptable.

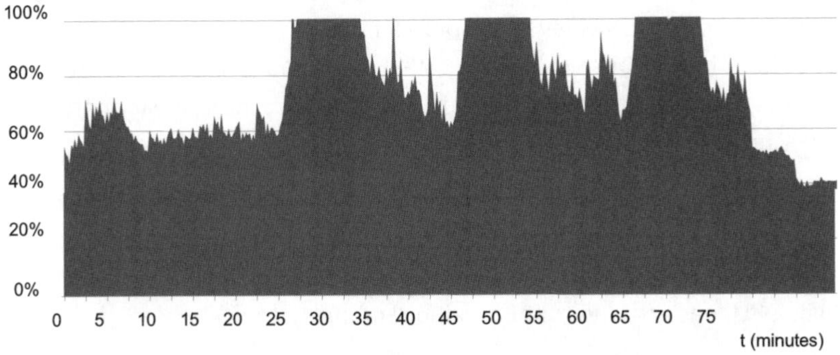

Figure 4.3 CPU load with an average value of approximately 80 %

Experience shows that the employees in business departments in enterprises are less interested in the average response times per hour than in how long, based on their subjective perception, they have to wait "yet again." Therefore, based on the required response times, the system must be designed in such a way that a specific medium-level CPU load is not exceeded, in order to ensure that load peaks don't turn into prolonged 100 % plateaus.

Queue theory

Queue theory[4] shows that the relationship between the response time and the CPU load is non-linear in character, and this is backed up by practical measurements (see Figure 4.4).

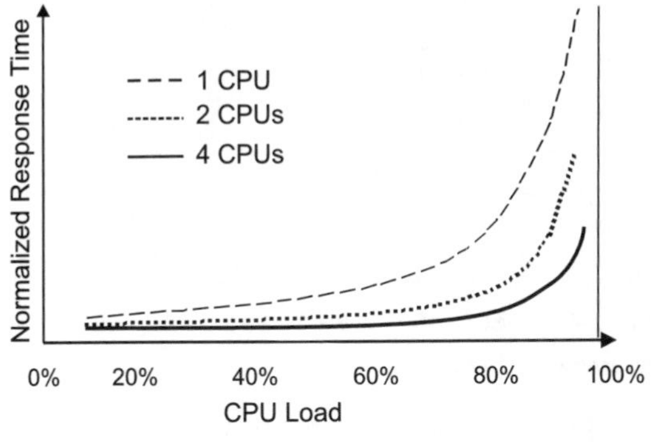

Figure 4.4 Relationship of Response Time to CPU load

Previous analyses have shown that only systems with more than one CPU and a low load can achieve anything approaching a linear relationship between the response times and the CPU load. In such systems, the

4 Broch G. et al.: *Queuing Networks and Markov Chains. Modeling and Performance Evaluation with Computer Science Applications*. John Wiley, New York 1998.

response time was approximately two seconds, when the average CPU load was 70 %. To achieve a response time of one second, the average CPU load has to be reduced to 50 %. For average loads of more than 70 % , the response time starts to increase in a non-linear pattern to unacceptable levels.

However, more recent analyses at the SAP-HP Competence Center (see Figure 4.5) show that response times of less than one second can be achieved in state of the art multiprocessor systems, even with relatively high CPU loads (thought not on all operating systems).

Measuring the average CPU load

The SAP Solution Manager uses the maximum of the daily averages over the last three weeks to specify the maximum CPU load of an SAP system. The hourly values between 10:00 a.m. and 1:00 p.m., and between 2:00 p.m. and 3:00 p.m., are used to calculate the average daily CPU load. Transaction ST03 shows the response times that were measured in the last full week.

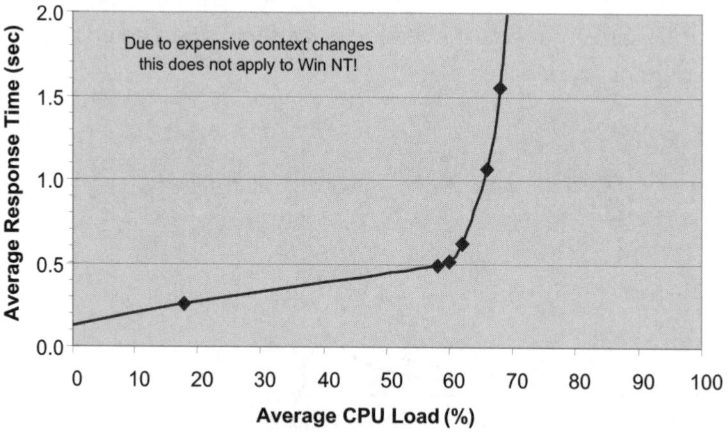

Figure 4.5 Response Time Versus CPU Load (Recent Measurements)

4.6 Main Memory Requirement

Every user who is logged on to a mySAP Business Suite solution is allocated a certain memory space in the SAP application instance and in the database main memory. Therefore, a certain amount of the main memory is always allocated to the logged-on user, regardless of whether he or she is currently active. If the memory requirement of an SAP system exceeds the physical main memory space that is available, the operating system starts shifting the code and data that was not used for some time to the hard disk (this process is referred to as *paging* for single memory pages, and as *swapping* for complete processes).

How to avoid paging and swapping

Both of these processes have a negative effect on system performance. Usually, paging rates of more than 20 % of the physical main memory per hour are regarded as critical. Therefore, the cause of system performance problems may not be the CPU, but under- sized main memory, because high levels of paging strain the CPU. Experience shows that removing the main memory bottleneck can also solve the problem of the CPU bottleneck.

You should always ensure that main memory is adequately sized, especially when dealing with an APO liveCache. Otherwise, the liveCache shifts data to the data devices, which is basically the same as paging. Even a memory-resident database like liveCache also stores data to the hard disk (data devices space or log devices space). Therefore, a high-availability (HA) concept can be implemented, which uses the data devices space or the log devices space if a system crash occurs.

In a production system, the maximum allocated main memory can be calculated using the instance configuration (buffer, number of processes, allocated memory for user data, and extra allocated memory for user data). In the project planning phase, it should be estimated on the basis of the number of concurrent users in the system and the modules in use.

In systems that mainly process batch jobs, the volume of documents and a standardized load factor can be used to calculate a hypothetical number of users and thus the main memory requirement.

Measuring the main memory requirement

After the go-live, Transaction ST02 can be used to monitor the actual main memory requirement of the SAP system, and Transaction ST04 can be used to monitor the main memory requirement of the database.

Last, you should not forget that the operating system, auxiliary programs, agents, and so on, all require their own share of main memory.

Database instance

The main memory requirement for the database consists of the requirement of the database kernel and that of the various database buffers, plus the shadow processes that process the work process requests. There is usually also backup software. If the database runs on its own machine, there will also be the operating system requirement to consider.

However, note that the Quick Sizer only considers the requirement of the database itself, and it also assumes that the setup of the SAP system has been optimized. It does not consider complex SQL statements that lead to complicated store operations (large table joins and so on). If extensive customizing is planned, additional storage requirements for the database server should be factored in to the calculations.

Application instance

When an SAP application instance is started, the first thing that happens is that the SAP application code is loaded from the database to main memory, and the various buffers are created. The size of the main memory required for this purpose depends on the number and type of the solutions.

In the past, with 32-bit systems, there was often no other choice but to load only one application module per application server, in order to save some main memory. Fortunately, with 64-bit systems, this kind of inflexible configuration is no longer necessary.

Besides this fixed part, there is also a variable part, which depends on the number of concurrent users and the modules in use. Between 5.2 MB and 10.4 MB of main memory are reserved for storing the user context of each user who is logged on to the system, regardless of whether a specific user is active.

The SAP Quick Sizer specifies a minimum and an optimum main memory size. With the minimum size, users with a low level of activity in the system are excluded from the memory calculation, and their contexts may be swapped out to the paging file.

Multiple application server instances

In addition, the number of application servers is not factored into these calculations. For every application servers, the operating system and a constant part for the application code and the buffers must also be taken into account for each individual server. For example, if the optimal memory size for the application is 8 GB and you want to deploy four application servers, it is not sufficient to install 2 GB of memory on each server. Because approximately 1 GB of memory is required on each individual machine for the application code, buffers and the operating system the total main memory requirement in this case is 3 GB per application server (giving a total of 12 GB rather than the original 8 GB). This also applies to all partitioning technologies that run multiple instances of the operating system on one machine.

Reasons for extreme memory requirement

In practice, there are systems that require an extremely large amount of main memory per user. The reasons for this are usually bad user habits, such as: too many open windows, each with long lists; multiple parallel long-running programs; not restricting selections and other searches; badly-written programs; extremely large requests and bills of material, and many more.

A well-trained user will avoid displaying unnecessarily large lists and data sets, for example, by using appropriate restrictions when selecting the data. At the other extreme, a user who is unaware of the effect of his actions on the system will, at the worst, run several unrestricted selections at once ("Because it takes so long!"), thereby consuming a large part of the memory space required for his work.

4.7 Hard Disk Capacity

Capacity and throughput (I/O) are the most important parameters for dimensioning the disk subsystem (I/O throughput is dealt with in the next section). The application servers require only disk capacity for the operating system and the paging file. The standard internal disks are sufficient for this in most cases. The same is true for the database server plus some extra disk space for the SAP software (usually less than 15 GB).

However, the main factor that influences the actual requirement for disk space capacity is the data that is generated by the business processes. This data is stored in the relational database in several thousand tables.

Retention period

The amount of disk storage space required for this data is directly proportional to the quantity of documents that is created and to the amount of time for which the data has to be stored in the system before it is (hopefully) removed, either by being archived or deleted. This time period is referred to as the retention period. Unfortunately, the number and size of the documents generated in a year is difficult to predict. Therefore, one uses the rule of thumb that a concurrent ECC user with an average level of activity usually produces approximately 450 MB of documents in a year. The SAP Quick Sizer also takes into account the varying number of work days in different regions.

These estimates can only be regarded as a rough starting point, however. Data growth can be in the region of several GB per day, especially in the retail industry. Therefore, it is the task of Capacity Management to monitor data growth, so that the capacity of the disk subsystems can be extended in a timely fashion as required, in order to handle the data growth.

Database housekeeping

In many cases, inadequate system configuration and insufficient maintenance can also cause the database to grow at an alarming rate. Therefore, it is worth remembering that certain data can be removed from the system after a relatively short time (spool and log data, for example). Also, the indexes of tables that contain lots of changes should be re-built or defragmented once a week. The SAP Service Marketplace contains a very good guide to minimizing and compressing data.

4.8 Units of Measure for Application Load and System Throughput

While the size of main memory and disk space can be specified in simple megabytes, gigabytes, and terabytes, with system throughput, we first have to define a way of measuring it that can be used to specify the performance requirements of the business processes, independently of CPU type, computer technology, and manufacturer.

SAPS: the horsepower of an SAP system

System throughput refers to the transaction volume that is processed in a given period of time. SAP has developed the *SAP Application Benchmark Performance Standard* (SAPS) unit of measure for system throughput, based on the SD benchmark. One hundred SAPS correspond to the standard processing of 2,000 order items per hour, which requires 6,000 user interaction steps (screen changes) or 2,400 Sales & Distribution (SD) transactions. SAPS can therefore be regarded as the horse-power of an SAP system. Having said that, SAPS has as much in common with the practical usage of the SAP Sales & Distribution module as horsepower does with the strength of an actual horse.

SAPS is release-independent

The SAPS unit was initially created to measure application load. Application load in SAPS is release-independent; in other words, 100 SAPS are always equal to 2,000 order items per hour, regardless of the release of the SAP system. The dependency between SAPS and the Solution Release becomes relevance when the SAPS are used as a unit for the possible performance of a server. Due to the fact that the resource consumption of the SD-module rises with nearly every SAP release, a given server can process fewer order items per hour with newer releases. The number of SAPS the server can be counted is lowering accordingly.

This result in the paradox situation, that in spite of more and better functionality provided with every new release, in principle the "consumed" number of SAPS of a 1,000 user SAP System does not change from release 3.1 to ECC as long as you don't change anything but the release (i.e. no changes in customizing, usage of functions and so on). However the system landscape that was able to support these 1,000 users with release 3.x might only be able to support 530 users with release ECC 5.0 because the more and better functionality consume significant more CPU power.

Figure 4.6 shows the performance increase of servers certified and benchmarked for SAP over recent years, which has exceeded by far the increase in performance requirements of the applications due to the tremendous advance in technology.

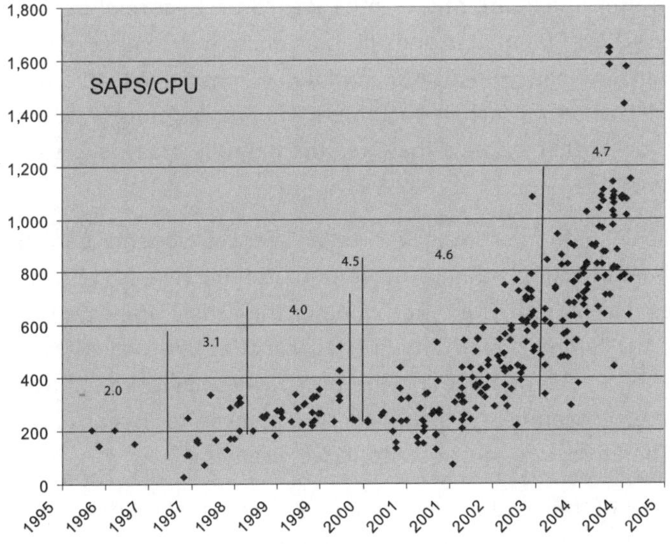

Figure 4.6 SAPS per CPU in the Certified Two-Tier SD Benchmark (Without regard to Multithreading and Hyperthreading)

The system throughput or the server capacity in SAPS, as specified by the hardware manufacturers, is the same as the application load in SAPS that can be processed when the server is working under a full load. The SD benchmark is therefore used to measure and certify system capacity. Under this benchmark, load is applied to the server up until the point at which response times are just under two seconds. With the two-tier SD benchmark, the database and the SAP application are run on the same server (centralized system).

This definition also applies to the required system capacity that is calculated by the Quick Sizer. In other words, the Quick Sizer calculates the load in SAPS, plus a certain amount for non-benchmark like load, so that the average CPU load of the target system stays at a tolerable level (and not at 100 %).

4.9 Sizing SAP NetWeaver Systems

With SAP NetWeaver, several SAP solutions are usually involved in every business process scenario. There is therefore little point in asking for a NetWeaver system to be sized in the standard way, as a separate sizing process is required for every solution involved in each scenario (which is why there is no sizing questionnaire for NetWeaver).

Larger user populations

Because each user in an enterprise can be logged on to several components at once via the portal, it is difficult to estimate the number of concurrent users in each component. Also, additional transaction load can be caused by external users, such as customers who are ordering goods on the Internet, or partner systems that are automatically ordering just-in-time deliveries.

The most reliable method of sizing SAP NetWeaver components is still by estimating the transaction volume. The important thing here is the quantity of requests to be processed, not whether the orders originate from sales staff or the Internet. Note that in this scenario, peak loads are no longer restricted to the number and the physical capacity of employees and a customer is even less willing than an employee to accept longer wait times. Therefore, you must plan for large reserves.

In the context of the Enterprise Services Architecture (ESA), system designers also have to consider what influence that resource requirements of Composite Applications will have on the various solutions whose functionality is accessed in the system.

The following sections are intended only as an overview, and describe the main parameters that influence the system design of each SAP NetWeaver component.

4.9.1 Enterprise Portal

A CRM scenario is the basis of Enterprise Portal sizing. In this scenario, a sales employee logs on to the CRM entry page, and then navigates to the overview pages for activities, account management, and acquisitions, each with four iViews.[5]

To design a portal server, you first have to estimate the number of users that will log on in the space of an hour, as well as the highest number of concurrent active users per hour. When calculating the distribution of activity of concurrent users, the Quick Sizer assumes that 60 % of users initiate a function in the portal via a mouse-click every 600 seconds, 34 % do so every 180 seconds, and 6 % do so every 30 seconds (these periods are the "think time").

For Content Management purposes, an estimate is required of the percentage of mouse-clicks that call up Content Management functions. If the TREX component is used, an estimate of the terms searched for per hour is required. This assumes that only whole words are searched for.

4.9.2 Mobile Infrastructure

Synchronization resources

The SAP NetWeaver component for Mobile Services is different from the usual sizing schemas in that the users don't execute their transactions online in a mySAP solution, but off-line on a mobile device (such as a PDA or laptop), and then synchronize this device once or twice a day with the back-end system. Therefore, response time in the classic sense is not important here. However, in some circumstances, the back-end system must process hundreds of transactions (similar to a batch process).

A white paper[6] is available in the SAP Service Marketplace that gives the measurement values in tabular form for designing the Mobile Engine and the mySAP ERP or SAP CRM systems for various scenarios.

4.9.3 Business Information Warehouse

While the focus of an OLTP system such as mySAP ERP or CRM is on processing lots of relatively small transactions, the system load in an analytically oriented OLAP system such as SAP BW is mainly due to the creation of a relatively small number of large reports and analyses. Therefore, it is not only the number of users that determines the processing load in SAP

5 For more information, see Note 519077.

6 Sizing mySAP Mobile Business.

BW, but also the type of queries, and the number and complexity of the InfoCubes and ODS objects.

Loading and transforming

Another feature of SAP BW systems is that the process of loading and transforming data from the source systems to the BW system can cause very high loads. In some BW systems, this load can exceed the load caused by user queries. Therefore, it is important to specify how many data records have to be handled per load process, and the time-window that is available for this purpose. You should also clarify whether the load processes run in parallel to normal operations, or whether time-windows are available for this purpose when the system load is low.

User types in BW

User types in BW depend on the number of navigation steps[7] per hour and their weighting:

- An Info User simply requests predefined reports and usually executes one navigation step per hour. The quantity of data involved is low.
- An Executive User uses OLAP functionalities and executes 11 navigation steps per hour to navigate in reports.
- A Power User analyzes the data using all possible criteria and uses ad-hoc reports. This type of user executes 33 navigation steps per hour and accesses large quantities of data.

Query types in BW

The type of query also has an effect on the system load. There are three types of query that are important for sizing purposes:

- Report Viewing usually does not provide any navigation options, or only very restricted ones. All the data is read from optimized aggregates.
- In OLAP Analysis, queries are used that allow "slicing and dicing" to a greater extent. During navigation, most of the data is read from aggregates, though these are not always optimized.
- Data Exploration uses queries that are not usually supported by high-quality aggregates, and therefore often have to access detailed data, thus absorbing significant resources on the application server.

In principle, every user can use every query type. However, experience shows that 80 % of Information Consumers perform Report Viewing and only 20 % carry out OLAP Analysis, while Executive Users use Report

---

7 A navigation step comprises several interaction steps (for example, drilling down) in reports and corresponds to approximately nine user interaction steps in the SD benchmark.

Viewing and OLAP Analysis in equal measure, and Power Users almost exclusively use Data Exploration.

InfoCubes

An *InfoCube* is a description of a self-contained data set (from the reporting viewpoint), such as a data set in a particular business area. The number of dimensions and the quantity of the data that each one contains must be estimated for every InfoCube. Every InfoCube can have up to 16 dimensions and 248 key figures per dimension.

For sizing purposes, the sizing experts have to estimate the number of data sets that are loaded when the InfoCube is first created, as well as the data sets that are loaded regularly for updating purposes (periodic load). The sizing process has to take into account the fact that the data set usually increases in size over time, and the total number of *periods* (uploads) that will be contained in the InfoCube.

A *dimension* is a group of related classification keys (characteristics) such as color and model. *Key figures* are values or quantities, such as turnover, fixed costs, sales quantity, and number of employees. Besides the key figures stored in the database, it is also possible to define calculated key figures such as turnover per employee, percent difference, and profit margin.

Design-dependent sizing

The design and granularity of the InfoCubes have a considerable effect on the size of the database and on system performance, as the following simple example shows. For an analysis of the sales figures for 12 branches of a store, each with 1,000 articles, the attributes in question could be article and time of sale. If we assume that the 1,000 articles to be analyzed can be divided into 10 groups, we get the following figures for an analysis over 300 selling days or 45 weeks in the year:

- Article group and week = 10 × 45 = 450 entries
- Article and week = 1,000 × 45 = 45,000 entries
- Article and day = 1,000 × 300 = 300,000 entries
- Article, day and branch = 500 × 300 × 12 = 1,800,000 entries

This dependency of system size on design is typical of OLAP systems, and also applies to the APO in mySAP Supply Chain Management (mySAP SCM), for example.

Operational Data Store

The objects in the Operational Data Store (ODS) are used for detailed analyses of current data sets to support decisions in everyday operations. Unlike the multidimensional data storage used with InfoCubes, the data in ODS objects is stored in flat, transparent database tables. An ODS object contains a key (such as a document number and a document position) and data fields, which, as key figures, can also contain character fields (such as "customer").

Ratio of DB to App-server capacity

In the data analysis process, the BW database is subject to a much greater load than in normal business processes. This is why the ratio of the processor capacity of the database server to the total capacity of the application servers, which is typically 1:4 to 1:3 in OLTP systems, changes to 1:2 to 1:1 in BW. Therefore, up to 50 % of the system resources are used by the database.

4.9.4 Exchange Infrastructure

The processes that are the most important for designing a SAP Exchange Infrastructure (SAP XI) system are those that occur on the Integration Server. Routing and mapping XML messages, in particular, are complex operations that have a considerable effect on system performance. Note that the SAP Exchange Infrastructure always has to be a Unicode system, as the Internet protocols it processes are Unicode-based.

CPU requirement

The most important pieces of information for deciding on CPU resource requirements are estimates of the number and size of the XML messages in the system. The ratio of the CPU load on the database server and the application server is approximately 1:4, and database processes use approximately 20 % of the total CPU capacity.

Main memory requirement

The main memory requirement depends on the number of parallel processes and the size of the XML messages. As long as the messages don't exceed 1 MB in size, no detailed main memory sizing is required. Three megabytes of main memory should be allowed per process for larger messages, four times the message volume for asynchronous processing, and nine times the message volume for synchronous processing. More than 20 times the message volume may be required for mapping or content-based routing, depending on the mapping type.

Hard disk requirement

By default, the Exchange Infrastructure stores only asynchronous XML messages in the database. Therefore, if synchronous messages are used, this has to be set explicitly. Logs and traces are written on the file level. Once they reach a certain size, these are compressed and stored centrally. Experience shows that a compression factor of 45 % is a good average in these cases, although messages that mainly contain text have a considerably higher compression factor, and messages that already contain compressed binary data have a correspondingly lower compression factor.

Messages are usually stored twice: once before processing and once after processing. To minimize the disk space requirement, you can set a retention period. Once this period expires, the data is archived and subsequently deleted from the system. The default retention period for disk sizing is usually one day. If messages need to be stored for debugging purposes or even longer, the disk space requirement increases as needed.

4.9.5 Master Data Management

To dimension the SAP Master Data Management (SAP MDM) system, the number and size of the master data records are of central importance in the design of the disk space. For the CPU and main memory requirements, the number of newly created, modified, and deleted master data records per day, and the number of systems to which the MDM system is connected, are the important factors.

4.10 Sizing mySAP Solutions

The central parameters for sizing SAP R/3 and the ECC as core components of the mySAP ERP solution have already been described in previous sections. Therefore, we will not repeat them here.

4.10.1 Customer Relationship Management

Another typical OLTP system is mySAP Customer Relationship Management (CRM). In this case, too, user figures can be used to dimension the various scenarios. The most important thing here is to estimate the peak loads, although this is especially difficult with Internet sales scenarios.

Internet sales

Users of Internet sales scenarios can be divided into two main groups:

- Most users simply browse through the product catalog at first, in order to get the information they need. This mainly causes increased load on the Web server.
- A relatively small number of Internet sales users then place items in the shopping basket and order products, which causes increased load on the CRM server (and increased cash flow for the company).

Opportunity and activity management

Another important area in terms of resource requirements is opportunity and activity management. An *opportunity* in this context refers to the interested party, his or her requirements, the available budget, the potential turnover, and the estimated sales probability. The frequency with which an opportunity is displayed or modified is important for estimating the system metrics, since this has a considerable influence on sizing. Activities are usually subsequent actions, such as a follow-up phone call after the first customer contact. These are frequently processed and modified.

Customer Interaction Center

User-based sizing of the Customer Interaction Center (CIC) assumes that the bulk of the transaction load originates mainly from opportunity management, activity management, and so on, and that the IC causes only a certain amount of additional load. Therefore, the users must be entered in the SAP Quick Sizer, in the IC itself, and in each business transaction. In this process, note that sales orders, for example, also have to be considered in Internet sales and in opportunities.

4.10.2 Supply Chain Management

The most frequently used component of mySAP Supply Chain Management (SCM) is the Advanced Planner & Optimizer (APO). The planning activities in APO are basically large batch processes that are influenced by the quantity of elements to be processed, the level of detail, and any relationships to other elements (as is the case with bills of material).

Users in APO?

Therefore, APO does not have user-based sizing like other components. The number of users is simply factored into the CPU calculations.

The most important processes in APO are requirements planning, supply network planning and production and detailed planning. The main factor that influences the processor capacity is the time window (in hours) that is available for planning and optimization runs. The shorter the time window for the planning run, the more CPU capacity that is required. The CPU requirement is therefore inversely proportional to the processing period.

As with BW, data structures in APO are based on InfoCubes, which are stored on the hard disks of the database. Therefore, here again, as in BW, the size of the database is determined by the design and granularity of the InfoCubes.

Characteristics combinations

SAP APO also has a main memory-resident database—the liveCache. The main factor to consider when designing the liveCache is the number of possible characteristics combinations, of which the most optimal should be identified. A characteristic in this context is a planning object, such as a product, a customer, or a location. A characteristics combination, then, is exactly what it implies: a combination of different characteristics. A common combination is product-location-customer. In APO, all existing characteristics combinations are stored, but this does not include all *possible* combinations of all existing characteristics.

Key figures in the liveCache

A *key figure* is a value or a quantity, such as turnover, sales quantity, or production quantity. Accessing key figures in the liveCache is a faster process than in an InfoCube, but increases the main memory requirement of the liveCache. Another important parameter is the number of planning versions that have to be stored in the liveCache. If, for any reason, this parameter should double, it can cause the main memory requirement of the liveCache to double as well.

Planning horizon

A time series is created in the liveCache for every characteristics combination and every key figure. The size of the time series depends on the number of periods (such as weeks or months). Other criteria that affect the main memory requirement are the planning horizon (days, weeks, months, quarters, years, or update period) and how far back in time the historic data should go that is stored for forecasting purposes. When a combination of these criteria is selected, the data is always stored in the form of the smallest criterion. For example, if the planning horizon is two years and the data is to be stored in weeks in the first two months, and thereafter in months, 104 periods are required, as the smallest criterion in this case is weeks.

Sales orders and planned orders

The more orders there are, the more main memory that the liveCache requires. For sizing purposes, the relevant factors are the average number of components, processes, and work steps per process. Different activity types are assigned to the different activities, such as "produce," "set up," "tear down," and "wait." Although the liveCache deletes finished orders, these orders are still kept in SAP R/3 until the bill for the order has been paid. For this reason, there are usually more sales orders in SAP R/3 than there are in APO.

With its Global Availability to Promise (G-ATP) component, APO provides a cross-system availability check function that uses a rule-based strategy to synchronize supply and demand. Unlike availability checks in classic ERP systems, G-ATP allows you to create availability queries across multiple R/3 instances. It carries out multilevel component and capacity checks, both in real time and in simulation mode. These checks are run on data stored in the liveCache in order to ensure the required level of performance. The system can handle simple checks such as product availability, as well as complex checks, which include anything up to scheduling a production order. As the number of parallel queries and their complexity increases, so too does the required CPU capacity.

Another point to think about is the CPU requirement for the interfaces between APO and the back-end systems. CPU capacity is directly related to the size of the data set and the size of the window, so that a larger data set with a small window requires a greater number of CPUs. Note here that the CPU load in the R/3 system increases by up to 30 % during the initial data transfer via the interface between R/3 and APO. Therefore, we recommend that you schedule this upload outside of peak hours.

4.10.3 Supplier Relationship Management

Self-Service Classic Procurement

The Self-Service (Indirect) Classic Procurement solution enables employees to order goods, such as office materials, from a predefined catalog. Once the order process is complete, the shopping basket is sent as a sales order to the SAP R/3 Material Management (MM) module, where it is further processed. Therefore, the orders and any follow-on documents also have to be entered in the Quick Sizer for the R/3 system.

Standalone Procurement

The whole procurement process in the Enterprise Buyer Professional (EBP) takes place in the Standalone Procurement scenario. The shopping basket and any follow-on documents are created and processed locally. Therefore, no separate Material Management system should be required, although accounting functions do have to run in a back-end system.

Plan-Driven Procurement

In the Plan-Driven Procurement scenario, products and service orders are created via planning functions such as production planning, APO, and the Project System. Because the purchase requisitions thus generated still have to be confirmed by a buyer, the sizing process for this scenario is also largely user-based.

Supplier Enablement

In the Supplier Enablement scenario, suppliers can make their products available directly in the buyer's system. There are two different sub-scenarios involved, each of which requires a different sizing approach. With Supplier Self-Services, the whole procurement process takes place in the SAP Enterprise Buyer Professional, and the shopping basket and any follow-on documents are created locally. Alternatively, an inbound delivery can also be created in SAP R/3 Materials Management (MM) via a shipping notification.

SAP XI and IDoc technology are used for communication between the various systems.

4.10.4 Product Lifecycle Management

mySAP Product Lifecycle Management (mySAP PLM) is an independent solution, but not a component by itself. mySAP PLM uses primarily project management and quality management functions from R/3 Enterprise and ECC. The number of users is therefore taken into account in the sizing processes for the PS, PP, PM, and QM modules.

The Knowledge Warehouse infrastructure can be used for storing and distributing files that require a large amount of disk space (scanned files, CAD drawings, video files, and so on). Files can also be stored in the R/3 database; however this increases the size of that database.

The sizing process for mySAP PLM cFolders is based on the average size of the files and the number of downloads per hour. The main memory requirement is determined by the number of parallel processes and the size of the document. The estimate of the disk space requirement is based on a compression factor of 10–50 %.

4.11 Deciding on the Server Configuration

Once you have estimated the overall resource requirements for the business processes, you then need to design a hardware system that can handle these requirements. Basically, the goal is to create a computer system that can cope with every individual customer situation and that combines the required computing power—SAPS), main memory, and disk space—with the lowest possible total cost of ownership, while simultaneously fulfilling all other conditions (sufficient addressable memory, flexibility, stability, downtime, security, and so on). The system also has to have enough reserves for any future increase in load and be easy to extend (scalability). Considering the bewildering range of products offered by the hardware manufacturers, this is no easy task.

Benchmark tests

Because it is impossible to test every possible combination of computer configuration with the functionality in every mySAP component, the performance of the various systems must be determined by using benchmark tests. SAP provides scripts for all the main scenarios in the mySAP solutions, which every hardware manufacturer can use to carry out these tests. All certified SAP benchmarks are made publicly available on the Internet.[8]

8 Go to *http://service.sap.com/benchmark*.

The OLAP trap There is an unsolved problem with the Quick Sizer: It outputs all the required system capacities in SAPS, regardless of whether the sized application has an online transaction processing system (OLTP) or an online analytical processing system (OLAP) load profile, and all system manufacturers use only the SD benchmark to measure their systems (with some rare exceptions) and to determine the possible system capacity in SAPS. However, this benchmark is definitely OLTP in character. Thus, the system capacity calculated with this method is suitable only for designing OLTP applications.

This can cause problems if OLAP applications are run using configurations optimized for an OLTP load. Extreme care should therefore be exercised when OLAP systems are sized.

Three-tier benchmarks With a three-tier architecture, no SAP processes are usually run on the database machine. Up to 160 application machines were used for the actual processing of the business logic in some high-end benchmarks. With these benchmarks, the proportion of application computers in the overall system capacity is between 89 % and 94 %, depending on the hardware platform. Even though this means that the actual processing of the SAP software takes place on a host of (usually smaller) application servers, it is always the database server that is praised in the marketing of the hardware manufacturers.

Two-tier benchmarks With a centralized system, on the other hand, the database and the SAP software run on the same machine. Even though the SAPS values for a two-tier system are not as impressive as those for a three-tier system, a two-tier benchmark still yields much more meaningful values for real-world installations, as with this kind of configuration, not all resources on the tested hardware architecture are reserved exclusively for the database and the actual business processes are also included. Therefore the results of two tier benchmark are used to determine the sizing tables for sizing.

Benchmark and reality There is one underlying assumption about the SAP system at the heart of all benchmarks: it is optimally tuned. On a well-tuned system, there are no resource-intensive SQL statements that cause large quantities of read operations (queries for large tables, and so on) on the database. Therefore, on such systems, only a small portion of the processor capacity of the whole system is required for the database and thus the database machine. Benchmarks therefore do not take into account reports, batch jobs, and in-house developments.

However, in practice, SAP systems are seldom optimally tuned. Reports and in-house developments, in particular, make extensive use of queries for large tables and place an extreme load on the database. Therefore, the relative load on the database server is considerably higher than is the case with a benchmark.

Formula 1 racer versus multi-function vehicle

A high-end benchmark has about as much of a relationship with reality as does a highly-tuned racing car on a high-speed track has in common with a standard trailer truck on the highway. The problem with system dimensioning is the same as attempting to approximate the performance data of a multifunction vehicle from the data from a Formula 1 race, and at bandwidths that range from that of a sports car to a heavy load truck. One should not attempt to compare the results of a benchmark directly with a normal end-user system.

Sufficient database reserves

Even if sufficient reserves have been allowed for, you still have to expect that adjustments to the system landscape will be necessary after the system goes live, despite all the estimates and calculations. The most common reasons for this need for further adjustments are unplanned changes and extensions to the system that "just come up" during the implementation. Once a system is up and running, the staff in the business departments are usually eager to use the many functions of the mySAP components to an even greater extent.

We have learned from experience that most hardware bottlenecks occur on the database server. IT systems that are constantly extended and refined, and the increasing amount of in-house development, push the ratio of application load to database load in the direction of the database. Consequently, experienced sizing experts are designing larger database servers for good reasons. Unfortunately three tier benchmarks don't help because the issues which cause the bottlenecks in the real world are not tested in such a benchmark.

However, including extra CPUs in the system from the start can be an expensive option, as this is an upfront investment that may not be used until later on, plus some system downtime is necessary while they are built into the system. However, there are two ways to avoid this initial cost.

One way to avoid this initial cost is by taking advantage of the option that many manufacturers give customers, of "activating" CPUs later if they are needed. A small pre-payment is required when setup in the system and then the full payment for the cost of these CPUs is only due once they are put to active use.

The other way to avoid this initial cost is to use any CPUs that are installed on the database server but are not currently required for database purposes for the application instead, thus putting them to much better use. This is because dialog and batch processes run fastest on a centralized system. As the database load increases, an extra application machine can then be purchased at the appropriate moment in order to relieve the database machine.

Like before, you should purchase as few machines as possible for this purpose, but they should be powerful ones. A smaller number of machines reduces the amount of administration work required and improves load distribution.

However, before you resort to purchasing extra hardware, you should first exhaust all options for optimizing the system. Settings that are less than ideal, program errors, and untidy programming can all cause hardware bottlenecks, even if the sizing is 100 % correct. Therefore, we strongly recommend that live systems be checked regularly by experienced performance experts with access to the appropriate tools. This is the only way to ensure that system settings are optimized and that optimal use is made of the available resources. We know from experience that, systems that contain a high proportion of in-house development benefit from these recommendations.

4.12 Guaranteed Performance?

Every business department naturally expects that the IT infrastructure will provide the level of performance established in the SLAs at all times. However, all parties involved have to understand that the performance of an SAP system can be guaranteed only if certain conditions are fulfilled.

As you can see in Figure 4.5, response time is a variable that depends on the ratio of the transaction load to the available resources. Therefore, a fixed response time can be guaranteed in an SAP system only if the transaction load is also fixed.

This situation is analogous to that of a truck on the road. While the manufacturer of the truck can guarantee that the truck engine has a certain horsepower (or kW), the trucks speed still depends on factors such as the load it is carrying, and the incline and the condition of the road it is using (as well as the skills of the driver). Similarly, computer hardware manufacturers can guarantee the SAPS of their computers, but cannot make any promises regarding the response time of the system, since the transaction load and user behaviour usage is unknown (as well as the skills of the administrators).

The network also affects response time

Also, the manufacturer of a computer system can only vouch for the performance parameters of that part of the infrastructure that he manufactured and delivered. The network itself rarely comes under the area of responsibility of the computer manufacturer. Demanding a guaranteed response time for the end user's PC is therefore akin to demanding a guaranteed road trip time from a truck on the highway without taking into account factors such as road works, traffic jams, and the weather. Therefore, response times of the intranet of the company in question can be ensured only if a guaranteed quality of the data transfer is thoroughly implemented throughout the network.

Unrealistic expectations

Demands for a guaranteed response time on the Internet are completely unrealistic, as in this case, not even the route that the data packages will take is known. If a connection should happen to pass via a satellite on a geostationary orbit, the signal transfer time alone will add an extra half-second to the response time.

Response time grows with the "weight" of the transactions

The unpredictability of the capacity requirements of business processes, however, has a much greater effect than the aforementioned technical conditions. The sizing process is based on measurements taken in a benchmark test, which can cover only a fraction of the functionality available in an SAP system. Adding extra, generalized estimates to the main calculated estimate is the only way of allowing for the influence of customizing, reports, background jobs, and hot spots. These generalized estimates are based on average values for systems with a normal level of customizing. Experience shows that systems with an above-average level of customizing can differ greatly from these values.

Response time grows with the size of the database

Response time necessarily increases along with the size of the database. This is especially true of reporting functions, but it also applies to operations such as online availability checks and price determination. To return to our truck analogy, this is the same as an increase in the load during a trip. The condition and incline of the road are equivalent to the number of users and transactions in the system. Customer extensions correspond to potholes, and user exits correspond to detours.

Therefore, as a rule, a hardware manufacturer can promise a particular response time only if the customer guarantees that the system load will not exceed a specified value. Even this kind of assurance is possible only for transactions whose execution time does not depend on the size of the database. For new developments, extensive modifications, and in-house developments, a stress test is unavoidable. The stress test then serves as the basis for determining the required system performance, which can then be verified in an acceptance test. However, all involved parties should understand that this kind of test requires a certain degree of effort and may take some days to complete.

Basic price and service price

The SLAs with the business departments should have a price adjustment clause that pertains to system load. This clause can be based on the CPU load measured using operating system tools or the SAP Solution Manager, for example. With this model, if the system load, and hence the response time, increase due to a rise in user numbers or the transaction volume (or a badly written ABAP program), so does the service price for the business departments.

With this approach, the IT department is automatically in a position to extend the system resources in order to handle the higher system load, without the need for long discussions about whether these measures are necessary. The basic price, then, covers routine system operation and the necessary investments in maintaining availability. This situation is similar to the established billing processes for energy, gas, and water supply, where the amount of the bill depends on the recipient's amount of utility usage.

4.13 How Reliable Is Sizing?

Considering all the "unknowns" mentioned in the previous sections, you may justifiably ask "How reliable are the SAP sizing algorithms when it comes to estimating the actual resource requirements of a system?" It was precisely this question that prompted one of the authors to set up a study as part of a Master's thesis, in collaboration with the Technical College in Furtwangen, Germany, with the goal of comparing actual measured system loads with the loads estimated in a sizing process.[9]

In this study, over 255 EarlyWatch and 140 GoingLive reports from live systems were analyzed. These reports were made available by customers

9 *Statistical Analysis of Resource Demand of Standard Software Solutions*. Master's Thesis of Syed Meraj Ahmed, supervised by Prof. Bernadin Denzel and Dr. Michael Mißbach.

to the SAP HP Competence Center within the framework of upgrade sizing and migration sizing processes.

Table 4.1 shows the percentage of SAP releases, databases, and operating systems used in the study.

EarlyWatch reports	Release 3.1: 44 (20 %) Release 4.0: 28 (13 %) Release 4.5: 50 (22 %) Release 4.6: 103 (45 %)
GoingLive reports	Release 3.1: 20 (13 %) Release 4.0: 30 (22 %) Release 4.5: 20 (13 %) Release 4.6: 72 (52 %)
Databases	Oracle 7.2.4: 15 % Oracle 8.0.5: 40 % SQL Server 7: 25 % Informix 7.31: 16 % ADABAS 7: 4 %
Operating systems	HP-UX: 50 % Linux: 20 % Windows: 20 % IBM zOS: 5 % IBM AIX: 5 %

Table 4.1 Data Used for the Comparative Study

The study determined the CPU capacity, memory, disk space, and the growth in occupied disk space for every data set, both at the time of installation and in actual use. These values were then linked up to the number of users and the correlation coefficient was determined. This statistical measure shows how closely values are related, or whether there is any relationship between them. For values of the correlation coefficient close to 1, it should be possible to determine the required values from the number of users, although this is unlikely for very low values.

Additionally, a standard user-based sizing with an average load factor was carried out for each area to be measured, and the results were represented in diagrams as a straight line plus measurement points. Figures 4.7 to 4.12 show some of the results.

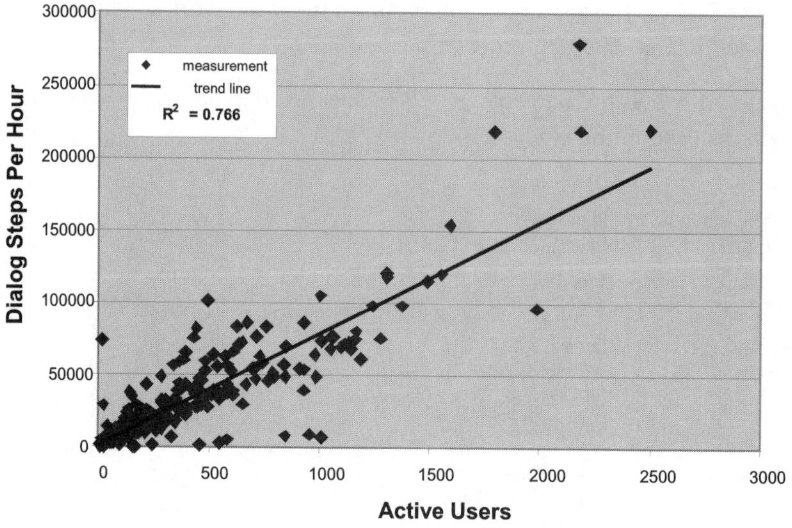

Figure 4.7 Ratio of Transaction Steps to the Number of Users

The user-based approach to sizing assumes that the number of transactions per hour can be calculated from the number of active users. As Figure 4.7 shows, the correlation coefficient here is 0.76, and so we can be reasonably sure that this assumption is correct.

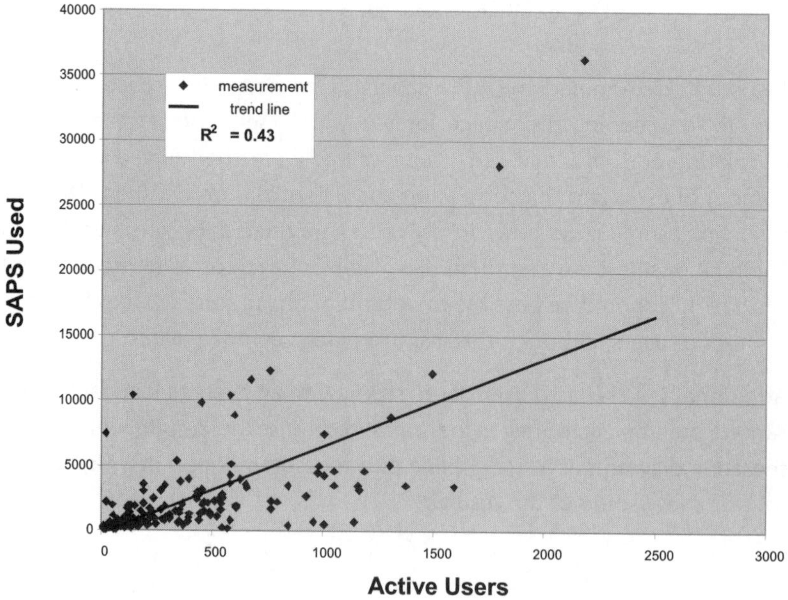

Figure 4.8 Ratio of SAPS to the Number of Users

If we compare the CPU resources that were actually used with the number of active users in each system at the time of the measurements, the correlation coefficient drops to 0.43 (Figure 4.8). However, this is obviously due to a small number of extreme values. As shown in a detailed analysis, all these values are from industry solutions, parts of which are very different to the standard solutions.

Figure 4.9 shows the same diagram after the measurement points from industry solutions were eliminated. As we can see, the vast majority of the measurement points now lie within a scatter band of plus (+) or minus (–) 7,500 SAPS.

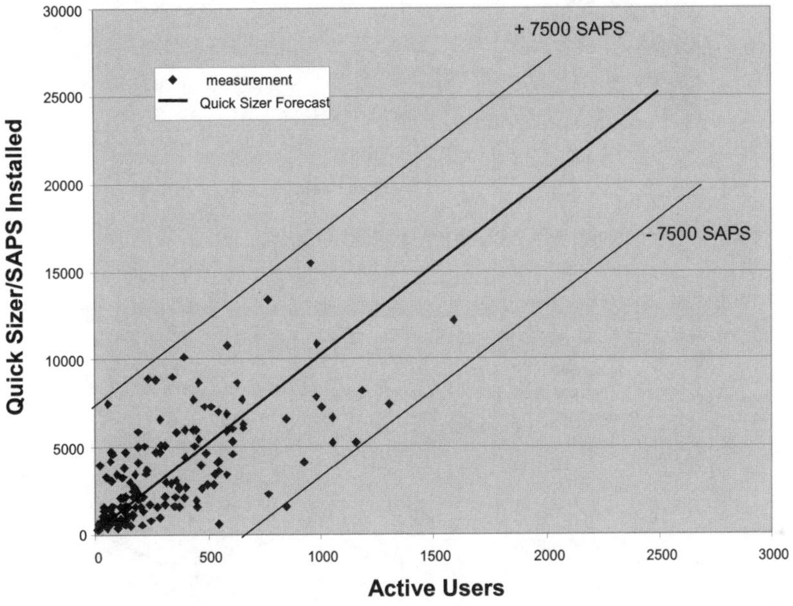

Figure 4.9 Used SAPS Versus Number of Users, with Forecast

Figure 4.10 shows the amount of main memory used compared to the number of active users. The scatter band here is a relatively narrow one with a high correlation coefficient of 0.72.

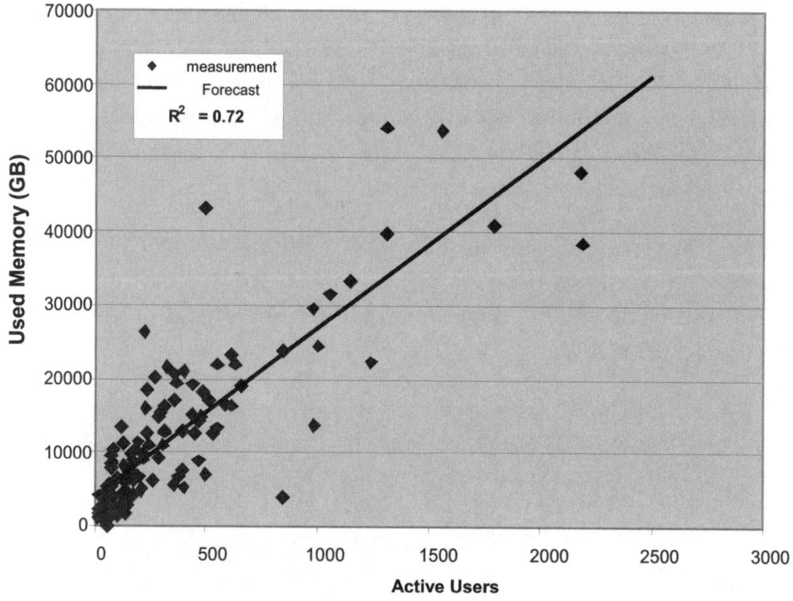

Figure 4.10 Main Memory Usage Versus Number of Users

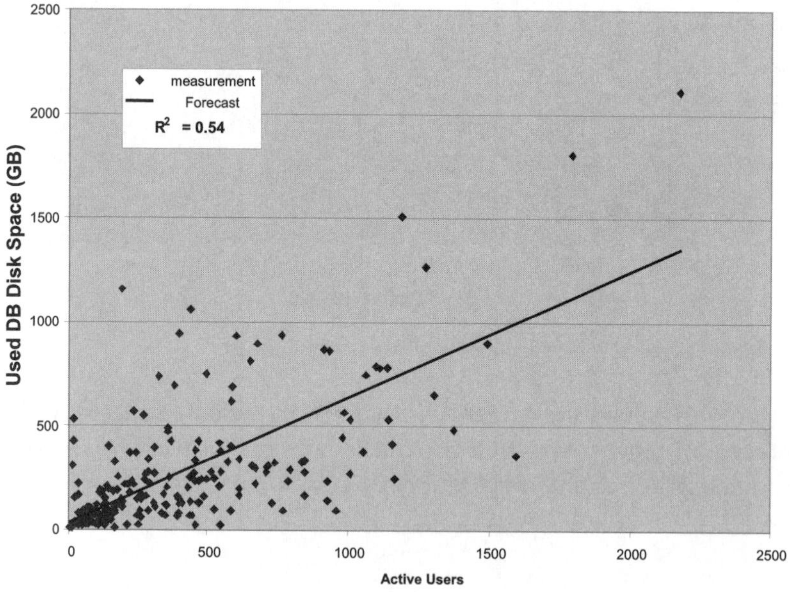

Figure 4.11 Disk Space Used Compared to Number of Users

Figure 4.11 shows the ratio of disk space used to the number of active users. The wider scatter band here, with a correlation coefficient of 0.54, is caused by the different retention periods. Lastly, Figure 4.12 shows the relationship between the growth in disk space and the number of users. Here, too, the few "strays" are due to industry solutions.

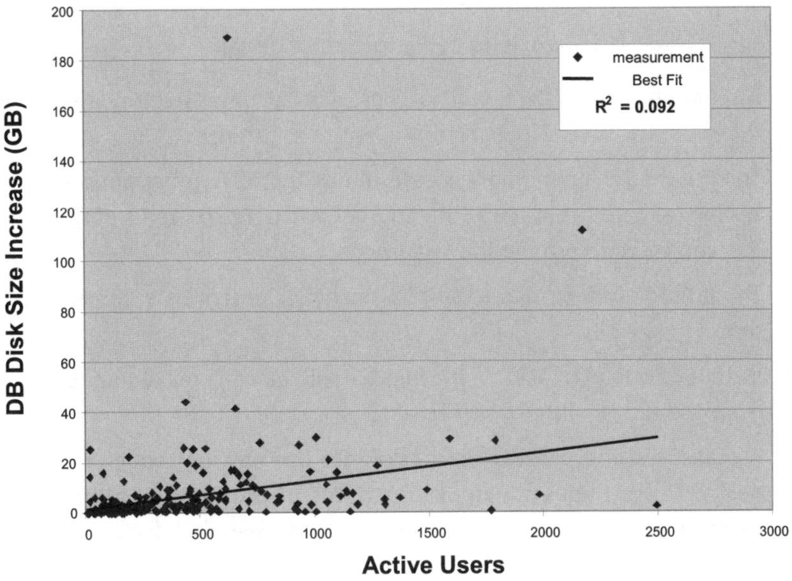

Figure 4.12 Growth of Disk Space Versus Number of Users

> **Feedback welcome**
>
> SAP and the Competence Centers of its partners go to great lengths to provide a realistic basis for system designs. However, it is simply not possible for them to operate live SAP system landscapes under real-world conditions. Therefore, the values provided in most cases are the result of benchmark tests. Any recommendations made are also based on knowledge gained from our experience with problems that have been escalated and special cases; however, you should note that measurement values from "normal" live systems that are operating satisfactorily are underrepresented. We would therefore be happy to receive real-world measurements from readers. This information would then be used anonymously to expand our existing pool of knowledge and experience.

4.14 Summary

In the course of the study, it was established that the instruments provided by SAP and its partners can estimate the performance requirements of a standard SAP system relatively well. If the industry solutions are put aside for separate analysis, the measured values lie within a scatter band of only plus or minus 7,500 SAPS. Considering the many different unknowns, this is a surprisingly good result.

The following basic principles apply to system design:

- An under-sized system will, at best, cause unsatisfactory response times, and at worst, jeopardize the entire enterprise.
- The required main memory is determined by the number of users who are logged into the system. The number and usage patterns of the concurrent users determine the system load.
- The ratio of system load to system resources determines the response time.
- With a CPU load of 100 %, throughput will be at its maximum, but the response times will be unacceptable.
- A realistic sizing process must take into account hot spots and load peaks. This includes any uneven patterns of distribution in the usage patterns per day, at the end of the month or year, and during seasonal peaks.
- It is impossible to estimate in advance the system load caused by in-house developments. If the quality of the ABAP or Java code is bad enough, the capacity of even the largest computer can be exceeded. Therefore, a quality assurance system is part of every standard SAP system landscape.
- Even with the most sophisticated sizing methods, it is not possible to reduce the required CPU performance and the size of main memory for a given transaction load.
- Because the business processes in an enterprise are constantly changing, the performance requirements of the SAP infrastructure are likewise constantly changing. A system configuration that is as flexible as possible, has adequate reserve resources, and the option to extend the system are required to ensure that the system can adapt successfully to changing requirements.
- Correct sizing is still not a guarantee of permanently satisfactory performance. Live systems should therefore be regularly optimized by experienced performance experts with the appropriate tools.

5 SAP System Platforms

Server, operating system, and database platforms

Although the platform, that is, the technical infrastructure, for the various SAP solutions is usually equated with the physical computers on which the software is installed, it is actually made up of several interacting levels. Figure 5.1 shows the individual components of a SAP system platform.

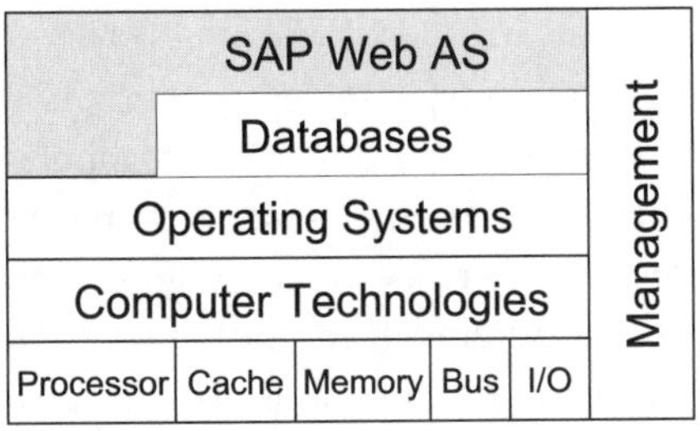

Figure 5.1 Components of an SAP System Platform

Selecting the platform

The software for mySAP business components is programmed as much as possible (with certain restrictions) in a way that is independent of computer technologies, operating systems, and database software, in order to make the software independent of the technologies provided by the various platform vendors. The customer can then select the platform that is best suited to his or her requirements. This decision depends on technical criteria plus the existing skill of the IT team, although many times a well-planned system is disregarded and replaced because of a company management decision.

Because only the SAP Web Application Server (Web AS) and the database are platform-specific, all SAP components that are based on the Web AS can run on all platforms supported by SAP Web AS. Figure 5.2 provides you with an overview of all the currently supported system platforms.

PAM

This platform-independence, however, does not apply to certain (non-Web AS) components, and restrictions also apply to the computing technology used and the possible combinations of SAP application release, operating system, and database. The SAP Product Availability Matrix (PAM)[1] contains details of which components are available with which releases on which platforms.

1 Go to *http://service.sap.com/pam*.

Databases

IBM DB2			Informix	Microsoft SQL Server	Oracle	SAP DB/ MaxDB
/UDB	/400	/390				

Operating Systems and Computer Architectures

Unix								Windows		Mid-range	Mainframe	
HP Tru64 UNIX	IBM AIX	HP-UX	HP-UX	FuSi Reliant Unix	SUN Solaris	Linux	Linux	MS Windows Server 2003		OS/400 iOS	Linux	zOS
Alpha	Power PC	PA-RISC	IA-64	MIPS	SPARC	IA-32	IA-64	IA-32	IA-64	AS/400 iSeries	zSeries	zSeries

Figure 5.2 System Platforms for SAP Web AS

Although low-range and, increasingly, mid-range server systems have become mass-produced goods, the specific properties of the technologies in question should still be carefully considered in relation to mySAP systems, as there can be significant differences between systems. This applies especially to higher-performance systems. If the system eventually reaches its limits and has to be replaced later on, this is certainly possible, but does involve system downtime and a certain amount of work.

This chapter describes the hardware platforms, operating-system platforms, and database platforms that can be used with mySAP, and explains the important selection criteria for capacity (throughput), performance (response-time behavior), scalability, availability, and last but not least, the total cost of ownership (TCO).

5.1 Computer Technologies for mySAP

There is a whole range of hardware platforms for operating mySAP, which differ from one another in terms of their architecture, the number of processors they support, the system buses they use, and the input/output technology (I/O architecture) employed for handling communication with external storage systems. The providers of these platforms include companies that also have their own processor technology, such as Hewlett-Packard and IBM, plus a wide range of providers that use either Intel processors or processors from other manufacturers.

HP Hewlett-Packard focuses on two areas: standard systems with Intel Xeon and AMD Opteron processors for small to medium-sized servers; and Itanium processors for high-performance computers with Linux, Windows, and HP-UX that function as consolidation platforms for entire SAP NetWeaver and mySAP system landscapes. HP also provides other computers based on the PA-RISC and Alpha families of processors, and offers long-term support for these, in order to enable the operators of these platforms to make the switch to Intel standard systems at a time and pace of their choice.

IBM provides a wide range of very different platforms: the zSeries and iSeries (previously S/390 and AS/400 respectively), its traditional large-scale computers and mini-computers; the pSeries (previously RS/6000), its UNIX systems; and the xSeries, its Intel standard servers. The computers in both the iSeries and the pSeries have processors from the PowerPC processor family. xSeries computers are available with AMD Opteron, Intel Xeon, and Itanium processors. **IBM**

Sun provides UNIX computers that are based on the SPARC processor family. However, in the near future, these systems will come with SPARC-64 CPUs developed by Fujitsu-Siemens rather than SPARC processors developed by Sun. Sun also provides another platform for mySAP in the form of servers based on AMD Opteron (with Linux only). **Sun**

There are also several providers that offer computers exclusively based on AMD Opteron, Intel Xeon, and Itanium processors. In recent years, vendors from countries that include India and China have had their Itanium computers certified by SAP.

5.2 Processor Architectures

The architecture of the CPU can have a major effect on the performance and reliability of a mySAP database or application machine. Besides obvious parameters such as the clock rate, other factors such as the scope and number of the statements processed per clock cycle, the size and structure of the cache memory, the speed of individual data paths (buses) to main memory and the interfaces, and the throughput of these paths also determine the performance of an individual CPU. The ability to automatically correct bit errors (along with thermal stability) is essential to ensure the reliability of the whole system.

The first commercial large-scale computers were based on the Complex Instruction Set Computing (CISC) architecture. These computers contained a relatively large set of complex commands at CPU level for processing the program code. The early CPUs of the Intel 32-bit processor family were classic examples of this kind of architecture (although Intel has since started using many of the design principles of the RISC processors). **CISC architecture**

IA-32 The Intel and Intel-compatible processors available on the PC mass market usually have only one CPU. Only the clock frequency and the capacity of the graphics engine matter in this market.

However, Intel also provides processors for high-capacity multiprocessor systems, such as those required in commercial applications (the Xeon processor is a good example). These high-end processors (and the chip sets that go with them) highlight differences in terms of the cache memory and the number of CPUs that can be used simultaneously in a standard multiprocessor system.

Usually, Intel brings its faster processors to the high-profit workstation market first. However, these processors don't support Intel's multiprocessor specification (MPS), to which distributed I/O interrupt-sharing and some other functions belong. This is why the clock frequency of the multiprocessor systems always lags behind a little. For higher clock frequencies, we have to turn to the Pentium4 uniprocessor chips, followed by the Xeon DP chips, which support two CPU servers, and lastly to the Xeon MP chips, which support servers with more than two CPUs.

Opteron and EMT64 AMD Opteron processors bring 64-bit extensions to the world of IA-32. However, to enable you to use these extensions, suitable operating systems, databases, and SAP kernels must be developed first. The same thing applies to Intel IA-32 processors with an EMT64 64-bit extension. Sixty-four-bit capability means that 64-bit data lengths and memory addresses can be processed. With Windows Server 2003 SP1, Microsoft plans to make x64 the third operating system platform that it supports.

RISC architecture For a long time, the superscalar 64-bit Reduced Instruction Set Computing (RISC) architecture was the touchstone for all high-powered UNIX computers. RISC deliberately reduces the instruction set, thus making it extremely fast to process. Therefore, even complex tasks that comprise several RISC instructions can be processed faster than they could on a traditional CISC processor.

"Superscalar" means that the CPU has between four and eight pipelines, in which multiple instructions per clock cycle can be processed in parallel. However, because the program does not know that it is being parallel-processed, the program code has to be checked during the program execution in order to establish which parts can actually be parallel-processed. When developing the parallelization unit, the designer must use all of his or her skills and expertise to create effective branch prediction. This also highlights the limits of the superscalar RISC architecture, as the space requirement for the parallelization unit on the chip increases exponentially if the number of pipelines grows.

EPIC architecture

The well known Moore's First Law can be used to describe how processor capacity increases. According to this law, the rate of progress in microelectronics means that processor capacity doubles approximately every 18 months. The less well-known Moore's Second Law states that the cost of the necessary production equipment also doubles at the same rate (Figure 5.3).

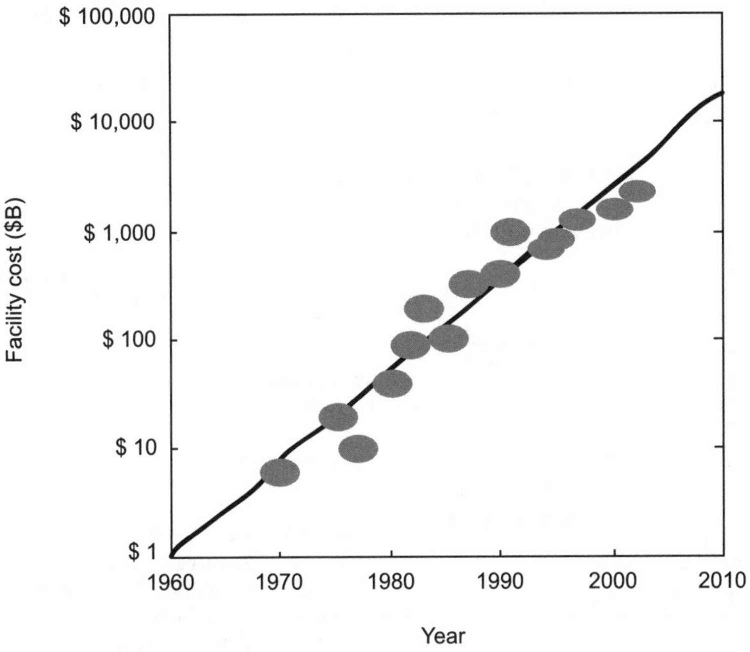

Figure 5.3 Moore's Second Law of Processor Development

HP and Intel collaborated on developing the Explicit Parallel Instruction Computing (EPIC) architecture, with the intention of increasing processor capacity even further while keeping costs down. The principle of EPIC is to optimize the parallelization process as early as the source code compilation stage and to issue explicit instructions for processing the code to the processor via a corresponding set of commands. The code can therefore be processed much faster. SAP provides EPIC-compiled components for HP-UX, Windows, and Linux.

Compiler quality is the key

A central factor in the speed of an EPIC system is the quality of the compiler that is used to parallelize and optimize the machine code. There is a different compiler for every operating system, which explains why SAP software runs at different speeds on the same hardware with different operating systems.

Because SAP supports several operating systems for Itanium processors, there is no dependency between hardware and operating system, and the infrastructure is therefore more flexible. For example, mySAP solutions can run in parallel on Windows, HP-UX, and Linux on a high-performance machine in different partitions.

With the EPIC architecture, Intel has made the transition to 64-bit systems and storage addresses for the first time, a step that had been achieved in the UNIX world some time ago. This step removes the restrictions on Windows and Linux in terms of the size of the addressable main memory.

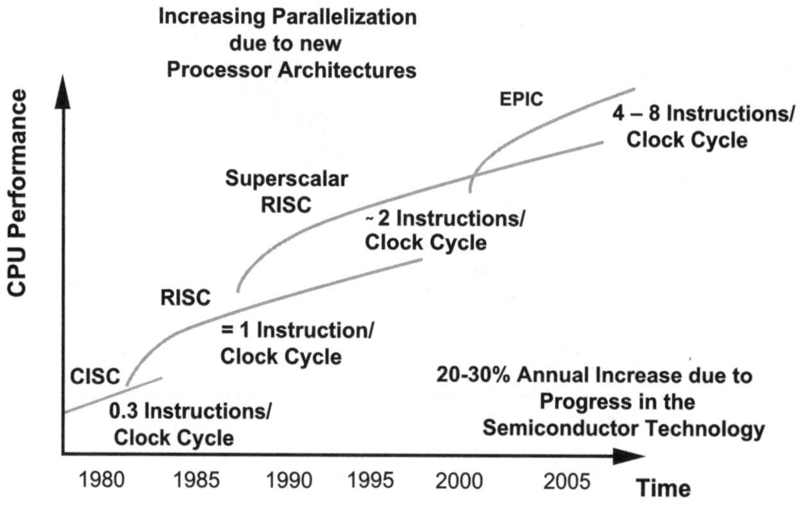

Figure 5.4 Developing Processor Architectures

Multicore and multithreading

Increasingly more manufacturers are equipping their CPUs with multicore and multithreading technology, with the goal to further increase their computing power.

Multicore means that multiple complete CPU cores are implemented on each chip. The cores usually have to share a level 2 or level 3 cache.

Multithreading refers to the capability of a CPU to process instructions from more than one process at the same time. Therefore, you can use more instruction units per CPU without the risk that they are blocked due to insufficient parallelization. This pushes back even further the limits of the parallelization problems mentioned above. With EPIC architectures, this limit is much higher, thanks to the better parallelization in the compiler.

Multicore and software licenses

Software manufacturers handle licensing for multicore and multithreading in different ways. While at SAP, licensing is usually separate from the number of CPUs, Oracle, for example, specifies one license per core. Microsoft requires licenses for SQL server and Windows per processor socket, regardless of the number of cores. This rule also applies to the processor limitation of the various Windows releases (Standard Edition, Enterprise Edition, and so on).

5.3 Main Memory Architectures

Besides the processors, the architecture and size of main memory and the cache are the central factors in the capacity of a computer system for SAP. While the data (and the program code) in main memory is available to all the processors in a computer, the cache memories are intended to increase the performance of the individual CPUs. Reliability, along with speed and size, is a central criterion in selecting a memory technology for enterprise-critical mySAP components.

Main memory

Just like processor capacity, there can never be too much main memory when it comes to SAP. Dynamic Random Access Memory (DRAM) chips are usually used for main memory. These are located in a storage module or on a storage circuit board. To minimize the time that it takes to access main memory, the individual data bytes are always distributed across multiple storage modules (interleaving). This makes it possible to parallelize access and thus to significantly increase system throughput, especially in multiprocessor computers. However, with this method, new main memory can be added only in fixed blocks of storage modules, in order to preserve the fixed number ratios necessary for interleaving. The number and combination of memory modules for optimal interleaving can differ from module to module, so the manufacturer's documentation should always be consulted.

More main memory versus more read cache in disk systems

When using read caches of disk subsystems with SAP applications, you should note that SAP applications with an Online Transaction Processing (OLTP) system load profile use high-level random access, while read caches on disk subsystems are optimized for streaming access with relevant look-ahead algorithms. You will notice that the maximum achievable hit rate on an SAP system on a disk cache does not usually exceed 60 %. Therefore, to significantly increase this performance, you should ensure that the database buffer is dimensioned to be large. The database manages the data in its cache according to its content and not according to its storage location.

However, you should assess this in each individual case. An array that is well equipped with caches can yield considerable performance gains for write operations to the cache, and the read-ahead mechanisms for sequential I/O can greatly enhance performance, especially in Online Analytical Processing (OLAP) applications such as SAP Business Information Warehouse (SAP BW). Also, by combining several small I/Os into a smaller number of large I/Os, you reduce the number of disk head movements. All this has a positive effect on performance. However, these effects can be fully achieved only up to a certain cache size. Once this size (which is different on every system) is exceeded, the benefits quickly level out, and the money would be better invested in main memory.

Cache memory

Memory Latency, that is, the time required to call a data row from main memory, is around 50 ns on small systems, and an average of at least 200 ns on systems with several dozen processors. The cycle time of one of the latest processors, on the other hand, is less than two ns. Thus, a processor often has to wait longer for data from main memory than it takes for the data processing itself.

Therefore, fast caches are used to accelerate the supply of instructions and data to the processor. There are many different kinds of cache (L1 to L3), depending on the structure of the cache memory in the system architecture relative to the CPU. The farther away the cache memory is from the processor, the longer the access times. Therefore, L2 and L3 cache memories have to be larger than L1 cache memories, in order to achieve any kind of worthwhile effect. Larger cache memories cache larger code segments and data records, which has a particularly positive effect with databases.

In general, it is safe to say that all tasks that store data to the cache can be processed very quickly. If the task at hand is a large one, or if it requires a large amount of data that is not stored in the cache, processor throughput decreases considerably.

Cache hierarchy

Primary or level 1 (L1) caches are physically located very close to the processor core and have the same clock frequency as the CPU. The latency time is therefore usually the same as just one CPU clock cycle. This makes L1 caches extremely valuable in terms of system performance. However, large primary caches do require considerable space on the chip. Because of connection lengths and signal runtimes, there are physical limits to the size of L1 caches.

An L2 cache has a longer latency time, even if it is on the same chip. In this case, the signal runtimes to the processor core are usually five to six CPU cycles.

L3 caches have signal runtimes of more than 10 CPU cycles. Various manufacturers implement extremely large L3 caches on external chips. These caches can even be used by multiple CPUs simultaneously, although the latency times in these cases are correspondingly longer.

5.4 Error-Tolerant Memory

If the structures of the memory chips (and also those of the CPUs) are very small, even natural alpha rays or cosmic radiation can cause memory bit errors. Electrostatic discharge and material defects can have the same effect. There are now special coatings that protect against alpha rays, but with cheaper products the substances used in the chip production process may not be sterile enough and thus may themselves emit radiation. Needless to say, there is no protection against this self-created radiation in the chip.

The more memory, the more errors

The increasing size of memory exacerbates this problem. With main memory of 1 TB, the likelihood of a breakdown is 256 times greater than with main memory of 4 GB. Therefore, for enterprise-critical SAP applications, we strongly recommend that you use only error-tolerant memory that can recognize and correct errors before they cause program crashes or, worse, inconsistent data. This kind of memory, known as Error Checking and Correction (ECC) memory, uses extra parity bits to identify errors in individual bits and to correct these errors, if necessary.

ECC is now included in almost all systems. However, its mechanisms cannot prevent a complete memory chip from crashing. The latest memory chips are several bits wide and therefore the part of a data word that they cover is often too large. So, if the chip crashes, it is impossible to correct this problem. To remedy this situation, technologies such as Chip-Spare (Hewlett-Packard) and Chip-Kill (IBM) enable you to avoid system crashes in these cases. The data is distributed across the memory chips in such a way that the ECC mechanisms can survive a breakdown of a whole memory chip.

There are now also servers on the market that provide hotplug memory with RAID backup, using parity mechanisms like those employed in a Redundant Array of Independent Disks (RAID). This technology allows whole memory modules to be replaced (if they crash, for example) without any interruption to normal operations. This option comes at a price, however: RAID-1 requires double the amount of memory. RAID-5 systems are only 1.25 times as expensive, but with this option a certain amount of performance has to be sacrificed to parity calculation.

5.5 The System Bus

The system bus is the connection between the processors, the memory, and the I/O sub-systems. It is one of the critical design elements of a computer system, because it is this element that can limit the maximum capacity and scalability of the system. Scalability is a particularly important factor for the database in an SAP system, since the database cannot be distributed across multiple computers without a loss of performance. No attempts to rectify this situation to date have produced satisfactory results. The most recent attempts to implement parallel databases, such as Oracle 9i RAC, are focused more on creating the highest possible availability rather than on scalability.

Standard SMP systems

The simplest symmetrical multiprocessing (SMP) systems have a bus architecture in which the processors use a shared bus to access main memory. A bus (from the Latin omnibus, meaning for all) is available to all processors simultaneously. In this kind of system, all processors attempt to access the memory via the bus, independently of each other. This design approach makes the programming involved simpler and is described as "shared everything" (Figure 5.5).

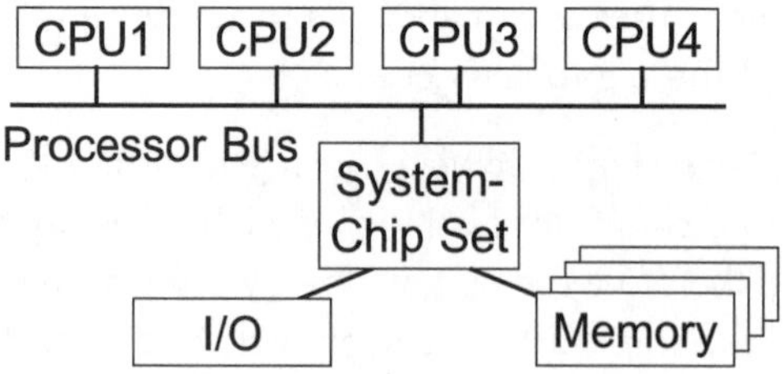

Figure 5.5 Bus-Based Multiprocessor Architecture

However, because the bus can handle only one data transfer at a time, the CPU often has to wait for the bus. Anyone who has ever seen an orderly queue of people at a bus stop in Britain can imagine the procedure of a bus system: There is no pushing, and everyone waits his or her turn. The scalability of these kinds of systems deteriorates as the number of CPUs increases. In other words, every additional CPU increases the overall capacity by an ever smaller amount (but it still costs the same).

Waiting for the bus

Multibus and crossbar technologies remove these restrictions. In systems with up to eight CPUs, it will suffice to use two buses, each with four processors, with a memory interleaving factor of at least four.

In larger systems, extremely fast crossbars are used. These are similar to hard-wired cross-rail distributors in communications engineering. However, contrary to network switches, no data packets are forwarded. Instead, an individual (temporary) data bus for every existing storage bank is activated for every processor, as required. This technology is a key element to improve the main memory throughput and the scalability of the overall system. The bandwidth and latency time of the crossbar switch are the central parameters in a crossbar system.

Crossbar SMP systems

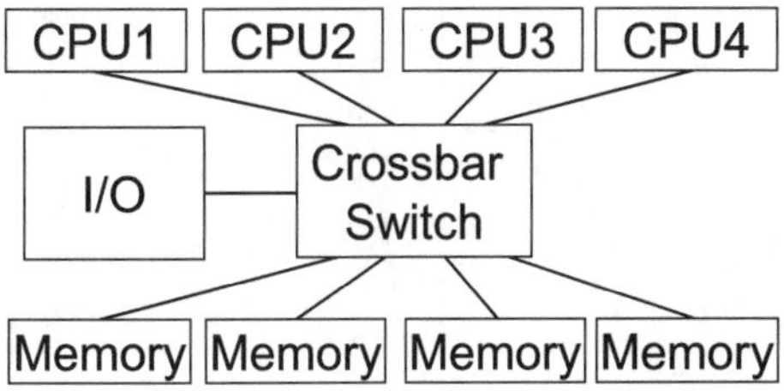

Figure 5.6 Crossbar-Based Multiprocessor Architecture

The key skill in system design is providing a processor with enough memory and I/O bandwidth for it to deliver its maximum throughput. The main problems here are ensuring the coherency of the cache, and managing access conflicts in main memory. Also, once eight CPUs or more are involved, the costs for the central switch become excessive. Therefore, in reality, the scalability of SMP systems has its limits.

Multilevel crossbar

One way out of this cul-de-sac is ccNUMA technology. ccNUMA is short for cache-coherent non-uniform memory access. This kind of system usually consists of cells, each with (usually) four CPU slots, its own memory and I/O interface, and a local crossbar switch. In turn, the crossbar switch of each cell has an interface to one or more superordinate switches, which connect the cells to a larger system (Figure 5.7).

ccNUMA

In a multilevel crossbar switch system, the latency time of memory access in a local cell is shorter than the time it takes to access the memory of another cell. The software has to take this into account in order to fully exploit the scalability of the ccNUMA architecture.

HP-UX, Tru64 UNIX, and Windows Server 2003 all contain similar ccNUMA optimization algorithms. With regard to databases, Oracle, DB2 and SQL Server are all optimized for ccNUMA. SAP applications are optimized by the operating system.

Thus, crossbar systems provide a very high level of performance and scalability (see Figure 5.8 further below in this chapter). Benchmark tests have returned capacities of up to 100,000 users and over 500,000 SAPS in these systems. However, they are most often used as consolidation platforms for multiple SAP solutions.

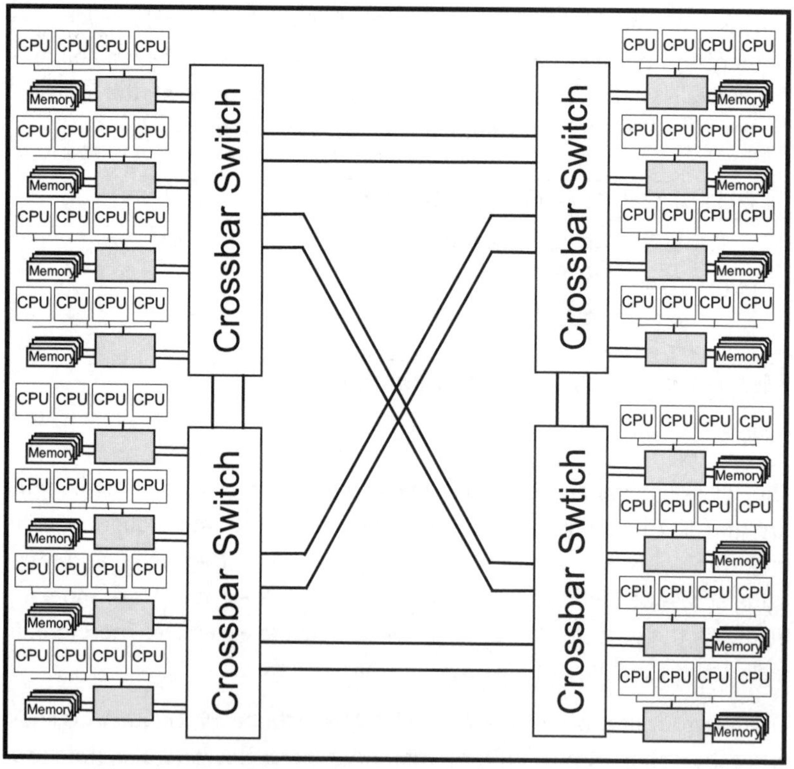

Figure 5.7 ccNUMA or Multilevel Crossbar Switch System

5.6 I/O Architectures

The input/output (I/O) subsystem of a computer has the job of setting up connections to hard disks, network cards, and other peripheral devices. In this area, the PCI industry standard and its follow-on technologies have become established for most SMP computers. Standard interface cards can thus also be used for high-performance computers.

Classic PCI

The PCI bus supports both 32-bit and 64-bit buses with clock frequencies of 33 MHz and 66 MHz. The transfer rates are thus 133 MB/s and over 500 MB/s, respectively. While 32 bits (33 MHz) are more than adequate for fast Ethernet network cards, we advise you to ensure that there are enough 64-bit (66 MHz) slots to connect to hard disk subsystems, especially where FibreChannel cards are used.

PCI-X

PCI-X, a follow-on technology of PCI, has even higher throughput rates, with an average of between approximately 700 MB/s (133 MHz) to 1,000 MB/s (266 MHz). It usually has only one slot per bus. However, as a parallel bus, PCI-X has to cope with differences in the signal runtimes of the individual connections (known as "jitter"). For this reason, if the clock rate is very high, the connections can be only a few centimeters long. PCI-X has thus brought about the end of parallel PCI buses.

PCI Express

PCI Express, the first generation of a serial I/O technology, uses bundles of serial transfer connections. Different transfer rates are possible, depending on the size of each bundle. Bundles can contain between one (PCI Express x 1) and 16 connections (PCI Express x 16). PCI Express x 4 can achieve ca. 1 GB, while PCI Express x 8 can achieve approximately 1.9 GB. The fact that bundles of different sizes can be combined means that the I/O bandwidth can be distributed very flexibly. Therefore, it's very easy to design servers with the correct number of slots and the appropriate bandwidth.

A small number of slots

Nowadays, the trend for the number of slots to have is as few slots as possible while drastically increasing the throughput per slot via new technologies. Only large database servers (those with more than eight CPUs) require more than two 2 GB FibreChannel cards for throughput reasons. The same applies to the network; that is, with Gigabit Ethernet and especially with 10 GB Ethernet, more than two interfaces are required in only extreme cases.

This concentration of slots is contributing to the increasing use of combo cards, which allow multiple FibreChannel and Ethernet interfaces to be implemented on one card. When using these cards, you always have to be aware that redundant interfaces are implemented on physically separate cards; otherwise, if one card crashed, so would all the redundant connections.

Servers with four CPUs can therefore function perfectly with six PCI slots, while larger models still have many slots. However, more often than not, these slots are required so that dedicated I/O cards can be provided for multiple partitions, rather than because of the bandwidth.

Supporting hot-swap PCI slots for the sake of system availability is a central criterion. With hot-swap capability, interface cards can be swapped without the need to shut down the computer. However, this only makes sense if the systems are designed to include redundancy. The operating system has to support hot-swap PCI, since it is the operating system that has to deactivate the driver and switch off the electricity supply to the PCI connector during the swap process.

InfiniBand

The InfiniBand architecture, which was promoted for a long time as the successor to Ethernet and FibreChannel, has failed to make much of an impression in the commercial IT market. Its areas of application are basically restricted to networking computer clusters in the technical research field (High Performance Technical Computing, HPTC).

5.7 Blade Servers

Blade servers are highly-compressed "plug-in" servers. They do not have their own power supplies or network components; rather, they are connected to the outside world by being inserted into special space-saving racks. These racks contain centralized power supplies for all blades. Integrated network switches are then automatically connected to the blades via the rack. The user-friendly management tools provided enable efficient management of the system.

The following are the advantages of blade systems:

- High performance density—Thanks to the way they are constructed, blade servers take up only a small amount of space in the rack. Therefore, their computing power per square meter of shelf space is much higher compared to normal rack-mounted servers.
- Low electricity usage—Because the power supplies are centralized, their capacity can be more finely matched to the actual energy usage. Also, less excess capacity is required for the high availability of the power supplies.

- High reliability due to rack-integrated network connections—That annoying and awkward "cable spaghetti" is a thing of the past, since the connections to the rack-integrated network switches are established as soon as the blade is inserted into the rack.
- Straightforward management—Manufacturers usually provide tools with the servers that make it straightforward to install and monitor the servers, and even replace a faulty blade. This is facilitated by automatic installation of a replacement blade ("rip and replace").

Blade server versus conventional server

Blade servers are always compared to conventional, extremely flat servers (called "pizza boxes" because of their shape), and the comparison does not always work in the blades' favor. The following are the disadvantages of blade servers:

- If the number of blades is between 10 and 20 (depending on the individual system), the basic investment in the blade infrastructure does not make financial sense.
- Scalability is usually restricted to a maximum of four CPUs.
- Because of their extremely high density in terms of performance, blades cause a high level of heat dissipation that must be take into account for the air-conditioning systems to handle.
- Requirements for several I/O cards and special I/O cards: While some blade servers have one or two PCI slots, most blade concepts are designed so that the I/O connections integrated via the backplane are sufficient and no additions are needed.
- Requirements for several local disks and downtime-secure local disks: Some blades have between two and four (maximum) hot-plug hard disks and one integrated RAID controller. Anything more than that has to be implemented via the network or SAN. Local tape drives are not available for blades.
- For readers mainly interested in the management tools: In many cases, blades will not be required, as these tools are already available for conventional computers. For example, Hewlett-Packard provides its "Proliant Essentials" tools for managing blade servers and conventional industry-standard servers (the extra blade functionality is basically restricted to identifying and replacing faulty blades).

5.8 Operating Systems for mySAP

After SAP developed the R/2 system for large computers (mainframes), AS/400 mini-computers were originally intended to be the platform for

R/3, which was aimed at small to mid-sized companies. However, it became clear during the course of the development work that the AS/400s available at the time did not have enough capacity for R/3. At short notice, Hewlett-Packard provided SAP with first-generation RISC-based UNIX computers, on which R/3 could run with the required performance.

Since the first SAP customer went live with R/3 on HP servers at the beginning of the 1990s, HP-UX has gone on to become one of the most predominant UNIX operating systems for SAP, this statement is based on the number of user installations. SAP now supports many other UNIX variants, including Sun Solaris, IBM AIX, Siemens SINIX (later Reliant UNIX) and Digital UNIX (now HP Tru64 UNIX). Some years later, support for Microsoft Windows Server, the new AS/400 generation and 1999 Linux also came on stream. In the later 1990s, support for OS/390 mainframes was also introduced. Support for HP-UX, Windows and Linux on Itanium servers came on stream in 2003.

UNIX The various UNIX versions are closely connected to the hardware of each provider. However, in order to remain manufacturer-independent, SAP goes to great lengths to ensure that it does not use any proprietary features of the UNIX version in question. SAP assumes that the manufacturers ensure the compatibility of their operating systems with the various computer systems. This is why SAP certifies only the operating system from each manufacturer, and not the individual servers on which the operating systems are installed. The following combinations are supported:

- HP-UX on HP 9000 and HP Integrity servers (HP-UX on Hitachi hardware is supported for SAP products only in Japan).
- HP Tru64 UNIX (previously Digital UNIX) on HP AlphaServer.
- IBM AIX on IBM and Bull hardware.
- Sun Solaris on Sun and Fujitsu-Siemens hardware. SAP supports Solaris on SPARC hardware only. Solaris on IA-32 or Opteron is not supported.
- Siemens Reliant UNIX on Siemens hardware. SAP supports this platform up to Release 4.6C. Customers who want to use Release 4.7 have to migrate to another platform.

Windows SAP R/3 has been available for Windows operating systems since 1994. Windows is now used in over 50 % of all SAP customer installations. Because Windows systems can comprise components from various manufacturers, SAP requires certification for every series for production systems, including the main storage circuit board, the processors, the chip sets in the system bus, and the primary I/O controller (in order to involve the manufacturer in the support to some degree). SAP guarantees support only for certified servers. The certification process is carried out on SAP's behalf by AddOn Systemhaus (previously by IXOS), and the certificates are published at *http://www.addon.de/pub/index.asp*.

Currently, computers by Acer, Bull, Data General, Dell, Egenera, Fujitsu-Amdahl, Fujitsu-Siemens, HCL, HP, Hitachi, IBM, Intel, Langchao, Mitsubishi, NEC, Samsung, and Unisys are certified (although for some manufacturers, only a few servers are certified). Since Windows Server 2003 was released, SAP R/3 is also supported on 64-bit Windows for Itanium-based servers; Bull, Dell, Fujitsu-Siemens, HCL, HP, IBM, NEC, Langchao, and Unisys are currently certified.

Linux

The Open Source operating system Linux is the newest platform for mySAP components, and has been available for use with SAP since the end of 1999. Currently, the SuSE and Red Hat distributions are supported on AMD Opteron, and Intel Xeon and Itanium. SuSE is also supported on the pSeries and the zSeries. Red Flag is supported only in China.

LinuxLab

To promote the use of Linux, the LinuxLab was set up in Walldorf, Germany, the location of SAP's global headquarters. Besides SAP, engineers at the LinuxLab include employees from HP, IBM, Dell, Fujitsu-Siemens, SuSE, Red Hat, and other companies. The LinuxLab has produced the extension to the Linux kernel, among other things, with which up to 64 GB of memory can be addressed with Xeon processors. This illustrates one of the strengths of the open-source philosophy: This extension was made available to the Linux community on the Web in a relatively short period of time.

SAP and Linux: Who releases what?

The release procedure, however, is somewhat complicated. This is because Linux does not "belong" to anybody[2], and thus nobody has or attains overall responsibility of the combination of hardware, operating system, and application. The Linux distributor, the hardware manufacturer, SAP LinuxLab, and SAP final assembly have to release every SAP component. A solution is considered released only once it has run through four stages:

2 This is the reason why Suse and Red Hat are called distributors rather than producers or vendors.

- The Linux distributor releases combinations of Linux distribution, Linux kernel, and CPU architecture (such as IA-32, IA-64, Opteron/Intel64, Power). The release is documented on the website of the Linux distributor in question.
- The SAP LinuxLab releases combinations of CPU architecture, Linux distribution, Linux kernel, SAP Web AS, and the database. The release is documented on the SAP LinuxLab website (*www.sap.com/linux*).
- On the LinuxLab website, the hardware manufacturers document the combinations of Linux distribution and server configuration released by the Linux distributor or the hardware manufacturer (these can time their releases jointly or independently). This release is usually independent of the Linux kernel, but may contain restrictions on the kernel versions.
- SAP final assembly releases combinations of SAP products or solutions and Web AS versions. Tests are carried out on a spot-check basis on more than one CPU architecture, but not usually on all. The release, however, applies to all CPU architectures, provided that no problems were detected in the tests. The SAP Product Availability Matrix (*service.sap.com/pam*) contains details of releases and restrictions[3].

Linux for enterprise-critical applications

Thanks to the legendary stability of Linux and the availability of professional support (albeit fee-based) of manufacturers such as HP and IBM, the basic conditions for using Linux in enterprise-critical applications are already fulfilled. Many customers use Linux as an SAP application server, or for development and training systems. However, the cluster support necessary for use as a database server in live SAP systems had been lacking for a long time. This gap has been filled by Steeleye LifeKeeper, and the porting of the widespread HP Serviceguard cluster solution to Linux. Therefore, Linux can now support cluster arrays with up to 16 servers.

Linux does not mean cheap

Companies often mention cost-cutting as a reason for changing to a Linux system. However, cost-cutting is often confused with cost elimination in this case. Linux is actually no more "free" than Windows or UNIX. In professional use, guaranteed support is the most important thing in a license, and for good reason. So, with SuSE and Red Hat, while customers don't pay for the operating system on the CD-ROM, they do pay for the accompanying right to have support for operating system-related problems. This can cost anything between a few hundred and over a thousand dollars per server per year. This cost is understandable, as the Linux dis-

3 Access for SAP customers and partners.

tributors have to hire specialists so that they can offer 24x7 support with short reaction times; and these services aren't free.

What is special about Linux is that its source code is fully open, so it can be viewed and monitored by anybody, and can be further developed by the Linux community on the Web, but it is not a "free lunch." If you aren't familiar with the cultural norms of the Linux community, you should exercise caution. It's easy to learn to rely on the community to solve any problems that occur, quickly and expediently, and to forget that not many Linux programmers have a server with eight CPUs and 32 GB of memory under their desks.

zOS

SAP also supports the classic IBM mainframe computers of the zSeries on the zOS operating system. However, the SAP standard kernel is not available on MVS[4] as native EBCDIC[5] code.

In a heterogeneous configuration, the mainframe serves as a pure database server on which no SAP code runs, deploying UNIX or Windows machines as application servers. In both cases, only IBM DB2 can be used as a database platform. Parallel Sysplex configurations are possible, even though their high availability potential cannot be reached with SAP applications, because there is no backup for the enqueue server. Based on previous experience, the performance of R/3 on mainframes is not very good, and analysts rate this solution as a relatively high-cost one.

OS/400

SAP has also supported IBM computers in the iSeries (previously AS/400) with OS/400 as their operating system since powerful 64-bit technology was introduced for these machines. Only the DB2/400 database from IBM can be used as the database platform in this case. Up to Release 4.6, the SAP kernel was available as an EBCDIC implementation for OS/400. In this case, the SAP system data was also stored in EBCDIC format. From Release 4.7 on, however, only ASCII is supported. The procedure necessary for migrating from EBCDIC to ASCII is based on a database export/import and is basically the same as a platform change.

Heterogeneous systems

To keep system maintenance and management as simple as possible, we recommend that you run a homogeneous system configuration in which the database server and the application server use the same type of operating system. Due to the multilevel system architecture, however, heterogeneous platform landscapes are also possible. The only technical prerequisite for these heterogeneous systems is that a database system client

4 Multiple Virtual Storage.

5 *Extended Binary-Coded Decimal Interchange Code.*

library is available to the operating system of the application computer (and that you can find a manufacturer who is willing to provide support for this).

In heterogeneous systems, it is advisable to set up both the live system and the test system with the same configuration. For example, it has to be possible to check all patches for the operating systems, the database, and the SAP kernel, and all other programs (such as backup software) on the test system.

UNIX and Windows systems

One potential benefit of a heterogeneous system landscape that is made up of a UNIX database server and several Windows application servers is the combination of the unsurpassed stability of UNIX for the database and the lower investment costs of the Intel-based application servers. However, the savings made by purchasing cheaper hardware can be quickly eroded by the additional costs of the staff involved in overseeing two fundamentally different operating systems.

Because the Network File System (NFS), which is widely used in the UNIX world, is not available for Windows, additional software is required to ensure that files can be used by both systems, if the database and the SAP central instance are running on the UNIX machine. The most common product for this purpose is Samba, which is available as freeware and provides file and printing services in the NetBios protocol for Windows clients.

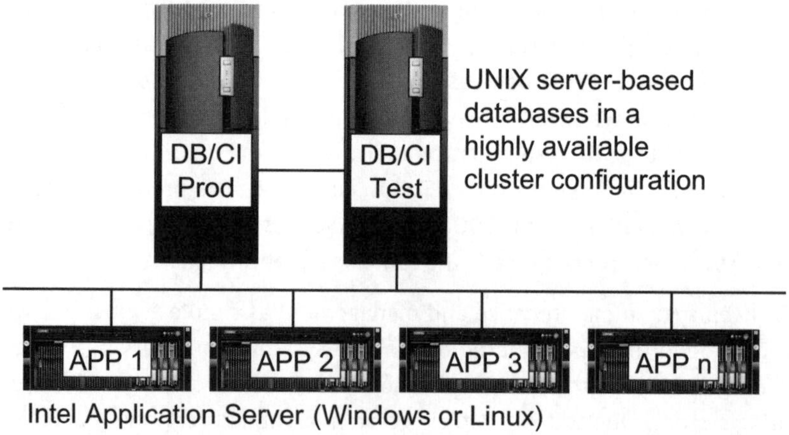

Figure 5.8 Heterogeneous Environment with the Database or Central Instance (or both) on UNIX, and the Application on Windows or Linux

If only the database runs on UNIX and the R/3 central instance runs on a Windows server, no additional software is required. From the point of view of the SAP application, this is a homogenous configuration. However, with this configuration, the single points of failure (SPoF) of the SAP system also apply to the UNIX platform (database) and the Windows platform (central instance). Therefore, to ensure availability, clusters are required on both platforms. To accelerate upgrades to R/3 releases, an extra, temporary central instance is required on the UNIX server when files are copied or imported.

The SAP Change and Transport System (CTS) also functions in a heterogeneous environment. However, the line-end characters are different in UNIX and Windows text files. Consequently, Windows must be configured in such a way that files are written in UNIX format. If file names are used in in-house ABAP programs, the correct UNC notation *server*\ *share**directory*) or UNIX syntax (*/directory*) must be used so that the files can be accessed.

UNIX and Linux systems

A combination of a database server with a commercial UNIX server, and Linux application servers is worthwhile mainly on large systems whose scalability requirements exceed the capabilities of Linux. There is not much difference in the administration of the different UNIX versions. Also, the NFS protocol is already implemented in the operating system, and the file formats and naming conventions match up.

32-bit Windows and 64-bit Windows

A combination of Itanium database server and Xeon application servers is possible if the systems are reaching the 32-bit limit. SQL Server even supports combinations of 64-bit production databases and 32-bit shadow databases. This combination is also regarded as heterogeneous.

5.9 Databases for mySAP

SAP has deliberately decided not to develop a database system specially for R/3. Instead, R/3 supports the relational database management systems (RDBMS) of various manufacturers. In order to remain manufacturer-independent, SAP goes to great lengths to ensure that it does not use any proprietary features of the database in question. The customer can then select the database that is best suited to his or her requirements. Besides technical criteria and the question of how to best leverage the existing expertise in the enterprise, the factors that must be considered in selecting the database are the availability on the various hardware platforms, and the license price factored in the SAP license fee.

Oracle The first R/3 implementations used Oracle as their database system. It became the most popular SAP database (using the number of installed systems as the unit of measure). Oracle is available on most UNIX platforms, including Linux, and on Windows (both the 32-bit and the 64-bit versions). For Itanium, there are EPIC compilations for Windows, Linux and HP-UX.

DB/2 DB/2 from IBM is available on most UNIX platforms, including AIX, HP-UX, Solaris and Linux, on Windows, and on IBM zSeries mainframes and iSeries mini-computers. However, note that DB/2 for zSeries or iSeries is a different database from DB/2 on AIX or Windows. For Itanium, there are EPIC compilations for Windows and HP-UX.

Informix Informix from IBM is also available for AIX, HP-UX, Solaris, Linux and Windows. SAP does not support Unicode, among other things, with Informix.

SQL Server Microsoft SQL Server is available only for Windows (32-bit and 64-bit). There is a 64-bit EPIC version for Itanium processors. Thanks to its close integration with the operating system from the same manufacturer, SQL Server can use special proprietary functions such as TCP/IP via Windows sockets. Therefore, there is no need for the CPU of the database server to process the IP stack, and the latency time is significantly reduced. SQL Server can also handle thread scheduling.

MaxDB MaxDB is also available on most UNIX platforms, including Linux, and on Windows. This database was previously known as SAP DB, which SAP developed from "Adabas D" by Software AG. SAP then transferred all rights and obligations associated with SAP DB to the Swedish company MySQL AB. This company now sells the database as Open Source software under the name MaxDB. MaxDB is the basis of the APO liveCache and the Content Server.

5.10 System Performance and Scalability

There are two dimensions to evaluating the capacity of server systems: scalability and performance. The former determines how many users or transactions a server can handle simultaneously. The latter determines how fast an individual task can be processed (in other words, the response and batch runtimes).

OLTP and OLAP loads As described in previous chapters, there are two different load profiles in business applications: OLTP and OLAP.

The main feature of Online Transactional Processing (OLTP) is a relatively large number of transactions that read or write a relatively small amount of data. OLTP loads are highly parallelized. The measurement criterion for this load profile is system capacity, and a relevant benchmark for this load profile is SAP SD.

The main feature of Online Analytical Processing (OLAP) is a relatively small number of transactions that read or write a relatively large amount of data. OLAP loads do not lend themselves to parallelization. The measurement criterion for this load profile is performance, and a relevant benchmark for this load profile is SAP BW.

OLAP-type loads are becoming more common in SAP systems. For example, besides the typical examples of SAP BW and SAP APO, industry solutions and end-of-month and end-of-quarter closings also have OLAP load profiles.

When is scalability important?

Scalability refers to the maximum limit to which a system can be extended or added to. High scalability is most important for database servers, because while an SAP application lends itself well to being distributed across multiple application servers, distributed database technology still has some performance problems.

Also, highly-scalable servers can be used to implement consolidation scenarios in which as many SAP systems as possible are located on one server.

ccNUMA scales best

Figure 5.9 shows the scaling behavior of the various design approaches described in Section 5.6. As you can see, ccNUMA systems have almost linear scalability.

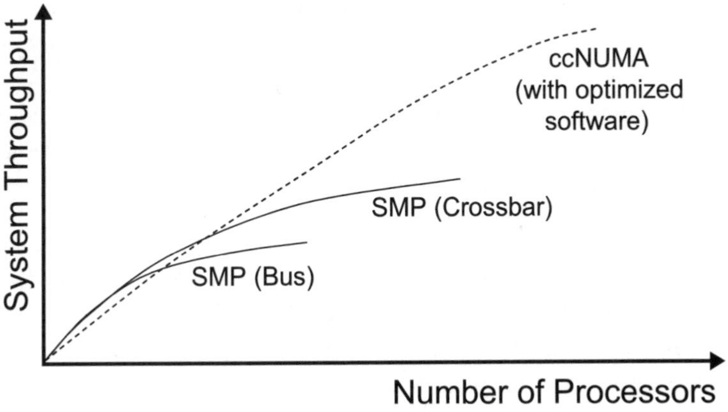

Figure 5.9 Scalability Behavior of Various System Architectures

When is performance important?

Performance is a measure of the speed with which an individual task can be processed. Performance is therefore vital in all tasks that cannot be parallelized and in which the runtime is critical, such as batch jobs, queries in SAP BW, planning runs in APO, and the heavy-load transactions with long runtimes that occur, particularly in the industry solutions. In general, performance is more important with OLAP loads than with OLTP loads.

Because SAP systems are tending more and more towards OLAP loads, you should always check whether the application contains runtime-critical processes. In this case, we recommend that you compare the OLAP performance of the available server types, in addition to the normal sizing process (which takes into account only the OLTP load profile, as explained in Chapter 4). Otherwise, a situation may arise where SAP BW users complain about long response times, or runtimes are too long for the batch windows, although the load itself is processed successfully.

OLTP specialists and other benchmark tricks

Some platforms may achieve excellent results in OLTP benchmarks, but not in OLAP benchmarks. OLTP can be optimized by an extremely large L3 cache, which is often located outside the CPU chip because of its size. However, the relatively high latency time of an external cache has little effect in OLTP benchmarks.

Caches that are simultaneously used by multiple CPUs tempt some benchmark experts' creativity. For example, there are SPECint benchmarks in which only one of eight CPUs was active during the benchmark run. Thus, eight times the cache capacity was available to this one CPU. However, this kind of configuration has little to do with real-life situations.

Individual CPU performance is key

Individual queries and batch jobs usually run on a single CPU in SAP application systems. In other words, multithreading is not used. Runtime-critical loads should therefore always be processed on the server of the system landscape with the fastest CPUs.

Databases such as Oracle, SQL Server and DB2 can distribute OLAP-type queries that read a lot of data across multiple CPUs. The capability to parallel-process queries is mainly beneficial to SAP BW. Typically, however, fast CPUs are preferable for parallel queries, too, as more work is required to sort the data for these queries.

More cache memory versus more CPU

Some processor types are available with L2 caches of different sizes. Intel Xeon processors, for example, come with 1-MB, 2-MB, and 4-MB L2 caches. Tests on 4-CPU and 8-CPU systems show that system throughput improves by between 8 % and 15 % if the cache size is doubled. In some cases, it may make sense to invest in larger caches rather than in more CPU capacity. Large L1 caches are even preferable.

5.11 Memory Addressing

Like almost all enterprise business applications, the SAP solutions depend on a relatively large amount of main memory. We have to keep in mind that several hundred users or even over one thousand users in an SAP system may be using memory resources concurrently. Keeping user contexts, data, and program code in the memory mainly serves to reduce response times. The SAP Web AS, for example, buffers the user context in the fast main memory in order to avoid slower disk accesses when the work processes switch between simultaneously active users. However, the memory does not have to be only physically present; it also has to be logically addressable (otherwise, the system cannot do much with the expensive memory modules).

Practical experience

A main memory that is too small will have much more serious effects on performance than will a processor capacity that is too small.

Since we have already discussed the physical properties of the various memory architectures, we will now look at the architectures that are available for logical memory access.

32-bit SAP kernel and the 4-GB limit

The number of users that can work simultaneously on a server without affecting the performance of the server is determined by the available memory. Memory requirement depends on the number of users and their behavior in the business processes. Even if not a single user is logged on to the system, a certain basic amount of main memory (~700 MB for Release 4.6, including operating system) is still required for the caches and the buffer.

On a 32-bit computer, a maximum of 4 GB (2^{32} bits) of main memory can be logically addressed, which the applications must share among themselves and with the operating system. In reality, significantly less memory is available to the SAP application than the theoretical 4 GB, since every operating system reserves a certain amount of memory for itself.

The fragmentation of the operating system core and the application address space also use up logical address space, which further decreases the amount of memory available to an SAP process. Depending on the operating system architecture, the 32-bit versions of the various 32-bit Windows and UNIX versions make between 1.8 GB and 3.8 GB of address space available to the application.

However, the rate of progress in processor and system architectures has meant that even computers with relatively few CPUs can easily handle more users than is possible with 32-bit addressing, because of the memory limit of 4 GB. Of course, as the functionality of a software system grows, so does the main memory requirement.

Unicode needs 64 bits

As described in Chapter 3, the increasing globalization of markets is making the implementation of Unicode a must in increasingly more enterprises. Also, the general usage of Internet protocols, which are all based on Unicode, will mean that most cross-enterprise software solutions will be Unicode-based in the mid-term. For example, SAP Exchange Infrastructure (SAP XI) already comes as a Unicode system only.

With the transition from single-byte code pages to multi-byte Unicode, the memory requirement increases accordingly. Unicode systems therefore usually require a 64-bit platform.

liveCache needs 64 bits

SAP recommends the use of 64-bit platforms[6] for the APO liveCache. Thirty-two bit platforms are no longer supported from SCM 4.1. Also recommended for SAP BW are 64 bits if BW is used for more than just simple reports.

64 bits with UNIX

What is now available for all UNIX operating systems supported by SAP are 64-bit Web AS and 64-bit databases. In these cases, you just have to ensure that no old 32-bit versions are used, because a 32-bit program cannot use more than 4 GB, even on a 64-bit computer.

32 bits with windows

"Classic" Windows implementations provide the application with an address space of 2 GB (the remaining 2 GB are reserved for the exclusive use of the Windows kernel). You can increase this limit to 3 GB by setting the `/3 GB` switch in the *boot.ini* file.

6 SAP Note 622709.

36 bits with AWE

Intel Xeon CPUs, however, have four additional address lines, with which a total of 64 GB of memory (2^{36} bits) can be addressed (Intel Extended Server Memory Architecture, ESMA). However, the operating system and the applications have to use special mechanisms to access these additional address lines. Microsoft introduced Address Windowing Extension (AWE) with Windows 2000 for this purpose.

To differentiate between Windows versions, this functionality is released in stages. Windows Server 2003 supports 4 GB of memory in the Standard Edition, 32 GB in the Enterprise Edition, and 64 GB in the Datacenter Edition. Therefore, databases that support AWE can use up to 64 GB on Xeon systems.

However, because there is no 36-bit SAP kernel, the individual work processes are still restricted to 3 GB. On the other hand, because an R/3 system consists of multiple work processes (each of these is a separate Windows process), multiple 32-bit processes with different contexts can be run on Xeon machines. You should note, however, that the Windows memory technology used for this has a negative effect on performance.

64-bit Windows

The critical point has always been the addressing limit of 3 GB per work process. Systems with large databases (and thus also large SAP buffers), many SAP modules, SAP industry solutions, and "creative" in-house developments are particularly sensitive to this limit. SAP BW, SAP SEM, and Unicode systems are especially demanding when it comes to memory.

With the introduction of the 64-bit Itanium processor family, 64-bit Windows is also available as an EPIC implementation. This removes all the restrictions mentioned above. An ever-increasing number of enterprises therefore use 64-bit SAP systems on Windows.

Opteron and EMT64

With its Opteron processors, AMD extended the low-cost standard CPU architecture to 64-bit memory addressing, and Intel did the same with its EMT64 Xeon processors. Both processor families enable you to use 32-bit (standard Intel x86) and special 64-bit operating systems, databases, and SAP applications (subject to availability: SAP Web AS from NetWeaver '05, Microsoft Windows Server 2003 from SP1, and Microsoft SQL Server from Version 2005). The Itanium-based 64-bit operating systems from Windows and Linux are not compatible with the operating system that is required for this kind of 64-bit architecture. A significant difference between Opteron and EMT64, and the Itanium-based 64-bit architecture is the native capability of the former to execute conventional 32-bit applications without an emulation layer on the processor. This means that many software manufacturers allow 32-bit x86-based software to run on a 64-bit operating system with AMD Opteron/Intel EMT64. Microsoft, for example, supports the x86 version of SQL Server 2000 on Windows Server 2003 SP1 x64.[7] However, the benefits of a 64-bit address space can be enjoyed only with special 64-bit software for this platform (although a mixture of 32-bit and 64-bit software was used in benchmarks).

36-bit Linux Intel Extended Server Memory Architecture support for Linux was implemented in the LinuxLab in Walldorf. An address space of 64 GB for 36-bit databases is thus available on Linux with Xeon processors. However, because there is no 36-bit Web AS, the aforementioned limits apply to SAP applications.

64-bit Linux The introduction of the 64-bit Itanium processor family meant that a 64-bit Linux operating system was now available. This is now being used more and more for SAP.

64-bit SAP kernel Now that 64-bit processors, 64-bit operating systems, and 64-bit database software are finally available, the 64-bit SAP implementation has finally freed itself of the restrictions on memory addressing.

However, this doesn't mean that the requirement for memory modules will increase. On the contrary, the physical memory that is required for a specific number of users and a specific module combination can be directly and efficiently addressed with the 64-bit kernel. Memory management was also significantly improved in the 64-bit implementation in order to accelerate hardware-based memory operations (users report increases in batch job speeds of 15 % to 30 %).

It is now also possible to cache large database tables in main memory, because of 64-bit technology. From the viewpoint of the operating system, databases are a single application. Therefore, their addressable memory is restricted to the size that the operating system makes available for each application (unlike the whole virtual space).

Because of its support for a much higher number of users per computer, the 64-bit kernel is now a prerequisite for server consolidation.

7 x64 is the Microsoft designation for this operating system. The name differentiates this system from the conventional 32-bit world, and IA64, which is the Itanium-based 64-bit operating system.

Even if data sets in the terabyte range can be more easily managed with 64-bit technology, the need for a document archiving concept cannot be overemphasized.

Migration

Migrating from a 32-bit to a 64-bit system takes only a few hours, because only the executables (kernel binaries) are exchanged, and the application logic is not involved. Therefore, no data export or import is required. Only the disks have to be "reassigned" from the 32-bit to the new 64-bit system.

Combinations of 64-bit and 32-bit computers are also supported, although you should note that the administrative work required to maintain two different code versions is greater than that for a homogeneous environment. With the current pace of technical and economic development, you should expect that the price difference between 32-bit and 64-bit systems will soon level out. Therefore, there will be no particular benefit to using mixed systems.

5.12 Summary

The selection of a system platform for mySAP components depends on many conditions. Besides technical and organizational factors, costs are also a major consideration. The most important recommendations in this chapter include the following:

- System platforms must be certified by SAP. With UNIX, only the operating system must be certified, while with Linux and Windows, the hardware also has to be certified.
- When selecting an operating system, consider the following: scalability, stability, ease of management and maintenance, and availability of established, error-tolerant solutions.
- Of the available processor architectures, superscalar EPIC and RISC architectures have the highest capacity (this is important for batch jobs that cannot be parallelized).
- The following applies to memory architectures: Use the largest possible caches, as close to the CPU as possible (as well as a sufficiently large main memory). CPUs with large and slow third-level caches are optimized for OLTP. A large main memory requires a 64-bit architecture.
- Only systems with error-tolerant ECC main memory and cache memory should be used for enterprise-critical applications.

- Multiprocessor systems (SMPs) have become the standard architecture at all performance levels. In many architectures, besides the operating system, the bandwidth of the internal system buses is a limiting factor. In these cases, crossbar-based systems provide the best performance. In very large systems, multilevel crossbar architectures are the most effective (ccNUMA).
- Even medium-sized SAP installations can easily require more main memory than can be logically addressed in a single 32-bit system. Therefore, a comprehensive 64-bit implementation should always be used, where possible.

6 Data Storage for SAP Systems

A strategic resource

In a knowledge-driven society, a company's most valuable commodity, next to the experience of its employees, is information. Storage subsystems are therefore strategic resources, and the availability of stored data is a critical factor for achieving success in business.

Depending on the business processes involved, productive SAP systems can generate enormous data quantities, which need to be accessed with minimal latency times. Contrary to what SAP does for servers and operating systems, it does not certify storage subsystems. However, SAP does share its experience and provide recommendations as technical notes (white papers).

The first section of this chapter discusses the typical read/write cycles of business applications, as well as disk drive performance parameters. It also introduces the different technologies for connecting disk drive subsystems to the computer.

The section on scalability and information management introduces an innovative design for improving the performance of storage subsystems and argues that effective archiving is essential to manage data growth. Finally, you will find a few tried-and-tested practical tips for designing the setup of disk drive subsystems for SAP infrastructures.

6.1 The "Files" of an SAP System

The data of an SAP system is managed by a relational database management system (RDBMS) and stored on the hard disks of the storage subsystem. In addition to the actual data files, a large number of other files are also needed, all with their own specific tasks and requirements.

The database server instance manages the read/write accesses (input/output, I/O) for the SAP application on the database files. For every request from the application, the database system determines whether the data is already stored in the main memory (cache hit), or needs to be fetched from the storage system first (cache miss). In the context of an SAP system, a database is just an intelligent I/O program that provides structured access to data.

Data files and index files

A company's actual business data stock is stored by the SAP system's database instance in data records, which are made up of tables. Depending on the business processes involved, productive SAP systems can generate enormous data quantities. For this reason, indexes are used to locate individual data records faster. The use of index tables (and secondary indexes) can take up a significant proportion of storage capacity. Practical experience shows that in a typical Enterprise Resource Planning (ERP) system, two thirds of disk space is filled with data and one third is filled with indexes. In some cases, the indexes are even bigger than the assigned tables.

The logical units for data storage are called "tablespaces" for Oracle and DB2, "dev space" for MaxDB, and "log spaces"/"data spaces" or "log files"/"data files" for SQL Server. Even if the descriptions and architectures for these files are different for each database producer, the basic structural principles are largely identical.

What happens if a new data record is written to the database?

A lot more happens in this process than you would think. First, the record is written to the rollback area, so it can be "rolled back" if necessary. Only then is the record written to the data table. Next, every index for the table must receive a new entry. To do this, the correct position for the entry must be found in every index (this is a read access). The system searches through the index tree until it finds the correct free position. Finally, the record must still be written to the transaction logs (online logs) so that the database can be recovered.

Operating system and swap area

All SAP servers, whether they are application servers or database servers, must have sufficient disk drive space for the operating system and swap space (swap space for UNIX, paging file for Windows). Generally, less than 2 GB is needed for the operating system (OS). The amount of disk capacity necessary for the swap space depends on the size of the main memory. Typically, the swap space should be at least twice the size of the main memory, or at least 20 GB. If the disk space for swap is too small the system will stall, however the performance of a system swapping more than 20 % of the main memory will be unacceptable anyway. For availability reasons, the disks for operating system and swap should always be mirrored (RAID-1).

Program files

The program files (executables) for the database and the SAP Web Application Server (Web AS) each use up to 1.5 GB. When starting the server OS, the database, and the SAP application, the corresponding executables are loaded to the main memory. After that, the system very rarely accesses this disk area. Apart from upgrades, the system rarely writes to these files. For this reason, these files can easily be stored with others, without affecting I/O performance. In clusters, however, the SAP kernel files must be stored on separate disks in certain failover configurations.

Log files

All databases supported by SAP protocol log the write accesses to the data files (transaction logging). The log files are extremely important for recovering the database after a crash. After the system has been restored from the tapes, as it was at the last full save, the dataset log files are used to repeat all the operations carried out after the last full save—recovering the system to the point in time just before the fatal failure.

In this context, the extreme importance of the log files is clear. A backup is of little use if you don't have every single log since the last save. If just one log is missing, then you can no longer recover the database consistently (a recovery of the system to the point in time of the last full backup which may be days or weeks ago is not feasible in practice). Therefore, you must always store archived log files separately from data files in order to prevent the loss of both sets of files if the storage medium fails.

It also makes sense to store log files and data files on separate disks for performance reasons. Log files require mainly sequential read and write accesses, so the disk has a heavy workload. Storing log files together with data files usually has a noticeable effect on performance. The exceptions to this rule are high-performance storage subsystems that have a large, mirrored cache. In this case, the log files are first written to the cache and then asynchronously to the disk. This reduces the workload for the disks.

The log files are saved to tape at regular intervals (archiving mode). In Oracle, for example, the logs for this are divided into two types: Online logs (redo) and offline logs (archives). The offline log is archived while the online log is defined. For security reasons, all these disks should be mirrored.

Rollback files

Rollback files are used after a failure in order to return a database to a consistent state. To do this, all transactions interrupted by the failure need to be rolled back. In productive SAP systems, the rollback areas are used extensively.

Rollback segments are extremely write-intensive, so it's easy to create I/O bottlenecks. Oracle and SQL servers store the rollback information as part of the data files. Informix and DB2 use a separate storage area (rootdbs and retrieve_log respectively), while MaxDB stores it in the log dev spaces.

With the introduction of Oracle 9i, the manual handling of rollback tablespaces that was previously required has been replaced by "Undo" tablespaces. These tablespaces are managed automatically by Oracle, so manual tuning is no longer necessary to avoid the feared "snapshot too old" error.

When setting up a high-performance system, the undo tablespaces for the data, index, and log areas should be stored separately. The same applies to other database systems that also store "before images" on the disk system in order to roll back an interrupted transaction, or to ensure consistent reading.

Write-Intensive Database Areas

Besides the rollback area, the temporary (temp), transaction, and archive log areas are the most write-intensive areas of a database. Each of these areas has special requirements.

The archive log area is particularly critical. To avoid the feared "archiver stuck" message, you usually configure the database so that every completed log is immediately written in duplicate to a central backup system and then deleted from the disk.

This means, however, that the system always writes and reads to the same place in the file system (it writes the archive log and then immediately reads it again and deletes it). Without striping across several disks, this can easily lead to massive I/O problems.

The SAP system also writes log files (for example, for batch input, background processes, work process logs ("developer traces") and so forth). You cannot optimize write operations using SQL tuning; you can do so only by tuning the logical structure of the disk subsystems, as described below.

Temporary data

Temporary files are required for sorting, indexing, and combining operations for which the database main memory is not sufficient. This can easily create an I/O bottleneck if insufficient disks are available to manage these write-intensive processes.

6.2 Read/Write Accesses from the Application Perspective

The number and type of hard disk drives have considerable influence on the performance of a disk subsystem. Vendors are eager to emphasize the maximum capacity of their storage subsystems. However, these values are only achieved with the largest possible hard drive types. An SAP system requires both capacity and performance in the form of high I/O throughput. However, there are physical limitations to the ideal combination of maximum capacity with maximum speed (and minimum price). It is therefore important to adapt the number and build type of the hard disks according to the access model and the type of data to be stored. These can differ a great deal depending on the application used.

Standard file sharing

On a typical file server, the I/O profile of the disk system consists of a mixture of random and sequential accesses. Disk access is random when you're searching for data. Access is much more sequential when files are being read or written to a file server's disks.

Typical files include text processing documents, presentations, and spread sheets, but SAP application servers also have this type of I/O profile. Because disk performance is higher for greater sequential I/O requirements, a few, large disks can guarantee sufficient performance.

OLTP applications

Online Transaction Processing (OLTP) applications such as mySAP ERP or mySAP CRM create millions of small random disk accesses (these are usually in 8 KB blocks for SAP databases). Therefore, the system performs often considerably more read operations than write operations. For R/3 systems, a ratio of 80 % read accesses to 20 % write accesses is typical. Depending on the components used and the adjustments made, other ratios are also possible (for example, when importing large files in batch mode).

> **Real-life Example**
>
> For cost reasons, a company with a small CRM system decided to store data on two standard computer internal disks. Although the computing power and disk capacity were more than sufficient, there were massive performance problems during productive operations due to insufficient I/O performance.

In particular, batch jobs for updating customer data created such heavy I/O conflicts, that they could no longer be completed over the weekend. Measurements (SQL trace) indicated that the individual read accesses had completely satisfactory response times (good usage of the DB cache), but that the time for a commit (the final write access) was extremely long. Because all the data in the system is retained in the same physical location, it was not possible to distribute the different database areas in order to optimize performance. Problems of this kind can only be solved by migrating the database files to the striped volumes of a central disk system.

OLAP applications

Online Analytical Processing (OLAP) systems such as SAP Business Information Warehouse (SAP BW) or SAP Advanced Planner and Optimizer (SAP APO), usually transfer large data quantities.

A SAP BW is operated in different modes, which generate the different types of I/O operations.

- Overnight, the SAP BW data set is updated, during which new data is imported from source systems. The import is a 100 % sequential write operation with large I/O operations—essentially a large copy operation.
- The copied data is then inserted into the different InfoCubes. Because the data is not sorted in advance, this phase consists of many random write accesses. There is usually only a narrow window of time for this session. Along with the processor and main memory resources of the BW database server, the disk subsystem here represents a possible bottleneck, especially for the transaction logs and the index update.
- During the day, users perform queries or create reports. This is often extremely read-intensive for the disks. If complex reports are being created, causing existing tables to be resorted, combined, or linked to new tables, then there are also a lot of write accesses. A large number of ad-hoc queries from InfoCubes also generate write accesses to the temporary database files.

6.3 Read/Write Performance from the Physical Perspective

Performance can be characterized as the number of I/O operations that a hard disk can perform per second (IOPS), and is generally published for the "random I/O" (usually referring to 2 to 8 KB I/O size). For "sequential

I/O," throughput in MB/s is used (usually referring to 64 KB I/O size). Another important performance feature is the I/O response time (latency) in milliseconds.

Rotational Seek Time

An increase in the drive rotation leads to quicker access to the data on a track or a cylinder (Rotational Seek Time), thereby reducing the response time. By increasing the track bit density, you not only increase the storage capacity, but the I/O performance as well, as more information per time unit is covered by the read/write head.

Burst Transfer

To further increase performance, most hard disks have a local cache memory, which can be accessed with the full speed of the I/O channel (burst transfer). Sophisticated algorithms attempt to predict which data will be accessed next, and this data is copied from the hard disk to the cache in anticipation of this action.

For hard disk arrays, this cache memory is used along with Tagged Command Queuing as a read memory. This enables you to reserve pending I/O operations for several servers, akin to a type of parallel processing. The write cache for the disks is usually deactivated, in order to avoid data losses in the event of a failure.

When specifying the IOPS rate for a disk, you must specify the data block size. The bigger the data block transferred, the more time required, and the less IOPS a disk can perform (transferring a block of 128 KB takes longer than transferring a block of 8 KB).

Table 6.1 indicates the performance of disks typically used for characteristic SAP-OLTP requirements (random access, block size 8 KB, 80 % read, 20 % write accesses). I/O accesses with 64 KB were assumed when estimating the sequential throughput per disk. The values in productive environments can deviate due to other I/O profiles.

Speed of disk drives	Estimated SAP-OLTP IOPS rate per disk	Sequential read/write accesses (MB/s)
5,400 RPM	45	6/3
7,200 RPM (1st generation)	60	7/4
7,200 RPM (2nd generation)	70	9/5
10,000 RPM (1st generation: 4–9GB)	90	12/6

Table 6.1 Disk Drive Performance

Speed of disk drives	Estimated SAP-OLTP IOPS rate per disk	Sequential read/write accesses (MB/s)
10,000 RPM (2nd generation: 9–300GB)	110	15/9
12,000 RPM	125	18/12
15,000 RPM (36–146 GB)	140	50/40

Table 6.1 Disk Drive Performance (cont.)

Disks: Size or Speed?

Technical development of disk systems in recent years has concentrated primarily on increasing track bit density. This has achieved significant increases in capacity. However, the maximum rotation speed is subject to physical constraints and cannot be constantly increased. As the disk capacity increases, so do the number of head movements needed in order to find the data. The bigger the disks get, the slower the accesses to it inevitably become.

Regardless of this paradoxical behavior, the advantage of a large number of disks lies in the fact that several I/O operations can be performed in parallel simultaneously. Example: The system needs to read from two tablespaces simultaneously. Using two small disks leads to sequential read accesses in the best case, while a single large disk results in fairly intensive head movements.

6.4 Availability from a Data Perspective

For all company-critical applications, data security is of vital importance. Data security has two aspects: security from unauthorized access and security of physical availability. Even if only for legal reasons, data must not be lost, but the existence of the company itself is increasingly dependent upon the availability of the information it stores.

The systems available for storing large data quantities are all electromechanical in nature (hard disks, tapes, and so on) and are therefore always subject to the wear and tear of the mechanical components. In modern hard disks, the read/write head hovers just over the surface of a rapidly rotating storage medium, in an operation that is comparable to a jumbo jet flying no more than a few centimeters over the ground. In the case of "chip removing information processing," or physical contact, data loss always occurs. In the worst cases, the head crash will destroy all the data on the hard disk.

To guarantee data availability, SAP therefore requires a certain level of redundancy in the storage subsystems for productive systems, regardless of the additional required data backup to tape.

However, redundant storage of all data (mirroring) is not always possible for larger SAP systems for economic reasons. Therefore, different methods have been developed to ensure data integrity without duplicating the entire storage capacity.

Storage Subsystems

Even if disks are now big enough to store all the SAP data from a smaller SAP system on a single disk, for the sake of performance and availability, this would not make sense. However fast a disk, it can only read or write one data record at a time—even if a disk with Tagged Command Queueing can virtually perform several I/O operations simultaneously (externally at least).

This is why disk arrays are used for productive (and quality assurance, QA) systems. In a disk array, I/O is run in parallel and is therefore accelerated considerably. There are also many reasons to avoid installing the disks that are used for storing the data files on the database server itself, which explains why the machines reserve disk capacity for only the operating system and the swap space. Capacity for the data files is provided by a high-performance, external disk subsystem.

Redundant Array of Independent Disks

In general, RAID systems have become established for SAP systems. RAID is the acronym for Redundant Array of Independent (or Inexpensive) Disks. Strictly speaking, RAID is a procedure for making an array of separate physical disks appears to be a single disk from a logical perspective.

The RAID principle can be applied in different ways, which have different effects on the performance, availability, and net capacity of an array of disks. The different RAID designs are called RAID levels, and are numbered from 0 to 6 (or 10), where only levels 1, 5, and 6 (or 10) are relevant for SAP systems. When the disk array is controlled via the operating system, this is called a software RAID. When it is controlled via the storage subsystem controller, this is a hardware RAID.

Just a Bunch of Disks A disk array with no RAID level is called "Just a Bunch of Disks," or JBOD). JBODs can still be used for the database of an SAP development or test system; however, using them for productive SAP databases would be counterproductive from a performance perspective and, without a software mirror, reckless in terms of availability.

RAID-0 striping Striping involves distributing the data across the individual disks of a disk array so that performance is considerably increased compared to a single large disk. If, for example, the file with data records A, B, C, D, E, and so on is stored on a single disk, the individual data records can be read only one after another from the physical disk. If the individual data records are distributed evenly across all the disks, as displayed in Figure 6.1, then data records ABC, DEF, GHI, and so forth can each be read simultaneously from all disks.

A redundancy-free stripe array of this type has a RAID level of 0. Up to a point, the more disks in the array, the faster the RAID-0 array becomes. However, the probability of failure increases with the number of disks. Therefore, RAID-0 provides high throughput, but zero security.

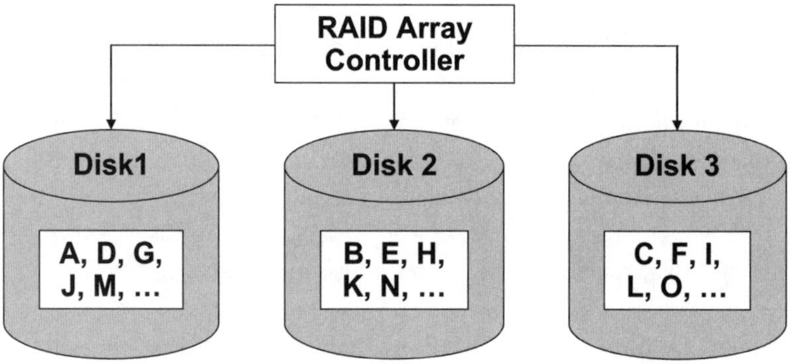

Figure 6.1 Distribution of Data Stripes A, B, C, D, E, G, H .... for RAID-0

Two key figures are used in striping—the stripe size (or width) and the number of stripe columns.

Stripe size The physical stripe size is also called the stripe width. This should not be confused with the stripe itself, which the operating system uses when formatting a striped file system. The file system stripe must not be bigger than the physical stripe on the disks. Otherwise, this generates more disk accesses than necessary. Therefore, designs using "stripe everywhere" can contribute to a loss of performance, because the actual file system striping is extremely CPU-intensive.

If the physical stripe on the disks is too big, the disk cache will soon be filled with superfluous data fragments (I/O chunks). If the stripe value is too small, the number of disk accesses increases dramatically, which has a negative effect on performance. For this reason, the stripe size should reflect the I/O requirements of the application as closely as possible. Many modern disk arrays implement methods to determine sequential I/O. Choosing a stripe size which is to small can prevent this algorithm from working.

An SAP database server has both large sequential I/O operations (paging/swapping of the operating system and transaction logs), as well as small, random I/O database operations. For sequential I/O, stripe sizes between 32 KB and 256 KB are appropriate. Usually, 64 KB is selected. Some array controllers can even generate stripe sizes of several MB. For small, random I/O, the physical I/O block size is usually selected, although values of up to 64 KB can also be used here (depending on the array controller).

Stripe columns

This value specifies across how many disks striping is being performed. This is always fixed for RAID arrays, and is specified or predefined when creating the stripe sets. Some volume managers, however, allow any number of additional disks to be added to a stripe set (restriping) or by adding integral multiples of the number of stripe columns.

RAID-1 mirroring

For RAID-1, the data is mirrored on two disks. RAID-1 combines maximum performance with maximum physical availability, although double capacity is required. Consequently, it is usually only the relatively small files that are mirrored with RAID-1 for operating systems, SAP program code and database logs. Although the term duplication is often used with RAID-1, duplication is a software RAID solution where two I/O cards are used on one server.

Because standard RAID-1 uses only two disks, capacity is relatively restricted. Solutions that combine RAID-0 striping with RAID-1 mirroring are called RAID-0/1 or RAID-10. The advantage lies in the combination of the speed of large striping arrays with the high availability of mirrored disks.

For RAID-1 and its variants, it is possible to read different data simultaneously from both sides of the mirror. When writing, however, the same data is written simultaneously to both halves of the mirror. Performance when writing to a disk is therefore half of what it is or would be when reading. An R/3 system with a typical I/O ratio of 80 % read operations to

20 % write operations therefore has a 20 % higher performance requirement compared to a RAID-0 or JBOD configuration (80 % + 2 × 20 % = 120 %). For write-intensive applications such as SAP BW, the relative performance requirement increases further.

RAID-5—distributed parity

As in mirroring, RAID-5 does not prevent the failure of individual disks, but can restore the data stock of the defective disks independently. To do this, the system stores additional (parity) information, which enables you to reconstruct the data on a damaged disk by using the data from the undamaged disks in the array (see Figure 6.2). Contrary to duplication of the required disk capacity when mirroring, RAID-5 only needs additional disk space for the parity information.

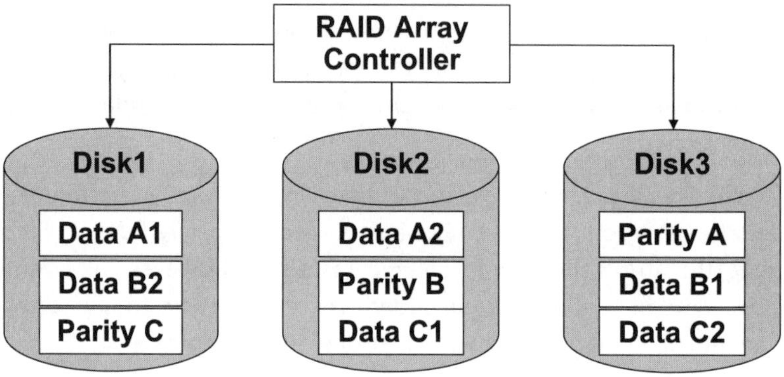

Figure 6.2 Striping with Parity in RAID-5

Through the even distribution of data and parity bytes to all disks (so called rotating parity; no dedicated parity disk like RAID-4) on a RAID-5 array, the system can read from all disks with no loss of performance. When writing, however, up to 1.8 times more physical I/O operations are required for RAID-5 than are required for RAID-0. Because RAID-5 takes up considerably less gross capacity compared to mirrored disks, there is still a favorable relationship between performance, availability, and costs.

At least three disks are needed for a RAID-5 configuration. Data recovery is only possible if just one disk fails, therefore, most RAID-5 systems have a reserve disk (hot spare disk), which is automatically included in the disk array in order to promptly ensure redundancy again. Then, the storage subsystem automatically issues a message to the management system so that the defective disk is replaced as quickly as possible. However, this requires the implementation of a management system and configuration of the event "disk failure." Many hardware manufacturers therefore offer a "call-home" feature as standard, which automatically informs a service center via modem/Internet when critical events occur.

In the unlikely, but not impossible, event of a simultaneous failure of several disks, all data is lost. The more disks combined in a RAID-5 array, the greater this risk. Consequently, RAID-5 should not use more than eight disks. If you need bigger storage capacity than a RAID array can provide, the disks in several RAID groups are combined. Some manufacturers therefore use RAID-5 groups of a fixed size, while other manufacturers provide variable sizes within specific limits. Common fixed RAID-5 implementations use three data disks plus one parity disk (3D+1P) or seven data disks plus one parity disk (7D+1P).

Today, modern RAID-5 implementations are almost as fast as RAID-1 systems, thanks to cleverly designed parity and cache mechanisms.

RAID-6—distributed parity stored in duplicate

RAID-6 is the same as RAID-5, except the parity information is stored in duplicate on two disks (double parity RAID). This increases the fail-safe security by 100 % (with RAID-5, a maximum of one disk can fail; with RAID-6, two can fail). First RAID-6 implementations use six data disks plus two parity disk (6D+2P) and therefore have the same amount of overhead like a RAID-5 with a 3D+1P setup.

Software RAID

Most UNIX derivatives and Windows support different RAID levels with standard I/O interface cards. Several I/O controllers can be combined within a RAID group. Combinations of software and hardware RAID setups are also possible, such as a software RAID-0 with a hardware RAID-1 or RAID-5.

Software RAID solutions are cost-effective, but they place additional load on the CPU of the database server. For RAID-1, this additional load can usually be disregarded for normal operation. Performance problems can arise, however, when the defective disk is exchanged and then needs to be resynchronized. In some systems it is no longer possible to start the server if the first SCSI-disk of the software-RAID-1 array has failed.

Even during normal operation, software RAID-5 has a noticeable effect on the CPU. When reconstructing a disk, the loss in performance is even greater.

Hardware RAID

With hardware RAID, the work-intensive management of the disk array is performed by the processor of the Disk Array Controller (DAC). This can either be installed internally as a PCI card in the server (iDAC), or externally in the storage subsystem (eDAC). A typical iDAC has a non-volatile memory (NVRAM), which stores stripe and RAID configuration information.

An important advantage of systems with eDAC is that the stripe and RAID configuration information is stored outside the server, which makes it considerably easier to set up a failover to another server. These failovers are mainly used on high-performance storage subsystems. Redundant disk array controllers enable load distribution and remove single points of failure (SPoF) in the I/O path. RAID-5 parity calculation is done by the XOR operation between data and old parity. Some vendors use XOR chips directly on the disk others XOR engines on backend adapters.

Real-Life Experience

When optimizing performance, many companies have very positive experiences with a combination of horizontal and vertical striping. This involves a storage array with several RAID-5 groups distributed across as many physical disks as possible. The server operating system sees each of these RAID groups as individual hard disks that can be combined into a volume group. The individual logical volumes are then striped again by the operating system's Logical Volume Manager (LVM).

This ensures the optimal distribution of data to the physical disks, verifying that the workload is spread evenly across all the disks. This makes it possible to completely avoid hotspots. However, with this method, volume groups can no longer be increased in small GB increments. Depending on the configuration of the storage array, several GBs must be assigned to achieve optimum horizontal and vertical striping.

Virtual arrays

Some storage subsystems are equipped with disk array controllers that are capable of independently optimizing disk performance. This is done by creating logical RAID groups and "leveling" all traffic across all disks (members) of the logical group. This reduces the administrative load for the disk subsystem. When using virtual arrays, remember that you can still recover the database when the entire virtual array fails. To ensure that this is possible, you must store the database log files separately—both logically and physically.

6.5 File Systems

A file system simplifies file management, but it is not absolutely necessary for storing data files. If disk systems are being used in their "raw state," these are referred to as raw devices.

File systems with buffered I/O

Windows, the Unix File System (UFS), or High Performance File System (HFS), as well as the various Journaling File Systems (JFS), use the file system buffer of the operating system in the main memory for I/O operations. The copying of data to the memory can affect server performance if many small I/O operations are being performed.

The additional I/O buffer memory also uses valuable main memory space. On the other hand, repeated reading of data can be performed from the file system buffer. Sensible sizing of the file system buffer and intelligent I/O options such as "sequential read ahead" (that is, prefetching data) or "sequential release behind read/write" (release and rewrite of the buffer to disk after read/write) can, however, achieve improved performance for a buffered file system with certain I/O setups.

But usually, the SAP database has its own buffer, so that the data is actually stored in duplicate. Another disadvantage of the file buffer system is that a system process—called "sync daemon"—is required to write the changed pages of the buffer back to disk. This runs periodically (roughly every 60 seconds), creating short-term high I/O load and using CPU performance.

This lower level of performance is offset by easier data management in the file system. The SAP database files are displayed in the file system and can be managed and saved using the same tools as all other types of files. It also provides a certain level of protection from user errors (deleting or unmounting data carriers, forgetting to save files, and so forth).

The advantage of a Journal File System (JFS) is quick recovery after a system failure. Before the file systems can be remounted, you must conduct a file system check. In a JFS, this is accomplished very quickly, since there is a record of every unfinished transaction and only files system structures corresponding to these transactions have to be verified. Without this information, the whole file system must be checked. This can be quite time-consuming in SAP systems with databases that approximate the size of terabytes.

File systems with unbuffered I/O

Raw devices are quicker, because there is no overhead from function calls to the file system. No additional buffer memory is needed, the applications can be written directly to the data carrier with no additional delay. Raw devices are therefore advantageous in areas with a high write-rate (logs, rollback, temp). If you need high I/O rates, you should consider asynchronous raw disk I/O. However, areas that are primarily read areas do not enjoy any particular benefits from the use of raw devices.

With an asynchronous raw disk I/O, the application is responsible for data integrity. It can never write simultaneously to the same block (most databases support a block at (data) record level to guarantee data integrity). With a synchronous raw disk I/O, the write accesses are serialized, making the process slower.

There are, however, many programs that allow you to manage raw disk systems, however, for disks without a file system, this would prove to be rather complicated. Furthermore, not all backup programs can be used.

Therefore, increasingly more operating system manufacturers enable you to completely deactivate the buffer cache when you are mounting your file systems (AIX JFS2 or Solaris UFS), or bypass it from a configurable I/O size (VxFS). Direct I/O systems provide a direct I/O-API option. This creates an ideal combination of the performance of unbuffered raw devices with the advantages of a Journal File System (JFS). The saving of main memory also benefits the SAP system.

In addition, nearly all Unix manufacturers now provide an "asynchronous I/O" option for both buffered and unbuffered I/O. The application that prompts an I/O does not wait until the operation has ended, but is informed when the I/O operation has ended. This type of I/O is implemented either as a core enhancement or as an application program interface (API).

6.6 Disk Array Caches

Generally, all disk arrays have a cache memory. Some vendors use one pool of memory for read and write caching, others use a separate pool. This considerably improves the performance of the disk system, since data transfer from cache memory is much faster than transferring data from a disk. However, due to frequent random accesses, read operations in typical OLTP applications usually don't exceed a hit rate of 60 %. The greater effect can be seen in the write cache, because the database does not have to wait for confirmation of the write request from the physical disk. Instead, the confirmation of the write operation occurs directly after the data is saved in the cache. After this, the data is written from the disk array controller to the disk (destaging).

To prevent data loss in the case of a cache error the write cache is either mirrored or intelligently striped across multiple physical components and parity-protected. Cache batteries must provide power for many hours or even days to keep write cache data during a power outage until power is provided again and destaging from cache to disk can happen. Some vendors use a special disk area to save the write cache in a power loss event.

The disk write cache is normally disabled. Otherwise additional power would be required to save data from disk cache to disk itself.

Cache size

The optimum size of the disk array cache depends on the main memory of the database server. If the database server has enough memory for data buffering, the disk cache is used only to accelerate write accesses to the disk. In this case, the cache size is determined by the number of physical I/O operations that a disk system can achieve per second and by the stripe size. A disk system with 12 physical disks, 125 IOPS, and 64 KB stripes, for example, needs 96 MB write cache (12 × 125 × 64 KB), provided that destaging is performed before the new write I/Os arrive. Here, more cache would not significantly increase performance. Some arrays limit the write pending amount of data to avoid filling up the cache or use ceilings where destaging takes precedence over new host IO.

If the database in a very large SAP system does not have sufficient memory of its own to save the data buffer, a sufficiently sized cache memory can serve as a secondary "read buffer" for the database.

Database cache versus disk cache

In our experience, a large database cache is preferable to a large disk cache. The database application has a logical view of the data, and manages its cache with the knowledge of which data is frequently required. The disk system, however, has only a physical view of the data and can merely guess at which data is usually required based on fixed algorithms. Furthermore, a disk system must meet the requirements of a file server in the same way as it does for a database system, but with completely different requirements for the I/O processes.

Write through or write back?

The write cache of the disk system can be operated in write-through or write-back mode. Some arrays are even able in defining this behaviour on a per LUN base. The write-through mode is the safest, but also the slowest. The write request is only considered to be completed when the data has been physically written to the disk. Practically this destroys the write cache advantage.

The write-back procedure (also referred to as the copy-back procedure) is the quickest method. A write request is considered to be completed as soon as the data is on the cache memory of either the file system (buffered IO) or in the disk array cache (direct IO). The system does not wait until the data is actually written to the disk.

However, a write cache in write-back mode circumvents the safety mechanisms of the database system. Upon receiving confirmation from the memory subsystem, the database assumes that the data is also saved physically to the disk. If there is a power failure or a cache memory error before the data is written to disk, data loss will be unavoidable. In the worst case, the entire database will be inconsistent and therefore unusable. Consequently, write-back caches for company-critical SAP systems must be mirrored and provided with a backup power supply!

6.7 Data Replication

Additional copies of operating data are required for many purposes. For example, the quality assurance (QA) system requires an up-to-date copy of the productive database.

Offline backups are not suitable because the interrupt production for hours which is impossible in a 24x7 environment. Online backups are helpful but have often have a performance impact on the SAP system. Some backup vendors use techniques to offload the backup operation to the array/SAN (like "third party copy" or "serverless backup") or to dedicated backup servers ("off-host backup").

You can create physical copies via the operating system using volume manager copy functionality. This can, however, damage the performance of the SAP database server. Most storage subsystems therefore have suitable functions for data replication.

points-in-time copies

In large databases, physical copying of the entire data stock would take several hours and the source database would not be available for productive use. It is sufficient, however, to make a single physical copy and then synchronize it at regular intervals (points-in-time) with the productive data. In this case, only the changes made since the last point-in-time (deltas) need to be copied, thereby reducing the update time to a few seconds. After synchronization, the mirrors are "split" again and are available independently for production, testing, and backups.

Virtual snapshots

Complete copies of the database require corresponding additional disk capacity, however. The snapshot procedure allows additional, virtual copies to be created without the need for a great deal of extra disk capacity. The productive disks are frozen in a snapshot. This snapshot then serves as the shared basis for several virtual copies.

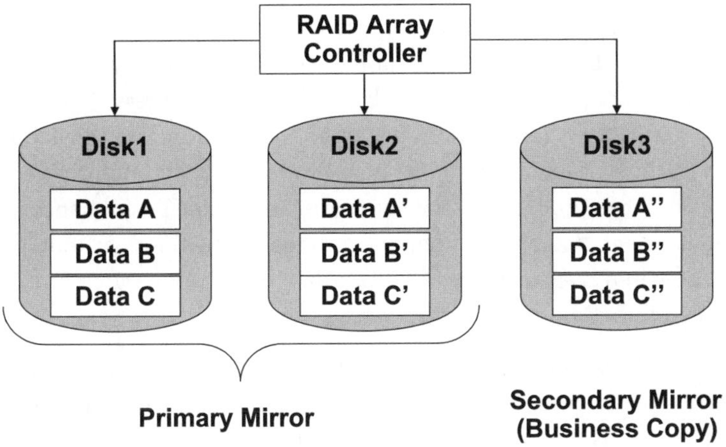

Figure 6.3 Additional Data Mirror for Data Replication

The data changed and inserted in the different copies is stored separately for each copy. After the snapshot, both the productive database and the virtual copies exist only as links to the original database and the delta files. Additional virtual copies can be created from the snapshots at any time.

Because shared data usually represents the majority of the data, snapshots can save a lot of physical disk memory. However, this advantage diminishes over time as the deltas increase in size.

When read accesses are made to the shared data stock, the different copies compete with the productive database for the disk I/Os. This can reduce the performance of the productive SAP system. Virtual copies provide no additional layer of security and therefore, cannot be used for error tolerance and disaster scenarios.

Remote replication

Where there is a high security requirement, particularly for disaster scenarios, data needs to be mirrored to a remote location. Again host (volume manager or other replication software), array or nowadays even SAN can be utilized for remote mirroring synchronously or asynchronously. In the synchronous procedure, the remote mirror is carried out immediately. In the case of array based replication the database server receives the commit from the remote storage system. In the asynchronous procedure, the remote copy is made only after the commit from the local storage system. In asynchronous procedures, you should ensure that the data at the remote location is consistent; otherwise, the database can no longer be used.

Synchronous mirroring

With synchronous mirroring, it is important to remember that light in a fiber optic cable travels at a maximum of 200,000 km/sec. This means that transfer over a distance of 100 km increases the access time to a piece of data by 1 ms (purely transfer time). Another aspect is the bandwidth of the line, as load peaks must be factored for synchronous mirroring. Asynchronous procedures, however, use the average performance. It has actually been established that synchronous procedures cannot be usefully operated over distances of more than 60–100 km. Greater distances need to be bridged asynchronously.

Asynchronous mirroring

The main advantage of asynchronous mirroring is that the distance has no negative effect on performance. The main disadvantage of asynchronous procedures is the potential data loss in the event of a system failure. All the data not committed by the remote system would be lost. Systems that must be mirrored over large distances are therefore first mirrored synchronously over a short distance, before being mirrored synchronously for the rest of the distance. This procedure is also called a multi-hop procedure.

6.8 Connection Technologies for Disk Subsystems

Several different technologies are available for connecting the hard disk subsystem to the database server(s). The following section describes the specific properties of these technologies when used with SAP systems.

UDMA

Ultra Direct Memory Access (UDMA,[1] also referred to as Ultra ATA) was developed for PCs with a single hard disk. UDMA is definitely the cheapest disk connection solution on the market. However, it was optimized

1 A further development of the Enhanced Integrated Drive Electronics standard (EIDE) which, in turn, was developed on the basis of the IDE standard used in early PCs.

for sequential I/O operations with very few disks. For that reason, it is not suitable for SAP databases with multiple simultaneous I/O operations.

SATA

Another piece of drive technology originally developed in the PC market is Serial Advanced Technology Attachment (SATA)[2]. This market segment also defines the relatively low I/O performance and sensitivity to vibration, temperature, or shock. Large capacities make SATA drives attractive for areas such as archiving in near-online operation, storage of reference data with low-level access, snapclone procedure, and backup. We would not recommend using this technology for areas with high I/O requirements and data that must be available 24/7.

SCSI

Servers use Small Computer System Interface (SCSI). SCSI provides greater performance due to parallel operation of several hard drives (and other peripheral devices) on one data bus. The constant progress of developments aimed at increasing throughput has created many different standards varying electrical and mechanical specifications.

SCSI Standard	Max. throughput(MB/s)	Bus-width (Bit)	Bus frequency (MHz)	Max. bus length* (m)			Max.** number of devices
				SE :	HVD	LVD	
SCSI-1	5	8	5	6	25		8
Fast SCSI-2	10	8	10	3	25		8
Fast Wide SCSI	20	16	10	3	25		16
Ultra SCSI (Wide)	40	16	20	1,5	25		8, 16
Ultra2 SCSI (Wide)	80	16	40		25	12	16
Ultra3 SCSI	160	16	80			12	16
Ultra3 SCSI 320	320	16	160			12	16

* SE= Single-Ended, HVD = High Voltage Differential, LVD = Low Voltage Differential
** SCSI-Host-Bus-Controller contained as a device

Table 6.2 Comparison of Different SCSI Specifications

The throughput values listed in Table 6.2 are gross values. Due to the administration overhead of the SCSI protocol, the effective data transfer rates are approximately 25 % lower. Consequently, for example, a data transfer rate of around 60 MB/s is realistic for Ultra2 SCSI.

2 A further development of the Advanced Technology Attachment standard (ATA).

The many incompatible standards with different cables and plugs can soon turn configuring SCSI components into a real nightmare. The maximum bus length is defined by the electrical parameters and the type of scheduling, as well as the frequency of the SCSI bus. The higher the frequency, the shorter the maximum length of the SCSI bus.

Single-Ended-SCSI (SE) is the cheapest and is therefore used in most Intel-based servers. High-Voltage Differential SCSI (HVD) supports more devices over longer lengths of cable, but is more expensive. Low-Voltage Differential SCSI (LVD) is backwards compatible and signal compatible with SE-SCSI. When used with SE devices, however, six meters is the maximum cable length, and 12 meters is only possible when using Ultra2-LVD devices. This SCSI variant has become generally established for servers. The relatively low bus lengths make all SCSI variants unsuitable for storage consolidation and increased availability designs.

Because SCSI is a bus system, the entire bus is interrupted when you exchange a SCSI device. For interruption-free operation, the SCSI interfaces must be set up with redundancy.

Do Not Combine Disks With Other Devices on a SCSI Bus

Using relatively slow devices such as CD-ROM drives or tape drives, along with fast disks can create performance bottlenecks. Some Ultra-LVD adapters switch all the devices on a bus to a slower mode, even if the bus has only a single SE device. Consequently, an SE-SCSI CD-ROM or tape slows down the fast Ultra-LVD disks. To optimize performance, we therefore recommend that you run disks on separate SCSI buses, rather than with other peripheral devices.

Fibre Channel As the name implies, Fibre Channel (FC) was originally based on fiber-optic technology. Now, FC can also use coaxial and shielded twisted pair cables (STP). Unlike SCSI (a parallel protocol), FC is a serial protocol. FC connections have a send and receive port, and operate in "full-duplex" mode (that is, you can send and receive simultaneously). The transfer rate is usually specified in gigabits per second (Gbit/s). The technology standard is currently 1 and 2 Gbit/s, but 4 Gbit/s has just been introduced and 10 Gbit/s is "just around the corner". With 2 Gbit/s, you get a send rate of approximately 200 MB/s and a receive rate of 200 MB/s to equal a total of 400 MB/s. The considerably increased range, in particular, allows FC connections to physically separate the database server and the disk subsystem, creating the basis for storage consolidation, error-tolerant solutions, and storage networks.

Originally, FC was designed as a high-speed standard for local networks. Instead, the network industry combined the technologies and protocols designed for FC with the Ethernet standard for gigabit Ethernet.

Transfer rate	Single mode fiber optic, (9 µm)	Multi-mode fiber optic, (50 µm)	Coaxial cable (copper)	STP cable (copper)
100 MB/s (1 Gbit/s)	10 km	500 m	50 m	28 m
400 MB/s (2 Gbit/s)	2 km	175 m		
Fiber optic cables (62.5 µm) for FDDI systems are also supported. This reduces possible transfer distances, however.				

Table 6.3 Maximum Distance for Fibre Channel Connections

For every cable and connection type (fiber optic, coaxial, STP cable,), there is a specific GBIC (1Gbit/s), SFP (2 Gbit/s), or XFP plug-in module (4 Gbit/s). Contrary to SCSI, computers and subsystems using Fibre Channel can have more than one connection.

Fibre Channel Fabric

Like Ethernet, Fibre Channel has also developed from a passive, shared (used by all devices at the same time) medium to an active, switched medium. Logical ring topologies (Fibre Channel Arbitrated Loop, FC-AL), in which several devices share the available transfer capacity, are no longer what's hot in the world of fiber optics. Fibre Channel switches enable a networked topology, or "fabric." This forms the basis for high-performance storage networks.

A SAN based on FC switches provides every connection with full transfer capacity, just like a point-to-point connection. Also, with a SAN, the transfer capacity is not significantly reduced over long distances (approximately 10 % for 10 km).

Practical experience shows that it is generally advantageous to use the SAN to store all the data belonging to an SAP system on central storage systems. In such a setup, the local disks on the computer only contain data that the operating system needs. Besides increasing effectiveness (for example, better usage of storage capacity and improved performance of I/O-intensive applications), this also makes it possible to move entire SAP systems from machine to machine in an adaptive computing scenario. Basically, only a VGExport and VGImport are necessary to start the system on a new server.

In a SAN, all computers can access all disks. Service data centers (ASP), in particular, must be protected by appropriate security measures from unauthorized access to data via the SAN. SAN security products are available at different levels (operating system, FC fabric, or storage level). High-performance storage subsystems can be subdivided into logical subunits, each with its own set of access authorizations.

FC Disks

FC drives are as robust as SCSI disks and have the same capacity, however, they have a different access mode, which allows you to control considerably more disks via a controller. Also, you can transfer data from the disk to the server at FC speeds.

The FC drives are accessed directly via the Storage Area Network (SAN) using the FC controller in the storage array. This controller places (mostly) redundant FC-AL rings around the connected disk arrays, ensuring FC speeds to the disk.

iSCSI Because of these advantages, SANs are installed in most data centers. However, the number of FC adapters, hubs, and switches built for this purpose remains far below the number of Ethernet adapters, hubs, and switches for Local Area Networks (LANs), because a company naturally has more PCs and laptops than it does servers and storage subsystems. Because less of them are produced, components for FC are correspondingly more expensive than the components for Ethernet, which are built and bought in bulk.

With this background, iSCSI was developed as a cost-effective alternative. iSCSI uses the IP protocol to transfer SCSI commands via standard Ethernet components. The SCSI commands are embedded in an iSCSI protocol unit, which is packaged within a TCP protocol header and sent via the LAN (and WAN) like a typical IP package.

The recipient device of the package deletes IP and TCP headers, unpacks the SCSI command, executes it, and uses the same method to return the requested blocks (which have been read from the hard disk or tape drive). At the same time, the IP package can even be routed in the same way as any other IP package.

For greater performance, implementation of the iSCSI protocol must be built into the hardware, which takes over the coding and decoding and packs and unpacks the data directly in a TCP header. This also relieves pressure on the host CPU. However, some of the price advantage is lost when you use such specialized iSCSI host bus adapters.

You must also consider longer latency times compared to a SAN, because LAN protocols were developed for communication over relatively long distances where latency is not the largest issue, while SAN is optimized for short-distance high-speed communication.

In addition, data transfers via a common LAN compete with the other applications for bandwidth. For database operation over IP dedicated switched gigabit Ethernet segments are mandatory, so that normal user traffic does not damage performance.

Therefore, iSCSI is far more practical for applications that don't need the quickest possible response times. A high-performance SAN infrastructure is also indispensable for company-critical application databases that must ensure maximum data throughput with minimum latency times.

Fiber Channel over IP

In contrast, the Internet Fiber Channel Protocol (iFCP) and Fibre Channel over IP (FCIP) standards also provide the option to transfer Fibre Channels via IP networks. This makes it possible to couple FC-based SANs via Wide Area Networks (WAN). Due to high latency times, solutions of this type are not suitable for synchronous data mirroring, but they are ideal for remote backup and asynchronous data mirroring (which are needed in disaster recovery scenarios).

Network Attached Storage for SAP?

Network Attached Storage (NAS) is the name used to describe hard disk arrays (so called filers), optical drives, and tape devices that use the IP protocol to provide a file system on storage level. (iSCSI also use the IP protocol, however the access is through the local file system on the server). These types of NAS systems enable you to use the existing LAN (and WAN) infrastructure for storage consolidation as well.

If a NAS is used to store the data, the database server uses the client component of the file transfer protocol, NFS (Network File System) for UNIX and CIFS (Common Internet File System) for Windows to access the data. Running databases over NFS is supported by SAP as long as the database software vendor supports the storage system. The usage of CIFS to run databases is not supported by SAP.

Therefore the performance of a NAS infrastructure is determined by the performance of the NFS client and the TCP/IP stack running on the server and the performance of the NAS system. It is essential to use a dedicated switched gigabit Ethernet segment to connect the database server to the storage system.

Since the NFS client and the TCP/IP stack run as additional software layers performing the I/O, an increased CPU usage compared to a FC infrastructure will be observed (typically 5 %–15 %). In return no local file system and volume manager on the server is necessary, since these software layers run on the NAS system. I/O latencies mainly depend on the quality of the NFS client and NAS system.

Enterprise NAS systems typically use a proprietary operating and file system, which have been optimized for database operation during the recent years. The same is true for the NFS client and the TCP/IP stack, where extensive performance improvements and optimizations for database operations have been achieved.

For very large SAP systems an FC infrastructure is still the best choice. For all other SAP systems running on UNIX the usage of NAS and NFS is a suitable alternative to FC. The advantages of NAS are mainly the simplified storage and storage infrastructure administration and therefore the lower costs compared to a FC solution.

6.9 Sizing Storage Subsystems

Dimensioning the storage subsystem does not only involve the trivial part of calculating the number of disks needed to provide the necessary storage capacity, it also involves the more complicated part of estimating the number of disks necessary to ensure the required number of I/O operations per second (IOPS).

Every SAP system has its own I/O profile. Due to the many influences of factors such as application and database version, customer-specific SQL statements, reports, and batch runs, sizing founded on the users currently logged on can only be an extremely rough estimate.

From the disk system perspective, a distinction is made between net I/O requests from the SAP database server to the storage subsystem (front-end IOPS) and the resulting gross I/Os to the individual disks (back-end IOPS).

You can use benchmarks and measurements of productive SAP systems to derive rules for dimensioning storage subsystems, provided that you do your evaluations from the perspective of the disk system rather than that of the CPU.

Front-end IOPS

SAPS	Disk number	Disk speed	IOPS for 8 KB	IOPS	IOPS per SAPS*
4,544	30	7,200	60	1,800	0.40
13,520	58	10,000	85	4,968	0.37
23,600	60	10,000	110	6,600	0.28
24,800	64	10,000	110	7,040	0.28
* Estimated number based on published reports from HP, IBM, and DataGeneral					

Table 6.4 Correlation of SD Benchmark and Performance of Storage Subsystem

However, the benchmark has no sequential I/Os. The database activity is reduced to as few read accesses as possible, and there is only one write operation (a DB checkpoint) in the whole benchmark.

Rule of Thumb for Front-End IOPS

In productive systems, a rough analysis gives values between 0.5 and 0.6 IOPS per SAPS (Release 3.1 to 4.5B, Oracle, 8 KB block size). This allows the required IOPS to be more realistically estimated for a specified SAPS value. A SAP system that needs to reach 10,000 SAPS at 100 % workload should be assigned with a storage system that can process between 5,000 and 6,000 IOPS.

Influence of the cache size

The size of the read/write memory (caches) also plays a role when dimensioning a storage subsystem. The bigger the read cache, the greater the likelihood that the data searched for is already in the cache, and doesn't need to be read from the slower disks first (cache hit rate). The bigger the write cache, the better the physical writing of data to the hard disks can be optimized.

High-performance storage subsystems have very large cache memories (several dozen GB) and therefore a comparably high cache hit rate. Medium-sized subsystems have smaller caches (a few GB), while smaller models may have no cache at all. In these cases, all I/O requests are forwarded directly to the much slower disks.

Unfortunately, there are no general rules on how many I/O requests can be satisfied directly from the cache of a storage subsystem. The hit rate is also influenced by the type of application. In traditional OLTP systems with a large number of small I/O accesses, the cache algorithm has very little chance of forecasting which block will be requested next. For this reason, the cache hit rates in Online Transaction Processing (OLTP) systems are most often extremely low. Online Analytical Processing (OLAP) applications, conversely, frequently read large data quantities that are well suited for the look-ahead algorithms of the disk systems. Table 6.5 indicates the effect of the hit rate on the IOPS.

SAPS	IOPS per SAPS	Front-end IOPS	Back-end IOPS	
			0 % hit rate	60 % hit rate
10,000	0.5	5,000	5,000	2,000

Table 6.5 Back-end IOPS Depending on Cache Usage

> **SQL Tuning and Cache Quality**
>
> Just one inefficiently written SQL statement can cause the database to read in full several times (that is, a full table scan) all data records of the relevant table. This then causes overflows in all caches sequentially along the data path (disk system cache, file system cache, database cache) thereby deleting the important cache data. Depending on the layout of the database, this could create such a heavy workload for all the disks, that a 1,000-user system can be reduced to a one-user system.Therefore it is mandatory to optimize SQL statement so that tables are not read in full (that is, a full table scan).

Back-end IOPS

The important factor when estimating the back-end IOPS (in addition to cache usage) is the RAID level. The additional I/O operations required for redundant data retention create an overhead, the size of which depends on the ratio between read and write operations. In RAID-5, it also depends on the parity logic (disk or controller logic) and the number of disks. For systems with standard disk array controllers, a small cache and a typical OLTP I/O model, can generally assume an overhead of approximately 20 % for RAID-1 and 80 % for RAID-5 on the front-end IOPS. High-performance storage subsystems and other I/O models provide different values. Table 6.6 indicates the affect of the RAID Level and Cache Usage on the ration between Back-end and Physical disks IOPS.

Back-end IOPS	Cache usage	Physical disks IOPS		
		RAID-0 (+0 %)	RAID-1 (+20 %)	RAID-5 (+80 %)
2,000	60 %	2,000	2,400	3,600
5,000	0 %	5,000	6,000	9,000

Table 6.6 Disk IOPS Depending on RAID Level

Number of disks

You can now use the back-end IOPS and IOPS values of the hard disks, installed in the disk array, to determine the number of disks necessary to manage the I/O requests of the SAP systems. The mirrored disks for the operating system and the protocol files are also added to this number of disks. The number determined in this way is a minimum value. If more disks are needed for capacity reasons, this benefits the I/O operations. If this number is not met, the I/O operations encounter a bottleneck.

Table 6.7 indicates how many hard disks (each with 110 IOPS) are needed to handle the I/O requests of an SAP system with 10,000 SAPS according to the rule of thumb mentioned above for Release 3.1 to 4.5B with an Oracle database configured for 8 KB block size. The faster the disks, the fewer disks required.

Back-end IOPS	Cache usage	Back-end disk IOPS		Number of required hard disks	
		RAID-1 (+20 %)	RAID-5 (+80 %)	RAID-1	RAID-5
2,000	60 %	2,400	3,600	22	33
5,000	0 %	6,000	9,000	55	82

Table 6.7 Recommended Number of Disks for R/3 Production Systems

This extremely simplified design can be applied to optimized R/3 systems with only a few adjustments. The more reports created or additional data loaded, the more disks needed (in extreme cases, 2 to 10 times more).

Log files

You need to consider both I/O requests for the data files and I/O requests for log files of the database system. The size and I/O requirements of log files in SAP systems depend on the number of transactions and the database system used. In productive systems, logs are usually written in duplicate to different drives and different tapes (to ensure data security), before they are deleted from the disk. This means that the I/O requirement for the log saving process is twice as high as for the log writing process.

The values range from less than 100 MB per hour for small SAP systems to several hundred MB per minute in large installations. Different industry solutions can produce even higher values in certain circumstances. Loading large batch input files always leads to a large data flow for log files. (For example: POS upload in IS-Retail.)

In extreme situations, the entire bandwidth of the I/O connections is used up. In this case, the write cache may fill up faster than the log files can be written to the physical disks. This means that the only solution is to provide more disks to enable the upload to be performed in the time allotted.

During archiving, the logs must be read fast enough to keep up with the speed of the tape drives (streaming). Reconciling the I/O performance of the disks with the tape drives is also very important for recovering the system. Current tape drives achieve a speed of 10 MB/s, high-performance drives such as LTO-3 reach a speed of 30 MB/s and greater. If the system is reading in parallel from two tape drives, a sequential write speed of 20 MB/s or higher would be needed. For this alone, three to four fast disks and fast I/O controllers are necessary to keep up with the incoming data flow.

An online backup creates an even greater number of redo logs, as the current transactions are not written to the data files of the database, but to the redo logs. Because full redo logs are copied to the archive area, the archive area is also constantly loaded with write operations. Simultaneously, the high read activity demanded to back up the archive log can bring the database to a standstill if the database archiver cannot complete its work on time due to disk bottlenecks. For these reasons, the archive log is always saved after the database, and not at the same time.

Table 6.8 indicates the typical sequential I/O activity that is generated when writing and saving the log files, and the number of disks that are needed for this activity with different system sizes.

System size	Transaction volumes	Data flow log files	Number of disks
Small	2 MB/min	33 KB/s	2–4
Medium	60 MB/min	1 MB/s	4–8
Large	200 MB/min	3.3 MB/s	8–12

Table 6.8 Recommended Number of Disks for Log Files

Tip

Oracle databases generally deploy four redo log groups with two "members" to which the system writes simultaneously. If a redo log group is full, a redo log switch is made to the next redo log group.

Then the database archiver copies the first member of the full redo log group to the archive log area. In order not to create a bottleneck in a large installation, the currently active redo log group should not have any members on the disk to be read by the archiver. For this reason, five disks should be used for the standard setup of four groups to two members and mirrored archive logs.

Disk 1 contains the original, that is, the first member of redo log group 11 (the groups are numbered 11, 12, 13, and 14). Disk 2 contains the second member of group 11. Disk 3 contains the first member of redo log group 12, and disk 2 contains member 2 of group 12. Disk 1 contains member 1 of redo log group 13, and disk 2 contains the second member of group 13. Disk 3 contains member 1 of redo log group 14, and disk 2 contains member 2 of redo log group 14.

Because the redo log groups are always numbered sequentially (that is, 11, 12, 13, and 14), this distribution ensures that each disk is written to by only one data flow at any given time, while another disk is only read. This avoids any competing read/write accesses to a disk. Disks 4 and 5 contain the original and the mirror of the archive log. A disk failure does not lead to loss of redo or archive logs.

Number of I/O channels

Next, you must determine the number of I/O channels (SCSI or FC) needed to manage the I/O throughput between the database server and storage subsystem.

When doing this, you should consider that the usable transfer rate of different I/O technologies is considerably lower than the theoretical bandwidth due to management overheads.

At the simplest level, the number of channels can be determined by dividing the total I/O rated performance of disks for data files and log files by the performance of the selected I/O channel type. Thirty-two disks, each with 15 MB/s, for example, would require a transfer performance of 480 MB/s. This would require four Ultra-3 SCSI connections or six FC-100 MB connections. This assumes, however, that all disks will achieve their maximum sequential read rate of 15 MB/s. In fact, however, this is a rare occurrence.

Very different values are determined only if you consider the number of I/O operations that can be achieved for small random accesses (the typical access model for relational databases). Thirty-two disks, each with 10,000 U/min and 110 IOPS, with I/O blocks of 8 KB, require an I/O throughput of only 30 MB/s (32 × 110 IOPS × 8 KB). In this case, a single Ultra SCSI connection or FC connection would suffice. In practice, however, this hardly ever happens.

One option is to divide the disks according to their usage onto disks that are mainly read-access or write-access sequentially (for example, log files), and onto those with random accesses (data files). For example, four disks with a maximum read rate, two disks with a maximum write rate, and 26 disks with an access model that is typical for OLTP. With typical values for disks with 10,000 revolutions per second, this gives an I/O throughput of approximately 100 MB/s [(4 × 15 MB/s) + (2 × 6 MB/s) + (26 × 110 IOPS × 8 KB)]. This would require two Ultra2-SCSI or FC. While this provides a certain amount of redundancy, it also halves the system performance when an adapter fails. For this reason, we recommend an additional adapter.

6.10 Structuring Storage Subsystems

Together with the physical parameters such as the number of I/O channels and disks, the logical structure of the database files also influences the performance of the SAP system. Optimizing the disk and file structures helps to prevent I/O bottlenecks that would increase response times. The bigger a system and the greater the transaction volume to be processed, the more important these measures. (For detailed information on database structures, see the publications by the SAP Advanced Technology Group).

The objective of optimization is to reduce latency time for read or write accesses. The goal for read accesses is an average value below 2 ms. Modern hard disks require less than 10 ms in order to react to a query. Normally, however, you can access data in the main memory in less than 1 ms. The read access time is therefore influenced by two questions:

- Cache hit rate: Is the data already on one of the different cache memories of the database (SGA), of the file system, or of the storage subsystem?
- Disk I/O: If not (cache miss), how quickly can the requested data be read from the disks, considering waiting times, due to competing I/O requests?

For an average value below 2 ms, hit rates of over 90 % in the read cache are required. Because this rate cannot be allowed to increase indefinitely, you will need to configure the available disks in order to avoid the creation of read request queues as much as possible.

Asynchronous write requests usually go directly to the disk cache. This ensures that the response times for read/write accesses are always below 2 ms. Synchronous write requests (log, rollback, and other critical data) are handled by the database as physical I/O operations. If the disk cache is full, or the write-through cache is used, this data must be written directly to the disks before the database can continue processing. This can also cause delays due to queues, which can be reduced by optimized configuration.

Traditional structure

In the last century, storage subsystems were equipped with relatively small, slow disks. The following recommendations apply to these systems:

- Set up the data files and index files for a tablespace on separate disks (for Oracle, for example, data file *PSAPBTABD* on one disk and index file *PSAPBTABI* on another disk).
- Use separate disks for archive log files, rollback files, and temporary files.
- Isolate tablespaces with high I/O numbers (hotspots) on separate disk arrays.
- Use mirrored disks for files with high I/O amounts.

Figure 6.4 provides a simplified illustration of this kind of structure. The emphasis of this structure is to separate files or tablespaces with high access profiles.

A database structure of this kind must constantly be analyzed and optimized, because during productive operation, the I/O bottlenecks (hotspots) are moved from one disk to another. Moving tables with high access profiles to a new tablespace, or a new tablespace to a disk with a low access profile is usually only a temporary solution, however. Managing a large number of independent disk areas is very labor intensive.

The next step

Disks on offer today are considerably faster (higher revolution speeds) and have much greater storage capacity. Also, RAID-5 implementations have become almost as fast as RAID-0/1 systems.

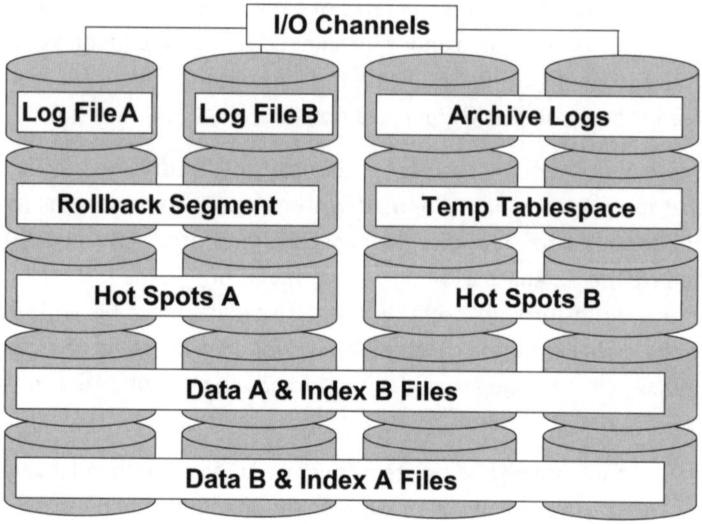

Figure 6.4 Traditional Distribution of Files

Using modern disks when configuring a storage subsystem according to the traditional model (a lot of independent disk arrays with RAID-0/1) results in a lot of unused storage capacity. Because you don't usually have as many disks as necessary for the optimum configuration, isolating the different files can actually cause the I/O bottlenecks that it was intended to prevent.

The challenge when structuring an SAP storage subsystem is therefore to ensure optimized I/O performance with the least possible number of disks. The solution lies in using less logical data volumes and as many physical disks as possible. There are various options, depending on the database, the operating system, and the storage array management software.

In the structure displayed in Figure 6.5, separate disks are provided for only the log files (for data security reasons). All the other disks are used for data files, index files, rollback files, and temporary files. The distribution reduces the influence of I/O bottlenecks on individual disks across the whole storage system. Administration and free space management is considerably simplified, since you no longer have to worry about a logical storage area.

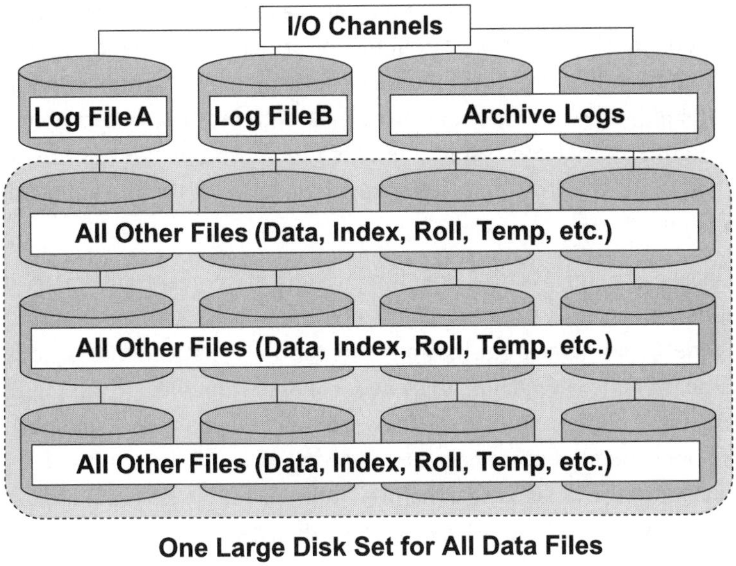

Figure 6.5 File Distribution via Striping

Hardware striping

Block I/O striping is often considered to be the ideal procedure for distributing data to several disks to achieve a good distribution of I/O load. The use of a single, large stripe set across all disks is beneficial for sequential I/O operations, particularly during initial upload. But small, random accesses are also processed effectively by this type of configuration. Stripe sizes from 8 KB to 256 KB or greater can be used. Block sizes of 64 KB are the most common.

In some cases, striping can cause problems with read-ahead caching or prefetching algorithms, if you create a software striping with Logical Volume Manager (LVM) across several RAID groups. The small striping blocks mean that the array controller can no longer recognize sequential read processes as being sequential, because LVM creates small read commands one after the other on different RAID groups. This clashes with the prefetch algorithms of the array controller, which can then wreck the cache memory.

Usually, however, hardware striping is easy to configure and independent of the operating system. Block striping with block sizes of 4 MB or greater has produced very good results. At hardware level, striped disk areas can be used by the database as raw disks, or formatted with a file system.

Striping via operating system

Systems with Logical Volume Manager (LVM) can also use the extent-based design for distribution of files. This method uses storage blocks of

4 to 16 MB (even bigger for AIX), which are called extents. Extent-based distribution mechanisms have good performance for random I/O accesses and are therefore useful if disk subsystems don't support hardware striping (see Figure 6.6), or if used in addition to hardware striping. This also ensures that the system benefits from the advantages of read-ahead and prefetch algorithms of the new generation disks for sequential I/O accesses.

Extent-based striping via the operating system has several advantages. The I/O workload is distributed relatively evenly across all host adapters, I/O channels, and "logical" disks. Implementation is relatively simple; due to a database restore which enables new configuration with renaming of the data files, without the need for a complete export and reimport. Because only one file system needs to be monitored, and the auto-extend functionality of the database can be used, administrative tasks are limited to adding new disks when disk capacity is exhausted.

Database extent-based distribution

With extent-based distribution, it makes sense to leave file management to the database. This type of distribution can achieve high performance levels with raw disks, in particular. The set-up design can be used for storage subsystems that don't offer hardware striping, and this procedure is independent of the hardware and database system. Microsoft SQL Server is an exception. This database works best with stripe sets, which are provided by the Windows operating system or the hardware.

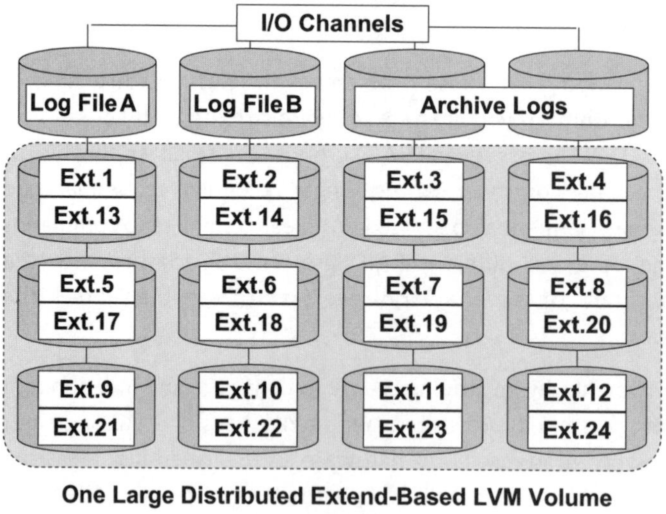

Figure 6.6 Extent-Based Data Distribution

Logical Disks

Today, RAID groups are almost always partitioned into logical disks when used in traditional RAID arrays (see Figure 6.7). In the frontend, these logical disks are then made available to the host as Logical Units (LUNs). For the server, a LUN of this kind looks like a physical disk. Large RAID groups with large hard disks (146 GB and soon even bigger), consist of many such units. You must therefore design the disk array backend carefully for SAP systems. For example, two OLTP systems using logical disks in the same RAID group can soon damage performance. In this case, it's preferable for a productive system to share a RAID group with less I/O-intensive consolidation or test systems.

Storage virtualization

Just like computer systems, modern Enterprise Virtual Arrays have well developed virtualization mechanisms. The physical processes no longer need to be adjusted manually, as they all run automatically. Instead of setting up the RAID sets across a few hard disks, an Enterprise Virtual Array uses larger storage units (disk groups) to write the data itself as distributed units with corresponding parity. These groups are called virtual RAIDs (Vraid), and can be selected as Vraid0, Vraid1, and Vraid5. The large numbers of hard disks (up to 240) in a disk group create very quick volumes that automatically provide the best performance.

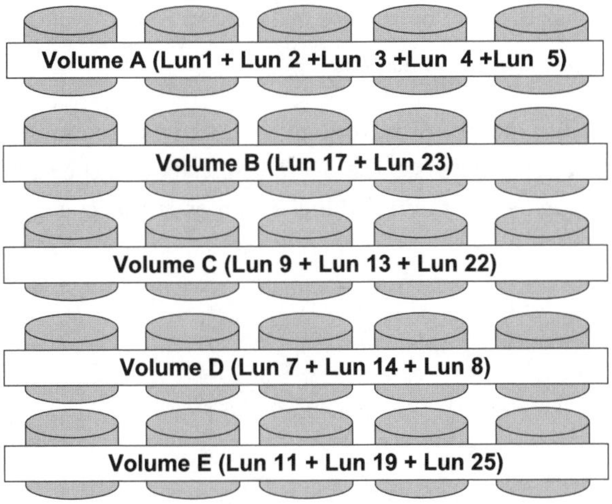

Figure 6.7 RAID Partitioning in Traditional Storage Systems

Automatic performance optimization (or leveling) enables distribution of RAID sets across several dozen hard disks, enabling a much higher number of spindles than in traditional RAID sets. The virtualization procedure also determines the optimum performance of the corresponding configuration and makes the necessary adjustments. Therefore, it is no longer necessary to spend time experimenting with numbers of drives, RAID set sizes, block sizes, and other factors of performance optimization. The Virtual Array simplifies management and guarantees optimum performance.

Virtualization also makes it possible to represent different Vraid levels on a disk groups so it is no longer necessary to set up RAID-5 sets with different numbers of disks (see Figure 6.8).

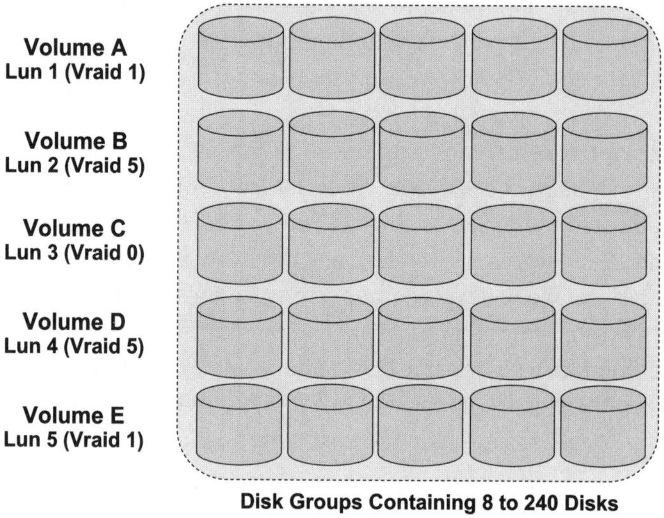

Figure 6.8 Partitioning in the Enterprise Virtual Array

Dynamic expansions of disk groups

You can even dynamically expand a disk group in productive operation by simply adding hard disks. This increases the overall capacity and speed of the disk group. The capacities of the individual volumes is not changed (see Figure 6.9).

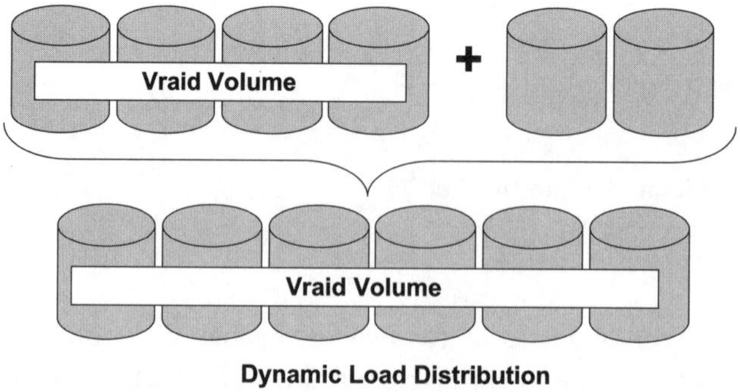

Figure 6.9 Increasing the Size of Disk Groups with Enterprise Virtual Array

You can also increase the individual volumes during productive operation. The only restrictions are set by the different operating systems. An increase to any size is possible, from 1 to 2,048 GB (see Figure 6.10).

Dynamic volume increase

In traditional RAID sets, the capacity of a volume is, however, determined by the hard disk size and the RAID level, and is a multiple of the disk capacity. It is usually only possible to increase a traditional RAID set by disassembling the set and then reassembling it. The data must also be restored. You should note that this data restore is not performed when increasing the size of Vraids.

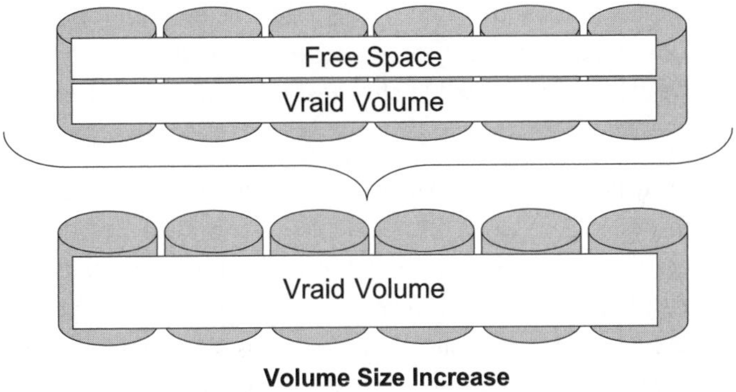

Figure 6.10 Increasing Volume Size in Enterprise Virtual Array

Another new aspect is that dedicated hot spare disks are not required. Instead, reserving a hot spare area in the disk group ensures further processing in the event of disk failure. The data is recreated in the reserved area (see Figure 6.11).

Hot spare area

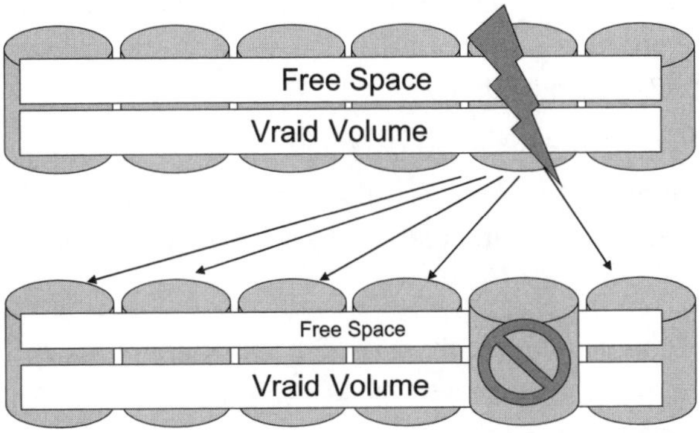

Figure 6.11 Hot Spare Mechanism in the Enterprise Virtual Array

Along with FC hard disks, which are connected to two paths each at 2 Gbit/s, cheaper hard disk technologies have become established in FC storage systems, such as parallel and serial ATAhard disks (as described above). Because they have different ports from FC hard drives, they require special insertion slot casings within the systems. Also, the PATA and SATA connections are only possible on a single path. FATA disks combine the advantages of the FC connection and lower price without additional investment in hard drive casings.

Business copy

In addition, Enterprise Virtual Arrays enable you to replicate the productive databases (business copy). In addition to physical copies, snapclones and vsnaps (vector-based copies) are also available.

Snapclones are copies that can be used immediately. The vsnap functionality allows you to create "capacity-free" copies. The disk group only needs to have the capacity for possible changes; reservation is not necessary.

Continuous access

While business copy is a replication within the storage system, copies can be created synchronously or asynchronously over long distances during continuous access on a "failover" array. If the replication partner is not available, the recently written data is stored chronologically to a write history log space. As soon as the replication partner is available again, all changes are replicated chronologically, so that the target system contains a consistent data set.

Alternatively, there is a fail-save mode, which does not allow any writing of data if the replication partner is not available.

6.11 The Other SAP Servers

When optimizing a storage subsystem for an SAP system, the focus is on the file systems of the productive database server. However, other servers also belong to a mySAP system landscape.

Application server

The application servers in the SAP system simply provide computing power and main memory for the SAP application. Basically, the hard disks are only needed to boot the computer and for the swap area (swap space or paging file).

For application servers, two internal disks in RAID-1 configuration are sufficient. Not only does mirroring increase availability, it also improves I/O performance for the swap area.

Development system

In development systems, while we recommend that you use certain measures to increase availability (consultants are expensive), note that high I/O performance is seldom needed from the disks. Therefore, a simple disk system should suffice for development systems. Because disk performance is not of paramount importance, large block-based hardware stripe sets can be used. However, the files in the development systems can also be stored in an Enterprise Virtual Array within a storage consolidation framework. There, they improve capacity usage without significantly influencing the I/O quota. Furthermore, they can also be used (as mentioned above) in traditional RAID arrays as "I/O low-intensity fillers" for RAID groups that already host logical devices of an I/O-intensive productive system.

Quality assurance system

A test system generally requires the same disk storage space as the productive database server, but not necessarily the same I/O performance and availability. In this case, you could save costs by copying the disk layout of the productive database to larger and therefore fewer disks.

Nevertheless, it makes sense to have the same storage subsystem available for the quality assurance system as for the productive system. This is because a quality assurance system is often used to carry out stress or mass tests (for release change, archiving, and so on) in order to predict runtimes in the productive system. This requires an appropriate level of I/O performance.

Here too, we recommend that you store the files in an Enterprise Virtual Array as part of storage consolidation, and use the additional disks to improve the I/O performance for the productive system.

Business Information Warehouse

In an OLAP system like SAP Business Information Warehouse (SAP BW), the different I/O model creates different disk system configuration requirements than for an OLTP system like R/3, ECC, or CRM. When reading the data from the source systems, the large numbers of sequential read accesses generate a high I/O load, requiring more disks than in an OLTP system. During the online analysis phase, however, the storage subsystem requirements are not very great. Nevertheless, temporary files are used intensively with corresponding I/O requirements. From this, we can draw the following recommendations:

- Block-level striping is more effective than extent-based striping, especially when importing data.
- The main memory of the SAP BW database server should be as large as possible, in order to store a great deal of temporary files without swapping files to the storage subsystem.
- If there is no other solution, the temporary files should be distributed between as many disks and I/O controllers as possible.

- RAID-0/1 is more effective than RAID-5. Hardware striping is the most effective.
- The segmentation of the transaction log to increase security is not as important as in R/3.

Advanced Planner and Optimizer (APO)

The same rules apply to SAP Advanced Planner and Optimizer (SAP APO) databases and application servers as to R/3 and SAP BW systems. The liveCache needs only a few, very fast disks for the operating system, application, and logs. The liveCache database is contained in the main memory and is not on the disk. Concurrently, the pages changed in the data cache must be written to the disk at regular intervals (to the save points). However, no high demands are placed on the disk system, as long as the server has sufficient memory.

6.12 Consolidating Storage Subsystems

In the field of business applications, there are increasingly higher investments in storage subsystems than there are in computer hardware. As in other areas of IT infrastructure, savings can also be made in storage subsystems, especially in management through consolidation of all storage resources into a few high-performance storage subsystems.

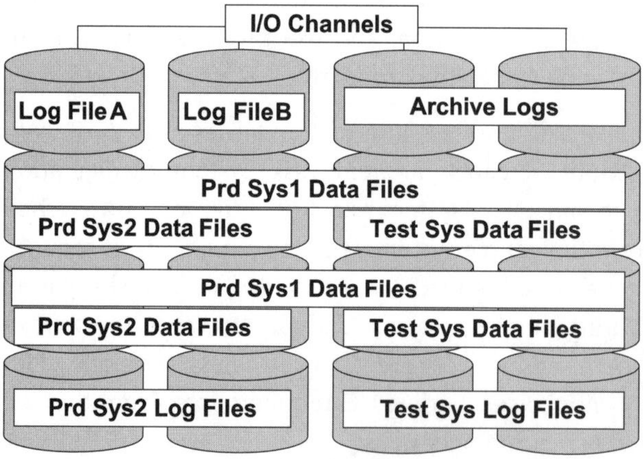

Figure 6.12 Configuration for Shared Usage of the Storage Subsystem by Several SAP Systems

Above all, in a mySAP infrastructure in which every component has its own database, we recommend that you store the data in a consolidated storage subsystem. Figure 6.12 provides an example of the disk configuration of a consolidated storage subsystem for a large and a small productive mySAP component, a quality assurance system, and a development system.

6.13 Data Archiving

In an economic system where the main objective is to constantly increase growth, data sets must also inevitably continue to grow. For this reason, when designing an SAP system, in addition to performance and security, you must also consider scalability of the storage design. However, because even the largest storage subsystems will eventually reach their upper growth limits, an archiving concept must be included right from the start.

An unlimited data increase also has negative consequences for the performance of an SAP system, as large database tables can significantly increase response times. The total size of the database also influences the amount of time needed for backup and reorganization tasks, as well as the amount of administration required.

Just deleting older data from the SAP system database, however, is generally not an option. First, the historic data represents a valuable information resource that can contribute to future developments. Secondly, there are legal regulations governing the retention of business data and documents.

Legal regulations previously stipulated the retention of tax-relevant documents for up to 10 years. In countries like Germany tax-relevant documents that have been created or received electronically must not also be available for inspection online.

Archiving—a Term With Many Meanings

The term *archiving* often has several meanings in a company. From an IT perspective, it often means data backup to tape or reorganization of the data stock. From a database perspective, it means the deletion and combination of data areas in a table in order to reduce storage space usage.

For the accounting department, it means the provision of data and printed lists for inspection by external auditors and tax office representatives.

The term is also used a great deal with document management. In many companies, incoming documents are scanned and archived immediately, in order to enable a paper-free workflow. Outgoing documents such as delivery notes and invoices must be archived for legal reasons. Here, electronic archiving means saving space, time, and cost by optimizing the processing chain.

The actual meaning of *archiving* in an SAP context is the transparent swapping out of data from the productive database of an SAP system.

SAP Archive Development Kit

With the Archive Development Kit (ADK), SAP provides a tool that can extract data records in its business context, so called business objects, that are no longer needed online from the database. The documents to be archived are first copied from the database, combined, and compressed by a factor of five (the compression rate can vary between different data types). The documents are deleted from the database only when the consistency of the archived data has been verified in the external storage system (two-step commit). The ADK ensures that SAP users can still access the documents (although it takes slightly longer), which are stored as external archive files. Entire archive files or individual documents should only be reloaded in exceptional cases, (that is, very soon after archiving, when no system changes have been made). Reloading a long time after archiving can create an inconsistent database, since not all semantic changes can be eliminated and then reconstructed.

Info structures

Depending on the customer requirements and the standard access methods to archived documents, additional functionality will be provided by SAP in order to complement the data access to archived data. This can be done through the definition and creation of info structures.

These info structures are an index for archived data. Creating these archive info structures, however, generates additional entries in the database, so you must be careful to choose the number and scope of the info structures in order that archiving does not place more, rather than fewer, demands on the database. The definition of the info structures will be done by the owner of the corresponding business documents.

The Archive Development Kit ensures, that only business objects can be archived (extracted) which are not active in the business process anymore. Before the archiving process starts, a number of verifications will be performed, such as—status of the document, are there dependencies to other documents, retention time check, etc.

Data Archiving in context of SAP is the only archive scenario, where SAP creates Archive Files in a file system. In order to access archived information, SAP requires access to the file system, where the Archive Files have been generated.

Data archiving

Though the documents, which have been archived and stored in the Archive Files, are not active in the current business process anymore, there might be different access requirements over time. Therefore, the Archive File management needs to be incorporated into a long term storage strategy. This ensures that Archive Files will be managed according to their business relevance and will be made available whenever it is required by the business.

For Data Archiving only, a Hierarchical Storage Management (HSM) System might be taken into consideration. The interface between SAP and HSM will be the file system; therefore no application integration is required.

Information Lifecycle Management

HSM solutions, which are also part of HP's Information Lifecycle Management (ILM) solution portfolio, use several storage levels to store the archived data on the most appropriate storage medium.

Several types of media with special properties are available for the storage of archive files. In addition to hard disks, which ensure fast online access, CDs, DVDs, and magneto-optical data carriers are the main contenders, providing a long data storage lifecycle. When you are legally required to store data, you must also ensure that the data has not been changed. You can do this by using non-rewritable CDs and DVDs (Write Once—Read Many, WORM).

There is also a possibility to manage SAP Archive Files by already available long term data management solutions. However, it needs to be carefully analyzed, which requirement needs to be met by that solution (legal requirements, etc.)

Alternatively, Archive Files can be managed by a certified Content Server for SAP. Content Servers are required to archive documents (scanned images, etc.) and will be eventually linked to an SAP transaction. Content Server might be taken into consideration to manage Archive Files, if the SAP Archive strategy covers more than Data Archiving.

You can also guarantee the unchanged status of data on disks. Content Addressed Storage (CAS) systems use software that stores the archived objects on the storage medium along with a unique key. This key is then managed in an archiving system such as IXOS[3], HP Globasoft Infolife[4] or EMC Documentum[5], for example. CAS systems can be contacted via IP, and communicate with the archiving system via an XML-style API.

6.14 Summary

This chapter focused on the structure of the files generated by an SAP system and on the storage subsystems needed to store business-critical data securely and efficiently. The most important points for the implementation of high-performance and robust storage solutions are:

- The I/O activity model of the SAP component is important for the performance and setup of a storage subsystem.
- Always save the log files that are necessary for a system recovery on a separate disk.
- You can use Point-in-Time and Snapshot technology to make additional copies of the productive database for offline backups, data analysis, and so forth, without significantly damaging the productive system's performance.
- Dimensioning storage subsystems is not just a question of capacity, but also of the necessary number of disks and I/O channels for high performance operations. The number of disks and I/O channels is determined by the I/O profile of the different components.
- Because SAP application servers don't store data, they don't require any separate storage subsystems.
- Consolidation of storage subsystems is a tried-and-tested means of reducing administration costs. A mySAP system contains many components, each with its own database, which can be consolidated in a high-performance storage subsystem.
- Data archiving must be considered from the very beginning of an SAP project. At the very least, the archiving project should be started just as the initial problems of an SAP implementation project are being resolved.

3 Go to *www.IXOS.com*.
4 Go *to www.digitalinfolife.com*.
5 Go *to www.documentum.com*.

7 High Availability SAP Systems

Availability and error tolerance as prerequisites for Enterprise Services Architecture

The solutions in the mySAP Business Suite represent some of the classic business-critical applications in a company. This applies even more to the SAP NetWeaver components, in which business processes are integrated across many interconnected SAP systems. Increasingly, systems of customers and vendors are also part of this network. Implementation of an Enterprise Services Architecture (ESA) means that there will be no non-critical systems anymore, because any application could potentially be used by a mission-critical business process implemented as a composite application. The breakdown of any component could therefore lead to anything from the partial paralysis of a company to its complete collapse.

Performing open-heart surgery on the company

Managing a productive SAP system can be compared to open-heart surgery, since it is usually the core of all business data processing in an enterprise. For a business process to function correctly, all the participating systems must run smoothly. Remember: Any process chain system can only be as strong as its weakest link.

From solo player to team player

There are many reasons that might prevent a system from being sufficiently available. These range from unacceptable performance due to poor management, to total system failure due to force majeure (acts of God). But insufficient interaction with other systems in a NetWeaver system landscape also means non-availability of complete business processes. In order to provide the required level of business process availability within ESA, we must therefore turn good solo players into great team players.

We are always open!

Unfortunately, maintenance windows remain unavoidable for hardware and software repair. In a globalized economy, however, these planned downtimes must be minimized. Today, even medium-sized companies often have a worldwide sales network, and we are always in the middle of peak business hours somewhere on the planet. With different time zones and cultures, there is often no common denominator for weekends and holidays. SAP systems must therefore be guaranteed to operate 24 hours a day and seven days a week. Therefore, measures that ensure continuous availability of SAP systems are the most important security investment that an IT manager can make.

7.1 Downtimes

In reality, there is no IT system that is always available. The time frames in which the system is not operational fall into two categories: planned and unplanned downtimes.

There are many possible reasons for both types of downtime. Different studies indicate that "people and processes" cause by far the most downtime events, whether directly, through incorrect actions, or indirectly, through faulty programming and poorly planned operating procedures (see Figure 7.1).

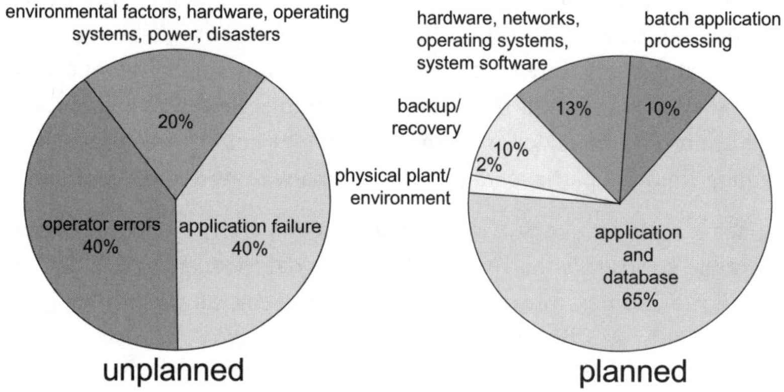

Figure 7.1 Causes of Non-availability (Gartner Group 2001)

Unplanned downtimes IT systems have unplanned downtime due to the all too common shortcomings of hardware, software, and the data center environment. The causes range from memory overflow, due to a software error, to failure of a database server, because of an overheated CPU (after a fan failure due to mechanical wear and tear), to natural catastrophes such as earthquakes or floods.

The worst-case scenario for an IT infrastructure would be the loss of an entire data center. As most catastrophe scenarios consider the possibility of a fire, data centers are usually well equipped to combat fires with fire extinguisher systems. Ironically, water damage is the main cause of data center downtimes in central Europe. Flooding from a burst water pipe or a cloudburst can be just as disastrous as a large fire.

Soft disasters In addition to the loss of a data center through these "hard disasters", you should not underestimate the effect of "soft disasters" such as the loss or corruption of data. Unlike the loss of a data center, which can be mitigated by good planning, it is impossible to predict the downtimes created by data loss or data corruption. Here too, the measures taken during a disaster cannot always be covered by an emergency plan. They often require a creative response and well-trained personnel, as well as the right service partners, to ensure that problems are handled in a structured and directed manner.

Unplanned downtimes are particularly critical, because they tend to occur at the worst possible time. Besides the worst-case scenario, failures in sub-areas and unacceptable response times can also lead to unplanned downtimes. As we already mentioned, the failure of a single system can paralyze a large proportion of the business processes in a closely interconnected NetWeaver environment, a situation that approximates a worst-case scenario.

Planned downtimes

As well as downtimes resulting from unforeseen component failures, there are also downtimes that can be planned for, even if they are just as undesirable. Some of the typical reasons for planned downtimes are configuration changes to the operating system, database, and application, importing support packages and patches, profile management, and CPU and memory upgrades.

Paradoxically, planned downtimes also occur due to measures intended to increase system availability, for example, data backup. Consequently, you should use one of the strategies described in Section 7.15 to minimize the downtime for the backup.

The window closes

Years ago, maintenance windows tended to cover an entire weekend or more. Today, many SAP systems often have only a few hours per month or even per quarter. In extreme cases (for example, Internet Sales), the available time is limited to once or twice a year. The goal of measures intended to increase availability is therefore not only minimizing unplanned downtimes, but planned downtimes as well!

7.2 What Is Availability?

The availability of an SAP system can be defined as the period during which the corresponding application can be used for the intended purpose, such as performing business transactions. More precisely, it is the time for which the system is operational and effectively available, compared to the time for which it should have been available.

Here, it is important that we make a precise distinction between the availability of the IT system and the availability of the application. While the IT department can influence application availability to a certain extent, there are limits how much the IT staff can control the degree of availability. If the application deletes a table in the database, the IT department can restore the table; however, they have no influence on the cause of the table being deleted in the first place. For this reason, it is very important to distinguish between IT and the application itself when drawing up Service Level Agreements (SLAs).

System availability is often expressed as a percentage of a specific period (for example, one year). An availability of 99 % would indicate an average of 3.6 days of downtime over a period of one year. An availability of 99.999 % would indicate an average of just five minutes downtime in the same period.

The Availability of the Overall System is Smaller Than the Components

The overall system availability is calculated by multiplying the availability of the individual components. The result is that the total system availability is always less than that of the individual components. Example: Two connected components each with an availability of 99 %, have an availability of around 98 % (99 % × 99 %). That is on average over one week of non-availability per year.

7.3 What Level of Availability Is Required?

Unfortunately, high availability has its price. All solutions for backing up data and operational availability require additional investment. These investments must, however, be viewed as a form of insurance. You accept a considerable amount of expenditure as security against an event that you hope will never happen. When evaluating the different high-availability solutions, you shouldn't think in terms of how much availability the company can afford, but in terms of how much downtime can the company allow?

National business legislation on control and transparency adds another dimension to the topic of availability. The authorities of some countries have defined rules for the ways in which listed companies must report the risks of their IT systems. Also, according to such regulations, management boards, supervisory boards, and business leaders can all be made personally responsible for damages arising if insufficient precautions were taken to address possible risks. This even extends to any failure to mention IT weak points and risks in the reports (for example, if an investor suffers financial damages as a result). Also, within the framework of the new guidelines for equity capital (Basel II), financial institutions pay more attention to the IT security measures employed by their borrowers.

Therefore it is mandatory to define the necessary level of IT availability in writing in the form of a Service Level Agreement (SLA). This may sound trivial, but many companies still don't use service level agreements. Internal customers (for example, the line of business departments and higher management) often avoid these kinds of documents, because they define not only what service levels must be delivered to the business departments but also what these departments are not entitled to. When requirements that were not previously clearly defined ("the system must run constantly!"), are properly documented along with the accompanying costs, then the line of business departments are forced to say good bye to many services they used to get for "free".

Risk analysis, and cost/usage analysis

It is obvious that because of cost restrictions, IT departments cannot always provide what their customers want, but they can usually give them what they need. To properly understand the fine distinction between want and need, you must consider the effects of non-availability within the framework of risk-analysis and estimate the financial consequences. You can then determine the budget that can be made available for the technical measures that need to be taken: The maximum amount spent for IT infrastructure availability should be below the cost of a breakdown of the IT infrastructure for the enterprise as a whole.

Case Study: a Tolerable Failure

Let us assume, no work is carried out over the weekend in the production IT system of a medium-sized company. Operation finishes on Saturday at 12:00 p.m., and the first employees are back at their workstations on Monday at 7:00 a.m. End-of-week closing activities require one hour; the backup requires another three hours. During the period from 4:00 p.m. on Saturday to 7:00 a.m. on Monday, the SAP system is not operational and any failure during this period has no effect on production processes. The same applies to overnight processing, which is completed by 10:00 p.m. at the latest. Because a system failure during these times causes no damage to the business, these periods are not included in our budget for security measures.

If there is a system failure during normal operating times, production can still continue for another day. From the second day onward, production comes to a halt and the company starts to lose about one million dollars per day. From this case example, we can deduce that the system must be restored within one day, and a budget of up to one million dollars is available in order to ensure this system repair. This is more than enough to cover a support contract guaranteeing repair within one working day.

Case Study: Around-the-Clock Operation

A similar company is a component supplier for the automobile industry. Customers send orders online directly to the SAP system twenty four hours a day, seven days a week (24/7). If the system cannot process an order within an hour, there is the danger of a production line stoppage for the customer and a multimillion dollar financial penalty for the supplier.

In this case, 24/7 operation is required, and the maximum acceptable downtime makes a failover solution absolutely indispensable.

When are the greatest damages caused?

When calculating the costs of downtimes, you should not assume that these downtimes occur during normal operation. Rather, you must ask yourself how much a system failure would cost if it occurred during year-end closing, for example, or during the Christmas sales season, or, worst-case scenario, just after the start of a big marketing campaign.

Even if the production lines can still be operated in emergencies without the SAP system, but a just-in-time (JIT) customer insists on an electronic delivery note from the SAP system, then even in this case the lack of communication can also lead to significant damages within a short space of time.

7.4 How Much Performance Is Necessary in an Emergency?

This question should be considered for the following two cases:

- Failover upon failure of a server, storage system, and so forth
- Disaster in the event of the loss of an entire data center

Failover cases usually require between 70 % and 100 % of the capacity that is necessary for normal productive operation. With a well planned strategy, this can usually be achieved with a reasonable investment.

To achieve 100 % system performance in the event of a disaster, you need twice the investment, because all components (computers, storage subsystems, networks, and data center infrastructure) must be available in duplicate. During normal operation, these resources are not used (on standby). Due to the enormous costs that this solution entails, companies are considerably more willing to operate with fewer resources for a limited time after a disaster.

Halving CPU resources means halving the number of users

One of the objectives of SLAs is therefore to define, together with the line of business departments, the minimum performance level that must be guaranteed even in the event of a system failure. For the reasons explained in Chapter 4, line of business departments and higher management must understand that halving the CPU performance, for example, does not simply double response times, it rather means that only half the usual number of users can work on the system and only half of the transactions can be processed to prevent response times from becoming completely unacceptable. Main memory for database servers in particular can also not be reduced a great deal; otherwise, tasks such as batch jobs would not be able to run in the required time because the database buffer would be too small. In particular, the APO liveCache cannot be reduced at all.

Emergency operation

Considering all these factors, the line of business departments involved must provide an estimate of which business processes are essential during emergency operation, and which processes can be deactivated temporarily. Partial or complete deactivation of non-productive SAP systems and the redirection of their system resources into productive operation is also worth considering.

Only after ruling out any operation that is not absolutely necessary for company-critical business processes, can you use this estimate to design an appropriate high-availability scenario and justify the budget that you need for it.

7.5 What Level of Stability Is Required?

Availability and stability are often confused, but they are two different factors. While availability means that the infrastructure must be available to the required extent, stability determines whether the business processes also run as required. The availability of a system is therefore just one of the requirements for its stability.

What your company's line of business departments actually require from IT is the highest possible levels of stability in company-critical applications. A system with slightly poorer performance is more acceptable than an unstable system that continuously disrupts the business process flow.

From the integrated system to distributed systems

SAP R/3 as an integrated system was always able to represent all significant important business processes within a company. As long as the availability of the R/3 system and its interfaces to external systems could be guaranteed, the stability of the business processes was also ensured.

With the evolution of SAP solutions to NetWeaver and then to ESA, this central approach has developed increasingly into a distributed system in which most business processes are represented across several systems. Company boundaries are no longer an obstacle; logistical processes across several companies have since become the norm.

Therefore, interaction between the systems involved is a key criterion for the stability of the cross-system business processes (see Figure 7.2).

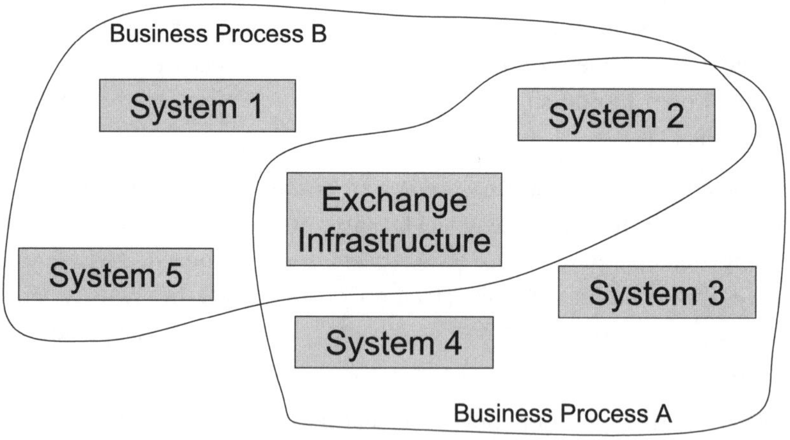

Figure 7.2 Distributed Systems and Business Processes

Interfaces

When coupling transaction-based systems, the main challenge is to ensure data consistency for all interfaces. Unfortunately, project teams often install "fair weather" interfaces. These interfaces function perfectly as long as no system failures occur. If a failure occurs in a network, for example, causing an interruption, you may lose all synchronization between the systems connected by the interfaces.

Robust interfaces with ALE

Application Link Enabling (ALE) is the classic SAP solution for ensuring stable data exchange between the different solutions in the mySAP Business Suite and also other non-SAP systems. The tools provided by SAP enable you to maintain consistency in all systems connected via ALE. Central ALE administration is imperative for a group of systems connected in this way in order to avoid conflicts between different system administrations. SAP also provides the necessary tools to implement this kind of administration.

Exchange infrastructure

With NetWeaver, SAP provides the Exchange Infrastructure (SAP XI) as a central data hub between all the solutions in the mySAP Business Suite and third-party systems. SAP XI centralizes administration and the flow of interface data. This approach makes it easier to ensure the consistency of interface definitions and data between many different systems. However, this centralized approach also turns the XI into a central Single Point of Failure (SPoF).

7.6 Avoiding Downtime

As you can see, a NetWeaver/mySAP system landscape can comprise a wide range of logical and physical components. SPoF occurs where there is only one instance of a particular component and the failure of that component would also indicate a system failure or damage to the system.

Holistic approach is mandatory

For a holistic approach, you must consider all the components relevant to the corresponding business process. As always, the weakest link in the chain determines the availability of the business process. A data center that is prepared for all disasters is of little use if users can no longer contact the data center because its only telecommunication connection has stopped working. Besides the SAP system landscape itself, you must therefore also consider all the systems that deliver or consume information (for example, inventory management systems, time management systems, laboratory data entry systems, and shop-floor systems, but also connections to systems in other companies and especially the Internet).

Cross-system data consistency becomes key

You must also consider these interconnected systems in terms of cross-system data consistency. In the past, resetting a single R/3 system an hour due to restoring and recovering its database could be resolved by a phone call to the line of business departments to search their paper baskets for the documents and run the now lost transactions of the last hour a second time. With today's cross system business processes exchanging thousands of transactions without any human interaction even a "time travel" backwards of a few minutes for a single system can create several days of post-processing work. In some cases, large data quantities must be compared manually and corrected as necessary.

To frame the issue think of a business process where a CRM system sends customer orders to an ECC system which processes the financial portion and then forwards the process to an APO system which takes care of delivery. If, in such a inter-connected system scenario, the ECC system has to be reset in time, the goods may be delivered (by the APO system), but the bills are never sent to the customers because the ECC has virtually never received the orders from the CRM system. If, on the other hand, the APO system fails, the customers get the bills from the ECC for goods which will never be delivered because the setback APO system never received the orders.

7.7 Components of High Availability

Data center environment

A professionally run data center with the right environment is the basis of maximum system availability. This environment includes a redundant power supply and air conditioning, as well as sufficient fire protection.

Categories for Data Centers

The Uptime Institute[1] is seen as being the industry's guide on data centre infrastructure. The institute defines 4 categories of data centres. Each tier has various infrastructure resilience requirements. Tier 1 being the lowest and Tier 4 being the highest. Tier 4 is very expensive to build and there are only a few in the world.[2]

Hardware components

The first technical measure for minimizing unplanned downtimes is to use high-quality hardware components. Where possible, these components should be able to intercept internally any subcomponent failure. Examples include Error-Checking-and-Correction (ECC) memory with chip spare technology or storage subsystems with Redundant Array of Independent Disks (RAID) protection. System components with no built-in error tolerance should be duplicated wherever possible (fans, power supply, network interfaces, and so forth).

Operating system

Operating systems for business-critical applications must ensure a maximum level of stability. They should support the use or activation of

1 Go to *http://www.upsite.com/*.

2 Go to *http://www.upsite.com/TUIpages/whitepapers/tuitiers.html* for these definitions.

redundant system components (for example, online addition and replacement of failed network and SAN interface cards). As far as possible, you should be able to make changes to the system configuration and parameters during productive operation (for example, adding hard drive space and activating on-demand CPUs).

Data security and network operation

Other measures are also needed to ensure data integrity and system performance, as described in this chapter. Local and remote networks, as well as the operation of all components, are described in Chapters 11, 12, and 14.

Application quality

Company-critical applications such as SAP are usually equipped with mechanisms for quality assurance (QA) and for ensuring stable operation. Knowledge of and full utilization of these mechanisms is a prerequisite for high availability. The application's SPoF must also be recognized. In the event of a breakdown, failover or restart mechanisms must seize control in order to quickly restore operation.

Manufacturer support

Last but not least, you should obtain adequate service coverage from the hardware and software manufacturers. Even redundant components must be replaced quickly upon failure in order to restore redundancy as quickly as possible. You should try to avoid software errors proactively by importing the latest patches. Quick and competent software support must be readily available in the event of a failure.

Figure 7.3 summarizes the levels that have to work together in order to provide the highest system availability possible to provide the necessary stability for mission critical business processes.

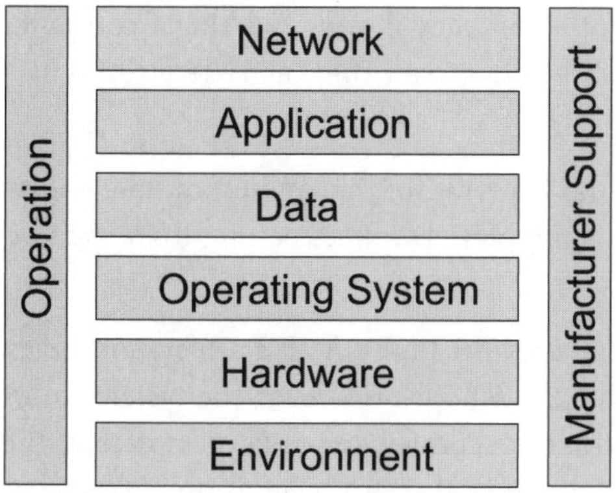

Figure 7.3 Components of Business Process Availability

7.8 The Proper Environment

The term environment entails everything you need to operate an IT system. This includes sufficiently sized and secured rooms, as well as power supply and air conditioning. Company-critical systems naturally have very high requirements. Breakdowns due to environment-related factors are relatively rare, but can have dramatic consequences, which is why these considerations play an important role in the risk analysis.

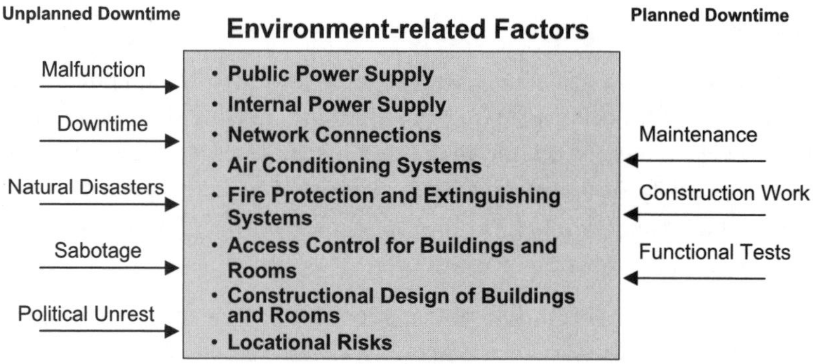

Figure 7.4 Factors Influencing the IT Environment

Unplanned downtimes due to environment-related factors

To operate correctly, IT infrastructures require ample space, energy supply, and cooling, as well as access to communication connections. These infrastructures are at risk for fire and water damage, but they are also vulnerable to unauthorized manipulation. Furthermore, the various units and power supply installations are all subject to the unavoidable reality of mechanical wear and tear.

Total loss of all systems

If the entire IT infrastructure of a company is kept in a single computer room or data center, a serious breakdown can affect all IT services. A natural catastrophe can lead to a total loss of all systems.

Because a company cannot usually survive for the amount of time necessary to create and reassemble a complete IT infrastructure, there are two options:

Mobile emergency data center

Large hardware manufacturers provide transportable emergency data centers that can be onsite within a few hours. However, the systems must then still be configured according to company-specific parameters, the applications must be installed, and the data must be imported from tapes (provided the tapes are still readable). The company site needs to maintain a dedicated site with the necessary power and data network connections ("data hydrant"). Often forgotten, all the necessary processes to bring such an emergency data center into production must be exercised on a regular basis.

Distribution of resources to several locations

In many cases, housing some of the computers in a suitable room in a different building will suffice. If necessary, a properly equipped cellar or container can be used. The only prerequisites are the correct power supply, air conditioning, and the ability to monitor all environmental parameters remotely, there is no need to have employees in these rooms. You must ensure that the computer rooms are located far enough apart to make certain that both locations are not affected by the same disaster.

At a minimum, we recommend that you distribute the IT resources between different fire sections in a data center to guard against possible fire damage. At companies with a greater risk of fire (for example, a petrochemical industry), greater distances must be used. To protect against water damage, do not place both sub-data centers underground. At least one center should be located higher up in the building.

Clusters between continents

Companies in areas prone to earthquakes or hurricanes should maintain even greater distances between the data center locations (continental clusters). The same applies to politically unstable areas.

It should be possible to operate all the machines in the data center remotely, without actually needing to enter the data center. This ensures that normal operation can continue, even if the data center cannot be physically accessed.

Real Life Example: The Police Block the Data Center

At one of our customers, an administrator in the data center had a heart attack. The police blocked all access to the data center until they had completed their investigations. During this time, nobody was allowed to enter the data center even to change the backup tapes. A tape library that allows remote data backup would have been a good investment in this case.

Planned downtimes due to environment-related factors

Planned downtimes due to environment-related factors are usually a result of maintenance work on the power supply or air conditioning, or building work. They can also be attributable to functional tests, which are carried out to test the measures taken to protect against unplanned downtime.

Real Life Example: Attention to the Main Emergency Switch!

When they arrive at a fire, firefighters are trained to switch off all electrical equipment before they even start to fight the fire. It is therefore instinctive for them to press all the emergency off switches immediately before they even establish whether they're dealing with a false alarm. If you're certain that there is no fire (false alarm), post somebody to the emergency-off switches and tell them not to let the firefighters press them!

Setting up an error-tolerant IT environment require a great deal of practical experience, and should be implemented as early as the risk analysis stage. You must not only consider the spectacular and obvious disaster scenarios, but the many hidden causes for breakdowns as well. Consequently, in conducting a risk analysis, you should not take anything for granted. At this point in the process, you must apply Murphy's Law: Anything that can go wrong will go wrong, and always when you least need it.[3]

7.9 Hardware Infrastructure

Like all other software solutions, mySAP and NetWeaver components should be installed and operated on stable and high-performance computers, storage subsystems, and network components. The sum of these components is called the hardware infrastructure.

RAS philosophy

The RAS philosophy is an industry approach to describing the reliability, availability and serviceability of a computer system. Under this philosophy, hardware manufacturers spend a lot of time and money to provide, through careful construction, robust products, high-value components, and a 24-hour test run before delivery (burn-in). However, in reality, there is no hardware that never fails and never needs to be maintained.

For this reason, a risk analysis must also search for all Single Points of Failure (SPoF) in the hardware. As for the environment-related factors, this risk analysis must look for ways to address known risks by using redundancy and organizational measures.

3 Go to *http://www.edwards.af.mil/history/docs_html/tidbits/murphy's_law.html*.

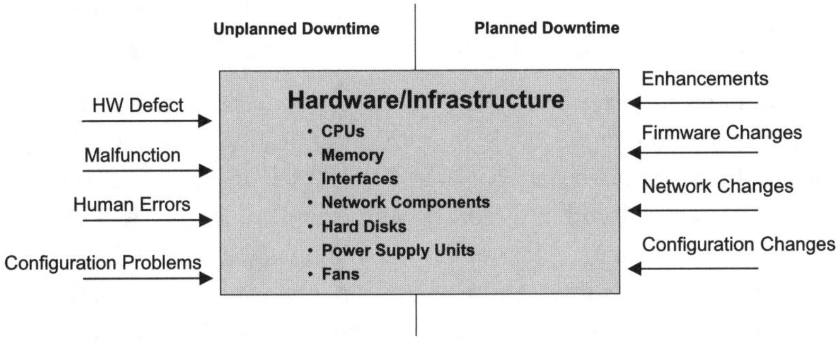

Figure 7.5 Factors Influencing the Hardware Infrastructure

Mitigating component failures

The first step towards minimizing unplanned downtimes due to hardware failure is to use high-quality components. However, because you cannot guarantee that a technical system will never break down, computers and storage subsystems for company-critical applications have a built-in error tolerance. Built-in redundancies, for example, Error Check and Correction (ECC) memory or RAID protection for hard drives, provide a tolerance for subcomponent failure.

Components that don't have these kinds of built in redundancies must be duplicated if necessary. Today's high-value computers therefore tend to have several redundant fans and power supplies (which should be plugged into separate power sources). Also, computers for productive SAP systems should generally always be equipped with redundant interface cards for Local Area Networks (LAN) and hard drive subsystems (iSCSI or Fibre Channel, FC), so that the SAP system can continue to be operated if one of the relatively inexpensive components fails.

ECC RAM

Processors (CPUs) and the main memory are considerably more critical hardware components in a server. Mission-critical SAP systems should therefore only be operated with error-tolerant ECC RAM. A CPU that has been recognized as defective should be able to be deactivated during productive operation if the error threatens to cause an immediate crash. At the very least, the operating system must be able to isolate defective CPUs or sections of memory after a restart, allowing system operation without the use of these components.

External hard disk systems

Similar recommendations also apply to storage subsystems. All systems provided for storing large data quantities (hard disks, CD, MO, DVD, tape drives, and so on) are electro-mechanical in nature and their mechanical components are therefore subject to normal wear and tear. Chapter 6 describes the worst-case scenario if the read/write head comes into contact with the hard disk, namely that all data on the disk will be destroyed.

Mirrored or striped?

To guarantee data availability, SAP therefore requires a certain level of redundancy in the data storage for mission-critical systems, regardless of the additional required data backup to tape. Even if the data availability can be guaranteed within a storage subsystem using the RAID designs described in Chapter 6, redundancy must generally also be provided for the entire storage subsystem and the paths toward the storage subsystems; otherwise, this too, would represent a Single Point of Failure.

You must also not forget the different active network components (switches and routers) when considering availability. Here too, solutions for ensuring availability are based on the redundant configuration of LAN and WAN connections, as described in detail in Chapters 9 to 12.

Recognize and replace failed components immediately!

All systems with redundant components must be monitored so that any component failure can be recognized and the failed component be replaced as soon as possible. Service technicians frequently encounter situations where an operator has failed to notice multiple components failures in a system until it finally crashes when the redundant components also fail. In order to keep the period of reduced redundancy as short as possible, you should replace failed components immediately.

Modern hardware systems are equipped with monitoring systems that can recognize potential problems early on. You should take advantage of these options to proactively remove potential problems before they can develop into real ones.

Planned downtimes for hardware maintenance

Due to urgently needed system configuration changes and resource expansions, planned downtimes occur much more frequently than does maintenance work. The architecture of the SAP systems supports the addition of resources during productive operation by allowing application servers to be added to the system landscape without any need to interrupt system operation.

Where there are sharp fluctuations in capacity requirements, the solution of adding and removing application servers has its limits. Before removing an application server, you must ensure that all users have logged off and that all batch jobs have been completed. If the database computer resources are no longer sufficient, then the whole SAP system must be stopped for the database system upgrade.

7.10 Operating Systems

The stability and scalability of operating systems are important factors when guarding against the downtime of company-critical applications. Operating systems for computers have their own level in the risk analysis. SAP also places a great deal of importance on this area. For this reason, it supports only systems that have been installed on SAP-certified operating systems.

Certified operating systems

To avoid problems with the interaction of operating systems and I/O card drivers from different manufacturers, SAP also certifies each combination of computer and interface cards for Windows and Linux systems. In the other operating systems supported by SAP (HP-UX, HP Tru64 UNIX, Solaris, AIX, OS/400, OS/390, zOS), certification of individual computers is not necessary, because the manufacturers are responsible for interaction between all the components. Storage subsystems are not certified by SAP in general.

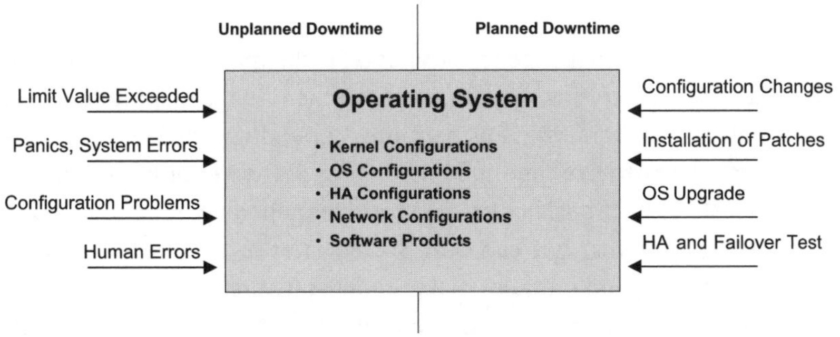

Figure 7.6 Factors Influencing Operating System Stability

Unplanned downtime due to operating system failures

Operating systems for business-critical applications must guarantee a minimum level of stability. When manufacturers develop operating systems, they spend a great deal of time and money on comprehensive quality assurance measures and tests. However, despite all the care taken with the many millions of lines of code, you cannot completely rule out errors. After the operating system has been released, if any errors are found that could cause a failure, the manufacturer provides a patch to eliminate the error. Over time, therefore, system stability increases (until a new release with new features brings new errors of its own).

Patch strategy

To profit from these continuous improvements, users must receive preventive information on the errors and be provided with the patches. This is usually guaranteed in the form of a maintenance contract. Along with the option to receive patches, you can also benefit from the knowledge of the operating system manufacturer, as they will regularly consult with you to check your operating system for known errors.

You can then patch your systems at regular intervals in a controlled manner, instead of waiting until an error necessitates an upgrade or a patch. Running these patch sessions every three months has proven to significantly improve operating system security and stability. Otherwise, the enterprise runs the risk of constantly encountering errors that have long been recognized and removed.

Real Life Example: No Time to Patch

At one of our customers, the line of business departments don't approve a maintenance window to import patches to the SAP system for more than six months due to "urgent" projects, until suddenly an error that had been known for four months led to a system crash.

In reality, the main challenge for businesses is the multitude of configuration options for operating systems, enabling them to be adapted for every conceivable requirement. Furthermore, operating systems can be expanded with software modules and drivers. Software for hard disk mirroring, clusters, data backup, or monitoring is generally not contained in all operating systems, but can be installed later as required. The large number of drivers and modules makes these software installations quite a complex task. In a worst-case scenario, it can cause unwanted conflicts with drivers from different manufacturers.

No screensavers!

For this reason, only components released by the operating system manufacturer absolutely necessary to run and monitor the application in question should be installed on a server for a mission-critical SAP solution. A screensaver, for example, has no place on computers used for company-critical applications.

Tainted Linux Kernel

This paragraph deals with the "tainted kernel" problem in Linux systems. A tainted kernel occurs when software components that are not published as Open Source are included with the Linux kernel. In this case, a flag is set automatically in Linux indicating this situation. SAP does not provide support for these systems. Before analyzing and eradicating the problem, the kernel must be returned to its original state.

An SAP system needs specific configuration of the operating system parameters. As the system load grows with the resource requirements, the operating system parameters must also be adapted accordingly. Otherwise, the application is bound to fail when the system exceeds the specified parameter limits. Therefore, it is important to monitor the "usage" of these parameters during productive operation. When changing operating system parameters in cluster configurations, it is essential that you follow the rules of change management very closely; i. e changes have to be applied at all nodes in the cluster. This problem has been eliminated in configurations where single system images are used.

Monitoring usage of operating system parameters

Tools such as the HP Change Alert Monitor ensure availability by automatically monitoring all configurations and resources for changes. Because the Change Alert Monitor not only keeps the current status, but also stores older versions in its documentation system, you can also compare the system status before the change.

Automatic change registration

All configuration work on computers hosting company-critical applications requires good planning. The corresponding documentation and advice from the manufacturer should be read and all possible interactions should be considered before carrying out any actions. In terms of change management, you should never perform a change on the production system first. Instead, you should perform all actions on a test system first, with a configuration that is identical to and a data volume that is as comparable as possible to that of the production system. In particular, this applies to big changes, such as an operating system release change.

Never run on the production system without testing!

To prevent the same bugs from constantly causing failures, all information on failures must be collected for evaluation. When system crashes occur, a crash dump is usually written. This must be stored together with trace files and log files after a crash, and before the failed system is restarted. If the system crashes again due to a subsequent error, this information is overwritten and lost for the error analysis. The time and effects of the failure must also be documented.

Paradoxically, measures performed on the operating system to minimize unplanned downtimes lead to planned downtimes. You must schedule enough maintenance windows to enable you to import the latest bug fixes and patches. When selecting an operating system for an SAP installation, you should already be considering how often the manufacturer usually provides bug fixes and patches. Many operating systems only need to be patched once a year and also allow you to change parameters during productive operation without restarting. Hardware components

Planned downtimes due to operating system maintenance

can also be activated (Instant Capacity) and exchanged (Online Addition and Replacement, OLAR) during productive operation. This significantly reduces the maintenance window required for operating system maintenance.

Security patches

This does not apply to patches that are intended to plug security gaps in the operating system in order to guard against viruses and worms (security patches). If you don't want to see your company mentioned in the press as another victim of a worm or virus attack, you should not delay implementing these security patches.

While any operating system can be attacked, some of the more commonly used operating systems are attacked more frequently. Selecting an operating system that is seldom attacked can therefore increase availability.

7.11 Failover Systems

The preceding chapters describe components that can be duplicated to provide redundancy. For technical reasons, however, you cannot provide multiple units for all components. If this is not acceptable, redundancy must be provided in the form of a fail over cluster for entire servers or storage systems.

Clusters cannot prevent a server from failing, but they can minimize the downtime by quickly switching to another server that is still functioning. Clusters must be implemented and managed carefully so that they don't cause failures by themselves. Regular courses and training for the IT team are therefore an important part of a failover solution. Failover clusters only protect the system from hardware or software failures, not from database inconsistencies or other logical failures like unintentional deletion of files.

Computer clusters

Failover solutions for computers automatically switch applications to another "adoptive computer" (adoptive node) as soon as the primary computer fails. The replacement computer must activate an IP address associated with the application so that the applications can be accessed transparently via the network.

If the clustered computer up is a database server, then access to the storage subsystem must be switched to the replacement computer. This is one of the reasons why the database files should not be stored on the internal disks of a computer, but rather on external storage subsystems.

To perform an automatic failover, the cluster software must be able to recognize a computer failure. The software packages installed on the individual computers of a cluster constantly query each other in order to establish health. This query process can be compared to a heartbeat. If a heartbeat stops, then the cluster software on the "surviving" computers assumes that the queried system is "dead" and adopts that computer's tasks and resources.

Heartbeat

During this process, you must ensure that only one of the cluster computers has access to the resources at any given time. The entire process—from recognition to restart—usually takes less than one minute. If just a single application stops reacting (but the server remains active), the cluster software restarts the application on the same server.

Figure 7.7 illustrates the principle of a clustered SAP system. The system is divided into two resource groups that can each be processed on a separate computer operating normally.

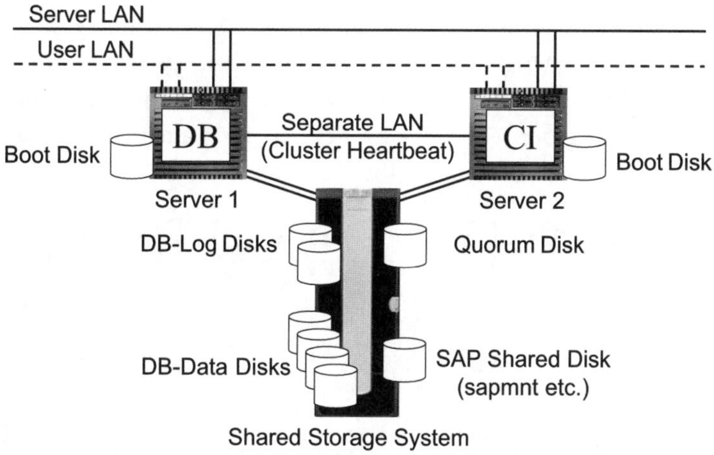

Figure 7.7 Basic Configuration for an SAP Cluster

A fundamental problem for all failover solutions, including manual failover solutions, is the so called split-brain syndrome. This is the situation whereby, for example, two nodes in a cluster stop receiving a heartbeat from each other due to a network failure, and therefore assume that the other node has failed. If the adoptive node would attempt to get access to the disks and start the database with the virtual IP address while the primary node still actively runs the application, data corruption and an inconsistent database would likely result. This is one of the very situations that clusters are programmed to avoid.

Avoiding stalemate situations: Quorum disk

The way this is accomplished is by use of a so called "quorum device," often times a disk or LUN. Because there is only one active quorum device in the cluster, the "surviving" node is the node which is assigned the quorum device (which is why a quorum disk is also called a voting disk, since it ensures a clear majority). This avoids any stalemate situations.

Heartbeat network The bandwidth required for the heartbeat is very low, but the network used should have a very high availability level. Even if most of the clusters on the market can use any of the available networks between the servers for the heartbeat, we recommend that you set up a dedicated heartbeat LAN, which will still work, regardless of whether or not all the other networks have been compromised (for example, by broadcast storms). Redundant heartbeat LAN's—i.e routing the heartbeat over more than one LAN—are also highly recommended.

As you learned in Chapter 3, with the SAP Web Application Server (Web AS) for the database and the ABAP central instance, Java Central Services have also become a Single Point of Failure. These services must also be made highly available via the cluster. All resources belonging to a service (such as processes, disks, IP addresses, and so forth) are therefore combined in a resource group. So, in the event of an error, a complete group is always moved to another node in the cluster.

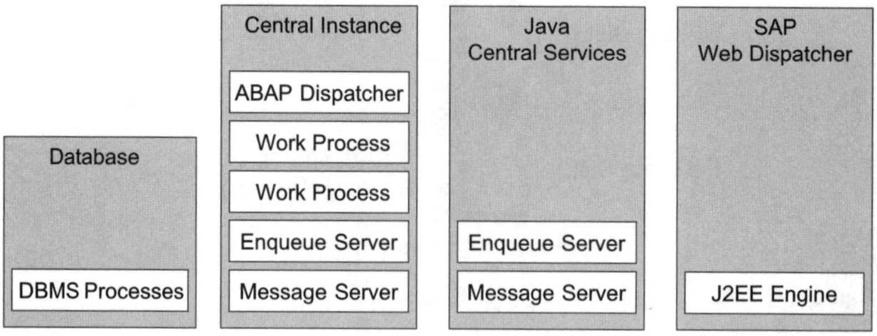

Figure 7.8 Single Points of Failure in SAP Software

Database failure When a database server fails, you must always consider the possibility that the main memory still contains transactions that have not yet been saved to the storage subsystem. This could cause a loss of consistency in the transactions. For this reason, databases are implemented in a way that transactions are either carried out in their entirety, or not at all. To achieve this, rollback information is written for any transaction.

As soon as the database is available again on the adoptive computer after the failover, it uses the rollback information to reverse processing for all open transactions. Also, all completed transactions are written back to the data files that had not been changed by a save/checkpoint before the crash. This "instance recovery" usually takes only a few seconds in an OLTP system, but, in extreme cases, it could take several hours if very large transactions need to be rolled back.

Rollback in the background

To ensure that employees can start working again as soon as possible, even for long roll back runs (usually large batch jobs that do not send any SQL commit work statements for hours), most database systems provide a rollback in parallel with productive operation. This means that the database is restored to operation quickly, even though it's with reduced performance while the rollback is still running in the background.

Because the database instance started on the adoptive computer has still the same network address, the SAP application instances can create the necessary connections automatically as soon as the database is operational again (DBRECONNECT).

Distributed Databases

In database systems that are distributed across several instances on different computers (for example Oracle9i Real Application Cluster, 9iRAC), the recovery process is restricted to the transactions involved in the instance that is lost. This takes a fraction of the time required in a standard recovery scenario.

With RAC, a Transparent Application Failover (TAF) is performed. The Web AS instances reconnect to one of the surviving Oracle instances, where new shadow processes are started for these Web AS instances. Also, since the predominantly read database accesses for SAP systems are continued, the failover is to some degree transparent for end users and batch jobs. There is no re-login after a TAF. However, even when using RAC technology, all "non-committed" transactions on the failed database server are lost.

Failure of the central instance

When the (ABAP) central instance (CI) fails, it is restarted automatically on the adoptive computer by the cluster software and is available again within a few minutes. Users who were logged in to the CI must log in again, however. Their user contexts are lost.

Failure of Java Central Services

The Java Central Service can also be made available again quickly after a restart on the adoptive computer. Unlike the central instance, users cannot be logged on to Java Central Services.

Loss of lock tables Because all lock information is lost during a failover of the central instance and Central Services, data consistency can only be guaranteed by restarting all application servers. Some may try to use the TRANSACTION_RESET function to try to avoid restarting application servers. This process is not 100 % secure and should not be used.

Replicated enqueue Starting with Web AS Release 6.40 a "Replicated Enqueue Server" is available which replicates the lock data synchronously to the failover computer. In the event of an error a new enqueue server can be initialized on the adoptive computer by the cluster software, which creates a new lock table from the replicated data. Therefore, the application instances don't need to be restarted. Only application-specific cluster solutions (such as HP Serviceguard Extensions for SAP, for example) can support Replicated Enqueue.

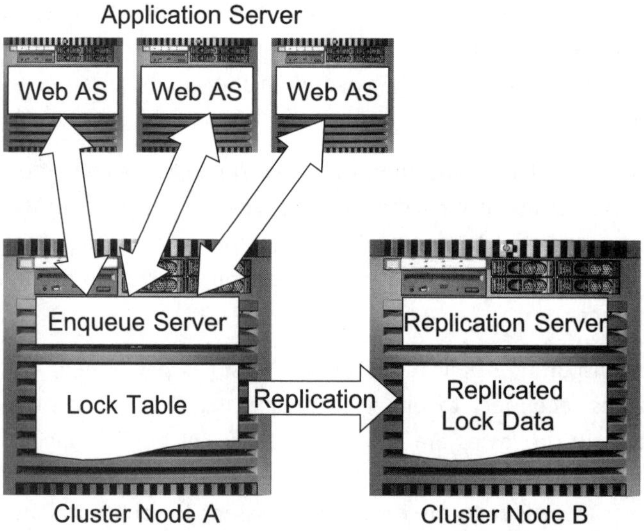

Figure 7.9 Replicated Enqueue Server

Failure of an application instance Pure application servers are not Single Points of Failure and are not usually included in the cluster configuration. If logon groups are defined in the SAP system and are used by users to log on to the system, then these groups are automatically distributed to the remaining application servers when users log on again after a computer failure. The SAP system has a built-in error tolerance as long as at least one application server is available at any one time.

However, all open transactions are lost to users who where logged on to the defective application server. The batch jobs on this machine are terminated. When programming your own batch jobs, you should therefore ensure that they can be restarted. Even an error-tolerant central instance cannot prevent the loss of open transactions on a defective application server.

7.12 SAP Cluster Configurations

Figure 7.10 displays some possible scenarios for SAP systems in error-tolerant clusters.

- **Scenario 1:** The database and Central Instance/Java Central Services are run on different computers during normal operation. When one of the machines fails, both resource groups run together on the remaining machine. In this case, the failover path is bidirectional. In this scenario the system capacity in terms of supported users and transactions is reduced accordingly by the amount of resources of the failed system.
- **Scenario 2:** A shared group with all Single Points of Failure is transferred uni-directionally to an application server. In case of a failover the system capacity as a whole is reduced accordingly by the amount of resources of the failed system. To grant full capacity in case of an emergency, a pure standby system must be used as adoptive system.
- **Scenario 3:** In this last situation, the QA system also acts as a standby system (dual use). The test instance is automatically shut down by the cluster software in the event of a failover, in order to provide enough capacity for the productive system. In this scenario no performance reduction with a negative influence to the business processes will happen.

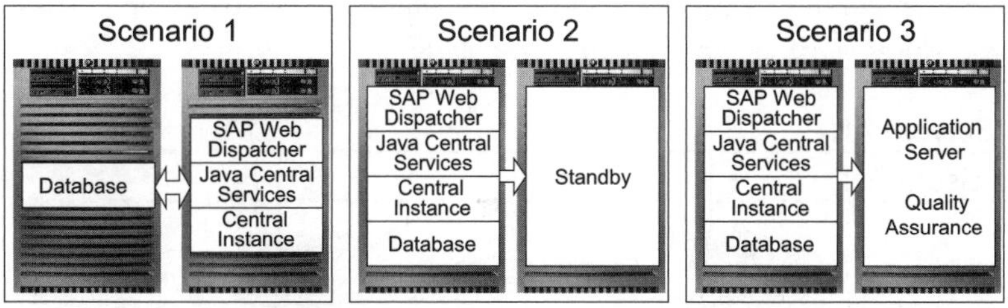

Figure 7.10 Examples for Failover Scenarios

These scenarios and many others are possible with cluster systems such as HP Serviceguard and HP Cluster Manager for Windows SAP systems. In principle, the SPoF for several SAP systems can be distributed across up to 16 cluster nodes. In the event of a failover, the distribution of services and paths to the individual failovers must be planned to meet the requirements of the individual systems.

With Windows, SAP currently supports only a part of Scenario 1 in general. Only systems under a special HP support contract are approved by SAP for scenarios 2 and 3, and also for consolidation scenarios as described in Chapter 15 (see "Failover for Windows" later in this chapter).

The sportive variant: manual failover

The failover principle can also be applied manually, without cluster software "by hand". You just need a storage subsystem and two computers with near identical hardware. Because the identity of a system is stored on its boot partition, when one of the machines fails, you can simply connect its disks to the reserve computer and restart it. However, you must be able to operate both machines using the same system configuration (especially regarding drivers for the I/O cards). During normal operation, the reserve computer can also run a application or test server that can be deactivated in an emergency.

The speed with which the failover can be carried out depends on how quickly a administrator can run down to the computer room or the technician can arrive onsite. Success also depends on whether the technician performs all the tasks correctly while working at considerable speed. We therefore recommend that you implement a color-coding system for the correct insertion slots, and provide clearly visible instructions onsite. Also, technicians should practice the manual failover procedure regularly.

In a SAN, this type of failover is possible without the need to disconnect and reconnect the disks. The disks can be assigned to another computer by reconfiguring Selective Storage Presentation (SSP) or zoning. These procedures must also be practiced regularly.

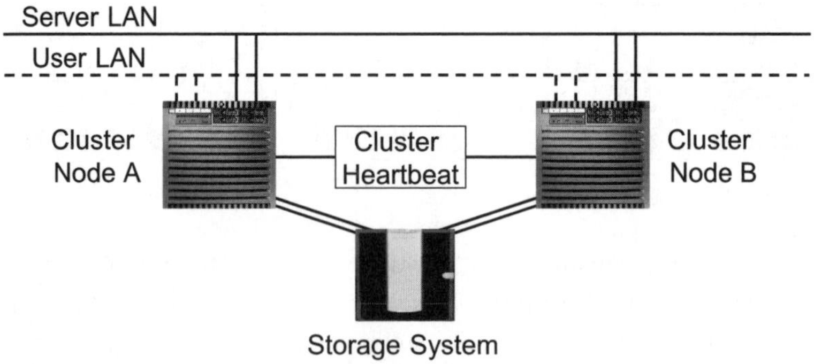

Figure 7.11 Local Cluster

Minimum cluster

Figure 7.11 represents the minimum variant of a cluster. Here, both cluster nodes and a storage system are housed in the same computer room. This configuration, however, provides only security against the failure of a computer, not the loss of the storage system, or of the computer room.

Campus cluster

To protect against the loss of an entire data center, some of the computer capacity and a mirrored copy of the data should be installed in a second computer room, which must be in a different building on the company campus.

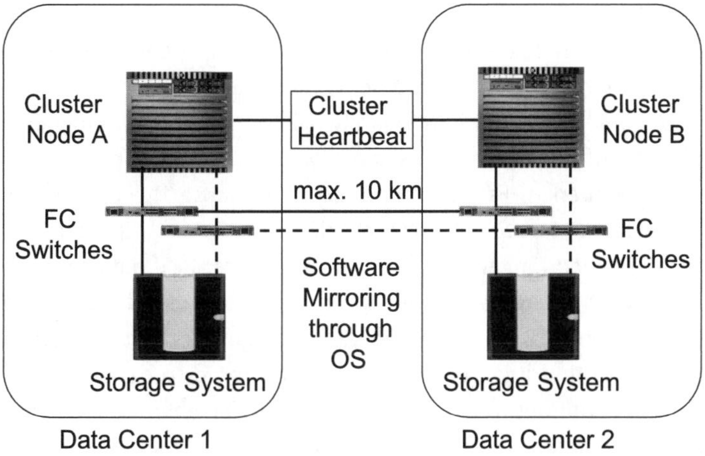

Figure 7.12 Campus Cluster

The individual computers in cluster systems can be distributed between data centers as required, as long as the heartbeat is run via an IP subnet and disk subsystems can be mirrored via a SAN.

When using fiber-optic cables, distances of up to 10 to 20 km are possible (see Figure 7.12). While distances of over 20 km are technically possible, the signal runtimes between the mirrors increase significantly and can affect SAP system performance if you're using synchronous mirroring.

Quorum with two cluster nodes

In a configuration with two cluster nodes, an automatic switch to the failover node cannot always be guaranteed. The quorum (or voting) procedure described above, which all current clusters use to avoid a split brain, can create situations where the "surviving" components cannot determine whether the other part of the cluster has actually failed. In these cases, you must intervene manually.

High-performance and cost-effective mirroring

To avoid additional costs for storage-based data mirroring, data mirroring can be performed using software (Logical Volume Manager, LVM). The

LVM (integrated with HP-UX and other Unix Systems) distributes the read processes between both mirrors and therefore uses the disks of both storage systems. If one of the two storage systems fails, the SAP system will still be up and running.

Windows and Linux systems do not support host-based mirroring in a cluster. Therefore, storage-based mechanisms must always be used for these operating systems. In this case, the SAP system does not continue to run automatically if a storage system is lost. Instead, you must intervene manually.

Rolling disaster

In some unusual failure scenarios, data mirroring with operating system resources can risk corrupting a database. It can create a "rolling disaster," where a data center does not immediately fail completely, but individual components die off (and sometimes come back to life temporarily) in an unpredictable sequence. Failed components can cause the connection between the data centers to fail. For example, data center 1 is productive, but written data is no longer replicated in data center 2. If data center 1 fails, data center 2 will take over operations without the last data being written to data center 2. In more complex configurations, it is possible that only a part of the disk areas is no longer mirrored to data center 2, while mirroring continues to work for another part. Takeover by data center 2 would completely corrupt the database. If you want to prevent these situations, we recommend using a metro cluster described in the next section.

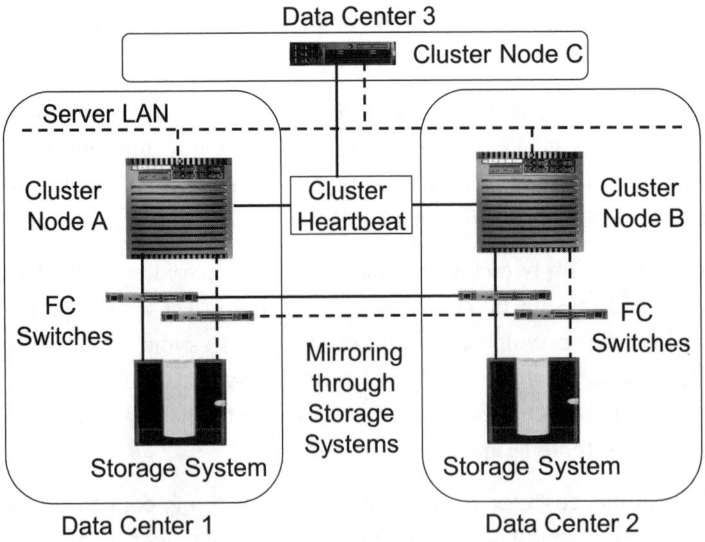

Figure 7.13 Metro Cluster

Metro cluster The metro cluster provides maximum availability with automatic disaster recovery in the event of the loss of a data center due to all conceivable causes. The following measures also make this solution superior to the campus cluster solution:

- Placing an arbitrator node in a third data center prevents any stalemate situations in the quorum mechanisms. The arbitrator node requires very few resources, so a small server will suffice. The arbitrator node itself can also be configured for high availability.
- Data mirroring carried out synchronously with storage resources (for example, Continuous Access with HP's XP or Enterprise Virtual Arrays, Symmetrix Remote Data Facility with EMC). These arrays have algorithms that prevent data corruption through "rolling disaster."
- Coupling HP Serviceguard and storage systems performs a failover on both server and storage in parallel. This ensures that the SAP system can still perform a failover without the need for manual intervention in the event of the loss of an entire data center.

As for the campus cluster solution, the maximum distance between the data centers is determined by the range of the connection between the data centers and the latency time during synchronous writing to both storage subsystems. The I/O cycle is only completed when the caches of both storage systems have confirmed the write process. This can affect performance over longer distances.

Continental cluster In some cases, even the distances possible with a metro cluster (up to 60 km) are not sufficient for the security requirements of a company. This is particularly applicable if the company is located in an area that is prone to hurricanes, or if it is in a geologically unstable area, such as the San Andreas fault in California. These companies need cluster configurations that span countries or continents.

Over these kinds of distances, I/O operations can no longer be performed synchronously. Therefore, continental clusters are based on asynchronous I/O. Considerable bandwidth is required between the data centers. Nevertheless, many companies that require this level of disaster protection use continental clusters.

Failover for Windows Microsoft Cluster Servers (MSCS) have a few more restrictions than do UNIX systems. The computer systems must be certified by SAP and must have successfully passed Microsoft cluster certification.

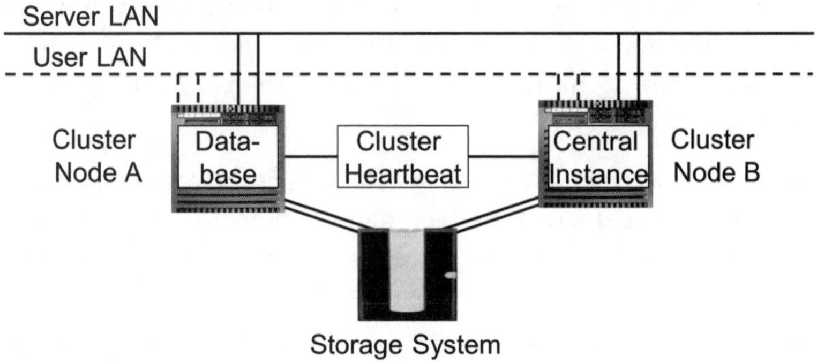

Figure 7.14 Windows Clusters Supported by SAP

At the time this book was printed, SAP currently supported only a two-node cluster as shown in Figure 7.14. In this configuration, the database runs on one node and the central instance runs on the other node. Additional systems or application servers in the cluster are not supported.

You should note that both computers must also be in a domain with Windows Active Directory Services. A Microsoft cluster server cannot be installed in a workgroup configuration. Because SAP recommends a separate domain for SAP administrators, this restriction does not make much difference. The cluster nodes must not be configured as domain controllers.

Together with Microsoft, the SAP HP Competence Center has developed the "HP Competent Cluster Service." This service provides the installation and support for multi-node, multi-instance SAP clusters on Windows. This cluster solution covers nearly all the scenarios possible under UNIX. Implementation and support for these scenarios is provided together with the HP Service organization. SAP tolerates these types of clusters, as long as the system manufacturer supports them. The detailed support process can be seen in OSS note 826119.

In the past, restoring a system after a disaster was not a trivial task, because MSCS was based on disk signatures. Therefore, the disk signatures on the physical disks had to correspond to those in the Windows registry, in order to ensure that the cluster functioned properly. Now, NTBackup copies disk signatures and the cluster configuration, so that a shared disk crash is no longer a problem.

Failover for APO

In principle, all the methods described for increasing availability can be used without restriction on all SAP solutions based on standard Web AS.

As demonstrated in Chapters 1 and 2, there are other components where this is only partially true, or simply not the case.

An example of this is the SAP Advanced Planner and Optimizer (SAP APO) because, besides the typical database instance found at any system, the liveCache, implements a memory-resident database instance.

The data in the APO system is distributed between the APO database and the liveCache; some data is stored redundantly, other data only exists in the liveCache. The liveCache has its own logging mechanism, which writes savepoints to the disks at intervals of a few minutes, without waiting for the open transactions to be completed. This means that processes in areas such as Demand Planning, SNP Time Series, and all planning versions are backed up. Transaction simulations and simulation versions are not logged. Consequently, simulations are lost in the event of a hardware failure and must be performed again.

There are two options for ensuring availability:

- A standard cluster for APO and liveCache; downtimes between 15 and 90 minutes can be expected for this option.
- A "hot standby" liveCache; where the liveCache is replicated by shipping the log files. This ensures that the liveCache is available again within minutes.

For reasons of performance, there is no two-phase commit between the two databases. Changes are committed separately in both. Therefore, automatic point-in-time recovery is not possible. After a failure, special reports (SMQ1, SMQ2) must be run to identify inconsistencies to be repaired manually.

Optimizer, IPC etc.

Components that don't store any data of their own, such as APO Optimizer, must simply be provided in a redundant configuration. The same applies, for example, to the Customer Relationship Management (CRM) components Internet Pricing and Configurator (IPC). Here too, it will suffice to install at least two instances on separate machines and register them in the mySAP CRM or ERP system. These instances provide load balancing, thereby ensuring availability.

Dimensioning clusters

As we mentioned previously, dimensioning computers in a cluster depends primarily on the level of performance that must be guaranteed, even after the failure of a component based on a Service Level Agreement (SLA). You need to assess the various failure scenarios and determine whether the resulting loss in performance can be tolerated, or whether it has to be bolstered with reserve capacity.

Today, because of the enormous growth in processing power over recent years, just two computers are usually sufficient for the database and SAP applications of large, productive SAP installations. However, without taking further measures after a failover, this leaves only 50 % of the processing power. In a consolidated central system, no application servers are available for the failover. In this case, we recommend that you use a sufficiently dimensioned test system as an adoptive node.

50 % capacity means a maximum 50 % of users can access the system

Still, the memory setup on the failover computers is even more important than the CPU performance. While poor CPU performance "only" leads to drastically lengthened response times, low memory resources lead to extremely poor performance because of high swapping/paging rates. In other words, the SAP system continues to run, but it is practically unusable. In an emergency, a main memory that is reduced by 50 % also means that only 50 % of the users can log on. For these reasons, organizational measures must be taken in order to ensure that only company-critical transactions are performed during these periods.

This justifies the need for careful planning and testing. In some cases, database and application instances can be provided with special profiles for a failover scenario so that they can operate with less memory, but still only a reduced number of users and transactions can be supported. If such a low-service level is not acceptable for the line of business departments, the necessary budget must be made available to provide the necessary additional resources, for example through temporary capacity solutions.

7.13 Cluster Consistency

Even clustered systems can fail as the result of a user error. "A common mistake people make when trying to design something completely foolproof is to underestimate the ingenuity of complete fools."[4]

Also, all solutions intended to increase availability are bound to increase the complexity of the system landscape. In a failover cluster, you must use the same exact environment on all cluster nodes (system parameters, file systems, authorizations, and so forth), in order for the application to start and to function smoothly. In a Cluster, every application package is

4 Douglas Adams (1952–2001): *A Hitchhikers Guide to the Galaxies.*

like a special key that must fit exactly to several locks. If you need to change the application (the key), exactly the same modification must be made on all locks (the nodes).

If you can't deliver "bullet-proof" Change Management, there's always the risk that changes only on one "side" of the cluster will be carried out and not on the other. During emergencies, this can mean that the "fail" works for sure, but maybe not the "over"!

For example Operating system parameters that are maintained differently on the computers in a failover configuration can cause the SAP application to fail after the failover. During normal operation, however, these differences will usually remain unnoticed.

Inconsistencies of this kind can occur in:

- Directory and file structures
- Operating system and SAP core parameters
- Shared memory segments, swap space
- Symbolic links
- Authorizations
- Network configuration
- Spool configuration
- Security settings
- NFS links
- User and group configurations

"Simple" and other catastrophes

Depending on the type of inconsistency, two possible situations can arise during a failover. With the simple version, the application cannot be started on the failover computer. This type of inconsistency can be easily recognized by failover tests and repaired as necessary.

With the sneakier version, the application starts to run, but not at full performance. This effect can only be recognized during a real failover of the productive system.

Changing parameters without a failover test

Often, the memory parameters for the database are increased incrementally, without carrying out a failover test. In the event of a failover, the database on the failover computer has increased memory requirements initially, in addition to the processes already running there. This often leads to more main memory being allocated than is physically available. Consequently, the system is practically paralyzed due to extensive swapping. If a failover test had been carried out, this problem would have been recognized, and either more memory would have been provided, or the parameters would have been modified to meet these new requirements.

Failover test

The typical procedure in a failover test is to simulate a failure of the primary computer and to start the application on the replacement computer. If you can then log on to the system, the test is considered to be successful. Generally, these tests are performed four times a year, or after every major change.

If the computers and the data centers are set up in exactly the same way (including the network connection to the users), the failover test can be performed without a fail back. In this case, production remains permanent on the previous failover computers, and only the roles are exchanged.

If a fail back is needed after the test, you must ensure that the application cannot be used productively again, immediately after the failover. Otherwise, before the fail back, you must ensure that no users are logged on to the system and that no batch jobs are running.

Problems with interfaces

Unfortunately, switchover tests can cover only some of the functionality. Interfaces in particular cannot usually be tested. Therefore, starting up an R/3 system on the failover server does not necessarily guarantee that the printing, faxing, archiving, or data exchange will also work.

Real Life Example: Insufficient Failover Test

At a mechanical engineering company, an R/3 system was being used to provide planning data to a CISC-based control computer in manufacturing. The control computer and the SAP system were being run on clusters. The cluster functions were tested regularly.

At 10 a.m. one work day, monitoring reported the failure of an SAP computer. After automatic failover, the SAP system was available again after about 10 minutes, and users could continue to work without any problems. A few hours later, however, manufacturing had ground to a halt, because planning data was no longer being transferred to the computers.

An analysis showed that a program that was supposed to fetch the data from the SAP system had no authorization to do so. Apparently, the corresponding entry for the control computer was missing in the security profile of the SAP server that lists all the computers with access authorization, the reason being that the control computer had been replaced a few months ago. When this was done, the old computer and the new computer were run in parallel for a short period to allow all the applications and configurations to be transferred. To enable this transferral of data, the new machine was assigned a new name and a new network ID, both of which were configured on all the computers in the system, except the standby computer for the SAP system.

This did not cause a problem during productive operation, because the primary computer was correctly configured. The missing authorization was not noticed during the failover tests, because no production data was transferred during these tests.

Cluster Consistency Service for SAP

To avoid these kinds of problems, SAP HP Competence Center has developed the Cluster Consistency Service as an automated, rule-based monitoring system. At regular intervals, this tool collects and compares all the parameters required for a secure changeover from all computers. This can amount to several thousand parameters per SAP system.

Every inconsistency recognized is logged with a detailed explanation of the consequences to be expected and reported via standard alarm interfaces such as SNMP-Trap, pager, email, or SMS.

This information can also be used for automated documentation of the cluster. This provides the administrator with a tool that proactively detects and analyzes sources of errors, before they can develop into a problem. Cluster Consistency Service works with internal rules that are based on many years of know-how from experienced cluster specialists.

Permanent monitoring

The permanent monitoring of inconsistencies in the cluster configuration ensures a secure failover. Contrary to a failover test, permanent monitoring not only ensures that the application will start on the reserve computer, but also that the connection to all other solutions in the mySAP Business Suite are working correctly. In theory, this proactive monitoring of the cluster can replace maintenance windows for failover tests to a large extent. Many of our customers are enabled by Cluster Consistency Service for SAP to reduce the time windows for test fail over from four per year to a single one.

Single System Image Cluster

In a Single System Image Cluster (SSI), all nodes share a common file system and a common operating system installation. This means that every cluster node automatically has the same data view, operating system, devices, and users. Any change made to a cluster node is automatically reflected in the whole cluster. This design prevents inconsistencies from arising due to changes that cannot be reflected on all other nodes.

On the other hand, the shared installation is also a limitation. A computer administration error immediately affects all the nodes in the cluster. Patch imports usually also indicate downtime for the entire cluster.

Implementing the SSI cluster design therefore represents an enormous technical challenge. For example, all locks on any object must be managed across the entire cluster, requiring a Distributed Lock Manager. Due to various technical restrictions, SSI clusters are limited in the number of nodes they can have and how those nodes are distributed. Not least of all, the maximum distance between the cluster nodes is limited to a few kilometers.

Of all the SAP-relevant system platforms, only HP Tru64 UNIX offers an SSI cluster. For the most part, the other platforms provide a cluster-wide file system.

7.14 Data Backup

Chapter 6 describes how you can use storage systems to secure data against physical loss. Unfortunately, none of these measures can also ensure logical consistency. Even systems with storage systems that are mirrored over several kilometers are not immune to software errors, because these errors are written immediately to both storage arrays.

Backing up logical consistency

Data that is changed below SAP transaction level by hardware failures, software bugs, and especially human error creates an inconsistency. This means that the data can no longer be relied on, making the entire database unusable for a business application, even if the data itself is available.

An inconsistency can be caused by technical faults (for example, corrupt database blocks due to bit errors in the data buses), as well as programming errors (for example, overwriting the wrong table), or human errors (for example, importing a transport to the wrong system, or inadvertently deleting a tablespace).

Importing a tape backup and recovering the database (Restore and Recovery) is the classic, and often the only, method for saving an inconsistent system. With the ever-increasing size of databases, the time required to do this is becoming more of a problem.

Shadow databases

Solutions based on a logical copy (shadow) of the database, in addition to a cluster solution, provide another option for protecting company-critical data.

The shadow-database principle is based on the fact that productive databases constantly log all transactions in log files, which are archived so that a consistent data set can be restored after a crash. But in addition, the log files can also be transferred to a second database (log shipping). This second database is set to run in recovery mode. This way the second database performs all the transactions of the primary database with a time delay. It therefore represents a logical copy (or "shadow") of the productive database (see Figure 7.15).

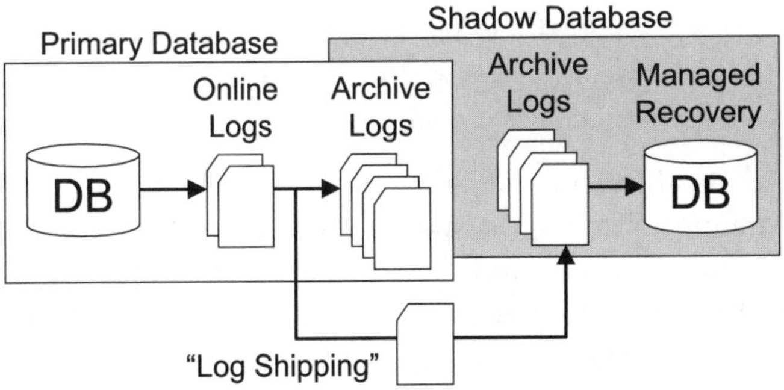

Figure 7.15 The Shadow Database Principle

When the consistency of the primary database is lost, the shadow simply needs to be activated to serve as a replacement. Because there is no need to import the tape backup, the recovery time is shortened considerably. Because only archive log files are transferred to the shadow database, however, recovery is only possible up until the last completed log switch, if the productive computer is also no longer available at operating system level or disk level (that is, for a recovery from tape). If the online log files of the primary database are still available, then these can be copied from the productive computer and run on the shadow computer. A possible solution here would be to replicate the online log files via the storage hardware.

After activating the shadow database, the SAP application servers must log on to the new database computer. This can be performed automatically via reconnect, provided the IP-address of the database server has been transferred to the shadow database.

Excluding logical errors

Shadow databases avoid logical errors that occur in physically mirrored systems, which destroy the integrity of the data on the mirror at the same time, since on a Shadow database all write processes in which errors of this kind can arise are performed again completely separately in the shadow database.

Even bugs in the database software can be intercepted quite easily, because the data files are written by different processes than those that write the log files. If the database writes a corrupt block to a data file, the corresponding information in the log is most likely correct. If, however, the data file is correct and the log is corrupt, then the shadow database terminates the recovery process because of the corrupt log. In this case, although the shadow database needs to be recreated, it still recognizes in time that the log is corrupt. If the log had been included in the data backup, and the database was later restored using this log, recovery would have been interrupted at that point.

Logical errors created by user errors or software errors in the application are, however, transferred to the shadow database. Because the shadow database always runs asynchronously at a planned time interval that is slightly behind the primary database, log shipping can be stopped before the error destroys the shadow. For this reason, the interval is set for up to 24 hours, in order to provide enough time to react. Selecting the time delay is always a delicate balance between providing as much time as possible to notice an error in production, and the shortest time feasible for the activation of the shadow database. In extremely critical systems, this is an impossible compromise to reach, so there are cases of systems running several shadow databases with different time delays.

Distance and network bandwidth

The distance between the systems is unlimited, because log shipping is not time-critical. This means that shadow database configurations can be run on separate continents without any problems. When setting up the shadow database, however, you will need to reserve enough bandwidth to ensure that the database can be copied to the shadow version within the required time. Alternatively, this copy process can be performed by transporting data on tape. Once the shadow database is up and running, only the bandwidth to copy all logs in time is needed.

The machine running the shadow database does not need to be as high-performance as the primary database machine, because it does not have to deal with any load peaks while running in recovery mode. After a failover, however, less performance will be available for productive operation.

Caution, data loss is still a problem!

One of the main disadvantages of shadow databases is that data is always lost in the event of disasters due to the asynchronous nature of the process (all the archive logs that had not yet been transferred). Data that is outside the database is not replicated by the shadow database either. Therefore, a shadow database cannot replace a full failover solution, but should ideally be used to complement such a solution to guard against logical errors.

It is also possible to mirror the online and archive logs physically across the locations. This process ensures the availability of the logs containing the data for all completed transactions on the recovery side. They can then be imported manually into the shadow database. Data in the file system (for example, transport directory) should then also be mirrored across the locations in this way.

Another advantage of the shadow database is that it checks all logs created. The continuous recovery of the shadow database means that the system is always checking whether the logs are working. If a log is incorrect, the system terminates the shadow database, issues a warning, and prompts you to look for the cause of the error. The shadow database must then be recreated.

Backing up the shadow database

Shadow databases can be stopped at any time without affecting production. For this reason, offline backups of the shadow database can be made at any time. This is often a valuable alternative to split-mirror backups, if you need to make a data backup without affecting production. Exports for consistency checking can also be made from the shadow database without affecting production.

Brtools or Libelle

With the exception of Informix, you can set up shadow databases for most database types used with SAP. The database management tools provided by SAP, brtools, support the creation and operation of a shadow database. However, brtools are subject to certain functional restrictions when it comes to shadow databases. Tools from Libelle,[5] for example,

5 Go to *www.libelle.com*.

make it much easier to set up and operate shadow databases efficiently. These tools have the following advantages:

- You can set up the shadow database at the press of a button (or via Script). Compressed copying to set up the shadow database with several parallel processes, dynamic process increase/decrease. Configurable package sizes (for optimum network load). Support of "Copy via Pipe" (with MS SQL, DB2, MaxDB).
- Failback after failover at the press of a button.
- Tracking of DB structures upon structural changes, recognition of newly added data files, mappings when file systems are different.
- Failover of IP address, with switch of entire SAP system (CI/DB) to the standby computer when required. The application servers don't need to be reconfigured.
- Monitoring of all processes on both sides. Alarms issued upon deviation from normal status.
- The time interval between log switches can be configured, and changed dynamically (for example, depending on time or week day).
- FSShadow for replication of all files important to the application that are not in the database (for example, transport directory, */sapmnt* directory, IDocs, profile).

7.15 Backup/Restore and Recovery

Despite the various options of modern storage systems for storing data in various versions as snapshots, clones, and replicas, you still need a solid backup strategy. This is because, for reasons of space, clones can usually be stored in only one or two versions. Tape is still the classic medium of choice, especially for storing older versions for revision.

The critical path: Restore and Recovery

In general, the backup infrastructure should be backwards planned (that is, you should consider the critical path for restore and recovery first). If you know how to follow this path securely and within the required amount of time, the backup procedure can be based on this.

Quick Recovery with Shadow Database

All SAP certified databases use transaction logging so that the data can be restored after a crash by recovering the transactions logged in the redo logs; however, this redo process takes a lot of time. If, for example, you import a tape backup that was created 24 hours ago, the system must then redo all the logs created in this period in order to bring the database back to its current status. Even if this generally takes less time than is needed to create the logs, redoing them can take longer than importing the tape backup.

If Restore and Recovery cannot be performed within the required time, you should consider using a shadow database. Because the shadow database always runs at a set interval "behind" the productive sytem, you can estimate the recovery time precisely.

Redo logs

For a successful recovery, all redo logs since the last imported backup must be available without exception. Even if only one log is lost, usually, you cannot return the database to its current state using Restore and Recovery. Therefore, the logs are often called a database administrator's "crown jewels."

To guarantee availability of the redo logs, you should take advantage of the database option to write two copies of the logs in parallel. Backing up the log disks with RAID systems does not make this second copy superfluous. Also, every log should be backed up to tape in duplicate, on different tapes, with different drives.

Disk Space for Logs

An SAP database writes several GBs of archive logs per day. The usage level of the archive file is a critical indicator, because an overflow that prevents redo logs from being transferred to the archive can cause the database to freeze (archive stuck) or worse. When restoring all the required logs from tape to disk, you should also ensure that there is enough disk space to store all the logs created in a 24 to 48 hour period.

Online or offline backup?

In the past, a database would often be backed up when it was inactive over night, or during the weekend (offline backup). Now, however, with a global economy, there is hardly any window of time during which the databases of productive SAP components can be deactivated. For this reason, today data is usually backed up during productive operation (online backup).

From the data security perspective, offline backups are also no longer absolutely necessary. The exceptions that confirm this rule are:

- Before a large change to the application (importing lots of transports) or before upgrading the database or SAP software, an offline backup should still be performed.
- If a log is lost during productive operation, then a backup must be created immediately; otherwise, the gap in the log chain will make it impossible to recover the current status.

Interruption in the log chain

- The log chain can, however, also be interrupted by activating a shadow database, for example, since this resets the log sequence numbers.

To avoid the risk of data loss in these cases, you should create an offline backup. When performing an online backup, you should consider that transactions can still be executed during the backup, and these transactions will be lost if the disk crashes before the backup is completed.

Because the window of time for these particular tasks is often very narrow, the backup should take as little time as possible. The solution here can be the creation of snapshots/clones, or simply, to stop the shadow database. If the upgrade is unsuccessful, the shadow database is activated with the old data status.

Quick backups

Online backup technology (and fast tapes) means that the backup duration is no longer critical; however, online backups can greatly influence the performance of a productive database due to the high I/O requirements. The faster the data is read in order to shorten the time needed for the backup, the greater the effect on productive database performance.

The criterion when considering quick backups or restores is therefore the database size. You'll save yourself a lot of time, work, and hardware resources if you can keep your database small through constant archiving.

Local backup

In the simplest possible configuration, the tape drives are connected directly to the database computer via SCSI or FC connections (see Figure 7.16). Here, the data flows from the storage system disks via the main memory of the database computer to the tape systems. Local backups can also be used in cluster configurations. In this case, every computer can save its data to the shared backup system. You should ensure that both cluster members do not attempt to access the same tape drive.

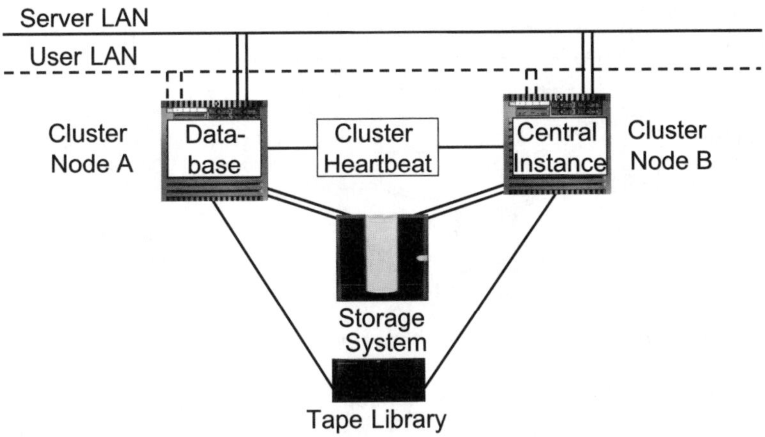

Figure 7.16 Local Backup Configuration

A local backup places considerable strain on the resources of a productive database server. Even if the online backup is performed during periods of low workload, it can still have a negative effect on the performance of the SAP system. Therefore, an additional CPU should be provided per tape drive. Main memory and I/O capacity should also be expanded accordingly. You should note that locally connected tape drives cannot be accessed by other systems.

Network backup

The data on several systems can also be backed up together with the files needed for booting the application servers via a local data network with a central backup solution. The advantages of a network backup solution include central administration and shared use of a tape library.

Because large data quantities must be moved during backup and recovery, we recommend that you provide a separate, virtual Gigabit Ethernet for the backup (see Figure 7.17). The operating system and backup software must be configured so that the data is transferred via the correct network in each case.

This variant also has the disadvantage of heavy workloads for the database server during the backup process. Consequently, a network backup is often used only for systems with lighter workloads, such as development, test, or training systems.

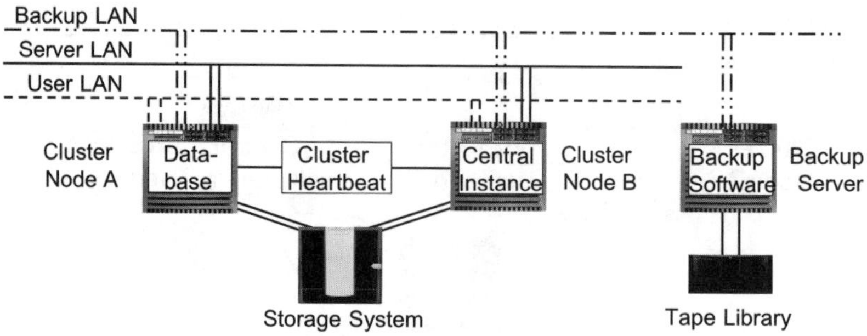

Figure 7.17 Network Backup

SAN backup

It seems reasonable to provide all database servers with direct access to the tape library via the Storage Area Network (SAN). This enables you to perform backups without having to go through the shared data network. Furthermore, all database servers can share the tape library. The backup server in Figure 7.18 is used only to manage the backup processes.

In practice, however, mixed systems using SAP backup and network backups are often implemented. In this case, the backup server also saves the data from the less critical systems via the network. Here too, the backup process affects database performance.

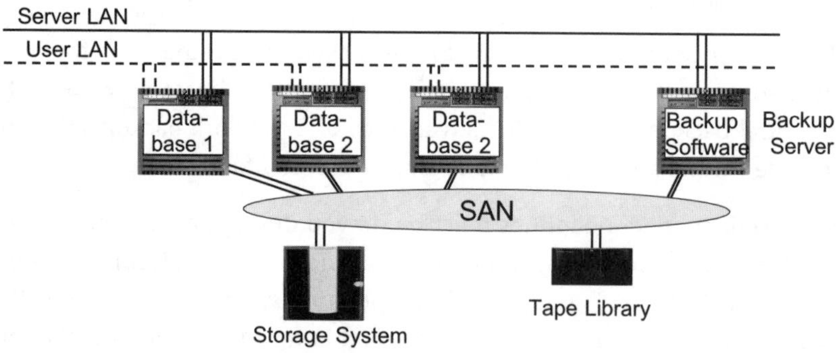

Figure 7.18 SAN Backup

Zero-downtime backup

The downtime when backing up a productive SAP database can be reduced to practically zero using replicated data mirrors (clones or split mirrors), or frozen dataviews (snapshots). The technologies for this are described in Chapter 6. The data backup is performed by the decoupled mirror, or the snapshot mounted on the backup server and saved to tape. Decoupling of the mirror/creation of the snapshot takes but a few seconds, and the database only has to be kept in backup mode for this short period.

Most high-performance storage systems and backup software certified by SAP (for example, HP Data Protector and Veritas NetBackup) support zero-downtime backups. The solutions on the market are usually integrated with the SAP-backint interface, allowing the backups to be scheduled in SAP CCMS.

Another option for creating backups without affecting the performance of the productive system is to use a shadow database, which can be stopped and backed up offline without any problems.

Tape systems

Magnetic tape is still the most widely used medium for storing large data quantities. Compared to all other storage media, it is the cheapest per gigabyte (although FATA systems are catching up). When choosing tape technology, as well as capacity, the main consideration is read/write performance. This is because the data volumes to save are constantly increasing, while the time allotted for backups is constantly shrinking.

In the past, the capacity and especially the read/write performance of the various magnetic tape technologies were relatively low. The advent of Linear Tape Open (LTO), however, means that tape solutions can now meet the requirements of large SAP systems (see Table 7.1).

Tape drives	Capacity (GB)	Throughput (MB/s)	Throughput (GB/h)
DAT 8/DDS-2	4	0,5	1,8
DAT 24/DDS-3	12	1	3,6
DAT 40/DDS-4	20	3	10,8
DLT 40 or 4,000	20	1,5	5,4
DLT 70 or 7,000	35	5	18
DLT 80 or 8,000	40	6	21,6
LTO, 1st generation	100	15	54
LTO, 2nd generation	200	30	108
LTO, 3rd generation	400	80	288

Table 7.1 Capacity (without Compression) and Transfer Rates for Current Magnetic Tape Technologies

Tape drive manufacturers often specify the transfer rate and maximum capacity for a compression ratio of 2:1. In our experience, however, the data of a productive SAP system can be compressed even further.

Backup to tape or disk?

With the introduction of FATA disks, affordable backups to disk are almost within reach. Backups to disk have two advantages:

- Disks break down less often than tapes and can also be protected against breakdowns more easily (with RAID technology).
- With disks, data can be accessed in any sequence. When performing a tape backup, you have to consider the structure of the data on the individual tapes in order to achieve the required performance during the subsequent restore.

For these reasons, you should think about this alternative, at least as the first stage of a two-stage backup. Backup software such as HP Dataprotector, for example, supports two-stage scenarios of this kind, in which a backup generation is written to disk in the first stage, and then copied to tape for longer storage in the second stage.

System recovery at the press of a button

When a computer breaks down completely, system recovery is usually a very time-consuming procedure. First, the installation media must install an emergency operating system (Disaster Recovery Operating System) on the replacement computer, to enable recovery of the original operating system configuration from the tape backup. Only then can the system begin to restore the database itself.

To accelerate this process, tape systems from various manufacturers provide One Button Disaster Recovery (OBDR). During this process, the firmware on the tape drivers emulates a bootable CD drive. In this way, the computer starts recovery of a virtual CD image that contains the original operating system configuration with all drivers and the backup software. By using HP-UX with Ignite/UX, you can employ this technique to restore a system disk in one to two hours.

Restoring mySAP system landscapes

Cross-system data consistency is essential to back up and restore entire mySAP system landscapes. The following scenarios can arise:

- A system is deactivated for some time by a "recoverable error." This scenario is annoying, since the SAP system can no longer be accessed by users; however, it is non-critical in terms of cross-system data consistency. Importing the last backup and rerunning all logs will suffice. The system is not reset, but a full recovery is performed up to the last transaction.
- During an upgrade or other large change to the system, all systems should be able to be reset to a previously known point in time. Because all the systems are out of operation before the upgrade or

change, a backup of all systems ensures data consistency across all systems.

- Resetting a system to any given point in time. Because this means that interface data exchanged with other systems after this particular point in time can no longer be traced, you must reset all the systems.
- If all systems need to be reset (because of data loss or inconsistency across several systems, or data loss in one system with far-reaching consequences for other systems), then the most recent backups are restored and a Point-in-Time recovery is performed for all systems by rerunning logs. Even if the backups are consistent across all systems, the result of the Point-in-Time recovery will be inconsistent. This is because despite precise recovery of the individual systems, due to a lack of synchronization at application level, the status of the individual systems will always differ slightly.

Technologies that synchronize the status of all operational databases by using checkpoints and then freezing them (federated backup), in order to create a snapshot/clone of all databases, are not necessary for these scenarios. They can, however, be useful if consistent copies of the entire system landscape must be generated to create test systems. Federated backup is described in documentation from the SAP Advanced Technology Group.[6]

A hitherto unsolved problem is that there are no cross-system synchronization or checkpoint mechanisms, therefore, consistency can only be guaranteed for the time of the backup, and not for the recovery to any given point in time after this backup.

System copies in mySAP system landscapes

Test systems are regularly set up as copies of the productive system. However, the job is not done by just installing a copy of the system from the tapes of yesterday or deploying split mirror technology. What you get in such a case is a clone which can't be used as a test system. To convert the clone into an individual you must generate a new System ID (SID), change IP addresses, and a whole bunch of other things. Without tools, creating a test system entails a great deal of manual work and usually takes almost a full working day to complete.

The use of technologies such as HP System Copy Service for SAP significantly reduces the overall runtime for a project of this kind. The System Copy Services (SCS) tools can be used to create a test system from a clone

6 Go to *http://service.sap.com/atg.*

of the SAP system generated via Split Mirror. This is done in a few minutes and is achieved via automated modifications to operating systems and SAP parameters (SID, services, users, hostname, and profiles).

In a mySAP system landscape in which the individual system parameters are constantly interacting, however, copying the systems individually and generating the corresponding test systems is only sufficient for isolated test scenarios. This is because this approach negates cross-system data consistency. To create a valid environment for testing system interaction, you need to make a consistent and simultaneous copy of the entire mySAP system landscape.

You should also consider that SAP has introduced the Logical System with ALE and mySAP products in particular. Every client has its own Logical System that uniquely identifies it within the overall SAP landscape. When data is exchanged via ALE, this data is identified using the ID of the logical system of the issuing system. This is an "origin ID" that prevents master data from an external system, for example, from being changed in the "recipient system."

7.16 Application

Unplanned downtimes due to application problems

It is important to remember that the programmers who write the code for company-critical applications are only human. Despite all their efforts, it is impossible to rule out the possibility of errors in millions of lines of code. Application errors range from complete system failure to partial breakdown or gradual loss of service. As shown in Chapter 1, SAP provides a cleverly designed Quality Assurance (QA) system. This can only take effect, however, if its mechanisms are also applied consistently. This is especially relevant to customer "home-grown" developments.

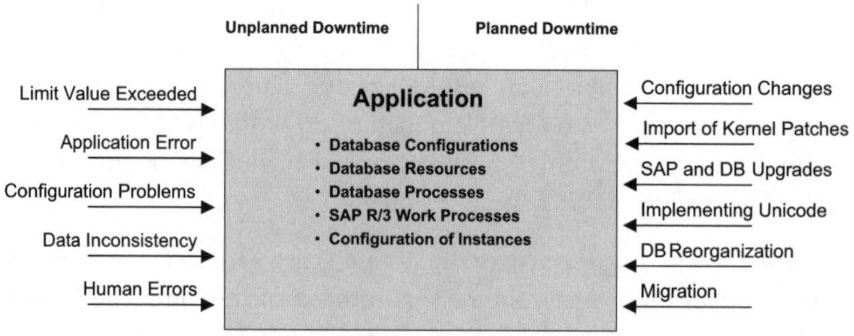

Figure 7.19 Factors Influencing the Application

Real Life Example: ABAP Code Causes Unexpected Interactions

A customer created his own report and imported it to an R/3 system. After developing the ABAP code, he carried out function tests in the test system, but only had time to test the functional part of the ABAP code and not the way it interacted with the rest of the system. During productive operation, and only in a very specific configuration, an error in the execution logic caused the ABAP program to delete all the data records in a 1 GB table that contained the most important company data.

Because the error was only recognized at 5 p.m. and the last data backup was carried out at 2 a.m. the previous night, a database restore would mean losing all the work performed that day. Instead, a massive overnight effort was made to install a copy of the productive system on the free hard drive areas with the last data backup. The affected table was copied to the productive system.

In a similar case, a report at an engineering and construction plant deleted 40,000 out of 50,000 bills of material. To restore them in full, a completely separate production system had to be created in which the redo logs could be run. Since then, the customer now has a three-system environment!

Practical experience shows, that many application problems can be traced to more trivial causes. For example, you can often find a relationship between software instabilities and certain performance requirements.

Real Life Example: Daily Crash

The SAP system of a company regularly crashed every morning between 8 a.m. and 9 a.m. After some root cause analysis, it turned out that the large numbers of users who were logging on to the time management system in the morning had created a parameter overflow.

In addition to low parameter settings, problems at the lower levels also affect the application. If, for example, the archive file system of an Oracle database is 100 % full, the database freezes, which then causes the SAP system to freezes. You cannot even log on to the R/3 system any more in this case.

EarlyWatch and GoingLive service SAP provides GoingLive and EarlyWatch services to check systems before productive operation start and during ongoing operation. You can use EarlyWatch sessions to check the workload on database servers and application servers, as well as the settings of the SAP instance, the database, and the operating system. The GoingLive service also provides a "sizing plausibility check," and checks important module-related (FI, CO) or system-related (EBP, APO, EP) Customizing settings. These services are provided by SAP within the framework of a maintenance contract. Among other things, this service issues warning messages and optimization proposals when it recognizes critical workload situations and badly chosen parameter settings.

Holistic analysis EarlyWatch sessions, however, only see SAP systems from the SAP perspective. They have a restricted view of the operating system, servers, and hard disk systems. Therefore, potential problems may not be recognized or they can be incorrectly interpreted by a generalist without knowledge about the specifics of the hardware platform. For this reason, different hardware manufacturers provide proactive services that analyze the entire system, including all of its components, on a regular basis. Through its service partnership with SAP, Hewlett-Packard can have the same experts run both EarlyWatch and the hardware-specific services.

Planned downtimes at application level are needed if configuration changes require a restart of the SAP instances. These usually only take a few minutes, as they do not necessitate rebooting the computer. For this reason, parameter optimizations and patch imports should not be postponed, because planned downtimes help to minimize unplanned downtimes.

In practice, when using HP-UX, for example, a patch cycle of three months for firmware, HP-UX patch bundles, SAP support packages, R/3 kernel patches, and Oracle patch sets has proven successful.

Legal patches This does not, however, apply to patches resulting from changes to the legal framework (legal change patches). These patches must be included by the stipulated date, at the latest.

Migration When you change hardware platform, operating system, or the database, you must perform a "heterogeneous migration" that involves exporting/importing the database. There are exceptions that make a platform switch possible by using simpler tools:

- The switch from HP-UX/PA-RISC to HP-UX/Itanium does not require a migration.
- The switch from Windows 32-Bit to Windows 64-Bit (Itanium) and from Linux 32-Bit to 64-Bit (Itanium) does not require a migration either.
- For the switch from HP Tru64 UNIX to HP-UX/Itanium, Hewlett-Packard provides the HP Smooth Transition Method that makes the transfer possible with considerably less downtime and costs than a standard migration.

From EBCDIC to ASCII

If SAP R/3 is being used on OS/400 while using EBCDIC code, then you must perform a transfer to ASCII code during the upgrade to R/3 Enterprise, as SAP no longer supports EBCDIC code from R/3 Enterprise onward. This transfer is performed using SAP migration tools. In terms of the procedures used, it is comparable to performing a platform change.

Implementing Unicode

From R/3 Enterprise on, SAP provides optional Unicode support. In terms of the procedures used, transferring an SAP system to Unicode is comparable to a platform change (export/import).

7.17 System Operation

Technology alone is not enough; we still need people to monitor and use it. Therefore, SLAs must also be defined for the services provided by people. This applies both to services provided by your own employees (insourcing) and also to services provided fully or partially by external service providers (outsourcing or out-tasking).

Is shift work needed?

In this context, you must also define the times during which these services must be available. Operating an SAP system landscape 24/7 requires the constant presence of personnel, and therefore shift work. This is, however, the most expensive way of operating a system and it is particularly difficult to find qualified IT specialists who are prepared to do shift work in the employment market. You should therefore carefully consider at exactly which times you need staff to be present and when you can afford to have people on call and use suitable monitoring tools with event notification.

Can you do everything with your own staff?

Small companies, in particular, are often not in a position to provide the dedicated staff necessary to carry out the different tasks. It is also important to remember that even the most talented "all-rounder" can never have expert knowledge in every area. Even an employee with the best possible training, high motivation, and meticulous work habits, cannot perform all tasks at the same time with the same degree of attention. Even if employees cannot avoid it, it is in the best interests of the company's smooth operation to restrict multitasking by IT employees to sensible levels. This is because in addition to insufficient qualifications and a lack of communication between employees, overwork by IT personnel is one of the main causes of errors.

Considering the availability and stability of company-critical applications, companies (especially small companies) should therefore at least consider the sensible alternative of bringing in third parties to deal with system operation tasks that cannot be covered by the company's own personnel. Our book *SAP System Operations* (SAP PRESS 2003) describes the different aspects of this kind of "outtasking."

On-the-job knowledge transfer

Administrator training and experience with the systems is a frequently neglected factor. "On-the-job" training is a tried-and-tested procedure for the effective training of administrators. This involves having the system fully installed and operated by experienced Basis consultants from a service provider, while the company employees are introduced to their new tasks with "on-the-job" knowledge transfer. This ensures a supervised transfer from the experts to your own team, whose members may not necessarily have been capable of performing all the tasks at the start of the process. Experience shows that this prevents some standard beginners' errors, and hands-on experience with the company's own system is a far more effective way of learning than the usual classroom training.

7.18 Summary

SAP systems are centralized, company-critical applications. Companies need to be able to rely on their availability. This requires a holistic approach that covers all the areas of the SAP infrastructure, in order to minimize both planned and unplanned downtimes.

Availability

Using the techniques described in this chapter, you can ensure extremely high levels of availability. Customers report a total of one hour of unplanned downtime over a period of four years with 45 HP-UX systems. Table 7.2 displays an example of SAP systems for a large insurance company, and the availability that can realistically be provided in all circumstances.

SAP instance	From	To	Days runtime	Minutes downtime	Availability
ISRE	1.10.1999	1.1.2002	823	480	99.9595 %
FI	1.10.1999	1.1.2002	823	485	99.9591 %
HR	1.10.1999	1.1.2002	823	365	99.9692 %

Table 7.2 Availability of SAP Systems at an Insurance Company

This data has been derived from the company's downtime database. The calculations include all breakdowns affecting hardware, operating systems, backups, and data center power supply (several power outages).

Measures

The following is a list of the required measures sorted by topic.

Measures to avoid environment-related breakdowns:

- Distribute computers, storage subsystems, and network components between at least two fire sections or buildings.
- Provide redundant power supply, air conditioning, and connections to Wide Area Networks (WAN).
- Measures to protect against fire and water, unauthorized manipulation, and theft.
- Monitoring of all the environment parameters of a computer room with connection to the monitoring system.

Measures to prevent downtimes due to hardware defects:

- Use of qualitative, high-value components
- Redundant interface cards for productive SAP systems
- Storing data files to redundant, external hard disk subsystems with a suitable RAID level
- Redundant setup for networks
- Sufficient reserves to provide additional performance, options for adding resources quickly

Measures to prevent downtimes due to the operating system:

- Stability, good design, and the option to exchange components during operation (instant capacity, OLAR)
- Analysis of operating system parameter "usage"

- Correctly spaced intervals (not too long) between maintenance windows (depending on the operating system release and patch levels, and its susceptibility to attacks)
- Regular checks at SAP Service Marketplace (SAP notes) and manufacturer bulletin boards

Measures to prevent downtimes due to application problems:

- Consistent Change Management (no patches can be imported to the production system without testing)
- The logical consistency of the data should also be ensured using a shadow database, where possible
- Implementation of preventive support concepts, regular use of the EarlyWatch service, and services from the hardware manufacturers as part of a holistic approach

Organizational measures against downtimes:

- The availability requiriements must be agreed in writing in a Service Level Agreement with the customer
- When deciding on a budget, you should not discuss the level of availability that the company can afford, but the amount of downtime that it cannot afford
- Even the most expensive high-availability solutions are useless if they are not maintained regularly and users are not trained in how to use them. If the knowledge about the usage of those solutions is not sufficient, they might not only malfunction in case of an incident, they even might reduce the availability of a mySAP system. Without proper maintenance and training, availability of the system will be drastically reduced

8 Presentation Layer and Output Management

The interfaces to the most important part of an SAP NetWeaver infrastructure—the users

This chapter concentrates on the most decentralized parts of an SAP NetWeaver infrastructure, the interface to the users (as well as the printers and other output devices). Due to the low cost of the individual devices, the importance of the frontend for the infrastructure is often underestimated. Even if most companies already have PCs at their workplaces, laptops and PDAs for the external sales force, and printers in their departments, the front-end infrastructure can still account for just 10 % of the value of the SAP hardware, according to a study from Gartner Group. The share of daily operating costs can be even greater, especially if the complexity of the front end landscape increases over time due the increase variety of desktop types or operating system versions deployed.

Despite the much-touted vision of the paperless office, companies are still floundering in a mounting flood of paper. The accurate and timely making available of business documents is still a critical factor for a company's business processes. Without a carefully planned printing strategy, you can expect problems ranging from poor printer performance to annoyed customers being reminded to pay invoices that they never received.

The first section of this chapter discusses the advantages and disadvantages of the different SAP user interfaces. The second section explains the different solutions for form and output management for SAP systems.

8.1 Frontend—The User Interface

Within SAP architecture, the presentation layer is the interface for interaction between the system and the most important person in the SAP system, namely, the user. The inclusion of a Graphical User Interface (GUI) with R/3 was revolutionary at a time when most applications still used "amber on black" text-oriented terminals.

The classic SAP GUI design was characterized by its objective of providing professional users with the perfect interface for performing business transactions. Experienced users can quickly access any of the required system functions by entering short transaction codes. However, the classic SAP GUI was still rather cryptic for less experienced users.

Release 4.5 saw the redesign of the SAP GUI by well-known design experts. The use of tabs, table controls, and context-specific buttons simplified navigation considerably. The number of screen changes for the individual business processes was also significantly decreased.

Different GUI architectures

SAP provides a series of different technologies and architectures for technical implementation of the user interface.[1] Above all, members of the classic SAP-GUI family differ as regards supported platforms and the installation location.

SAP GUI for Windows environment

The official name "SAP GUI for Windows Environment" is usually shortened to "WinGUI." This is the most frequently used version of the SAP GUI, and it runs on standard PCs with the various versions of Windows. With OLE interfaces and ActiveX Controls, the SAP GUI for Windows provides a deep level of integration with Windows applications such as Microsoft Office. The recommended CPU level for the WinGUI generation is usually at the upper level of the PC generation at the time of development. For Windows 2003, for example, you require at least Pentium 233 MHz, although 500 MHz is recommended. For main memory, at least 64 MB is required, but 256 MB is preferable if other MS Office applications are to be started in addition to the SAP GUI. The disk space requirement (110–510 MB) is non-critical with contemporary hard disk sizes. Most customers are deploying the SAP UI with Pentium IV processors and above with 500 MB–1 GB of main memory.

mySAP Supply Chain Management (mySAP SCM) requires different SAP GUI components from SAP Advanced Planner and Optimizer (SAP APO) 3.0, and these components are different yet again in R/3 4.6. Apart from small, limited projects, a company should always use only one SAP GUI version. SAP recommends using newer versions of the SAP GUI with older SAP releases. When upgrading the SAP application, it is not imperative to upgrade the SAP GUI as well if you're using a backwards-compatible kernel. However, we don't recommend using an older SAP GUI with a newer R/3 release.

You can install the WinGUI from the SAP Presentation CD, or via the network. Just as when you update the server, you should also schedule tests when changing the WinGUI version, especially before you start the cor-

1 You can find additional information on SAP's GUI strategy at *http://service.sap.com/ui*.

responding rollout. These tests should determine whether the other PC applications work with the new SAP GUI version, and whether all SAP application areas continue to run without any problems.

SAP GUI for Java Environment

The "SAP GUI for Java Environment" was developed in order to guarantee platform independency for the user environment. This user interface (usually just called JavaGUI) can be used to access mySAP components from any device that can run Java.

This technology is based on a combination of Java and C++; the proprietary ActiveX-Controls from Windows have been replaced by JavaBeans. This provides support for business graphics and file transfers. Integration with MS Office is restricted to displaying and exporting, however.

Installation via email

Users can install SAP GUI for Java on their computers simply by clicking on a URL (browser-based installation), which can be sent via email, for example. This uses existing C/C++ libraries on the terminal for network communication, file transfer, and so on. The JavaGUI uses the same bandwidth-minimized SAP GUI protocol as the WinGUI to communicate directly with the SAP Web Application Server (SAP Web AS).

WinGUI and JavaGUI are installed and executed on a PC, or a laptop as independent programs. Because the graphic for the user interface is provided locally, only a few lines of ASCII text need to be transported via the network for each transaction. For this reason, SAP uses the least network resources of all business applications. On the other hand, both the installation and maintenance of distributed SAP GUIs are relatively labor-intensive. The relative large size (200–400 MB) of SAP GUI for Windows and SAP GUI for Java requires relative extensive installation time, distracting users from their work while the process is completed.

Business Explorer

In addition to standard SAP GUIs, SAP Business Information Warehouse (SAP BW) also provides two additional user interfaces for analyzing the data stored in BW.

Business Explorer Analyzer (BEx Analyzer) is installed locally on the user's PC as an add-on to Microsoft Excel. This means that the user can also use the standard Excel functionality and interface for complex analyses in BW with filtering, drilling, or slicing and dicing.

If you want to analyze data using the browser as a frontend, you can do this using a Web application created with BEx Web Application Designer specifically for the report in question. This provides the same analysis options and features as does BEx Analyzer, without the need to install software on the user's PC.

> **Internet Graphics Service**
>
> SAP Internet Graphics Service (IGS) is integrated with SAP BW and enables data output from SAP systems or other sources as graphics (or non-graphical ouput) in a browser or the SAP GUI. This enables you to create informative business graphics (for example, including maps or geo-coded information). IGS can create raster graphics (GIF, JPEG, and so on), as well as vector graphics (for example, VML and SVG).

WinGUI in the browser?

You can also access WinGUI and BEx Analyzer using a browser, if these interfaces are provided centrally via a Citrix Presentation Server (Citrix CPS) to a Microsoft Windows Terminal Server (WTS). The WinGUI and other Windows applications are executed 100 % on the server. The PC simply transmits the user's keyboard entries and mouse clicks to the server. An Independent Computing Architecture (ICA) Client installed on the PC provides a network protocol that has been optimized in terms of bandwidth and performance. This can be used to significantly reduce bandwidth requirements in areas such as BW and APO (see Chapter 9).

The ICA client components (ActiveX Control Elements or Java Applets) can be installed from the Web server using the MetaFrame Web interface—a free Citrix MPS component. With MetaFrame XP Presentation Server, Citrix provides an expansion for WTS that can be used to enable applications installed on the server to also use the local PC resources (local hard disk, printer, clipboard, serial and parallel port, etc.).

Because the WinGUI is executed on the server and only minimum capacity is required to display it on the client, the WinGUI can also be used on older PCs that would not normally have sufficient CPU and main memory. The lower hardware requirements for the terminals, however, do translate to higher requirements for the terminal server.

Because several users can access the programs independently, you only need to install and maintain the programs in one place, creating a significant reduction in operating costs. For this reason, SAP uses Citrix for its own systems.

GuiXT

If necessary, the GuiXT add-on allows the SAP GUI to be adapted. Screen elements can be added and changed (images, logos, and so on). Changes to the layout have no effect on the application logic. You should, however, keep in mind that bitmaps are used to mask the input fields. These bitmaps are static and do not adjust when a user changes the font size in the SAP GUI.

If even the expanded GuiXT functionality cannot meet special requirements, SAP Automation enables you to develop alternative user interfaces. This allows applications such as Microsoft Office, Visual Basic, or IBM Lotus Notes that function as OLE controllers, to execute SAP GUI functionalities.

8.2 The Future—Web Dynpro

The presentation logic for current Web applications is generally based on server page technology along with Tag Libraries. These programming models are very common, especially on end user-oriented Web sites. These sites impress their visitors with perfect visual design and numerous graphics.

Browser-based applications often lack the ease-of-use of PC software, however. There is usually very little help or support for entering data in the correct format, for example. Web applications generally do not consider local conventions or settings, and therefore, force the user to enter the date in a certain format that may be alien to his or her way of thinking. For example, the US "month, day, year" format can be extremely confusing for European users, for whom the usual format is "day, month, year." In particular, errors are handled so badly that users who make an incorrect entry must re-enter all of their data.

All these drawbacks are addressed by Web Dynpro technology, which is based on the design principles developed by SAP with the dynpro technology.[2] However, it uses completely new technology that is specifically tailored to Web applications. Web Dynpro runs on the SAP Web AS and no additional coding is required for the client.

Separation of layout and content

SAP Web Dynpro technology is based on the Java Server Page (JSP) programming model, which separates the user interface from content gener-

2 The dynamic program (dynpro) concept originally stems from R/2.

ation. Designers can use this technology to change the entire page layout without changing the underlying dynamic content. When generating Web sites, JSP uses a mixture of HTML and Java programming code. Compared to typical Web development tools that are based exclusively on the server page programming model, Web Dynpro technology requires only a fraction of the time and costs for design, development, and maintenance required by other Web applications.

The strict separation of layout and content in Web Dynpro makes it possible to support location-independent rendering (generation of the screen content). Depending on the capacity of the terminal, an HTML page can be rendered either on the server or the client. High-performance devices such as PCs can be used to add content to the page using XML and JavaScript. If you're using devices such as PDAs or cell phones, which don't provide client-side scripting or XML transformation processing, the server generates the HTML page before it is sent to the browser. There is no need to change the application code or the presentation code. Device recognition functions are provided to more easily support the many different devices and browsers. SAP provides a tag library for rendering the user interface, the control flow, and internationalization.

Tag Libraries

Developers can use Tag Libraries to develop user interfaces that use standard technology for Web design and Web development, such as HTML, XML, Java, and Cascading Style Sheets (CSS), without needing to delve too deeply into the details of this technology. In short, Tag Library is a collection of reusable codes in mark-up languages such as HTML or WML. It enables Web applications to be reused and ensures a consistent design.

Flicker-free images

Constant reloading of pages in traditional browser applications is annoying for most users. Web Dynpro technology only changes the necessary sections of the screen, providing a predominantly flicker-free screen.

In WorkProtect mode, Web Dynpro applications prevent unsaved entries from being lost accidentally if users navigate to another portal page.

The client-side eventing supported by SAP Enterprise Portal (SAP EP) means that Web Dynpro applications can exchange data both with each other and with every required iView with Portal Content (BSP, ITS).

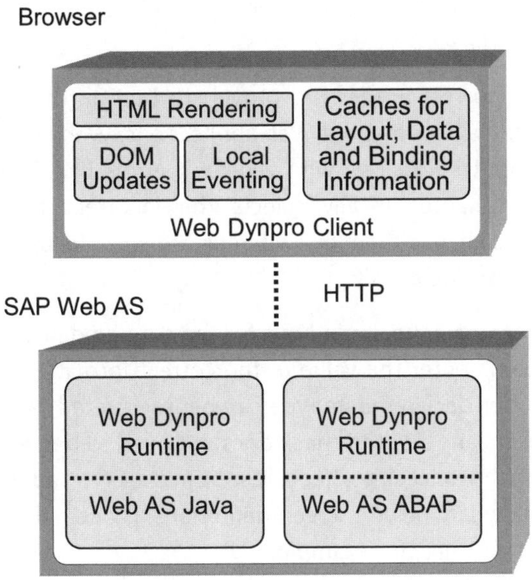

Figure 8.1 Web Dynpro Architecture

Roundtrip and bandwidth optimization

To win acceptance from end users in particular, the architecture required needs very little bandwidth and very few roundtrips between the frontend and the servers in order to ensure the quickest possible response times. When using Web Dynpro technology, therefore, the effective utilization of cache memory and preloading plays a pivotal role when improving response times. Views or layout definitions can be stored (cached) and reused in the local PC's memory or hard disk. This requires less bandwidth and improves performance. Furthermore, Web Dynpro has a data mechanism that calls only the updated content.

Internationalization

All parts of a Web application can be displayed in internationalized and country-specific form. An application can be enhanced with country-specific views, in order to take into account the cultural background of the user as well as culture-specific aspects such as writing direction (that is, left to right or right to left). Language-specific names for input fields can be displayed automatically using the translated texts contained in the Data Type Repository. Text data or language-dependent images such as icons are managed centrally in the Internationalization Repository and linked to the translation tools.

Customizing

During customizing, the user interface is adapted onsite at the customer location without changes being made to the business logic. Typical examples include inserting company logos, adapting the layout to reflect the corporate identity, and entering default values. Web Dynpro also provides a catalog of wizards with different customizing procedures for typical changes to the user interface.

Handling error messages

The correct response to incorrect entries has proven to be one of the most difficult aspects of the development of Web applications. Web Dynpro provides automatic input help along with a default error- handling mechanism. Error handling automatically selects the incorrect field entries and helps the user to change them by switching the input focus to the incorrect fields and proposing entries.

The input check can, for example, be carried out for the data type in the field to ensure that the users enter the value in the correct format. The metadata that represents this declared data type can be interpreted with client-sided scripting. This means that the check does not need to be performed on the server, which noticeably affects response times. In addition to data types, metadata can include screen definitions, process flow or dialog flow, and validation rules, for example.

Web Dynpro also uses the browser's scripting functions for other areas, for example, for setting input focus, as well as supporting a range of input devices (that is, a mouse, keyboards, touch-screen, barcode scanners, etc.).

The Web Dynpro technology therefore closes the gap between typical Web development tools and the need for a professional, low-maintenance user interface for business solutions.

Standard for new applications

SAP uses Web Dynpro for Java as a strategic development platform for the user interface for new applications. In fact, SAP is currently developing new Web applications, based to a large extent on Web Dynpro. For example, Employee Self Services (ESS) is founded on Web Dynpro for Java and SAP Enterprise Portal 6.0. Web Dynpro for Java is also used for larger functional enhancements to existing applications.

Web Dynpro for ABAP

For existing, ABAP-based applications, SAP is developing a Web Dynpro for ABAP to protect customers' investments. Using a migration tool, standard ABAP Dynpros can be converted into Web Dynpros for ABAP. The converter translates the metadata and creates Web Dynpro event handlers to emulate the ABAP flow logic. However, a certain amount of manual operation is unavoidable for the conversion. Web AS is, however, also able to emulate existing ABAP Dynpros within a Web Dynpro session using the integrated SAP Internet Transaction Servers (SAP ITS).

The technology can also be used by NetWeaver customers for in-house developments. With the adaptation of "Portal Styles," applications developed with Web Dynpro technology can be integrated seamlessly with the "look and feel" of the SAP Enterprise Portal, and can use Web services provided via the SAP Exchange Infrastructure (SAP XI).

SAP GUI is not obsolete

SAP still supports the locally installed GUIs for Windows and Java across many existing applications. Web Dynpro and SAP GUI will therefore continue to coexist as independent concepts for quite some time. New applications, however, are developed extensively with Web Dynpro.

8.3 Mobilization—Online and Offline

Online access via cell phone

The simplest option for mobile communication with SAP applications is online access to existing SAP functionality using technologies such as GPRS, GSM, or UMTS. Synchronization is not necessary, since the data is accessed in real time. However, many browsers on mobile devices do not understand "real" HTML, and cannot process scripting. With SAP's mobile architecture, however, it is possible to generate every required markup language (for example, cHTML, HTML 3.2, WML, or VoiceXML), although this requires a wireless gateway.

Adjusting to device-specific capabilities

With device recognition and device-independent Tag Libraries for ABAP and Java, SAP Web AS makes it possible to adjust Web applications to the specific capabilities of the device-browser combination. You can use the Device Wizard to add further mobile devices to the database.

SAP Console

The SAP Console product provides a third option for mobile, online data entry in the SAP application. It is generally used in warehouse management, but also in production sites or other areas of logistics. This supports mobile radio scanners that use mobile transactions from the SAP application. Users who connect to the SAP application via SAP Console work in real time with no middleware and no need for synchronization.

SAP Mobile Infrastructure

In some cases, it is not possible (or necessary) to make entries online, and connection costs are generally not insignificant. For scenarios in which no permanent connection is possible or required, SAP NetWeaver provides the SAP Mobile Infrastructure (MI) described in Chapter 1.

The standard programming model for the user interface in the SAP ME Client Component is Java Server Pages (JSP). Java APIs are used for data synchronization, storage (persistence) and reading and writing replicated data.

The SAP MI Client requires a minimum of 64 MB of RAM and enough hardware resources to support Web and database servers. The recommended minimum storage capacity is approximately 3 MB. The Java-based client in SAP MI can run on any operating system that supports Java 1.1.4 (currently Windows 32-bit operating systems such as Windows XP, Windows 2000, Pocket PC and with some limitations Linux).

The offline applications are installed centrally via the user roles in the portal. Therefore, the administrator can assign every user device with the applications that are specific to that user's tasks. This is done centrally, and the applications are installed automatically to the mobile devices at the next synchronization.

8.4 Output for mySAP

For the foreseeable future, we can expect the concept of a paperless office to remain wishful thinking. Consequently, support for daily business processes must include reliable print solutions. In addition to the traditional hardcopy printout, a mySAP system can use many different forms of alternative output media (for example, email, fax, and so on), thus we use the general term "output."

Although output appears to be only a secondary function for business processes, it is often irreplaceable, even in the Internet-based economy. In many cases, printing is a time-critical process (for example, manifests and shipping papers that must be included in a delivery before the truck can leave the loading bay).

With geographically distributed business processes and an increasing number of output options, the area of output is becoming increasingly complex and ever more critical for the smooth operation of a business. Nevertheless, this area is overlooked or taken for granted in the initial phase of most SAP projects.

Experience shows, however, that about 50 % of calls to helpdesks involve printing in some way. The damage is even worse however if nobody notices that an invoice or delivery note has not been printed at all.

For this reason, robust output management makes an important contribution to the reliability of the entire IT infrastructure. In the context of company-wide communication management, modern output control integrates form, spool, and output management.

8.4.1 Spool Management

From the very beginning, the SAP system was developed for multi-platform implementations. One of the objectives was to shield users from details specific to the operating system, including the area of print spoolers. Consequently, Web AS has its own spool work processes (and a spool database).

Spool work process

The spool work process has three different tasks. The first task is formatting the application data for printing. The second task is transferring the print request to the actual printer spooler and checking the print status. The third task is managing and reorganizing the spool resources in the system. In order to process all of these tasks in parallel at any time, you must ensure that at least two or preferably three spool processes are initialized in the system.

The spool work process in turn uses the spool system of the computer involved in the print process. After creating a print request, the spool work process transfers the print data to the operating system spool process. The print request is then managed completely by the operating system spooler. A spool request without the "Print immediately" attribute is only output when it is explicitly released. Spool requests transferred from the SAP spool system to the spool system of a computer can no longer be deleted by SAP output control and are marked as "Completed."

Spool request and output request

The core concept of a print document is the keystone of the SAP spool system. While some spool systems recognize only print requests, the SAP spool system can make a distinction between spool requests and output requests. Spool requests are documents that are sent to the spool system, but are not yet output to a printer or another device. Output requests instruct the SAP spool system to transfer the data in a spool request to a distinct printer or fax.

TemSe

The SAP spool system stores spool requests in the temporary, sequential database (TemSe). The TemSe database is not a separate database, but a part of the application server. However, the data in the TemSe database is stored in tables in the database. The TemSe can be stored in a file to accelerate the spool process, but the data then no longer has the transaction security of the database, which means the spool requests could be lost in the event of a crash.

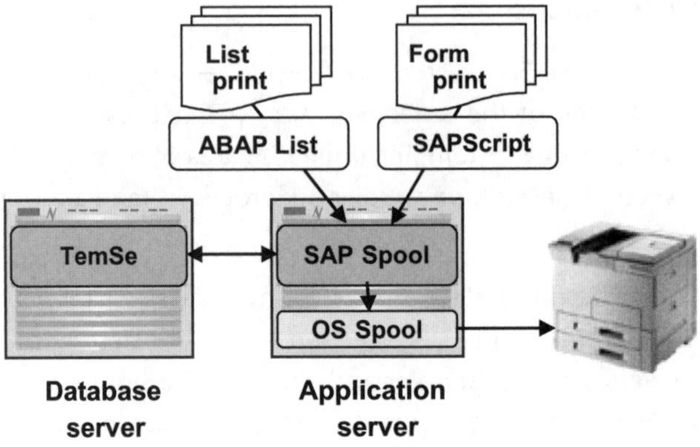

Figure 8.2 Data Flow in the SAP Spool System

To ensure stable operation, permanent reorganization of the spool requests is vital; otherwise, the number range for the spool request numbers would be exhausted and the growth of the TemSe in the database would cause problems.

As well as the SAP spool system, the TemSe database is used by a few other SAP components as an all-purpose storage area for temporary documents. This includes applications such as SAPcomm and SAP ArchiveLink. The background processing system also stores batch job logs in the TemSe database.

A spool request can have several output requests. Each of these output requests can be output to another printer with a different number of copies. However, the device type attributes and formatting attributes of the original spool request cannot be changed, because the data in a spool request (for SAPScript documents) is already defined specifically for every device type and every format.

A spool request and the corresponding output request are generally automatically deleted after successful printing, but can also be saved. If an error occurs, the spool request, the order request, and the corresponding log are retained in both cases.

Local and remote spooling

The SAP system also differentiates between local and remote spooling. From the SAP perspective, the terms "local" and "remote" are defined from the point of view of the SAP system. "Local" means that you can access the printer via the operating system of the application server on which the SAP spool process is executed. Remote printing uses the spool services of a "remote" computer. In this context, "remote" refers to anything that does not belong directly to the SAP system.

Spool Retention Period and Reorganization Cycles

When creating a print request, a user can define the spool retention period. If he or she specifies nine days, this translates to an infinite retention period. The only "workaround" to avoid a infinite growth of the TemSe through the configuration of the spool reorganization jobs at the operating system, so that the print request is still deleted. If you really need an unrestricted time-limit to access certain print requests, this must be achieved within the framework of an archiving solution. You cannot do this within the confines of the TemSe.

The reorganization cycles (spool retention period) for the print requests should be harmonized with the reorganization cycles of the jobs. If print requests are deleted earlier than jobs, for example, it is possible for a job to refer to a print request that no longer exists, or, worse, it can refer to the wrong print request if the spool request number is reused for a new request after the old one has been deleted.

8.4.2 Form Management

Forms are the lifeblood of any bureaucracy. Even in a globalized economy, printouts are needed. At the very least, customs documents and freight manifests still need to be printed on paper (or even worse on carbon copies). For these reasons, forms are usually the main type of output in mySAP systems.

ASCII text

Documents are output from the SAP system in their most basic form as unformatted ASCII text. A few simple formatting commands (spaces, separators, and so on), and operations (subtotals) are available for reports and list printing. For forms, pure ASCII text is not usually adequate.

Documents such as quotations and invoices, which must be sent to customers, must conform to the guidelines of a company's corporate identity. In addition to pure text, forms usually also contain graphics; especially print elements such as company logos and bar codes. Quotations, purchase orders, delivery notes, and invoices also usually contain standard texts, such as the terms of business and delivery and other small print.

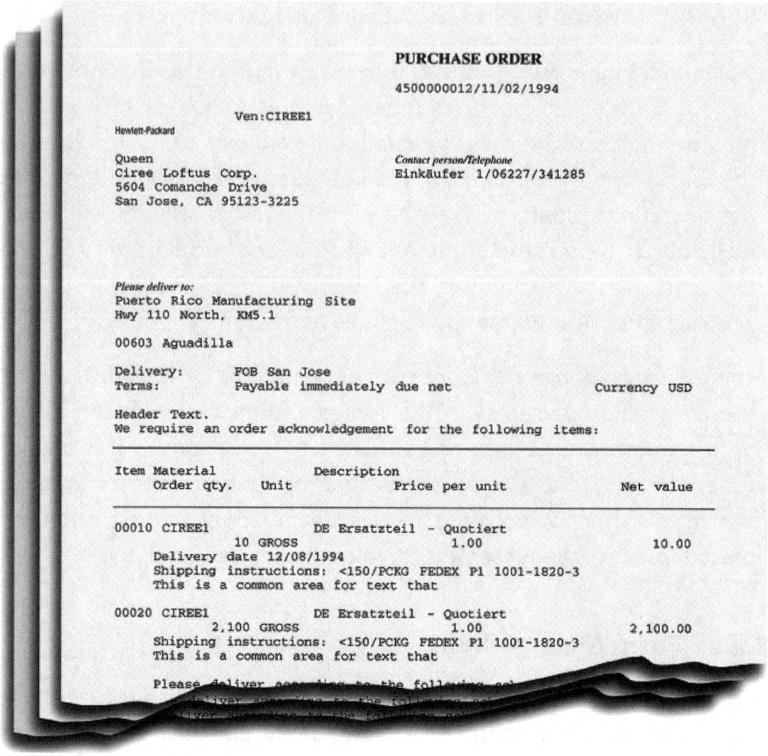

PURCHASE ORDER

4500000012/11/02/1994

Ven:CIREE1

Hewlett-Packard

Queen
Ciree Loftus Corp.
5604 Comanche Drive
San Jose, CA 95123-3225

Contact person/Telephone
Einkäufer 1/06227/341285

Please deliver to:
Puerto Rico Manufacturing Site
Hwy 110 North, KM5.1

00603 Aguadilla

Delivery: FOB San Jose
Terms: Payable immediately due net Currency USD

Header Text.
We require an order acknowledgement for the following items:

Item Material / Order qty.	Unit	Description / Price per unit	Net value
00010 CIREE1		DE Ersatzteil - Quotiert	
10	GROSS	1.00	10.00

Delivery date 12/08/1994
Shipping instructions: <150/PCKG FEDEX P1 1001-1820-3
This is a common area for text that

Item Material / Order qty.	Unit	Description / Price per unit	Net value
00020 CIREE1		DE Ersatzteil - Quotiert	
2,100	GROSS	1.00	2,100.00

Shipping instructions: <150/PCKG FEDEX P1 1001-1820-3
This is a common area for text that

Please deliver according to the following ...

Figure 8.3 SAP Standard Print Output

Electronic form solutions for SAP can be divided into internal designs such as the SAP standard tools SAPscript, Smart Forms, and "interactive forms based on Adobe software," and software that formats the print requests outside of the SAP system. The external solutions can be divided into printer-based and server-based designs. These solutions all have their own specific advantages and disadvantages.

SAPscript

With SAPscript, SAP had already provided an integrated form editor early on in its development. While the options that SAPscript provides are almost unlimited, it does require a deep understanding of ABAP programming. Because formatting is performed in the SAP system itself, the SAP Web Application Server must provide the necessary resources.

Smart Forms

From Basis Release 4.6C, SAP provides Smart Forms to simplify the form creation and maintenance process. This is a much more user-friendly solution than SAPScript.

The Smart Forms solution provides simple graphical tools that substantially reduce programming costs. Form Painter can be used to create the form layout via Drag&Drop. You can use Form Builder to define the form logic without having to use a script or programming language. Smart Styles are used to define paragraph and character formats. Maintenance is carried out in Style Builder.

You can also perform migrations from SAPscript forms. Just like SAPscript with the Raw Data Interface (RDI), Smart Forms provides an open interface to external applications (XML for Smart Forms, XSF). Forms created in Smart Forms can be converted into HTML or XML using a conversion tool. So, in addition to printers and faxes, Smart Forms also supports email and publication via the Internet.

From SAP NetWeaver '04 (SAP Web AS 6.40), new developments are created using "interactive froms based on Adobe Software". Both SAPscript and Smart Forms are still fully supported.

Interactive forms

For this latest form solution, SAP has used its partnership with Adobe to provide a new form solution that focuses on interactive form usage. Therefore, forms can also be used for data entry. The core of the solution is Adobe's Portable Data Format (PDF), which contains all the form data in XML format.

For this, the form design tool Adobe LiveCycle Designer, is included in the development environment for ABAP (ABAP Workbench) and Java (SAP NetWeaver Developer Studio, NWDS), which allows user-friendly formatting of the form layout. SAP Web AS contains Adobe Document Services as a runtime component, which mainly uses a form template and system data to generate a PDF document, or to extract the data entered in the form by the user from the PDF document.

Inclusion of electronic forms with input fields in Web Dynpro applications facilitates the transition from paper-based to automated business processes. Using the free Adobe Reader application as an editor, end users can enter the required information in a PDF document and transfer it directly into the system.

ABAP integration was designed for the area of mass printing in particular. It is based on the principles of Smart Forms, especially with the separation of data procurement and form logic. A Wizard is provided for migrating forms created in Smart Forms.

Printer-based forms

Printer-based and server-based form solutions represent alternatives to form creation in the SAP system. Modern laser printers usually have their own processor and non-volatile memory (Flash-DIMM or Flash-SIMM), so software can also be executed. Printer-based forms use the printer resources to link form templates stored in the non-volatile memory with unformatted raw data. Therefore, you only have to transmit the raw data via the network, rather than the entire form with all its formatting instructions.

In this way, an order form, which takes up about 55.6 KB with its formatting, can be reduced to 4 KB. This reduces the network traffic by 93 %. When changes are made, the form templates themselves only need to be transmitted to the printer once. Where a company has a lot of printers, however, it is not exactly easy to implement central form management when using printer-based forms.

Buffering Print Data

If print data is output directly from the SAP Web AS to the printer (without first passing through an intermediate print server), performance problems can arise if the printers do not have enough buffer memory. As soon as the buffer is full, the spool work process can only forward the data at the relatively low rate at which printing is performed. In the interim, all other output requests for this spool work process must wait. If the system cannot communicate with the printer, then the spool work process must wait until the connection is interrupted when the time limit is exceeded. Only then can the spool work process start to process other output requests.

Server-based forms

Beyond a certain number of printers, however, form solutions with dedicated servers are more appropriate because of the central management aspect. Just as for printer-based solutions, this solution drastically reduces the network load on the SAP Web AS. However, the required bandwidth between the form server and the printer remains high. Consequently, subsidiaries with a high printer workload should install dedicated form servers in the local networks to save valuable Wide Area Network (WAN) bandwidth. Because the server buffers the output flow, standard printers can also be used without additional memory.

Of the many server-based form management systems available, we will now introduce a few tried-and-tested options in the SAP environment.

Advanced volume printing

HP Advanced Volume Printing (AVP) enables Microsoft Word for Windows to be used to format SAP printer output. This allows users who are confident with Word to create forms for SAP printer output. AVP uses the SAP output data flows to create Word documents that can be printed with the normal standard letter function.

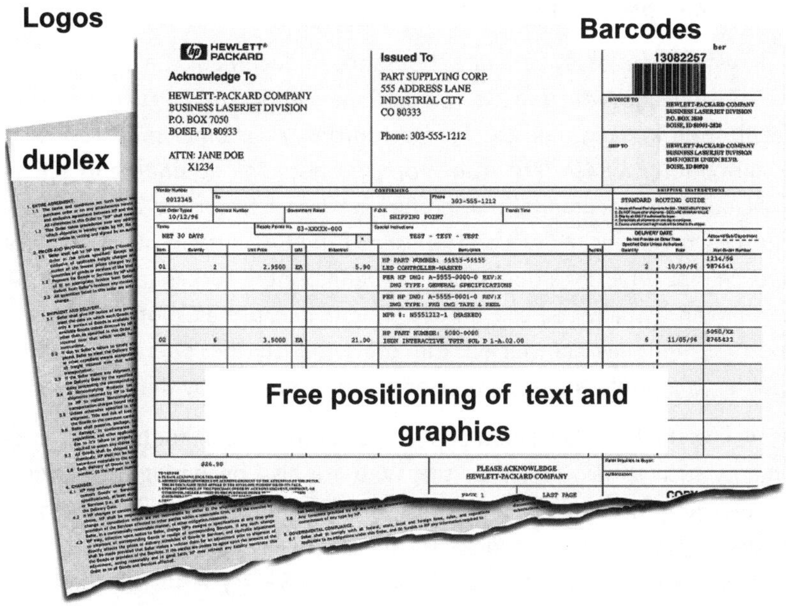

Figure 8.4 SAP Printer Output with a Form Management System

Adobe Output Pack

Adobe Output Pack for mySAP enables you to position field objects anywhere on forms using graphic form design tools. The SAP data is then formatted on the printer server. This enables you to modify the appearance of the individual documents dynamically via the data. For example, an invoice can be changed automatically to reflect the actual size so as to match the number of line items. Also, values such as totals can be calculated from the data flow, or the forms can be sorted according to any data fields (by zip code, for example).

Your Company Should Have as Few Different Types of Printers as Possible

For every type of printer that you want to access from an SAP system, the corresponding printer drivers must be installed on the system to ensure that a form on an HP LaserJet appears exactly the same as it does on a Kyocera, for example. The more printer drivers on your system, the more system management this entails. To ensure that adding a new printer type does not lead to unpleasant surprises, new printers must be tested to verify that all hard copies print as expected.

8.4.3 Output Management

SAP systems can easily generate thousands of documents on a daily basis. For most business documents, it is extremely important to guarantee successful printing and delivery. For each order, a customer must receive a confirmation, invoice, etc.—no more, no less. The accurate and timely availability of documents is therefore a critical factor for a company's business processes. However, the user in the SAP system has no way of determining whether a document has been printed successfully unless he or she can actually see the printer. This is because as soon as the SAP spool system has transferred the print job to the operating system spooler, the print request can no longer be controlled by the SAP system.

Alternative output media

As well as the traditional hard copy, other output media for business documents such as fax, email, or the Web are also becoming increasingly important. In these cases, it is critical that you determine whether a document has actually reached its recipient. Any number of printers and other output devices can be configured in an SAP system. The challenge in SAP output management is to output the right document in the right place at the right time and in the correct format.

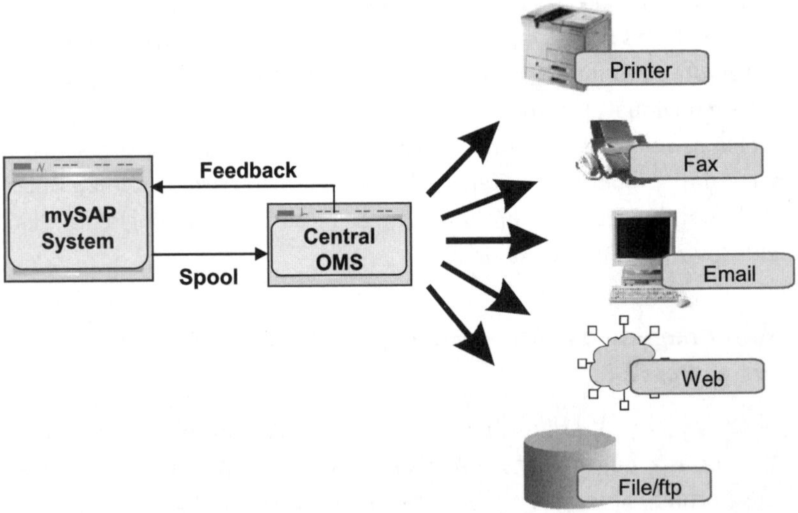

Figure 8.5 Information Flow in an Output Management System

These requirements are met by output management systems (OMS), such as HP Output Server for SAP. With BC-XOM, SAP provides a dedicated interface, through which the SAP spool work process can transfer output requests directly to the OMS. Because the OMS circumvent the operating system spoolers, you also eliminate a potential source of errors.

The OMS manages and controls the entire document provision process for printouts, faxes, email, or Web documents independent of output medium or device. Systems such as HP Output Server have certain characteristics that are of particular value in the environment of a mySAP infrastructure.

Confirmation to the user

One of the main advantages of an OMS is the confirmation of the status of the print job to the SAP spool work process, or to the system administration and the helpdesk. With a plug-in for the mySAP components and corresponding Remote Function Call (RFC) connections, the system uses an asynchronous status feedback to create a closed "control loop" in which it is always possible to determine whether a document has actually been output.

Users can also control (pause, cancel) their output requests when these requests have already left the SAP spool system and have been taken over by the external OMS.

Automatic reaction to printer errors

For mission-critical documents or output devices, the OMS must be able to react automatically to breakdowns in order to guarantee the making available of important documents under all circumstances. If, for example, a printer fails in a delivery warehouse that is critical to the goods delivery process, then the documents can be diverted to an alternative printer without delay. If that is not possible (for example, if a local print server is defective), then the central OMS sends an email to a PC in the warehouse. If that fails too (for example, if the network connection to the delivery warehouse is interrupted), then a local fax device can be used as an additional fallback level for the printer. If that also fails, then the warehouse can be informed of the breakdown via SMS.

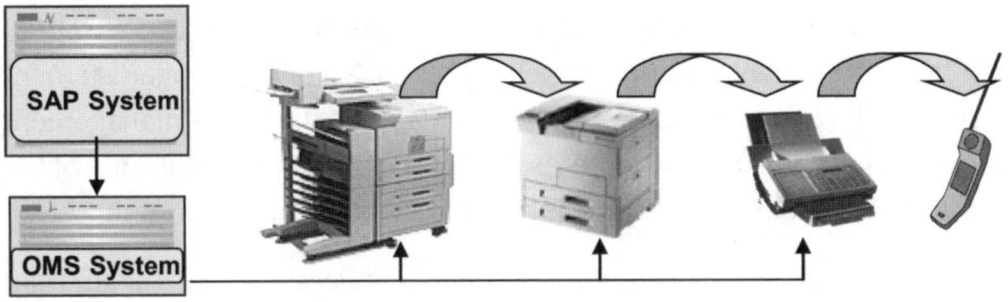

Figure 8.6 Automatic Rerouting of Output in the Event of Printer Breakdowns

The output management system also monitors all confirmations created by output devices during document output. This enables the system to send job-specific warnings to users and administrators. You can use a plug-in to integrate monitoring of the OMS directly with OpenView. This enables system administrators to use output event evaluation, process monitoring, log control, and end-to-end tracking.

Another advantage is that the storage of the output data formatting in the OMS means that separate printer drivers don't need to be installed and maintained separately for each operating system (Unix, Windows) and application (SAP, etc.). Furthermore, you only need to configure output devices once in output management systems.

Format transformations

HP Output Server is also able to automatically convert document data into formats that printers or other output devices understand. First, this saves you the trouble of having to define different forms in SAP for different types of printers. Instead, you can use a generic "device type" for many different types of printer. If the printer is replaced by another model at a later time, then the OMS must be adapted, but no changes need to be made to the SAP system.

Accounting function

Printouts also represent a cost factor that is usually dramatically underestimated by most company employees. The effect of the countless email printouts and hundreds of pages of lists that end up in the wastebasket after being glanced at only once can't be understood. In our experience, direct appeals to employees rarely help. Greater cost-awareness is usually only achieved with cost transparency.

Because ideally all documents pass through the output management system, accounting functions should also be involved in output. With the HP OMS accounting functions, the amount of output can be calculated in terms of workload per individual device, per user, or per department. This is especially important if the company IT department functions as a service provider and must account for services provided.

Integration of server based forms management systems

Any SAP customer running an OMS like HP Output Server can also benefit from the advantages provided by a server based forms management system with regards to bandwidth savings. Even if the forms management software is installed in remote sites, HP Output Server can still control the whole delivery path of the documents to the point of the printer.

To achieve this, the forms management software will be called from within the Output Server queue, which will also be installed and running on the remote server. In this way it is made sure that the SAP spool work process is at any time aware of the latest state of the output job; even though it might have been handed to other systems.

The output management system can be used to flexibly define additional document workflows. The options range from a simple document reuse—e.g. for storing it in a short-time archive on a web server—to an integration with systems that often exist in parallel to SAP in a global infrastructure. An other example is the distribution of selected pages from a large report to various recipients, depending upon the contents of the report and the business roles of the recipients.

Modeling of complex document workflows

Even if an OMS is implemented in the scope of an SAP project, there is no reason to limit its use to the management of SAP output. The biggest business benefit will come from an integration with all other applications in the enterprise. Consistent output management takes care of all parts of the information flow where data, information and documents are delivered, independent from whether the data source from a mySAP system or an other application.

Use of the OMS beyond SAP

8.5 Summary

Despite the vision of a paperless office, business processes usually generate a certain number of business documents that must be created, using many different types of media and in many different types of format. A carefully planned and managed, reliable front-end and output infrastructure is therefore indispensable for the successful operation of a mySAP system. The most important points are:

- The GUI standard for new applications is Web Dynpro. Strict separation of graphics and content enables flicker-free images and the optimization of roundtrips and bandwidths. In WorkProtect mode, Web Dynpro applications prevent unsaved entries from being accidentally lost if users navigate to another portal page.
- The Web Dynpro technology can be used by NetWeaver Customers for customer developments. With the adaptation of "portal styles," applications developed with Web Dynpro technology can be integrated seamlessly with the "look and feel" of the SAP Enterprise Portal and can use Web services provided via the SAP Exchange Infrastructure.
- The traditional, locally installed SAP GUI is still supported to provide experienced users with an interface that enables them to access any required system functions by entering short transaction codes.

- Along with SAP GUI, SAP BW also provides BEx Analyzer as an add-on to Microsoft Excel. BEx Web Application Designer can be used to create Web applications that allow data to be analyzed in the browser.
- The SAP system has its own spool work processes that use in turn the spool system of the operating system. After transferring the print data to the operating system, the print request is managed by the operating system spooler. You cannot pause or delete a job or a confirmation via SAP's output control.
- Documents are output by the SAP system in its basic ASCII text form. Forms in the SAP system can be created with SAPScript and Smart Forms, for example. This requires a profound knowledge of ABAP programming and possibly additional products.
- The current solution for creating forms in the SAP system is "Interactive Forms based on Adobe Software". In addition to the form print functions covered by SAPScript and Smart Forms, this enables electronic forms to be used for data input and linked with automated business processes.
- Form management systems, in which formatting is performed on a dedicated server or directly in the printer, reduce the workload on the SAP Web AS and the network. They also provide additional functions ranging from output medium-specific formatting to output language-specific formatting.
- Output Management Systems ensure correct document provision in complex, geographically distributed systems. The system confirms successful output, or informs the user in the event of a breakdown. We also recommend integration with Accounting and System Management.

9 Network Requirements for SAP

Building the link between users and Enterprise Services

In this chapter we step into a "parallel universe" with respect to the field of server systems running SAP applications. We call it a parallel universe because the technology, the terminology, as well as the vendors for networking technologies are almost all different from those of the server-computing infrastructure. Because these worlds are different, many companies create a separate department for the network infrastructure and management, more or less isolated from the department responsible for the operation of business applications like SAP. This isolation often leads to islands of job responsibility, whereas a clean integration across both is key for running interconnected solutions. In most cases, the "server guys" take for granted sufficient network bandwidth and availability, whereas the "net guys" know nothing about the specific demands of the applications. The result is the well-known finger pointing whenever trouble occurs within an integrated system.

Network architecture, although critical to the success of distributed business application software, is often not considered until very near a system's implementation. This may lead to a configuration that does not adapt to performance and availability requirements. The network sizing, configuration, and setup can play a major role in the success of an SAP system. As mentioned in a previous chapter, sizing methodologies for SAP systems depend on benchmark results. However, the response time in an SAP benchmark test is determined without consideration of the access network. Therefore, the numbers do not consider any network transmission delay to the user's PC. If a bottleneck in the network is causing the transactions not to propagate quickly enough, the performance of the system may be in jeopardy. It is therefore worthwhile to consider how the correct network infrastructure can contribute to the success of a business-critical system such as SAP.

The tempestuous development of network technologies over the last decades has settled various problems regarding the interconnection between the different layers of a SAP system landscape. With the availability of switches in the local networks, bandwidth requirements of SAP system landscapes no longer represent a problem for local networks (LAN), besides the questions regarding availability for business-critical applications. However, this is not the case when connecting SAP users to the central SAP systems via Wide Area Networks (WAN). Here, despite new technologies and the liberalization of the telecommunications market, bandwidth is still a relatively scarce and therefore expensive commodity.

To explain the requirements of high-performance data infrastructures so that even those not considered "specialists" could benefit, we will first explain some of the technology basics that may seem self-evident to "networkers." A discussion of the famous OSI seven-layer networking model, however, will be avoided as much as possible. Instead, the pros and cons of the available networking technologies will be discussed and recommendations will be made with respect to SAP systems.

Rather than present a complete network tuning methodology, which is beyond the scope of this book, our intention is to provide basic information on some widely applicable techniques for optimizing applications like SAP, deployed over networks. With special focus on high-availability, we will also discuss some "side" areas that may be of interest even to experienced network professionals. This include topics like cabling and building equipment, down to grounding and lightning protection. Principles will first be highlighted in order to make the recommendations for the successful operation of "mission-critical" business applications like SAP.

As with the computing and storage infrastructure topics, the following chapters present the SAP network infrastructure with respect to performance (response time), total cost of ownership (TCO), and ability to support mission critical applications (availability). In addition, the various factors influencing network response time are presented. This particular chapter covers the characteristics of SAP network traffic. The formulas shown in this chapter, however, are only intended to demonstrate the relationship between the parameters. In the chapters following, the demand SAP applications place on the different parts of a network infrastructure is discussed in detail.

9.1 The Influence of the Network on Performance

As we mentioned previously, the productivity of a user in online transactions and analysis systems, such as SAP NetWeaver and the other components of mySAP Business Suite, are seriously affected by the response time.

Chapter 4, introduced the technical factors influencing the response time of an SAP system from the technology side. From that, some rules for sizing SAP server systems were presented. However, the benchmark test results used for sizing take only the influence of the network connections between database and application server in three-tier architecture into account. In addition, the load generator servers that simulate users during benchmark are attached on the same high-speed network as the SAP system under test, eliminating many of the network delay issues in a more real-world configuration. The influence of the local- and wide-area network connections between users and SAP system in the real world is therefore not considered when dimensioning SAP systems.

What Benchmarks don't test

From the user perspective, response time is made up of the following components:

Response time

- Time for the user's request to reach the SAP Web Application Server (SAP Web AS) via the network
- Time that the SAP system needs to process the request
- Time for the response to return to the user via the network
- Time to render the screen content on the end user device (front-end)

Because the request and the response are usually transmitted along the same path over the network, the following equation applies for the response time to the network interface of a terminal:

$$t_{A(GUI)} = t_{A(Sys)} + 2 \times t_{t(Net)}$$

The parameters of this equation are defined as follows:

- $t_{A(GUI)}$ = Response time as measured at the network interface of end user device
- $t_{A(Sys)}$ = Response time as measured at the network interface of the SAP Web AS
- $t_{t(Net)}$ = Total duration of the unidirectional data transfer over the network

This formula is only intended to clarify the relationship between the parameters and does not consider other factors, such as the system response usually has a greater data volume than the user's original entry. It also omits the processing time at the end user device and the fact that many roundtrips are required if there are many interactions.

With a speed for electrical or optical signals that is 70 % of the speed of light, the length of the transfer route can be disregarded in most cases. The runtime for a connection between the east and west coasts of the US is only 65 to 75 ms, for example.

Transcontinental connections can, however, lead to significantly longer runtimes. This applies to connections between Europe and Asia in particular, because parts of these connections take long diversions to avoid an overland route when possible. Some of the data traffic between Europe to Singapore, for example, travels via an underwater cable that runs around the tip of South Africa. The network distance between Europe and a location in China can therefore be more than twice the actual distance.

With satellite connections, the signal must always take a route of at least 22,370 miles to the geosynchronous orbit of the communication satellite and back. This results in a roundtrip delay of at least 480 ms for the satellite link alone.

This can cause problems for an outsourcer or internal service provider who thoughtlessly promises a response time of one second, without first specifying at which the location. Even if, as shown in Chapter 5, response times of less than 300 ms are possible with modern 64-bit CPUs, the bandwidth must also be set up correctly to avoid bottlenecks. Despite all of these real and potential problems, the additional costs incurred are often significantly lower than the operation of an additional data center.

High speed = high bandwidth

There is a paradoxical effect that the signal runtime on a high speed network connection is not higher than on any other network, a signal sent via a gigabit Ethernet connection at 1,000 mbit/s is not travelling quicker than when it is sent via a standard telephone connection with 9,600 bit/s. However, the transfer frequency of a high-speed connection is considerably higher. This means that the signals that transmit the data are much more "tightly packed."

Therefore, with high-speed networks, the number of data packages that can be transferred per time unit is increased rather than the speed of the signals. High speed therefore really means high bandwidth. And bandwidth is the data transfer performance provided by a connection. The actual time to transfer a complete data package is during the time period that begins when the first message bit is received in the network and ends when the last bit leaves the network. In connections with low bandwidth, it takes longer to transfer a complete package.

A network connection can only be as fast as the section with the lowest bandwidth. For example, it takes almost a quarter of a second to transfer 1,500 bytes via a 64kbps connection. It takes two to three seconds to transfer a queue with several 1,500-byte packages. If one of these queues contains an SAP data package, the response time will increase accordingly. During high-traffic periods, delays caused by queues can make up a significant portion of the response times experienced by end users. Giga Ethernet "data highways" in the data center are of little use if user connections to the data center are made over bumpy country roads.

A connection is as fast as the link with the lowest bandwidth

Timeout

The connection between the SAP GUI and the message server is subject to a timeout; the default is 10 seconds. This also applies to the dispatcher. For WAN connections, for example, this value can be increased directly in SAPlogon via the environment variable TDW_TIMEOUT.

Active and passive components

While bandwidth is an important parameter, it is not the only one. In addition to the required network bandwidth, the transfer duration of packages across the network is also important for system performance. A network typically comprises of different types of transfer devices. The cables and their accessories are called passive components. Devices that ensure that data arrives at the correct recipient are called active components.

Active components are usually specialized computer systems that lead data packages down the correct channels, make changes to addressing, and perform other processing tasks. The other tasks can include protocol conversion, filtering, compression, and encryption. In some cases, the package must also be processed. The time required for this processing creates delays, which are dependent on the performance of the active network components.

Latency time

The time delay caused by active network components during the processing and forwarding of data packages is called the latency time. En route from the user to the SAP system and back, every data package passes through several network devices or nodes, each of which adds their own individual latency times.

If the inbound buffer of a network device overflows due to a work overload, the TCP/IP protocol requests a repeat transfer of the data packages. This creates a further delay.

This creates a (simplified) relationship between the parameters that influence the transfer times:

$t_{t(Net)} = V_{Data} / B_{min} + RTT \times N_{RTT}$

The parameters of this equation are defined as follows:

- ▶ V_{Data} = Data volume to be transported in bits
- ▶ B_{min} = Bandwidth of the slowest connection within the transfer channel in bit/s
- ▶ RTT = Round Trip Time in seconds (total time for trip to target system and back)
- ▶ N_{RTT} = Number of round trips

Figure 9.1 provides an example of the distribution of network times in relationship to system response times of a real life SAP system.

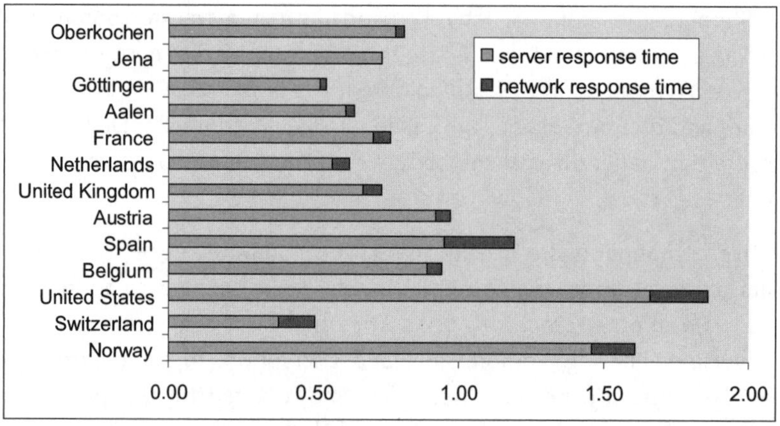

Figure 9.1 Relationship Between System Response Time and Overall Response Time (with kind permission of the Schott/Zeiss company data center)

The higher function levels of an active network device can be executed as an application on a computer with several network cards. These "software-based" gateways, firewalls, and routers have relatively high latency time. Typical examples in an SAP system are the SAP Internet Transaction Server (SAP ITS), the SAP router process, and SAP Gateway.

With typical network components, special hardware is used to achieve minimum latency times. Due to the complex tasks that they must perform, hardware-based routers also tend to have higher latency times compared to switches. The golden rule for all online-based applications is: Routing where necessary and switching where possible!

Ping and Traceroute

The easiest way to analyze network connections is to use the programs provided with every operating system: ping and traceroute (tracert for Windows). However, these measure the *Round Trip Time*[1] (RTT) for an empty IP package,[2] while usage data generally consists of several IP packages. For this reason, the package loss rate is another important parameter. Because lost packages must be transferred again, loss rates of more than zero greatly increase the transfer time.

With NIPING,[3] SAP also provides a program for analyzing network connections. Unlike the standard PING command, NIPING works in TCP socket layer, which is also used by SAP application programs. Therefore, you can also use NIPING to find errors arising from TCP and socket implementation on the platform. You can also use NIPING to measure the throughput and long-term stability of LAN and WAN connections.

Ping and his relatives are perfect for estimating the expected delay rates and the quality of the network connection at the start of a project. For more detailed analyses intended for solving problems, however, you need professional tools.

Network Monitoring

It is possible to constantly monitor the current system status using SAP Solution Manager. This monitoring is, however, restricted to SAP-internal processes, database objects, and operating system areas directly connected to these processes and objects. It does not, therefore, provide a global overview of the connected systems and networks.

1 Because RTT is usually measured via ping, it is also often called the *ping time*.

2 Empty IP packages are used to isolate the latency time from delays created by transfer capacity. The latency time is constant for a network connection, while the delays depend on the package size. However the size of the pakets is a paramter you can set, you can also test for example 1500 byte packets (Option `-l` under windows).

3 See SAP Note 500235.

Network management systems, such as HP OpenView Network Node Manager, support system administrators in monitoring and controlling the network infrastructure. Information from different network levels is correlated automatically so that the administrator can quickly identify the actual cause of a problem (root cause analysis).

9.2 Network Influence on Costs

The network infrastructure does not only affect performance, it also influences the cost of an SAP system in terms of both initial investment in the infrastructure and ongoing operating costs.

Costs of Bandwidth

In this context, bandwidth applies in particular to network connections that extend beyond the company's premises. These connections must usually be rented from telecommunications companies. Despite competition within the telecommunications market, over the long term, costs for providing transfer capacity and line rental can exceed the investment made in the entire SAP system hardware. For this reason, we recommend that your estimate of bandwidth requirements is as realistic as possible at the very start of an SAP project, so that you can negotiate the prices for telecommunications connections with as little time pressure as possible.

On the other hand, you must also consider the costs arising from insufficient network performance, since the loss of working time caused by long response times is also a cost factor.

The required bandwidth is determined by the data quantity that must be transferred via the network per time unit. This is never constant, however. With an increasing number of users and the inclusion of additional functionalities in new SAP components, the required bandwidth is also increasing.

Network Management

Due to the wide range of parameters, estimating the bandwidth requirements of an SAP system is no simple matter. Regular analysis of network usage enables you to adapt the available bandwidth to actual requirements before bottlenecks are created. You can also use these analyses to create forecasts of future bandwidth requirements.

Different systems and services are available for network monitoring. The problem here is not so much the installation of measuring devices or agents, but rather the configuration of filters, and interpreting the measured data volume and traffic relationships.

Correct analysis of measurements requires specialized knowledge and experience with networks. Therefore, HP, for example, provides a special service for monitoring and optimizing SAP networks.

9.2.1 Bandwidth for SAP Servers

In the past larger SAP systems generally had to be designed with a three-tier SAP system architecture with separate database servers and application servers because of the limits to CPU performance and addressable memory. Even if actual technology allows executing most SAP solutions in a single server, the advent of blades introduce the concept of dedicated database and application servers with all the specific technical drawbacks again for the benefit of lower initial hardware costs.

In such three-tier architecture, database and application servers have to exchange data over a network. The amount of data that is required to perform a business transaction is usually greater than the amount of data that is displayed on the user's device. Consequently, the quantity of data transferred between the SAP application servers and the database server is much greater than the amount of data transferred between the application servers and the user's device.

Switches versus server network

In the past, a separate "server network" was usually installed for three-level system architectures in order to avoid network bottlenecks. The "Fast" and "Giga" Ethernet switches available today can provide dedicated connections between the servers, so a separate network is rarely needed to connect SAP servers. However still the rule applies that all servers in a SAP system landscape should be in the same network segment without routers in between[4] (due to high latency when routing between the segments).

IP stacks increase the latency time

IP stacks play also a important role when ensuring the lowest possible response times for users. With each data exchange between the separate database server and application servers, every data package must pass through the different logical layers of the IP stacks of both servers, in order to get from the CPU of one server to the CPU of the other server.

4 Called a "flat network", because there are no hierarchical levels.

Even with Giga Ethernets, this can create mentionable latency times, which can have dire consequences for system performance.

The lowest latency times can only be achieved if you do not separate the database and application, and therefore avoid the need for any network connection. This means that all instances of SAP systems are consolidated on a suitably equipped computer, as a so called "central system."

A central system halves latency time

In this case, data exchange between the application instances and the database instance is performed via the operating system's internal Inter Process Communication and is therefore much faster than via IP stacks. Experience shows that consolidation of this kind can halve system response times in systems with equal resources. Users report that consolidated SAP systems running on Itanium computers in productive operation can easily achieve response times of 100 milliseconds.

Layer-3 Switching

Layer-3 switching is not true switching; rather, it is extremely fast routing. It enables easy division into different subnets (for example, for backup and transfer of offline logs). Even if it does not increase bandwidth, it can improve stability, especially in large company networks. With this solution, communication with the backup system, which can sometimes create a heavy workload, does not affect normal traffic for the application. Also, in the event of an error, there are fewer places in which to search for a network problem. However, for a clean implementation, you usually need to restructure the IP address setup.

9.2.2 Bandwidth for SAP Users

SAP GUI

Among other things, the traditional multilevel R/3 architecture was developed to reduce the required bandwidth for data traffic between application computers and terminals to the lowest possible degree. This is how SAP managed to enable the operation of a modern graphical user interface 15 years ago, when data lines usually transferred at a rate of 9,600 bits per second. This was achieved by transferring only the information content, while the locally installed SAP GUI provided the graphical content. Graphical formatting is performed on the terminal. In addition, the data traffic is compressed.

An Interaction Step (IS) is defined as a user interaction with the SAP GUI that triggers the sending of a request to an application server and a corresponding response to the SAP GUI. The result is a change in the screen template displayed by the SAP GUI. One dialog step can involve several network roundtrips between the application server and the user interface. The characters entered by the user are not sent to the application server immediately, but only after data release. This allows you to edit entries on the SAP GUI.

LSC Option

From Release 4.6, you can use the Low Speed Connection (LSC) flag for connections with low bandwidth. Upon activation, menus are transferred only when called. When displaying lists, the system transfers only the lines of lists visible on the screen. Background images (depending on the application), among other things, are not transferred, and field and input history are not available.[5] This reduces the required bandwidth, because it reduces the data volume to be transferred. The bandwidth is also reduced because the data transfer is distributed across several steps. SAP recommends that you use this option specifically for WAN connections. In the standard system, the LSC option is deactivated.

Type of information

The data quantity to be transferred also depends on the type of information called by the user. If, for example, a text needs to be edited, then the entire text must be transferred to the terminal in one chunk. When downloading large tables, the network load depends naturally on the quantity of the data contained in the table.

If a option list is displayed to the user, the quantity of data transferred in the individual dialog steps depends on the number of records stored in the database. With very long lists, however, a function integrated with list control ensures that only a part of the list is transferred immediately. The rest of the list is transferred only when the user scrolls down through the list.

In addition to normal dialog steps, data will also be transferred when the user opens a menu, for example, since these menus are only called from the application server when they are required. The progress-display bar in the SAP GUI status bar is controlled by the application server, which also cause data transfer (can be deactivated if the connection is slow).

5 SAP white paper "Front End Network Requirements for mySAP Business Solutions."

Keep Alive

To prevent resources in the SAP system from being blocked by users who simply switch off their PCs without logging off the system, the application server sends keepalive data packages to the SAP GUI when no transactions have been performed for a specified amount of time. If there is no reaction within 40 seconds, the session is terminated. You can define the wait time using profile parameter *rdisp/keepaliv*. A value of 0 deactivates the mechanism (default: 1,200 seconds).

SAP in the browser

In addition to the traditional, locally installed SAP GUI for Java and Windows, as well as the Business Explorer (BEx) of SAP BW, SAP NetWeaver also provides SAP Enterprise Portal and Web Dynpro, which require only a browser as user interface. The other browser-based solutions (SAP GUI for HTML and the Business and Java Server Pages, BSP/JSP) are not being further developed.

Windows Terminal Server & Citrix Meta Frame

As we described in the Chapter 8, the Citrix Presentation Server (CPS) along with the Windows Terminal Server (WTS) enable you to exploit the full functionality of SAP GUI for Windows (WinGUI) in a browser or a dedicated Citrix ICA client[6] without needing a local installation, or significant resources on the frontend.

Instead of generic dynpro traffic between the SAP Web Application Server (Web AS) and the presentation server (the SAP GUI or the browser on the frontend), only the user's keyboard and mouse input are transferred between the browser and the WTS/Citrix server, as well as the delta for graphical output in the form of a bitmap (the data volume exchanged between the WTS/Citrix server and the Web AS is the same as the data volume exchanged in a completely normal WinGUI installation because the WinGUI is executed on the WTS/Citrix server).

The network load when using WTS with Citrix therefore depends on the number of keystrokes and mouse movements during the individual dialog steps, and the number of pixels that change between two screens displayed. Depending on the SAP solution installed, results range from an increase of roughly 20 to 30 % compared to WinGUI with R/3, to a reduction by one tenth with BEx Analyzer.[7] The main advantage is the rel-

6 Caution: The Citrix ICA protocol uses its own TCP/IP ports, which are blocked by some firewalls.

7 According to *Accelerate your SAP Deployment*, Webinar on SearchSAP.com (August, 2003).

ative "evenness" of the ICA data flow compared to SAP GUI, which helps to "flatten" peaks in workload.

Web Dynpro

We do not yet have any measurements and practical experience of the network load created by Web Dynpro applications. Based on the technical design, we can assume that productive operation will generate a network load somewhere between that of a locally installed SAP GUI for Windows and the WebGUI, because only the content needs to be transferred. The first time you log on, however, you can expect a period of high network load while the data required for the graphical display is loaded to the front-end cache.

Online Documentation

Because a local installation of SAP documentation requires disk space and additional work to update every single workstation, the online documentation can be installed on a central documentation server that all terminals can access.

Because the SAProuter cannot, however, forward any requests to the documentation, you must use HTTP proxy servers that allow indirect access. Together with the SAProuter, the proxies can be installed on the same computers.

To prevent access to online documentation from overloading any of the remote connections, local documentation servers can also be installed at the remote locations.

9.3 Network Load Caused by Different SAP Applications

As mentioned in Chapter 4, the resource requirements of the different solutions in the mySAP Business Suite depend on a large number of parameters that can differ widely from company to company.

Compared to the transaction-oriented (OLTP) SAP R/3 and SAP CRM systems, analytical (OLAP) mySAP solutions such as SAP Business Information Warehouse (SAP BW) or SAP Advanced Planner and Optimizer (SAP APO) transfer considerably more data per request over the network. The geographical data display in APO Supply Network Planning (SNP), for example, can increase the network load by two to three times.

In the white paper "Front End Network Requirements for mySAP Business Solutions"[8] by Susanne Janssen, SAP presents the results of network load measurements made for different SAP applications. This white paper is updated at regular intervals to include new technical developments and observations.

At this point, it is important to emphasize again that benchmarks only reflect a very small part of the full range of SAP functionalities, and cannot therefore replace measurements of your own company-specific implementation.

9.3.1 SAP Business Information Warehouse 4.0

Compared to the transaction-oriented (OLTP) solutions like SAP R/3 or SAP CRM, analytical (OLAP) mySAP solutions such as SAP Business Information Warehouse (SAP BW) transfer considerably more data per request. As a rule of thumb, the data load that is five times greater than for OLTP systems. On the other side, these systems have relatively few users compared to OLTP systems.

Two different user interfaces are available for data analysis in the SAP Business Information Warehouse (SAP BW). Each interface creates different levels of network load:

- **Business Explorer Analyzers (BEx Analyzer) installed on desktop PC**
  BEx Analyzer covers a wide range of evaluation options, from tables to formatted reports, to interactive analyses with functions such as filtering, drilling, or slicing & dicing. BEx Analyzer can be used to call data with different levels of granularity—from detailed information to highly aggregated information. Embedding in Microsoft Excel provides the user with a familiar environment.
- **Browser-based SAP BW Web queries**
  These are created by the BEx Web Application Designer and provide the same options as BEx Analyzer, but without the need for a local installation. Statistical information is stored in the browser cache so it only needs to be transferred once. You can also display graphical elements, which increases network load accordingly.

You can expect different network loads, depending on which user interface you use. The network load consists of a fixed amount and a variable determined by the number of (Excel) cells to be displayed. With SAP BW

8 Available to partners and customers in SAPnet: *http://service.sap.com/network*.

Web Query, you can limit the size of the table to be transferred by setting a "cut-off" value. Cells beyond this value are only transferred if the user scrolls down.

The use of Citrix reduced the network load for BEx Analyzer with Microsoft Internet Explorer 5.5 SP2 from 30.5 KB to 3.5 KB[9].

9.3.2 SAP Advanced Planner & Optimizer

Demand Planning and Supply Network Planning

The network load generated by SAP Advanced Planner & Optimizer (SAP APO) as a central component of mySAP Supply Chain Management (SCM) depends both on the functionality used and, to a great extent, on the number of cells to be displayed. In our experience, the most interactive processes are changes to planning figures in Demand Planning and Supply Network Planning (DP/SNP), as well as optimization of the sequence of production orders in the planning table. Depending on the requirements of the individual users, both transactions transfer a large quantity of data to the frontend.

The data volume to be transferred may be greater than that for an R/3 Enterprise transaction, but it is still within the size of a typical website enhanced by interactive visuals. The geographical data display in APO Supply Network Planning (SNP), however, can increase the network load by two to three times compared to a OLTP system.

APO also allows scrolling on the front-end, without the need to transfer data via the net every time. This also means that the first time the function is called, more data must be transferred.

With Citrix, the network load of APO with SAP GUI 4.6D was typically reduced from 200 to 66 KB when the function was called for the first time and 13 KB[10] for the subsequent dialog steps.

9.3.3 mySAP Customer Relationship Management 4.0

As discussed in chapter 2, the SAP CRM solution can be deployed with several different scenarios, each with its own set of requirements for the network infrastructure.

Interaction Center

From a network perspective, the call-center solution "Interaction Center (IC)" , is the most demanding component of mySAP CRM in terms of network resources, because it is extremely interactive and because the

9 See footnote 5 in this chapter.
10 See footnote 5 in this chapter.

employees, who are usually evaluated by "calls per hour," are very sensitive to long waiting times.

Older measurements made in CRM Release 3.1, along with Citrix, provided a reduction in network load of 21.2 to 3.3 KB per dialog step with SAP GUI 6.20 and of 20.1 to 10.5 with Microsoft Internet Explorer 5.5 SP2.[11]

Analysis of the Network Load

The SAP Computer Center Management System (CCMS) transaction ST03N can be used to display the data volumes transferred between the application server and the frontend, as well as the number of roundtrips per dialog step.

This transaction can be called via the menu: **Administration · CCMS · Performance menu · Workload · aggregated Statistic Records (local)**, or directly by entering `/nST03N11`. You need the appropriate authorization and the WinGUI to execute the transaction. The button above the top left window (Workload) is set to **Administrator**. Change this in expert mode. The window on the left now displays a list of servers. After selecting a total and the required period (for example, one month) the system aggregates the required statistics and displays them in the window at the bottom left (**Analysis overview**).

To view statistics on the network behavior of individual transactions and reports, select: **Transaction profile · Standard, and** then, in the window on the right in the transaction profile, select: **Task type · Dialog**.

To determine the kilobytes transferred per user interaction, the values in column **Ø Input (Avg. number of bytes sent to the application server)** and column **Ø Output (Avg. number of bytes sent to the frontend)** need to be added together.

You derive the average number of roundtrips from the values of column **# Trips (Total number of roundtrips between frontend and application)** and column **# Steps (Total number of interaction steps between frontend and application)**. For the average number of roundtrips per interaction step, you add **# Trips** and **# Steps** together and divide them by **# Steps**.

11 See footnote 5 in this chapter.

Transaction ST03N also provides statistics on the number of bytes read from the database, as well as information on front-end PCs.

You can also use the Statistical Records (STAD) transaction to access the same information as ST03N, since both transactions use the same information sources. For more information on the network load in Web environments, see SAP Note 578118.

9.4 Estimating the Required Bandwidth

With the wide use of "Fast" and "Giga" Ethernet switches in local networks, it is not normally necessary to perform detailed analyses of LAN connections, since systems usually have sufficient resources.

This is not the case when connecting employees and subsidiaries, who must access the servers in the data center via long-distance data connections (wide area network, WAN), or when SAP services are being provided from an outsourcing data center.

When setting up these WAN connections, it is a question of which resources must be provided in order to guarantee the response times (and availability levels) required in the Service Level Agreement (SLA). Alternatively, it is a question of the response times (and availability) that can still be achieved with a specific budget.

When sizing network connections, it is not enough to define network load as the data volume to be transferred. Generally, network resources are defined by bandwidth, that is, the maximum possible gross throughput per time unit (in kilobits or megabits per second).

Don't Confuse Megabits and Megabytes!

While the byte and its multiples are normally used as the unit of measure in computing, the unit used in messaging and network technology is the bit, representing the smallest possible information unit. The following applies: 1 byte = 2^3 = 8 bit. Confusing the two can lead to serious miscalculations. Furthermore, a Kilobyte is normally 1,024 bytes, where a Kilobit is typically 1,000 bits, and similar differences exist for Megabyte and Megabit.

9.4.1 Bandwidth for the User Connection

As mentioned in Chapter 4, the main factor of uncertainty when dimensioning a network connection is the frequency with which the users access the system (that is, the behavior of people who use IT technology add value to the business). After sending a request, the user must also mentally process the information delivered by the system, which requires a certain amount of "thinking time."

The fewer the users, the less regular the network load

Because user don't hit the ENTER button evenly spaced in time, they can cause characteristic peaks in network load. This effect becomes even more pronounced when fewer users are working via a connection. Larger user numbers create a more levelled "statistical" distribution of transactions. However, practical experience shows that there is always some "spikes" in the activity profile over the day[12], depending on the employees' activity profiles.

As displayed in Figures 9.2 to 9.4, heavy transmission workload is bound to lead to longer response times. Just as we found with computer systems in Chapter 4, experience shows that average network load should not exceed 70 % of the available bandwidth for WAN connections.

To estimate the required bandwidth between the application server and the user devices, SAP provides the following formula for dialog transactions, which includes the most influencing factors in the form of common numerical factors:

$$C = X \times N \times D \times 0.25$$

The parameters are defined as follows:

- C = Bandwidth required for the connection [in kbps]
- X = Data volume transferred per dialog step [in KB]
- N = Number of users active simultaneously
- D = Average number of dialog steps per minute and user
- 0.25 = Numerical factor

Take X=1, N=1, D=1, which means 1 Kbyte is transferred every minute, 8,192/60 = approx 150 bits/sec. The formula results in 0.25kbps, so this is consistent with a max utilisation of 60 %.

12 And also some "holes" due to the fact that users tend to have lunch at the same time.

Based on the practical experience of the authors, you should consider the following when using this formula:

- This formula only describes purely SAP GUI-related dialog operation. It does not consider data transfer for printers, graphical display, uploading or downloading, as well as the use of X controls, iViews, and XML.
- The factor only applies for a large number of users. For small numbers of users (less than 20), you should use a numerical factor greater than 0.5.
- The formula only provides the requirements for SAP data traffic. You must also consider additional workload created by other applications (email, Web browsers, access to a file server, etc.) when estimating required bandwidth. We therefore recommend that you set the performance capacity to twice the result of the formula.

As mentioned previously: Due to the many factors involved, you can only get reliable figures for the actual implementation by using measurements from a comparable reference implementation.

Rules of Thumb for Bandwidth Requirements for Users

From practical experience, the following values have proven useful when making rough estimates:

- for OLTP (R/3, CRM, SRM etc.):
  - 10–12kbps per WinGUI and JavaGUI user (without download)
  - 50–90kbps per WinGUI and Portal user (with compression)
  - 15–20kbps per browser with Citrix & Windows Terminal Server
- for OLAP (BW & APO): multiply bandwidth by five (or expect response times that are five times longer)

9.4.2 Bandwidth for Print and Other Output

With mySAP components, the spool work process controls document output. Network load is influenced not only by the amount of data sent but also where the spool work process sends the print data for further processing.

Printers and faxes, for example, which are connected directly to the application server, do not create any data traffic on the network. Therefore, it is advisable to install printers directly in the data center for large scale (mass printing or faxes) or sensitive print requests (payroll).

Rule of Thumb for Print Jobs per User

HP reports that productive R/3 systems using HPOS create an average of four print jobs per named user per day, each with an average of two to three pages.

Usually, printers are set up so that users don't have to walk far to get their printouts. With remote connections, you must pay special attention to the bandwidth requirements of the different SAP printout options.

Output device

In a SAP context, the so called output device is the SAP "printer driver." It contains device-specific information that is required to format data, which is to be output on a specific printer or fax device. This formatting information increases the volume of the print data.

Size of the print request

Every output request contains information on the selected output device, the format type (portrait, landscape, two-sided or single-sided printing, etc.), as well as the resolution. For small print requests of only a few pages, this overhead is relatively large when compared to the output data. For a single page, the overhead volume can be as large as the reference data volume. Therefore, documents that are formatted in the same way should be printed together whenever possible. A 10-page full print request creates only a 10 % overhead load on the network.

Coupling type

Selecting the output device determines the "printer language." In the same way, selecting the so called coupling type defines the protocol used for transferring the print data. The SAP system differentiates between local and remote spooling. From the SAP perspective, the terms "local" and "remote" are defined as follows. "Local" simply means that the printer is accessed via the operating system of the application server on which the SAP spool process is executed. Remote printing means that the spool services of another computer are used. A so-called local printer may still be on a distant location.

From a network perspective, local printing only occurs if a printer is physically connected to the printer port of the computer running the SAP spool process. All other cases involve transferring print data via the network.

The spool work process can access all print systems that can work with the lpr/lpd protocol (Line Printer Requester/Line Printer Daemon). Communication is based on RFC 1179, which was first used on the Berkeley System Distribution (BSD), the "Great Granddaddy" of all Unix systems.

This protocol can be used to transfer data formats such as PostScript or HP PCL. Line Printer Requester/Line Printer Daemon transfers the print data in uncompressed form via the network. The data volume therefore comprises the number of characters to be printed, plus the overhead of the print request.

Windows, however, does not usually provide the lpd protocol. SAP has therefore developed SAPLPD, its own lpd program for Windows, which is installed with WinGUI. SAPLPD contains a few enhancements to the lpd protocol, such as encryption with SAP Secure Network Communication (SNC), connection via the SAProuter, and data compression. Body text can be compressed at rates of up to 3:1. **SAPLPD**

Frontend Print provides a coupling type that can communicate with the printers that are not defined in the SAP spool system. This transfers the output data to the Windows PC via the WinGUI. SAPLPD transfers the data to the Windows printer driver. In Frontend Print, unlike in typical printing, the document is formatted in the dialog work process of the user. For this reason, Frontend Print is only suitable for the occasional printing of small documents.

As mentioned previously, in most cases "naked" ASCII text does not usually meet standard business requirements. In day-to-day business with customers, documents such as quotations and invoices, for example, must meet the requirements of the corporate identity. Orders, for instance, must often be printed with the terms and conditions of business. The large quantity of redundant data and format information that is transferred to the printer every time one of these documents is printed can seriously overload the network. Chapter 8 describes different methods for reducing the network load when printing forms.

Rules of Thumb for Bandwidth Requirements for Printers

Printer performance is usually measured as the maximum number of pages that can be output per minute (pages per minute, ppm). This can be used to estimate the bandwidth that a printer would need to print continuously. For example, a 25-ppm printer with 60 kb per page to be printed results in the following:

$$C_{Print} = 25 \times 60 \text{ kbit} / 60 \text{ s} \approx 25 \text{ kbit/s}$$

A 32-ppm printer HP LaserJet 8100N, for example, would create an a maximum network load of 28kbps.

9.4.3 Other Network Loads

Batch jobs

In non-consolidated architectures, batch jobs performed within a SAP NetWeaver system landscape can create heavy network loads between the database server and the application server, since there is no pause or "thinking time" between the processing steps. However, this does not affect WAN connections because as a rule database and application servers must be installed in the same LAN. Another situation arises if external programs communicate with the SAP system via Remote Function Call (RFC).

Bandwidth for CPI-C connections

The SAP Common User Programming Interface-Communication (CPI-C) protocol forms the basis for connections between mySAP components, as well as other computer systems.

Using the CPI-C protocol, data is transferred in "character" format in packages of up to 30 KB in half-duplex operation; there is no data compression. The protocol generates an overhead of approximately 10 %, as well as an additional 2 KB per connection. This can be used to create the following formula for estimating the required bandwidth:

$$C_{CPI\text{-}C} = 8 \times (2 \times N_{Connection} + 1{,}1 \times V_{Data}) / t \text{ in kbit/s}$$

The following applies:

- $C_{CPI\text{-}C}$ = Bandwidth required for CPI-C [in kbit/s]
- $N_{Connection}$ = Number of connections
- V_{Data} = Usage data [in kbits]
- t = Transfer time [in seconds]

Bandwidth for RFC connections

Calling functions on other computers (RFC) forms the basis for business processes spanning multiple mySAP components as well as other computer systems. SAP Remote Function Call (RFC) is a communication layer developed by SAP that is built on CPI-C (not to be confused with the Internet standard, which is also called RFC). There are several types of RFC data transfers:

- Synchronous RFC (sRFC)—The RFC client waits for the feedback from the called function before the program can continue.
- Asynchronous RFC (aRFC)—The RFC client continues with its program without waiting for the feedback of the called function.
- Transactional RFC (tRFC)—The called function is processed only once in the target system, even if the function is called several times due to an interrupted connection.

- Queued RFC (qRFC)—The call is placed in a queue and then transferred to the target system together with other function calls.

Depending on the characteristics and time distribution, the volume of data traffic generated by RFC can be greater than that generated by user transactions. Because the RFC interface is a logical layer above CPI-C, the network loads generated by RFC and CPI-C accumulate. In an RFC function call, the application data is compressed, before it is sent via the network. However, RFC generates its own protocol overhead for registering the connection, calling the function module, and so on.

Protocol Overhead

The registration process creates an additional load of around 1.2 KB. With RFC servers registered on the gateway, about 3 KB of additional data is transferred than for programs that are started on the gateway. When using transactional RFC, you should expect an overhead of about 600 bytes per function call.

When a connection is being created, login data and various system parameters are exchanged (for example, codepages). This creates a network load of about 2.5 to 3.0 KB per connection. An existing connection can be used to call several function modules in the same target system. It is not necessary to log on to the SAP system again. For this reason, the network load is less when you transfer a group of previously combined IDocs, rather than when you transfer the IDocs individually.

Depending on how much the data to be transferred can be compressed, the RFC overhead can make the transfer data volume even greater than the payload data volume. The compression factor of the payload data depends on the data content. With IDocs, for example, table lines are filled to the end of the line with spaces. For this reason, IDocs including RFC overhead can be compressed to 30 to 40 % of the original data. Text data using any type of characters creates in spite of compression a data volume of 90 to 100 %. Binary data, which has already been compressed, creates a data volume that is 10 % greater. Typically, the overhead can be disregarded from a data volume of 100 KB.

Heartbeat, Backup & Recovery

Along with the actual SAP system, other supporting applications also create workload for the network (for example, software agents for management systems, the "heartbeat" for the cluster solution, and so on). The heaviest workload, however, is generated by backup (and recovery) of the database. With large databases, a separate backup network is highly recommended.

9.4.4 Practical Example

In business practice, when connecting branches and individual "remote users," the main question is "How much bandwidth does a remotely connected employee need?" rather than "How much network load does an SAP system generate per user?" This is because the WAN connections don't only carry SAP data, but also email, Internet content, and file transfers, for example.

In many companies, 5 to 20 kbits per user with a minimum bandwidth of 64 kbits has proven to be a reliable rule of thumb. The additional applications using the connection are a more important factor than which SAP GUI is used. Practical experience shows that you can expect a ratio of 30 % for interactive communication (SAP GUI, Citrix, and so forth) and 70 % for email, Web, and file transfer, for example.

The first example shows the workload for a domestic Internet connection with approximately 10 to 15 SAP users via a VPN tunnel (IPsec). The subsidiary is connected to the Internet via an ADSL line with 768/128kbps, while the head office has 2mbps Internet access. Thanks to a PacketShaper[13] at the head office, SAP access is satisfactory even without Quality of Service (QoS).

Figures 9.2 to 9.4 show how much data traffic is characterized by workload peaks when a system has relatively few users.

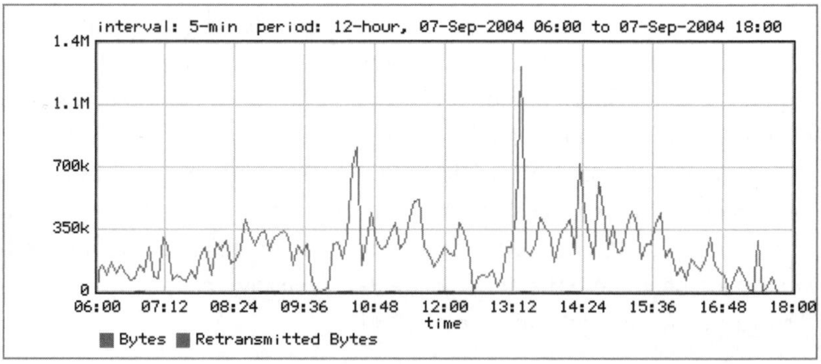

Figure 9.2 Downstream Data Traffic for 15 Users

13 Go to *www.packeteer.com*. PacketShaper enables you to prioritize SAP in WAN links, so that the email sent, or FTP downloads performed concurrently, don't slow down the SAP query.

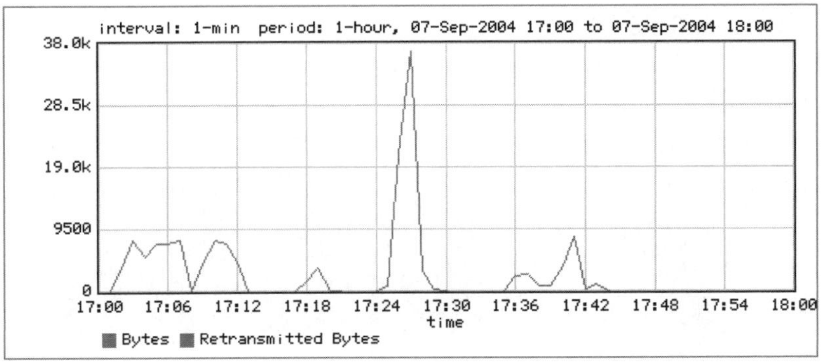

Figure 9.3 Upstream Data Traffic for 15 Users

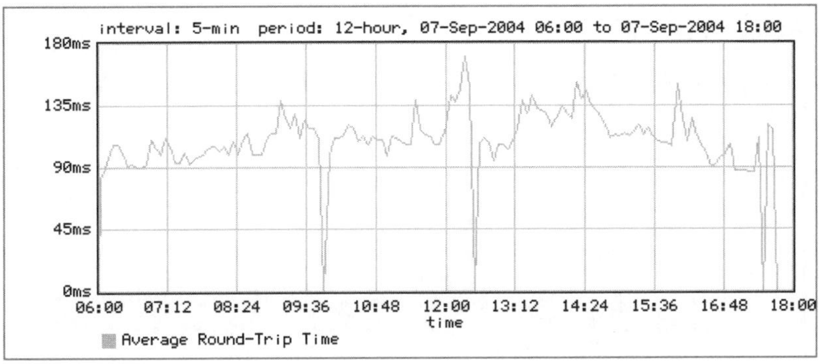

Figure 9.4 Distribution of Roundtrip Time via Internet VPN

The second example demonstrates the network characteristics of a company with about 400 users working simultaneously and connected to a service data center via a 64-Mbit line (see Figure 9.5). This solution also uses PacketShaper to prioritize the SAP traffic and to perform evaluations.

During peak hours (9:00–12:00) on a normal working day (Thursday), the average bandwidth usage is 2 kbit/user, while the average peaks in workload are around 800 kbit. The peak values are therefore about two to three times larger than the average value, which means we can assume roughly 5 kbit per user to enable "fluid" work processes. This value is also reflected in our experience of other locations with more than 20 SAP users. Where there are fewer users, you should plan for more bandwidth per user.

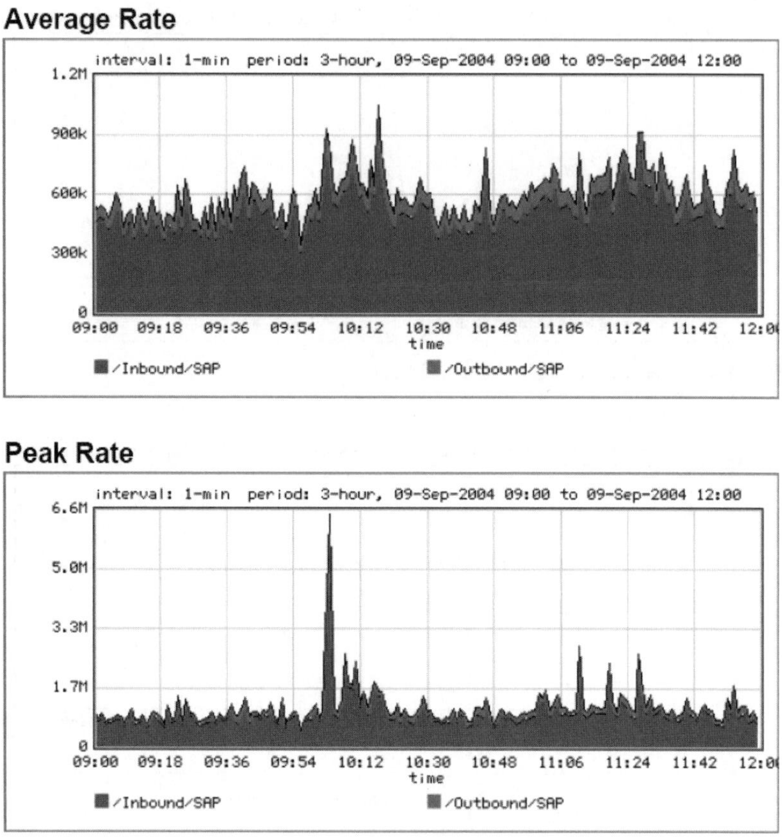

Figure 9.5 Average Workload and Peak Workload for 400 Users

9.5 Network Influence on Availability

End-to-end availability is mandatory

At the start of this book, we discussed the importance of the availability of computer and storage subsystems in a company-critical system like mySAP. In a global economy, the users of such systems are also distributed over the globe in most companies. Connections between central computer systems and the users devices must be equally reliable in order to guarantee overall operation of the system. It is therefore end-to-end availability that is important, not just availability of the central components of a data center IT infrastructure.

If a document is not received properly in a mySAP solution due to an overloaded or faulty network, then the SAP system blocks the transaction until the problem has been solved. The SAP system indicates that the data is incorrect, but the transaction block must be removed manually by the system administrator.

With increased integration of the value chains between companies, reliable connections are becoming more important. Above all, however, it is the use of Web services between companies that have made network availability an extreme important factor.

Holistic approach

A holistic approach is therefore important for highly integrated, multilevel systems such as the different mySAP components. As discussed previously, overall system availability is the product of the availability of the individual components involved in the connection (where there is no redundancy). The consequences of this effect on the availability of the entire system can be demonstrated in a practical example (see Figure 9.6).

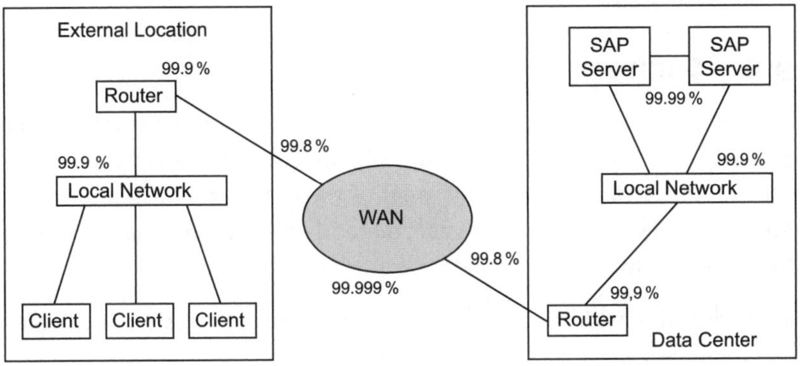

Figure 9.6 End-to-End Availability in the mySAP System

To simplify the task of estimating end-to-end availability of the infrastructure, we will not consider cabling and the availability of terminals. With a Unix cluster configuration for the server infrastructure, it is generally possible to achieve an availability of 99.99 %. This corresponds to an unplanned downtime of less than one hour per year.

Provided high-quality devices are used, the availability of components in the local network (including the router) is the same as that for Unix servers without failover (99.9 %). The interconnected network infrastructure of the telecommunications provider is generally set up to guarantee availability of 99.999 %. For the leased line between customer locations and their core network 99.8 % availability is a good number. Without redundancy the End-to-End availability of the connection between a user in a remote office and the Sap system in the data center can be calculated as 99,18 % (= 0.9999 × 0.999 × 0.999 × 0.998 × 0.9999 × 0.998 × 0.999 × 0.999)

Although this is good value compared to the 95 % for PCs, this means that for the user in the remote office the SAP solution will be unavailable for more than 71 hours per year. This somewhat theoretical calculation is backed up by our practical experience that connections in Central Europe tend to go down on average nine times per year, each for about four hours.

If a downtime of four hours is acceptable for a company-critical application, then no further measures are required. If not, then the following chapters will introduce methods for ensuring the required availability for all parts of a network infrastructure. As for computer systems, it is not a question of how much availability your company can afford, but of how much downtime it can allow.

9.6 Summary

The network infrastructure also affects the response time, the availability, and therefore the productivity of the SAP system. In the chapters that follow, we'll describe the different areas of the network infrastructure. The following checklist summarizes recommendations for minimizing latency time and bandwidth requirements:

- Wherever possible, all the computers in an SAP system landscape should be installed in a local network.
- In switched networks, a separate server network is generally not necessary for performance reasons.
- To avoid latency times in the IP stack, the database and application should be consolidated on one computer where possible.
- Use network components with latency times that are as low as possible.
- When setting up a WAN, you must determine the required bandwidth for every location, in terms of the number of users and their activities.
- Rules of thumb for OLTP (R/3, CRM, SRM, for example):
    - 10 to 12 kbit/s per WinGUI and JavaGUI users (without download)
    - 50 to 90 kbit/s per WinGUI and Portal user (with compression)
    - 15 to 20kbps per GUI with Citrix & Terminal Server
- Rules of thumb for OLAP (BW & APO): Multiply bandwidth by five, or expect response times that are five times longer. You can also use Citrix to achieve significant reductions here.

- The minimum bandwidth of an SAP connection should not be less than 56kbps.
- Additional load for Unicode: Latin-1 < 7 %, Japanese ~ 15 %, exotic languages 25 %.
- Bundle print requests; avoid PostScript.
- Use coupling type SAPLPD; avoid Frontend Print.
- Transfer queued IDocs with qRFC.
- Monitor networks and regularly analyze data flows.
- Due to competing applications (file transfer, email, etc.), set capacity at twice the amount specified by the formula.

10 Logical Network Architectures and Network Security

A Question of Protocol

In this chapter, we'll discuss the logical structures that are required for the implementation of SAP system landscapes in open network systems, as well as the measures necessary to secure the systems against attacks through these open network systems.

In the previous chapters, data security was discussed in the context of measures taken to ensure against a loss of data. In this chapter, data security is discussed in the context of the protection of data against unauthorized access. This additional meaning has come about because the combination of the Internet, standard software, and standardized operating systems does not just open undreamt of options to integrate information, but also untapped opportunities for their unauthorized use as well.

Cross-company business processes and collaborative scenarios require that the company networks are increasingly open to the external world. This is exactly the point at which problems arise between the security experts, who would rather seal off everything, and the project managers, who would prefer to leave everything open. The people in IT operation, who only want to ensure a high degree of service quality, are caught in the middle.

In the first part of the chapter, we'll deal with the SAP-specific names and addressing conventions as well as the specific network services that are necessary for access to SAP systems.

For reasons of redundancy, as well as ensuring the necessary performance, host systems for SAP are generally equipped with several network connections (multihomed host). The second part of the chapter is therefore dedicated to the resulting requirements for configuration.

In the last section, we'll look at the problem of load distribution across several application hosts and the specific problems that result from the encryption of the data flow. This finally leads to the concept of multilevel security zones.

10.1 Logical Network Structures

Since the introduction of R/3, connectivity between the different parts of an SAP infrastructure is based on standard Internet protocols. TCP/IP is a synonym for an open network structure. The success of the Internet demonstrates how much foresight went into this decision.

Due to the multilevel architecture, a large quantity of data packages constantly runs through the network between a variety of hosts. Similar to cars moving in traffic, all of this data uses the same routes. However, for data networks, there are no "road maps" that the data packages can use to navigate their way through the labyrinthine paths of the network.

This means that certain processes are necessary so that the data packages can find the correct route, and the individual network components can forward the packages along the correct path. In addition, you need a method to identify the destination addresses clearly and a schema indicating how to assign these addresses. The address and naming structures required for this must be established before installing the SAP systems. Subsequent changes are costly and cause interruptions to the running operation.

10.1.1 IP Address Concepts

In the early days of the Internet, when address space appeared to be unlimited, very large address blocks were generously allocated to individual organizations. Because of this transgression, born out of a lack of foresight of the turbulent development of the Internet, a bottleneck of globally unique IP addresses became a dangerous possibility.

Private address spaces

Since then, the use of private address spaces has generally been implemented according to RFC 1918 as the most practical solution to this problem. These private IP addresses must only be unique within a company. By default, Internet routers are set so that they don't transfer any IP packages from private address spaces. This means that the addresses can be used simultaneously by different companies. This gives medium-sized businesses the opportunity to implement a global network infrastructure, the likes of what you see in a large international corporation.

Network Address Translation

However, this also eliminated the exchange of data between companies using private address spaces. This problem was subsequently solved by Network Address Translation (NAT). NAT exchanges the private IP addresses of the data packages with one or more public IP addresses and vice versa. The implementation generally occurs via the router that serves as the gateway between the public and private networks.

A purely static 1:1 implementation, however, has the disadvantage that you require a public address for each private address so that the data packages can find their respective destinations. You can bypass this problem by assigning an individual TCP or UDP port to the connection in addition to the IP addresses (Port Address Translation, PAT).

You can compare this to the telephone system of a company that has its own official phone number, plus specific extensions for its individual employees. Contrary to this, after ending the connection, the TCP port is released again and can be used for another connection.

This way, it is generally sufficient to have a small number of public IP addresses, which are provided by an Internet Service Provider, ISP. This means a private network can be connected to the Internet via thousands of nodes.

However, this means that the initial point of a connection cannot be clearly identified anymore. While this does not pose a problem for communication with the end devices of SAP users, for server-to-server communications, there is no alternative to the 1:1 allocation, because at any time a unique allocation of the communication partner is necessary.

For SAP data exchange through NAT there are a few specific problems. By logging on to the central instance of an SAP system, the message server sends the IP addresses of all application instances of the system back to the end device. These addresses are used by SAP GUI to create a connection to the server that causes the smallest workload. The connection attempt through SAP GUI then ends up at the official IP address and hence leads to nothing.

You can circumvent this problem by setting up additional logon groups or, better still, by using two SAProuters. One router is available in the Internet and the other router is available on the intranet. The user only needs to be able to specify the IP address of the outer of the two SAProuters.[1]

NAT and RFC

When an SAP system calls functions on another computer by SAP Remote Function Call (RFC), NAT again creates problems, if the RFC cli-

1 You can find details on the configuration in the SAP white paper "Network Address Translation in the SAP Environment," which is available for partners and customers in SAPnet.

ent has an official IP address, while the gateway and the RFC server are part of another network. This problem can be solved by enhancing the file gw/alternative hostnames in the instance profile of the SAP system.[2] This ensures that the IP address assigned by the router can be identified by your own host.

DHCP The Dynamic Host Configuration Protocol (DHCP) automatically executes the network configuration of hosts. This feature is primarily used for the administration of workstation on local networks and for dial-in connections. DHCP automatically assigns an IP address from a list of available IP addresses, which are defined by the network administrator. This means that the same computer is assigned a different IP address after each restart, or every time someone logs onto the network. You can also instruct the DHCP server to assign a specific IP address to certain hosts by using their MAC address.

You can operate SAP end devices with DHCP and change IP addresses if no SAP services such as gateways or dispatchers run on them. Because the SAP servers save the name and address of the network for the individual connections, when using DHCP, the following points must be taken into account:

- Name resolution is buffered in the SAP system. This can lead to incorrect entries in some protocol files when the IP address is assigned to another device. In the user overview (Transaction SM04), however, the correct name is displayed, which is determined in the application server when logging onto the SAP GUI.
- Printers can then only be addressed by the complete DNS name (provided the name resolution is functioning).
- Even though front-end PCs or workstations work with DHCP, fixed IP addresses are imperative for SAP servers, print servers, and network devices (these IP addresses can be virtual however).

10.1.2 Name and Address Resolution

Computers can work better with numbers, while people can generally work better with words. As people like to assign descriptive names to things in their environment, it is only natural that a computer also is assigned a name. The computer name or host name is a logical name for

2 See SAP Note 0148832.

the computer itself and is configured in the operating system. The operating system identifies itself and its host by the host name.

Host names

In the SAP system, the servers also have host names. The host name for SAP servers is used at many points, for instance, for installation, in the start scripts, and for communication between the servers. The host name must therefore receive its final value before installing the SAP system. A subsequent change is relatively difficult. The length of the host name in an SAP system is limited to a maximum of eight characters.

You should therefore create a flexible naming concept in the ramp up to an SAP implementation. It is advisable to select a host name for the SAP system different from the name of the server on which the system is installed. This allows you to shift SAP systems to another server at any time without having to perform configuration changes.

Full qualified domain name

You can freely select the host name by taking into account the rules of Internet naming conventions.[3] Letters of the alphabet (A to Z), the minus symbol (-), and the digits (0 through 9) are permitted. However, the last character cannot be a minus character. There is no differentiation between uppercase and lowercase letters. The period (.) cannot appear as a part of the host name, it can only appear in the full qualified domain name. The length of the full qualified domain name (for example, *r3app01.company.com*) can have a maximum of 60 characters.

Generally, the full qualified domain name should always be used, even though this is not really necessary if a company has only one domain. Using the full qualified domain name allows you to avoid name resolution problems, if, for example, the domain structure is changed during an active directory implementation.

In particular, when creating printer queues on the operating-system level, the problem arises that you can only enter a specific number of domains in the file *resolv.conf*.

Furthermore, for definitions of RFC destinations, you should always enter the entire DNS name instead of the IP address (see checkbox in Transaction SM59). Otherwise, as the system buffers the address, you would have to delete the RFC destination when making a change to the destination address and then recreate it.

3 See RFC 952 and 1123.

Host names and IP names

Similar to the host names, the numeric addresses can also be translated by descriptive IP names. Each IP address is then usually assigned an IP name that simplifies the treatment of IP addresses. The IP name is the name by which the network adapter is identified on the network. This IP name is often incorrectly referred to as the host name. Only if a computer has only one network adapter are the host name and the IP name generally identical. In this case, a unique relationship exists between the logical host name and the IP name (or the IP address).

Name services for SAP systems

Because the network devices can only manage numeric addresses, the IP name must be assigned IP addresses using a name database. The use of a local host file or a naming service such as Domain Name System/Service (DNS) or Windows Internet Naming Service (WINS) are among the established methods.

Address resolution

The translation of an IP or host name in an IP address is referred to as a resolution. Most frequently, an IP name is resolved to an IP address. For an SAP system, the resolution in the opposite direction is also necessary (and is referred to as reverse lookup). An SAP system places different demands on the IP name and address resolution:

- All IP names must be resolved by all hosts in an SAP system in identical IP addresses and vice versa (carrying out a resolution in the IP name–IP address–IP name sequence must result in the same name).

Alias name

- The IP name cannot be an alias name. In Windows, the sequence of the network adapters must be properly configured in the system.
- The *localhost* name must be resolvable (typically the corresponding IP address is 127.0.0.1).
- For RFC or CPI-C client programs that are externally connected with the SAP system, no resolution of the client computer's IP address is required. The same goes for the RFC server programs, which are registered on the gateway or can be started via an SAP GUI. Exceptions are the gateway security functions that can be activated in the file *secinfo.*
- The SAP gateway can start RFC or CPI-C server programs on another computer. In this case, a reverse lookup must be feasible. If the RFC destinations are configured with the computer names, the IP name resolution must be ensured.
- Printer or print server names must be resolved on the SAP server. For print servers, it is not a requirement that the names of the printers themselves can be resolved. For front-end printing, there is no name

resolution required since the existing connection between application computer and SAP GUI is used.

- When starting the SAP system, a reverse lookup of all network adapters that are integrated in the computers is performed. The system also attempts to resolve the addresses for all end devices with SAP GUI, and for all RFC and CPI-C client hosts into names. These resolutions are carried out so that readable names instead of numeric IP addresses are displayed in the monitors and in the system log.

Reverse lookup

Name and address buffering

The SAP system has its own network interface (NI), which is used by SAProuter and for CPI-C and RFC. The NI saves the results of the name resolution and the reverse lookup in a special buffer. This means the operating system only has to perform the resolution once. In order to ensure that changes to the IP names or IP addresses are effective in the system, SAP recommends that you restart the system, because just manually deleting the buffer does not include the message server.

In order to ensure that the name resolution functions correctly, we recommend that you use the nslookup command. It is available in the command line mode of Windows and as a UNIX command. The nslookup command checks both the resolution and the reverse lookup.

10.1.3 Name Resolution Methods

Resolving a computer name into an IP address is comparable to calling the directory assistance to inquire about a person's phone number. In this context, there are several procedures that can be configured in the operating system.

Host files

Host files represent the simplest and most reliable solution. When making entries, you must ensure that the IP name (which corresponds to the host name) must be entered as the first name after the IP address and not as an alias (second name). In UNIX, the file is called */etc/hosts* and in Windows, it is *C:\WINDOWS\system32\drivers\etc\hosts*. Additionally, Windows also contains the file lmhosts in the same directory that performs the name resolution for WINS. Since all information for name resolution is available on the computer, no network access is necessary. The costs involved in maintaining host files on every server consistently can be quite high when there are numerous computers in a system landscape. Therefore, this method is not recommended from a network point of view.

Network Information Service

With Network Information Service (NIS) a master server provide the central directory for name resolution. Since an access to the NIS server is necessary for every resolution, high availability, short response times, and careful planning of the NIS system are requirements for a seamless operation. In order to enhance availability and performance, additional slave servers can be implemented in addition to the master server.

Windows Internet Name Service

The Windows Internet Name Service (WINS) is suitable for pure Windows environments. It cannot be used to resolve the host names of a UNIX system, because it assigns NetBIOS names to the IP addresses. Even if it is easy to implement and configure, it is more suitable for smaller, Windows networks with flat structures.

Domain Name Service

The Domain Name Service (DNS), which has evolved to become a defacto standard, can support large, complex hierarchical network structures with many hosts. In fact, the entire Internet uses a single DNS infrastructure for name resolution. Availability and response time considerations are the same as those discussed for NIS.

Because the configuration and maintenance is relatively complex for DNS, careful planning is particularly important. Errors in DNS cause massive performance losses, or even total failure. If the DNS server is not available, no new connections can be established in the network. Therefore, at least one backup DNS server should be available on the network, for which all the configuration data and error-tolerant network connections between the DNS server and the SAP system are replicated. Alternatively, you can run a DNS server on any server with SAP systems.

DNS zone file

All name domains of a company (for example, *sales.company.com*) must be specified in the zone file of the DNS, and a name server must be installed as the primary name server for this zone. In addition, a zone file is required for all network domains for reverse lookup.

However, not all computers have to be entered in the zones. The most important thing is that the zones exist. If, for example, no client computers need to be resolved, the zone files for the network and name domains of the end devices can remain empty.

For security reasons, requests for internal names or addresses should not be referred to external name servers (for example, to the Internet). You can ensure this if the DNS cache files only contain root name servers that are located on the local network.

10.1.4 SAP Servers with Several Network Cards

A server with more than one network card is referred to as a multihomed host. There are various reasons for equipping the servers of a productive SAP system with more than one network card. However, this can cause problems if it is possible to access a multihomed host from different subnetworks via several network addresses. Then, it becomes clear that the assignment of the server is no longer unique.

Separate server network?

In the past, it was necessary to provide a separate "server" network in order to connect the database and the application servers. This network used to be physically separated from the general or user network. The reason behind this separation was the insufficient performance of the shared network topologies where all hosts had to share the same bandwidth. Consequently, the SAP systems had to be equipped with a network card for the server network and a second one for the general user network (dual homed).

In this case, however, there are two possible paths between the SAP application and the database server. For this reason, static entries in the host files had to ensure that the server communication really took place through the server network. Furthermore, in Windows, the sequence of network cards must be strictly defined before SAP is installed. The necessary configurations are explained in detail in the SAP white paper "Network Integration of SAP Servers" which is available to partners and customers in SAPnet.[4]

Due to the increased use of fast and gigabyte Ethernet switches, the network bandwidth bottlenecks were eliminated. From a performance perspective, generally a single gigabyte Ethernet adapter is sufficient for approximately 4,000 users. Therefore, today, it's usually no longer necessary to have a separate server network from a performance standpoint.

However, for reasons of availability, there should be at least two network cards installed in each SAP server to avoid a single point of failure (SPoF). In order to avoid broadcast storms due to network loops (see Chapter 11 for more information) and the difficulties of a layer-3 multihoming, the manufacturers of network cards provide different methods.

Adaptive fault tolerance

For Adaptive Fault Tolerance (AFT), one network card is configured as active and all others are configured as standby. A common MAC and IP address is used for all network cards. The standby cards are in standby

4 Go to *http://service.sap.com/network.*

mode, but data is only transferred if the active network card is defective. A load distribution is not possible with AFT.

Adaptive load balancing

In Adaptive Load Balancing (ALB),all network cards send data, but only one of the cards can receive data. This card has the only layer-2 server address that is recognized by all clients. If this network card fails, another one assumes its identity. Therefore, load balancing in ALB only occurs for the outgoing traffic but not in the incoming direction.

Link aggregation

For link aggregation, several parallel connections are bundled between network devices and hosts. The network cards of a connection that are bundled to a group are addressed through a common, virtual IP address. Therefore, the host can be identified by a unique assignment to the host name. Consequently, it is no longer necessary to configure static routes manually on every server. In addition, the SPoF, which is represented by a single network card, also disappears.

A disadvantage of link aggregation is that only parallel links can be bundled to the same network switch. The single point of failure is therefore shifted from the network card to the network switch. HP Auto Port Aggregation (APA) can configure active standby links to different switches. However, in this mode, only one bundle transfers active data. Balance Suite from NSI software[5] supports the configuration of link aggregations through several switches for Windows.

Switchover configurations

In Chapter 5, different concepts were introduced to ensure the smooth operation of business-critical applications. For all these solutions, the end devices must be able to find the substitute host after a failover. Two processes can be used here. In this context, either the "identity" consisting of IP address and host name is transferred with the applications, or virtual IP addresses are used. This ensures that the user machines always find an SAP server after the switchover.

The standby server host names and the IP addresses of the failed servers are assigned during the identity transfer. In this case, no particular configuration is necessary for the SAP system since the host name and the IP address of the productive and standby servers are identical. However, only one computer can be active at a time on the network.

For cluster solutions, each system generally has virtual IP addresses and names. In the event of a system failure, a server adopts the virtual IP

5 Go to *http://www.nsisw.com*.

address and the virtual IP name of the failed server from the cluster. In the SAP system configuration, only the virtual IP name is used.

The virtual host names are used in all profile parameters within an SAP system. These virtual names and addresses must be located in the host file or in the DNS so the end devices can reach the application hosts. The "real" host names of the physical servers are not used in the SAP profiles. This configuration is also described in the SAP white paper "Network Integration of the SAP Servers."[6]

Today, many SAP customers work primarily with virtual addresses, regardless of whether the system is in a cluster. The configuration files of the SAP systems contain only the host name. The systems are exclusively called by their DNS names. The host name of the server is not used. Thus, when you exchange a host, you don't have to reconfigure the SAP system (or the SAP systems). If all the data exists in a Storage Area Network (SAN), no data should be copied. The vgexport and vgimport commands will suffice, because they enable you to do an exchange in approximately two hours.

10.1.5 Identifying the SAP Data Traffic

SAP applications use Transmission Control Protocol (TCP) ports exclusively when communicating via networks. User Datagram Protocol (UDP) is used only for internal communication on the same host. Typically, several processes or applications run simultaneously on one computer. That's the reason why an IP data package transfers a socket or TCP port number, in addition to the target address of a computer, to identify the session or application for which the data is supposed to be provided.

TCP ports

For some SAP services, the port numbers are defined as fixed. Mostly, they are determined by a variable. This also ensures the operation of several instances of the application on one server. In many cases, the instance number of the Web AS instance is part of the TCP port number, and the three letters of the SAP system identifier (SID) of the SAP system are a component of the service name. In this way, the data traffic of different SAP components can be identified. The well known TCP Ports are,

6 However, the Enterprise Portal stores the real host name of the server in its config files.

for example, published in SAP white paper "TCP/IP Ports used by SAP Applications," which is available to partners and customers in SAPnet.[7]

SAP Web AS and Port 80

In contrast to the Internet standard, which always specifies Port 80 for HTTP, when installing the SAP Web AS, a port number must be configured in the form "80NN" (or "443NN" for HTTPS) (NN stands for the instance number of Web AS), so that the server can be started. For servers that are to be accessed from the Internet, this value should be changed accordingly after the installation, or a proxy server should be used.

The port schema provides a maximum of seven server processes per instance for J2EE. However, if this is not sufficient, the schema can be easily modified in order to permit more processes.

10.2 Load Balancing and Availability

The architecture of the SAP system allows you to install several Web AS instances of a SAP NetWeaver or mySAP solution on several hosts. This allows you to distribute the system load to several servers. On the other hand, this grant some redundancy for business-critical systems. Solutions for load balancing and increasing the availability basically use the same mechanisms.

To grant a single point of access to the system you usually need an additional component called a "load balancer". This device accepts incoming requests and directs them to one of the application servers

The classic ABAP part of the SAP Web AS provides the SAP Message Server as an integrated mechanism for load balancing. Applications that use a standard Web browser as a user interface, however, require other methods for load balancing and failover as well as grant a single point of access.

Client-based load balancing

Using a load balancer is not the only way to accomplish Web server load balancing. Even the client can be used for load balancing; this case is called client-based load balancing. When logging onto the system the client first contacts a load balancing device and request, to which Web application server Web AS it should connect.

7 Go to *http://service.sap.com/network*. For general information on assigning ports, go to *http://www.iana.org/assignments/port-numbers,* which is the official address for the assignment of port numbers, domain names, and so on.

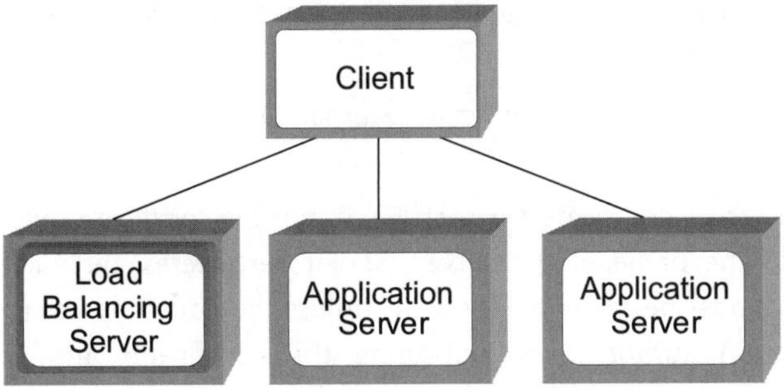

Figure 10.1 Client-Based Load Balancing

The following two processes are available for this:

- For redirects, the Internet address (Uniform Resource Locator, URL) of a host is replaced by the Internet address of another host.
- For DNS-based methods, the IP address of a host is replaced by the IP address of another host, as a result of name resolution.

Redirection

As for classic SAP GUI processes, during a redirect, the SAP Message Server determines which application host is best suited to serve an additional user. This decision is based on the relative strengths of the application host and the number of users who are already logged on to this computer. The strength of the application host is determined by the number of processes configured on this host and by other factors as well.

In addition, the Message Server considers whether the requested function runs on the ABAP or the Java part of the Web AS. Redirection is not limited to the SAP Message Server. If other load balancing mechanisms that support redirection already exist, SAP Web AS can be integrated into such an infrastructure.

Drawbacks

Today, the redirection mechanism is the norm even for security critical Internet applications such as electronic banking. One of the benefits of client-based load balancing is that no additional hardware is required. It does however have certain disadvantages:

- Users become annoyed because the redirection is shown in the URL display field of the browser. This can lead to questions regarding whether the server is correct, or the session was captured by a hacker who would steal confidential information.
- If users set browser bookmarks on an application host, they cancel the entire load balancing process. If this host is then not available at a par-

ticular time, the user can no longer log onto the system (at least not via the bookmark).

- Each individual host requires official external DNS names and IP addresses.
- You require a server certificate for each host and this certificate must correspond to the name of the server. Server certificates are quite expensive and must be renewed annually, unless the company has its own certification authority. Administering the certificates and IP addresses requires much effort.
- Redirection is not particularly suitable for the Firewall mechanisms, because they refer to the internal names of the application servers. Although you can resolve the problem by rewriting the redirection response in the firewall or reverse proxy, this is not the best solution.
- A new authentication is required for every redirection. Although this can be avoided by cookie-based authentication, the cookies must be distributed to all hosts of a DNS domain.

What all this means is that load balancing with redirection for connecting users through the open Internet is generally not advisable. For access from the company intranet, where security aspects, IP addresses, and expensive certificates are of little or no importance, load balancing through redirection can be a suitable solution despite certain disadvantages.

Round-robin DNS

Another simple load-balancing mechanism uses the domain name system. Here, contrary to normal practice, the DNS server does not assign a single fixed IP address to the network name; instead, the network names are assigned the IP addresses of the available application servers from a pool "in sequence" (round robin).

Round-robin DNS can actually be used with the SAP Web AS; however, the users are not automatically redirected to another host if their application server fails, because the name resolution is usually performed only during logon. The users must then restart the browser and click on the Refresh button.

To ensure that users are not assigned to malfunctioning systems, a mechanism must be implemented that regularly checks the availability of the application hosts and, if necessary, removes their IP addresses from the pool. In addition, there are problems with the session persistence, if users access the system through a proxy server.

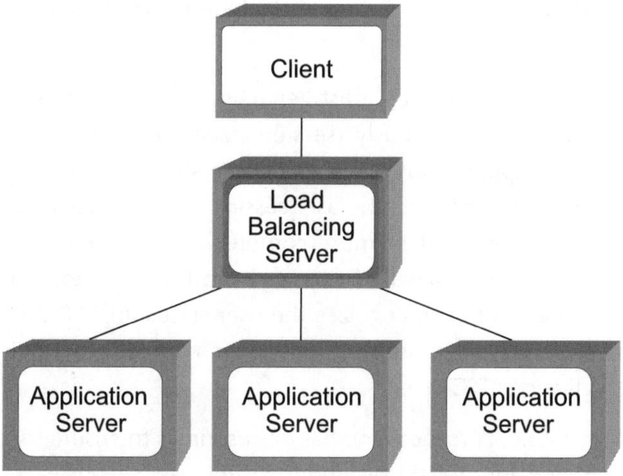

Figure 10.2 Load Balancing with Dedicated Load Balancer

Load balancing systems

The disadvantages referred to can be avoided through software or hardware-based load balancers such as LocalDirector from Cisco. There are also various routers and switches that are available with the corresponding functionality. However hardware load balancers come naturally for a price.

An excellent example of a cost free software load balancer is the SAP Web Dispatcher which receives the incoming requests and transfers them to a suitable application host.

This ensures that there is a central access point (single point of access) to the system with an official name for the service. An official IP address and a Secure Sockets Layer (SSL) server certificate are sufficient to reach all application hosts. Since the same URL is always displayed to the users, they can use it as a bookmark.

With the help of a session cookie, the SAP Web Dispatcher can always forward all the requests of a particular user to the same application instance, as is necessary in stateful applications (see below).

In general, the SAP Web Dispatcher is installed on a host in the demilitarized zone (DMZ). Since it represents a SPoF in addition to being a single point of access, it should be backed up by a cluster configuration.

Stateful Web applications

A distinction is made in programming models for Web applications between stateless and stateful programs. The stateless model is sufficient for applications for which each user request is independent from the previous one. For stateless applications, each request can then be assigned to another host without a problem. Examples include browsing in catalogs, or selecting an individual article.

More complex applications, however, must generally be able to remember what the user has done previously (session persistence). A typical example of this type of applications is the electronic shopping cart in a Web shop. For business transactions, the user session can also lock database objects or include the result of more complex requests. For such applications, each request must always be assigned to the same application host, because only this host recognizes the user status. In SAP Web AS, session persistence is implemented by the so called roll area, which is also the case with classic SAP GUI.

HTTP is stateless

However, HTTP is a stateless protocol and has no resources to ensure that requests that follow one another always find the same user session.

Therefore, if the first user request creates a user session on an application host, the load balancing mechanism must ensure that all subsequent requests are sent to this host as well. Otherwise, not only would the user context get lost, because the other hosts don't know the user, but, furthermore, a newly structured second session wouldn't be able to use any database objects that were locked or kept active by the first session.

Cookies and URL rewriting

Using session cookies, applications can recognize which session a request belongs to. A cookie is a small text string that the server sends to the browser to identify the session and that the browser, in turn, resends with each subsequent request.

As an alternative to cookies that are not permitted in some companies due to security reasons, the application can also insert a session identifier in the URL in the HTTP header and can send this to the browser (URL rewriting). SAP Web AS supports both methods.

Load balancers can use the session identifier in the HTTP header and mapping between the session cookie and the assigned application hosts, in order to balance stateful applications. It is even easier when you use SAP Web AS, because it uses the host name of the application host as a component of the session identifier.

However, this also means that the load balancer must know the structure of the SAP session identifier in order to ensure session persistence. Alternatively, many hardware-based load balancers insert their own session cookies in the HTTP data flow. This method, of course, fails if the use of cookies is deactivated on the browser.

The problem with encryption

With the Secure Socket Layer (SSL), a safe, encrypted tunnel is drilled from the client device through the potentially unsafe Internet. In the conventional use of SSL, the entire data flow, including the HTTP request header, is encrypted for security reasons. This is also recommended by SAP, since the URL session identifier or session cookies are used to authenticate the subsequent requests after logging onto the SAP system. If, during a transfer via an Internet connection, a session URL or cookie is stolen by scanning the data flow, it can be used for unauthorized access to the system.

The essential question regarding load balancers is where this SSL tunnel actually ends. Both cookies and URL session identifiers work only with HTTP in plain, un-encrypted text. Therefore the SSL network connections must be terminated at the load balancer, in order to use cookies or URL session identifiers for session persistence through the Internet.

Client IP address

In principle, the user's IP address could also be used for identifying the session. However, this is only the case when one user is working on one host and this same user starts only one session. This method, however, causes problems if the connection runs through a proxy server, because the proxy server replaces the IP addresses of all users with its own address. Although the proxy server can differentiate between the individual user sessions, this would cancel the load balancing; the load balancer would always forward all users that arrive in the system through a proxy to the same application host. (Some Internet providers use proxy load balancing between different proxy servers, resulting in the same users being dynamically assigned different IP addresses during a session.)

A further disadvantage is that the load balancer doesn't detect a break in the session and, therefore, unnecessarily keeps the connection open.

SSL session ID

The SSL session ID method was developed to enable encrypted end-to-end connections for stateful applications. Unfortunately, the duration of an SSL session does not correspond to the user session. For security reasons, the browser terminates the SSL session after a certain period of time and starts a new session, regardless of whether the user session has been ended.

A TCP session can also be terminated at any time. For this reason, the TCP port cannot be used instead of the IP address, because of the stateless HTTP that opens a new TCP session with a new port. Therefore, neither SSL session ID nor TCP ports are suitable methods to secure session persistence through encrypted connections.

This leaves two methods to ensure session persistence through encrypted connections with SSL:

- Terminating the SSL connection to the load balancer and using a session ID to secure persistence
- End-to-end SSL encryption from the browser to the application server and using the client IP address

Selecting a method that meets the requirements your company depends on your security concept.

10.3 Security Aspects

In this section, we examine ways to ensure the security of SAP Web AS against unauthorized access through the network. A detailed description of topics such as firewall technologies, recognizing attacks (intrusion detection), or security on operating-system levels, however, would exceed the scope of this chapter.

10.3.1 User Authentication

The data traffic in business applications is inherently confidential. Therefore, data must be protected against unauthorized access (if it involves personal data, protection against unauthorized use is a legally imperative). However, the defense against unauthorized access is not the only aspect that is integral to ensuring security. In addition, you must make certain that the authorized users can also be securely authenticated by the system.

Authentication via cookies

SAP applications enable the authentication of sequential requests via cookies. This also means that users must log on only once with a user name and password, in order to access various mySAP solutions (so-called Single Sign-On, SSO). But, if someone eavesdrops on such a cookie during the transfer, despite encryption, it can be misused.

X.509 certificate

Authentication can also occur through X.509 certificates. On the Internet, an X.509 client certificate acts as a digital identity card and is also referred to as a public key certificate. The threat of eavesdropping is eliminated here through a combination of this technology and SSL encryption.

SSL encryption

The general rule here is that all Web AS applications that require a user authentication also demand SSL encryption. Exceptions to this rule are public catalogs or Web pages for search engines.

SSL versus VPN

In addition to SSL, the necessary security can also be implemented through a *classic* Virtual Private Network (VPN). In this context, VPN gateways (firewalls or routers) encrypt and authenticate authorized networks (intranets). This option is completely transparent for SAP services and is, in particular, suitable for remote client access (remote access VPN), or for communication between SAP servers (site-to-site VPN). Load balancing is not a problem for a classic VPN, because the data is decrypted by the load balancer.

Terminating SSL in the load balancer

SAP Web Dispatcher can either terminate an SSL connection or forward it to the application host (end-to-end SSL). Terminating the SSL session in the load balancer has different advantages in comparison to forwarding an SSL connection. Processing SSL places a considerable load on the CPU. The load on the application hosts is reduced if the decryption is already done on the load balancer.[8] Session cookies or URLs can be used to ensure session persistence. Authentication can be implemented on the load balancer, for example, with data from a company's Lightweight Directory Access Protocol (LDAP) directory (early authentication). The requests can be checked and filtered by the load balancer for viruses and attacks.

The termination in the DMZ, however, means that communication between the load balancer and SAP Web AS occurs in plain text and is susceptible to being eavesdropped on by a potential intruder. In addition, the intruder could also usurp an authentication token and pass himself off as an authorized user.

Subdivided DMZ

Such risks can be countered by subdividing the demilitarized zone (subdivided DMZ) and using an intrusion detection system and efficient security management.

As an alternative, the load balancer can also encrypt the connection to SAP Web AS through SSL. The ostensible man-in-the-middle attacks can mostly be eliminated by using SSL client certificates for authentication between the load balancer and SAP Web AS.

If the SAP Web Dispatcher is to terminate the SSL connection, it must have a security environment. For this, the SAP cryptographic library must be installed on the Web Dispatcher since it contains the necessary secu-

8 With SSL accelerators, the decryption process can be accelerated substantially.

rity information for using the SSL protocol. The SAP Web Dispatcher must also have a key pair and a public key certificate in order to use the SSL connection.

User authentication with X.509 certificates is not possible, because the connection to SAP Web AS must be terminated in order for the user to log on.

Several names for a system

The server certificate of a Web server must be issued for the host name in the URL, which the client uses to access the server. When using end-to-end SSL encryption, all servers that are accessed through a load balancer are called through the same host name. This means that they can all use the same server certificate.

Problems arise if a system landscape must be accessible from different networks, for example, from the Internet and intranet, or in an application service provider (ASP) from different customer networks. In this case, every instance of SAP Web AS can have only one server certificate. Thus, for every URL and for every certificate, a separate server pool must be established (Figure 10.3).

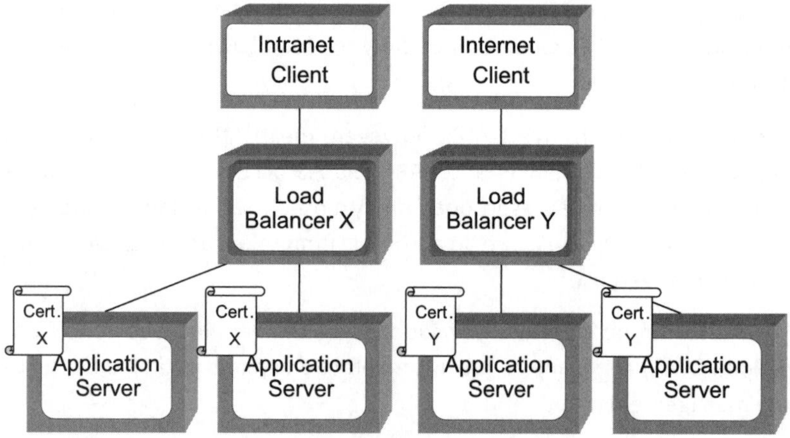

Figure 10.3 Server Certificates for End-to-End SSL

If the SSL connection is terminated at the load balancer, then this load balancer is the owner of the server certificate, and the requests can be distributed to all the application hosts (Figure 10.4).

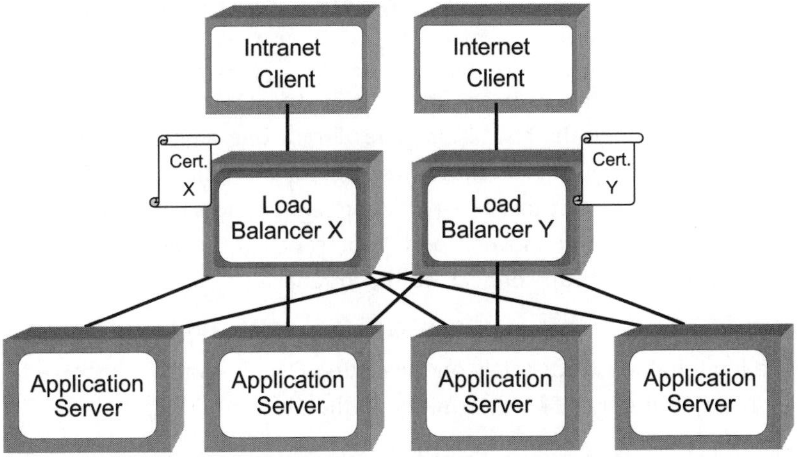

Figure 10.4 Server Certificate for Termination at the Load Balancer

As described above, the decision as to where the SSL encryption is terminated is essential for the security architecture. Here, all variants have specific advantages and drawbacks that must be taken into account. Therefore, there is no one definitive recommendation.

10.3.2 Demilitarized Zones

The Internet opened up inconceivable methods of communication with customers and business partners. However, opening internal SAP systems for free access from the global network also released uncounted methods for their unauthorized use. Each system which is connected with the Internet must therefore be protected by firewalls against unauthorized access.

Firewalls, much like their real-life counterparts, separate the different parts of a network infrastructure to ensure that the threat of unauthorized access does not move from one segment to another.[9]

Unfortunately, you can't set the filters in such a restrictive manner so as to block all potentially dangerous threats as this would also block all desired accesses by potential customers and business partners. Therefore, state-of-the-art security concepts are based on a multilevel architecture.

Attacks from the Internet

In this context, a separate network segment is implemented between the potentially hostile Internet and the intranet that is regarded as friendly,

9 Names such as bastion host or gatekeeper are no longer in use as their functionality has been integrated into the firewalls.

which, in military-like language, is referred to as the "demilitarized zone," DMZ.

Even if in diagrams such as Figure 10.5, the DMZ is always shown between two (logical) firewalls, in general, only one physical firewall system is necessary. This is because firewalls such as Checkpoint FW-1 or Cisco PIX have at least three network ports: one port is connected to the Internet router, one or several ports represent one or more DMZs, and one port or port group connects to the intranet.

Between ports, all data flows can be filtered in any direction, analyzed, and limited. It depends solely on the setup of the firewall if a package filter is set, or if only HTTP is permitted in the different DMZs.

The only hosts that are then installed in the different DMZs are those for which access from the Internet cannot be blocked. Examples of this are Web and mail servers and application proxies for other applications that are located on the internal network. An SAP Web dispatcher is not necessarily situated in the same DMZ as the mail relays or the Web servers.

Web dispatcher as an application layer gateway

In general, SAP application hosts should not be located in a DMZ, because of security reasons, and their names and IP addresses should not be found on the Internet under any circumstances. All requests must therefore run through an application layer gateway in the DMZ. This task can also be executed by the SAP Web Dispatcher (Figure 10.5).

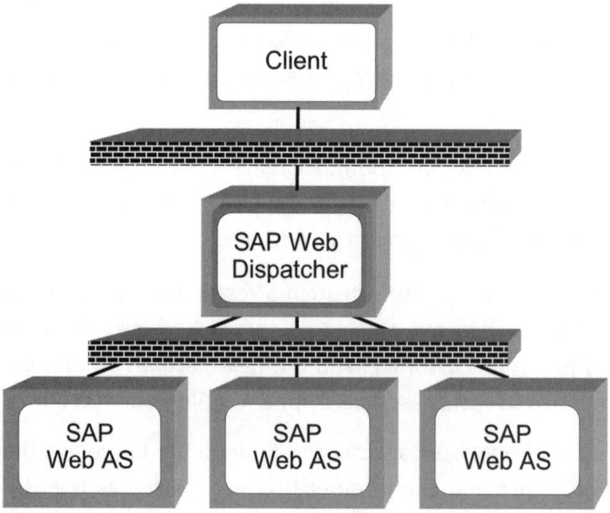

Figure 10.5 SAP Web Dispatcher as an Application Layer Gateway in the DMZ

Installing a firewall between the application hosts and database hosts is only minimally beneficial for security, because the SAP Web AS requires full access to all databases. Since this would considerably disturb the system performance, we do not recommend that you use such a configuration.

It makes more sense to install an additional firewall between the NetWeaver systems, which are available over the Internet, and the mySAP solutions, which map particularly sensitive business processes (FI, HR, and so on) (see Figure 10.6). The security systems that are arranged in successive order increase the difficulties that a potential attacker must overcome in order to encroach on protected systems. Despite the increased management effort, the firewall systems should be from different manufacturers, so a security gap (for example, because of a missing SW patch) in one system does not compromise the other system. This multilevel approach ensures that a potential attack is limited to a small part of the system.

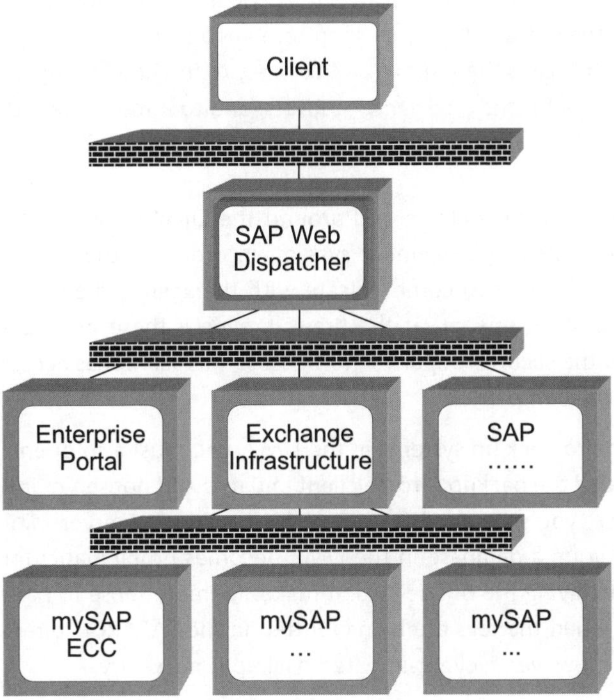

Figure 10.6 Second DMZ and High Security Network

Be aware that DMZs place several additional requirements on the system operation that don't occur in a closed intranet.

No DNS in the DMZ In order to protect the internal naming structures, it is best to work in a DMZ with a host file and not with a DNS. When changes are made here, the address maintenance must be done in all host files (which is easily forgotten).

Firewall Rules and Addresses

Firewall rules are combinations of IP addresses and ports. Here, connections can be permitted or blocked. If you have implemented a concept where the systems are not addressed through the host names of the server, but through the functional, logical address of the system, you may encounter an unexpected problem. The system in the DMZ addresses the back-end system via the function address which, in turn, responds with the host IP address. This address is, however, not generally stored in the rules table of the firewall, which means that communication is denied by the firewall. If you have also stored the server address in the rules table of the firewall, this can result in another problem at a much later stage. That's because the problem occurs when it's time to replace the server. The server then receives a new address (the function address remains the same). It is then easy to forget to maintain a rule in the firewall for the new server address (and to remove the old one).

System monitoring The hosts, routers, and firewalls in and around the DMZ must also be monitored by the system management system. In order for the central system management server to communicate with the agents, the corresponding ports must be opened at the firewall, even if these ports are seen as critical by the security department, because this server has access to all systems in the company.

Data security and backup In order to also be to back up systems in the DMZ, you must also open a port in the firewall if the backup is to be client initiated and not server initiated. In this case, you should prefer simple file backups to server-initiated ones. Backing up a database in the DMZ becomes problematic, for example, when archiving the offline logs. It makes far more sense to back up immediately, when the logs are being written in the SAPARCH directory. To this end, however, a client-initiated backup is necessary.

Designing redundant firewalls Although firewalls are largely displayed as brick walls in schematic diagrams, in reality, they are specialized hosts which, like all technical systems, can fail. To avoid single points of failure, firewalls, like routers, should be designed as redundant.

All servers installed in the DMZ should be "hardened" against attacks,[10] so that only the absolutely necessary ports are opened (as is the case with most software systems, the Web AS is wide open to attack after installation). While only a few ports are required in an ABAP application server, this number increases with each new project in SAP Web AS.

"Hardened" systems

As DMZs are critical protection mechanisms that defend the company network against unauthorized attacks of any type, each change to these protection mechanisms must be critically checked and authorized by those responsible for security. Since cross-company processes and collaborative scenarios increasingly tend to perforate the firewall over time, the security goals must be established at the very beginning of a project. This is imperative if you want to avoid an endless discussion, when the security concept you have to implement for a business process is not compatible with the company's general security policy.

Change management

10.4 Summary

Before implementing an SAP system, you must first set up a hierarchical IP address and naming concept. The increased opening up of businesses to the outside requires rethinking in companies. The security requirements must be examined at an early stage in the project and kept in mind. The operation concepts must be changed so as to ensure that, despite increasing security requirements, a stable operation can still be guaranteed. The requirements include the following:

- A clear translation of IP names into IP addresses (address resolution) and vice-versa (reverse lookup) must be possible, either by host file DNS or WINS.
- The use of a backup domain name server is highly recommended.
- SAP frontends can generally be operated with Dynamic Host Configuration Protocol (DHCP).
- If several SAP Web Application Servers are installed for an SAP system, load balancing can be achieved by redirecting the Internet addresses or DNS-based methods.
- Due to the problems with client-based load balancing, the use of a load balancer such as the SAP Web Dispatcher is recommended.

10 For operating systems, the respective manufacturers provide all the necessary information.

- Since SAP transactions generally require a session status, the load balancing mechanism must ensure session persistence.
- This leads to the fact that an encrypted SSL Internet connection must be terminated at the load balancer. If this is not what you want, you can only achieve load balancing by using the classical Internet VPN approach (encryption on OSI layer 3).
- To ensure security against attacks from the Internet, a multilevel security concept—with at least two firewalls and a DMZ in between—is advisable.
- The firewalls and load balancers must also be redundantly designed to avoid single points of failure.
- Load balancers and dispatchers should not be located in the same DMZ as mail servers and relays, or Web servers.

11 Local Area Network Solutions

SAP NetWeaver solutions on the internal data highway

Network infrastructures installed on a company's premises are called local-area networks (LAN). Modern LAN technologies are capable of providing extremely high bandwidths on an area of several square miles.

When our first book on SAP infrastructures was published,[1] many company networks were still based on proprietary terminal-based applications with their own cable and plug types, bus systems based on coaxial cables, and architectures that were built from hubs and bridges. With the advent of SAP, cabling and network technology often had to be completely redone.

Since then, a unified infrastructure based on full switched Ethernet fiber optics, or twisted pair cables, RJ45 plugs, and hierarchical architectures from department and backbone switches has become standard, which is in keeping with the requirements of SAP solutions.

This chapter will therefore deal with only those aspects of local networks that pertain to the end-to-end availability of SAP systems. For example, these include technical characteristics that are often ignored such as lightning protection and electric potential equalization. When planning new buildings or approving the facilities in rented buildings, we advise you to read the corresponding chapters in the book mentioned above.

At the same time, mobile network technologies have undergone further rapid development. Therefore, we have devoted a specific section of this chapter to the characteristics, and the advantages and disadvantages of the wireless network.

Bandwidth demand for end users

Today's LANs are integrated data highways that transport a variety of data flows. These data flows can be divided into three categories: business-critical, time-critical, and other data traffic. The average bandwidth requirement of a typical client application is:

- SAP GUI: 1.5kbps (depending on the content)
- VoIP: 12kbps (depending on the compression)

1 Mißbach, Hoffmann: *SAP Hardware Solutions—Servers, Storage, and Networks for mySAP.com*. Prentice Hall 2000.

- Web browser: 30kbps (depending on the content)
- MPEG video: 1.45Mbps (depending on the compression)
- File transfer: many Mbps but not time-critical

If you compare the bandwidth consumption of these typical online activities, you'll notice that an SAP system, when contrasted with all applications, creates the least amount of data load on the network. Since only a few users use SAP and video-on-demand simultaneously, a bandwidth of 10Mbps is more than adequate for the individual end-user connection.

The individual data flows are merged at the work group level. For 12 to 24 users, a bandwidth of 100Mbps will generally suffice. The data flows are merged a second time at the building level where a multiple of 100Mbps or 1,000Mbps is required as a bandwidth. In the computer center, this bandwidth is then distributed with 100Mbps or 1,000Mbps connections to the server systems on which the applications run.

Fast, Gigabit, and more Ethernet

Optical and electrical signals are subject to various negative effects on their path. As these effects increase in proportion to the product of frequency and distance, the achievable bandwidths and range of communication lines are subject to physical limits. Therefore, increasing the signal frequency alone will not help you to attain a higher bandwidth. Special encoding algorithms must ensure that the signal that was originally put into the medium on the sender's side can be correctly reconstructed from the signal that contains added noise on the recipient's side.

Fast Ethernet and Gigabit Ethernet could only be developed so quickly, because existing tried-and-tested coding algorithms could be reverted to. Fast Ethernet is based on technologies that were originally developed for Fiber Distributed Data Interface (FDDI), according to ISO 9314. For Gigabit Ethernet, the encoding algorithms of fiber channel (see Chapter 7) where adapted. Meanwhile, even switches with 10 gigabit uplinks are no longer considered exotic.

11.1 High Availability for Local Networks

As already discussed, the local network architectures generally used contain several points of failure regarding both the active components and the cable connections. The worst-case scenario is represented by a failure of the central backbone. This is similar to a blackout for the entire company. A disruption at the work group level affects the work of an entire department.

Beware of loops!

In order to achieve high availability of local networks, it is apparent that all cable connections and active components should be redundantly designed. Unfortunately, for Ethernet networks, this is not always possible because redundant connections would generate loops in the data path, which must be avoided under all circumstances within a broadcast domain.

To understand this problem, we must look at the functionality of switches. A switch learns the addresses of the hosts which are reachable through its different ports from the transferred packets that arrive at these ports. In an internal address table, the switch saves information regarding whose hosts can be reached via which connection.

When a data packet arrives at a port, a check is performed to verify whether the destination address already exists in the address table. If this is the case, the packet is forwarded through the corresponding connection. Otherwise, the switch replicates the packet through all its connections, with the exception of the connection through which the packet was received. This means that target hosts, which had been unknown until this point, can be reached, and due to their response, the address table can be updated. This is exactly where the problem of redundant configuration lies, as shown in Figure 11.1.

In this example, there are two potential paths from computer a to computer b, which, in each case, lead through a connection to switches 1 and 2. What happens if computer *a* sends a packet to computer *b*, but computer b is not yet listed in the address tables of either switch?

1. Computer *a* in network Segment A transfers a packet. Both switches learn that computer *a* can be reached through connection 1.1. or 2.1, and broadcast the packet through all the other connections as they do not yet know the address of computer *b*.
2. Thus, there are two identical packets in Segment B. Because both switches are connected with each other via Segment B, these packets also reach both switches *cross-over*, then through connection 1.2 or 2.2 respectively. Since the packet still contains computer *a* as the sender, both switches learn that computer *a* suddenly seems to be located in Segment B.
3. As computer *b* is still not recognized, the packet is once again replicated through connections 1.1 or 2.1 into Segment A, from which it originates and is then duplicated. As the switches do not know each other and each switch continuously broadcasts the packet into the other segment, an endless loop is generated.

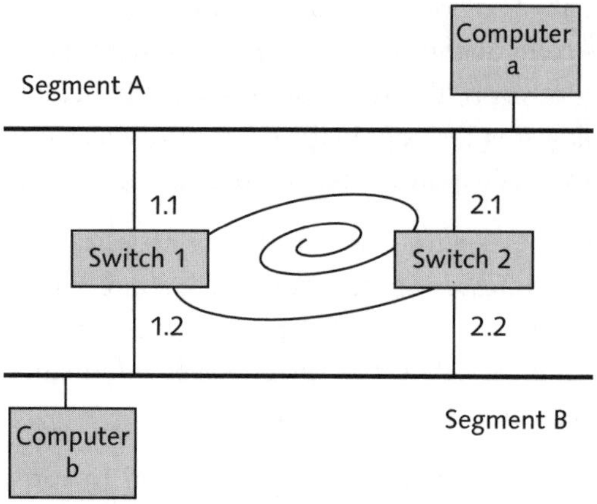

Figure 11.1 Network Loops caused by Redundant Paths

Broadcast storms and network meltdown

Due to the endless replication of the broadcast packets, the loop creates an avalanche effect. In a short space of time, one of the feared broadcast storms floods the network. In such a situation, no more communication is possible as the broadcasts use up the entire available bandwidth. This causes a network meltdown. The PCs connected are so strongly overloaded with interrupts that the systems freeze, which disturbs the entire data processing. For this reason, you should definitely avoid starting loops within a broadcast domain.

Spanning tree

To solve this problem, Radia Perlman developed the spanning tree algorithm (IEEE 802.1D). Switches exchange information using the spanning tree protocol, in order to recognize parallel paths. These paths are then shut down in sequence until only one is left. The remaining loop-free paths result in a tree structure that spans from the data center to the end devices, which is why it is called a spanning tree.

The disadvantage of the spanning tree process is that in redundant processes only one link can be used for data transport, while all other links are switched to standby mode. Investments in these cables and connections are therefore not exploited until there is a breakdown. In the event of a breakdown, the necessary recalculation of the spanning tree is also a relatively time-consuming process. During this time, the connections don't forward any more packets.

Modern switches limit broadcast storms

Therefore, the spanning tree concept doesn't play an important role anymore. Modern switches have mechanisms that limit broadcast storms. These mechanisms are based on the assumption that typically a certain ratio between user data and broadcasts is not exceeded. In the case of a broadcast storm, those broadcasts that go over the limit are distorted. You should, however, implement such mechanisms with caution. On the one hand, there is the danger that good broadcast packets could also be eliminated; on the other hand, the danger exists that a real broadcast storm could be disguised. In both cases, problems that are difficult to identify can emerge.

11.1.1 Link Aggregation

Different manufacturers provide different technologies that can bundle several 100Mbps or 1 Gbit/s connections (link aggregation). For the operating system, the bundled connections represent a single logical interface with a single MAC and IP address. Due to this aggregation, the load is distributed to the parallel connections. This provides higher performance and redundant paths. If a connection breaks down, the data traffic is automatically transferred to the remaining connections within the bundle.

However, link aggregation supports only parallel point-to-point connections between two devices. This means the switches that are linked through link aggregation still represent single points of failure. In addition, the different cables of a bundle are generally placed in the same position so that they're exposed to the same potential risks and can be simultaneously destroyed.

11.1.2 Highly Available Network Clusters for Business-critical Applications

Installing redundant cables and switches for each important work center in a company would lead to exorbitantly high costs and immensely complex configurations. An alternative approach, (which was developed by one of the authors) is based on the view of the business functions in a enterprise to design highly available networks for business-critical applications.

Human redundancy

From this hands-on approach, you can assume that a high availability is essential at the department level, but for individual work centers, a certain downtime can be tolerated. This is because at the department level there is always a functional redundancy since each user is assigned a substitute for leave, sickness, and so on. This substitute is often the colleague at the next desk. Even if the substitutes themselves are not there, the employee whose connection to the SAP system is disrupted can use the colleague's PC (or the colleague's connection wall socket). This fact can be used to grant also that work will be done even in case a network device is going down.

Rules for network clusters

In order to avoid SPoF on the business functions level, network clusters must be configured according to the following simple rules:

- An employee's PC that fulfills an important business function should never be connected to the same network switch as that of his or her substitute.
- For this reason, every network cabinet must contain at least two switches with separate connections (uplinks) to the data center.
- If possible, the connections should be executed on different paths.
- There must be at least two backbone switches installed in the data center (in different fire protection zones).
- Each clustered SAP server must be connected through separate network cards to these backbone switches.

Network clusters can most easily be implemented by intelligent patching, which consists of linking the end device connections on the patch panels of the network cabinet with the connections of the switches. You can generally assume that adjacent PCs are provided for employees with the same business functions that can mutually cover for each other. In order to meet the requirements of a network cluster, you only need to attach the end device connections with straight numbers on the patch panel to one switch and those with odd numbers to another switch.

When this concept is implemented methodically, single points of failure are avoided at the business function level as well as network loops and inactive standby connections. Network clusters can be implemented with plug & play components of any manufacturer.

Two simple examples illustrate the network cluster concept. In Figure 11.2, the sales departments PCs are located on the left-hand side and the logistics department PCs are located on the right-hand side.

- **Scenario 1:** One of the switches (or its uplink) in the sales department breaks down. Every other work center is dead, but the rest remain operational. In a typical network environment in which all PCs of the same department are connected to the same switch, the entire department cannot process any more orders.
- **Scenario 2:** One of the backbone switches in the data center breaks down. In half of the hosts the connection breaks down, but the rest, how-

ever, remain operational. If it takes too long to replace the backbone, switch cross connections between the switches can be used as a bypass.

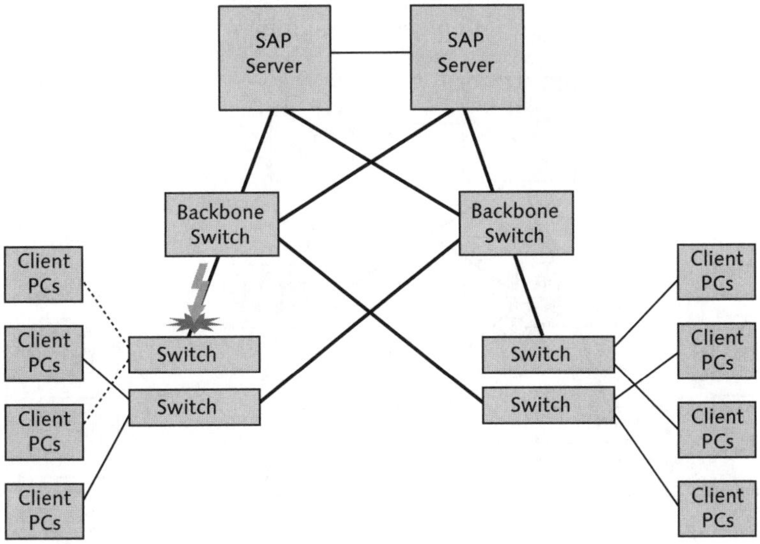

Figure 11.2 Highly Available Loop-Free Network Cluster

The network cluster concept ensures that at least one in every two PCs of a department has a connection to the SAP system at any time from a network perspective, and the business tasks of a department can be executed in any situation. The investments are the same as for a redundantly designed network based on the spanning tree concept. Alternatively, there is a network cluster but no convergence time, and the available bandwidth is substantially higher due to the utilization of all available links and connections.

11.1.3 Error-tolerant Meshed Networks

For a network cluster, even when a backbone switch or link breaks down (see Scenario 2 in the previous example), the operation of the enterprise can be maintained. However, in this case, up to 50 % of the work centers can lose their network connection. Due to switch meshing, the network cluster concept can be extended so that even the breakdown of a backbone component can be absorbed. This means that the local network is extensively error tolerant.

Switch meshing

Switch meshing is a technology originally developed by Hewlett Packard, which enables the creation of a completely meshed local network infrastructure without generating the risk of loops and subsequent network meltdown due to broadcast storms. Currently, other manufacturers implement this technology as well. All links and connections are always active. On the basis of load statistics, algorithms distribute the data traffic equally to all links and prevent broadcast landslides.

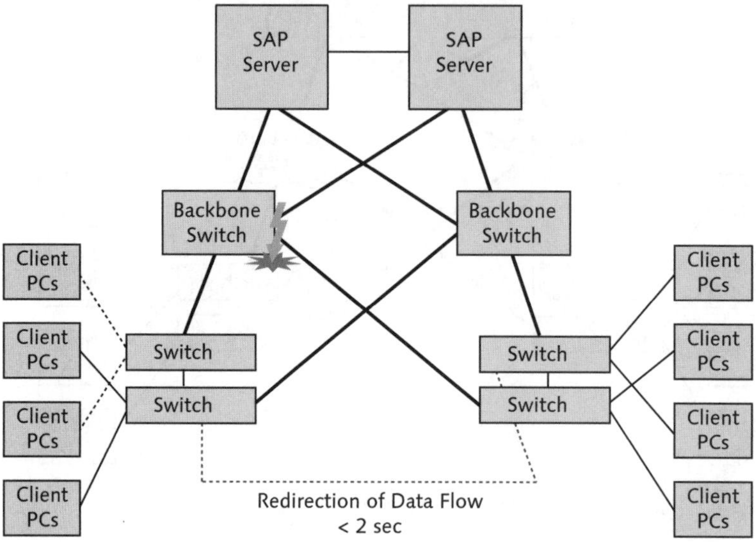

Figure 11.3 Error-Tolerant, Completely Meshed Network

If the "intelligent patching" described for network clusters is implemented with completely meshed switches, even in the case of a failing backbone component, the full operation of the network can be ensured. The switchover time in an SAP cluster test environment, after turning off a backbone switch, was under two seconds in a running operation. The switch took place transparently for the application and user without losing any transactions.

UPS Units Are Also for Network Cabinets

To ensure the availability of the SAP infrastructure, in areas where there are more frequent voltage fluctuations, Uninterrupted Power Supply (UPS) units should be used. The ability of a UPS unit to filter and stabilize the power supply voltage is more important than bridging long power outages. A switching operation in the high-voltage power grid of the electricity supplier only causes the office lighting to flicker, but the switches and routers may restart and cause network downtime. However, USP units are also active components that must be monitored and maintained.

11.2 Wires and Fibers

Today, basically two cable types are used for local networks: lines with twisted pairs of copper wires and fiber optics cables. Both have types have advantages and disadvantages, because of their physical characteristics.

11.2.1 Copper Cables

The area of end device connections is generally based on twisted pair copper wires. This type of cable has existed since the first telephone signals were transferred. Throughout the years, on the one hand, the transfer frequencies have become much higher; on the other hand, there are essentially more sources of disturbance. Fortunately, twisted pair cables were also developed to the same extent. Therefore, we can say with assurance that twisted copper cables actually do meet the requirements of high-speed data transfers. Compared with optical fibers, copper cables are much easier to install and, consequently, are more cost-effective.

Copper cables—"lets twist again"

Twisted pair cable consists of two copper wires. Each wire is encased in its own color-coded insulation, twisted around one another. Multiple pairs are packaged in an outer sheath, or jacket, to form a twisted-pair cable. The twist of the cable is essential for electrical noise immunity and must go as near as possible to the connectors of the wall receptacles and patch-panels. By varying the length of the twists in nearby pairs, the crosstalk between pairs in the same cable sheath can be minimized. The typical nominal impedance is 100 ohms.

For data networks in companies, structured cabling in accordance with EN 50173-1[2], ISO/IEC, or EIA/TIA-568 category 5 onwards has become standard.

The decisive quality attribute for top quality data cables is the symmetry of the cable. Different twist lengths of pairs that are placed next to each other avoid crosstalk. In this context, it is important that the cables are not only symmetrically stranded but also precisely finished.

2 General requirements for application-neutral communication systems in offices (2003).

High Bandwidth is not Equal to High Frequency

There only appears to be a connection between the transfer frequency and the achievable bandwidth. By using highly developed signal encoding processes, all high-speed technologies such as Fast Ethernet and Giga Ethernet, as well as ATM, don't exeed 310 MHz as the transfer frequency. Technologies with higher bandwidth are based on fibre optic cables.

Shielded or unshielded?

Contemporary data networks operating with frequencies that are located in the middle area of the VHF radio band (Very High Frequency). The metallic conductors act like antennas for these frequencies, for receiving as well as for transmitting. STP cables contain a metal shield to reduce the potential for electromagnetic interference (EMI). EMI is caused by alternating electromagnetic fields from other sources such as electric motors, power lines, high power radio and radar signals but also by flickering fluorescent tubes in the vicinity that may cause disruptions or interference, called noise.

There are, however, a variety of shielding solutions for data cables. From the most simple aluminum polyester compound film, through combinations of tin-plated twisted meshwork and compound film, to expensive metal shields, you can find all possible constructions.

The names of the various shielded (Shielded Twisted Pairs, STP) and unshielded (Unshielded Twisted Pair, UTP) cable types are quite confusing. STP also encompasses Screened Shielded Twisted Pair (ScTP) and Foil Twisted Pair (FTP) cables. Within UTP, there are paradoxically also Shielded Unshielded cables (S-UTP) with a complete external shielding, but without individual shielding of the pairs.

STP cables

At first glance, STP cables appear to be immune to any interferences, because of their shielding. But, unfortunately, this is not the case. As the grounded shield also acts as an antenna and transforms the incoming interferences into a current, which induces a current in the signal wires in the opposite direction. As long as both currents are symmetrical, they eliminate each other. Any discontinuity in shielding or asymmetry in the currents between the shield and signal wires acts as a source for electronic noise. Therefore, STP cables are effective only if the entire link from one end to the other is continuously shielded and properly grounded. However, this can in turn cause severe problems by amperage flow over the shield in cases, where the electrical supply grid has no separated grounding.

For UTP cables, the physical shield is replaced by improved variations of the twisting as well as sophisticated filtering techniques in the network devices. Disturbances are equally induced in both conductors and therefore eliminate each other. Throughout the years, the UTP cables have constantly been improved so that they now fully meet the requirements of category 5.

UTP cable

Despite a heated debate over the years about the advantages and disadvantages of shielded versus unshielded twisted pair cables, a final conclusion has still not been reached. In Europe, STP is the main preference, not only to protect data signals against outside emissions, but because corresponding regulations require the protection of the environment against the emissions of data signals. UTP cables are used generally in the rest of the world. In any case, reliability is always determined by the quality of the cable manufacturing and proper installation.

Electromagnetic Compatibility (EMC)

Another factor to consider when choosing a cabling system relates to electromagnetic compatibility (EMC). In the U.S. and Germany, EMC regulations have existed for years. However, the implementation of the European EMC Directive 89/336/EEC in 1989 has refocused attention on EMC. With the increased amount of electronic equipment in the average workspace, EMC becomes increasingly more important. Excess radiation from one piece of equipment can adversely affect performance of another piece of equipment. EMC refers to the ability of an electronic system to function properly in an environment where several pieces of equipment radiate electromagnetic emissions. This means that every electronic system, which includes all copper based cabling systems, must meet this directive.

11.2.2 Fiber Optics Cables

A fiber optics cable consists of a bundle of optical threads (fibers), in which messages modulated onto light waves propagate along the direction of the fiber because of internal reflection. The reflection occurs due to the different refraction indices between the core and the coating. Fiber-optic network cabling is made up of at least two strands of optical fiber running parallel to each other in a plastic "zip-cord" jacket, or multiple fibers in a single jacket.

Multi-Mode Fibers

There are two different types of optical fibers: Multi-Mode Fibers (MMF) and Single-Mode Fibers (SMF). In this context, "mode" refers to the effect of spreading a light signal in an optical fiber, resulting in light-rays following different paths (or modes) down the fiber (modal dispersion). Multimode fiber (MMF), with a core diameter of 62.5μm allows a light signal to take various zigzag paths. This modal dispersion causes some light rays to arrive later at the end of the fiber. Due to the undesired runtime differences caused by these different modes, the range of MMF cables is limited to 1.5 miles (2 km).

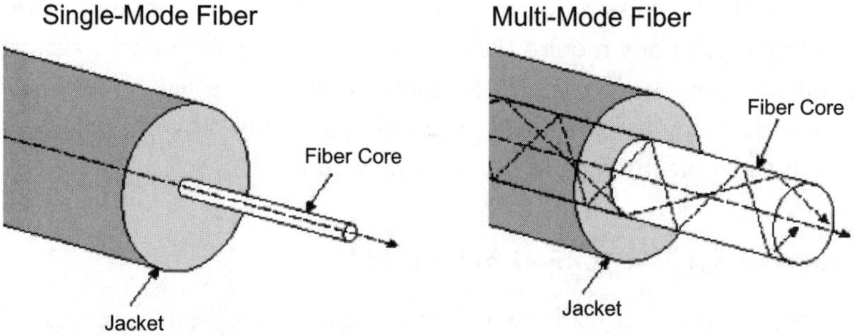

Figure 11.4 The Route of Light Rays in Single-Mode and Multi-Mode Fiber Optics Cables

Single-mode fibers

Single-mode fiber (SMF) with a core diameter of only 9 microns allows only one path for the light to take due to the fiber's very small diameter. Single-mode fibers and components are more expensive than Multimode fiber, but allow connectivity up to 12 miles (20 km). Cheap Plastic SMF fibers can be used only for very short connections, they absorb the light rays earlier because plastic is not as clear as glass.

Multi-mode fiber is designed for coupling light from low cost LED[3]-based transmitters. Single-mode fiber is only suitable for laser-based transmission.

There are varieties of connectors (FDDI-MIC, ST, SC-Duplex etc.) for MMF as well as for SMF. Be sure to use the same diameter and connectors throughout your infrastructure. Project deadlines are easily missed when plugs at fibers do not fit the active components, and adapter cables are not on hand.

3 Light Emitting Diodes.

Fiber optics cables can be used for all current network technologies. In comparison to network connections made of metal, fiber optic cables have numerous advantages:

Advantages of optical fibers

- Optical fibers enable a larger bandwidth than copper cables.
- Optical fibers are not sensitive to electromagnetic radiation and don't emit any by themselves. This means that all regulations are meet by default.
- Optical fibers are immune to lightning strikes and power line transients.
- Metal free Optical fibers cannot generate any ground loops.
- Optical fibers are much thinner and lighter in weight than metal wires.
- It is very difficult to tap eavesdrop on optical fibers without being noticed, making this very secure from electronic eavesdropping.

On the other hand, fiber optics cables also have some disadvantages:

Drawbacks

- Fiber optics cable connectors are high precision parts. An exact alignment of the fiber inside the connector housing and proper polish of the fiber end is crucial for connectivity quality.
- Installing connectors on site is time consuming and requires high precision work. The alternative of fusion welding strands with prefabricated connectors (called pigtails) on site needs expensive equipment.
- Together with the higher costs for the cable itself, the deployment of fiber-optic cable costs more than twice that of a category 5 copper connection. The "per port" price of active fiber optic components (hubs, switches, router modules) is typically twice the price of their copper counterparts. The prices for long range single-mode cables and components are even higher than for multi-mode
- Glass fibers are more fragile than wire and sensitive and age under the impact of hydrogen ions. They must therefore be protected against moisture through special coatings. However, this protective layer is also subject to aging.

Case Example: Mice in Cable Conduit

In a company, a complete administration building was suddenly without network based IT services. The reason behind this was a fiber optics cable that had been gnawed through in a cable conduit. Rodents like to build their houses in cable conduits, and their offspring like to test their teeth on the cables. Since fiber optics cables can only be spliced by using special tools, this led to a downtime lasting several days. Even rodent-safe cables and mousetraps are therefore investments that increase availability of enterprise service architectures and IT services in general.

11.2.3 Installation Guidelines for Cable Networks

Good craftsmanship, together with using high quality components, has a direct relationship to how long your cabling infrastructure will last. As mentioned before, high-speed data links have higher demands than plain-old telephone lines. To make matters worse, the effects of poor installation work may not be immediately evident!

Deformation or mechanical stress during installation causes most cable failures. Deformation changes the physical properties responsible for high frequency transmission. Even when the cable looks flawless from the outside, irreversible degradation of transmission properties is suspected when too much stress is applied to the cable. Mechanical stresses as well as temperature levels are part of the ISO/IEC 11801 standard "Generic Cabling for Customer Premises." The installation of network infrastructures should be dedicated to certified contractors, familiar to the special demands of data cabling.

However, even with equipment, which has been checked and conforms to the standards, problems still exist, as with increased demands on the networks, the reserves in the transfer parameters decrease.

Visual inspections

An example is the standard of fitting the data cables in the connection components. The standard for this does provide for a visual inspection, but this is rarely carried out. Generally, people content themselves with the test logs created by cable scanners. For instance, in distributor panels where the cable sections that have been stripped of the isolation are narrowly guided along the blank wire ends of the neighboring cable, this can lead to a short circuit between the wire and the foil shield if the latter changes, for example, because the temperature of the cabinet interior increases. During an acceptance test on cabling, it is therefore critical that you perform visual inspections.

With fiber-optic cables, you can run into problems later on as well, even if they have been installed according to the standards. Here the problems can mainly be found in the preconfigured plugs. These plugs are very sensitive to scratches, dust, and inept treatment when being mounted. We also recommend that you use a microscope when conducting checks. You can find additional information and further considerations when executing acceptance tests in Mißbach/Hoffmann,[4] which is also worthwhile reading for small changes or enhancements carried out by your internal electrician.

11.3 Potential Equalization, Grounding, and Lightning Protection

Frequently, sporadic disturbances and breakdowns occur in data networks without a clear reason. Connections become extremely slow, monitor screens flicker, assemblies burn through or after a thunderstorm, and entire facilities break down at once. Furthermore, individual employees may be marginalized, because strangely it is only always their PCs that go "mad."

In many cases, however, the real reason for these breakdowns can be found in the potential equalization and grounding. Apart from the data network cabling in every building, there is also cabling for the power supply. People often overlook the fact that these two cable networks are linked via the grounding, and massive disturbances of the data networks can occur if the power supply network is not designed as IT-compatible.

Potential displacements

In order to ensure an electricity flow, a wire (L) is required from the electricity source to the consumer, as well as a retracting wire (N). A third wire is stipulated as a ground wire or protective earth conductor (PE). As the 230V alternating current is tapped from a 380V three-phase network, this results in a 5-wire network or TN-S system with three conducting phases and a common neutral and ground wire for each phase.

The security function of the protective earth conductor is ensured, even if the protective earth conductor is connected to the neutral cable that is also grounded, and thereby forms a "combined" PEN conductor (that is, a retracting circuit (N) plus a protective earth conductor (PE)). Such cou-

4 Mißbach, Hoffmann: *SAP Hardware Solutions—Servers, Storage, and Networks for mySAP.com*. Prentice Hall 2000.

plings are permitted and are commonly used in building installations, because this means that a cable can be saved. This form of network is called a 4-cable network or TN-C system. This variant has no negative effects on the lamps connected, whereas, when connecting other electronic appliances, this can lead to considerable problems.

Interfering transmitters in the system

Since an increasing number of electronic pre-connection units are being used for fluorescent tubes and switching power supplies for computers, the current flow is not sinusoidal. Instead, it contains considerable high-frequency components. These can cause parasitic currents of several amperes, which results in a magnetic field that acts as if an irregularly functioning high-frequency transmitter is an integral part of the computer system.

To ensure a stable operation of the data network, an integrated 5-wire network with a clear grounding concept should be guaranteed. If necessary, a separate 230V power supply grid must be installed from the transformer of the sub-distributor. In this separate supply circuit, the neutral cable must not come into contact with the ground wire at any point (separate conduits for PE and N, so that no parasitic currents are possible through the data cables). The sockets for this network should be marked "only for IT devices." There should also be corresponding signs in the rooms of its installation to ensure that an inexperienced electrician does not create a connection between N and PE again.

Danger—high voltages due to lightning

In conjunction with a nearby lightning stroke, cable screens grounded on only one side, act as antennae into which high voltages are induced. The voltage will be discharged at the network board or the network socket, depending on where the disruption to the shield occurs. Even with a double-sided grounding due to the induction caused by a lightning stroke, a compensatory current flows in the data shield. This can lead to extensive destructions of the connected interfaces as a result of strong electric currents. Therefore, power sockets with integrated over voltage protectors are definitely advisable. The same is true for your house, where lightning bolts can induce voltage surges in the main telephone line, which destroy telephone systems and DSL routers, as one of the authors can attest from his own first-hand experience.

Parasitic currents through ground loops

Ground loops represent another cause of parasitic currents, and one often overlooked. In the network cabling system, problems with ground loops occur mainly when shielded twisted-pair cables (STP) are used between parts of a building complex. If these parts have different earth potential, parasitic currents of several amperes can flow over the shield if grounded on both ends. These ground loops can lead to a degradation of network performance, and even to a damage of network components.

When installing STP cables, you must ensure that grounding occurs only at one end of the grounded link. For UTP cables, ground loops are not an issue, because of the design of these cables. Fiber-optic cables are the most secure way of eliminating damage caused by parasitic currents of any type.

Fire Protection

The insulation of data cables generally consists of flammable synthetic materials, mainly polyethylene and PVC. To reduce the threat to people and material, Building Codes generally require cables that does not generate toxic fumes when burning, such as FEP (fluoro-ethylene polymer) in air ducts, air plenums, and other environmental air spaces.

In the event of a fire, these cables also don't generate corrosive gasesand the smoke gas density is considerably lower. Therefore, PVC cables are banned in building installations in an increasing number of countries.

It is for good reason that building insurers in recent years placed major emphasis on the issue of fire protection. According to the insurers, all cable conduits in ceilings that run at a right angle to an emergency route must have a full fire protection. This also applies to all later changes. You should therefore always ensure that the cable installations are in accordance with the regulations of the property insurers.

11.4 Wireless Networks

Wireless technologies in recent years have undergone rapid development in terms of both their bandwidths and their increased use. In 2004, 42 % of all notebooks were already equipped with Wireless LAN (WLAN) functionality, and, according to estimates from the IDC market research institute, this percentage will rise to 98 % by 2007.

11.4.1 WLAN Standards

Wireless local networks (Wireless LAN, WLAN) are defined in the norms IEEE[5] 802.11 and ISO CD8802-11. After an initial 2Mbps in the first

5 Institute of Electrical and Electronics Engineers.

802.11 standard without additional letters at the time, 802.11b followed with 11Mbps and 802.11g followed with up to 54Mbps (~30Mbps net) with three channels on the 2.4 GHz frequency. Some manufacturers already provide systems with transfer rates of 100 Mbit/s, with the assurance that modifications resulting from a standard that will subsequently be introduced can be imported in the form of a software update. Contrary to this, 802.11a and 802.11h each have eight channels in the 5 GHz band at their disposal. However, this band is also used by radar systems and earth observation satellites. A certain detection threshold in the interaction with Dynamic Frequency Selection (DFS) is supposed to ensure that these radar systems and satellites are not disturbed by WLAN.

The 802.11 alphabet

The 802.11 alphabet also knows a range of other letters, which reflect modifications made according to country-specific regulations or modifications made for functional enhancements.

For example, variant 802.11h was introduced to comply with the requirements of some European countries for a automatic adaptation of the transmission power (Transmission Power Control, TPC), which is supposed to further reduce the probability of interferences. Without TPC and DFS, 5 GHz radio networks in Europe can be subject to very rigid obligations that limit the operation to ranges of less than 20 meters in buildings.

The letters e, I, and f, are used for function enhancements. IEEE 802.11f defines the Inter Access Point Protocol (IAPP) for roaming between Access Points of different manufacturers. The 802.11i standard is supposed to protect wireless networks against unauthorized access by implementing encryption processes and user authorization. The 802.11e attempts to enable a prioritizing of certain applications such as voice-over IP (VoIP) in the WLAN. However, no bandwidth can be guaranteed here; rather, the access point tries to implement the different priority levels in as far as possible.

Standard 802.11a uses Orthogonal Frequency Division Multiplexing (OFDM) for transmission with up to 12 channels depending on the country, while standard 802.11b is based on Direct Sequence Spread Spectrum (DSSS). The development of 802.11g was made possible after the Federal Communications Commission (FCC) had released the OFDM technology in the 2.4 GHz band.

802.16a

In addition to the 802.11 family, the IEEE has ratified norms for even higher speeds. 802.16a or Wimax[6] uses the frequency range of 2 to 11

GHz for transfer speeds of 70Mbps with coverage of almost 30 miles, while 802.16b is supposed to enable even 134.4Mbps in the frequency range of 10 to 66 GHz. The Wimax Forum[7] aims to have an unlicensed band for 802.16a with 5.8 GHz and two licensed bands with 2.5 and 3.5 GHz. Other bands are to follow later. The radius of a cell should realistically be set to 20 miles, regardless of whether there are obstacles between the sender and the recipient. Market researchers expect a wide availability of these technologies by 2008.

A Practical Example of WLAN

In the feeder railway of a lignite mine, information about shunting tasks, the sequence of wagons, wagon data, and the currently covered length of shunting tracks is transferred to the handheld PCs of shunters and locomotive drivers via 802.11b WLAN.

To minimize the number of access points, the antennae were aligned along geographically defined lines of sight, and the locomotives were equipped with an access point repeater that ensures radio coverage for the shunter's handheld in the area of his shunting unit. In addition, the locomotive drivers enter operating data such as engine and compressor runtimes, or the fuel consumption directly through pocket PC and WLAN on the driver's console.

While using WLAN for mobile applications is indispensable, the rapid development of radio technologies to ever-increasing bandwidths and the growing use of laptops with integrated WLAN interfaces beg the question of whether avoiding cabling altogether, for stationary work centers as well, is a real possibility. There are, however, some constraints to consider that you won't typically find in the manufacturers' brochures.

Bandwidth is dependent on the distance

Due to physical laws, at a given transmitting power, the bandwidth is dependent on the distance. As you can see in Table 11.1, the rules are as follows: The larger the distance, the lower the actual bandwidth. For increasing frequencies, obstacles cause mounting problems to electromagnetic waves.

6 Worldwide Interoperability for Microwave Access, the corresponding name of the European ETSI is HiperMAN as this technology is generally regarded as suited for Metropolitan Area Networks (MAN).

7 Go to *www.wimaxforum.org.*

	11Mbps	5.5Mbps	2Mbps	1Mbps
Open country	70 yds. / 66 m	100 yds. / 91 m	135 yds. / 125 m	187 yds. / 171 m
In buildings	30 yds. / 28 m	38 yds. / 35 m	47 yds. / 43 m	58 yds. / 53 m

Table 11.1 Correlation between WLAN Coverage and Bandwidth

In addition, all WLAN protocols cause considerable overheads, so out of a bandwidth of up to 11Mbps, approximately only 7Mbps can be used for user data and this can only be reached when you are close to the transmitter (i.e., access point).

ISM band

Most WLAN products use the ISM (industry, science, and medicine) band in a range of 2.4 GHz. However, the transmitting power in the ISM band is limited to 500 mW so the highly sensitive medicinal diagnosis systems don't get disturbed. For this reason, mobile telephones that have an essentially higher output power must not be used in hospitals, and you should resist the urge to download your latest email to the computer via your cell phone while sitting in the waiting room of the intensive care unit. The low transmitting power reduces the range correspondingly. Similar restrictions also apply to the 5 GHz band.

In addition, a basic disadvantage of radio networks is that all participants must share the available bandwidth. It is precisely because the ISM band is license-free that it is also used by many other systems. Examples of other systems include the wireless control of erection cranes and the hobby area. RC cars and planes are therefore potential sources of inferences for WLANs. The Bluetooth short distance radio technology, which allows mobiles, headsets, handhelds, and printers to communicate with each other, uses also the 2.4 GHz ISM band. Even a microwave can pose a possible source of disturbance since it also often works in the 2.4 GHz range.

5 Gigahertz band

Like the 2.4 GHz range, the 5 GHz band is similarly utilized by radio applications. However, because of the higher number of channels, more users can share a radio cell.

All end devices share the bandwidth

All end devices set to a specific channel necessarily share the bandwidth. Therefore, the 11Mbps that exist on paper can easily become only 600 kbit/s in actuality, and even this cannot be guaranteed. In certain circumstances, this leads to drastically increased response times for an SAP user who is connected to an SAP system through WLAN if a coworker is currently loading a large email attachment on the same channel. If access points are used as radio bridges, the range increases but not the bandwidth as the traffic from the neighboring cell also has to be transferred.

Power users in fixed cabled network connections

In order to cover larger areas and user numbers, more cells must be installed. The access points required for this, in turn, need a conventional cabling, which means that you cannot avoid providing a fixed cabled network. Practice has shown the benefit of equipping power users with both stationary work centers and a fixed cable network connection, and a hotspot for the shared desk area in the office.

11.4.2 Installation Guidelines for Wireless Networks

In order to determine the locations for WLAN access nodes (so called WLAN basis station), the construction drawings for the building should be inspected for hidden metal constructions such as steal reinforcement and water pipes, which shield the radio waves like a Faraday cage and therefore disrupt the WLAN connection. But, even a larger number of people have a negative influence on the performance of a radio network (the high water content of human beings damp the radio waves). Due to starkly reduced prices for access points, you can simply install some of them on a trial-and-error basis.

Directional Antennae for Improved Radio Coverage in Warehouses

In warehouses and manufacturing, wireless mobile terminals with bar code readers are frequently used to compile data along with the mobile data entry interface of SAP Materials Management (MM-MOB).

The steel racks and the steel reinforced concrete walls in high-bay racking, however, absorb the transmitting energy of omnidirectional antennae. Directional antennae that radiate into the warehouse alleys can ensure a stable connection.

WLAN channel layout

Using the Direct Sequence Spread Spectrum (DSSS) technology, the IEEE 802.11b standard provides 13 channels for transmission; however, because these channels overlap each other, they can't be used in direct proximity (side by side). At the end, there are three triples (channels 1, 6, and 11; channels 2, 7, and 12; and channels 3, 8, and 13), which don't overlap each other.

This means that in an ideal scenario a maximum of three access points with a total bandwidth of 33Mbps can cover a room without any disturbance. Anyone can send and receive on a different frequency without any interference provided there's a sufficient distance between the sender and the receiver. To ensure complete redundancy, the radio field of an access point must also be covered by the radio field of a second access point.

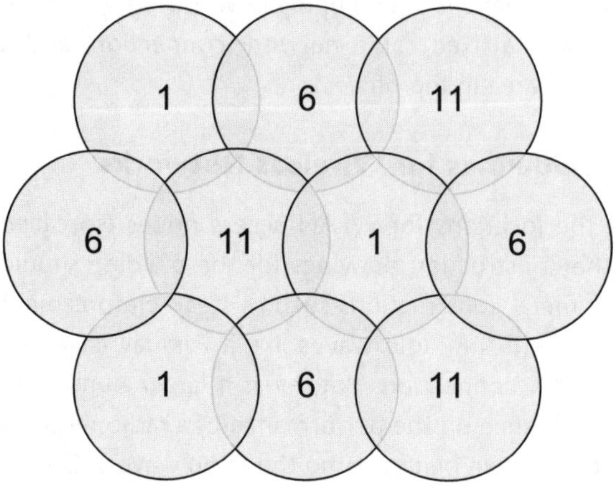

Figure 11.5 Channel Layout for WLAN

For larger WLAN installations, you must ensure that access points, which are situated next to each other, are configured with different channel numbers. Otherwise, they would mutually disrupt each other. Here you must consider that access points necessarily radiate through several floors. As the individual radio channels also partly radiate into neighboring frequencies, for instance, when node A transmits on channel 1, the directly adjacent access node B should be set to channel 6, and node C should be set to channel 11. Therefore a carefully designed channel layout is necessary for larger WLAN installations.

In larger office buildings that are used by several companies, there are also problems if the WLANS of individual companies overlap and thereby cause interferences. If services in the form of hot spots are provided for third parties, in some countries a concession is required, which is currently still free of charge.

WLAN—a paradise for hackers?

Experience has shown that many WLANs are insufficiently secured. According to a study by Ernst & Young from 2003, over 50 % of users do not change their default passwords to access points, 25 % configure the Service Set Identifier (SSID) in such a way that it reveals the network name, and in many cases, even the company name or the IP address. But, at least 48 % of WLAN users use a Virtual Private Networking (VPN) to protect their data. Only a third of users implement a firewall between wired LAN and WLAN. In total, WLANs are included in only 33 % of the companies in the technical and regulatory regulations for the security concept.

WLANs also Threaten Wired Networks

For companies, the growing use of notebooks with built-in WLAN connectivity increased the likelihood that the security of their networks was being compromised. The reason behind this was and is that badly configured notebooks function as WLAN access points when they are connected to a company LAN by cable without disabling WLAN functionality. In most cases users are not aware of this security hole and breach security unintentionally.

Hiding the SSID

In addition to encryption, the access procedure can also enhance security. Each WLAN has Service Set Identifier (SSID) as a name. So clients can communicate with the radio network, they must know this SSID and enter it when logging onto the radio network. In hot spots, the SSID is often sent out as a broadcast. If this is prevented, the clients must already know the SSID in order to be able to create any connection. All other participants are excluded from communication with this WLAN.

However, during the authentication process, each client sends the SSID in plain text to the access point, which can easily and most assuredly be eavesdropped on by an attacker. Unfortunately, this is unavoidable, because several different radio networks can exist within one footprint.

MAC-address access control lists

Some manufacturers have integrated access control lists (ACL) in their access points so they can only permit those clients with known MAC addresses to communicate in the WLAN. Although this excludes participants with unknown MAC addresses from using the network, this mechanism can also easily be overcome by attackers with simple methods. During communication in a radio network, the MAC addresses must be transferred unencrypted. This enables the attacker to tap valid MAC addresses, which they can then configure in their own WLAN cards by using the corresponding software.

Fixed keys do not provide sufficient security

Technologies like Wired Equivalent Privacy (WEP) which the key is stored in the access point and the notebook, generally do not provide sufficient security, because they can be relatively easily cracked by scanning the data traffic.

Therefore, we advise you not to implement any WLAN-based encryption; instead, you should establish a secured connection between the client and the firewall with a powerful IPSec encryption in a VPN. In addition, an overall concept from authentication, authorization, accounting, and encryption is necessary.

Security from end to end

In "typical" access point concepts, only the WLAN-side "air interface" of the access point is encrypted while the data in the cabled part is transferred unencrypted. So called WLAN switches can be positioned in such a way that their network port is logically immediately connected to the firewall or the VPN server. As data traffic on the cable route between the WLAN switch and the antenna systems is encrypted in the same way as in the air interface, security is guaranteed from one end to the other without the end user having to install a VPN client.

For big installations, a large number of access points means that configuration and administration becomes time-consuming and costly. These difficulties were overcome on classic, cabled networks by automatic, rule-based switching on network levels 2 and 3. For WLANs, there are corresponding concepts of Wireless LAN switching.

Wireless LAN-switching

To do this, a WLAN switch is installed (for example, from HP, Nortel, Extreme Networks, or Proxim), from which access points and access to the network can be administered centrally. Thus, the decentrally installed access points become pure antenna systems that convert only radio signals to Ethernet packets. The "intelligence" of the WLAN is concentrated in the wireless switch. In general, access points don't even need an IP address. Their power supply can be ensured through "power over Ethernet" according to the 802.3af standard, so that, apart from the Ethernet cable, no further installation is necessary.

For real mobile users, which roam within a WLAN network between the footprints of different access points, a wireless switch provides a single sign on (SSL) and roaming times that are typically under 30 seconds. However, strictly speaking, this is not the kind of roaming we know from mobile phones that roam between the networks of different providers. Instead, it is an interruption-free handover from one radio cell to another.

Furthermore, many WLAN switches offer functions such as automatic channel selection—where the layout of the radio cells is automatically optimized—and preemptive roaming (wireless load balancing).

11.4.3 Ad-Hoc Networks

Bluetooth

Ad-hoc network technologies such as Bluetooth[8] were developed to enable a dynamic connection establishment between mobile devices such as wireless DECT phones, laptops and PDAs. Recently, this list has been complemented by hands free speaking systems and headsets. Originally, the Bluetooth concept was only intended to replace the cables between the phone handsets and their peripheral devices with a radio connection. However, the user spectrum was very quickly expanded to include the world of the personal computer. The developed is controlled by the Bluetooth Special Interest Group.[9]

Network configuration on the fly

While WLANS require a fixed configuration, ad-hoc networks are based on a master-slave system where a master device controls the changing connections in a Piconet cell. As the type and number of devices in the cell can change unexpectedly, the routing protocol used by Bluetooth must be capable of dynamically reconfiguring the network "on the fly."

The designers of Bluetooth, too, have decided to use the license-free 2.4000 GHz–2.4835 GHz ISM frequency band. Since this band is already used by so many other wireless services, Bluetooth uses an Advanced Frequency Hopping Technology (AFH) to avoid interference problems, which have made life difficult for other ISM band users. The AFH concept uses 79 different radio channels from among which it switches 1.6 times per second. Thus, a channel is used only for 625 microseconds before the switch is made to the next randomly selected channel.

Bluetooth currently allows a transfer rate of up to 1Mbps which corresponds to a real throughput rate of approximately 720 kbit/s. Power management in Bluetooth is divided into three different performance classes: Class-1 devices work with 100 milliwatt (mW) and have a range of up to 110 yards (100m). Class-2 devices work with 2.5 mW and have a range of up to 10 yards (10m). Class 3 manages with 1 mW and reaches between 5 inches (10cm) and 1 yard (1m). This relatively short range has the advantage that the transfer channels are not blocked by Bluetooth devices operating from a greater distance.

8 Named after the Viking prince Harold Bluetooth, who unified Denmark, Sweden, and Norway in the 10th century.

9 Go to *www.bluetooth.com.*

11.4.4 Mobile Communications

For the mobile business applications, in particular, which are provided by SAP with its NetWeaver product, the data services of mobile communications providers are an interesting alternative for replication—that is, replication between the mobile client (mostly a Personal Digital Assistant, PDA), and the SAP Mobile Engine Infrastructure Server. The data quantities to be transferred are typically so small that the mobile technologies currently available have no problems with them. However, even these relatively small volumes of data, which are usually ignored when designing a network, can become an issue, especially when it comes to connection costs.

11.5 Voice—Data Convergence

One area in which the infrastructure consolidation has rapidly developed in recent years is the merging of voice and data services. After all, this is not very surprising because the transmission of information through electronic signals is really integral to both concepts.

All through one cable

One of the reasons why Ethernet has become more popular than technologies such as TokenRing was the development of 10BaseT by Hewlett-Packard, where, instead of coaxial cables (10Base2 and 10Base5), twisted-pair cables of category 3 could be used, which at the time corresponded to the existing telephone cables used in the US.

American-type phone cable consists of two pairs of separately twisted wires. Alternatively, the telephone cables predominantly used in Europe consist of four wires that are twisted together (see Figure 11.6). This structure results in a stronger crosstalk that obstructs a usage for the Ethernet.

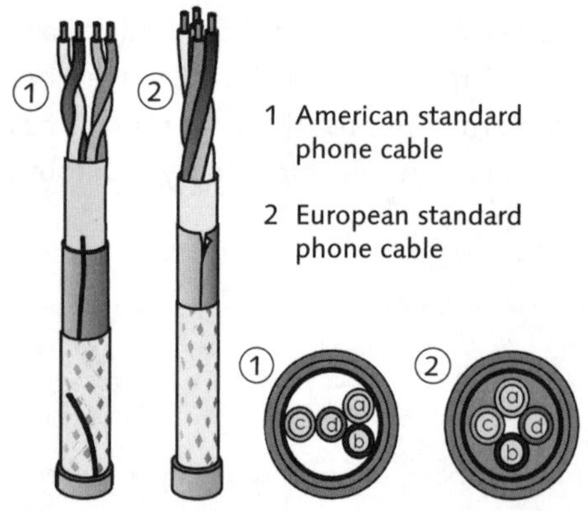

Figure 11.6 American and European Telephone Cables

Meanwhile, at least in company networks, the quantity of bytes for data transfers has exceeded that for voice communication by far. It is no longer about transferring data via a modem through proprietary telephone networks, but rather about transferring voice through open IP infrastructures (Voice over IP, VoIP). Here, one advantage is that, due to suitable compression algorithms (codecs), the necessary bandwidth for a telephone conversation is so low that it can be easily "saddled" on the normal Ethernet connection of an SAP user. However, the particular requirements of language services must be considered here, especially with regard to latency. Therefore, the use of VoIP technologies depends on the constant availability of Quality of Service (QoS) in the IP infrastructure of a company.

Power supply for IP telephones

Another important difference between language and data networks is that in conventional telephone systems the end devices are generally provided with the necessary operational voltage through the connection cable. Even if a PC with headset was perfectly sufficient (and offers substantially more functionalities), experience shows that users don't like to be without their familiar phones on their desks; admittedly, these phones don't have to be booted. These problems can be solved through patch fields, which superimpose a direct voltage on the high frequency data signals (Power over Ethernet, PoE) to supply power to the IP telephones. If, on top of that, the IP phones are also daisy chained into the connection of the PC, only one Ethernet connection per user is necessary.

Voice-data convergence needs high availability

In this way, the consolidation of voice and data transfer can drastically reduce the costs for the local network infrastructure. However, we know from experience that, in order for VoIP to be accepted by the users, availability must be guaranteed, which is akin to that of the familiar telephone, and it can only be achieved with the concepts described above.

11.6 Summary

Modern LAN technologies provide sufficient bandwidth to connect a large number of users to an SAP system. However, there are certain requirements to be considered regarding reliability:

- Design the network backbone as redundant, but be aware of the threats caused by network loops.
- Implement highly available network clusters and error-tolerant meshed networks together and patch intelligently.

- Do not forget to equip all network cabinets with an uninterrupted power supply.
- For connections between buildings and in the rising mains area, all fiber optics cables are required due to their lack of sensitivity to lightning strokes and ground loops.
- The quality of the installed cables and the proper installation has a significant impact on the performance of your network which is usually underestimated. The wiring of a floor or entire building is a major investment. Using low quality cables or unqualified installers can void this investment to a great extend, leading to significant cost in future. A wiring investment should be planned as carefully as a hardware investment project.
- The cabling for power supply also plays a pivotal role for disruption-free operation. Neutral wires and protection wires should never be used together (PEN); between building parts with different grounding potential, only fiber optics cables should be used.
- Radio networks are suitable for connecting individual mobile SAP applications. For large numbers of users, a distribution across several access points is necessary, which requires a well devised channel layout plan.
- WLANs must be integrated into the security concept of the company.

12 WAN and Web Connections

Global SAP services outside the company premises

In today's globalized economy, increasingly even medium-sized companies establish their subsidiaries and branches on a worldwide scale, and these have to be linked with the central SAP systems over large distances. In many cases, the majority of SAP users are not based in the same location as the data center. For that reason, the individual local area networks (LANs) must be connected via a wide area network (WAN). If SAP services are provided by an external data center (outsourcing or application service provider), the entire communication flow between the users' computers and the SAP application hosts takes place via WANs.

In addition to these LAN-WAN-LAN connections, there is a growing demand for the integration of home offices and mobile computers in the company network. This is due to an increase in the mobility of the workforce, as well as the growing flexibility of work models. Furthermore, it has become a standard requirement for each company to get connected to the global village of the Internet.

High costs

As companies usually are not the owners of the telecommunication lines, they very much depend on the services of telecommunications providers. Despite the strong competition in the liberalized telecommunications market in Europe and other parts of the world, a WAN bandwidth is generally still a relatively expensive resource when compared to a LAN.

For intercontinental connections, in particular, the running fees for remote connections can represent an essential part of the operating costs of a company-wide SAP system. To minimize these costs, companies usually strive to "buy" a bandwidth that is as low as possible. For this reason, WAN connections represent the weakest element in a network infrastructure in terms of throughput. The use of appropriate technologies is then supposed to ensure a smooth operation of business processes.

WAN connections as a availability risk

In terms of system availability, the WAN connection represents the "umbilical cord" of the connected location. If the connection fails, the affected branch no longer has access to the SAP applications. If the connection between the data center and the telecom service provider dies, none of the subsidiaries and remote users will be able to access the SAP system.

In the context of Supply Chain Management (SCM), Supplier Relationship Management (SRM), and Customer Relationship Management (CRM) scenarios, the Internet connection is mandatory to communicate with customers and suppliers. Therefore, the connection to the Web must be available 24 hours a day, as peak business time always exists somewhere in the world. This is especially true if you deploy Web services, where an entire business process can be blocked because a service is not available. Therefore, one of your top priorities should always be to avoid creating a situation that results in the simultaneous breakdown of all your Internet connections.

WAN connections as a security risk

The option to access SAP systems through the Internet opens a potential back door to sensitive data. News about an enterprise portal that has been hacked or paralyzed is unwanted public relations for every company, which is why you should focus also on security when it comes to Internet connections.

In this chapter, we will therefore describe the infrastructure of an SAP WAN network with regard to performance (response time), total cost of ownership (TCO) and the support of business-critical applications (availability), as well as the security, adaptability, and convergence characteristics integral to maintaining this infrastructure.

Despite the vast technical progress that we have seen in recent years, which has led to a complete digitalization of communication networks in many countries, Internet and broadband connections still can't be taken for granted in some countries and areas. Particularly in places where wages are at the lower end of the scale, the telecommunications infrastructure does not always reflect the latest standards. Therefore, we will briefly describe how you can integrate locations into an SAP system, for which there is no modern infrastructure available. In the final section of this chapter, we'll introduce various high-availability concepts for WAN connections.

However, we will not delve into greater detail about the architecture of a WAN and the configuration of routers, since this would exceed the scope of this book. Apart from that, any discussion of WAN architecture should be launched by an experienced expert. Instead, we'll provide you with an overview of the pros and cons of currently available WAN technologies.

12.1 WAN Technologies

WAN connections represent the communication paths between geographically distributed sites of an enterprise. Telecommunications service providers, in turn, offer various different technologies for the transfer of IP data packages that can be used to transfer SAP data.

The following section briefly describes these different technologies. In addition to the characteristic latency times and system stability, the criteria that you should also consider when selecting a technology are the characteristic cost structures.

12.1.1 Leased Lines

No adaptiveness

Leased lines are the classical medium for remote data transfers. They provide a permanent point-to-point connection at a predefined bandwidth. The problem is that this bandwidth cannot be exceeded. Consequently, networks that are based on leased lines usually cannot adapt to new requirements at short notice. For that reason, the capacity of a leased line should be designed in such a way that it provides some room to maneuver when it comes to a maximum data load, so that the required response times can be met.

Costs

The price for leased lines depends on the transfer rate and the distance, regardless of how often and to what extent the connection is actually used. Compared to other WAN offerings, leased lines provide the lowest latency times at the highest cost.

12.1.2 ISDN

For Integrated Services Digital Network (ISDN), a multiplex technology is used, which makes it possible to provide several transfer channels in a single line.

BRI and PRI

A basic ISDN connection (Basic Rate Interface, BRI provides two so called *B channels* with a transfer rate of 64kbps each, as well as a D channel with 16kbps. The B channels can be bundled to provide a bandwidth of 128kbps.

In Europe, a primary multiplex connection (Primary Rate Interface, PRI) comprises 30 B channels and one D channel with a transfer rate of 64kbps each. By channel bundling, a bandwidth of 1.984Mbps can be provided (E1, in Germany is referred to as S2M). In the US, a PRI contains only 23 B channels with a bundled bandwidth of 1.536Mbps (T1).

Costs and availability In addition to the basic fee for ISDN, you also incur costs for the time of use and the distance. Contrary to the analogous technology with ISDN, it doesn't take even half a second to establish a connection. Routers generally utilize this characteristic to release a connection when there is no data to be transferred for a certain period of time (short- hold mode). As soon as a new data package arrives, the connection is reestablished automatically. Even though this process can take several minutes with channel bundling, ISDN-based connections can be adapted to changing requirements relatively easily, provided there are sufficient capacity reserves available. ISDN is virtually available around the world; however, nowhere else is it as widespread as it is in Europe.

12.1.3 DSL

You probably know the digital subscriber line (DSL) technology as a means for fast Internet access from your desk at home. But, for companies, DSL is a cost-efficient alternative to leased lines connections in terms of connecting to the backbone of the Internet when you implement a virtual private network (VPN).

During the transfer, DSL and ISDN benefit from the fact that, under favorable conditions, the bandwidth of the common copper lines that are used in telephone networks can be utilized far beyond the 4 KHz needed for speech transfers, and up to 1.1 GHz. However, generally, you should keep the following in mind: The higher the transfer rate, the smaller the range of coverage.

Range of coverage In general, you can use copper cables to bridge a maximum distance of approximately 3.5 miles (5.5 km); with asymmetrical DSL (ADSL), it's not more than 2 miles (3 km); and with the high-speed variant DSL (VDSL), it's just 1 mile (1.5 km) to the next point of presence (PoP) of the telecoms service provider. For longer distances, you need fiber optics lines.

Basically, DSL technologies are divided into symmetrical (SDSL) and asymmetrical (ADSL) processes. These concepts refer to the ratio of transfer rates used in the two channels.

The advantage of ADSL when connecting to SAP end users is that when using a locally installed SAP GUI or Enterprise Portal, the data flow to the user is essentially higher than in the opposite direction.[1] SDSL has certain

1 SAP White paper *Front End Network Requirements for mySAP Business Solutions*, which is available to partners and customers in SAPnet (*http://service.sap.com/network*), contains examples of the relationship between upstream and downstream.

advantages when it comes to LAN coupling. Here, transfer rates of up to 2.3Mbps are possible for both the download and the upload.

Costs

Apart from the costs for the devices and a basic fee, there are also costs for the on-line time. However, there is a growing tendency in the market to provide a flat rate. Because DSL is almost always used for accessing the Internet, the distance is irrelevant.

12.1.4 X.25

The X.25 standard of the International Telephone Union (ITU) defines a protocol which data can be reliably transferred through qualitatively bad lines. However, the integrated error-correction functions generate a large amount of protocol overhead. With an available bandwidth of between 9.6kbps and 64kbps, X.25 is completely outdated, but it is still available almost everywhere in the world.

12.1.5 Frame Relay

Frame relay refers to the forwarding of data packages (frames) through transmission node hosts (relay). It may sound paradoxical that such a network offers permanent virtual connections (PVC) and switched virtual connections (SVC). A permanent virtual connection is a predefined connection where the destination does not change. The advantage of this is that the connection is permanently available. A switched virtual connection, on the other hand, provides connections to different destinations that are established on request by the end devices.

The frame-relay protocol also has error recognition. However, there is no error-correction function available, and frames containing errors are simply deleted. With TCP/IP, this is not a disadvantage, because functions in TCP are implemented for a renewed transfer of those data packages containing errors and those packages that are missing.

Committed information rate

Frame relay is a very effective protocol for data traffic between SAP users. For each virtual connection, a specific data rate can be determined, which is referred to as a Committed Information Rate (CIR). The CIR is the bandwidth guaranteed by the frame relay provider, however it can be exceeded if there are currently unused capacities available on the frame relay network. The maximum bandwidth is then finally limited by the capacity of the (permanent) connection between customers and frame relay providers, as well as by the providers' contractual conditions.

During times with low network utilization, more data packages can be smuggled into the frame relay network than are guaranteed by the CIR. The "additional" data packages are, however, marked by a specific bit. If the data packages that have been selected in this way come into an overloaded connection, they are deleted without much ado.

Costs When compared with a leased line, higher latency times occur in the frame relay. Frame relay connections are mainly charged according to the CIR, the transferred data volumes, and the distance between the network points. In addition, there is a once-in-a-lifetime installation charge and monthly fees for ports and PVCs.

12.1.6 ATM

ATM (Asynchronous Transfer Mode, CCITT I.361) has its roots in phone technology and, for this reason, is a Consultative Committee for International Telephone and Telegraph (CCITT) norm. In this context, asynchronous means that no specific synchronization signal—such as in traditional multiplex technology—is required, because the ATM cell current generates the synchronization.

ATM was developed so that language, data, and video services could be operated in a standard technology via local networks and wide area networks as well. The different requirements for language, video, and data communication led to certain compromises, which, in turn, resulted in specific disadvantages.

Quality of Service In order to ensure quality of service (QoS), time-critical language and video data have priority over other data. QoS is one of the most important performance characteristics of ATM. However, the QoS algorithm also ensures that the connection isn't established at all, if the network is so overloaded that the necessary quality of service cannot be guaranteed.

While the triumphal procession of Fast and Giga Ethernet, along with its unbeatably low device costs, has ensured that ATM is not widely accepted in local networks, many telecommunications companies use ATM in their wide area networks and offer corresponding WAN services.

The advantages in using these services for SAP are a higher speed in contrast to frame relay, along with the bandwidths and service classes adapted to meet the requirements of the respective application.

Costs ATM, however, is relatively expensive when compared with frame relay. In addition to the initial installation charge, there are also monthly costs for ports and SVCs, depending on the bandwidth used and the distance that exists between the network points.

12.1.7 Internet

Basically, the Internet is the merger of a variety of individual networks of different Internet Service Providers (ISP), which are capable of transporting IP packages. The confidentiality of SAP data connections on the "public" Internet is ensured through the concept of a VPN described below.

The advantages of the "network of networks" as a transport medium for SAP data is the global availability and the unbeatably low costs. However, on the Internet, the transfers of business-critical transactions are in fierce competition with megabytes of colorful images, MPEG videos, MP3 music, and voice over IP data.

In our book on SAP infrastructures[2] which was published in 2000, we advised against using the Internet for connecting the end users to the SAP data center. This recommendation was based on runtime measurements that proved a relatively large distribution and frequent loss of packages, which meant that a consistent response time behavior in a service level agreement (SLA) could not be guaranteed by deploying the Internet for SAP traffic.

A good example

As actual measurements of runtimes on the Internet demonstrate, many things have happened since with regard to Internet infrastructure. For example, for the connection to a popular online bookstore[3] in Australia, it takes a signal runtime of between 320 and 340 ms through the path Hamburg—London—Singapore—Brisbane, with an average value of 330 ms and without any data package loss. Admittedly, this online store also has a powerful connection to the network of his ISP.

Bad example

In comparison to this online store's impressive network connection, here's a frightening example of the connection to (another) provider in Hong Kong, which is also routed via Hamburg—London—Singapore. Here, the values are between 395 ms and 561 ms, with an average value of 481 ms. However, there is a 25 % loss of data packages. Since this data must be retransferred, this results in at least a doubling of the time it takes for the information, which is compiled from several data packages, to be completely transferred. In this example, the analysis shows that the

2 Mißbach, Hoffmann: *SAP Hardware Solutions—Servers, Storage, and Networks for mySAP.com*. Prentice Hall 2000.

3 Go to *www.4wdbooks.com.au*.

problems were definitely caused by an insufficient connection of the local ISP to the connections that form the backbone of the Internet.

Experience shows that a powerful ISP connection is required in order to establish a powerful VPN connection. The problem are not originated only in the capacity of the local connection and the quality of the ISP's own network , but also in the capacity of the transitions points to other ISP networks.

In general, Internet providers cannot guarantee any service levels outside of their own network. When selecting an Internet Service Provider, you should not only consider the capacity, quality, and range of coverage of the selected ISP, but the provider's connections to other ISPs and their network quality as well.

For example, it is insufficient for an US enterprise connection to offices in Europe and Asia to rely on an ISP with a powerful network in the US; rather, you should also ensure that the ISP has an established partnership with an ISP's in Europe and Asia who is equally powerful, a principle called peering.

Costs The strength of Internet VPNs is that they are essentially more cost-effective than any other kind of connection. Costs generally only arise for the data volumes transferred, regardless of the distance. However, there are also costs for the local loop, that is, the connection to the point of presence (PoP) of the ISP using the aforementioned technologies. In international traffic, the costs are about 70 % less than those of frame relay.

Weakness The weakness of Internet VPN lies in the lack of the ability to prioritize, so that the timing of a transfer will depend generally on the principle of best effort. Using the Internet as a transfer medium for SAP applications is therefore only advisable if higher response times are acceptable, or a provider has technologies that can ensure a corresponding service level across the entire connection distance.

12.1.8 Multiprotocol Label Switching

In Multiprotocol Label Switching (MPLS), the data is not addressed using the IP address, but by using labels that specify both a path and a priority. Since analyzing labels takes less time than does reading a complete IP address, throughput and speed increase.

QoS on the Internet The big advantage of MPLS is that it is completely independent of the transport medium. This means that the QoS can be guaranteed, even across different technologies between the Ethernet, frame relay, or ATM. However, MPLS is only available in private IP networks. Most telecommunications companies that offer MPLS use three to four service classes, the highest being reserved for voice and video. In the middle class, the application data is transferred with response times that are defined by SLAs. Other data such as Web downloads and emails are provided by MPLS according to the best-effort principle if the capacity is available on the ISPs network.

In providing flexible bandwidths and fixed service classes according to the requirements of the respective application, VPN combines the advantages of the Internet with the qualities of ATM on the basis of MPLS. MPLS is generally only provided with the relevant access routers, which will be centrally managed by the provider.

Costs

However, quality comes with a price. In addition to the initial installation charge, there are also monthly charges for ports, bandwidth used, service classes, and the distance that exists between the network points. Currently, MPLS offers the most cost-effective price-performance relationship, after what is offered by the Internet. However, MPLS is not available in all countries.

An example of what is technically possible

As an example of what is technically possible, the following table documents the latency times of an connection with MPLS and very large bandwidths for the local loop from a data center in Hamburg (2 × E1 connection, i.e. 4 MB bandwidth):

New Jersey/US (2 × T1 connection)	90 ms
Austin/US (1 GB trunk connection)	103 ms
Rio/Brazil (T1 connection)	230 ms
Santiago/Chile (10 MB bandwidth)	240 ms
Hong Kong (3 × T1 connection)	295 ms

For such a network that has been designed for VoIP and video conferences, you would pay approximately $120,000 per month. For a global MPLS network with approximately 100 locations, some of which have 34MB connections, the costs are about $350,000 per month. In general, the necessary bandwidths for the SAP data traffic and, therefore, also the costs, are reduced by at least a factor of 10 compared to the example above.

12.1.9 Satellite Connections

Stable and reliable terrestrial connections are not available everywhere in the world. In such cases, communication satellites are a tried-and-tested medium for SAP data transfer. The necessary antennae dishes with a diameter of between one and several meters, however, require a license in some countries and cannot be installed in every location.

Very small aperture satellite

With the help of modern communication satellites, antennae dishes with a diameter of only 1 yard to 2.6 yards are possible (Very Small Aperture Satellite, VSAT). With an available bandwidth of up to 2Mbps, there is sufficient room for the connection of SAP systems. Tests that were carried out in the SAP HP Competence Center proved the appropriateness of VSAT links for the SAP data traffic. The costs for VSAT connections depend on the needed bandwidth and not on the distance. There are two types of connections: One connection is a transparent fixed connection (SCPC) with a fixed bandwidth, which is comparable to a leased line. The other connection consists of a shared medium (TDMA) that corresponds to DSL.

Speed of light as a limit

The primary disadvantage of commonly used satellite systems derives from the distance to geosynchronous orbits, which is at least twice the global circumference of 22,700 miles (36.000 km). Even at the speed of light, a signal latency of approximately 480 ms for a round trip occurs. In addition, latency is caused by the electronics of the transmitter equipment. As a result, when you use a satellite connection you must provide for approximately 560 (SCPC) to 700 milliseconds (TDMA) for each round trip between the server and the user.

One to two roundtrips per R/3 transaction

In all R/3 releases, the transactions with WinGUI or JavaGUI generally require one to two roundtrips so that they are still suitable for satellite connections. A few transactions require two or three roundtrips, which means that you must expect a response time here that is on the limit of what is acceptable.

Several specific transactions, however, require considerably more roundtrips. Some functionality in human resources (HR), as well as the APO cockpit and others are among them. You can determine the number of roundtrips from the display in the SAP GUI status bar.

Due to the limitation of the speed of light, transactions that require more than two to three roundtrips yield response times that are greater than two seconds in all applications. Therefore, they are only suitable for satellite connections if the users are prepared to accept this under the given conditions. However, a sufficient bandwidth in the terrestrial connections should also ensure that no additional delays are caused.

Bandwidth Management in Global Networks

Due to the massive extensions to fiber-optic networks, you could easily get the impression that the bandwidth in the networks of the large providers that span the globe is no longer subject to any restrictions. In reality, however, this is the result of constant sophisticated bandwidth management. For example, the administrators in the network control centers have always kept an eye on CNN so that in case of a disaster, the sufficient bandwidth for the camera teams flown in will be available in the corresponding part of the world.

12.2 Strategies for Cost Optimization

In the long run, a WAN is the most expensive part of a network infrastructure, because they cause running costs. Nevertheless, the available bandwidth should not be too small.

Peak loads

The necessary network bandwidth is determined by the data quantity that must be transported through the network per time unit. However, the data quantity is never constant. Like the distribution of activities of the SAP users, the SAP data traffic via typical WAN connections also shows different maximums at different times of the day. In addition, there can also be seasonal peak loads.

The challenge lies in dimensioning the WAN connections so that they can manage the varying network loads in an optimal way. If the connection is dimensioned too large, the company pays for bandwidth, which is rarely used to its full extent. If it is too small a dimension, the data packages accumulated, are lost and are unnecessarily re-transferred. This, in turn, leads to high response times and ultimately to lower user productivity, which, of course, is not wanted, especially at peak times.

Data packages lost are transferred again

An overloaded connection also causes an overflow of the input buffers at the network nodes. TCP/IP then causes a new transfer of the data package that was "lost," which further worsens the situation.

Telecommunications Markets: From Monopoly to Competition

The deregulation of the national telecommunications markets in the countries of the European Union and other parts of the world has caused the telephone costs in theese countries as well as the costs for long-distance connections to drop dramatically.

However, in the local exchange area, the situation looks far different. Here, the entire cabling infrastructure is owned by the former national telecoms that still have a monopoly. This leads to the paradoxical situation that the costs for a leased line of just a few miles between the customer location and the connection point (POP) can be several times the costs for the subsequent frame relay or Internet connections that span over thousands of kilometers.

Optimal use of WAN bandwidth

The following section primarily deals with methods in order to utilize the WAN connections as efficiently as possible. To do this, the specific properties of modern routers can be used to optimize the transfer of data flows.

12.2.1 Filtering, Spoofing, and Compression

The main function of a router—and that is also where its name stems from—is to determine the best possible routes to transfer a given data package in a meshed network. In addition to this function, modern routers provide a wide spectrum of functions that can be used to optimize the WAN connections.

To determine the optimal route, a router must analyze the entire address information of a data package. This information can also be used to filter out "unnecessary" data packages in order to reduce the protocol overhead and to prioritize the important data.

By using access lists, you can define which data packages are permitted to pass a router interface and which are not. This means that you can ensure that only the data packages that are required in the destination network are transferred via a WAN connection. However, you must use caution with this tool as it can lead to network disruptions.

Muzzle for gossipy LAN protocols

The various different LAN protocols can be quite chatty. Each protocol sends special data packages in intervals of a few seconds to the end devices in the network in order to notify them of available resources and services (service advertisement), for example, which host is still active (keepalives). Although these data packages can be easily filtered out by a router, they are also required under certain circumstances in sub-networks. Using so-called Spoofing, a router can regenerate the data packages at one end of a WAN connection which its partner has filtered out at the other end. At larger intervals, both routers exchange information on which packages were "seemingly to be transferred." By using spoofing, the network overhead, which is transferred through the WAN connection, can be drastically reduced without affecting the functionality of the local networks.

Router as a proxy server

The use of a router as a proxy server for address resolution (proxy ARP) works in a similar way. As the router analyzes the physical (MAC) and logical addresses (IP) of all data packages that run through it, it can also answer an ARP request directly by itself, without the request having to be transported through the WAN connection.

SAP data is already compressed

In addition, routers can also compress the data packages, and decompress them again at the transition point to the LAN. Therefore, larger data quantities can be sent through a WAN connection than would nominally go through it. However, the SAP data flows are already efficiently compressed and therefore cannot be further compressed. In addition, the on-the-fly compression of the data also utilizes a large portion of the router's CPU. An overloaded router will lead to increased latency time which quickly consumes the benefits achieved through the increased bandwidth.

12.2.2 Bandwidth on Demand

When a defined load of a fixed WAN connection is exceeded, routers enable you to turn on additional dial-up ISDN connections. By doing this, they increase the available bandwidth to meet the current requirements (bandwidth on demand or dial on demand. These temporary connections are automatically released again as soon as the load decreases. In this way, the available total bandwidth is constantly adjusted to reflect the actual requirements. This makes it possible for you to design the fixed connections in accordance with the average requirement, without peak loads affecting the operation. However, the costs for the additional ISDN channels can be pretty high.

12.2.3 Data Prioritizing

In WAN connections, the data packages of SAP systems must compete with other applications for the available bandwidths. In contrast to flat networks whose layer-2 switches handle the data packages equally, layer-3 switches and routers can handle the data packages differently, depending on the applications for quality of service.

"Well known" TCP ports

To grant quality of service, the router sorts the approaching data packages in queues with different levels of priority using the IP address and the "well known" TCP ports of the SAP system. For example, in correspondence with the prioritization settings in the router, the data packages of the SAP dialog traffic can always be sent through the WAN connection before the print data. In this way, acceptable response times can be ensured, even with a higher load in the WAN. This is the ideal solution for connecting the SAP user groups to where the data volume fluctuates most, for example, due to print jobs.

Since Release 4.5, SAP also supports the Winsock2 GQoS API in Windows 2000, for QoS signaling with the resource reservation protocol (RSVP). The well-known TCP ports and policy locator strings necessary for RSVP are published in the SAP White Paper "SAP Software in Quality of Service Networks," which is available to partners and customers in SAPnet.[4]

Pros and Cons of Network Caches

By using caching devices in remote subsidiaries, you can reduce the data volume transferred by between 5 % and 95 %, depending on the user behavior. Experience has shown that savings are reduced with an increased use of the SAP system, so that higher values only occur if a user carries out just a few transactions per month. For those who use the SAP system intensively every day, there are only minimal savings.

On the other hand, caching devices represent a certain security risk, because they terminate the SSL connections. In such a case, the server private key must be stored in the caching device. Authentication on the basis of X.509 certificates is also not available.

4 Go to *http://service.sap.com/network.*

Therefore SSL is typically end to end so it can't use caches. For example, I pretty sure that my ISP runs a cache. However, I am also sure that when I do my online banking they are not able to cache any of the details. The browser forms an end-to-end SSL session with my bank's server. I can verify this by examining the certificate that has been issued to the bank and successfully authenticated by the server. The cache is not able to able to tamper with or eavesdrop on the connection.

12.3 Security Aspects of WAN Communication

Business systems such as SAP carry a company's sensitive data. Consequently, all unauthorized access to this data must be prevented. While the local networks are fairly secure against eavesdropping, the Internet connection is a potential open back door to business data. With some technical effort, it is possible to read the data displayed on a monitor screen from the other side of the street due to the high frequency emission. In fact, when using the Internet, you can read it from wherever you are.

Within the network of a telecommunications provider (not ISP), the confidentiality of data can be considered as more or less ensured due to the provider's security measures. An additional encryption is only necessary for particularly sensitive data, or in regions in which monitoring by government institutions, in particular, cannot be completely ruled out.

Data security through cryptography

For all connections that run through several providers and especially through the Internet, the security of data can only be ensured by using additional cryptographic methods.

Through the network connection between SAP GUI and the application hosts, all data is transferred, which the user enters or displays. This does not occur in plain text, but with a static key. For this reason, the encryption does provide protection against accidentally reading the data but not against serious attacks. If the confidentiality of data is really to be secured, the connections must be encrypted with more elaborated methods.

SAP Secure Network Communication

In order to be independent of the different national restrictions in relation to high-level encryption technologies, SAP have not implemented own security measures; instead, it provides an interface to the security products of other manufacturers. This interface is called Secure Network Communication (SNC).

SAP has certified various security products for SNC. Some of these systems have additional authentication methods such as smart cards or biometric processes. Users who log on to an SNC connection via SAP GUI do not have to undergo authentication in the SAP system with their user names and passwords.

SNC can also be used to set up a secure tunnel between two SAProuters. In this way, however, only SAP data is encrypted. Other data streams such as email messages cannot be secured with SNC. The connection between the application hosts and the database cannot be secured through SNC.

VPN tunnel for sensitive data

Virtual Private Networks (VPN) have become widely accepted as the most useful method for transferring sensitive data, in particular, over the Internet. Here for all data between the local networks of a company, a secure "tunnel" through the public network is established by encrypting the data packages at one end of the tunnel, and then packing it into other IP packages, and finally unpacking it again and decrypting it at the other end. Due to the packing, there is a slight increase in the data volume to be transferred.[5]

Cryptography and Authorities

The use of cryptographic processes by companies and private people is regarded as critical by various countries and is therefore frequently subject to legal restraints. It can be assumed that the key systems approved by these countries correspond exactly to the status that the responsible services can decrypt with their available ressources. To this extent, the authorities' approaches to key escrow reflect the growing difficulties of keeping up with the constantly improving encryption technologies. As with SAP software, no particularly strong encryption is used, and neither is it subject to the corresponding restrictions. Instead, strong encryption is only ensured with regard to external systems via the SNC interface. These external systems, in turn, are subject to the aforementioned restrictions that we just referred to.

Crypto-Boxes

To this end, dedicated devices can be used for encryption on the basis of specialized hardware (so-called crypto-boxes); access routers and firewalls with the corresponding functionality can also carry out this task. This means that the tunnel is transparent for all applications and users. Not only does this ensure that the SAP data is secure, but it also justifies

5 See also *Front End Network Requirements for mySAP Business Solutions*, SAPnet.

the case for file transfer, email, and other applications, and users in distant locations not having to go through an additional logon procedure.

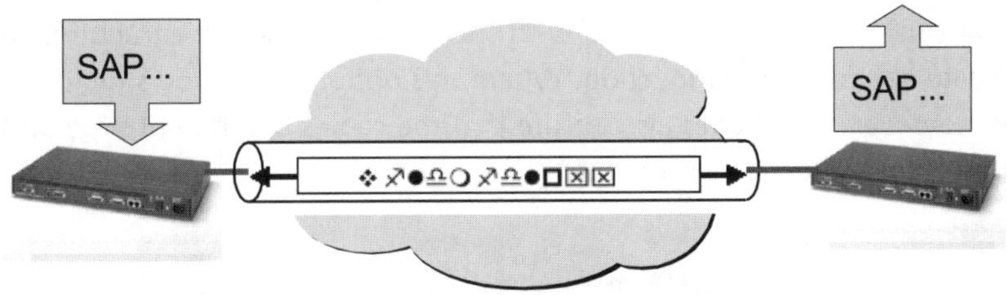

Figure 12.1 Encrypted VPN "Data Tunnel" through the Internet

VPNs are currently enjoying great popularity. However, they're not that easy to implement, especially if different devices are used at the end points. Because of the importance of data security, therefore, we believe that the configuration of VPNs should be carried out only by proven experts.

Setting "Idle Time-Outs" in Firewalls to Sufficient Length

During the entire time that a user is logged onto the SAP system, the SAP GUI maintains a TCP connection to the application server, even if the user has not made any entries for a long time. In order to ensure that this connection is not interrupted, there should be no "idle time-outs" set on the firewalls for SAP and none that are shorter than the usual lunch break.

12.4 Failure-Tolerant WAN Connections

Due to the business-critical character of SAP systems, more attention should be paid to the issue of high availability in WAN connections. For all users who are not connected to the same local network as the SAP servers, the WAN connection represents an "live-line." If this line is cut in two, no more business processes can be carried out. If SAP services are outsourced to an external data center or rented from an application service provider (ASP), the entire company is affected.

Although the highly-meshed core networks of the telecommunications providers always ensure a high degree of availability, WAN connections still remain the least reliable part in an SAP network infrastructure.

Dirty Last Miles

The reason for this unreliability lies in the connections between the sites of the companies and the Point of Presence (PoP) of the telecommunications provider. This so called local loop is often referred to as the "dirty last mile." This doesn't necessarily mean that the local loop is of bad quality, but that it is a single point of failure (SPoF). Only in a large metropolis you can find several providers with their own cabling infrastructures to create a redundant connection. Where this option exists, you should use it; however, you should also ensure that the cables of different providers don't run through the same duct.

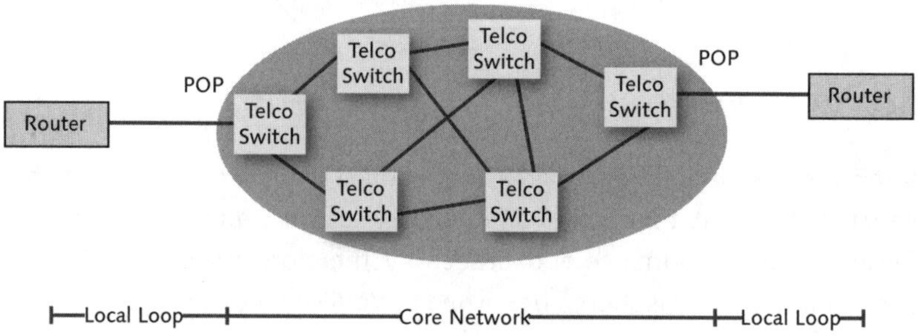

Figure 12.2 Single Points of Failure in a Typical WAN Network

There are different approaches to increase the availability of WAN connections, which are based on the capacity of routers to transfer data streams through several paths. From a router's perspective, all disturbances in the line can be bridged as long as an alternative path is available.

12.4.1 Redundant Hardware

As is the case with all complex devices, there can also be hardware problems in routers. For this reason, routers and their connections to each other should be redundant. In this way, the connectivity is also ensured even if an individual router breaks down.

UPS also for routers

Instabilities in the power supply are frequent sources of errors. A voltage transient that causes only a short flickering in the lighting can cause a router to reboot. We therefore advise you to stabilize the power supply of the routers by implementing uninterrupted power supply units (UPS), in order to secure the availability of the WAN connections.

12.4.2 Redundant Connections

To achieve high availability in a WAN, you need redundant connections. Without them, all other measures are only patchwork. However, in the area of the "dirty last mile," it's not always easy to find an alternative path.

A simpler and more cost-effective method is to use the capabilities of routers in order to establish additional ISDN dial-up connections when needed (bandwidth on demand). In addition to bandwidth-on-demand, this also results in a significant increase in availability. As soon as the router recognizes that in a specific location the primary connection is disturbed, it immediately establishes a backup connection through the ISDN network. However, this is only the case if the ISDN connections don't run through the same cable as the WAN path.

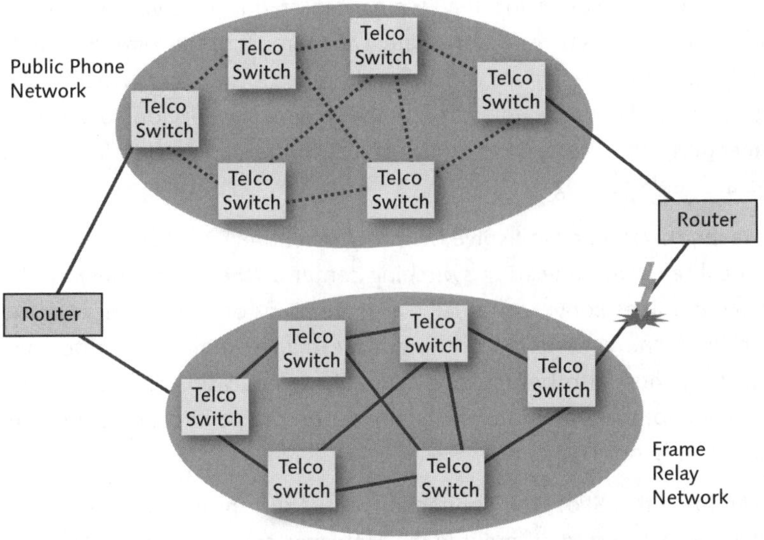

Figure 12.3 Bandwidth-on-Demand as a Backup for WAN Connections

Monitoring WAN Connections Through Network Management

If the ISDN backup connection has the same bandwidth as the primary line, then the switchover to the backup line is so transparent that it goes unnoticed. If the telecommunications provider doesn't notice the failure of the primary connection and therefore, doesn't correct it, the customer will get a surprise in her monthly telephone bill when she sees that the connection has been running for weeks through the ISDN dial-up connection. For that reason, we recommend that you monitor all WAN connections via a system management system.

Bandwidth on demand

Using bandwidth on demand as a safeguard against a failure of the primary connection is probably the most cost-effective solution, since, apart from the basic charges for the ISDN connection, no additional costs incur during normal operation. As soon as the primary network connection is available again, the ISDN dial-up connections are switched off. If, in addition, every single point of failure is eliminated in the hardware through a redundant design, the only weak point is that the ISDN dial-up connections run on the same cables and telecom switching centers as fixed connections in the local loop.

SPoF local loop

Disruptions to the connection from a subscriber's terminal to the PoP at the telecom provider's local switching center due to civil engineering works or natural disasters unfortunately affect most of the wires in a cable bundle. In countries where cabling within towns and cities is still a defacto monopoly of one telecom company, the only option to create a connection redundancy is to apply for a second main connection with a separate cable routing

SpoF local telco switching center

However, this still doesn't solve the problem entirely, because in this case the local telecommunication switching center as the place where all the connection lines converge remains a single point of failure. Because the switches in the centers are nothing more than complex computer systems, they must also be updated and restarted occasionally. In a worst-case scenario, the entire local switching center can be knocked out by fire or a lightning bolt.

Microwave link as a backup

To eliminate this SPoF, the connections must run through different local switching centers and different POPs. However, this solution can be quite expensive if a cable must be laid in the neighboring town. In this context, point-to-point microwave links represent an alternative that can be set up relatively fast and easily.

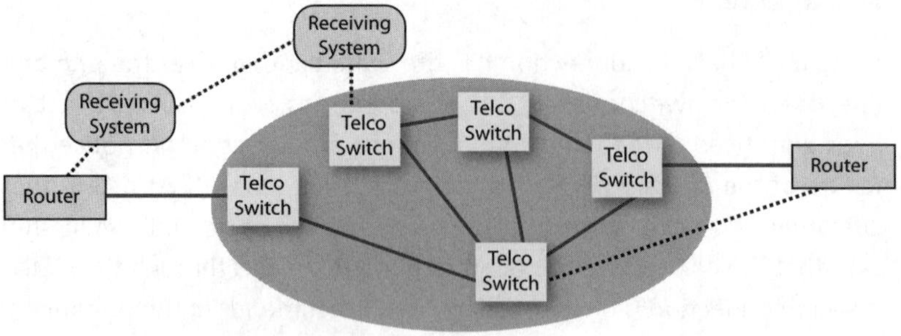

Figure 12.4 Redundant Connection to the Core Network of a WAN Provider Using Microwave Links

If neither cable nor microwave links are available, or any dependency on terrestrial connections should be avoided, VSAT connections can also be used as backups. This also fulfills the requirement that the backup path runs in a completely different direction than does the primary connection. The data goes directly from the backup router in the local network to a satellite dish, which is typically installed on the roof of the building. The general suitability of these systems for connecting SAP end devices was proven with tests at the SAP HP Competence Center.

Satellites as backup

Satellites are almost independent of terrestrial influences (excluding damages to the satellite dish caused by hurricanes or hail). There are actually short-term disturbances twice a year if the sun stands immediately in the extension of the satellite's "line of sight." These times, however, can be predicted with astronomic precision. Due to the independence of satellite systems of terrestrial influences, there is a very high availability. But, due to the long signal paths, a significant prolonged response time is the result. However, if the terrestrial connection completely breaks down, a poor response time is still better than no response at all from the SAP system.

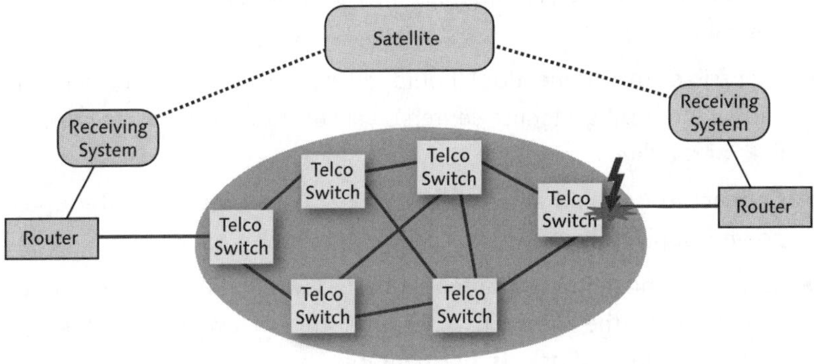

Figure 12.5 Backup Connections via Satellite

12.5 Summary

Wide area networks (WAN) ensure the connection between geographically distributed locations of a company. For WAN connections, bandwidth is a scarce and expensive resource when compared to local networks. Therefore, the rental fees for the remote connections can represent an significant portion part of the running operating costs of a company-wide SAP system. Most often, WAN connections are the weakest element in a network infrastructure in terms of bandwidth. This is also true for availability, because the WAN connection—as the IT life line of a location—represents a single point of failure.

The recommendations for an efficient and failure-tolerant WAN infrastructure can be summarized as follows:

- Regarding SLAs with telecommunications providers, do not just consider the bandwidth in the access channel; you must also consider those ISPs who make up the backbone of the Internet, as well as those providers that lead to other providers.
- For WAN connections, not only is a sufficient bandwidth important, but a low roundtrip time (RTT) as well.
- Avoid unnecessary data traffic through WAN connections as much as possible by using filters, spoofing, and proxy ARP.
- Prioritize SAP data using QoS technologies like MPLS.
- Always encrypt all data that runs through WAN connections.
- Either set very long idle time-outs in the firewalls, or don't set any.
- You should reserve redundant routers and connections to the connection node of the telecommunications provider and do so, at least in the data centers.
- If possible, the connection should always run through two separate paths (and local switching centers), via substitute cabling, microwave link, or satellite.
- Connect routers and all other network components to uninterrupted power supply units.
- Each ISP connection is a potential back door. For all systems that are connected to the Internet, a security strategy against unauthorized access and other attacks is indispensable.

13 Adaptive Infrastructures

Virtualization of infrastructures and services

As discussed in the first chapter, companies are forced to constantly adapt their business processes to the ever-changing requirements of the market. Because these business processes depend on the support of specific business applications, highly flexible and adaptive infrastructures (adaptive computing) have become a basic necessity for success in a competitive global marketplace.

However, adaptive computing can mean many things. It can be interpreted as dynamic load distribution, automation of software installation, updates to the virtualization of entire computer centers, or the automatic recognition and monitoring of resources. One thing all definitions have in common is the goal of enabling infrastructures to adapt flexibly to business requirements.

This chapter will show how the virtualization technologies introduced in the previous chapters can be used to design SAP infrastructures with maximum flexibility and to transform existing SAP infrastructures into flexible ones. In addition, we will describe the SAP Adaptive Computing Controller, along with the application service these infrastructures can use in order to form an integrated solution that incorporates the infrastructure and application. Finally, we will introduce 10 different use cases for adaptive infrastructures.

13.1 Reasons for Adaptive Infrastructures

More servers means more operational complexity

The development of business-critical applications for accounting and enterprise resource planning was characterized at first by central computer systems (mainframes). Client/server technology then made it possible to distribute the execution of applications to several computers.

More applications means even more complexity

As described in Chapter 1, the increasing diversification of SAP applications meant that the monolithic SAP system evolved into specialized applications. The bottom line is that each functional area in a company has its own company application.

On the infrastructure side, the implementation of specialized applications led to a multiplication of system landscapes to be operated and maintained. Independent servers with their own operating systems were to be provided for each application, and local disk-storage space with sufficient capacity had to be made available. This led to a large number of autonomous systems on the infrastructure level.

Heterogeneous landscapes

As individual applications were generally implemented as projects specific to certain business departments, a dedicated platform for each individual application was also purchased each time as a typical procurement practice. In many cases the hardware was selected by the business departments rather than the IT department. In the worst cases, outside consultants just recommend the hardware they were accustomed to from other projects.

As a result the empty space in the data centers, which had become available because the mainframes were dismantled, was quickly filled with the racks of the individual servers and storage systems. The IT operation found itself confronted with a heterogeneous zoo of different hardware and software systems that drove operating costs ever higher, even if each individual system by itself did lead to the promised savings. Figure 13.1 shows a typical example.

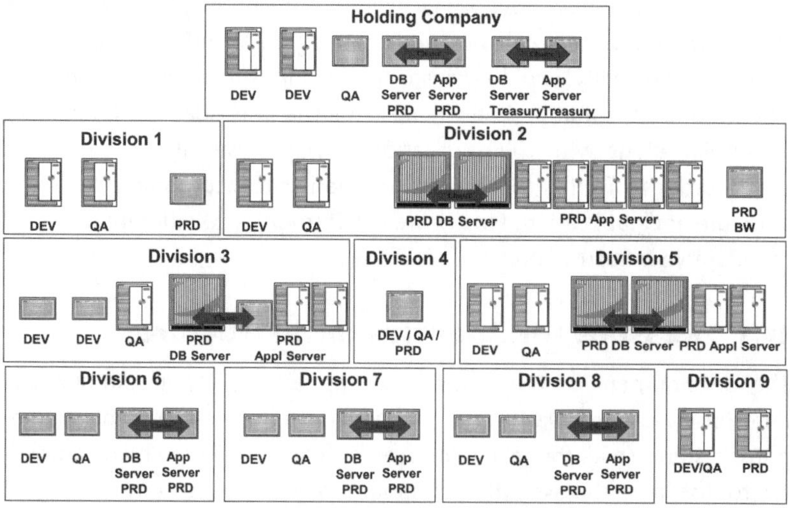

Figure 13.1 Typical Example of an Unconsolidated System Landscape

As shown in Chapter 4, the demands placed on the performance of an SAP system can increase because of the growth of the database, even without any additional use. In addition, end-of-month accounting and seasonal influences can lead to temporary strong fluctuations. In heterogeneous hardware landscapes, unused resources of an application can generally not be used for another application for technical reasons. Hardware exclusively reserved for a specific project often remains for the large part unused and produces nothing but ambient heat. This occurs because, where there is a fixed assignment of applications and system platforms, each individual application must have the corresponding reserves.

ESA

An Enterprise Services Architecture (ESA) substantially changes the situation. New business processes can be implemented in a few days with internal staff, without having to install new software components (or the requirement of "hired guns"), by using the concept of composite applications.

Applications that can be flexibly integrated or relocated in an infrastructure define specific requirements for the underlying hardware infrastructure. The sizing of the hardware infrastructure must be also adapted to the performance requirements of changing services in a few days. In order to enjoy the advantage of flexibility you must be aware of the fact that you have to pay a certain price. The positive aspect here is that hardware is constantly becoming cheaper, while the human effort—constantly becoming more expensive—is lessened due to the increased flexibility.

Some parts of an SAP system landscape are required only temporarily. This is primarily the case for non-production systems such as training and sandbox systems, but also for development and test systems that do not need to be constantly available for each mySAP solution for the entire year.

Fixed assignment versus agility

While the requirements of applications are changing ever more quickly, the procurement of systems usually involves the familiar processes of purchasing separate hardware for each application and only working with these until the cost of the hardware has been completely depreciated. Each change or enhancement is generally connected with a new, time-consuming budgeting and bidding process.

Due to the immense increases in performance in recent years, the smallest blade available on the market, which only has two CPUs, is capable of processing the load of more than 430 benchmark users. Even when taking into consideration all the differences between benchmark users and real users discussed in Chapter 4, we see that this performance is essentially higher than the requirement of many SAP systems, especially in medium-sized companies. In addition, there is the requirement that an SAP production system should have at least two CPUs.

This means that a fixed 1–1 assignment between SAP systems and servers would lead to a growing "round-up syndrome" between the SAPS values defined in sizing and those that can be realized technically. As CPUs only exist as units, this means you must always "round up" to the next nearest integer. While the performance requirements increase with the number of users and transactions along a constant curve, the performance offering must always follow a step function. This effect accumulates in relation with the number of systems you have. Table 13.1 shows an example of the difference between the number of CPUs actually required and the total figure after rounding up in a complete NetWeaver landscape.

Unsatisfactory low utilization of resources

Even if performance reserves result in flexibility within load fluctuations, this effect increases the low-level use of the CPU resources and presents a paradox: Although hardware costs are low, TCO is needlessly high. This effect is increased still by the new dual and multi-core technologies. Even here, you have to round up to the next whole chip number.

Component	Required CPU "number" according to sizing	Technical possible CPU configuration
ECC	8.1	9
BW	5.2	6
APO	4.4	5
CRM	0.6	2
SRM	0.4	2
EP	3.2	4
XI	2.1	3
Total	24	31

Table 13.1 Rounding-up Effect in a Typical Sizing

13.2 Virtualization of Hardware

In addition to standardization of processes on the company level and the harmonization of infrastructures, virtualization is the basic element of an adaptive solution and a way out of the round-up syndrome. Logically, all resources that are necessary for the operation of an application should be virtualized. If this principle is universally applied, it finally enables virtualized application services.

As a consequence of the immense increase in performance and above all the availability of 64-bit platforms, the problem of the constantly increasing number of computers with a constantly decreasing degree of utilization could be elegantly solved by consolidating several SAP systems on fewer but more powerful servers. The operation of several software systems in one common infrastructure (application stacking) led to the dissolution of the classic 1–1 relationship between software and hardware and to the virtualization of applications and resources.

Virtualization through consolidation

In addition to the simplification of the system landscape and the reduction of TCO, which are the aims of consolidation, a related side effect is the enabling of dynamic redistribution of the CPU and I/O resources, between the SAP systems which can be processed together on one server. The implementation of virtual IP addresses with high-availability clusters also enables the system operators to transparently move complete SAP systems between different servers.

Dynamic redistribution of resources

Regarding storage sub-systems, implementing storage area networks in the interest of storage consolidations involved new virtualization concepts that also led to the dissolution of the classic 1–1 relationship between software and hardware. Here again, in addition to reducing TCO, we see an increase in flexibility, thanks to the common use of storage capacity, with improved I/O performance by several SAP systems as a side effect.

In a way similar to the client/server model—where an application is distributed across several servers—virtualization means freeing yourself from the idea that one dedicated server and one dedicated storage system are necessary for each SAP system. Mainframe and UNIX operating systems have always been constructed to execute several applications simultaneously. Windows has also been capable of this for several years now. Even in a central system, the relational database and SAP Web AS are two separate programs that are executed together and at the same time. So the next logical step was to run several SAP systems on just one server. This principle has already been successfully practiced by many customers for years.

Control by partitioning

In the past, an essential argument against the operation of several SAP systems on one server was the justified fear that performance problems on one system could negatively influence other systems. If true, this meant that all service level agreements would also be affected. Depending on the manufacturer, operating system and hardware, several methods now are available for partitioning consolidated SAP systems, which under certain circumstances can be combined with each other (see Figure 13.2 below).

When designing consolidated systems, it is essential to achieve maximum flexibility with sufficient isolation and at the same time with a minimum of complexity. This is because unnecessary partitioning and virtualization technologies increase the complexity. Higher complexity increases the management complexity and the occurrence of errors, which in turn reduces the availability.

Process resource management

Competition among consolidated SAP systems for CPU and I/O resources of shared servers can be eliminated by active management of process resources.

Operating system enhancements such as the HP Process Resource Manager (PRM) for HP-UX and Linux, IBM Workload Manager for AIX, Solaris Resource Manager (SRM) from Sun, and HP Workload Management Pack for Windows enable individual program groups to dynamically allocate a percentage of the entire CPU and I/O performance.

PRM for instance simply enhances the normal scheduler algorithm of the operating system, which otherwise carries out this allocation according to a fixed "fair-share" schema. PRM allows the operator to set the rules of an individual schema according to the specific demand of the enterprise. This way, every SAP system stacked together with other SAP solutions on the same shared server can be granted an individual share of the total CPU and I/O resources.

Because the standard "fair-share" schema is completely transparent for the SAP system, PRM is also transparent for the SAP system and requires no additional resources by itself. As the assignment of resources can be changed dynamically, the resource distribution between the stacked SAP systems can be changed "on the fly" without restarting the application. This provides a flexible option for controlled load balancing between any individual mySAP components.

In addition to the flexibility and granularity, the largest advantage of process resource management for SAP is that only one operating system instance has to be installed, managed and maintained.

Virtual partitions

A number of platforms also provide the option of operating several operating system instances on one server. There is also the option of dynamically changing the resource distribution during the operation. On every virtual partition, several SAP systems can in turn be consolidated with PRM.

Independent operating system instances have the advantage that they can be booted independently from one another. Booting should be avoided as much as possible with productive SAP systems because of the downtime associated with this and the loss of the buffers. However, booting cannot be completely avoided in development and test systems. It is therefore advisable to create productive and non-productive SAP system stacks on separate operating system partitions. Virtual partitions enable consolidation of development, quality assurance, and production systems on one server.

VMware and Microsoft Virtual Server

VMware[1] ESX server allows several Linux operating system instances to be operated in parallel on one server[2]. Microsoft Virtual Server allows the same function for Windows, although the number of operating systems on a 32-bit system in both cases is narrowly limited if the application is to get its share of the addressable main memory. Therefore the PAE and AWE options described in Chapter 5 should at least be used for enhancements of the address space to 36 bits. The ultimate solution however is to deploy 64-bit technology.

Micropartitions and Virtual Machines

For HP UX, HP provides Virtual Partitions (called *v-pars*) as well as Virtual Machines. IBM provides Logical Partitions (called *l-pars*) and Micropartitions for AIX. For v-pars and l-pars the smallest possible partition is a single CPU. For micro-partitions, as for Virtual Machines, an additional abstraction layer was implemented (so called *Hypervisor*) to allow sub-CPU partitions. The Hypervisor acts as a basis operating system which can host several guest operating systems. For AIX this results in an additional resource requirement that increases with the number of Micropartitions. If the option of distributing I/O cards is used, you require a specific additional AIX instance with at least one CPU for the virtual I/O server, whereas IBM recommends two CPUs. This instance must be redundantly created for a high availability solution.

HP Virtual Partitions can operate without an additional virtualization layer. The software to control v-pars is only active at the start or if changes to the partitioning are executed. This means HP v-pars in normal operation require almost no system resources and like PRM no additional operating system instance.

1 Go to *http://www.vmware.com/*.

2 Regarding SAP support for VMware check SAP Note 674851.

Hard partitions The crossbar-based servers of some manufacturers provide the option of executing complete separation in different hardware partitions (HP n-partitions for HP UX, SUN Dynamic domains with Solaris). These form virtual independent servers within the server, which—as is the case with a blade frame—have nothing in common besides the cabinet, electricity supply and system management. In contrast to a blade system, the individual hard partitions can encompass several cells and therefore scale to very high performances.

An advantage of hardware in contrast to virtual partitions is the total "electric" isolation of the individual sub-systems from one another which allows different operating systems without a common interface layer to function (for example Linux, Windows, HP UX and OpenVMS for Itanium systems).

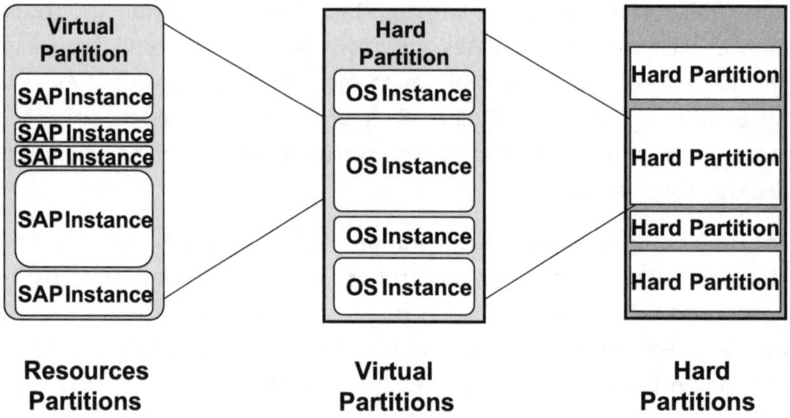

Figure 13.2 Partitioning Layers for mySAP Systems

Sense and nonsense of partitions In Figure 13.2, the "degree of isolation" increases from left to right, the granularity and dynamic in contrast increases from right to left. For process resource management concepts, the resources can be dynamically distributed precisely by percentage. For hard partitioning and dynamic domains, the resources must be redistributed in multiple CPUs and by rebooting at least the SAP system only.

The main disadvantage of hard partitions, dynamic domains, v-pars, and l-pars is that an operating system instance must be licensed, installed, monitored and maintained per partition. For Micropartitions, Virtual Machines, Microsoft Virtual Server, as well as Vmware, another operating system instance must be added.

From the point of view of TCO, several operating system instances on one server are generally counter-productive, given that every additional operating system instance not only brings additional licensing costs but additional operational costs. As a larger computer is more expensive to buy than several smaller computers that together provide the same performance, the savings to be achieved through consolidation lie in reducing the number of operating system installations that must be maintained.

This means, in the final analysis, there is not much point in cutting down a large, expensive server by partitioning into small (operating system) pieces.

Practical experience shows that process resource management concepts allow maximum savings with maximum flexibility and sufficient isolation. However, not all operating systems support the operation of different SAP releases with the same patch levels and possess the necessary stability.

Ressource reallocation without reboot

An important criterion for judging the different partitioning technologies from the point of view of flexibility is whether the change of resource distribution occurs dynamically in the running operation or if the application must be rebooted for this. Even if this can be achieved quickly, you lose the content of the buffer, which must be re-tuned. And if, before stopping the application, a user or batch job was still active on the system, transactions can even go missing.

Finally, it must be pointed out that there have to be sufficient resources available in all consolidation scenarios. However, if the available CPU or Memory capacity is too small, it is of little help to manage this by partitioning.

Financial Flexibility

Despite all the different technology to transfer system resources between SAP solutions, the performance requirements of a business application can overburden the resources of an installed system landscape for a short or long period. The solution of providing generous resources is beyond the scope of most limited budgets.

Hardware manufacturers in this case provide different instant capacity solutions, which permit the switching on of CPUs already installed "on-the-fly" without the need to reboot. Under the terms of this financial solutions, only the resources that are actually used here must be paid for. Further resources can be released in steps for an increased load, which must only be paid for at that point. Pure instant capacity solutions are however comparable to a one-way street, as the resources can only be added, not removed, but must also be continously paid for if the load sinks again.

If peak capacity is only needed temporarily for a few days in a given month or year (e.g at month's end closing or for seasonal peaks), temporary instant capacity allows you to switch on and off CPU ressources and pay only for the hours the additional CPU's are actually used, similar to using a pre-paid telephone card.

With pay per use and metered capacity solutions, all CPUs are always activated, and the actual CPU load is precisely measured to the second and calculated.

Adaptive data centers

Based on the virtualization of servers, storage and network resources, several platform manufacturers introduced concepts for adaptive data center infrastructures. These concepts allow for corresponding controller software to be used to dynamically allocate different corporate applications against existing resources (Figure 13.3). HP is counted among the first with the Adaptive Enterprise concept and this was followed by IBM On Demand, Sun with N1 and Siemens Fujitsu with Flexframe. All these concepts are based in principle on the same components and similar concepts:

- A pool of virtualized storage arrays on which the applications and their data can be stored on
- A pool of SAN switches which permits the establishment of virtual SANs
- A pool of servers which can be partitioned, on which the applications are executed
- A pool of LAN switches which permits the implementation of virtual LANs
- A pool of firewalls, proxy servers and routers to connect to the Internet via VPNs (Virtual Private Networks)

▶ A pool controller with a corresponding record of tools to implement, control and monitor the different pools

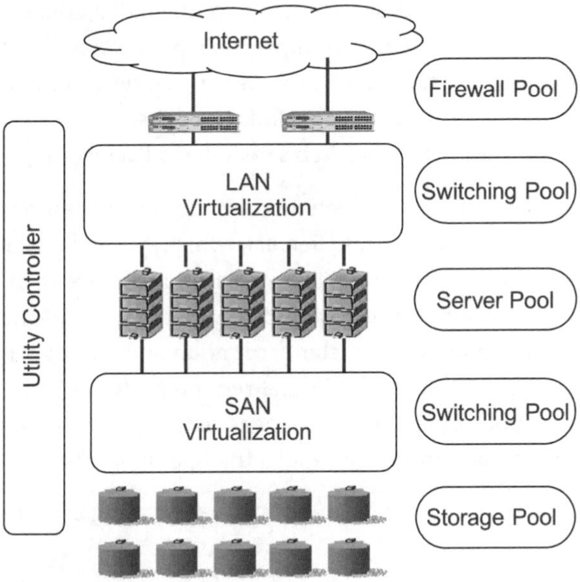

Figure 13.3 Data Center Virtualization Concept

As the concepts are mainly based on proven technologies that are transparent to the applications, the applications can operate unchanged. In cases for which application-specific adaptation is necessary (above all in the area of high availability), this is provided by the hardware manufacturers (for example the ServiceGuard extension for SAP, SAP Cluster Manager for Windows or the Cluster Consistency service by HP). However, these concepts are generally based exclusively on the hardware portfolio of the respective vendor.

In addition, these concepts are generally not capable of taking into consideration specific requirements of the applications. This is not only caused by the concepts of the hardware manufacturer but also that applications generally do not provide any interfaces for such adaptive infrastructures.

13.3 SAP Adaptive Computing

While our previous considerations focused on the hardware infrastructure resources, the concept of SAP Adaptive Computing is application-centered. The concept consists of a reference architecture and the SAP

Adaptive Computing Controller (ACC), which is supplied as a component of SAP NetWeaver.

Application services

The SAP Adaptive Computing Concept has the aim of operating application services in a virtualized hardware environment. Application Services are all components of an SAP system landscape, which can be automatically started and stopped. Components include databases, Web AS instances, and middleware components (Web server, Load Balancer etc.).

The virtualization of servers, storage and networks also forms the basis for the virtualization of application services. Servers, which the individual application services can accept, are compiled into a pool and are managed through central mechanisms. The standardized specification of the infrastructure means that the principle of standardization and homogenization is adhered to as much as possible. Centralized methods to distribute operating systems and configuration changes actively reduce the work involved in operation and therefore reduce the operating costs.

Adaptive Computing Components

Consider the basic architecture where, you will find the following components:

- The SAP Adaptive Computing Controller to control the application services
- A pool server to provide operating system images and configurations
- A server pool (consisting pool nodes which can execute the application services)
- A storage pool, in which the application services are installed

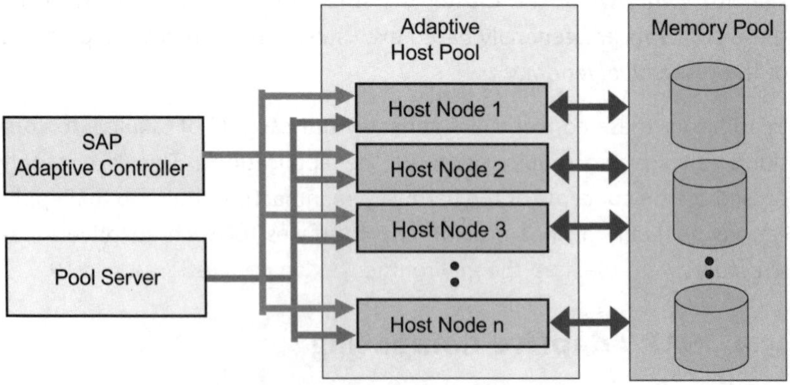

Figure 13.4 Overview of an SAP Adaptive Infrastructure

The ACC provides a browser-based user interface and is capable of starting, stopping and relocating SAP applications on pool nodes. However, it cannot directly control the hardware. For this task, it requires the tools of a pool controller provided by the hardware vendor. However, ACC and pool controllers can be installed together on one pool node.

SAP Adaptive Computing Controller

While the pool controller in an adaptive infrastructure is the central point for managing the resources and configurations for the operating systems, the SAP Adaptive Computing Controller is the central point for controlling the application in the adaptive infrastructure landscape.

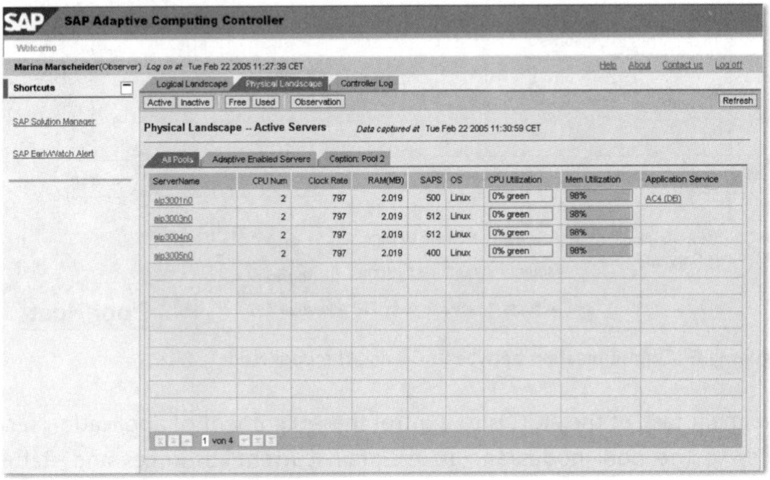

Figure 13.5 The ACC display for available CPU and memory resources of active pool nodes and their current utilization

Software Agents

From the SAP System Landscape Directory (SLD) the ACC receives information on the existing server resources, the so-called physical landscape. The following agents are installed on every node to control and monitor the pool nodes and these communicate with the ACC.

- *saposcol*—Determines the current load of a node
- *sapacoscol*—Transports the *Saposcol* data to the SLD
- *sapacosprep*—Sets up the environment of an application service
- *sldreg*—Registers a node in SLD
- Client Library from HW vendor—Routines to control OS and storage etc.

This means the ACC not only provides information on the configured application service—the logical system landscape—but also on the physical system landscape that executes the services.

These agents are automatically set up when installing the operating system and are automatically started when booting the system. Figure 13.6 shows the communication structure in detail.

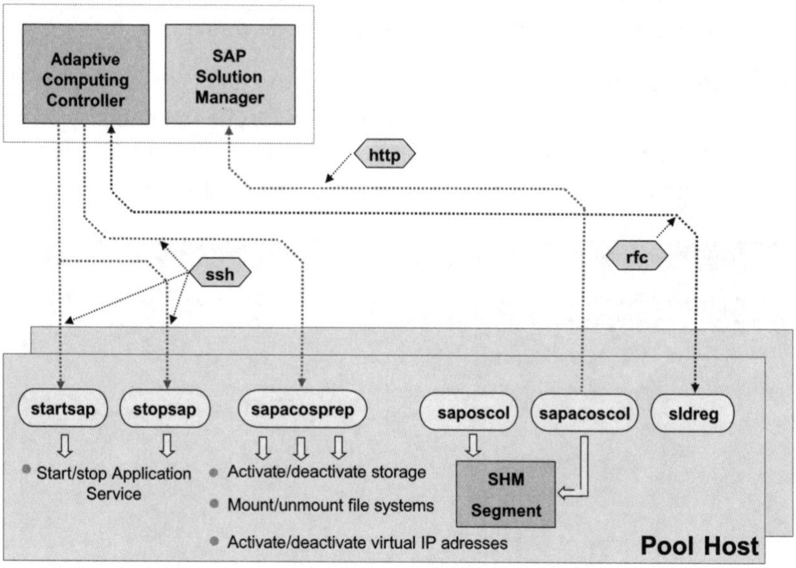

Figure 13.6 Communication between ACC and the Pool Node

The main task of the ACC is to control the assignment of application services to the pool nodes and to maintain current resources and status information on these assignments. If you supplement these tasks with central methods for data backup, spooling, network management and performance monitoring of all components, you get an adaptive system landscape which offers a high degree of automation and standardization.

Configuring the resource requirements of the individual services and the resources available on the different servers from the pool in the SAP Adaptive Computing Controller means that when transferring services a selection of the relevant servers can be predefined in a pool.

The performance specification of a server is established by a benchmark or certification test in each case while the performance requirement of a service is submitted as a result of a sizing and running performance analysis in the operation. Both specifications are stored during installation in the ACC.

13.4 Storage in the Adaptive Computing Concept

In order to automatically activate the application services on the pool servers, all of these nodes require access to the (virtualized) storage arrays, which provides the data of each respective service. The necessary storage virtualization technologies are available for NAS (Network Attached Storage) as well as for SAN (Storage Array Network). Both of these concepts have their own specific advantages and disadvantages.

Network attached storage

As shown in Chapter 6, the investment costs for NAS-based storage concepts using standard Ethernet components are relatively low but they can become bottlenecks for the database operation. NFS with UNIX provides all functionalities of a shared file system which are necessary in an Adaptive Computing environment. Therefore no additional hardware components and software layers are needed at the server level. SAP only supports iSCSI for accessing Windows systems on NAS, the CIFS protocol is not supported.

Even if in principle each storage array can be converted to a NAS by a "NAS head," the database operation through NFS generally requires at least hardware that is optimized for this (NAS filer).

SAN-based concepts require a connection to the storage area network for pool nodes, used for databases in addition to the standard network.

SAN storage

For storage area networks, the utilized storage of different application services are called via a storage ID which is translated by the adaptive implementation of the manufacturer (for example, ADAM by HP) into the activation of a LUN in the storage pool. The basic underlying technology is LUN masking or zoning in the fiber channel switches, which allow the use of any SAN storage as an industry standard. This means that existing infrastructures can be adapted for an adaptive infrastructure.

By using physical I/O, file systems, raw devices can also be used. Both types of access have been used for many years for applications in classic system operation. Only the activation of a LUN to a pool node comes additionally within the scope of adaptive computing.

Through use of a cluster file system, all data can be transparently provided to all pool nodes. Inconsistencies are therefore ruled out from the beginning. However, using this technology, which was developed for high availability, means that a cluster can encompass relatively few nodes. In addition, distributed file systems for adaptive computing are not available in all operating systems.

In a SAN concept, the database files exist in the LUN assigned by the application in the storage array. Operating system files, transport directories, instance profiles (logs), and other elements exist in a file system and are centrally mounted from the pool controller via NFS to the pool node. However, this file system can exist on the same storage array as the database files. A separate NAS filer is therefore not necessary.

13.5 Software Logistics

Several software solutions and technologies are available for provisioning the pool nodes with the necessary operating systems and application software. These solutions provide for updates and configurations, which can be implemented according to the specific hardware and operating system.

13.5.1 Provisioning of Operating Systems

In principle, the operating system could be installed locally in a traditional way on any pool server. In order to reduce the installation and maintenance effort, a central provision of the pool nodes with identical operating system instances is a keystone of the adaptive concept. These procedures also make the distribution of patches essentially more efficient.

Single system image

In a so called "shared netboot" concept, an operating system installation is adapted in such way that several computers can boot from it. This way, an identical copy of the operating system runs on every pool node (single system image). The advantage of this concept lies in the fact that changes must only be carried out at one point.

When configuring a new application service, all configurations relevant to the applications, including users, groups, and service ports, must only be executed in one operating system (usually that of the nodes, on which the ACC and pool controller are installed).

Shared Netboot Installation with Linux

With Linux, a standard installation is first carried out on the pool node on which the pool controller and ACC are installed. The necessary individual settings and operating system files of the pool controller and the other pool nodes are then stored in the */var* directory. All other files are then overwrite-protected in order to safeguard them from accidental changes by a pool node.

However, Linux does not write by default in the */var* directory. Therefore, for all files to which the operating system must write, there must be a manual, symbolic link created in the */var* directory. The files which must be individually written can differ with each release and patch.

In order to keep the necessary individualization regarding the CPU and memory resources and the driver configuration at as low a level as possible, netboot is generally used exclusively in standardized hardware environment whenever possible (e.g. blade servers).

The operating system copy standardized on all pool nodes also leads to problems if different NetWeaver components or mySAP solutions require different OS core releases, hot fixes or patch levels.

OS deployment

As an alternative; complete individual operating system installations can be created for individual nodes or node groups on the pool controller and its storage that are deployed when booting the nodes.

Like with netboot, the basic configuration must only be executed once on the pool controller. In contrast to netboot, node-specific configurations and settings can be considered as well as for application-specific settings, such as security.

This means that existing heterogeneous hardware landscapes can be integrated within an adaptive infrastructure and meet the performance requirements of the corresponding mix of systems. Maintenance on the operating system of a node (or node group) can be carried out independently of the pool controller. A mixed operation of different operating systems and versions can also be carried out without any problems.

13.5.2 Installing Application Services

In order to maximize flexibility, application services must be installed in a way so that they can be started on any node in the pool that has the necessary resources.

In a first step, the installation of the applications occurs using the standard methods with a suitable pool node. Then the configuration is adjusted for operation in an adaptive environment.

Installation Example

The following example describes the process for installation of a central system in an SAN-based infrastructure in a way, so it can be started on any node in the pool.

First a pool node is manually prepared for installation. A new LUN is created and activated on one of the virtual storage arrays for the application. For an NAS-based solution, the corresponding file systems are generated on the NAS device and mounted on the pool node.

In a shared netboot concept, the next step is to establish the configurations for the users, groups and service ports for the new SAP system in the operating system of the pool controller. In a deployment concept, only the NIS maps (Network Information Service) are updated for all pool nodes in order to activate the configuration change for user Ids, groups or service ports on all pool nodes.

Finally, a standard SAP installation (with sapinst) must be executed on the pool node. During post-processing in an SAN-based solution, all files and file systems which do not belong to the database must be exported to the central NFS server (i.e. copied). This step is omitted in an NAS-based solution.

Before the first start of the SAP solution, a service definition still must be created in the ACC. This configuration contains file systems, mount points, start/stop commands, and service names. In addition you still have to create a virtual IP address for the service in the solution manager.

For a single system image the central administration of the configurations that an application service (for example users, groups and service ports) requires functions implicitly. For a deployment solution the Network Information Service (NIS) is used for central administration of these configurations.

After completing these configuration tasks, you can start the service with ACC. SAP solutions, whose patch levels supports Transaction RZ70, register themselves at the start at the ACC. This functionality does require some basic configurations (e.g. definition of RFC destinations).

Managing an application service

After installation and configuration, each service can in principle be started on each node within the pool. Before starting a service, the ACC checks whether the selected pool node also has the necessary resources. In a central instance, ACC must also check if the database instance required for the application is already active. If not, the database will be started by the ACC. As is the case in every SAP system, any amount of dialog instances can be started, the necessary file systems will be mounted via NFS shares by the pool controller.

In order to allow several application instances to be started on one node, you can create a dedicated configuration with an individual, virtual IP address in the ACC for each instance which is to be started as an individual service.

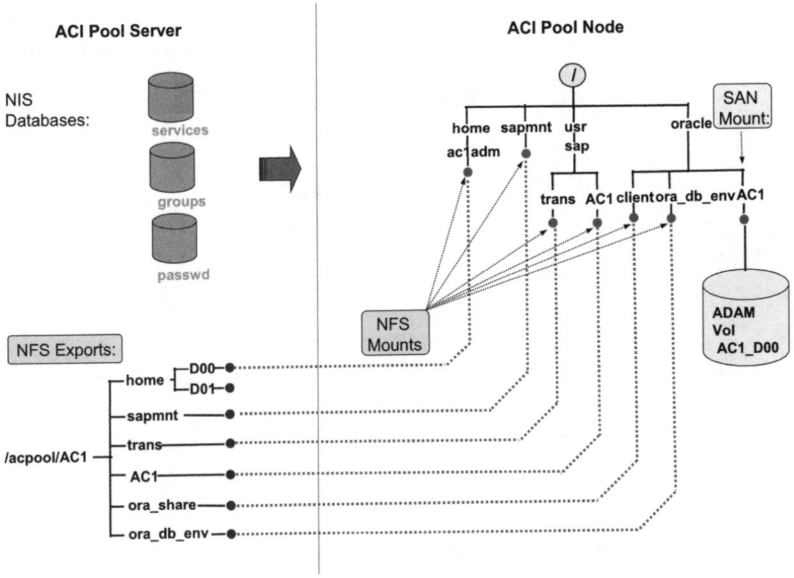

Figure 13.7 Mount Structure of an SAP Database Central Instance

Relocating an application service

An application service can be relocated as required during operation to another pool node. This is also in principle true even for databases and central instances. While relocating a database by stopping the instance, mounting the volumes on the new node and finally starting the database instance, all SAP application instances still running on other pool nodes are in a wait status. As the database is shut down in a controlled manner with no rollback necessary after the start, a relocation can be implemented in just under five minutes. This means no transactions in the SAP application instances are lost and the user context remains preserved so that it is not necessary to log on again. Throughout the duration of the relocation, the hourglass icon is displayed.

Here the parameter *rdisp/max_wp_runtime* (which defines from what point a program can be cancelled as a "user long runner") must not be set so low that there are no cancellations during the relocation.

In a central instance, a relocation to another node normally leads to a loss of the enqueue lock table. This means a relocation in the running operation is only possible with a replicated enqueue installation.

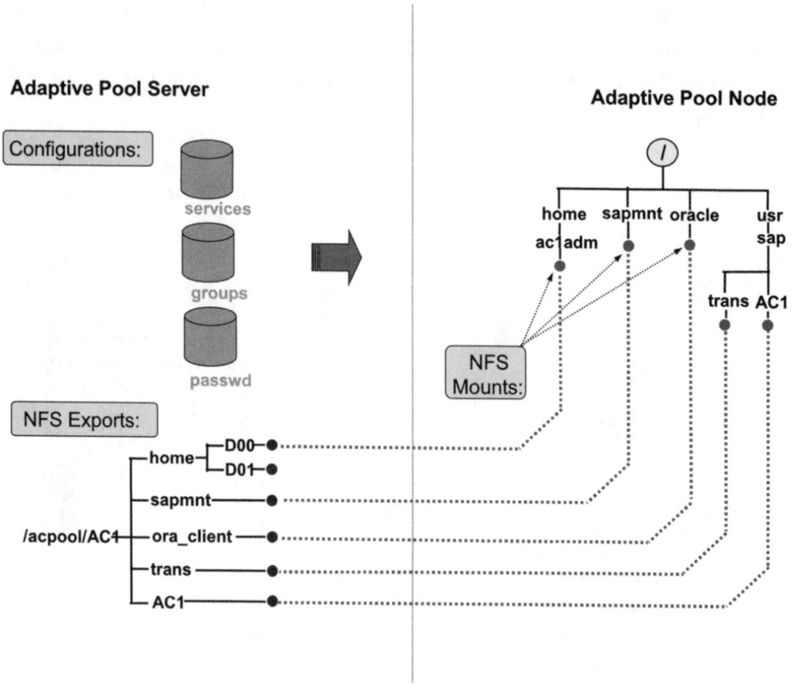

Figure 13.8 Mount Structure of an SAP Dialog Instance

Adaptive Computing and License Key

At 30 days after installation at the latest, a valid license key is required for operating any SAP system. This is also true for non-productive systems for development, quality assurance, and training. Costs are incurred for users, engines, and developers but not for the systems.

These license keys are only issued for the nodes on which the message server runs. As the key contains unambiguous parameters of the node (like burned in serial numbers of CPU and host buss adapter), any license key is only valid on this node. In a cluster solution, for each node on which the message server can run a distinct license key required. The request for the license key is an automated process[3], i.e. the license keys are distributed around the clock.

3 *http://service.sap.com/licensekey*.

If in the scope of an adaptive computing concept any system including the message server can potentially be operated on any pool node, a distinct license key must also be provided for any node. For a complete mySAP system landscape whose components should be operated on any node pool, you must therefore manage hundreds of license keys.

With the introduction of the SAP Adaptive Computing Controller, any number of license keys can be created upon request for a certain SID by SAP for the different nodes in an adaptive server pool.

13.5.3 Printing in Adaptive Infrastructures

As shown in Chapter 8, SAP applications print "indirectly" via the spooler of the local operating system. Thus the OS spooler must look after the transport details of the print job for a physical printer, whether it is a device which is locally connected, a network printer, or a print server.

For a single system image solution, all printers in an operating system spooler of the central pool controller must be configured so they can be used by the different application services on the pool nodes. A distributed printing solution can be used in a deployment solution which is already contained in many operating system. In both cases, the use of a professional output management system is recommended.

13.5.4 Availability and Adaptive Computing

With the dismantling of fixed assignments between software applications and hardware infrastructures based on virtualization technologies, the adaptive computing concepts become strongly similar to the clusters described in Chapter 7 in the way they guarantee availability.

As in a cluster, the systems in SAP Adaptive Computing are basically installed on disks in the network. The installations can be assigned to any server from a pool using scripts. By changing this assignment, SAP systems can be restarted at any time on another server.

This leads to the question whether you can generally avoid very complex high-availability clusters (HA clusters) to guarantee system availability, just by relocating an SAP service. A comparison of the two concepts however shows a number of decisive differences.

In the case of a typical HA cluster, the transfer occurs automatically after a hardware breakdown. As described in Chapter 7, it is mandatory to be

100 % sure that the primary cluster node is really broken down, and is not merely the keep-alive package has failed to reach its target because of a network disruption (so called split-brain syndrome). In addition, the configuration scripts of the cluster must specify which applications are started on which nodes and in which sequence. This is the only way that, for example, you can ensure that the database instances are started followed by the central instance followed by the dialog instances.

While an HA cluster solution automatically guarantees exclusive access to file systems of the application in the storage array, an adaptive computing solution requires that access to the file systems must be managed administratively (registration in the ACC controller: which pool node contains which application).

Failover by hand for adaptive computing

Attempts to automate these monitoring and failover processes led to the development of cluster software. As the next section shows, adaptive computing and HA cluster solutions can be combined in order to guarantee high flexibility and at the same time high availability without having to reinvent the wheel.

What is adapted and how?

The aim of adaptive computing is to adapt business processes quickly to changed basic conditions. However, there are significant differences here as to what is adapted and how and whether the adaptation is dynamically achieved in the running operation or statically achieved during booting.

In order to judge the different parameters, the following question is key: Is the concept compatible with the real business requirements?

In addition, there are the following questions:

- How is the operating system installed and maintained on the individual pool nodes in the necessary application-specific configuration (patches or updates)?
- How are the individual pool nodes supplied with the necessary individual network configurations?
- How are the different applications installed and maintained on the different applications on the individual pool nodes (patches or updates)?
- How are changes to the configuration planned, implemented and monitored?
- How is the performance of the individual nodes monitored?
- How is the service-level quality ensured?

- How can the requirements of the applications regarding operating system services and configurations (users, groups, services etc.) be ensured on all nodes?
- How are events entered and alarms executed?
- How do the interfaces of applications for typical IT services (such as spooling, backup/recovery, name resolution etc.) appear in an adaptive infrastructure?

There is also the question of how the adaptive capability is defined:

- Can the resources be relocated to different applications during the running operation without having to restart these?
- How long does it take for a change to take effect?
- Does this involve a loss in performance?

13.6 Adaptive Application Scenarios

Combining the different technologies described in this book with the SAP Adaptive-Computing Concept, brings forth a variety of practical application scenarios for the data-center operation that far exceed the pure starting, stopping, and relocating of SAP application services.

From many discussions with customers and developers, the HP SAP Competence Center has compiled 10 adaptive scenarios or reference cases with the aim of providing practice-oriented solutions for frequently emerging tasks. When describing the scenarios, it is assumed an SAN environment is in use. In a pure NAS system, NFS shares are used instead of LUNs.

Reference case 1: Adaptive deployment

In the most simple application case, exactly one SAP central system runs on every pool node. Figure 13.9 shows the virtual connection between the respective pool node and the assigned LUNs on a pool storage. The data files of a system are stored together in these LUNs. The executables of the database and the SAP application software reside in one shared file system.

The ACC can relocate every SAP system by stopping the services on a node, "redirecting" the LUN assignment to another pool node and start the service there. This means for example, a virtualized SAP instance can within a few minutes be removed from a two-way server and relocated to a four-way server if a higher capacity requirement emerges.

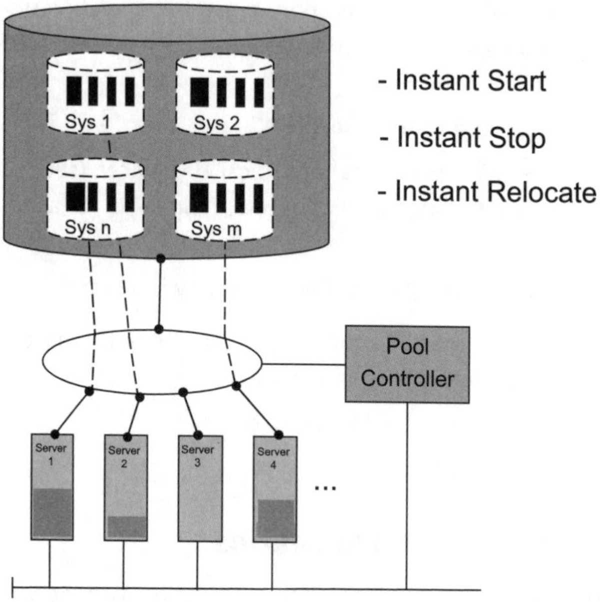

Figure 13.9 Reference Case 1—One SAP Central System per Node

Parking lot concept

The server pool can literally be regarded as a parking lot full of company cars, from which the ACC can call the necessary transport capacities as required; as a result this application scenario is also called the "parking lot" concept.

You can think of SAP instances that are not immediately required as being parked in the storage pool. This means, for example, that a training system does not clog node resources if there is no training taking place at this time. You can also visualize a parking lot concept as a number of SAP systems parked on the disk sub-systems and only being activated as required by the nodes. In order to get the full picture, keep in mind that there is also only one driver in each vehicle.

Reference case 2: System stacking

As described in further detail above, it is possible to easily consolidate several SAP systems on one operating system, whether that system is UNIX, Windows or Linux-based. This means the parking lot operation can be enhanced using the process resource management tools referred to previously so that several virtualized SAP instances can be operated per server beside each other (Figure 13.10). By avoiding the "rounding-up syndrome", the number of CPUs as well as the number of pool nodes required for a complete NetWeaver system landscape is significantly reduced and a better efficiency of the system is ensured.

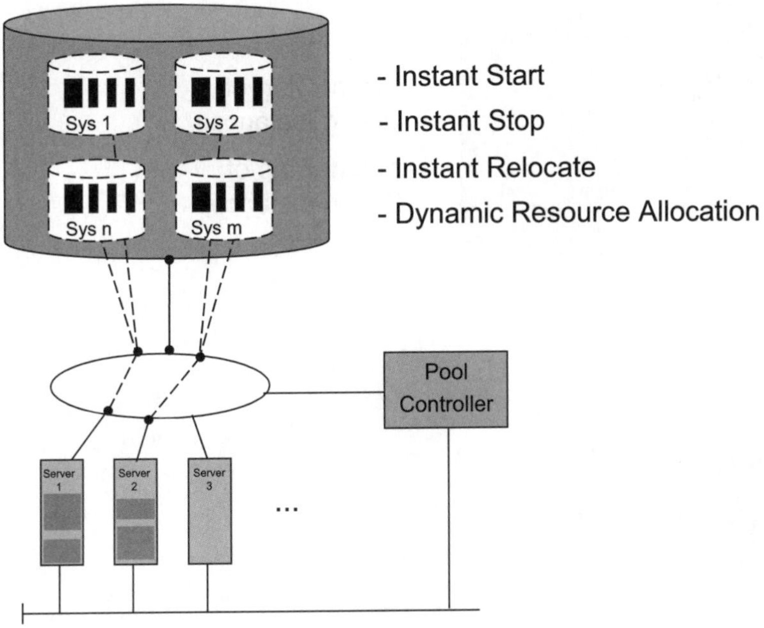

Figure 13.10 Reference Case 2—Several SAP Systems per Node

The individual systems can be started, stopped and relocated independently from one another here also. In addition, the resources between systems that run together on a pool node can be dynamically redistributed while the operation is running.

Reference case 3: Dynamic workload adaptation

If the capacity requirement of an SAP solution exceeds the individual pool node, then—as in every SAP system—additional Web AS instances can be started at any time on additional pool nodes. By starting and stopping additional virtualized application servers, a dynamic adjustment of the application resources can be obtained.

As Figure 13.11 shows only the operating system files are stored in the assigned LUNs. The database and application data are only required on the central instance.

This makes, for example, the resources of a training system available at night for batch jobs or at months end for salary calculation. This concept can also be enhanced to temporarily assign more application power to central systems which reside "outside" the server pool on a dedicated server.

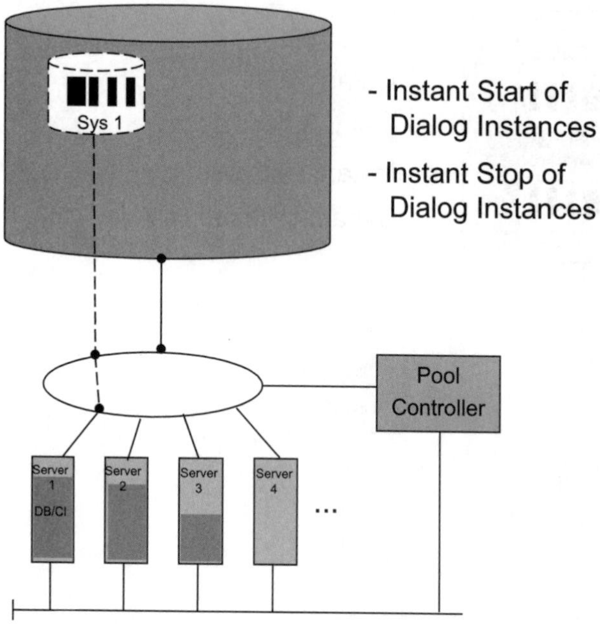

Figure 13.11 Reference Case 3—Additional Application Server

After the temporary load peak is processed, the nodes used as application servers can be returned to the resource pool after it is ensured that no user or batch job is active.

Reference case 4: Automatic generation of Test Systems

In daily operation, copies of individual SAP systems or entire system landscapes for quality-assurance tests, trainings and other purposes must be created on a regular basis. The creation of test clients using client copies is suitable only for small live clients as the duration of a client copy is in line with the size of the client. In addition, nobody can work in the live clients during the client copying.

SAP systems cloning

It is much easier to generate a quality-assurance system by "splitting" a mirror of the database file on the disk sub-system. However, an exact clone is generated here, completely identical to the production system (down to the SID-ID and IP addresses), which can't be used as intended for test purposes because of these identical SID-ID and IP addresses.

Considerable post-processing is necessary in order to convert a system clone into an individual that is usable as a test system. This post-processing comprises among others also the "decoupling" of the print spooler from the real printers; otherwise during a test run "real" invoices and delivery notes would suddenly be printed out. This manual post-processing generally takes at least half a day.

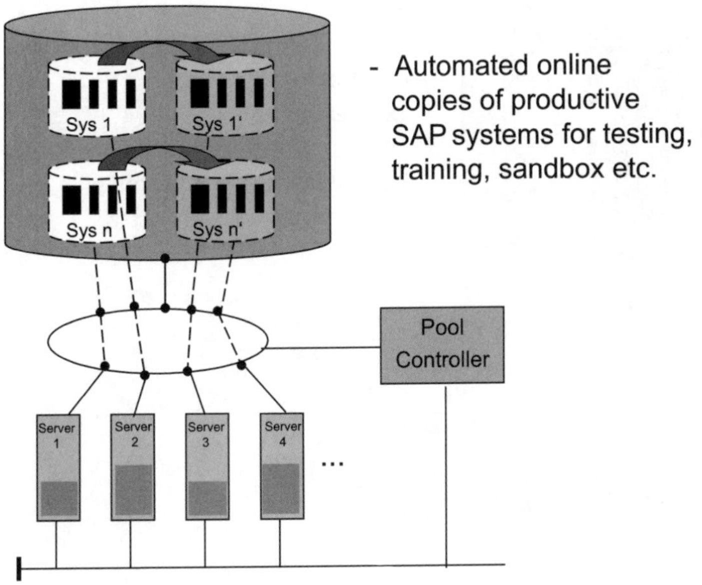

Figure 13.12 Reference Case 4—Homogeneous System Copies

System Copy Service for SAP

To ease the task of generating test and training systems the SAP HP Competence Center developed a tool called "System Copy Service" for SAP which automates and dramatically accelerates the processes for converting a clone of a productive system in to an individual quality assurance system (approximately 30 minutes for 1 Terabyte including splits, without changing the logical system names). This also dramatically reduces the time needed for upgrades and migrations, as all tests can be run in parallel to productive operation with most actual copies of the live system.

Reference case 5: Rapid backup/restore

In principle, the same methods and technologies are available for data backup in an adaptive infrastructure, as already described in Chapter 7. Therefore all the different "zero downtime" methods can be used in connection with virtual storage arrays to backup and restore the data of business processes spanning multiple SAP systems..

Data Backup in Adaptive Infrastructures

As shown in Figure 13.13, snapshots of all production systems are created at the same time, and can then be saved in sequence over a longer period of time on to tape. When there is a problem with an application in an emergency, the entire system landscape can be reset to a consistent baseline in order to grant the consistency of cross-system business processes (or only the system which has broken down).

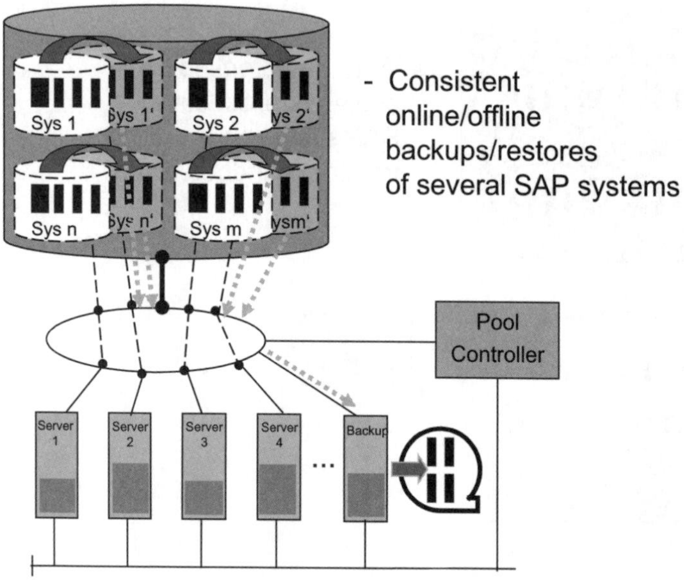

Figure 13.13 Reference Case 5—Zero Downtime Backup

Reference case 6: Adaptive software management

A further application scenario, in which daily operation benefit from the specific properties of an adaptive computing architecture, involves software-maintenance measures, such as importing and implementation of application-, database and operating system patches, service packs and updates.

As Figure 13.14 shows, an operating system patch can for example be automatically distributed from the pool controller to the system landscape after downloading from the manufacturer and passing the mandatory test on the quality-assurance system by single-system image or OS deployment.

There are two different scenarios here: In the case of netboot, the update occurs through the "golden image." In the case of OS deployment it occurs by an automatic update of the OS images through the corresponding tools. In both cases the patch must be tested on a separate node and released according to the rules of change management.

Reference case 7: Dynamic solution installation

An adaptive computing architecture can be dynamically expanded at any time by additional applications. New SAP products are first installed as standard on a pool node and then are made adaptive by generating a system image (SID package).

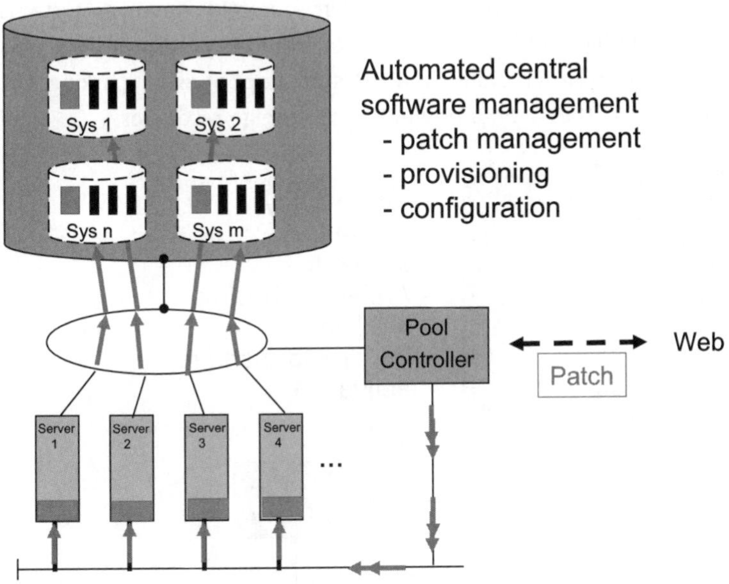

Figure 13.14 Reference Case 6—Rolling Patches

Existing systems operated on a separate environment can be transferred by a homogenous system copy into the pool, or simply by incorporating their platform in the pool and then generating a system image.

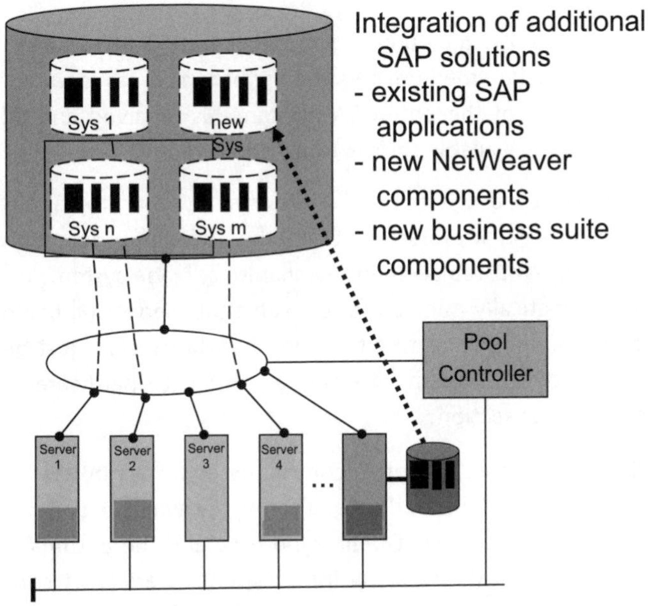

Figure 13.15 Reference Case 7—Enhancing the SAP System Landscape

Reference case 8: SAP system archiving

Another application scenario in the system operation involves systems that are only required in larger intervals for a limited period of time. You could simply "park" such systems in the storage pool as in "parking lot" Reference case 1. They would however clog storage resources.

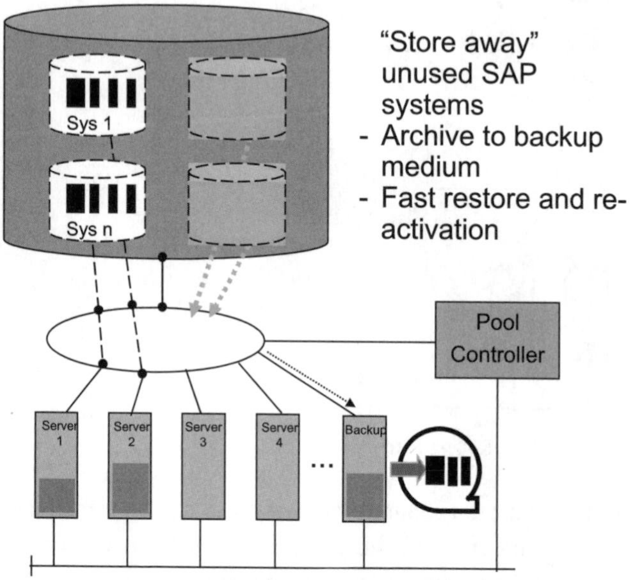

Figure 13.16 Reference Case 8—Archiving SAP Systems

As you can see in Figure 13.16, you can export virtualized SAP instances even completely to a backup medium and import them again as required. By exporting, the status of the entire SAP instance is archived and all resources are once again available for the other applications.

Reference case 9: Highly available system landscapes

When a pool node breaks down in an adaptive infrastructure, the applications can be relatively quickly relocated to another node after detection of the failure. Using rip-and-replacement mechanisms, blade systems for instance can be automatically transferred to a substitute server if a blade server breaks down. A node executing the Central Instance can't just be ripped and replaced because of the license key bound to hardware as described in the previous section.

As discussed above, a "simple" adaptive computing concept however is not sufficient to meet the established criteria for highly available systems regarding the safe avoidance of split-brain syndrome and the automatic error recovery of the application, taking into account a variety of constraints.

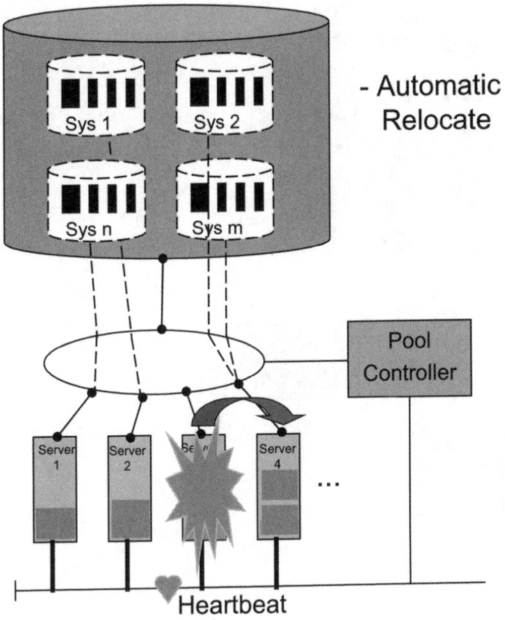

Figure 13.17 Reference Case 9—Highly Available SAP Systems

Adaptive computing should therefore not be a substitute for cluster solutions, even if it provides some hooks for such an approach. However, an adaptive infrastructure can be made 'highly available' by combining it with the existing proven cluster technologies described in Chapter 7. One option is to "cluster" systems "within" the adaptive pool concept, the other one is to provide highly available DB/CI systems which are run "outside" the pool on dedicated clustered nodes, with additional application power provided from the Adaptive Computing pool (scenario 3).

However you should also have a redundant storage and network switch pool (omitted in Figure 13.17 in the interests of clarity).

Reference case 10: SAP system database mover

For reasons of redundancy you would not operate an adaptive infrastructure for SAP production systems with a single storage system. However, it can also be necessary for business reasons to combine the necessary storage capacity from a pool of different memory sub systems.

In this way, SAP instances with low performance requirements can be operated on cost-effective storage. If the requirement for I/O increases, the SAP instance in this application scenario can be relocated to a more high performing storage (Figure 13.18).

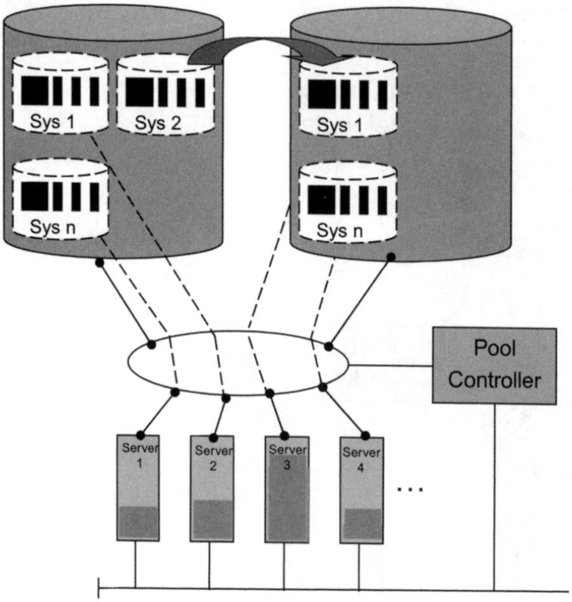

Figure 13.18 Reference Case 10—Relocating an SAP System to another Storage System

Value proposition

When deploying the adaptive computing concept, an infrastructure can be implemented that enables the physical system landscapes to adapt flexibly to the requirements of the company.

Figure 13.19 shows, within the scope of the 10 application scenarios, how effectively an adaptive infrastructure attains the goals of increased quality and agility of the system operation while at the same time mitigating the risks and reducing costs.

Be aware that during installation and planning the resources a higher degree of effort and complexity must be reckoned with here. If, for example, resources from training or development and test systems are systematically drawn on to process the month end, the increased flexibility of the system landscape paradoxically limits the flexibility of scheduling for training, development and testing.

In addition, exploiting the oft-mentioned advantage of an adaptive system landscape—implementing new applications without long lead times for budgeting and creating the hardware platform—means that the corresponding resource reserves must also be available.

	Quality increase	Risk mitigation	Cost decrease	Agility increase
Parking lot concept	◐	◕	●	●
Virtual services	◐	◕	●	●
Dynamic workload balancing	●	◐	◐	●
Dynamic landscape extension	●	◕	●	●
Rapid backup/restore	●	●	◐	●
Dynamic solution extension	●	◐	●	●
Adaptive management	◕	◕	◐	●
Archiving of unused systems	◐	◕	●	◐
High Availability	●	●	◐	◐
DB Mover	◐	◐	●	●

Figure 13.19 Value proposition of the Adaptive Application Scenarios

Avoid the Tragedy of the Commons

Here the IT department must pay up for resource reserves in advance and each new project must finance the "topping up" of the reserve capacities. Otherwise an adaptive infrastructure quickly becomes a self-service store where everyone moans about the too-scarce resources but where nobody is prepared to invest (known in economics as the "tragedy of the commons").

13.7 Summary

In contrast to the more technically oriented IT solutions, adaptive computing is mainly an organizational concept that also incorporates operational conception. This mainly involves abandoning the conventional 1–1 assignment of logical application servers and physical servers in favor of virtualized services as they were developed in the scope of consolidation and high availability concepts. This virtualization also comprises logical resources such as profile, IP addresses and node names in addition to the physical nodes, storage and network resources.

SAP Adaptive Computing Controller (ACC) works closely with the SAP Solution Manager and the System landscape Directory supplied with each SAP system. The ACC provides a browser-based user interface and is capable of starting, stopping and relocating SAP applications within a pool of computing and storage resources.

By using the virtualization technologies described, 10 application scenarios can be defined:

- **Parking lot concept**—Starting and stopping of *one* virtualized SAP instance on *any* hardware
- **Virtual services**—Starting and stopping of *several* virtualized instances on any hardware
- **Dynamic workload balancing**—(automatic) distribution of the dynamic workload across the infrastructure
- **Dynamic landscape extension**—(automated) creation of individual usable copies of productive SAP instances for quality assurance, training and other purposes
- **Rapid backup/restore**—solution-integrated backup-/restore process of the entire system landscapes
- **Dynamic solution extension**—The option of "gentle" migration of existing SAP system landscapes into the solution
- **Adaptive management**—methods to automate the distribution of patches, fixes, upgrades etc.
- **Archiving of unused systems**—Automatic removal (and renewed installation) of a virtualized SAP instance
- **High Availability**—The option to operate the virtual SAP instances in a highly available manner
- **Database mover**—Relocating an SAP system on another storage system

Following the development path of applications and the resulting IP landscapes with their typical requirements, adaptive computing is a logical and evolutionary expansion.

14 IT Service and Application Management

Of management and men

SAP NetWeaver and the mySAP components enable the integration of business processes across enterprise boundaries. However, the wide range of components and the large number of sub-systems in question have brought about an unavoidable increase in the complexity of the IT infrastructures involved in operating these processes.

At the same time, the fact that the systems are connected to the Internet has made availability requirements more demanding. Customers who order goods or services on the Internet are simply not willing to accept downtime or lost transactions. This, in turn, places more demands on the team of system administrators responsible for the performance, stability, and security of the infrastructures. What is more, these ever-increasing requirements have to be fulfilled by an staff that is usually pared down to the minimum. Therefore, to support the employees of an enterprise with their daily tasks, enterprises require system-management tools and processes that provide reliable control over these increasingly complex system landscapes.

System management systems help to ensure the availability and performance of IT infrastructures by constantly monitoring the key performance indicators. Where necessary, they carry out proactive measures based on these indicators. The goal is to identify and remove potential resource bottlenecks before they have any noticeable effect on daily operations and thus cause a violation of the service level agreement. If a system fault occurs, management systems help to minimize the consequences and duration of the fault supporting fast root-cause analysis. Ideally, the management system can also react to faults itself and trigger the necessary measures automatically.

Besides daily business operations, functional areas such as the help desk, system configuration, change management, and service-level management also have to be supported. In these cases, it is advisable to have not only individual solutions for every area, but also to implement a comprehensive overall solution.

However, while highly developed technical systems can turn data into information, only human beings can turn information into knowledge. No system, no matter how sophisticated, can replace the treasure-trove that is the experience of the employees themselves. Even the most powerful SAP infrastructure is of little use without well-trained staff to put it to optimal use.

This chapter uses examples to provide an overview of the most important IT management topics in the NetWeaver environment. The particular characteristics of this environment are due to SAP's implementation of a service-oriented architecture, the Enterprise Services Architecture.

Consequences of an Enterprise Services Architecture

In an Enterprise Services Architecture (ESA), all processes are integrated and their interaction is largely automated. This means that enterprises can enjoy real-time information (Gartner calls this the "Real-Time Enterprise"). Complex procedures and processes do already exist in "conventionally"-structured software systems, but these are by no means as closely integrated with each other as is possible with the NetWeaver components.

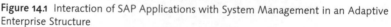

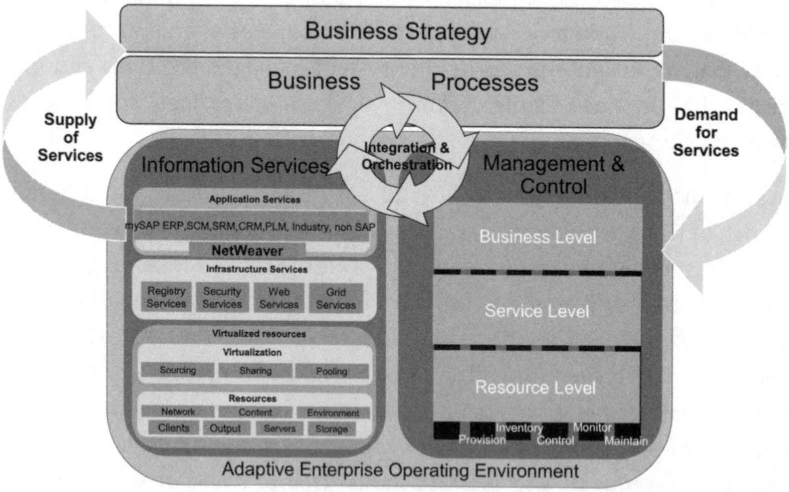

Figure 14.1 Interaction of SAP Applications with System Management in an Adaptive Enterprise Structure

As a result of this close integration, closed loops are created between the business processes and the IT systems, and all the systems influence each other within these loops. Figure 14.1 shows the interaction between enterprise strategy, business processes, IT management, and application services, plus the virtualized resources of an adaptive IT infrastructure.

Conventional organizations have these closed loops too, but they consist to a much greater extent of human beings.

The automated closed loops in a real-time enterprise can be very sensitive to unexpected changes, sometimes with unexpected results. This is because human common sense, which is part of the process in conventional enterprises, has been dispensed with here in the name of agility (and cost-cutting).

In an ESA, the business processes are not system-specific; they run one after the other through the systems that are best able to process them. Thus, all the systems that are involved in the system network have to be considered as a whole; no one system in an ESA is self-contained. In terms of business processes, every system is dependent on the others. Correspondingly, if there is a problem with the performance of one system, this can have serious negative effects on the other systems.

All systems are enterprise-critical

In this kind of system network, the availability of every individual system is critical. This is because it is always possible that an enterprise-critical composite application uses the functionalities of any particular system.

There are also problems with cross-system data consistency when it comes to backups and restores. If an individual system has to be reset, this upsets synchronization with the other systems. The issue is not just restoring an individual system; it is ensuring the consistency of the data in the entire system network. In some cases, it may not be possible to reset a system without loss of transaction data. It is therefore essential to prepare restart scenarios to deal with these situations.

Adequate test system networks

Because these systems are so intensively networked, particular attention has to be paid to the quality of the software development. A test environment should be set up that mirrors the complex interrelationships of the productive systems.

Portals: Blessing and Curse

The process of rolling out a new portal is a typical example of the changing nature of the problems that occur in the operation of these kinds of systems.

For the end-user, the portal is a blessing: He no longer has to log on to multiple systems to access the tools of his trade, as the portal now offers him everything he needs in a personalized format.

On the other hand, he no longer knows which application he is working in, and this can cause problems with troubleshooting for the end-user help-desk staff. Previously, the user was always able to tell the support specialist on the phone which system was causing the problem, and so the support specialist knew where to look. With a portal, however, the end-user can only say that "something" is not working, and it is up to the support specialist to find out what system the user is using.

Troubleshooting is even more complex in an ESA. The cross-enterprise and cross-system business processes in this architecture involve an even greater number of IT components that have the potential to cause problems. Moreover, it is not usually obvious at first glance which component is at the root of a problem. To deal with this situation, the IT organization of a enterprise must prepare the necessary tools and processes to handle the problems specific to enterprise service architectures integrity. The key issues at stake are as follows:

- Cross-system availability
- Cross-system tests
- Cross-system data consistency
- Cross-system troubleshooting and performance analysis

14.1 IT Service Management Reference Model

In principle, operating an SAP system landscape or an ESA is no different from operating any other multi-user application. However, one distinction is that in enterprises, the availability of the mySAP solutions and the consistency of the data they contain is of fundamental importance for the business. Therefore, the same principles apply to these systems as generally apply to enterprise-critical applications in the Information Technology Infrastructure Library (ITIL).

The six ITIL planning levels

Originally developed by CCTA[1], ITIL is the most comprehensive and respected source of information about IT processes ever written. The library contains over 60 books, which can be divided into six planning levels, as described below.

- "The Business Perspective" deals with the strategic task of ensuring the ongoing availability of IT services, not only in everyday operations, but also in exceptional circumstances, such as terrorist attacks or virus out-

1 Central Computer and Communications Agency, Rosebury Court, St. Andrews, Business Park, Norwich NR7 OHS.

breaks. Measures to deal with these situations must guarantee the basic level of IT services necessary for the continuing business operation of the enterprise, should a crisis occur.

- The second topic, "Planning to Implement Service Management," deals with how to roll out IT service management using best practices. Among other things, it provides ideas on how to determine the current status, goals, and milestones on the path to ITIL-oriented service management.
- The third book, "Applications Management," describes the services and processes required in the life cycle of an application in order to ensure that the software is secure, stable, and is used in an optimal fashion. Planning, development, testing, and further development are all covered.
- The aim of the fourth book, "Infrastructure Management," is to provide an introduction to the planning and organization of an IT infrastructure. According to the ITIL, this includes hardware, software, and telecommunications solutions, all of which are closely connected to IT technology. The guide explicitly excludes industry-specific software, specialist software, and business applications.
- The central reference works for organization and management are books five and six, "Service Delivery" and "Service Support" They deal with the core processes of IT service management on which all other topics are based. "Service Delivery" examines which services are required to provide the user with the appropriate level of support. The book deals with topics as: Service Level Management, Financial Management for IT Services, Capacity Management, IT Service Continuity Management, and Availability Management.
- The book "Service Support" explains how to ensure that the user can access the services that he needs to perform his daily tasks.

Although the ITIL does not describe technical details such as the minimum size of a hard disk or the required throughput of a data connection, it does provide real-world-oriented advice. The ITIL defines organizational aspects and guidelines to do with IT, and the relevant processes are described in impressive detail.

The ITIL thus provides readers with a good overview of what a Best Practice entails and helps avoid the need for time-consuming internal discussions. Nonetheless, a lot of initiative is required to adapt it to the specific needs of an enterprise, as the ITIL does not provide any pre-defined optimal processes. It can therefore be said to present an ideal structure that then has to be tailored to the practical needs of each organization. In other words, the books describe the content, processes, and goals of an IT organization (the "what"), but not how to implement these in the real world (the "how").

ITIL and ITSM Therefore, there is nothing particularly different to note about operating an SAP infrastructure in a professionally managed data center. SAP-specific however, is that the system landscape is made up of multiple layers and a wide range of solutions and components. It was for this sort of distributed computer environment that Hewlett-Packard further developed ITIL to become the IT Service Management Reference Model (ITSM) (see Figure 14.2). Today, the ITSM is regarded as the industry standard for the professional operation of distributed computer environments.

Figure 14.2 Hewlett-Packard IT Service Management Reference Model

Within ITSM, the SAP-specific issues of authorization concept, quality assurance concept, and Solution Lifecycle Management are taken into special consideration.

IT organization The IT organization for the operation of mission critical SAP system landscapes can be roughly divided into four areas of responsibility:

- The application administration area is responsible for daily business. Tasks such as batch job scheduling, administrating user accounts, and administrating access authorizations all fall under this area. This area, in particular, is becoming increasingly complex in cross-enterprise collaboration scenarios and business processes.
- The application maintenance area comprises software logistics (SAP TMS, Patch Management, and so on), solving application errors ("fix-on-fail"), and reactive application optimization (Performance Tuning).

- The application help desk provides first-level support for end-user problems, assigns a priority to each problem, and forwards problem messages to the relevant expert team in the enterprise, to SAP, or to other support partners.
- The application monitoring team monitors the application to ensure that it fulfils the service level agreement.

IT is a service

The provision of information technology is a service that supports business departments in fulfilling their respective tasks in an enterprise. The type, scope, and quality of these services are described in service level agreements (SLAs) between all involved parties. In principle, it does not matter greatly whether these services are provided by internal sources (insourcing) or external ones (outsourcing).

Service Level Management

A service that has to be nearly 100 % available around the clock year round has to be organized differently than a service that is required only during normal business hours. Similarly, a system landscape that is required to guarantee very short response times, even under extreme loads, and to tolerate breakdowns of individual components, has to be designed differently than for example a training system. This also applies to the required degree of safeguarding specified in maintenance contracts with suppliers and technology partners. SLAs also define the basic conditions (number of users, number of postings, and so on) under which the services are to be provided. If these conditions are exceeded on an ongoing basis, the costs will have to be re-negotiated.

SLAs are often misunderstood as wish lists of the various business departments (along the lines of "it doesn't hurt to ask"), especially in enterprises with their own IT department. However, in reality, SLAs are the basis for the conception of the organizational processes and infrastructures in question and, of course, for the relevant costs.

The main benefits of correctly designed SLAs are as follows:

- They focus IT resources on what the (internal) customers need (and what they are paying for).
- They ensure that investments are needs-driven (in other words, they focus on what is necessary for the business, not on what is technologically possible). So they are in alignment to the KPI's (Key Performance Indicators) in the Business.
- They protect the investments of the business departments in IT.

Capacity Management Ongoing capacity planning is an important instrument for ensuring that the SLAs are adhered to. The goal of capacity management is to proactively avoid resource bottlenecks in the IT infrastructure. To this end, data has to be gathered that provides adequate meaningful information about the developments and trends to be expected.

The issue here is not only computer resources (such as CPU and memory), disk resources (such as I/O rate, data transfer volume, and data growth), and network resources (such as bandwidth load and number of packets), but also intangible resources, such as buffer size, tables, indices, and table spaces in databases, the number of reserved dialog processes and update processes on application servers, and the number of IDocs and work items in applications. This kind of data is equally important for the purposes of capacity planning and excellent early warning indicators for upcoming resource bottlenecks.

Availability Management Availability management includes all measures that are necessary to ensure the availability of an IT environment and the services it provides. This includes risk analysis (what can go wrong, with what probability, and with what consequences), organization of on-call duty, creating emergency plans, and organizing regular training in emergency measures.

Remember that a service can be disrupted by more than just hardware breakdowns: A badly-placed database lock can just as easily cause the service to come to a standstill.

Operations Management Operations management comprises all the processes and tasks that are necessary for normal daily operations, and ensures that the SLAs in these areas are adhered to. Besides the routine tasks associated with administrating SAP systems, solving small and large faults also comes under this area.

Incident Management Incident management involves all processes for handling incidents and unplanned events in normal daily operations. Only if a fault cannot be solved within the scope of Incident Management is it then defined as a problem.

In this case, the fault is escalated; in other words, it is forwarded to the relevant persons to be solved, in accordance with a pre-defined process. The reference model draws a clear distinction between incident management and problem management. While incident management acts reactively, the aim of problem management is to proactively prevent problems from occurring (or at least to occur again and again).

SAP systems process data that is often highly sensitive. As well as internal security requirements, legal conditions also have to be complied with, such as those set down in trade law, tax law, and data-protection law. Note also that compliance with these conditions will be checked by an external audit or a government tax audit. Therefore, there has to be a security management concept for the SAP systems. Besides measures for protecting data centers from unauthorized access, the most important element of this concept is the authorization concept, which controls access to data at the level of the operating system, the database, and the SAP system itself.

Security Management

Security in the context of SAP systems also includes safeguarding data consistency and ensuring the availability (backup and recovery) of enterprise data (availability management).

Change Management

Changes made without adequate preparation are among the main causes of system and service breakdowns. The main task of change management is to take into account the potential effects of a change to an individual component on the entire system. Change management is thus an important quality assurance instrument that plays a particular role in ensuring adherence to the SLAs.

ITSM process mapping for SAP Application Management

Figure 14.3 shows how service areas for SAP application management are assigned to the ITSM process categories.

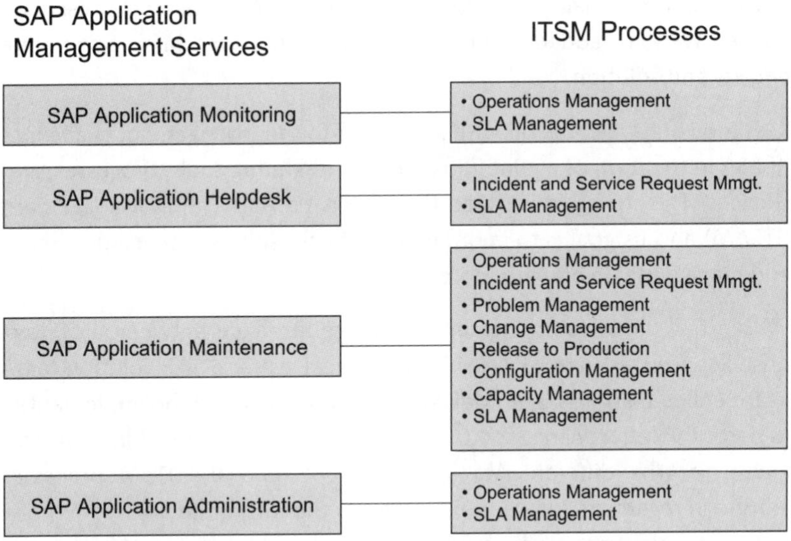

Figure 14.3 Assignment of SAP Application Management Services and ITSM Processes

Configuration Management However, there is little point in managing changes if the initial situation has not been clearly defined. Configuration management is therefore the "baseline" of change management. It involves documenting the system configuration for both hardware and software in a configuration management database (CMDB), as well as gathering all documentation relevant to operating the application. This includes, for example, support agreements with hardware and software manufacturers. Configuration management also provides information for inventory and budget planning.

> **Management Means "Taking Care of it"**
>
> In ITSM, the over-inflated term "management" does not refer to leadership tasks in the narrower sense; in this context, it should be understood in the sense of "taking care of things." Therefore the term "management" refers only to the technical infrastructure for operating SAP systems. The term "process" refers in this context to the sense of procedures and not software processes on a computer.

ITSAM initiative The components in the SAP Solution Manager provide many of the necessary functions for monitoring and controlling an SAP system landscape. However, to be able to monitor and control an entire IT infrastructure, including the underlying technology infrastructure (network, systems, databases, middleware, Web servers, and so on) and non-SAP applications, service-management tools and the ITSM processes described above have to be added to these functions in order to achieve a complete end-to-end solution.

SAP and HP have come up with an answer to the management challenges of ESA in the form of a joint initiative for integrating tools, processes, and services. This initiative is called the IT Service Application Management (ITSAM) and its goal is to coordinate ITSM consulting, service processes, and management software more closely.

Within this initiative an incident-exchange interface between an Enterprise Service Desk like HP OpenView ServiceDesk and SAP Solution Manager Service Desk has been defined, and SAP's part will be implemented as part of SolutionManager 4.0 in 2006. This will provide additional integration of the different Management tools and the ITSM processes around in regards to incident exchange. In the future the SAP Notes[2] system as it is right now will be fully replaced by SAP SolutionManager and

2 Former SAP Online Support System, OSS.

it's integrations to external tools on different level (Monitoring , Service-Desk, Adaptive Computing Controller, etc). This will help to better integrate SAP management tools and processes with non SAP related application management tools and tools to manage the SAP IT infrastructure.

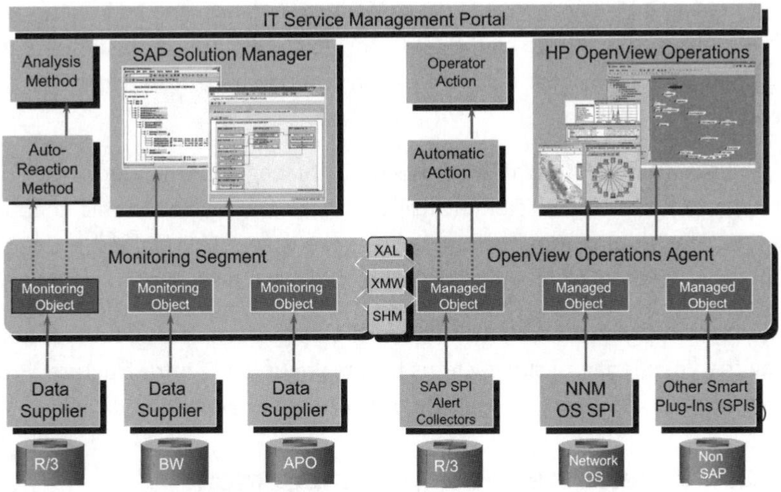

Figure 14.4 Integrated IT Service and Application Management Solution with SAP Solution Manager and HP OpenView Components

Figure 14.4 shows the technical integration of SAP Solution Manager and HP OpenView within the framework of an enterprise IT management landscape. To be able to fully recreate business processes, events in the SAP system landscape are transferred from the Solution Manager to OpenView, where they are then represented together with non-SAP-system events. This interface can also be used to add events from other applications or the network area, for example, to the graphics in the Solution Manager.

System Management Interfaces

Communication between the various tools is carried out via proprietary SAP protocols and industry standards that are supported by most enterprise system-management solutions. In total, there are more than eight SAP interfaces for connecting external IT management environments to SAP systems. One of the most important of these is the CCMS XMV interface for alert generation, which external tools use to transfer alert information to the Computer Center Management System (CCMS). The CCMS can then send this information to the Solution Manager Business Process Monitor. With the CCMS XAL interface, the communication goes in the other direction; that is, alerts generated by the CCMS are transferred to the enterprise system management system. Other interfaces are used to read information, such as syslog, batch, performance metrics, system status, data backups, and so on.

Using agents, system management systems can also read a whole range of other information about SAP NetWeaver and mySAP components, and thus can graphically represent the entire system landscape and document how the systems are configured (for example, which instances are started, how many dialog processes and batches are currently configured, and so on).

The user interfaces of the various system management solutions can be integrated into the SAP Enterprise Portal, as the figures in this chapter show. The system administrators thus have access to a unified interface that can be adapted to each user's individual requirements.

System management systems support the operations team with monitoring the wide range of sub-systems that make up an IT infrastructure. Predefined workflows ensure that the ITIL processes are adhered to.

14.2 Enterprise System Management

Similarly to IT infrastructure, the various topics within system management can also be divided up into separate management areas. One very important aspect, however, is that all the topics are integrated with an overlying system that provides reliable, cross-area management functions for the entire infrastructure from the viewpoint of the business processes. Isolated solutions may optimally cover an individual area, but are not integrated, and thus pave the way to finger-pointing between the individual areas.

Blanket monitoring

In an IT infrastructure, as in every complex system, the basis of efficient management is objective information. Only something that can be measured can also be controlled. Note also at this point that the management system has to cover all areas of the infrastructure; that is, it has to be an end-to-end system. There cannot be any "black holes" along the way from the application to the end-user's device. This kind of blanket monitoring is the only way to ensure absolute control (as we know from Orwell's 1984).

Nonetheless, it is still possible to lose sight of the central issues among the constant streams of information. Therefore, an enterprise management system has to be able to take the plethora of detailed information from the sub-systems and filter, condense it and correlate it with related information. The important factors here are not only traditional event correlation, which helps avoid "event storms", but also determining the effect of IT events on the business processes, with the aim of assigning priorities to the administrators' work.

Comparing current data with historical data helps identify trends. Graphical representations should be used to map trends, so that a clear overview is always available. Reports are also useful for documenting for customers and users the performance and availability of the IT infrastructure and the level to which SLAs are complied with.

System management concepts

Many manufacturers of servers and active network components provide software free of charge for monitoring and administrating their software (at a minimum, in a "pared-down" form). The management tools have benefits: They are usually free and are optimally designed to work with the system with which they are delivered.

However, these benefits can be a disadvantage at the same time, as the tools' functionality is restricted to the infrastructure and products of that one manufacturer. Therefore, these tools are not adequate for monitoring a multi-layer NetWeaver or mySAP infrastructure with a wide range of hardware and software components. For this reason, several manufacturers provide software systems that facilitate cross-application and cross-system IT infrastructure management. These systems are based on different basic concepts, each with its own strengths and weaknesses.

Top-down

"Top-down" concepts first implement an overlying management framework, and then integrate the various infrastructure areas into this framework. This has the advantage of a unified structure, and the disadvantage that a lot of time and effort has to be invested in creating the framework infrastructure before the system can be used. This can mean long-running roll-out projects.

Bottom-up

With "bottom-up" concepts, the individual components can be used independently of each other to manage the various areas of the infrastructure. The management modules can thus be gradually introduced into individual sub-projects and then integrated into the overlying management system. Experience shows that with this kind of gradual implementation, projects can be completed more quickly and the system is more widely accepted by administrators.

One thing that both concepts have in common is that they gather together information from the various sub-areas in one user interface that provides a unified view of the IT infrastructure. Regardless of the underlying concept, a system-management solution should always support the administrators without causing too much extra administration work. However, even the most sophisticated management software is of little use if it is not used. It is an unfortunate fact that many expensive management software packages gather dust on a shelf because the employees in question found it too complicated. In this case, a bottom-up approach using the free management tools provided by the manufacturers is still better than no system management at all.

Operations Management

Operations management involves the permanent monitoring (event and performance monitoring) of all parts of the IT infrastructure in order to ensure high-performance operations. Operations-management systems provide functions for centrally monitoring the various applications, computers, and networks, including databases, middleware, Internet services, and even SAP transactions.

Monitoring hardware components for infrastructures is usually based on the Simple Network Management Protocol (SNMP), which was originally developed for managing network components. As well as network components such as switches and routers, most other modern hardware components are also able to output messages about status changes in the form of SNMP traps. However, the SNMP protocol is not a particularly efficient or secure method of transferring management information. Not only does it use a lot of network resources, because of its high protocol overhead, but it also loses messages if there is currently no connection available to the management system. Therefore, secure communication on the basis of TCP/IP is preferable.

Systems and applications that do not themselves generate any SNMP messages can therefore "act through" software agents. For this to be possible, the management environment has to be able to provide appropriate agents for a large number of databases and business applications. As an example, Figure 14.5 shows a system in which an Internet service is monitored by HP OpenView agents.

This kind of monitoring by "autarkical" agents is becoming more and more established. The systems available on the market differ in terms of the built-in agent intelligence they use, which is important for ensuring that information is transferred securely, even if the connection to the management server is broken. Some management agents can correlate information, condense data, encrypt data, and ensure that duplicate messages are not transferred twice.

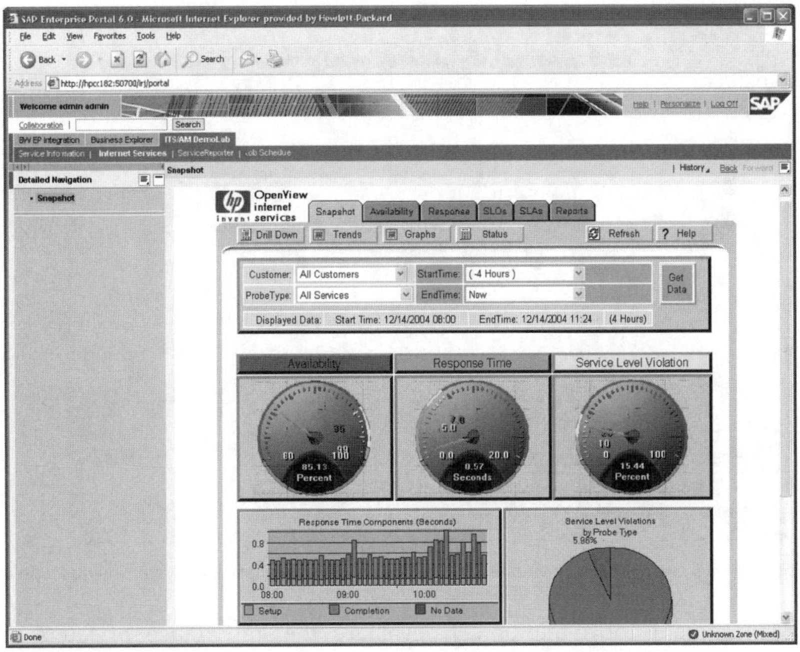

Figure 14.5 Performance Report for Response Times of an Internet Service

For SAP systems, another important consideration is that the software agents understand the SAP system architecture: for example, that different SAP releases can provide information at various locations with different names. Intelligent monitoring agents therefore adapt themselves to the peculiarities of each release.

The management system either receives messages directly from the various sub-systems (via a message interface or a log file), or it monitors key performance indicators (KPIs) from the sub-systems and generates alarms if specified threshold values are exceeded. Also, 'heartbeat polling' in the management system and 'keep-alive packages' in the monitored device check that the software agent is functioning correctly and that the general availability of the component via the network is satisfactory.

The messages are represented in the form of hierarchical service objects (see Figure 14.6). The degree of detail of this view can be varied, depending on the user profile.

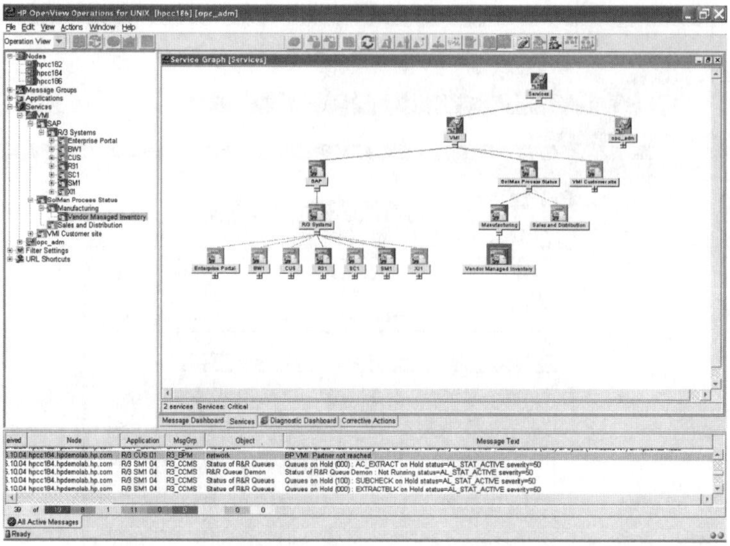

Figure 14.6 Automatically Created View of the Services in an SAP System Landscape

System management from the business perspective

Management tools traditionally evaluate the importance of faults in accordance with their severity. Thus, for example, a disk fault is classified as very serious. Similarly, with automatic monitoring, the fault report for the device in question or the resource is also given a high priority. However, from the business perspective, the priority level depends much more on how central to the enterprise the business process is that is supported by the service to which the disk in question belongs. Only from this kind of service-oriented viewpoint is it possible to effectively use the resources of the IT department.

This kind of business-process viewpoint is defined using a logical model in which the resources of a service and their dependencies are modeled in relation to each other. With this model, the "state of health" of a business process from the IT viewpoint and the effects of an IT fault on the functioning of the enterprise can be represented. The model is thus the basis of service-level management and monitoring.

Event correlation in Operations Management

Usually, an operator can process and complete up to 10 messages per hour. If the number of messages exceeds this rate, a situation tends to arise where the operator simply clicks away the messages or even completely ignores the message browser, with the explanation that, "It's always full of red alerts anyway."

This situation can be ameliorated by means of a function that automatically hides duplicate and secondary alarms. However, simple correlation mechanisms also hide similar-sounding error messages from the same source. Complex correlations, on the other hand, link multiple alarms from different sources.

An example of this is the evaluation of alarms in a cluster group. If one computer in a cluster fails, this does not represent a critical threat to the system, provided that the application can be automatically restarted within a set period of time on another computer.

However, configuring event correlations is not something that should be undertaken lightly, because these configurations have to be kept up to date on an ongoing basis. Red alerts displayed at the system management console should therefore really signal a highly critical situation and always trigger an instant reaction.

Application Operations Monitoring

The SAP Solution Manager covers many of the functions required to administer mySAP Applications and NetWeaver components. The Solution Manager monitors the most important SAP kernel and database parameters that can be called via the SAP GUI and the usual transaction codes. The basic services of the operating system in question are used for this purpose.

Although the SAP systems play a central role in the enterprise IT infrastructure, there are other applications that are just as important to the success of the enterprise, such as e-mail, document-management systems, in-house developments, other business applications, and the network infrastructure.

A business-process-oriented IT management environment should therefore be able to monitor all the important components of a system landscape and should be capable of being seamlessly integrated with SAP CCMS and the SAP Solution Manager. For external monitoring tools, SAP provides communication interfaces for CCMS and the Solution Manager. This ensures that the external software can exchange two-way information with the SAP solutions and transfer important SAP metrics. SAP also certifies monitoring tools by other manufacturers. This certification tells the customer that a monitoring tool can monitor SAP software and that it properly supports the SAP interfaces.

Besides the large applications, there is also a significant minority of smaller services whose role in the functioning of the infrastructure is less obvious, but just as important. Examples of such services are DNS, NTP, DHCP, Web servers, and firewalls. To monitor these kinds of services, software probes send simulated client requests to the services in question (for example, the DNS server or the HTTP Web server) at regular intervals, and also send corresponding messages to the system management system, where they are analyzed and graphically represented in context with the other applications. This process thus provides a unified view of all the applications and services in a mySAP infrastructure, including all integrated non-SAP applications and IT components.

Disasters Need Preparation Too

All the organizational and technical measures in the world will not help much if they do not act and interact as planned in a real-life situation. If a system cannot be re-started after a failover, it is often because some small detail has been overlooked. Just as with a firefighting unit, these kinds of disaster situations have to be regularly simulated in advance, both in the form of drills and of emergency exercises that are as realistic as possible. It is advisable to try out newly installed parts of the infrasturcture in these exercises before they are officially rolled out. These new parts could be a newly refurbished office building or a newly installed server landscape. If the deadlines are very tight, you should still use these opportunities to detect any faults, because Murphy's Law applies: The fault that you have not tested in the exercises will cause an emergency later.

Network Operations Management

Although the importance of the network connections between the individual components of a client/server architecture is obvious, in many enterprises the operation of the business applications and the network infrastructure are handled by separate departments. If an error occurs, then, each department often points to the other as the source of the problem. Therefore, highly integrated multi-level systems like the various mySAP components have to be handled as a whole. For this to be possible, the monitoring process for the network infrastructure has to be seamlessly integrated into Operations Management.

Network discovery and mapping

Because of the spatial distribution of the various network components and their sometimes complex interconnections, it can be difficult to maintain a clear view of the topology and the status of the infrastructure. Two central factors in evaluating a network management system are its degree of automation in identifying the topology (discovery) and its capability to represent the networks as clearly as possible (mapping). Besides the physical connections between network segments and components, the manner in which the logical structures (virtual LANs, vLANs) are represented is also important.

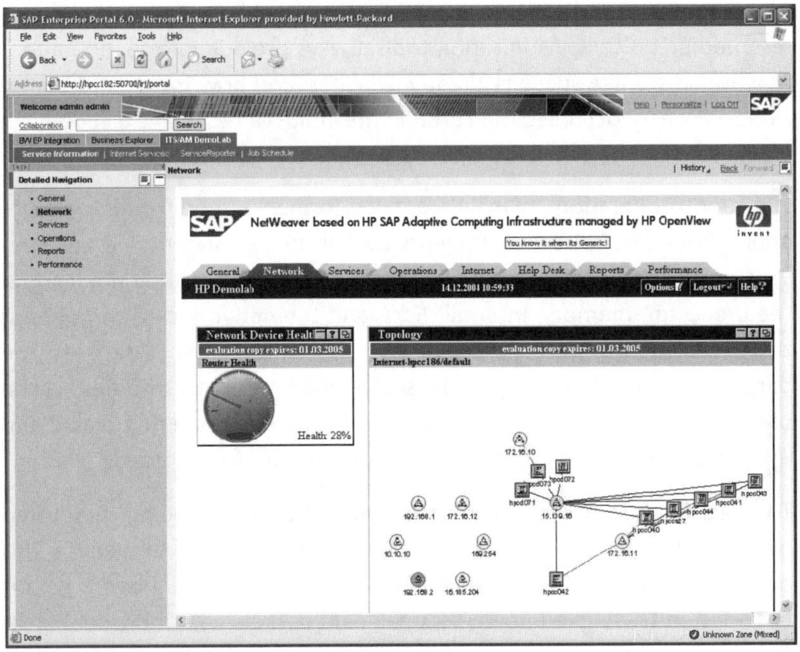

Figure 14.7 Automatically Generated Graphical View of the Network

Network Operation Monitoring

Besides the topology of the network, the management system has to be able to inform the administrator about the current status of the individual components. To do this, the system analyzes messages (SNMP traps) output by the active network components via the Simple Network Management Protocol (SNMP)

However, SNMP is not a secure protocol because, unlike TCP/IP, it does not confirm messages once they have been received. Therefore, if there is a problem with the transfer to the management system, the message is simply lost. If a component fails completely, then it is of course no longer able to send any messages at all. To prevent these situations, the Network Node Manager needs to check the status of all network components at regular intervals, in a process known as polling.

SAN management

Storage area networks (SANs) may be of even greater importance to the SAP systems that they provide with data than the local and wide-area networks. In SAN management, IT management solutions monitor not only storage area that is connected via fiber channel (fiber-attached storage—in other words, SANs), but also local storage areas (direct attached storage) and network-attached storage (NAS).

Also, the capacity of all storage components must be monitored and represented graphically. Monitoring tools always provide information about how much storage space is already allocated and how much of the allocated space is occupied. If certain threshold values are exceeded, an alarm is activated, which in turn triggers the relevant activities.

Application Performance Monitoring

Similarly to operations management, performance-monitoring tools use application-specific software agents to call up parameters that are relevant to performance. With servers, these parameters include the load on the processor, memory, internal disks, and the network card throughput that is assigned to each processor and application. With databases, the parameters include data growth, space reserves, sort attributes, cache usage, and so on. With mySAP systems, parameters covering dialog and update processes and end-to-end response times are recorded.

The agents store the collected data from the system being monitored over a certain time period (which can be set up to several weeks). This procedure is similar to the "black box" on airplanes. The network is thus not constantly weighed down by small data packets with individual measurements, as the measurements are called up only when required for analysis by the management system.

All the measurement data is collected, represented graphically, and correlated with the other data. This comprehensive, ongoing process of data collection by distributed agents makes it possible for administrators to recognize bottlenecks and trends early on. Also, the growth rates can be used to estimate future resource requirements and to then use this data as the basis for budget planning.

The increasing significance of the SAP Enterprise Portal as the SAP front end means that measurements have to be taken from the perspective of the portal. To do this, modern IT management environments use software probes that carry out relevant Web transactions and thus collect the required parameter data.

Network Performance Monitoring

From the performance point of view, the interesting thing about networks (besides the latency time) is the segment load or the data volume transported on a connection. Previously, to measure the segment load, a measurement system called a network probe would be installed. This probe counts all the data packets (and can also analyze them). Today, this counting process is done by the active network components, such as switches and routers, and the values are forwarded to the management system for analysis on request (Remote Monitoring or RMON).

The data collected by the various agents and RMON-enabled network components is then called up by the central management server and is condensed to form meaningful diagrams and graphics. For performance analyses and optimization, the management tool has to be able to correlate performance-related values from the various data sources in order to identify dependencies and causes.

Performance analysis and reporting

Beyond performance optimization, creating statistical evaluations as evidence of performance (for example, as proof of compliance with SLAs) is an important part of performance management. The important thing here for the business departments as end-customers is that they do not just get reports about the availability and response time of individual computers and applications; they can also see this data represented in relation to the processed transaction load (for example, with posting receipts, document volumes, and so on).

The various measurement data can be used for strategic development of the infrastructure, which is the planning part of infrastructure management, as well as to document the availability of the system and its performance within the framework of the SLAs (operational monitoring).

In strategic development, the main aim is to identify trends and bottlenecks, to balance the system load, and to gain information about the sizing of the SAP systems in the case of extensions or upgrades. Typical questions that may be asked in this regard are: Which transactions cause the most system load? What happens if thousands of additional delivery notes per day have to be processed? Are there system resources that are significantly more or less busy than the others?

Desktop management

The classic topics in desktop management (DTM) are software distribution (MS Office, SAP GUI, and so on) and the configuration of the terminal devices via remote access. Other issues that merit consideration are central license management and inventory management, that is, collecting information about the existing PCs and their software installations.

The Desktop Management Initiative (DMI) has created standards for this purpose. And these are used by solutions such as the Microsoft System Management System (SMS). These systems enable the administrator to carry out from one central work place all activities necessary for software maintenance, from installing complete software packages to a BIOS update, including booting up. This is obviously much more efficient and faster for the administrator than physically going to each individual user's work station.

According to a study by the Gartner Group, of the total cost of a workplace PC, 15 % is spent on procuring the machine, 14 % on administration, and 29 % on productivity losses due to the machine not functioning the way it should.

Within the scope of IT management, one of the tasks of Desktop Management is to ensure that the end-user has a fully functioning work environment. Desktop management is part of the "early-warning chain" and thus has to be integrated into the overlying operations management function, so that faults can be quickly identified and solved.

Job scheduling The term "job scheduling" comes from the punch card era, where it is applied to classic batch processing. The modern approach to this is often called business process automation. Integrated online transaction systems such as SAP R/3 Enterprise also need to initiate specific processes under defined conditions and to ensure that these processes are fully completed.

Typical job-scheduling tasks in an SAP infrastructure are for example: the day-end closing in the sales area; the so-called period closing program in materials planning (runs directly at the end of a posting period and posts the current stock level of a material as the closing stock of the old period and the opening stock of the new period); the payment run and reminder run (monthly in most enterprises); report updates (usually once a day after the day-end closing and often the cause of performance problems); and the vendor evaluation (weekly or monthly).

The important thing is always to ensure that the various interlinked batch jobs are processed within a defined time. The fact that the various mySAP components are asynchronously linked with each other and with external systems makes batch management even more important.

The SAP CCMS provides basic job-scheduling services that enable administrators to create and submit batch jobs for deferred execution. Job attributes such as class, status and target application server, along with scheduled start date and time can be set. Jobs can be set to run based upon the completion of another job, an event or a change in operation mode (from day to night, for example).

There are no facilities provided with CCMS to support more advanced dependencies between jobs, for example where the execution of a subsequent program is determined by the value of an output field set by a preceding job, possibly running on a remote system. It is not practical to integrate the execution of non-SAP tasks with SAP tasks using CCMS.

With CCMS, jobs are constructed to run one or more programs, with each program having parameter variants set. A new job needs to be created every time there is a requirement to run the same program with different variant settings. This can result in a massive proliferation of jobs within CCMS that perform almost identical functions, causing a major headache for Basis administrators responsible for managing SAP batch workload.

While it is possible with CCMS to build a job that contains multiple steps, the SAP work process dispatcher does not recognize a job by its separate steps. As a result, in the event of step 8 failing in a job that contains 15 steps, the job will need to be restarted from step 1. Although the application design might permit many steps running in parallel, each step within a multi-step job will be processed one after the other, in sequence as a single background work process.

Certain SAP applications, such as mySAP Retail, require the running of batch jobs that are reliant upon the input of multiple files transmitted from remote locations, (often referred to as batch input maps). SAP handles the processing of this data through the submission of a parent job, which spawns child jobs to manage each file. Only when all child jobs have successfully completed, can any following work be run. As the names of the child jobs are not known until the time at which they run, the only way that dependent work can be scheduled using CCMS is through the pre-allocation of sufficient time for all child jobs to complete. As well as being inefficient in terms of system resource utilization, additional problems can result when the transmitting of files is unexpectedly delayed.

To support administrators with advanced batch scheduling, various manufacturers offer SAP-certified scheduling tools and batch-management systems. From the SAP viewpoint, these can be classified into external multi-platform schedulers, such as Cronacle for SAP from Redwood[3], $Universe from Orsyp[4] and Tivoli Workload Scheduler (TWS) from IBM[5], and schedulers written in ABAP, such as Batchman and BatchControl, which are run on the SAP system itself.

To enable complementary software partners to control the invocation of SAP batch jobs, SAP provides the eXternal Interface for Job Background

3 Go to *http://www.redwood.com/index2.html*.
4 Go to *http://www.orsyp.com/*.
5 Go to *http://www-306.ibm.com/software/tivoli/products/scheduler-apps/*.

Processing (referred to as BC-XBP). The XBP interface offers a wide range of functionality that can be used to perform many functions, including submitting, status checking and canceling jobs.

In a co-development with Redwood, SAP integrated advanced job scheduling technologies as an integrated component of the SAP NetWeaver stack.[6]

14.3 Business Process Management

SAP was one of the first business software manufacturers to provide an integrated tool for managing its applications. This tool was the Computer Center Management System (CCMS). Now, within the scope of NetWeaver, the Solution Manager Business Process Operation (BPO) takes this to the next level, providing an integrated tool for managing business processes that run in an SAP application landscape.

Business Process Monitoring

As early as the blueprint phase, the business departments should, as a rule, model the business processes using business process graphics. The ARIS Tool Set from IDS Scheer[7] is often used for this purpose in combination with the SAP Implementation Methodology, which is part of Solution Manager. The Tool Set is of great value to model the business processes for the purposes of monitoring by department managers, using business-oriented key performance indicators (KPIs), such as the number of orders or their throughput time.

Tools such as ARIS cannot tell administrators where to look for a problem if a process is "stuck"; they cannot tell, for example, whether an order is not being fully processed because an IT component has broken down. Therefore, systems management enhances this business view by adding data from the IT infrastructure and integrated external applications and the Solution Manager by adding information from the SAP application.

This integration of the business view and the IT view makes it easier for administrators to identify the location of a problem. Also, because the business processes are connected to the IT infrastructure metrics, the IT department has a good overview of the effect a problem has on the business processes, and is thus able to assign it the correct priority.

Business Process Operation

Enhancing the IT view occurs through the addition of extra data (such as order ID and order volume)extracted from the individual applications by

6 Go to *http://www.sap.com/company/press/press.epx?PressID=4134*.

7 Go to *http://www.ids-scheer.com/*.

adapters, enabling the virtualization of the "health status" of a business process in the form of graphics and service level reports. Compliance with the Service Level Objectives (SLOs) can be easily monitored (for example, the average time period that elapses between arrival of an order in the system and delivery of that order).

The SAP Solution Manager obtains information about the status of the business processes from CCMS alarms. It is thus restricted to business processes that can be completely executed within the SAP environment. For the SAP Solution Manager PBO to be able to monitor the entire physical and logical system landscape, it needs to be connected to the system management system (see Figure 14.4 earlier). Corresponding certified plug-ins are available for this purpose. The products certified by SAP are listed on SAP's website.

Business Value Management

Tools such as HP OpenView Business Process Insight (BPI) take business process monitoring a step further. This tool has adapters which allow it to connect to all sorts of applications from different manufacturers, and the resulting combination of business-relevant data (such as number of pieces, monetary value, or processing time) with events from the infrastructure monitoring process (SAP, database, storage, network) actually allows conclusions to be drawn about the value of the goods that are currently affected by a problem in the IT infrastructure and therefore cannot be delivered.

The HP OpenView Smart plug-in for SAP also makes bi-directional communication possible, which means that information about the SAP infrastructure and the SAP application layer from the SAP Solution Manager can be integrated into an overlying HP OpenView BPI.

For the management of Service Oriented Architectures (SOAs) like SAP ESA and similar technologies, HP OpenView SOA manager was introduced. This software will not replace the other techniques but concentrates on the SOA layer; from there a drilldown to the other management components can be done to locate a problem.

The role of the service desk

The service desk is an important part of IT management. Unlike a help desk, it handles change, configurations, incident and problem management, within the framework of ITSM. A classic help desk is therefore a sub-set of a service desk.

A configuration management database (CMDB) is a central component of configuration management and thus an important function of the service desk. Therefore, most management systems provide tools that automatically scan the entire system configurations of all systems involved in process communication, and add this information into the CMDB (auto-discovery). Part of a holistic system management according to ITIL, the scope of a CMDB goes beyond the information available in the SAP System Landscape Directory (SLD) or Solution Manager SMSY.

Products such as OpenView Service Desk support ITIL-based service processes by means of built-in, configurable process and object definitions. These products can also be adapted to the specific requirements of an enterprise by means of best practices for service desks and SAP support methodologies.

Events can also be automatically transferred from the operations management environment to the service desk. Solution Manager Support Desk supports the transfer of trouble tickets (incident exchange). This way, the "trouble ticket" is forwarded via Solution Manager Support Desk to SAP if the enterprise IT department is not able to solve the problem. In future versions of the Solution Manager, the incident exchange interface to other management software will be available as Web service.

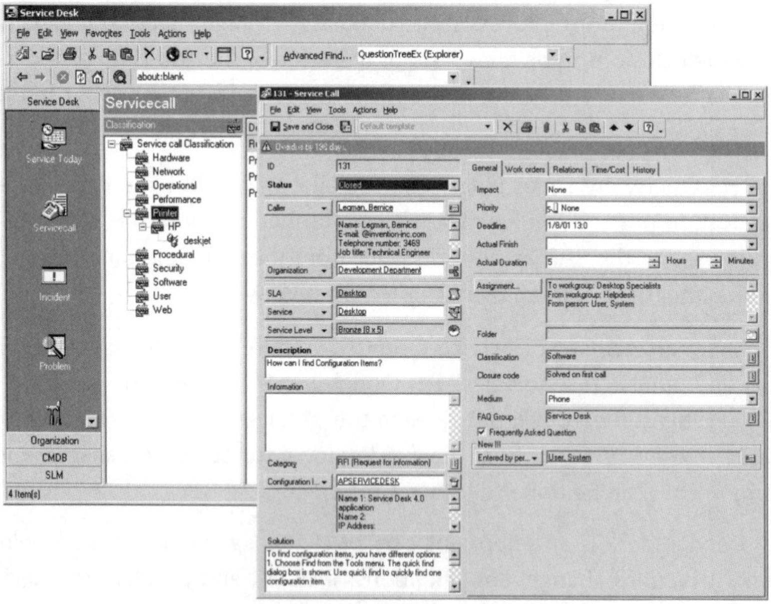

Figure 14.8 Example of HP OpenView Service Desk

For customers with HP support contracts, support center tickets are electronically transferred from SAP Support to HP and vice versa by means of exclusively integrated workflow processes between SAP and HP Support.

Other partners receive problem cases via specific processing queues in the SAP Workflow System.

RACI diagrams

RACI diagrams are an important aid in structuring ITSM processes. RACI stands for "Responsible, Accountable, Consult before doing, Inform after doing." These diagrams define in a clearly structured way who has overall responsibility, who has direct responsibility, who must be consulted in any decisions, and who simply has to be informed.

Incident management task	**Role and responsibility**					
	User	Help-desk mgr.	Help-desk agent	Probl. ana-lyst	Prob-lem-mgr.	System pro-vider
Receive change request	C	A	R			C
Create incident record		A	R			
Interrogate CMDB		A	R			
Priorize incident		A	R			
Check matching symptoms		A	R	C	I	
Check known error database		A	R			
Identify change objects		A	R			
Referral (internal/external)	I	A	R			R
Resolve incident at help desk	C/I	A	R		I	
Functional escalation	I	A	C/I	R	R	R
Hierarchical escalation	I	R	R	R	A	
Problem resolution	C/I	A	R	R	I	
Proactive activity	C/I	A	R	R	C/I	
Metrics accumulation		A	R		I	
Metrics analysis		R/C/I		R	A	
Set policies, procedures	C/I	R	C/I	C/I	A	C/I
Set thresholds	C/I	R	C/I	C/I	A	C/I
Produce management reports		A/R				
Manage escalation			C/I	R	A	C/I
Close call	C/I	A	R	C/I	C/I	C/I

Table 14.1 Example of a RACI (Responsible, Accountable, Consult, Inform) diagramm

14.4 Example of a Typical Application Scenario

This section describes a vendor managed inventory (VMI) scenario as a typical example of a cross-enterprise business process, in order to illustrate the relationships between the various persons, processes and systems involved in IT service management. The example will clearly represent the different persons involved and their specific requirements in terms of business-process management and systems management. It is therefore less concerned with the technical structure of the system management system or how the operation of the system is organized[8] than with the various people involved in ITSM processes.

What is VMI?

In a VMI scenario, the warehouse stock of a customer or retailer is independently maintained by the vendor or manufacturer. In many cases, the goods in question remain the property of the vendor and only become the property of the customer once they are removed from storage. Markets where this scenario is used include consumer electronics and car manufacturers that supply dealers with new cars and replacement parts.

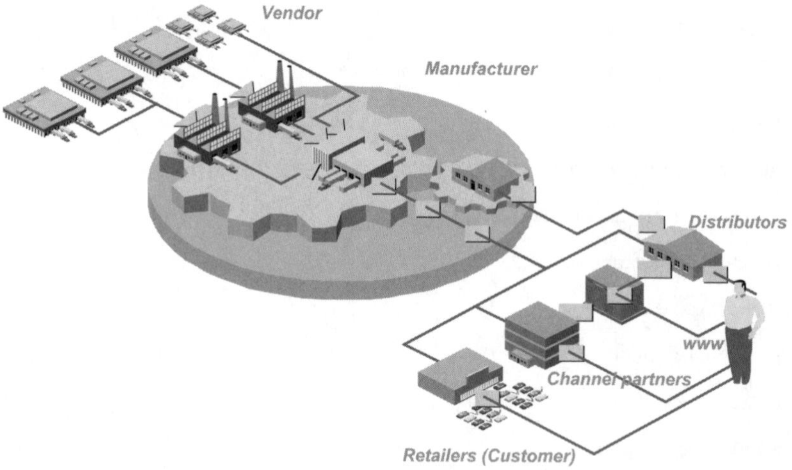

Figure 14.9 Simplified Representation of a VMI Supply Chain

In order to optimally control the capacities in the supply chain, the customer's requirements must be assessed on an ongoing basis. This process of assessment has to take into account special offers and seasonal changes in buyer behavior, as well as factor in and monitor the whole

8 You can find further information on this subject in our book, *SAP System Operations*, SAP PRESS 2003.

process of manufacturing the products on the vendor's side in conjunction with requirements.

If the available stock falls below a defined level on one tier of the supply chain, an automatic alert is sent to the relevant "upstream" vendor containing information about the decreasing stock level and potential bottlenecks. This information is highly critical for the whole manufacturing chain.

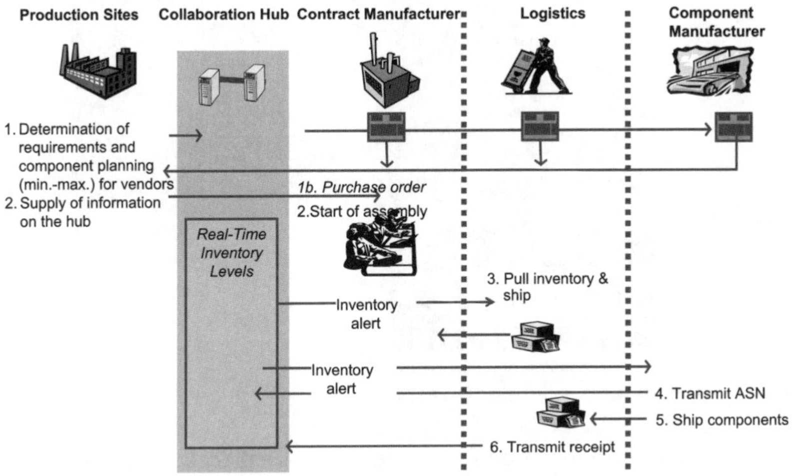

Figure 14.10 Typical Vendor-Customer Communication Process

Business to business communication

Figure 14.10 shows the information flow between the enterprises involved (producer, contract manufacturer, logistics service, and component manufacturer) in a typical SCM scenario (the central communication component is usually referred to as the hub).

In the SAP product portfolio, these kinds of scenarios are implemented on the vendor's side using the mySAP SCM component APO. mySAP ERP is also used for the business processing side. However, because this is a cross-enterprise scenario, customer-side systems such as mySAP SRM and other ERP systems are also involved in the business processes. Then there are also the relevant partner systems for logistical processing (haulage) and connecting systems with prior vendors.

The SAP Enterprise Portal integrates the users in the various enterprises, the SAP Exchange Infrastructure ensures that the different systems and services are properly integrated, and report generation is handled by the Business Information Warehouse.

Figure 14.11 shows the components involved and the flow of information between the processes and systems involved (albeit in highly simplified form).

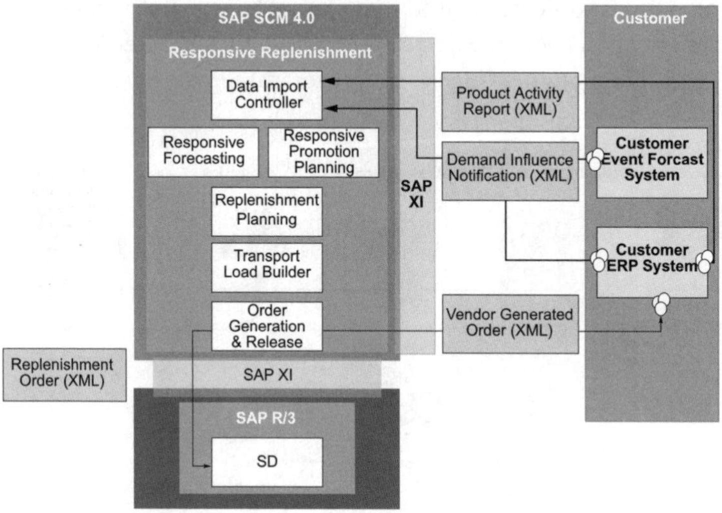

Figure 14.11 VMI Business Process Diagram

In this kind of business model, high demands are placed on the IT system to provide uninterrupted availability of the business processes. However, the IT department of one enterprise is not able to keep track of all the users and interfaces up and down the business process in these kinds of scenarios.

Figure 14.12 shows the relationship between the business processes and systems, and the ITSM processes and IT systems that are necessary to operate them (also highly simplified; for example, databases, networks, test systems and development systems have been omitted).

ITSM as a bridge between line of business department and IT

When it comes to operating business applications, employees who ordinarily have nothing to do with each other must work together. The element that these employees have in common is the business processes that they use or support. ITSM and the IT management tools that are based on them form the bridge between the line of business departments and the IT department.

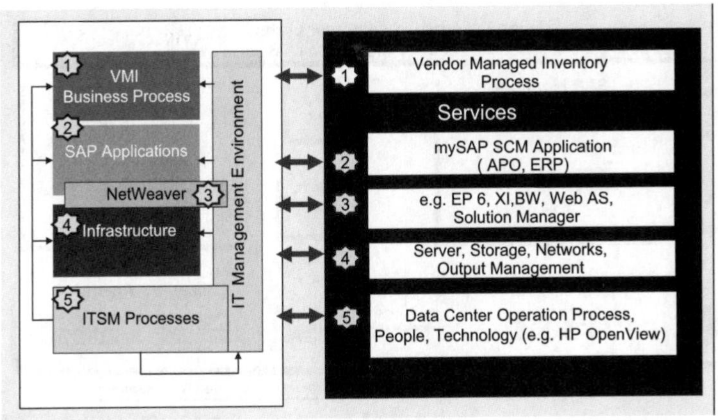

Figure 14.12 Relationship Between Business Processes and ITSM Processes and Systems

However, which roles are important for end-to-end management of business processes supported by SAP solutions? The head of a line-of-business department, for example, should be able to identify whether a fault is due to a problem with the process or a problem with the IT. He can then decide whether the fault lies within his department's responsibility or whether it is the responsibility of the IT department. The details about the type of fault, however, are of interest only to the specialist, although the lines-of-business departments are interested in the quality of the services provided by the IT department.

Same data from different user viewpoints

The important thing for the IT management concept in our example is to take into account the roles of the employees, their business activities and concerns, and the software that they use.

Bridge between business and IT

Collaborative cross-enterprise business processes like our VMI example require the interaction of a large number of employees from different parts of the enterprise. Even if the enterprise's own IT department does not know the names of the users at its vendors, logistics partners, and dealers, their different requirements in terms of information still have to be satisfied. The following paragraphs show how operational management provides the various user groups with specific information.

IT management

The system-management portal gives the CIO and his IT management team an overview of the status of the IT services for which their departments are responsible, plus additional information such as SLAs, fault statistics, and so on. For the purposes of change management, it provides an overview of all planned changes including risk assessment, authorization status, and status information for changes made.

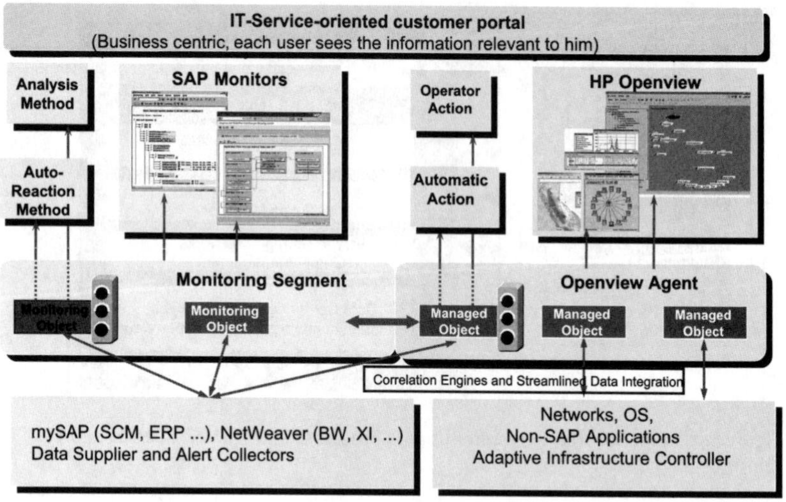

Figure 14.13 Integrated IT Service and Application Management Solution with SAP Solution Manager and HP OpenView Components

IT infrastructure team

The system management portal provides the specialists in the IT infrastructure team—which is responsible for computers, storage sub-systems, and networks, as well as output management—with access to the specific management tools for the various IT components.

Statistics about the infrastructure load caused by the business processes help administrators to estimate the effects of changes and the associated risks within the scope of change management.

SAP infrastructure team

The SAP infrastructure team is responsible for preparing the SAP system landscape. It is the interface between the SAP application and the IT department. In smaller enterprises, this task is usually covered by a group of employees in the IT infrastructure team.

These employees can use the portal to find all the necessary information and tools for operating the SAP system and the database instances in the SAP Solution Manager and the CCMS.

Within the scope of Operations Management, the staff in the SAP infrastructure team has to be able to identify the cause of a fault (root cause analysis). In other words, they have to be able to explain whether the SAP application, an in-house development, or a third-party program is the cause of the fault (for example a mailer or a job scheduler or non SAP SCM system). In our VMI scenario example, another difficulty is that not all parts of the process can be processed by systems within the enterprise. Therefore, it would be a good idea to know the employees "on the other side." Ideally, the employees in the enterprises in question have mutual access to each other's system management system and thus form a virtual combined team.

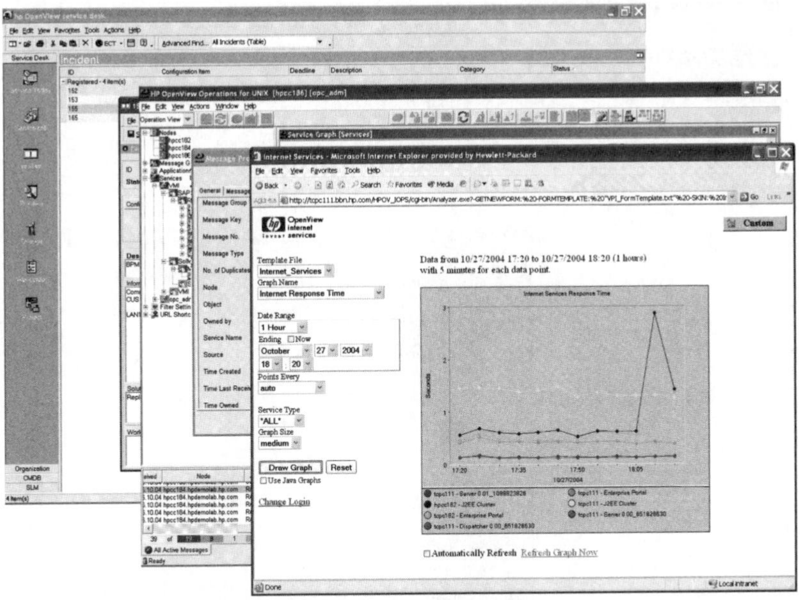

Figure 14.14 CCMS Drill-Down to Performance Metrics

Changes are planned interruptions

This applies especially to change management. In cross-enterprise business processes, every change to a system of one of the involved parties necessarily affects the partner systems (for example, changes to an interface). Also, the maintenance window has to be coordinated across enterprise boundaries. In the brave new world of enterprise services, purchased from the cheapest source in the global marketplace enabled by SOAP, the UN may have to designate a worldwide "patch day" in order to coordinate the maintenance window worldwide.

SAP Application Support team

The Application Support team is responsible for supporting the business processes "above" the SAP infrastructure and has the business competence required to do so. Even in small and mid-sized enterprises, this team does not usually consist of the same people as the infrastructure team; instead, it is made up of power users from the line-of-business departments. In large enterprises, this expertise is concentrated in a dedicated customer competence center. However, because the people responsible naturally cooperate closely with the SAP and IT infrastructure teams, they also use the relevant tools to classify problems.

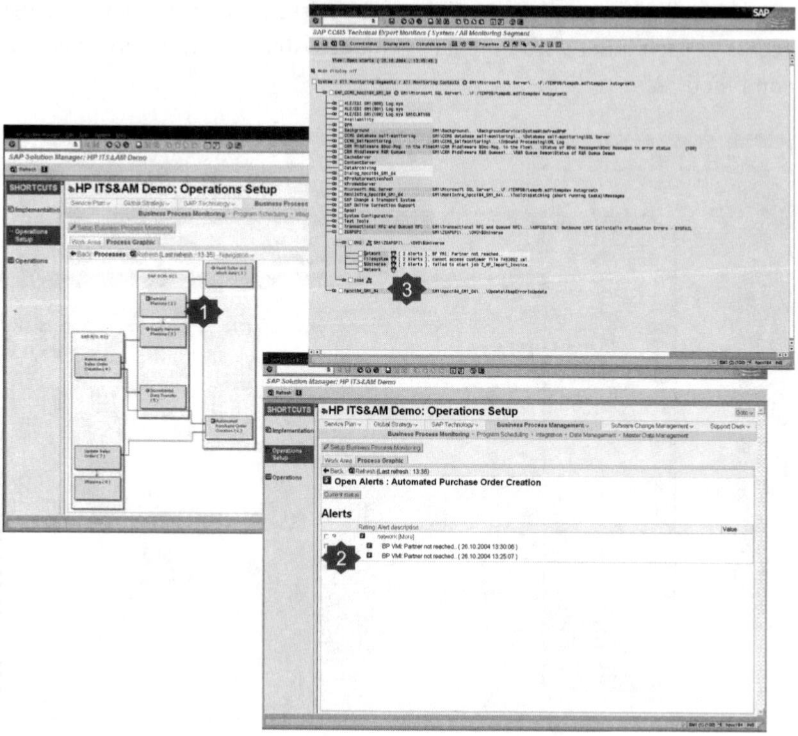

Figure 14.15 Solution Manager View of a Problem

Screen 1 of Figure 14.15 shows a graphic representation of the business processes in the VMI example, in the first level of the SAP Solution Manager. We can see the various steps of the business processes and that there has been a fault in one of these steps (by the red "lightning" symbol in the box). By drilling down to the Solution Manager (screen 2) and from there to the CCMS of the SAP component that caused the fault (screen 3), the application support staff can identify the cause of the problem (in our example, the connection to a vendor).

In this example, the information that the connection to an external process partner has been lost comes from HP OpenView. The integration of the system management system tool with the SAP Solution Manager simplifies and speeds up the root cause analysis process and thus prevents the "stab in the dark" approach, not to mention the all-too-common finger-pointing.

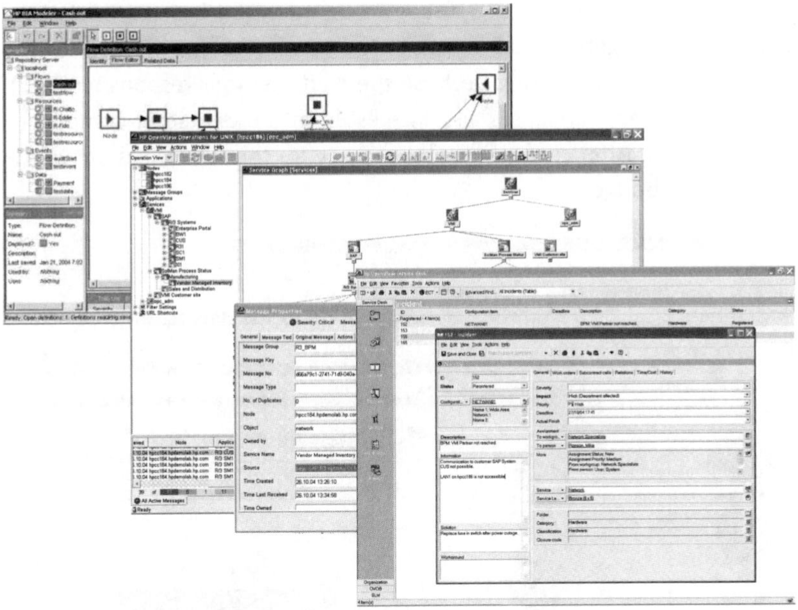

Figure 14.16 OpenView View of the Problem

Figure 14.16 shows the same problem, but from the viewpoint of the system-management system that is integrated by means of the SAP Enterprise Portal. Here, the employees on the SAP and IT infrastructure team get not only information about which component is currently experiencing a fault, but also which business processes are affected by the fault. This information is helpful if priorities have to be assigned to various measures (after all, it is not always the application whose users shout the loudest or who are highest up in the company hierarchy that is the most important one in an enterprise).

The application support specialists' requirements of the ITSM processes in operational management and change management are similar to those of the infrastructure support staff, only with more focus on the business processes. The important issues in this case are likewise monitoring availability, keeping up to date with upcoming changes, and being actively involved in the relevant processes.

Line-of-business management

The actual process owners and thus the ordering parties for the individual IT services are usually the managers of the line-of-business departments (in our example, the production planning manager and the purchasing manager). For one thing, the manager requires aggregated information and analyses for business processes (these are provided via SAP BW in our example), and he or she also needs to be informed by means of alerts when a process gets "stuck" (in our VMI scenario, for example, this could be a release that is missing because the staff member responsible is ill). For another, the manager is also interested in the degree of compliance with the SLAs. After all, he or she has to pay for the IT services out of the department budget.

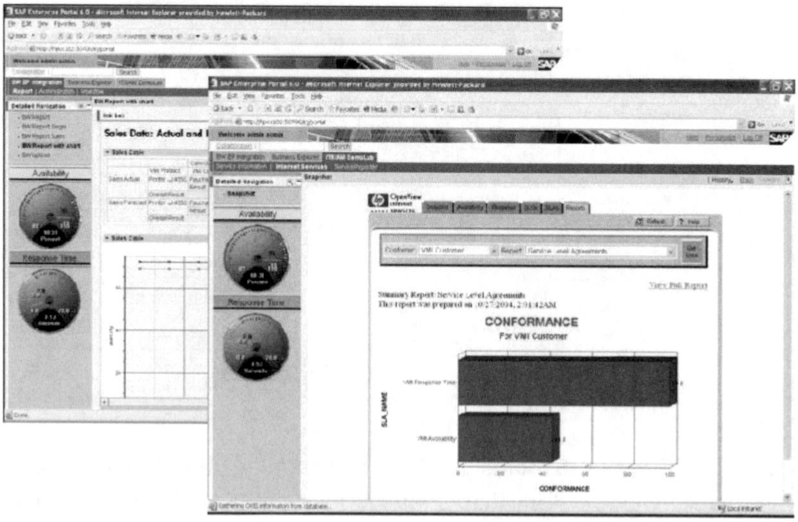

Figure 14.17 IT System Management View for Department Manager

To summarize, then, what a department manager wants from operations management is to be able to see the current availability and performance of the applications in use in his department in terms of how they affect the relevant business processes. He or she also needs information about the degree of compliance with SLAs. As the process owner, the manager is also actively involved in the change management process, as he or she has to approve all changes that have an effect on his department's applications.

Users in the line of business departments

Although it may be unexpected, users of the applications in the line-of-business departments are also involved in the ITSM processes. While production planners, purchasers (at the customer), salespersons (at the vendor), or developers (at a partner) of course work primarily with the specialist application relevant to their work, information about the availability of the business processes they use and any planned changes to these processes is also of interest to these employees.

When a fault occurs, the enterprise's employees not only need to know whether only individual business processes are affected and other applications can continue to be used, or whether the problem is a general one and they would thus be better off doing their filing until the problem is solved. They also need to know whether their business partners can still access the application.

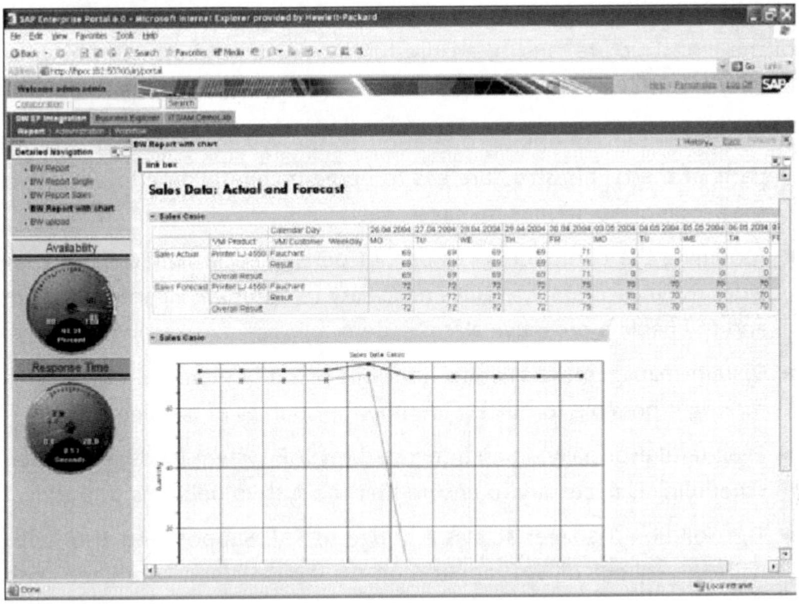

Figure 14.18 IT System Management View for End-Users

To get this information, employees should simply take a look at the end-user views in the system management tools via the SAP Enterprise Portal. This approach saves the end-user a lot of unnecessary "poking around" (during which the user could destroy the configuration on his computer, in the worst-case scenario) and the help desk a stream of phone calls.

Therefore, within the scope of operational management, end-users inside and outside the enterprise need information about the current availability of the services they use. In change management, all these users need to know about planned changes in good time. After all, these users are the ones who have to decide whether a change has had the desired effect, in other words, whether the application is back up and running properly and with the required level of performance.

It also makes sense to provide end-users with information about IT services, such as when a new PC will be delivered and installed on their desks.

14.5 Summary

Because of the large number of components in IT infrastructures, the complexity of these infrastructures and thus the requirements of system administrators are increasing. Management systems are therefore required in order to provide administrators with an overview and control of the infrastructure, and to ensure that business processes can be processed smoothly. The following are the most important points to note:

- To ensure the continuing operation of the systems, the status of all parts of the IT infrastructure has to be permanently monitored within the scope of operations management.
- Modeling the components as part of performance management provides the measurement values necessary to optimize the infrastructure and to enable a proactive alarm system.
- System-management systems filter out secondary problem messages, making it possible to quickly identify the sources of problems.
- Even (and especially) in an integrated mySAP system landscape, batch scheduling is necessary to ensure that the system operates smoothly.
- The Solution Manager acts as a bridge to SAP Support and also helps with the rollout of SAP application solutions. When combined with ITSM processes and enterprise management solutions, the result is a business process-oriented management solution for Enterprise Services Architectures.
- Technical systems condense data into information, but only human beings can turn this information into knowledge. Therefore, the in-depth knowledge of the employees in an enterprise cannot be replaced by any expert system, no matter how sophisticated.

15 SAP Operating Costs

"If you can't measure it, you can't manage it"

In the days of Internet hype, it often seemed that business concerns in IT projects were subordinated to the dictates of "time-to-market." Today, cost-benefit issues have regained their primacy. IT departments are under more pressure than ever, not only to prove their cost-effectiveness but even to justify their very existence, and in so doing to let their business unit be measured against and compared to external services.

It is for these reasons that many projects now focus on optimizing existing IT landscapes. A simplistic approach to cost management, based on a philosophy of "Just cut back on everything," is only a short-term solution. Experience shows that IT departments that strive simply for the lowest possible operating costs do not last long. This is because no matter how low the costs of an internal IT department, there will always be an outsourcer who can do it for less (or least, who will claim to be able to do so).

> *"IT departments that function simply as assistants to the line-of-business departments deserve to be outsourced."*[1]

The above quote is based on the realization that today IT departments have to make a concrete contribution to the success of the enterprise. Therefore, a task that is essential to the survival of IT teams is to work with the various business departments on an ongoing basis to initiate projects that result in measurable benefit to the enterprise.

This chapter presents various approaches how to determine the added value of IT departments and concepts for lowering the costs without jeopardizing the value. The first part of the chapter discusses a range of methods for investment analysis and cost-efficiency analysis. Building on this information, this chapter then shows how to create a total cost of ownership (TCO) analysis and also how to use this to create a benefits analysis. Only these kinds of costs and benefits analyses can provide an adequate basis for enterprise-level decision-making.

Be aware that this chapter is not intended as a detailed examination of the economics of business. It is intended only to provide tips for and

1 Andreas Kerbusk, CIO of STEAG and board member of the German-speaking SAP User Group (DSAG).

assistance with identifying cost factors, along with suggestions on how to use the various procedures and concepts.

15.1 The Benefits of IT

What is the value of IT?

Since the publication of the article entitled "IT Doesn't Matter"[2] by Nicholas Carr the value of IT investments in terms of the competitiveness of enterprises has been hotly debated. According to Carr, IT investments no longer add competitive advantage because IT has become commoditized, just as electricity became commoditized at the start of the last century and steam power the century before that. However, the reverse is also true; that is, an enterprise today that tries to operate without IT is as uncompetitive as companies without electricity or steam in the past.

IT matters!

We must remember that the enormous progress made by humanity since the invention of the hand-axe hundreds of thousands of years ago is mainly due to the continuous improvements made to tools. Excellent results are possible only with excellent tools, and in this sense IT is indeed of central importance in an enterprise's daily fight for survival.

Of course, simply setting aside a certain percentage of revenue for IT purposes is no guarantee of success. One should never lose sight of the fact that IT is first and foremost an organizational aid. IT, in the form of hardware and software, is the basis for innovative business processes, but innovation and running a good business are still the responsibility of the human beings involved.

15.2 IT Cost Structures

Studies show that in most cases, 75 % of IT costs are spent on staff and services, and only 25 % on software, hardware, and the rest of the infrastructure.

Operating costs structure

Before starting cost-benefit discussions, it is helpful to be clear about the various cost factors that arise in the operation of enterprise software solutions. In practice, it has been shown that the costs of operating an SAP system can be divided into eight main cost blocks (Figure 15.1).

The cost blocks can be further sub-divided into fixed item costs and performance-related variable costs, as well as infrastructure costs and staff costs.

2 Harvard Business Review, 5/2003.

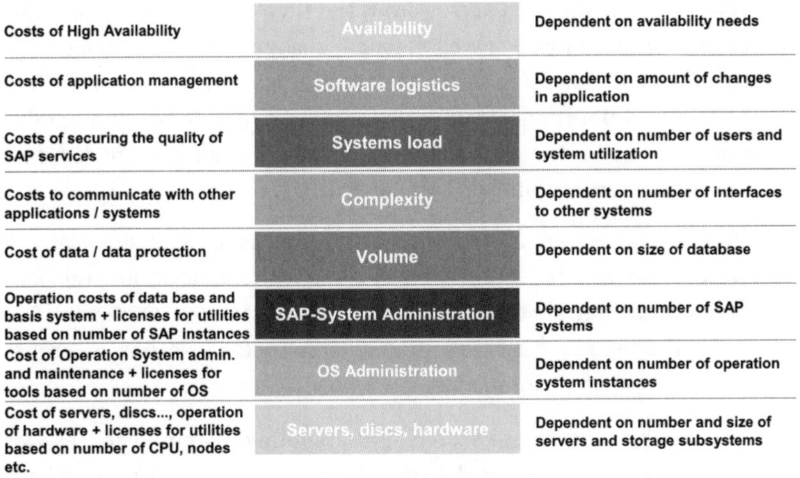

Costs of High Availability
Availability
Dependent on availability needs
Costs of application management
Software logistics
Dependent on amount of changes in application
Costs of securing the quality of SAP services
Systems load
Dependent on number of users and system utilization
Costs to communicate with other applications / systems
Complexity
Dependent on number of interfaces to other systems
Cost of data / data protection
Volume
Dependent on size of database
Operation costs of data base and basis system + licenses for utilities based on number of SAP instances
SAP-System Administration
Dependent on number of SAP systems
Cost of Operation System admin. and maintenance + licenses for tools based on number of OS
OS Administration
Dependent on number of operation system instances
Cost of servers, discs..., operation of hardware + licenses for utilities based on number of CPU, nodes etc.
Servers, discs, hardware
Dependent on number and size of servers and storage subsystems

Figure 15.1 The Eight Cost Blocks of Operating an SAP System

Fixed costs

Fixed costs include costs for operating the hardware (computers, storage, networks, HW related tools and so on), Operating System (OS) instances and SAP systems (monitoring, applying patches, SW related tools and so on). These are costs that are determined by the number of computers or systems.

Variable costs

Examples of performance-related costs are: system load and volume costs (which vary according to the transaction load and the size of the database); costs associated with complexity (number of interfaces to other systems); software logistics costs (which vary according to the frequency with which programs and their settings change), and availability costs (which vary according to the maximum permitted downtime).

Hardware platform

The costs of computers and storage hardware and of their operation obviously depend on the number of server systems and storage systems. These fixed infrastructure costs can be divided up as follows:

- Leasing and depreciation of hardware and operating system software.
- Manufacturer maintenance and repairs for hardware and operating system software.
- Network connection (cabling, LAN ports, SAN ports).
- Proportional costs of data-center infrastructure (space requirement, electricity supply, air conditioning, and so on).
- Proportional costs of backup software and system monitoring software, plus costs for their software agents.

The staff costs for this area accrue from the time spent on system monitoring and administration, as well as patch, change and fault management for the individual operating system instances and storage systems.[3] Then there are also proportional staff costs for system monitoring and administration and, again, the patch, change and fault management for data backup and system monitoring software.

Operating Operation Systems

A computer without an operating system is useless, a fact every user will be aware of when after the disk crash a service technician just replaces the disk (as covered in the SLA) but doesn't install the OS again. The necessity of operating systems also generates costs in relation to licensing, monitoring and maintenance.

In the past, the numbers of servers and operating system instances was equal. With technologies like dynamic domains, logical, virtual, and hard partitions (l-pars, v-pars, and n-pars) multiple operating system instances can be executed on a single server. Naturally the cost models must be adapted to these new developments.

Be aware that with technologies like VMware, Micropartitions and Virtual Machines you add another OS instance which hosts guest OS instances, which run in turn with the applications. This additional OS instance generates additional effort for monitoring and maintenance. Therefore you must evaluate the need for additional OS instances carefully.

While the costs for hardware and software can be calculated with relative ease based on key figures associated with the implementation project costs per named user like "invest per R/3 seat", the ongoing costs are not easy to determine. The reason is that typically few support specialists, are assigned 100 % to a single system environment or set of tasks. Few statistical numbers are published about the effort per server or instance.

Rule of Thumb

A non-representative survey of various customers showed a time investment of ca. 30 minutes per operating system instance per day for operations monitoring and performance tuning. This same survey also showed three to five days per operating system patch, including all preparations and post-patch work such as importing data and testing.

3 For more details on the necessary tasks in patch, change and fault management, please refer to our book, *SAP System Operations*, SAP PRESS 2003.

Basic operations of an SAP system

The actual daily operation of an SAP system is naturally one of the item costs that depend on the number of systems. By "SAP system" we mean the totality of all SAP Web AS instances and components of a solution plus the associated database instances.

In terms of hardware infrastructure, the only costs here are the proportional costs for data backup and system monitoring software plus the costs for their software agents.

The staff costs in this area can be divided up as follows:

- Database administration, including change, patch, and fault management for the database
- Administration of the SAP application software, including change and patch management (Support Packages, plug-ins, and so on), and fault management
- Proportional costs for configuring the system monitoring software

In practice, a frequently-used ballpark figure for applying database patches and SAP Service and Support Packages is three to five days per session, including preparation and post-patch tasks.

Load-dependent costs

Besides the fixed costs there are naturally other cost elements that depend on the size of the SAP system. The greater the number of users and, especially, the more transactions they generate, the more powerful the computing infrastructure has to be.

Also, as the number of users increases, so does the number of staff hours required for user administration and help-desk functions. Similarly, as the system load increases, so does the work required for performance optimization of application programs. Another point—frequently forgotten—is that the number of printers also tends to increase along with the number of users, and so more staff hours are required for output management, change management, and fault management for the printers.

Volume-dependent costs

As the volume of data stored on the hard disks increases, so too do the costs of leasing or depreciation of the necessary hard disk capacity. The costs for the required data backup capacity also increase at the same rate. Staff costs for database administration (tuning, reorganization, and so on) usually also increase in line with the database size.

Complexity costs

One cost block that is often underestimated is the cost of interfaces to other applications in a system group. These costs can be described as "complexity costs." The costs are incurred due to man hours spent on implementation, change, and fault management of the individual interfaces, and performance analysis and optimization.

In the case of batch-driven interfaces, there are additional costs for implementation and change and fault management of the job control system. The time and effort required for coordination with the owners of the other applications also incur costs.

The magnitude of the complexity costs obviously depends on the number and complexity of the interfaces in an application. Estimates put the figure at ca. $100,000 per interface per year.

Software logistics costs

Costs associated with software logistics depend on the number of production solutions that are required in-house development. The number of such solutions determines the staff costs incurred by the use of software modifications and components in test systems and production systems plus employing the correction and transport-management systems of the various solutions. Cluster testing and creation of training and test systems by means of homogeneous system copies are additional cost items.

Availability costs

Clearly, ensuring a specified service level in terms of system availability does not come for free. The costs in this area include those for maintenance contracts with short reaction times, plus the cluster software and reserve capacities, and also staff costs for on-call duty, among other things.

15.3 Cost-Efficiency Analyses

The requirement of any business investment is that the benefit must be higher than the costs in the long run. Every cost-efficiency calculation is based on the basic principle of costs and returns, or expenses and benefits. In terms of an IT system, benefits can be classified by three categories:

- Direct benefits are those that reduce current costs.
- Indirect benefits are those that reduce future costs.
- Non-quantifiable benefits are those that are immaterial or strategic, and those that have secondary effects, and so on.

The issue here is that it can be very difficult to objectively describe and evaluate the factors that influence the benefit of an IT system to the business. While the benefits of most activities related to core business processes can be directly and unambiguously calculated from the revenue made, this is not so simple when it comes to investments in IT.

Unlike goods and services, to which costs and revenue can be directly assigned, IT revenues can be expressed in concrete figures only in the case of outsourcing companies. IT departments share this problem with other "services" within the enterprise, from security guards to secretaries to management. However, IT shares an important trait with research and development, sales support, and even the finance department: Their costs do contribute at least indirectly to the profits of the enterprise. From this point of view, the IT department is in good company.

Indirectly or not, IT can have considerable influence on the profitability of an enterprise, as the following example shows. Let us assume that an enterprise with a revenue of $1 billion and 4,000 employees spends ca. 5 % of its annual turnover on IT (ca. $50 million). If this enterprise reduces its IT costs by 1 %, it saves $500,000. On the other hand, if IT is used to increase the productivity of the 4,000 employees by 1 %, the enterprise gains an extra $10 million. The problem in this case is to prove the increase in productivity in terms of dollars and cents.

However, the profit gained due to the purchase of a Lear jet, which helps make top management staff more flexible and saves them valuable time, is just as difficult to quantify. The best way to understand the benefits that IT brings is to imagine what things would be like if the services provided by the IT department were not available; for example, if all written communication was by letter and each letter had to be dictated, typed, and delivered by messengers.

15.3.1 Classic Investment Calculation

The classic investment calculation process analyzes the monetary effects of an investment and converts these effects into figures that express the value of the investment. The process comprises static and dynamic investment calculations and risk management. The benefits of the classic approach are its ease of use and transparency.

Static procedure

These techniques are used in cost comparison and profit comparison analyses, profitability analyses, and amortization analyses, among other operations. The aim of amortization calculation is to minimize financial risk. It is based on the assumption that as the reflux time of the capital and by association the capital tie-up period increases, so does the investment security. However, using this payback time as a measure of risk works only to a limited extent, because it ignores long-term (monetary) benefits.

Static procedures do not take into account relationships between functional areas, nor do they take into account future fluctuations in returns or the duration of use. Also, the results of the individual methods are difficult to compare, as every method returns different decision options for the same input parameters.

Dynamic procedures

Dynamic investment procedures take into account the whole life cycle of an investment. They do this by taking into account the yield over time of deposits and payments by means of accumulation or discounting based on a reference time. The best-known examples of this are net present value (NPV), internal rate of return (IRR), annuity methods, and return on investment (ROI). Although calculating the payment series for IT systems can be difficult, dynamic procedures are regarded as the most reliable key figures, due to their high level of transparency and clarity.

Sensitivity analysis and risk analysis

The classic investment calculation procedures illustrated so far assume that all values required for the calculation are already available. However, with long-term investments, the presence of risks can cause these values to change. A sensitivity analysis assumes that the initial values in a calculation will be liable to fluctuate above and below an estimated value. For this reason, it calculates the threshold values within which the investment seems to make financial sense.

A risk analysis works differently. It examines the risk structure of the result value. If we change the input values, we get the probability distribution of the result value. The nature of any change and its probability of occurring are determined by various environmental factors that have to be defined in advance of the analysis.

Multi-dimensional procedure

Besides criteria that have a monetary value, multi-dimensional procedures also take into account subjective values as target values. The focus here is thus less on cost-oriented issues than on benefit-oriented methods of analysis. The best-known procedures are utility analysis, extended cost-efficiency analysis, work system value analysis, and benefit analysis.

15.3.2 Return on investment

The Return on investment (ROI) compares the net benefits of an investment with the total project costs. ROI thus returns a key value that relates to the returns that will be made by an investment to the means required to acquire that investment. The following calculations apply.

- ROI = (benefit—costs) / costs = relative value of net benefit over the analysis period / cumulative costs
- Benefit = TCO saving + expected improvement in profit
- Costs = project execution costs + third-party costs

The result is a percentage value of the invested capital. As with all investments, the ROI should be greater than the interest return on the capital market. An ROI of 200 %, for example, means that the net benefit is twice as high as the total expected project costs. To put it another way, every euro or dollar that the enterprise spends results in a profit of two euro or two dollars.

This calculation does not take all the costs into account, however; it is based only on the direct implementation costs of the project, and not the total costs involving everything in conjunction with the project. During the course of an investment, the current value of the capital in question may change (due to the effects of interest rates, for example), and this also has to be taken into account in the calculation. Nonetheless, this method is suitable for estimating costs and benefits within the scope of a planned project and for calculating the effects of cost-cutting measures. However, note that ROI is not a standardized procedure; there are a number of different calculation methods.[4]

15.3.3 Total Cost of Ownership

The term "total cost of ownership" (TCO) originates not from business academics subject but from the Gartner Group, an IT consultancy firm. It refers to the total costs of operating IT systems. The aim of a TCO analysis is to create a complete description of the current costs of an IT infrastructure in a clear and comprehensible way, using a transparent cost framework.

An important consideration in a TCO analysis is that the emphasis be on "total". As we know, an IT investment consists not only of the expenditure on hardware and software, but also of many other cost elements that arise during rollout and operation. Therefore, all costs that arise during the life cycle of an IT application have to be taken into account. This includes not only direct costs, but also hidden costs and indirect costs. Costs are categorized into the following areas: hardware and software, operation, administration, downtime, and end-user operation.

---

4 Harrison, Ann: *Return on investment*. Computerworld 6/1999. *http://www.computerworld.com/news/1999/story/0,11280,36069,00.html.*

However, the TCO concept does not appear widely in business literature, nor is there a consistent definition of the term and the cost elements that it covers.

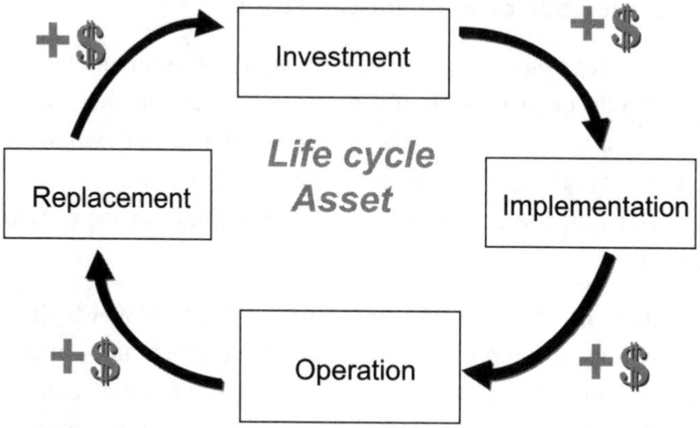

Figure 15.2 Life Cycle of an IT Solution

In light of the usual depreciation cycles for long-term investment goods, it is common practice to take a time period of three or more years for hardware investments. This period takes into account the repair and maintenance costs that arise after the guarantee expires. These can be significant.

Because TCO does not provide any information about the profit that may be made by a particular IT investment, the TCO figure can be used only to compare various options in a process of selecting new technology, evaluating projects, and comparing the experience of different industries.

TCO in practice

In practice, there are a number of variants of the TCO model, one of which is the Gartner TCO Manager for Distributed Computing. This model is used to determine the total operating costs of a client-server environment.

It takes into account hardware costs, including maintenance and service costs, and all running costs for operation, maintenance, and downtime. To perform the unique TCO analysis, one carries out an IT process analysis, the results of which are then incorporated into Best Practices. The Best Practices are standardized procedures defined by the Gartner Group that describe how the use of IT technologies can have a positive influence on total costs.

The process of gathering data in the categories: Change Management, Operational Management, Asset Administration, Customer Service, Training and Technology Planning, and Process Management for the purposes of a TCO analysis are divided into three stages: interviews and questionnaires, tool-based validation, and computer-based processing. The questionnaires gather information about the following areas:

- Company profile
- IT net worth values
- Degree of implementation of Best Practices
- Complexity of the system landscape

To create the company profile, the questionnaire contains 20 questions relating to the position of the company in terms of industry and size, and the type and number of IT systems. The Best Practices questionnaire contains 105 questions relating to the categories referred to above. The complexity questionnaire contains 32 questions.

The process of collecting data for the IT net worth values and representing these values in a structured way is based on the Gartner Group Chart of Accounts. The following categorizations are used in this system:

Category	Description	Information sources
Current hardware and software expenses	Costs directly caused by the purchase of hardware and software	Purchase and leasing contracts, budget protocols, inventory records
Current operations expenses (direct costs for system operation)	Costs for staff, support activities, service desk calls, and on-site service	IT budget, time recording, outsourcing and maintenance contracts, IT management, service desk records, IT organizational diagrams, HR payroll records
Current administration expenses (direct costs)	Recording administration work involved	Training schedules and logs, IT budget, procurement, training contracts, IT organizational diagrams, HR payroll record
Current end user operations and downtime (indirect costs)	Costs for peer and self-support, training, application development, employee satisfaction with IT system, productivity losses due to downtime	End-user survey, payroll records, end-user focus groups, end-user interviews, training manager

Table 15.1 Overview of Gartner Group Chart of Accounts

The questionnaire on IT assets is divided into 60 questions in the various categories. Questionnaires are also given out to end-users for the category Current End-User Operations and Downtime, in order to obtain a realistic picture of the situation within the enterprise. The unified chart of accounts ensures that all costs are taken into account, and it is therefore the initial basis for modeling, measuring, and optimization.

TCO team Support is required from various parts of the enterprise in order to provide the wealth of information needed for a TCO analysis. Besides an executive sponsor, Gartner also recommends that there be a core TCO team, consisting of a project manager and one specialist for each of the following areas: assets, finance, users, and operations and administration. Experts from the areas of procurement, human resources, service desk, training, vendor management, technology, business units, and development are also involved.

A TCO project usually lasts eight weeks. The actual time required can be longer or shorter, depending on how well the team works together, the priority assigned to the TCO project, and the degree of difficulty of gathering the data.

Regular TCO studies highlight the development of the cost structure within an enterprise and can thus help in selecting suitable IT projects. It is also possible to simulate the effects of IT investments on the TCO and thus to select the most suitable option from a range of investment alternatives.

However, Gartner advises companies against comparing its TCO analysis with those of competitors, as the key figures do not reflect the basic conditions in each case:

> *"Companies are like snowflakes—no two are alike."*[5]

It was for this reason that, in 2000, Gartner stopped publishing TCO figures.

One critical point is that a TCO analysis does not take into account the benefits of the infrastructure. The system landscape is regarded simply as a cost factor that does not contribute any visible benefit to the success of the enterprise. It has been shown in the past that the IT environment with the lowest TCO is not necessarily the best solution for a specific enterprise. Therefore, a TCO analysis should only be used to identify the

---

5 Bill Kirwin, Vice President Gartner Group.

possible costs of a technology project, and its results should be incorporated as a key figure into any other necessary analyses.

TCO benchmarking

As well as offering a TCO analysis service, the Gartner Group also provides a benchmarking service that compares cost structures with the Best Practices of other SAP customers in the same industry. In the benchmarking process, the figures are compared with the average from the peer group (that is, a group of customers with the same functionality (functions and modules), application requirements, infrastructure, and architecture).

Gartner claims that the database it keeps for this purpose is the most comprehensive and detailed worldwide.

The following questions are asked within the scope of a benchmarking study:

- Was the SAP rollout carried out at a similar cost to other rollouts in the peer group?
- Are the costs of the SAP projects in line with the market?
- Are the operational costs in line with the market?
- What is the total cost of ownership?
- What is the cost structure in the service area (SAP support)?

Figure 15.3 shows the result of this kind of study in terms of the project duration and costs of an SAP rollout. Figure 15.4 shows a comparison of the costs of the software, infrastructure, and maintenance costs.

Project Duration	Customer	Peer group
Planned project duration	48 months	36 months
Project duration		38 months
Project approach	Implementation in stages	Implementation in stages
Project Team		
Project team members	130	104
Department	42	38
IT	39	22
External consultants	48	44

Longer project duration and higher quantity of project resources compared to the peer group due to ...

Figure 15.3 Comparison of Project Duration and Resources

Investment costs	Customer	Peer group
Infrastructure	$340,000	$360,000
Server	$1,800,000	$2,800,000
Storage and backup	$2,200,000	$2,500,000
Hardware service	$675,000	$1,450,000
Total	$5,015,000	$7,110,000
Software costs		
SAP licenses	$6,500,000	$5,200,000
SAP maintenance	$1,380,000	$1,400,000
Other software	$682,000	$390,000
Total	$8,562,000	$6,990,000

Under-dimensioned hardware resources compared to the recommended sizing result in high enhancement costs in later years.

Figure 15.4 Comparison of Infrastructure and Maintenance Costs

The study also describes the reasons for any deviations from the average and indicates potential for improvement, where possible. This kind of benchmarking process takes approximately 12 weeks.

15.3.4 Other Tools

Several other consultancies besides the Gartner Group provide tools for identifying TCO and ROI.

e-Valuator

e-Valuator from the Winslow Consulting Group[6] collects and administers architecture and finance data to do with servers, storage, staff, software, and network infrastructure. The data collection process is mainly automatic, thanks to data collection agents and import interfaces to other programs. Additional data is obtained from a range of questionnaires and interviews, in which basic information about the enterprise and locations, and specialized information about hardware and software (such as date of procurement, performance specifications, licenses, and so on) is obtained. The data is stored in an Access database.

The integrated Decision Support Reporting Toolkit processes the collected data and uses it to create TCO, ROI and NPV calculations that that can then be used as the basis for asset management, investment, consolidation, and IT strategy decisions.

Thanks to its high degree of detail, the tool is well-suited to these purposes, and the data used is transparent and comprehensible. The benefit

6 Go to *www.winslow-consulting.com*.

of this method is that there is an add-on methodology for e-Valuator that supports the application right up to the design and implementation of a concrete business case.

ROInow! and TCOnow!

The company CIOview[7] provides two tools, ROInow! and TCOnow!, which create graphics-based comparisons of different investment alternatives and collect and represent graphically the total costs and the benefits associated with making an investment. It also provides a front-end for data gathering and heuristics methods.

Using the input it receives, plus market analyses and industry averages from IDC[8], the program calculates the estimated number of production, development, and quality assurance systems that will be required in the future, the storage costs per MB, the required staff numbers, and the expected system availability.

ITCentrix Server Consolidation Value Model

The ITCentrix[9] Server Consolidation Value Model was developed specially to determine the contribution of a server consolidation to the business value of the enterprise, and is restricted to this purpose.

The model brings together the costs, technology, and business value factors in order to create prognoses regarding the effects of a consolidation. Based on the TCO approach, the model adds the Availability and Flexibility modules to the operational costs established by the TCO analysis.

The model compares the costs of a consolidation with the benefits that it will bring to the enterprise. In this process, benefits that are difficult to quantify in financial terms are expressed in the form of cost savings and possible increases in revenue and productivity.

ITCentrix uses the Application Value Model to express problematic factors such as higher system availability and increased flexibility. The value of an IT consolidation is considered in terms of two dimensions: the business benefit and the benefit from the viewpoint of the IT department. The ITCentrix model quantifies data by expressing IT benefit in the form of increased employee productivity. The key quantity here is the turnover per employee.

"Home-made" TCO and ROI estimates

It is also perfectly possible to carry out your own rough TCO and ROI analyses using home-made methods. The following practical examples show how simple comparison calculations can be used to roughly estimate the total cost of ownership of various system configurations and the ROI.

7 Go to *http://www.CIOview.com*.
8 Go to *http://www.idc.com*.
9 Go to *http://www.ITCentrix.com*.

15.4 Reducing TCO by Consolidation

As shown in the first chapter, enterprises with mature SAP systems often have a whole range of heterogeneous system and computer landscapes that can incur relatively high operating costs if the resources are not used satisfactorily. This is especially true in situations arising from company mergers and acquisitions, where multiple production instances of the same SAP component may be running. The same situation arises when individual country or regional subsidiaries of a company run their own systems.

Chapter 13 described the various technical concepts for reducing the number of systems and servers as part of a consolidation process. We now want to examine these concepts from the point of view of TCO and ROI.

In the SAP area, there are many different types of system consolidation. The main differentiating factor between them is their cost-saving potential:

- Server consolidation (from client-server to centralized system)
- System consolidation (stacking multiple systems on a small number of computers)
- Logical consolidation (system merge to form multi-client system)
- Application consolidation (on NetWeaver and mySAP)

Where are savings achieved?

A logical consolidation on the application level is different from a purely technical consolidation (server or system consolidation) in terms of which cost blocks are affected, how they are affected, and what amount of work is required for the consolidation.

Figure 15.6 shows an example of which cost blocks can be expected to produce savings, and to what extent, in a situation where three separate SAP systems, each with its own system landscape, are consolidated to form one multi-client system. While savings can be made in the areas of hardware, complexity costs, software logistics, and especially system operation, the system load stays more or less the same, and there is usually only a relatively small reduction in volume.

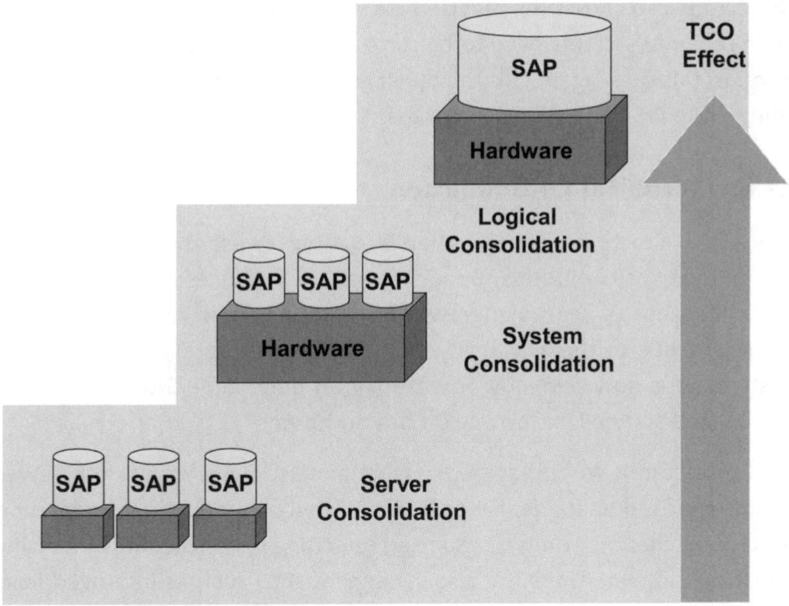

Figure 15.5 Stages of SAP Consolidation

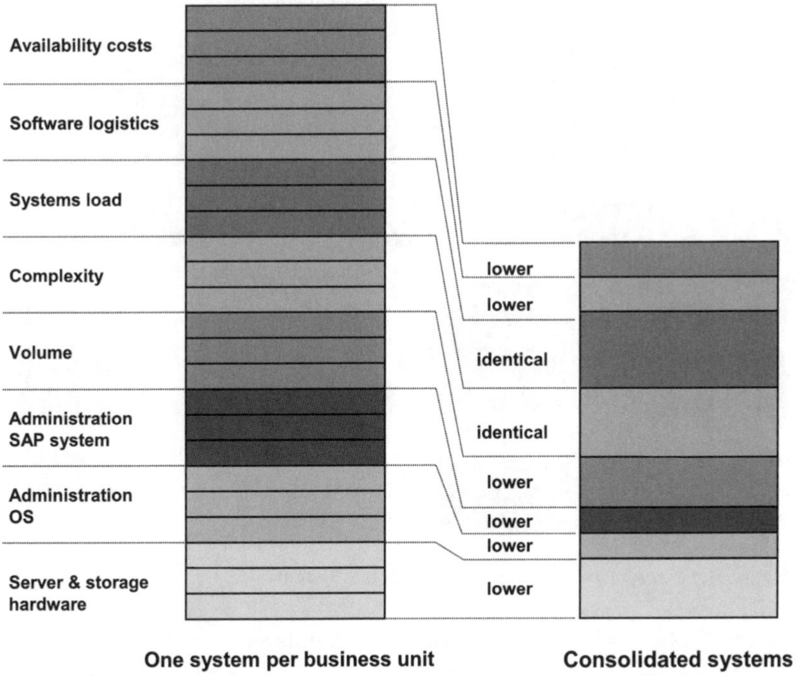

Figure 15.6 Savings Potential through Consolidation

The figure also shows the reverse case; that is, that costs increase if multiple separate systems have to be run for technical or organizational reasons. In this case, again, it is the much greater workload involved in operating more OS and SAP instances that has the biggest effect.

15.4.1 Technical Consolidation

The aim of a technical consolidation is to achieve cost savings by reducing the number of computers, operating system instances and storage systems. Because of the huge growth in performance in recent years, and especially due to the availability of sufficient address spaces with 64-bit systems, it is now perfectly possible to run quite large SAP instances as centralized systems exclusively on one computer.

Saving effects

This results in a whole range of saving effects. Every application server that is removed no longer has to be monitored or supplied with operating system patches, nor does it require an operating system license or a maintenance contract. There are also synergy effects, such as improved load distribution between the database and application instances. The fact that proportionally less memory is "wasted" on multiple operating systems and buffers is good news for shared memory.

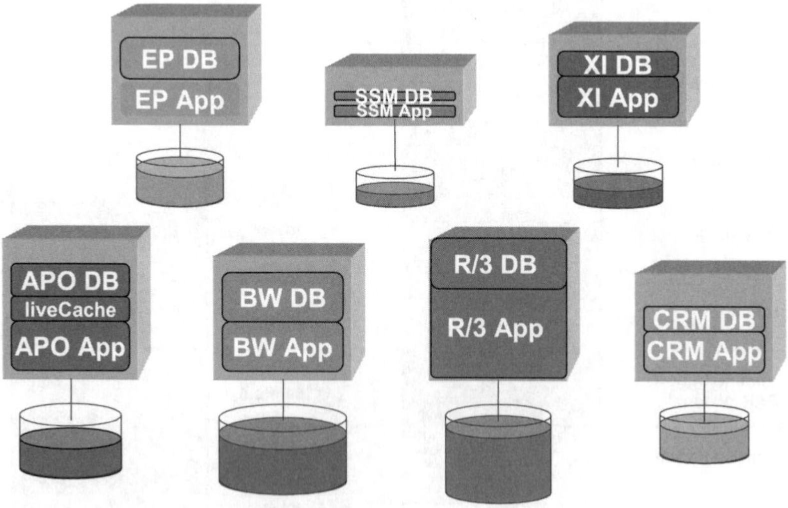

Figure 15.7 Server Consolidation to SAP Central Systems

Figure 15.7 shows a system landscape with different mySAP solutions and NetWeaver components. For the sake of clarity, development, test, and training systems have been omitted, as have the necessary measures for ensuring system availability.

However, this kind of system landscape is not very adaptive, because if one of these systems is under a high load, there is no way to share unused resources with other computers. Therefore, every single computer has to be designed to handle the maximum load of each application. Due to the rounding-up syndrome described in Chapter 13, the investment is used in quite an unsatisfactory way, which could be avoided by means of a configuration like that shown in Figure 15.8.

Static landscape

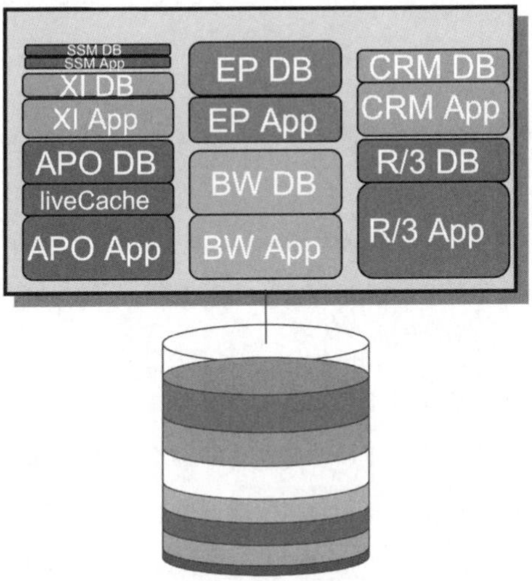

Figure 15.8 System Consolidation

Here, all SAP systems are installed on one computer and run under one operating system. This results in a better distribution of system load, as the load peaks on the various instances balance each other out.[10] Cost-saving potential also arises from the reduction in the number of computers that have to be monitored, supplied with patches, and maintained.

On the other hand, with larger computers, there are significantly higher costs for hardware, operating system licenses, and maintenance, as the prices of these computers usually scale more quickly than performance improves (however the potential discounts are usually also higher).

Practical experience shows that the savings made on maintenance costs alone as a result of a technical system consolidation mean that the amortization period is reduced to less than a year. Some studies even promise

10 SAP also supports the operation of several SAP systems with one common database instance; this is referred to as "multiple components—one database" (MCOD) or "SAP one Server" (S1S).

a reduction in TCO of 50 %-60 %, although savings of this magnitude are possible only with a great deal of administration work per computer.

One of the central benefits of a technical consolidation is that nothing in the applications has to be changed. Therefore, no coordination with the business departments or painful regression tests becomes necessary.

Because nothing in the SAP applications changes, only the hardware, operating system license, and maintenance costs have to be compared for a TCO analysis (Table 15.2).

	1st year	2nd year	3rd year	4th year	5th year
Depreciation of investment					
Hardware	\$200,000	\$200,000	\$200,000	\$200,000	\$200,000
Software	\$20,000	\$20,000	\$20,000	\$20,000	\$20,000
Operation					
Servers	\$25,000	\$25,000	\$25,000	\$25,000	\$25,000
Backup	\$10,000	\$10,000	\$10,000	\$10,000	\$10,000
SAP Basis	\$50,000	\$50,000	\$50,000	\$50,000	\$50,000
Database	\$10,000	\$10,000	\$10,000	\$10,000	\$10,000
Performance	\$10,000	\$10,000	\$10,000	\$10,000	\$10,000
Repairs and maintenance					
Hardware		\$95,000	\$95,000	\$95,000	\$105,000
Total	\$325,000	\$420,000	\$420,000	\$420,000	\$210,000

Table 15.2 Investment for Server Consolidation

15.4.2 SAP System Consolidation

As Figure 15.6 shows, much more can be saved if the number of duplicate SAP application instances is reduced through a process of logically consolidating systems to form a multi-client system.

Low operating costs

These savings are chiefly due to the significantly lower operating costs for the SAP system. Complexity costs are also saved because the interfaces between the various systems are removed. The scope of any software logistics savings depends on whether all clients can be transferred to a single development environment.

Table 15.3 juxtaposes the staff requirement for administrating 29 SAP instances that are distributed worldwide across several data centers with the investment required for seven instances in one centralized system. This assumes that a centralized SAP system requires 50 % less administration work than a distributed system.

	Distributed	Centralized
Number of instances	**29**	**7**
System administrator—SAP Basis	14	6
System administrator—Logistics	14	7
System administrator—Accounting	14	7
System administrator—Data Warehouse	14	7
Interface support	14	7

Table 15.3 Comparison of Staff Requirements

Logical consolidation is a consulting project

A process of logical consolidation includes the business processes and applications, plus any customizing required for each SAP system. This usually leads to a considerable requirement for consulting services, the scope of which can sometimes be the same as for a new rollout project. The business departments also have to be involved in the process, and detailed regression tests have to be carried out. Nonetheless, these projects are usually worth the investment.

In addition to the purely financial aspects, a logical consolidation has other benefits. For example, it makes unified maintenance and customizing possible, and it imposes consistency on master data and processes.

For example, transferring SAP Financial Accounting to one client with one company code per business unit in the group automatically makes cross-enterprise processes possible. In a non-centralized solution, interfaces would have to be used for this purpose.

Another benefit to a logical consolidation is the fast access to material stock information when all the companies in a group are mapped together to one client. In a cost-benefit analysis, you can represent these benefits by assigning a monetary value to the lower stock levels of a centralized approach.

This kind of logical consolidation can only succeed, however, if there is clear sponsorship of the project by management. The main issue here is the political punch of the management, because this kind of consolidation requires sacrifices in some areas of the enterprise.

Therefore, there must first be a clear strategy for the shared business processes, which is then reflected in the SAP model. There is no point in carrying out a logical consolidation if the enterprise does not have a consistent chart of accounts.

15.4.3 Application Consolidation

This book does not deal any further with application consolidation scenarios, as they depend too much on the individual situation in the enterprise. However, Table 15.4 uses an example of an international chemical company to show that an application consolidation based on mySAP solutions makes it possible to make significantly greater cost savings than would be the case with a "best-of-breed" approach, where applications from actual leaders in each relevant market are combined.

	mySAP solutions	Best-of-breed
Software licenses		3–4 times higher
Software maintenance		3–4 times higher
Integration costs	None	ca. $1–3.7 million
Support, upgrades	Less complex	Highly complex
Administration	Same as R/3	+ 2–4 FTEs
Management system integration work	Unified platform (Web AS)	Heterogeneous platforms

Table 15.4 Comparison of mySAP Solution and "Best-of-Breed"

15.5 Reducing TCO by Platform Migration

Migration consulting

In many cases, cost savings can be achieved by means of a change in system platform. However, note that this kind of heterogeneous migration is a project that requires a certified migration consultant (for approximate one week per system plus one half-day per interface), and that downtime is still unavoidable during the database import and export.

The following practical example uses real-world figures to show a comparative analysis of the TCO of two system platforms, plus an ROI analysis for a platform migration. Keep in mind that the figures apply only to this specific situation and should not be taken as generally valid.

Table 15.5 shows the annual TCO of a system platform that consists of a mainframe database and multiple Unix computers from the same manufacturer as application servers. Because the system has been up and running for several years, the hardware and the database have been depreciated to a symbolic value of 1.

Hardware maintenance costs for database and app. server	$700,000
Hardware depreciation	$1
Database software maintenance	$30,000
Database software depreciation	$1
Electricity costs	$46,000
Footprint (Space requirement)	$50,000
System operation (6 FTE employees)	$600,000
Total per year	$1,426,002

Table 15.5 Annual TCO—Mixed Mainframe / Unix Infrastructure

Table 15.6 shows the TCO of Unix infrastructure that was consolidated with the help of an Itanium system and that has a somewhat higher throughput.

Hardware maintenance costs for centralized system	$125,000
Hardware depreciation	$175,000
Database software maintenance	$23,000
Database software depreciation	$80,000
Electricity costs	$9,000
Footprint (Space requirement)	$25,000
System operation (3 FTE employees)	$300,000
Total per year	$737,000

Table 15.6 Annual TCO—Homogeneous Unix Infrastructure

Because the number, configuration and size of the SAP instances do not change, their associated costs do not change significantly either.

In spite of the significantly higher depreciation of the newly acquired hardware and database software, the considerably lower repair and maintenance costs for the hardware result in much lower annual operating costs.

Thanks to the reduction in the amount of system operations work brought about by the migration from a mixed environment with two operating system to a homogeneous environment with one operating system and considerably fewer operating system and application instances, the amount of administration work necessary is also greatly reduced.

Although this cost comparison suggests that migrating an SAP system to open system will lead to major cost savings, you should still always compare the investment costs with the savings potential in order to get a balanced view of the issue and to be clear about whether a platform migration will pay for itself, and if so, when.

Project costs

The expenses incurred by the migration project, such as those for external consultants and in-house services by the IT department, should always be taken into account. Any training costs made necessary by the platform migration should not be forgotten, nor should the fact that during the project, both platforms will have to be run in parallel. Only when all these cost factors are added up can we draw reliable conclusions about the cost-efficiency of this kind of project.

Table 15.7 contains the total operating costs of such a project, including the costs of the migration project over the expected operation period of the infrastructure.

	1st year	2nd year	3rd year	4th year	5th year
Hardware depreciation	\$175,000	\$175,000	\$175,000	\$175,000	
Software depreciation	\$80,000	\$80,000	\$80,000	\$80,000	
Hardware maintenance and repairs		\$125,000	\$125,000	\$125,000	\$125,000
Project costs—consulting	\$150,000				
Project costs—customer	\$80,000				
Training	\$25,000				
Total	\$510,000	\$380,000	\$380,000	\$380,000	\$125,000

Table 15.7 TCO Including Project Costs for Migration

The next step is to identify the value of the benefits. This figure is derived from the costs that no longer exist after the migration project (Table 15.8).

Benefits

	1st year	2nd year	3rd year	4th year	5th year
Repairs and maintenance	$200,000	$875,000	$875,000	$875,000	$875,000
Operation		$300,000	$300,000	$300,000	$300,000
Total	$200,000	$1,175,000	$1,175,000	$1,175,000	$1,175,000

Table 15.8 Savings Made Through Lower Repairs and Maintenance Costs

If we now compare the costs and benefits, we see the return on investment; that is, the point in time at which the costs are covered by the savings. Based on the above figures, this investment resulted only in cost benefits (Figure 15.9).

In this example, the mainframe migration will pay for itself on an open platform within 17 months. After this period, the full force of the cost savings will take effect.

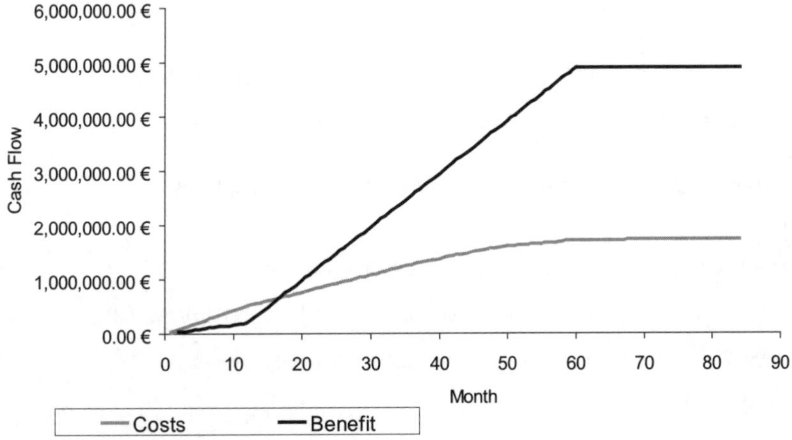

Figure 15.9 ROI of a Migration Project

Scale up—scale out

During the course of another project, the question was asked as to whether a heterogeneous distributed system landscape (scale out) on the basis of blade servers is more cost-efficient than a homogeneous consolidated system landscape (scale up).

Figure 15.10 compares both alternatives for a complete mySAP and NetWeaver system landscape, including development, test, and failover systems. In the consolidated system landscape, a computer is run with two partitions in order to separate production instances from non-production instances. If one of the computers fails, the missing resources are dynamically re-filled by temporary CPU. Distributed systems have a reserve computer that can fill any gaps that arise in the system landscape.

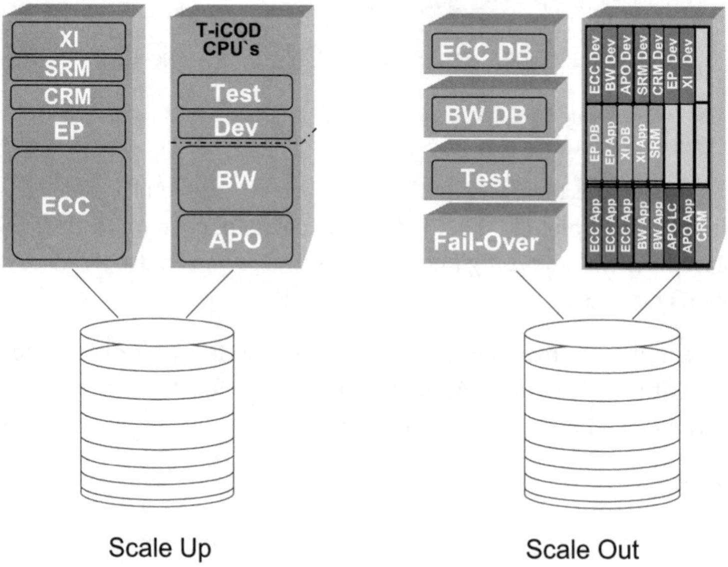

Figure 15.10 Example of a Scale Up versus Scale out Architectures

Table 15.9 compares the CPU count of both alternatives

SAP Solution	CPU for Scale Up	CPU for Scale out
ECC	8.1 DB/App (64-bit)	1x4 DB (64-bit)+ 3x2 app (32-bit)
BW	5.2 DB/App (64-bit)	1x4 DB (64-bit)+ 2x2 app
APO	4.4 DB/App (64-bit)	1x2 DB (64-bit)+ 2x2 app/LC (32/64-bit)
CRM	0.6 DB/App (64-bit)	1x2 DB/app (32-bit)
SRM	0.4 DB/App (64-bit)	1x2 DB/app (32-bit)
XI	4.3 DB/App (64-bit)	1x2 DB + 1x2 app (32-bit)
Test (shared)	3.4 DB/App (64-bit)	1x4 (64-bit) DB/app
Dev (shared)	2.6 DB/App (64-bit)	6x2 DB/app (32-bit)

Table 15.9 Scale up—Scale out

SAP Solution	CPU for Scale Up	CPU for Scale out
Failover	4.0 DB/App (64-bit)	1x4 (standby) (64-bit)
Total	2x16 CPU (64-bit)	4x4 CPU (64-bit) + 17x2 CPU (32-bit)

Table 15.9 Scale up—Scale out (cont.)

Blend syndrome

There is a tendency towards the well-known blend syndrome, which arises when a dedicated computer platform has to be set up for every mySAP solution and NetWeaver component. Load peaks can be dynamically prevented in the scale-up model by making changes to resource distribution; in the scale-out model, the same can be achieved by reallocating application computers. In the scale-up scenario, there would thus be two 64-bit computers, each with 16 CPUs. In the scale-out scenario there will be four 64-bit computers, each with four CPUs, and 17 blades each with two CPUs.

A cost analysis therefore has to take account of the fact that in a scale-up scenario, three operating system instances have to be licensed, administrated, and maintained, while in the scale-out scenario, there are 21 operating system instances. The main memory required by the operating system instances also has to be taken into account. In this case, because of the main memory requirements, the database servers of two mySAP solutions, and thus also the test and failover systems, had to be designed as 64-bit systems. Table 15.10 shows the average costs (rounded up).

CPU	Scale up	Scale out	
	64-bit	64-bit	32-bit
OS instances	3	4	17
Hardware	2 × 16 CPU	4 × 4 CPU	17 × 2 CPU
Hardware costs	$193,333	$96,667	$33,333
Hardware maintenance and repairs	$50,000	$25,000	$8,333
Operating system licenses	$14,667	$7,333	$5,667
Operating system maintenance and repairs	$19,333	$9,667	$19,000
Operating system administration	$18,000	$24,000	$102,000
Total	$295,333	$331,000	

Table 15.10 Cost Comparison of Scale up and Scale out per Year

The costs for administering the operating systems have been set at $500 for one man-day per computer and month. The computers are leased for three years.

You should also note at this point that the figures above apply to this example only and cannot be regarded as generally valid.

As the example shows, it is mainly the costs for administration and maintaining the operating system instances that have led to the trend towards system consolidation in recent years. However, if you have been able to significantly reduce your costs for operating system administration using the measures described in Chapter 13, this may in fact tip the balance back in favor of a system consisting of several small computers. The extent to which this solution is possible cannot be specified in figures at the time of writing because of the lack of real-world evidence.

The availability of 64-bit systems and dual-core CPUs for blades may also cause a general reconsideration of this subject.

However, the main benefits of an adaptive infrastructure cannot be reflected in a purely TCO-based analysis, as they are mainly non-quantifiable benefits (immaterial or strategic benefits, secondary effects, and so on).

15.6 Summary

Like every other part of the enterprise, the IT department also has to be able to prove the cost-efficiency of its investments. It is therefore not enough to simply provide IT services as cheaply as possible; the IT department also has to contribute in a measurable way to the success of the enterprise. However, it is not usually easy to objectively quantify the costs and benefits of an SAP solution in its entirety.

- Within the scope of a cost-efficiency analysis, the total operating costs of an SAP system can be divided into fixed costs, which depend only on the number of systems, and variable costs, which depend on the system throughput.
- Cost blocks that are often underestimated are complexity costs (costs incurred by interfaces) and software logistics costs (costs incurred by changes and quality assurance).
- The largest cost block in operating an SAP solution are the fixed staff costs for system monitoring and administration, patch, change, and fault management. Therefore, measures that reduce the number of

systems and the cost of operating them have the most cost-saving effect.

- The term "total cost of ownership" (TCO) was coined by the Gartner Group. It refers to the total costs of operating IT systems. TCO analyses do not provide any information about the profit that may be made from an IT investment.
- Return on investment (ROI) compares the net benefits of an investment with the total project costs. The result is a percentage value of the invested capital.
- The business literature does not provide a consistent definition of TCO and ROI. There are therefore different calculation methods for both.
- A TCO project usually lasts eight weeks. The actual time required can be different from this, depending on how well the team works together, the priority assigned to the TCO project, and the degree of difficulty of gathering the data.

Sources and Further Reading

Ahmed, Syed Meraj: *Statistical Analysis of resource demand of Standard software solutions*. Master's Thesis University of Applied Sciences Furtwangen (Germany), attended by Prof. Bernadin Denzel and Dr. Michael Mißbach.

Amor, Daniel: *The E-Business (R)evolution: Living and Working in an Interconnected World*. 2nd Edition. Prentice Hall 2001.

Anthes, Gary H.: *ROI Guide: Internal Rate of Return*. Computerworld, 02/17/2003, *http://www.computerworld.com/managementtopics/roi/story/0,10801,78524,00.html*.

Anderson, George W.: *SAP Planning: Best Practices in Implementation*. Sams 2003.

Berry, John: *ROI Guide: Economic Value Added*. Computerworld, 02/17/2003, *http://www.computerworld.com/managementtopics/roi/story/0,10801,78514,00.html*.

Hagemann, Sigrid; Will, Liane: *SAP R/3 System Administration*. 2nd Edition, SAP PRESS 2003.

Hewlett-Packard: *How to manage SAP Solutions with HP OpenView.* HP Whitepaper, *www.openview.com/sap*.

Hewlett-Packard: *Take control of your IT and TCO.* HP Whitepaper, *www.openview.com/sap*.

IBM Business Consulting: *SAP Authorization System. Design and Implementation of Authorization concepts for SAP R/3 and SAP Enterprise Portal.* SAP PRESS 2003.

McFarland Metzger, Sue; Röhrs, Susanne: SAP *R/3 Change and Transport Management: The Official SAP Guide.* Sybex Inc. 2000.

META Group, 4/99: *Enterprise Resource Management. Solutions and Their Value.*

META Group, 9/99: *Enterprise Application Ongoing Support Costs.*

Mißbach, Michael; Hoffmann, Uwe M.: *SAP Hardware Solutions—Servers, Storage, and Networks for mySAP.com*. Prentice Hall 2000.

Mißbach, Michael; Sosnitzka, Ralf; Stelzel, Josef; Wilhelm, Mathias: *SAP System Operations*. SAP PRESS 2003.

Oakland, John S.: *Statistical Process Control*. Heinemann Professional Publishing, Oxford 1989.

Oswald, Gerhard: *SAP Service and Support.* 2nd Edition, SAP PRESS 2004.

Prior, D.; Govekar, M.: *SAP Performance Management: Make an Informed Choice.* Gartner Research Note COM-19–0368, February 2003.

SAP AG: *Security Guide Vol. I-III. http://service.sap.com/securityguides.*

SAP Labs: *System Administration Made Easy, 4.6C/D*. Johnson Printing Service 2002.

Schneider, Thomas: *SAP Performance Optimization Guide. Analyzing and Tuning SAP Systems* 3rd Edition, SAP PRESS 2003.

Schneider-Neureither, Andreas; et al.: *SAP System Landscape Optimization*. SAP PRESS 2004.

Sheward, W.A.: *Economic Control of Quality of Manufactured Product*. Dr. Van Nostrand Co., New York 1931.

Stefani, Helmut (Hrsg.): *Archiving Your SAP Data. A comprehensive guide to plan and execute archiving projects.* SAP PRESS 2002.

The Authors

As a Senior Consultant of the SAP HP Competence Center in Walldorf, **Dr.-Ing. Michael Mißbach** is responsible for the development of flexible SAP NetWeaver and mySAP infrastructure solutions. His work mainly focuses on system consolidation, SAP for Linux, and network infrastructures. Prior to that, he worked as a Project Manager and IT Superintendent for ALCOA and implemented outsourcing and network projects for GE CompuNet. He studied Mechanical Engineering at the University of Karlsruhe, Germany, and received his doctorate in Materials Science at the Nuclear Research Center, also located in Karlsruhe. Michael lives with his wife and son near Walldorf, Germany. His spare time not occupied by authoring SAP books is spent building his extensive model railroad system and hiking.

Thomas Wagenblast is a Senior Consultant at the SAP HP Competence Center in Walldorf, where he is responsible for all aspects regarding the technology and architecture of SAP system landscapes. He studied Communications Engineering at the University of Applied Sciences in Esslingen, Germany, and then worked as a developer of hardware and software for telephone systems at SEL/Alcatel. He later worked for several years as a technology consultant in the presales area of various computer manufacturers such as Digital, Compaq, and HP. For the last eight years, he has worked at the SAP Competence Center. Thomas lives with his wife and three children near Stuttgart. Some of his leisure activities are playing the trombone, sound engineering, cooking, sailing and skiing.

Peter Gibbels is responsible for the definition, creation, and marketing of infrastructure, application management, and integration solutions in the area of HP Manufacturing and Distribution Industries. He started his professional career in 1975 in the telecommunications division at Deutsche Telekom, and then studied Tele Communications Engineering at the University of Applied Sciences in Aachen, Germany. Since 1984, he has had several positions at Hewlett-Packard. For 11 years, the focus of his work has been on SAP systems integration with a special emphasis on infrastructures, IT management, and integration in SAP implementation projects. Peter lives with his wife and two daughter in Aachen, Germany. His hobbies beside family life are gardening, acquiring tools to enhance his house, driving his motorbike, jogging, badminton, and technology (hobby railroad, digital slotcars).

As a Senior Consultant in the SAP HP Competence Center in Walldorf, **Jürgen Karnstädt** is responsible for the trading industry and for issues related to the interaction of IT and business. He has experience with the implementation of SAP modules and the design of large customer environments.

Josef Stelzel is an SAP Program Manager at Microsoft. Prior to this, he was Solution Architect at the SAP HP Competence Center in Walldorf. His work focuses on the development and implementation of adaptive SAP infrastructure solutions. His range of experience with SAP dates back to the early days of Release 2.2. As a consultant, he supported large corporations such as Opel, Hoechst, and Heidelberger Druck in the development of operating concepts and the creation of operating manuals. His hobbies include gardening and biking.

Index

D

M

N

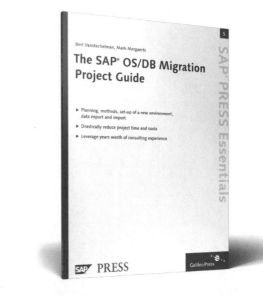

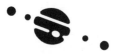

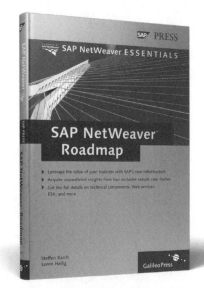

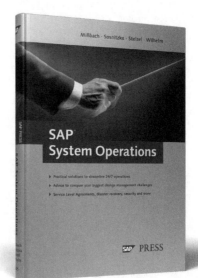

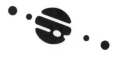

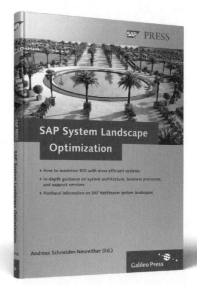

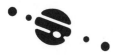